John Stuart Mill

and the

Religion of Humanity

John Stuart Mill
and the
Religion of Humanity

Linda C. Raeder

University of Missouri Press
Columbia and London

Copyright © 2002 by
The Curators of the University of Missouri
University of Missouri Press, Columbia, Missouri 65201
Printed and bound in the United States of America
All rights reserved
5 4 3 2 1   06 05 04 03 02

Library of Congress Cataloging-in-Publication Data

Raeder, Linda C.
  John Stuart Mill and the religion of humanity / Linda C. Raeder.
    p.   cm.
  Includes bibliographical references and index.
  ISBN 0-8262-1387-1 (alk. paper)
  1. Mill, John Stuart, 1806–1873—Religion.   I. Title.
B1608.R44 R34   2002
210'.92—dc21   2002017986

♾™ This paper meets the requirements of the
American National Standard for Permanence of Paper
for Printed Library Materials, Z39.48, 1984.

Designer: Jennifer Cropp
Typesetter: The Composing Room of Michigan, Inc.
Printer and binder: The Maple-Vail Book Manufacturing Group
Typefaces: Palatino, Garamond Classic, Garamond Condensed,
        Woodtype Ornaments

To my parents,

Evelyn and
Howard Maxwell

Contents

Acknowledgments   ix
Abbreviations of Mill's Writings   xi

Introduction   1
1. Early Influences: James Mill and Jeremy Bentham   7
2. The Spirit of the Age: Mill and French Immanentism   38
3. "Nature" and "Utility of Religion"   87
4. Sir William Hamilton and the Mansel Controversy   145
5. "Theism"   167
6. *On Liberty*   234
7. *Utilitarianism*   268
8. Consequences and Implications   320

Notes   345
Bibliography   377
Index   393

Acknowledgments

Thank you seems far too insignificant an expression to convey my gratitude to Claes Ryn. But for him and his devotion to creative freedom, the present work would not exist. I would also like to thank Robert Sokolowski for immediately recognizing the significance of Mill's religious aspirations for subsequent social developments, as well as David Walsh for leading me to Mill in the first place. I am indebted to the work of James E. Crimmins for providing me with the key to Mill, and to that of Joseph Hamburger for moral support.

I owe special thanks to George Carey and John Alvis for their thoughtfulness, insight, and generosity, as well as to Maurice Manring, Jameson Campaigne, John Lulves, Edmund Opitz, and Ellis West for their helping hands. Thanks to Gary Kass for his critical eye, sound judgment, and infinite tact. I would like to thank the following publishers for granting permission to reprint selections from the indicated works: Transaction Publishers (Oscar A. Haac, trans. and ed., *The Correspondence of John Stuart Mill and Auguste Comte*); University of Toronto Press (Joseph Hamburger, "Religion and *On Liberty*," in Michael Laine, ed., *A Cultivated Mind, Essays on J. S. Mill Presented to John M. Robson,* and "Mill and Tocqueville on Liberty," in John M. Robson and Michael Laine, eds., *James and John Stuart Mill/ Papers of the Centenary Conference;* and *Collected Works of John Stuart Mill*); Intercollegiate Studies Institute (Joseph Hamburger, "Individuality and Moral Reform: The Rhetoric of Liberty and the Reality of Restraint in Mill's *On Liberty*"); and Routledge (UK) (James E. Crimmins, "Religion, Utility, and Politics: Bentham versus Paley," in Crimmins, ed., *Religion, Secularization, and Political Thought: Thomas Hobbes to J. S. Mill*).

Thanks too to Laura Nyro, wherever you are, and to Judy Mollet, Boyanna Jacobson, Joni Dalton, Eva, Vincent, Audrey, Ben, and the two William Blakes, Peggy Hull, Kathleen Gibbs and Camille, Eileen Creane Phillips, Ursula Tafe, Helen Foggo, Sharon Donohoe, Amy Clyman, Joseph Baldacchino, Frau Irmgard Guth, and *meinem lieben Hansimann* for faithfulness and affection and for helping me maintain perspective. And, last but not least, thanks to my parents, Evelyn and Howard Maxwell, for everything.

Abbreviations of Mill's Writings

ACP   *Auguste Comte and Positivism*, Ann Arbor: University of Michigan Press, 1968.

Auto   *The Autobiography of John Stuart Mill*, ed. John M. Robson, New York: Penguin Books, 1989.

Corr   *The Correspondence of John Stuart Mill and Auguste Comte*

CW   *Collected Works of John Stuart Mill*

Ham   *An Examination of Sir William Hamilton's Philosophy*, in *Collected Works*, vol. 9

"Nat"   "Nature," in *Collected Works*, vol. 10

OL   *On Liberty*, in *On Liberty and Other Writings*, ed. Stefan Collini

Spirit   *The Spirit of the Age*, Chicago: University of Chicago Press, 1942.

"The"   "Theism," in *Collected Works*, vol. 10

"UR"   "Utility of Religion," in *Collected Works*, vol. 10

Util   *Utilitarianism*, in *The Utilitarians*, New York: Anchor Books, 1973.

I always saw . . . in the idea of Humanity the only one capable of replacing that of God. But there is still a long way from this speculation and belief to the manifest feeling I experience today—that it is fully valid and that the inevitable substitution is at hand.

—J. S. Mill to Auguste Comte

John Stuart Mill

and the
Religion of Humanity

Introduction

The extensive corpus of John Stuart Mill has been subjected to an equally extensive scholarly examination. There are numerous and thorough studies of Mill's contribution to moral and political philosophy, logic, political economy, and the methodology of the social sciences; his liberalism, utilitarianism, and feminism; his views on democracy, representation, education, and much else. Despite the wealth of scholarship devoted to his work, however, relatively little attention has been paid to Mill's views on religion beyond passing references to his "secularism" or "naturalism" in ethics. The neglect of the religious dimension of Mill's thought and activity is curious, and even remarkable, because what must be regarded as essentially religious preoccupations dominated Mill's thought and structured his endeavors throughout his life.[1] From beginning to end, religious themes abound, implicitly and explicitly, in his books, articles, correspondence, and diary. Neither Mill's philosophy nor his politics can be adequately comprehended without taking into account his religious views and purposes.

More particularly, what should be recognized for a proper appreciation of Mill's thought and legacy is the depth of his animus toward traditional transcendent religion, and especially Christianity, as well as the seriousness of his intent to found a new secular or nontheological religion to serve as its replacement. Mill was committed both to the destruction of what he regarded as a moribund and immoral Christianity and to the social establishment of what he regarded as the superior morality and spirituality embodied in the Religion of Humanity that he adopted, with revisions, from Auguste Comte.

At first glance, the attraction of a self-styled utilitarian rationalist such as Mill to the intense sentimental religiosity of Comte's Religion of Humanity seems peculiar, if not downright bizarre. Yet Mill's lifelong embrace of what he called this "real, though purely human religion," this "religion without a God," was one of the few consistencies in a philosophical career otherwise notable for its fluid eclecticism.[2] Indeed, as this book aims to show, Mill's commitment to the replacement of Christianity with

1

a Religion of Humanity was one of the chief purposes governing his philosophical endeavors throughout his life. Mill, generally regarded as the very type of the modern secular humanist, is more accurately characterized as the militant apostle of an intramundane "social religion," the substance of which, moreover, has been widely assimilated by modern Anglo-American consciousness.[3]

The neglect of the religious dimension of Mill's enterprise has shaped the present work in several ways. The first task must be to show what Mill himself believed, intended, and pursued and why this is essential to an accurate understanding and evaluation of his writings. The work is thus, in part, an effort at retrieval—a close study of the original sources. It was deemed essential to present a detailed exposition of Mill's explicit writings on religion, as well as the religious themes disclosed in his private correspondence and diary. The work is also an effort of criticism and analysis; certain of Mill's writings demand a critical response and are treated accordingly. The overarching aim is to explore the significance of Mill's religious thought and aspirations with respect to both his corpus and to subsequent social and political developments. It is argued that the material brought to light in this study requires a significant reevaluation of both Millian liberalism and the advanced or modern liberalism that derives from it.

The work explores two related aspects of Mill's engagement with religion: first, his specific views on religion and God; and second, his aspiration to found a new religion. Chapter 1 begins at the beginning, with a discussion of the two most significant influences on the development of Mill's religious thought and intent—James Mill and Jeremy Bentham. Contrary to Mill's famous assertion in his *Autobiography* that he grew up free from religious prejudice, the religious views he absorbed from his father throughout his peculiar childhood would shape and even determine his own religious convictions until the end of his life. Similarly, a discussion of the nontheological utilitarianism of Bentham is essential to an understanding of Mill's religious aspirations. As we shall see, Bentham's enterprise, like Mill's, involved the replacement of a transcendent or "theological" morality with a "purely human" equivalent oriented *exclusively* toward the temporal dimension of existence. Moreover, and even more directly to the point of this work, it was precisely this aspect of Benthamism that affected Mill with all the force of a religious conversion.

Chapter 2 explores Mill's engagement with French immanentism and especially his encounter with two French "secular messiahs," Henri de Saint-Simon and Auguste Comte. Both thinkers fully shared Mill's Benthamite aim—to replace what Saint-Simon called "celestial" ethics with a "terrestrial" equivalent. What Mill found in the French thinkers was a more radical elaboration of the positivist hostility to traditional religion that he had found so overwhelmingly appealing in Bentham. Equally important, Mill's French compatriots provided him with a philosophy of history that served not only as a rationale for, but as a further impetus to, his already well-formed intention to construct and establish a new "positivist" or nontheological ethics and society. As formulated in the Saint-Simonian/Comtean "law of the three stages," the task of the philosopher was to assist the transition from the obsolete theological and metaphysical states of mind (and society) to the newly emerging positivist state that was man's destiny and end. Moreover, Mill would find his final spiritual home in Comte's vision of a Religion of Humanity. Under Comte's influence, Mill came to believe that the long-awaited and "inevitable substitution [of Humanity for God] is at hand."[4] Mill never wavered in his conviction that, as he said, "[t]he best . . . thing . . . in Comte's [work] is the thoroughness with which he has enforced and illustrated the possibility of making *le culte de l'humanité* perform the functions and supply the place of a religion."[5] Although Mill's relation to Comte's thought was complex, he would bend his efforts toward the realization of this aspect of Comte's vision until the end of his life. Chapter 2 also examines Mill's correspondence with Comte. This is essential for an adequate interpretation of Mill's published writings, for it reveals that those writings are not always a reliable indicator of his true views on religion.

In Chapter 3 we turn to an examination of Mill's explicit writings on religion. We examine two of the essays that constitute his posthumously published *Three Essays on Religion* (1874): "Nature" and "Utility of Religion." These essays were composed more or less contemporaneously in the 1850s as complementary components of a set of essays Mill designed in collaboration with his wife, Harriet Taylor Mill. This set of pieces was intended as a concentrated summation of what the Mills regarded as their most important views, views they hoped would inform the thought of future thinkers. "Nature" was intended to undermine the deistic conception of a providential governance of the universe or, as Mill put it, the "irrational proviso of a Providence manifest in general laws."[6] It was also designed to complete Bentham's project of the destruction of the idea of natural law, that is, to dissever the traditional association of "nature" with lawful order, with the right and the good, with God. The essay is fascinating for the glimpse it provides into Mill's own experience of cosmic disorder and even terror in the face of that disorder. "Utility of Religion" is one of Mill's strongest public expressions of his intent to establish a new religion. The general purpose of the essay is to show that, contrary to common belief, traditional religion is not in fact necessary for the achievement of either personal or social happiness and well-being. Mill claims that all the alleged benefits of traditional transcendent religion may be attained by widespread subscription to his proposed intramundane substitute— the Religion of Humanity—and, moreover, that this new religion represents a decided moral advance over traditional Christianity. "Utility of Religion" represents Mill's synthesis of the views concerning religion that he absorbed from Bentham, James Mill, Comte, and Harriet Taylor and is one of his most important works on that subject.

Chapter 4 discusses Mill's participation in the Mansel controversy. Mill's conflict with Henry Longueville Mansel ostensibly concerned epistemology and, more particularly, the limits of man's knowledge of God. Mansel had argued that natural theology was incapable of establishing limits to the nature and attributes of God, a conclusion Mill would strenuously resist. The real issue, however, certainly to Mill, was not epistemological but moral: What incensed Mill was Mansel's claim that human nescience forbids human judgment of God and his ways. Mansel denied that human moral conceptions can shed any light on the moral nature or attributes of God. Human conceptions of goodness and justice, he argued, held by necessarily finite and limited minds, are utterly inapplicable to divine goodness and justice; thus the latter cannot be judged by human standards. Mill's response was the "famous outburst" that both shocked his contemporaries and significantly influenced the subsequent development of religious thought: "I will call no being good, who is not what I mean when I apply that epithet to my fellow-creatures; and if such a being can sentence me to hell for not so calling him, to hell I will go" (*Ham*, 103). Mill's defiance made the rejection of the traditional Christian God a matter of moral superiority and even necessity.

Chapter 5 examines the last of Mill's explicit writings on religion, "Theism," composed sometime between 1868 and 1870, in the evening of his life (Mill died in 1873). Although published in the same volume with the two essays discussed in Chapter 3, "Theism" is sufficiently distinct, both in tone and substance, to justify a separate treatment. The essay may be understood as a development of the tradition of English deism or natural theology. Mill examines and evaluates the traditional arguments for the existence of God from the perspective of science, in line with the "canons of induction" he formulated for his generation in *A System of Logic*. He claims to have found evidence for a god of a kind, a probable limited god, limited in power certainly and possibly also in wisdom and knowledge. Mill's limited and possibly inept god resembles the Platonic Demiurge. His new god, moreover, is a god who "really needs" man's help in the realization of his plans. Indeed, Mill's god is limited in such a manner that the achievement of order becomes, in effect, the exclusive responsibility of man. He is thus perfectly suited to assist the realization of Mill's overriding aim—the replacement of a theological orientation and morality with a purely human equivalent. The essay is also important for what it reveals of Mill's "conversion" strategy. His aim was to enlist the "supernatural hopes" and aspirations of Christians in service of the Religion of Humanity, for these, as he says, are so "excellently fitted to aid and fortify that real, though purely human religion, which sometimes calls itself the Religion of Humanity and sometimes that of Duty" ("The," 488). Mill's vigorous proselytizing on behalf of the Religion of Humanity in his final essay offers conclusive evidence that he remained committed to the establishment of the new secular religion to the end of his life.

Chapters 6 and 7 offer a reinterpretation of two of Mill's most celebrated essays, *On Liberty* and *Utilitarianism*. Both essays are shown to have been employed by Mill as crucial instruments toward the accomplishment of his two-pronged religious goal—the evisceration of traditional religious belief and the social establishment of the Religion of Humanity. Chapter 6 discusses the role Mill intended *On Liberty* to play in that process, namely, to engender the freedom of discussion that he regarded as essential to the final eradication of lingering theological belief. In Chapter 7, *Utilitarianism* is shown to be Mill's most developed effort at proselytization on behalf of nontheological utilitarianism. The aim, as Mill says, is to establish the principle of utility as "the ultimate source of moral obligations," that is, to substitute utility for the traditional transcendent God. The chapter presents a close examination of the text that aims to elucidate Mill's strategy in this regard and offers a critical analysis of some of the arguments that Mill employs.

Chapter 8 attempts to elucidate the significance of Mill's religious thought and aspirations for subsequent social and political developments. First and most important is the success of Mill's endeavor. The values and ideals embodied in his new social religion have, as noted, been widely assimilated by modern Anglo-American consciousness and constitute the ethos that has impelled the rise of modern liberalism. Second, Mill's successful promotion of a militantly intramundane social religion is in tension with the classical-liberal commitment to individual liberty and limited government. One consequence of this has been the transformation of Anglo-American liberalism from a philosophy of limited government to one of modern expansive government. Third, Mill not only elevates the "social" over the personal or individual but invests it with an intense religiosity. This has led to the sacralization of the political realm and a concomitant politicization of Anglo-American society. Finally, it is suggested that Mill's attempt to replace a theologically based ethics with a secular or "purely human" equivalent eviscerates not only the spiritual foundation of individual liberty and limited government, but the higher-law tradition essential to their preservation as well.

The Benthamite circle, centered on the charismatic figure of James Mill, liked to think of themselves as counterparts of the eighteenth-century philosophes they regarded as their spiritual and philosophical predecessors and guides. What Jacob Talmon remarks of the eighteenth-century philosophes—that they "were never in doubt that they were preaching a new religion"[7]—may be equally said of their self-styled descendants Bentham, James Mill, and, even more, of John Stuart Mill. For Mill would develop, more extensively than either his father or Bentham, one particular strand of the philosophes' speculation—their aim to establish a secular religion to replace the Christianity they rejected. Mill, like various other nineteenth-century thinkers, keenly felt the need for a new religious ethos to fill what was widely experienced as the spiritual vacuum that had ensued in the wake of the eighteenth century's critical attacks on Christianity. The concern was for social unity and a spiritual underpinning to social and political order. Thus Mill, like other descendants of the philosophes such as Saint-Simon and Comte, aimed throughout his life to formulate and establish a new spirituality and morality to meet the needs of the posttheological or positivist age. His aim was the aim of Bentham and Comte—the replacement of the traditional Western faith in a transcendent God with a purely human social religion whose ultimate end and value were conceived as an intramundane "service to Humanity." As this work will show, Mill was very far from the secular philosopher of the modern-liberal imagination. Leslie Stephen and other of Mill's contemporaries saw far more clearly than later interpreters the religious nature of Mill's enterprise. "Truly," said Stephen, "Mill was nearly qualified for a place among the prophets."[8] Perhaps in even greater truth, Mill should be regarded as he seems to have regarded himself—as a religious founder.

Early Influences
James Mill and Jeremy Bentham

A new religion would be an odd sort of thing without a name—
[I] propose . . . Utilitarianism.

—Jeremy Bentham, writing to a friend

I: The Influence of James Mill

The sanguine speculator can hardly forbear supposing that such
insight might be obtained into the means of producing mental
virtues, that we might make as many good men as almost as we
please.

—James Mill

In his *Autobiography*, John Stuart Mill recounts those formative influences he regarded as most significant for his "mental" development, including those that had a bearing on his religious views. Such influences are especially important in the case of Mill, whose unusual upbringing at the hands of his father, James Mill, has become almost the stuff of legend.[1] The importance that Mill attached to the subject of religion is indicated by his introduction of his formative religious influences in the second chapter of the *Autobiography*. The title of that chapter, "Moral Influences in Early Youth. My Father's Character and Opinions," also draws attention to the preponderant role played by James Mill in shaping his son's religious outlook. As we shall see, John Mill's religious thought, despite a certain amount of resistance, remained to the end of his days fixed in the groove cut into his mind by his father.

By any account, James Mill was a formidable figure.[2] Born in Scotland, he rose by dint of the qualities he admired in Martin Luther—"courage, activity, and perseverance"—from humble beginnings to a position of considerable influence.[3] Educated at the University of Edinburgh in the last decade of the eighteenth century, he was ordained as a minister in the Church of Scotland in 1798. James Mill, however, never served as a practicing minister. Unable to find a parish position in Scotland, the young man moved to London in 1802, where he eked out a living writing journal reviews. The success of his *History of British India* in 1817, a work of ten years' labor, secured him both a position and lifelong financial security at the East India Company. He, as did John Mill, held highly responsible positions at India House throughout much of his adult life, gaining firsthand experience in practical governance.[4]

In the *Autobiography*, John Mill tells of the enormous appeal his father held for the young disciples who gathered to hear him preach the utilitarian and philosophical radical gospel. His father's "personal ascendancy," says Mill, made him "as much the head and leader of the intellectual radicals in England, as Voltaire was of the *philosophes* of France" (*Auto*, 173). This is one instance where Mill, prone to exaggerate the virtues of persons he admired, seems to have made an accurate assessment. There is much testimony to the effect that James Mill was a charismatic figure. The young John Mill's compatriot William Ellis described how his early encounter with James Mill "worked a complete change in me. He taught me how to think and what to live for." Even more to the point of this study, James Mill, said Ellis, supplied him "with all those emotions and impulses which deserve the name of religion."[5]

The influence of such a person on his own son was enormous, not to say determinative.[6] Indeed, the young John Mill struggled to overcome the perception of his contemporaries that under his father's dominion he had become little more than a "'made' or 'manufactured' man, having had a certain impress of opinion stamped on me which I could only reproduce" (*Auto*, 126). All his life, Mill would struggle to establish his independence against his father's hegemonic sway, to become a person and an original thinker in his own right. Although an analysis of James Mill's influence on his son is beyond the scope of this work, it is not too much to say that his figure hovers in the background of all John Mill wrote and experienced. "My conscience," he would say, "always spoke to me in my father's voice."[7]

What is important for this study, however, is that sometime between 1807 and 1811, James Mill abandoned his Christian faith. The process had been gradual, manifested first in his loss of faith in revelation and later in his rejection of deism. Deism, or "natural religion," the rationalistic form of Christianity that rose to prominence in the eighteenth century, held that the Creator is known through natural law rather than through miracles and Scripture. According to John Mill (*Auto*, 49), the "turning point" in his father's movement away from Christian belief was his reading of Joseph Butler's *Analogy of Religion* (1736). Butler's aim was to defend the truth of revelation. To that end, he argued that a belief in the divine origin of the Old and New Testaments and the deistic belief in a God manifested through natural law must stand or fall on the same ground. Because natural religion and revealed religion are equally susceptible to rational criticism, both ultimately depend on faith. Apparently, James Mill went from accepting Butler's argument in support of both revelation and deism—it is as rational or irrational to believe in one as in the other—to a conviction that the argument could uphold neither form of religion. As his son put it, James Mill

> considered Butler's argument as conclusive against the only opponents for whom it was intended. Those [the Deists] who admit an omnipotent as well as perfectly just and benevolent maker and ruler of such a world as this, can say little against Christianity but what can, with at least equal force, be retorted against themselves. Finding therefore no halting place in Deism, he remained . . . perplexed, until, doubtless after many struggles, *he yielded to the conviction, that concerning the origin of things nothing whatever can be known.* This is the only correct statement of his opinion; for dogmatic atheism he looked upon as absurd; as most of those, whom the world has considered atheists, have always done. (emphasis added)

In this passage, Mill casts his father's loss of faith in a rather rationalistic light—he had found "Butler's argument . . . conclusive." In almost the next breath, however, he suggests that James Mill's ultimate rejection of Christianity hinged on something quite other than the compelling logic of Butler's argument. For Mill goes on to say that his father's rejection of Christianity, or "all that is called religious belief, . . . was not . . . primarily a matter of logic and evidence: the grounds of it were moral, still more than intellectual. He found it impossible to believe that a world so full of evil was the work of an Author combining infinite power with perfect goodness and righteousness. His intellect spurned the subtleties by which men attempt to blind themselves to this open contradiction" (*Auto*, 50). Mill's observation approaches the heart of the matter for both his father and himself. John Mill held throughout his life precisely the view he ascribes to James Mill in this passage. Moreover, he held it for a more or less identical "moral" reason. Neither of the Mills believed that a world as disordered and full of evil as the one they perceived could possibly be the work of a Creator simultaneously omnipotent and all-benevolent.

John Mill's own views will be extensively explored in subsequent chapters. At this point, let us direct our attention to Mill's curious failure to perceive a relation between the views "impressed" upon him throughout his childhood and his own mature views on religion. Throughout his life, Mill would characterize himself as peculiarly free of religious prejudice, having had the "rare" experience of being "brought up from the first without any religious belief. . . . I am . . . one of the very few examples, in this country, of one who has, not thrown off religious belief, but never had it: I grew up in a negative state with regard to it. I looked upon the modern exactly as I did upon the ancient religion, as something which in no way concerned me." Mill nonchalantly tells us, "History had made the variety of opinions among mankind a fact familiar to me." The suggestion is that he was as detached from, and objective about, the views held by his contemporaries as from the views held by the ancient Greeks. He found it "no more strange that the English people should believe what [he] did not, than that the men whom [he] read of in Herodotus should have done so" (*Auto*, 49, 52).

Mill's repeated insistence that he was peculiarly free of religious prejudice seems to have been based upon his not having been reared in accordance with conventional Christian teachings. (According to one of Mill's biographers, however, Mill's mother and her family were "averagely religious folk." All the Mill children were baptized and the daughters regularly attended church.[8]) In any event, as Mill also explains,

> It would have been wholly inconsistent with my father's ideas of duty, to allow me to acquire impressions contrary to his convictions and feelings respecting religion: and he impressed upon me from the first, that the manner in which the world came into existence was a subject on which nothing was known: that the question "Who made me?" cannot be answered, because we have no experience or authentic information from which to answer it; and that any answer only throws the difficulty a step further back, since the question immediately presents itself, Who made God. (*Auto*, 52)

Mill also tells us that his father gave him a religious opinion "contrary to that of the world," as well as something of the substance of that opinion. "Religion," James Mill had taught him, was "a great moral evil," indeed, "the greatest enemy of morality":

> The Sabaean, or Manichaean theory of a Good and an Evil Principle, struggling against each other for the government of the universe . . . [my father] would not have . . . condemned [as he did Christianity], and he . . . expressed surprise that no one revived it in our time.[9] He would have regarded it as a mere hypothesis, but he would have ascribed to it no depraving influence. As it was, his aversion to religion, in the sense usually attached to the term, was of the same kind with that of Lucretius: he re-

garded it with the feelings due not to a mere mental delusion, but to a great moral evil. He looked upon it as the greatest enemy of morality: first, by setting up factitious excellencies—belief in creeds, devotional feelings, and ceremonies, not connected with the good of human kind,—and causing these to be accepted as substitutes for genuine virtues: but above all, by *radically vitiating the standard of morals;* making it consist in doing the will of a being, on whom it lavishes indeed all the phrases of adulation, but whom in sober truth it depicts as eminently hateful. I have a hundred times heard him say, that all ages and nations have represented their gods as wicked, in a constantly increasing progression; that mankind have gone on adding trait after trait till they reached the most perfect conception of wickedness which the human mind could devise, and have called this God, and prostrated themselves before it. *This ne plus ultra of wickedness he considered to be embodied in what is commonly presented to mankind as the creed of Christianity.* Think (he used to say) of a being who would make a Hell—who would create the human race with the infallible foreknowledge, and therefore with the intention, that the great majority of them were to be consigned to horrible and everlasting torment. The time is drawing near, I believe, when this dreadful conception of an object of worship will be no longer identified with Christianity; and when all persons, with any sense of moral good and evil, will look upon it with the same indignation with which my father regarded it. (*Auto,* 50–51, emphases added)

For most of his life, John Mill's beliefs and attitudes concerning religion and God were almost indistinguishable from those he here ascribes to James Mill. The "impressions" made by his father's views left an indelible mark. The striking parallels and even identity between the religious views of the two Mills are obvious to even the most casual observer. Like his father, John Mill could find little evidence for either natural or revealed religion.[10] He too flirted with Manichaeism. He too regarded conventional Christian ethics as immoral. He too regarded the notion of a simultaneously omnipotent and all-benevolent God in "such a world as this" as a logical absurdity; he too was incensed by the vulgar Nominalist God of Will and Power. He too rejected "dogmatic atheism" and he too evinced deep hostility toward organized and dogmatic religion. John Mill too believed he knew something about the "genuine virtues" for which conventional Christianity substituted its "factitious excellencies."

"John Mill," says Ruth Borchard, "was always the worst possible judge of character."[11] He was also, it seems, rather deficient in self-knowledge, certainly with respect to his religious convictions and aspirations.[12] Mill seems to have regarded the religious beliefs he absorbed during his childhood and youth as simple objective truth, uniquely free of prejudice. This was pure self-deception. Mill was bound by certain granite prejudices against traditional religion, and especially against Christianity, almost from first to last.[13]

Making Good Men

Karl Marx was not the only nineteenth-century figure to declare that man makes himself, Nietzsche not the only thinker to conclude that God is dead. James Mill, the quintessential nineteenth-century self-made man, also seems to have been greatly concerned to obscure the Source of human existence.[14] As we have seen, John Mill tells us that his father had "impressed upon [him] from the first, that the manner in which the world came into existence was a subject on which nothing was known."[15] James Mill's concern to deflect attention away from the ground of existence was accompanied by a fanatical insistence on human self-making. In his view, success was achieved by personal effort and perseverance, strenuous labor, training of character, and the abhorrence of all personal or social dependency. More ominously, this view was accompanied by a passionate conviction of the utter malleability of human beings at the hands of human "educators."

James Mill's passion for the "self-made man" was grounded in the psychological and educational theories he imbibed from such sources as Helvetius, Locke, Hobbes, and Condillac. Man is a tabula rasa, a clean slate upon which the Educator may write what he will. Indeed, the elder Mill seems to have been inspired by such views to a vision of a brave new world of perfected men: "What important assistance should we derive toward the training of young minds to future eminence, had we the history of the intellectual progress of but a few of those who have risen to mental excellence minutely disclosed? The sanguine speculator can hardly forbear supposing that such insight might be obtained into the means of producing mental virtues, that we might make as many good men as almost as we please."[16] John Mill was not only his father's first experiment in this project of "making good men" but was himself thoroughly committed to the same end. His famous account of his mental development in the *Autobiography* was intended to provide the "history of . . . intellectual progress" necessary to assist "the training of young minds to future eminence" for which his father had called. The son fully intended to realize the father's dream of "making good men" and to do so by employing the associationist psychological techniques—the "means of producing mental virtues"—that the latter had advanced.

James Mill's Educator, like the Helvetian Legislator, is a godlike figure of almost unlimited power. Mill, like his sources, believed that all human attributes, characteristics, virtues, and vices are formed by education and environment, through the psychological association of ideas and sensory impressions. He believed that human nature is plastic, if not infinitely malleable. As Jacob Talmon explains, for Helvetius and his followers, "[m]an is a product of education. . . . How fascinated Helvetius was, by the power and greatness of the founder of a monastic order, able as he was to deal with man in the raw, outside the maze of tradition and accumulated circumstances, and to lay down rules to shape man like clay. . . . [Moreover, i]n a society from which the Church had been excluded and which treated social utility as the sole criterion of judgment, education like everything else was bound to be focused in the governmental system."[17]

This is the tradition that shaped the mind of the young John Mill. As he said, the firmest article of his father's faith was his "doctrine of circumstances": "the formation of all human character by circumstances," most of which are under human control (*Auto,* 95–96). The task of the Human Educator, Legislator, and Moralist is to so manipulate those "circumstances" as to form the proper "associations" between virtue and pleasure or vice and pain in the minds of their charges. This is to be accomplished through the skillful employment of the triumvirate of human powers—Education, Law (legislation), and Opinion—including the judicious distribution of rewards and administration of punishments. It was through such means that the utilitarian utopia, the greatest temporal happiness for the greatest number, was to be realized.

For James Mill as for Helvetius, Bentham, and other philosophes, "social" happiness and harmony were to be realized by the conscious reconciliation of personal or self-interest with the general or collective interest. This was to be achieved in the manner described: by "education," the construction of good legislation ("laws"), and the appropriate distribution of rewards and punishments.[18] It is essential to note that for James Mill, as for Helvetius, Holbach, Bentham, and their fellow travelers, the shaping of human behavior in service of the greatest happiness was, as a matter of principle, confined exclusively to the employment of *temporal* means and inducements. The leading idea, to which we shall return time and again, was, in Talmon's words, that

the temporal interest alone if handled cleverly was sufficient to form virtuous men. Good laws alone make virtuous men. This being so, vice in society is not the outcome of the corruption of human nature, but the fault of the Legislator. . . . [M]an is only a raw element in the edifice of social harmony. A legislation is possible under which none would be unhappy but fools and people maimed by nature, and none vicious but the ignorant and stupid. That such a society has not yet come into existence is due not to man, but to the failure of governments to form man with the help of education and proper laws.[19]

The problem, as James Mill and his predecessors conceived it, was that in the past education had been haphazard and the victim of false and pernicious (religious) views and precepts. The time was ripe, however, to acknowledge that all human happiness depended on education. As Talmon explains, "Men have in their own hands the instrument of their greatness and their felicity, and . . . to be happy and powerful nothing more is requisite than to perfect the science of education. . . . Legislators, moralists, and natural scientists should combine to form man on the basis of their teachings, the conclusions of which converge upon the same point. Governments have it in their power to rear genius, to raise or lower the standard of ability in a nation."[20]

Such was the all-encompassing mental environment of the young Mill. James Mill had impressed upon him the "fact" that he was nothing more than the product of his upbringing, "made" or "manufactured" in accordance with the "laws" of associationist psychology and the power and wisdom of his father. James Mill's environmental determinism and spiritual nihilism would permanently shape the mind and thought of John Mill. The son would defend a qualified form of "necessitarianism" or determinism against the "free-will theologians and philosophers."[21] He also shared his father's belief in the omnipotence of Education as a tool of spiritual formation. As he wrote in his diary in 1854, "In this age a far better ideal of human society can be formed . . . than at any former time. . . . The only means [by which to realize this ideal] is universal Education."[22] And such means, for John Mill as for James, were understood to entail the judicious wielding of the other human powers of Law and Opinion and the strategic employment of associationist training techniques. These were the tools by which John Mill hoped to create the virtuous men of the future of whom he, like his father, dreamed.

The Reign of Virtue

We have seen that one of the predominant themes of the religious training that John Mill received at the hands of his father was a passionate hostility to Christianity—the conviction that its God was nothing less than the "ne plus ultra of wickedness." One of the effects of this pronounced aversion was the Mills' unwillingness to recognize or admit the influence of Christianity, and especially Calvinism, on the formation of their own ethos and outlook. Both the Mills preferred to regard themselves as disciples of the pre-Christian philosophers, especially the Greeks. Thus, in the *Autobiography,* Mill portrays his father as an eclectic Greek, one whose outlook was shaped by Stoical, Epicurean, and Cynical elements. James Mill's

Stoicism, he says, was of the conventional sort—endurance in the face of privation and pain. The Epicurean element manifested itself in his father's utilitarian moral standard, "taking as the exclusive test of right and wrong, the tendency of actions to produce pleasure or pain." The Cynical element relates to the fact that James Mill "had . . . scarcely any belief in pleasure." More precisely, Mill explains, his father felt pleasure to be a greatly overrated value, not usually worth its cost, "at least in the present state of society." (It is striking that Mill never associated his father's mistrust of pleasure with the Calvinist mistrust of the natural man, a far more likely source of such a mistrust, especially in one trained in the Presbyterian ministry, than an intellectual Cynicism.[23]) Moreover, James Mill "never varied in rating intellectual enjoyments above all others, even in value as pleasures, independently of their ulterior benefits."[24] All of this is of interest in revealing the peculiar mistrust of the very "pleasure" that was ostensibly the ultimate end of the "greatest happiness" philosophers; hedonists they were certainly not. A more penetrating glimpse into the nature of Benthamite / Millian utilitarianism may be gained from Mill's remark that his father sometimes thought that life "would be worth having . . . [if it] were made what it might be, by good government and good education" (*Auto*, 55–56). The aim of Benthamite utilitarianism, certainly in the hands of the morally impassioned Mills, was not pleasure or happiness but virtue, the formation of "as many good men as almost as we please." As we will see, John Mill's proposed substitute for Christianity— a substitute that he conceived as the spiritual carrier of the greatest happiness principle—as he says, "sometimes calls itself the Religion of Humanity and sometimes that of Duty." Potential converts were forewarned.

There is a final aspect of James Mill's character that has a bearing on our study of John Mill and religion. Mill tells us of his father's contempt for "passionate emotions of all sorts. . . . The 'intense' was with him a byword of scornful disapprobation." It is significant, however, that despite his ostensible contempt for emotion, James Mill himself was among the most emotionally intense of philosophers. As John Mill observes: "[My father's] aversion to many intellectual errors, or what he regarded as such, partook, in a certain sense, of the character of a moral feeling. . . . All this is merely saying that he, in a degree once common, but now very unusual, threw his feelings into his opinions, which truly it is difficult to understand how any one, who possesses much of both, can fail to do. None but those who do not care about opinions, will confound it with intolerance" (*Auto*, 56–57).

All this could equally well be said of John Mill. The father's disparagement of the role of emotion in human existence engendered in the son a lifelong commitment to the conscious cultivation of sentiment. He would cling to a conviction that passion, strong feeling, and intense desire are not only essential ingredients of a well-formed and elevated human character but the spring of all virtue and the very constitution of conscience. Moreover, and perhaps more important, John Mill, following his father in this as in much else, "threw his feelings into his opinions" to such a degree that those feelings often governed, if not determined, the opinions.

On the Church

An account of James Mill's influence on his son's religious outlook is not complete without a discussion of his views on the Church of England. He and the other philosophical radicals regarded the British constitution as irremediably corrupt. This, they believed, was due to its thoroughly aristocratic character, its domination by an oligarchy of great landholders, and its two props, the Established Church and the law. Accordingly, the Benthamite war against the traditional British constitution in the name of democracy was directed against what James Mill called the British constitution's "two great provinces of abuse—Law and Religion" ("The Church, and Its Reform," 277). This entailed a continuation of Bentham's attack on the natural and common law as well as his attack on the Church of England.[25] The battle on the latter front was led by James Mill.

Religious skepticism had spread throughout the eighteenth century and become ever more virulent in the wake of the French Revolution. In England this led to various attacks upon the traditional alliance between Church and State. By the latter half of the eighteenth century, the Church of England had been substantially secularized and, as one scholar puts it, had become "for all practical purposes obsolete and impotent." The weakened position of the Established Church in English society led to its increasing dependence on the aristocracy, and over time the clergy came to be regarded as an integral part of the great landed interest. Clergymen were widely believed to devote more time and attention to worldly than to spiritual concerns. Reformers such as Bentham and James Mill saw the Anglican clergy as one of the chief obstacles to progress and reform. Clergymen, they charged, clung to indefensible dogmatic positions merely to maintain prerogative and privilege. The perceived degeneration of the Church and the condemnation of its dogmatic attitude went hand in hand with a growing skepticism of both the Church and its dogma.[26]

As will be discussed more thoroughly in subsequent chapters, a universal characteristic of the Benthamites, including the Mills, was what

Joseph Hamburger called their "policy of prudent concealment" with respect to the public expression of their unorthodox religious views.[27] The cultural context sketched above helps explain why, in dramatic contrast to their strategic silence on religion and God, the Benthamites felt perfectly free to attack the Church vigorously and incessantly. James Mill's article "The Church, and Its Reform" (1835; cited hereafter as "The Church") presents a concise and representative summation of the Benthamite position on the role of the Anglican Church in the English constitution. The article is instructive for the light it sheds on the attitudes toward established religion that John Mill absorbed during his childhood and youth and on the rhetorical strategies he learned from his father as well. It is thus worth examining in some detail, as it may be taken as a statement of John Mill's own settled convictions on the nature and role of the Established Church in England.[28]

The essence of the article is that the Church of England is corrupt beyond redemption:

> *[T]he present ecclesiastical establishment in England is a perfect nullity in respect to good, but an active and powerful agent in the production of evil.* . . . It has not the look, the colour, not even one of the outward marks, of an institution intended for good.
>
> The world, at least the Protestant world, needs no information respecting the abuses of the Romish church. That ecclesiastical establishment had been reared up into a system, most artfully contrived for rendering men the degraded instruments and tools of priests; for preventing the growth of all intellect, and all morality; for occupying the human mind with superstition; and attaching the very idea of duty to nothing but the repetition of ceremonies, for the glorification of priests. . . . [Furthermore, although other countries] struck off, some more, some less, but all a great part of the machinery, by which the Romish church had become the curse of human nature, the English clergy embraced that machinery very nearly as it stood, . . . praised it to the skies, and done whatever they could in the way of persecution against all who condemned it. . . . If the Romish establishment was not framed for the production of good, but was an exquisitely fashioned instrument for the production of evil, is it not certain that the English establishment, which consists of the same integrant parts, must very closely resemble it in its tendencies? ("The Church," 259–60, emphasis added)

In this pronouncement, one hears the voice not only of the Calvinist preacher but of the philosophe as well. James Mill and Bentham, like the philosophes they regarded as their predecessors, ultimately came to conceive of all traditional religion as mere superstition based on what Bentham called "imaginary fictions." John Mill was fully in accord with such views. He always regarded the defenders of traditional theology, especially as institutionalized in the Church of England, as the last crumbling pillar of the ancien régime.[29] One of his missions was to destroy their influence. This, he believed, was necessary to eradicate the "poisonous root"[30] of theology to which the remnants of the old political and social order clung and which prevented the growth of the superior and "purely human" morality he himself aimed to establish (*OL*, 51).

In the passionate rhetoric of John Mill's *On Liberty*, in its demand for the "living belief" only freedom of thought can allow, one hears again the voice of James Mill. The Anglican clergy, thundered James Mill, do nothing to "rais[e] the moral and intellectual character of the people." Their so-called worship is mere ceremony, their services "a merely mechanical operation, in which the mind has little concern." That is, Anglican religious practice fosters what John Mill would later call the "dead beliefs" of Christianity. Moreover, it not only promotes hypocrisy and dissembling, but also turns devotees into liars.

> [T]he repetition of creeds, . . . if it is not . . . purely ceremonial, . . . is something far worse: it is a forced declaration of belief—in other words, an instrument for generating the worst habit which can be implanted in the human breast—the habit of saying the thing which is not—the habit of affirming as a matter of fact, that which is not a matter of fact—the habit of affirming that a man is conscious of a state of mind, when he is not conscious of it. This is to poison morality in the very fountain of life. The fine feeling of moral obligation is gone in a mind wherein the habit of insincerity is engendered: nay, more—every man who is possessed of that fatal habit possesses an instrument for the perpetration of every other crime. Mendacity is the pander to the breach of every obligation. ("The Church," 260–61)

In James Mill's view, the Church of England was a den of vipers, deliberately keeping the populace in ignorance in order to maintain its own power. The Anglican clergy hated truth and stupefied the people with pointless ritual and "vapid commonplaces." The clergy were dull, lifeless, insipid: "[A]ll of them [are] defective, or rather utterly worthless, in moral teaching." They were also conniving and power-hungry. Indeed, they self-servingly distorted the image of God: "[P]riests, for their own ends, have perverted men's notions of the Divine character." They purposefully conveyed immoral conceptions of God—the "Omnipotent Author of Hell" (*Auto*, 51)—undermining the "idea of the Divine Being, as a being of perfect wisdom and goodness." They encouraged the "unmeaning ceremony" of prayer, which is a slur on the Divine Perfection:

> [Prayer conveys] the idea of a being very imperfect in both . . . wisdom and goodness. . . . [P]erpetually to be asking God for things which we want, . . .

implies the belief that God is imperfect both in wisdom and goodness. Telling God unceasingly of our wants, implies that he needs to be told of them—otherwise it is an unmeaning ceremony. Asking Him continually to do things for us, implies our belief that otherwise he would not do them for us; in other words, our belief, either that God will not do what is right, if he be not begged and entreated to do so—or that, by being begged and entreated, he can be induced to do what is wrong. ("The Church," 262–70)

Moreover, prayer was by no means enjoined by Jesus, but is rather the product of the "interested interpretation of priests." "Nothing can be clearer than [that Jesus himself] reprobated . . . all prayer . . . but secret prayer, and even that is not recommended." Indeed, Jesus said, "Your Father knoweth what things ye have need of, before ye ask him." One suspects that it is the dependency implied in prayer that made it anathema to such a self-made man as James Mill.

Finally, James Mill regarded the Anglican clergy as hatemongers, castigating dissenters as evildoers and causing division over inconsequential matters involving mere dogma and ceremony. Their prohibition of the questioning of religious dogma aimed to "prostrat[e] the understanding and the will," which, indeed, is "one of the desiderata . . . to the Church of England." All of this, pronounced Mill, is to "renounce the good of mankind as the grand principle of action, the main point of obedience to the will of God."[31] ("The Church," 262–65).

It is difficult to trace James Mill's influence on his son's religious views through their published writings because we cannot be sure the views expressed in those writings represent the Mills' true beliefs. We have alluded to the Mills' policy of concealment with respect to their religious views. As John Mill put it, his father's unconventional opinions on religion did have "one bad consequence deserving notice. In giving me an opinion contrary to that of the world my father thought it necessary to give it as one which could not prudently be avowed to the world" (*Auto*, 52). We will return to the issue of Mill's silence on religion, as well as the significance of this self-censorship for an evaluation of his published writings, in following chapters. For now, our interest is in highlighting the rhetorical strategies pursued by both father and son. We know that James Mill abandoned the Christian faith sometime around 1810. Yet in "The Church, and Its Reform" (published in 1835, a year before his death) he often speaks like a true believer. For instance, he refers to the "example of our Saviour." He describes the benefits that a "truly Christian pastor," properly trained in the "art of doing good," can bring to his parishioners. He appeals to God, the "author of all good, and the perfection of wisdom and benevolence," against the evildoing of His representatives who prohibit the questioning of religious dogma and the search for evidence to support religious truth: "Oh God! with what perseverance and zeal has this representation of thy Divine nature been maintained, by men who, with the same breath, and therefore in the spirit of base adulation, were calling thee the God of truth." John Mill would make similar, if less histrionic, appeals to a Christian belief he himself did not hold. Both the Mills appear to have developed the very "habit of insincerity" that the father so forcefully condemns in his essay. Neither was above the merely rhetorical employment of religious symbols and beliefs if such could usefully serve their overriding purpose of moral and political reform ("The Church," 271–88).

The Sin of Believing without Evidence

According to the gospel of James Mill, the greatest of all sins was "belief without evidence."[32] As he put it, "The habit of neglect of evidence . . . is the habit of disregarding the good and evil of our fellow-creatures. It is the habit of hard-heartedness and cruelty, on the largest scale, and rooted in the deepest part of the mind . . . of what is vicious and degraded in human character."[33]

The urgent demand for "evidence" was bound up with the Mills' mutual hostility to religious dogma. As James Mill wrote,

> The insistence of subscribing to religious dogma as a test of faith . . .attach[es] undue importance to uniformity of belief on points on which it is not necessary. [It] does nothing but create . . . a habit of forcing a belief; that is, of dealing dishonestly with [one's] own convictions. To hold out rewards for believing one way, punishment for believing another way, is to hold out inducements to resist the force of evidence. . . . [Forcing people to subscribe to religious dogma] is a mode of attaching belief to any opinions, however unfounded; and as soon as a man is thoroughly broken in to this mental habit, not only is the power of sound judgment destroyed within him, but the moral character does not escape uninjured. The man in whose breast this habit is created, never sees anything in an opinion, but whether it is agreeable to his interest or not. Whether it is founded on evidence or not, he has been trained to neglect. Truth or falsehood in matters of opinion is no longer with him the first consideration.
> *This is nearly the most immoral state of mind which can have existence in a human being.* . . . No other cause of criminal actions is of equal potency of this. (emphasis added)

To believe without evidence is not only unnecessary, dishonest, base, a sign of mental weakness and poor judgment, but, says James Mill, it is to lie.

[Inculcating religious dogma is identical to] suborning belief, using means to make it exist independently of evidence; that is, to make men hold opinions without seeing that they are true—in other words, to affirm that they know to be true what they do not know to be true; that is, if we may give to the act its proper name—to lie.

. . . [God himself] approve[s] in his rational creatures the love of truth. But the love of truth leads a man to search for evidence, and to place his belief on that side, whatsoever it be, on which the evidence appears to him to preponderate. . . . [Thus] the atrocity of giving men inducements to make a belief, which they have not derived from evidence.[34] ("The Church," 280–81)

As may be expected, such teaching engendered in John Mill an intense anxiety concerning the evidentiary basis of belief. With respect to religion, such anxiety issued in his preoccupation with scientific "proof" and "evidences" for the existence of God. God, he would maintain, must be regarded as a hypothesis. As such, the question of God's existence is subject to investigation by the same methods—the canons of induction that Mill formulated in *A System of Logic* (1843)—by which all phenomena are investigated. James Mill's teachings on the immorality of believing without evidence should be kept in mind as we examine Mill's "scientific" investigation of God's existence in later chapters.

On a State Religion

James Mill concludes "The Church, and Its Reform" by presenting his own model of a thoroughly reformed "State religion." This model highlights the collapse of the differentiation between the spiritual and temporal dimensions of existence that is such a prominent feature of the Benthamite view of religion. In the hands of the Benthamites, as in those of the French social or political religionists who were their guides and inspiration, religion becomes a tool of politics.[35]

The first attribute of James Mill's state religion is that such a religion would be universal:

[It would be a] church without dogmas and ceremonies. It would be truly a Catholic church. Its ministers would be ministers of good, in the highest of all senses of the word, to men of all religious denominations. All would share in the religious services of such a church, and all would share in the blessings which would result from them. This is the true idea of a State religion; and there is no other. It ought to be stripped of all which is separating; of all that divides men from one another; and to present a point whereon, in the true spirit of reverence to the perfect being, and love to one another, they may all unite. . . . [This religion] ought to be so contrived as to embrace, if it were possible, the whole population.

Second, the State religion would be administered by the government, which would be responsible for education, understood to involve the techniques of associationist psychology and oriented toward the realization of utilitarian moral ends.

> Ministers of Public Instruction . . . would be responsible for overseeing the provision of instruction, both religious and secular, within the local parishes. . . . [The local priests would be charged with] mak[ing] their people more virtuous and more happy . . . by assiduous[ly] endeavour[ing] to make all the impressions on the minds of their parishioners which conduce to good conduct; not merely negative, in abstaining from ill; but positive, in doing all the good to one another which the means put in their power enable them to do. ("The Church," 275–77, 288–89)

Incentives would be created to motivate the local clergy to be "useful," to help them achieve their assigned goals. For instance, "annual premiums [could be given] . . . to those ministers in whose parishes certain favourable results were manifested—in whose parishes there was the smallest number of crimes committed within the year—in whose parishes there was the smallest number of law-suits, . . . paupers, [and] . . . uneducated children" ("The Church," 289). James Mill also recommended communal meals on the ancient and early-Christian models to encourage "feelings of brotherly love." "Music and dancing, if regulated," might also afford "an important resource" for the attainment of this end. Finally, the clergy should arrange for Sunday lectures on various secular subjects—mechanics, chemistry, botany, health maintenance, and political and economic education ("The Church," 279, 293).

Mill's model, of course, owes much to Plato; both Mills idealized the ancient commonwealths as the very height of virtuous existence. It is probably unnecessary to note the relative disinterest in God.

II: The Influence of Jeremy Bentham

No monk ever adhered with more ascetic severity to the discipline of a monastery than did these Benthamites to the one purpose of their lives . . . the reform of the world.
                              —*Henry Reeve, "Autobiography of John Stuart Mill"*

John Mill's account of his mental history, as suggested, is marked by a curious lack of insight into the formative influences that shaped his mature religious convictions. One of the more dramatic indications of this lack of self-knowledge is Mill's revealing account of his "conversion" to Benthamism, which occurred in 1821 when he was almost sixteen years old. Mill tells us that his reading of the *Traités de legislation civile et pénale* (1802), Étienne Dumont's translation of Jeremy Bentham's treatise,[36] was nothing less than "an epoch in [his] life; one of the turning points in [his] mental history" (*Auto*, 66). This itself is somewhat surprising. Mill had of course been "trained as a disciple and prophet" of Benthamism—indeed, as a "utilitarian messiah"—almost since birth and this in the most rigorous and forbidding manner.[37] Yet Mill tells us:

> When I laid down the last volume of the *Traité*, I had become a different being. The "principle of utility" understood as Bentham understood it, and applied in the manner in which he applied it through these three volumes, fell exactly into its place as the keystone which held together the detached and fragmentary component parts of my knowledge and beliefs. It gave unity to my conceptions of things. I now had opinions; a creed, a doctrine, a philosophy; in one among the best senses of the word, a religion; the inculcation and diffusion of which could be made the principal outward purpose of a life.[38] And I had a grand conception laid before me of changes to be effected in the condition of mankind through that doctrine. (*Auto*, 68)

There can be no doubt that Mill channeled what are self-evidently, and indeed self-avowedly, religious aspirations into the realization of ideals exclusively temporal—the "improvement of mankind" through moral and political reform. The result was the investment of such immanent reform with religious—ultimate and salvific—significance. Mill's religious valorization of worldly "improvement" was, however, more or less a byproduct of his overarching end. As we have seen, Mill's ultimate aims were to replace theological morality with a "purely human" morality and to reorient traditional religious aspirations away from a transcendent God and toward an intramundane substitute—what Comte would call the Great Being of Humanity. This two-pronged end entailed a two-pronged strategy. First, theological morality was to be replaced by the nontheological utilitarianism that Mill adopted, with revisions, from Bentham. Second, spiritual aspirations were to be directed away from otherworldly concerns by the social establishment of the Religion of Humanity that Mill adopted, again with revisions, from Comte. Mill pursued these related aims with a single-minded tenacity from the time of his "conversion" to Benthamism in 1821 until his death. Indeed, as this work seeks to show, Mill's endeavor to substitute a purely human for a theological orientation was one of the governing purposes of his public career.

The *Autobiography* provides insight not only into the transformative experience Mill underwent in response to his reading of Bentham, but into the social and political significance it held for him as well. The vision inspired in the young Mill by Bentham's *Traités*, he says, was of a "vista of improvement . . . sufficiently large and brilliant to light up my life, as well as to give a definite shape to my aspirations." It was a vision of a world perfected through the widespread embrace of the "opinions" and "laws" expounded in Bentham's treatise[39] (*Auto*, 69).

What was it in Bentham's philosophy that had the power to strike Mill with the force of revelation? Mill explains:

> [I recognized that my] previous education had been, in a certain sense, already a course of Benthamism. The Benthamic standard of "the greatest happiness" was that which I had always been taught to apply. . . . Yet in the first pages of Bentham it burst upon me with all the force of novelty. What thus impressed me was the chapter in which Bentham passed judgment on the common modes of reasoning in morals and legislation, deduced from phrases like "law of nature," "right reason," "the moral sense," "natural rectitude," and the like, and characterized them as dogmatism in disguise imposing its sentiments upon others under cover of sounding expression which convey no reason for the sentiment, but set up the sentiment as its own reason. It had not struck me before, that Bentham's principle put an end to all this. *The feeling rushed upon me, that all previous moralists were superseded, and that here indeed was the commencement of a new era in thought.* (*Auto*, 67, emphasis added)

The conventional interpretation of this passage is that Mill was inspired by the realization that Bentham's principle of utility would permit the achievement of "rational objectivity" in moral theory and practice.[40] It is true that Mill, like Bentham, always regarded traditional morality, as well as its expression in natural and common law, as nothing but subjective preference in objective guise. Mill, like Bentham, found custom, prejudice, habit, and legal and moral traditions little more than "nonsense on stilts." Nor is there any doubt that both thinkers regarded the principle of utility as the sole objective moral or legal standard available or even conceivable. They certainly regarded the utilitarian enterprise as the introduction of rationality into the morass of subjective feelings that posed as moral law and were embodied in legislation.

This acknowledged, however, their self-interpretation should not be taken at face value. The principle of utility held far more significance for Bentham and, even more, for Mill than the introduction of an objective standard. Both law and morality would henceforth be entirely man-made, purified of theological and metaphysical superstitions and other alleged fictions. Perhaps most important, henceforth man and not God would be seen as "the ultimate source of moral obligations" (*Util*, 427). In short, the principle of utility (as interpreted by the utilitarian Moralist and Legislator) was intended by both Bentham and Mill to play the role in human existence heretofore played by God. For Bentham, "utility" replaced God in his role of Guarantor of social harmony and Administer of ultimate justice. In the hands of Mill, who, moreover, was mainly responsible for extending the principle of utility to the field of morals, utility became nothing less than "the ultimate source of moral obligations"—a source traditionally apprehended in the West as a transcendent God. Before embarking on an exploration of Mill's religious thought, then, it is essential to examine certain critical aspects of Benthamite utilitarianism—Mill's first "religion."

The Nontheological Utilitarianism of Jeremy Bentham

The notion that moral and political rules possess utility in some sense had of course been espoused by various thinkers prior to Bentham. Hume and Burke, for instance, suggested that inherited rules serve a function in preserving order and well-being in human society. As John Plamenatz puts it, their idea, explicit or implicit, was "that an institution's having lasted a long time is itself a proof of its utility, of its conduciveness to human happiness."[41] Thus, in their hands, prescription and prejudice assume a functionalist or utilitarian flavor. Although Bentham appealed to Hume as a precursor of his view that "the foundations of all *virtue* are laid in *utility*," Bentham took up the principle of utility in a far more comprehensive sense than Hume. It became in his hands a substantive ethical and legal theory, indeed, the "test and measure of all virtue," the ultimate principle from which both laws and morals, as well as the obligation to obey them, are derived.[42]

Utilitarianism as a formal ethical doctrine did not, however, originate with Bentham. Until well into the 1830s, the principal representative of the utilitarian outlook in England was not Bentham but William Paley, the conservative Anglican divine and Bentham's acknowledged rival. Paley and Bentham's utilitarianisms were in many respects identical. Both thinkers posited the "greatest happiness for the greatest number" as the ultimate end of moral action.[43] Both identified the good with the pleasant or the beneficial, the "beneficial" meaning that which is productive of happiness, and "happiness" meaning the excess of pleasure over pain. Finally, both believed that all pleasures are essentially alike, differing only in their degree of intensity and their duration.

There was, however, one all-important difference between the philosophies of the two thinkers, a difference, moreover, that defines the essence of Benthamite utilitarianism. Paley's utilitarianism depended for its coherence on the conventional Christian conception of a just God who serves as both Guarantor of order and Administer of ultimate or posthumous justice. It is precisely this conception that Bentham, and later John Mill, was at pains to undermine. What Bentham did, in effect, was to remove the very keystone of Christian utilitarianism—the assurance of divine or posthumous justice. The result was what Ernest Albee calls Bentham's "non-theological utilitarianism."[44] It is essential to grasp the significance of Bentham's move in order to grasp the nature of the utilitarian movement that was spearheaded and carried forth by the Mills.

To do so, it is necessary to take at least a cursory view of Paley's Christian utilitarianism. For Paley, the moral obligation to seek the greatest happiness for the greatest number is binding because it is required by the will of God. Virtue, he said, consists in "the doing of good to mankind, in obedience to the will of God, and for the sake of everlasting happiness."[45] As Plamenatz explains, there was for Paley only one "true utilitarian" in existence—God—for he alone desires the greatest happiness for all men for its own sake. Everyone else has more or less mixed motives. For although God has so contrived matters that his creatures do desire not only their own but the general happiness, they do so both because God has commanded this as a means to their personal salvation and because they are impelled to it by a "violent motive"—the fear of posthumous punishment.[46]

What is significant about Bentham's utilitarianism, then, is not his elevation of the greatest happiness principle to an ethical ultimate; this, indeed, had become something of a commonplace by his time. Various eighteenth-century Christian moralists, of whom Paley was the most influential, had already espoused a utilitarian ethic, one, however, essentially grounded in Christian theology. As James Crimmins writes,

> [I]t is still little appreciated that, for the most part, it was the religious version of the doctrine of utility which dominated English moral thought in the age before Bentham. Exponents of this theological variant, influenced by Locke's ethics with its deference to revelation, included George Berkeley, John Gay, John Brown, Abraham Tucker, and Edmund Law, among others. Even into the early decades of the nineteenth century it was the Cambridge Divine William Paley (1743–1805) who was most often toasted as the standard-bearer of the general doctrine, not Bentham.[47]

Such Christian utilitarians acknowledged self-interest as an important motivator of human action and regarded the pleasurable or painful consequences of any action as, in some sense, the test of right and wrong. But traditional English utilitarianism had developed within a largely Christian context, and the expectation of posthumous rewards and punishments was assumed to figure prominently in the utilitarian calculus of self-interested actors. Bentham's chief significance is not his promotion of utilitarianism per se but that he tore utilitarianism from its transcendent context. As we have seen, his purpose was to establish an utterly secular, nontheological, strictly human ethic to replace the theologically based ethic he regarded as fiction and nonsense. As a result of his efforts, and even more those of his disciples the Mills, utility became the "cornerstone of [the] new secular philosophy in the eighteenth and early part of the nineteenth centuries."[48]

Bentham and Paley engaged in a self-conscious rivalry for the ear of their contemporaries. Paley's *Principles of Moral and Political Philosophy* appeared, to great acclaim, in 1785. Bentham feigned indifference but delayed publication of his own work, *Introduction to the Principles of Morals and Legislation,* until 1789 when the interest sparked by Paley's work had somewhat subsided. At times Bentham seemed to regard Paley as an ally in the struggle to gain the acceptance of utility as the criterion of morals and legislative policy. At other times he regarded him as an enemy or at least as a "false brother," and this for Paley's conservative tendencies not only in religion but also in politics and law. At such times Bentham would castigate Paley as "an apologist for the status quo, a founding member (along with William Blackstone) of the 'everything-as-it-should-be-school.'"[49]

Paley's political conservatism was bad enough, but even worse was his religious orthodoxy and his defense of the Church of England.[50] Bentham was sometimes willing to regard Paley as one of his precursors, one who had discerned the fundamental motivations of human beings and learned to associate pleasures and pains with the goal of general happiness. In Bentham's view, however, Paley had failed to get it quite right and this because of the religious dimension of his thought. Bentham insisted that Paley's Christian assumptions were not and could not be justified by the strict standards of utility. And this, let us repeat—their radical divergence on religion—is what marks the crucial difference between the two utilitarianisms and isolates the essence of Benthamite utilitarianism. As Crimmins puts it, in Paley's thought it is "the basically theological constructs of . . . ethics which remain dominant," while Bentham's object is to remove such constructs from ethical considerations. And, Crimmins adds, it is this divide—between the theological and nontheological orientation of the two utilitarianisms—that provides the "substance of the contrast" between Paley's and Bentham's doctrines of utility.[51]

John Stuart Mill's utilitarianism is well known. Less widely understood is the nature of that doctrine as he inherited it from Bentham, that is, its self-consciously and essentially antitheological thrust. This is what must be grasped for a proper understanding not only of Mill's utilitarianism but also of his thought in general and his religious thought in particular. All were governed, if not determined, by an identical and profound antitheological intent. We have seen that Bentham's treatise on morals and law affected the young Mill with the force of a religious conversion. The reason for this, one may suggest, was not the treatise's promise of "rational objectivity" or even its satisfaction of Mill's "strong relish for . . . classification," as Mill himself suggests[52] (*Auto,* 67). What seems to have struck Mill with the force of a conversion was the possibility of replacing what he called theological morality with a purely human counterpart. It was *this* possibility, surely, that offered him the vision of a "new era" in morals, one, that is, radically divorced from traditional theological constraints and radically reoriented toward the intramundane dimension of existence. Moreover, it was this same possibility that would later draw Mill to the very home of radical immanentism—to France and to Auguste Comte. Mill's aim was precisely the aim of Bentham and of Comte—to eviscerate the traditional conception of a transcendent God and all that such a conception implies for ethics, politics, and personal and social life. As said, the essence of Bentham's "new religion" of utilitarianism was its virulent antitheological intent. Mill would undergo a similar, and perhaps even more dramatic, "conversion" experience under the influence of Comte, whose positivist religion had a similar impetus. This is the aspect of Benthamite utilitarianism and Comtean positivism—their mutual antitheological intent—that must be grasped in order to comprehend Mill's contribution to the development of Anglo-American philosophy and politics.

Bentham's Analysis

That Mill's "conversion" to Benthamism was principally due to the latter's antitheological immanentism is also indicated by the second of Bentham's works that profoundly influenced Mill's developing outlook. "[O]ne of the books which . . . produced the greatest effect upon me," he tells us, was the *Analysis of the Influence of Natural Religion on the Temporal Happiness of Mankind,* which the sixteen-year-old Mill read at the direction of his father (*Auto,* 71). This work, which was published under the pseudonym Philip Beauchamp, was actually composed by the lifelong Benthamite George Grote, based upon Bentham's unpublished manuscripts.

The main theme of the *Analysis* is quintessentially Benthamite: Religious belief, contrary to conventional supposition, is not useful to society.

John Mill's own argument against the social usefulness of religion in "Utility of Religion" (written between 1850 and 1858) is essentially an elaboration of this work. Not only the structure but much of the substance of Mill's essay is taken directly from the earlier publication.

The acknowledgment of the social utility of religion had become a commonplace by the time the *Analysis* appeared in 1822. Both heterodox and orthodox thinkers agreed that religion, however true or false, is essential to the maintenance of morality and thus of social and political order. Religious skeptics had long employed this argument for the utility of religion as an implicit attack on the truth of Christianity; after all, as Mill would point out in "Utility of Religion," if a doctrine is true, the question of its utility is moot. On the other hand, the argument for the social utility of religion had assumed increasing significance among orthodox Christians in the wake of the growing religious skepticism that followed the French Revolution. This, then, is the context that dictated Bentham and Grote's, and later Mill's, strategy in their efforts to undermine traditional Christian belief. The overthrow of inherited religious views required the storming of one of the last bastions of orthodoxy—the claim for the social utility of its beliefs.

The *Analysis,* then, aimed to undermine the conventional belief in the social utility of traditional religion. A second and related aim was to undermine the traditional Christian belief in and expectation of divine justice—the notion of man's ultimate accountability to God. Because the cultural and legal context of the times prohibited the direct expression of anti-Christian opinions, Bentham and his disciples could pursue their antitheological aims only indirectly.[53] Unable to openly attack the Christian notion of a final judgment (or, in utilitarian jargon, the "posthumous religious sanction"), they instead denied its efficacy in regulating human conduct. This strategy involved the evaluation of traditional religious belief by strict utilitarian criteria.[54] The aim was to determine whether or not such belief—for instance, the belief in a final judgment—was "useful," that is, whether it contributed to "happiness in the present life." As Bentham/Grote put it, the object of the *Analysis* was "to ascertain, whether the belief of posthumous pains and pleasure, then to be administered by an omnipotent Being is useful to mankind—that is, productive of happiness or misery in the present life . . . [and whether] religion, considered with reference to the present life, is not beneficial but pernicious, not augmentative but destructive of human happiness" (*Analysis,* 3).

The *Analysis* begins by stacking the deck in favor of the utilitarian position by defining religion in utilitarian terms: Religion is the "belief in the existence of an almighty Being, by whom pains and pleasures will be dispensed to mankind, during an infinite and future state of existence." The *Analysis* argues that religion, and especially the expectation of divine justice, creates a balance of pain over pleasure and is thus, by utilitarian criteria, an obvious disutility to humanity. The reasoning is as follows: Man's lack of knowledge of the hereafter does not permit him to determine the limits of pain and pleasure in the afterlife. This lack of knowledge inevitably generates fear, for fear is the "never failing companion and offspring of ignorance." Fear produces pain, and pain is always a stronger sensation than pleasure. Thus the expectation of a posthumous existence must create a net balance of pain. The afterlife will be conceived as a state of suffering rather than of enjoyment. Religion is therefore not conducive to earthly happiness: "[N]atural religion will to the majority of its believers materially aggravate the disquietude occasioned by the prospect of death" (*Analysis*, 3–8). If utilitarianism is an adequate guide to human conduct, it is suggested, the wise will abandon religious belief posthaste.

The Posthumous Sanction

We have seen that Bentham's nontheological utilitarianism was developed in conscious opposition to the theological utilitarianism of Paley. Paley's Christian utilitarianism involved certain orthodox assumptions: It is God's will that all men be happy, all men should contribute to the fulfillment of God's will, and all men have the ability to know what contributes to that end. Finally, and most important for our study of Bentham and Mill, there is the assumption that all men possess an immortal soul and will be judged on a future day of reckoning, when good will be rewarded and evil punished.

As Crimmins explains, the latter element was central to Paley's moral thought and decisive for his utilitarian ethics. For it was the notion of a final judgment beyond time and space that reconciled the apparent conflict between self-interest (seeking one's own good) and the general interest (seeking the good of others), thus providing a solution to what had been one of the chief problems of eighteenth-century ethics. Without such a judgment acting as a restraint on personal self-interest, there was no guarantee of harmony between self-interest and the general interest, an essential assumption of utilitarian philosophy. As Crimmins explains the Christian utilitarian position:

> The harmony between the private interests of the individual and those of his associates is based on the necessity that each man take into account in all his thoughts and deeds his own eternal happiness. And the teachings of Christ dictate that each individual is responsible not only for his own spir-

itual well being, but (toward this end) also for the temporal well being of those about him. . . . To "be good" means that we actively pursue the happiness of others whenever it is within our power, for only by so doing can we secure our own happiness in the most encompassing sense of this term: eternal happiness.[55]

Moreover, the conception of a final judgment provided Paley's ethics with a moral sanction readily apprehended by his readers. Indeed, as we have seen, the notion of a final judgment was the linchpin of Christian utilitarianism. For this reason, it became a chief target of the apostles of nontheological utilitarianism.

Bentham was of course well aware of the appeal of the Christian utilitarian view to his contemporaries. The strategy he adopted was to oppose it on both metaphysical and moral grounds. With respect to metaphysics, Crimmins explains, "[Bentham's m]aterialism and nominalism dictated that the ideas of the soul, of a future state, and of an allseeing omnipotent God were fictions irreducible to 'real' entities. . . . [His] descriptive theory of language, with its attendant classificatory and paraphrastic techniques, . . . [aimed to show] that these ideas, lacking physical referents, could not be made intelligible to the human understanding."[56] Bentham's second, related, strategy would be of greater importance to the development of Mill's approach. The aim was to show that the very notion of behavior regulated by the prospect of posthumous pleasures and pains was immoral. Not only was such a preoccupation base and servile but, worse yet, it caused people to be selfishly concerned merely with their own personal salvation and not with the good of the whole.

The role played by the posthumous sanction in Christian utilitarianism has been emphasized because it is key to understanding why this aspect of Christian belief was singled out for attack by the Benthamites. Bentham and the Mills insisted strenuously and repeatedly that the posthumous rewards and punishments that constituted divine justice were both impotent to regulate human behavior and morally pernicious, appealing to the selfish desire for mere personal salvation. As James Mill explained:

What would be thought of a legislator, who should ordain, that the punishment of murder and theft should not take place till twenty years, or so, after the commission of the crime; and that, for the distance of the time, compensation should be made in the severity of the punishment?

[Legitimate] punishment is employed by virtuous men for the prevention of hurtful actions. But what is the use of punishment when the time of action is gone by, and when the doom of the wretched victim is fixed for ever? . . . It is said that the apprehension of [God's] punishments is a restraint on men during their lives. But to make this allegation is only another mode of

ascribing imperfection, both intellectual and moral, to the Supreme Being. . . . It is a certain and undisputed principle, that proximity of punishment is necessary to its efficiency. ("The Church," 268)

No other article of the Benthamite faith was more vigorously asserted
than the inefficacy and immorality of the "religious sanction." Indeed,
said Bentham, one can gauge the moral health of a community by the extent of its belief in man's ultimate accountability to God. When the
posthumous religious sanction was "the sole antidote depended on for
the care of every moral ill, morality was [then] at its lowest ebb: and as
morality improves, . . . [it] in proportion sinks to neglect."[57]

Let us return to Mill's claim that Bentham's attack on the utility of religious belief in the *Analysis* "produced the greatest effect upon me." What
seems to have affected Mill so profoundly is the denial of the efficacy of
religious sanctions in general and of the posthumous religious sanction in
particular. Mill learned from Bentham that the principal argument for the
utility of religious belief—that such belief was essential to maintain
morality and thus social order—was misconceived. Bentham maintained,
on the contrary, that the apparent efficacy of religion in encouraging
morality was in truth merely a result of its beliefs and maxims being inculcated from childhood, impressed upon the growing mind with all the
force and power of parental and religious authority. The *Analysis* thereby
provided Mill with what would become one of his leading principles—
that *any* system of ideas, rules, and values, if inculcated from childhood
by authority, could have the same power over the human mind and behavior that traditional religious beliefs and practices had heretofore
achieved. Mill's views in this regard will be discussed in detail in Chapter 3. For now, we will note that Mill, following the argument of the *Analysis*, would always insist that Public Opinion, shaped by the other triumvirate powers of Education and Law, is the actual power behind the
merely apparent efficacy of religion in regulating human conduct.[58] By
denying the governing efficacy of the religious sanction and relocating it
in public opinion, Mill could claim that *any* system of opinion, enforced
"from infancy" (*Util*, 436) and at the behest of authority, could achieve the
governing control of human behavior heretofore erroneously ascribed to
religion. Such a view permitted Mill to assuage the fears of those wavering believers, increasingly common in his day, who clung to religion because they feared its wholehearted rejection would undermine the foundations of morality. Mill employed Bentham's argument to persuade such
readers that the abandonment of Christianity would not weaken the nec-

essary ground of social and political order because religious belief, in fact, had never been the effective governing force of personal or social conduct.

The second aspect of the *Analysis* that affected Mill was its repudiation of the efficacy of the posthumous religious sanction. This conception would play a central role in Mill's own religious thought and aspirations and was crucial to his plan to establish a new intramundane religion. The Benthamite / Millian attack on the posthumous sanction was also an indirect attack on the notion of divine justice. In order to establish a purely human morality, it was essential to eviscerate the traditional sense of accountability to a transcendent God. Lingering otherworldly allegiance would undermine the authority and power of the human sanction the Benthamites offered in place of the allegedly ineffective and immoral religious sanction. It would also prevent a full-bodied commitment to the new Religion of Humanity that Mill intended as a replacement for Christianity. In short, the denial of the efficacy and morality of the posthumous sanction was central to Mill's religious goals. Theodore Fantl observes that "it is this rejection of the utility of the religious sanction that marks the really far-reaching change brought about in the conventional utilitarian calculus by Bentham and carried on by the Mills."[59]

The Human Legislator and Moralist

It is appropriate to close this account of the Benthamite attack on transcendent justice by highlighting Bentham's proposed replacement for the religious sanction—Legislation. In Christian utilitarianism, God was the Guarantor of harmony between individual self-interest and the general interest. Benthamism removed this guarantee and replaced it with the conscious reconciliation of particular and general interest through the human construction of "law" (legislation). The task of the utilitarian Legislator, then, is to devise the rules that will realize the social harmony formerly realized by an orientation toward a transcendent God. The all-knowing and godlike Legislator ensures public happiness under the non-theological utilitarian dispensation, therein replacing the God of the Christian dispensation. Fear of the Legislator's penal sanctions replaces the allegedly immoral and selfish fear of a transcendent God. It is worth emphasizing in this context that, despite their strident condemnation of the posthumous *religious* sanction for its immorality and promotion of selfishness, none of the utilitarians condemned behavior regulated by fear of the *human* sanction as selfish or immoral. Indeed, quite to the contrary, fear of the penalties imposed by either the penal sanction (law) or the social sanction (public opinion) was regarded as central to the shaping of human conduct in accord with the new utilitarian ethos. John Mill included the fear of the "internal sanction" of a socialized conscience among the means by which behavior would be shaped in accord with the new humanitarian social ideals. Again, the actual if implicit target of the Benthamites was the conception of divine justice administered by a transcendent God—not behavior shaped by "inducements," by the anticipation of rewards and punishments per se. Indeed, the psychological theory advanced by the Mills was based precisely on "giving men inducements." The associationist psychology that underlies Benthamite and Millian utilitarianism is roughly equivalent to what today is called Skinnerian behavioral conditioning.[60] Behavior was to be shaped by a system of human rewards and punishments whose aim was to create the proper "associations" between virtuous behavior and pleasure and vicious behavior and pain. The principal motivation was fear of punishment, as the sensation of pain was regarded as vastly more efficacious in shaping behavior than that of pleasure.[61] In order to achieve the shaping of behavior in line with the human sanctions proposed by the utilitarian Educator and Legislator, the inconvenient supernatural inducements held out by the Christian God had to be eliminated.

Bentham's chief concern was the application of the principle of utility to legislation. As Crimmins observes, the "probing of the deficiencies of religion as an agency of social welfare . . . was integral to [Bentham's] endeavour . . . to establish the primacy of legislative science as a means to advance the happiness of the greatest number."[62] In Bentham's scheme of things, the utilitarian Legislator becomes the human replacement for God. John Mill, as we have seen, extended Bentham's nontheological utilitarianism into the area of moral philosophy. Accordingly, Mill enacts a similar transfer of authority from a transcendent God to a human equivalent; he, more explicitly than Bentham, grants such authority to the human Moralist. Indeed, Mill's proposals are more radical than Bentham's—Mill would have the "principle of utility" honored not only as the guiding principle of legislation but as "the ultimate source of moral obligations." There can of course be nothing beyond an ultimate source. In Mill's hands, the principle of utility, interpreted in line with the preconceptions and ends of the utilitarian Moralist, becomes functionally equivalent to God. We will return to this issue in the examination of Mill's *Utilitarianism* in Chapter 7.

The Benthamite Religion

Ethical and social thought in the West is generally regarded as having undergone a gradual process of secularization throughout the eighteenth and nineteenth centuries. The term *secularization*, however, is often employed carelessly, and, as Jacob Viner observes, "is liable to deceive." Viner defines secularization as a "lessening of the influence . . . of ecclesiastical authority and traditional church creeds, and a shifting of weight from dogma and revelation and other-worldliness to reason and sentiment and considerations of temporal welfare."[63] By such a definition, Benthamism must certainly be regarded as an important aspect of the secularization process. Viner's definition, however, is itself somewhat misleading, at least with respect to Benthamism. For the notion that secularization represents a "lessening" of the influence of religious authority, creeds, and the like fails to capture the essence of secular or nontheological utilitarianism. Bentham and his disciples were not mere passive carriers of a more or less autonomous process of social change but, on the contrary, energetic and indeed militant activists determined to undermine, if not eradicate, the traditional theological orientation of the West and the social and political order it sustained. The following passage from John Mill's diary conveys the urgency with which he went about his "business" of "regenerati[ng] the world":

> In a militant age [such as his own], when those who have thoughts and feelings to impress on the world have a great deal of hard work to do, and very little time to do it in, and those who are to be impressed need to be told in the most direct and plainest way possible what those who address them are driving at—otherwise they will not listen—it is foppery to waste time in studying beauty of form in the conveyance of a meaning. . . . The regeneration of the world in its present stage is a matter of business, and it would be as rational to keep accounts or write invoices in verse as to attempt to do the work of human improvement in it.[64]

Bentham's "declared aim," in the words of Crimmins, was to "extirpat[e] religious beliefs, even the idea of religion itself from the minds of men."[65] As Leslie Stephen observed, "[T]he utilitarians clearly recognized [that] Utilitarianism . . . logically implied the rejection of all theology."[66] Nevertheless, the Benthamites not only infused their allegedly secular ethics with a quasi-religious spirit but, as Bentham himself acknowledged, also intended their philosophy as a "new religion," a this-worldly substitute for the otherworldly religion they regarded as superstitious nonsense. As Bentham wrote to a friend in 1801, "A new religion would be an odd sort of thing without a name—[I] propose . . . Utilitarianism."[67] John Mill would go even further in this direction. He bent his prodigious efforts and talents, inspired by all the moral fervor of his essentially religious nature, toward the social establishment of his new "religion without a God" (*ACP*, 133). The aim was to capture the spiritual energy traditionally channeled toward a transcendent God and personal salvation and reorient it toward the attainment of collective salvation through an intramundane "service to Humanity." The Benthamites, and especially Mill, not only brought the most intense spiritual energy to the propagation of their new creed but invested their "secular" ethics and ends with *ultimate* value. Benthamite and Millian utilitarianism, in short, was itself regarded and experienced by its devotees as a new religion—secular, social, political, intramundane—a fact expressly acknowledged by both Bentham and Mill.

The intraworldly character of the Benthamite "religion" is, then, not an accident but its very essence. Again, the whole point of Bentham's enterprise was to replace the "fictions" of transcendent religion with strictly human substitutes. Indeed, Bentham grew more virulently antitheological over the years, eventually seeking, as Crimmins puts it, to eliminate "even the idea of religion . . . from the minds of men." Benthamism, in short, was far from the easygoing and tolerant, if atheistic, hedonism it is sometimes made to appear. It was a militantly this-worldly ideology that was self-consciously developed in radical opposition to the transcendent Christian religion. What Bentham and his followers such as the Mills created is yet another variant of the secular or social religions invented by the eighteenth-century philosophes whom they regarded as their precursors and guides.[68] And the Benthamites, like their predecessors, "were never in doubt that they were preaching a new religion."[69]

Bentham's positivist method was not the only aspect of his teaching that made it easy for Mill to move from Bentham's new religion to what would become Mill's final spiritual home—the new religion of Auguste Comte, the Religion of Humanity.[70] Mill's early conversion to Bentham's nontheological utilitarianism, with its elevation of the greatest temporal happiness of the greatest number to the ultimate end of human existence, also made for a relatively easy transition to the full-fledged Religion of Humanity that Mill would embrace until his death. Comte's Religion of Humanity partook of the essence of the Benthamite religion—its radical antitheological impetus. It shared other fundamental attributes of Benthamism as well. Both "religions" championed an "altruistic" or "social" ethic in service of a strictly worldly end conceived as obligatory, ultimate, and all-encompassing—service to the Great Being of Humanity.[71] Both were regarded by their adherents as a moral advance over the "selfish" Christian aspiration for personal salvation. Both deliberately eclipsed transcendence by, in effect, elevating an intramundane abstraction, whether conceived as "humanity" or "utility," to the position of God.

Comte's Religion of Humanity, in short, embodied essentially the same aspirations and ends as Bentham's greatest happiness principle. It is thus not a coincidence that Mill would undergo an even more profound "conversion" experience under the influence of Comte. For under that influence, as Mill told Comte, he came to feel that the "inevitable substitution [of Humanity for God] is at hand."

The Spirit of the Age
Mill and French Immanentism

Today, I believe, one ought to keep total silence on the question of religion when writing for an English audience, though indirectly one may strike any blow one wishes at religious beliefs.

—*J. S. Mill to Auguste Comte*

I would be filled with hope if I believed the time had come when we could frankly hoist the flag of positivism and succeed, shake off every shred of the doctrines of the past (except for their historical value) and refuse all concessions, even tacit, to theories of the supernatural.

—*J. S. Mill to Auguste Comte*

What needs to be underscored in a study of Mill and religion is the emphatic antitheological intent impelling his philosophical and political activity. The messianic fervor of such nineteenth-century social saviors as Henri de Saint-Simon and Auguste Comte has long been recognized.[1] Indeed, neither Saint-Simon nor Comte made a secret of his aim—to usher in a "new world" defined by its opposition to the allegedly obsolete theological and metaphysical states of the human mind and society. The terminology varied—Saint-Simon would have his "terrestrial" New Christianity, Comte his "positivist religion" or Religion of Humanity—but the aspiration was identical; all of the "secular religions" formulated by the French messiahs were variations on the same theme. As Frank Manuel puts it, they all "represented . . . a deflection of love from the God of the Christians to mankind and a transfer of interest from the future of the immortal soul to man's destiny on earth."[2] They all preached a gospel of innerworldly social and political salvation.

The hostility to traditional religion in post-Revolutionary France was far more rabid than the growing skepticism that characterized English society during the same period. Such a climate made it relatively easy for a thinker like Comte expressly to declare his antitheological aims and intentions. Mill, on the other hand, confronted a cultural environment less congenial to the overt expression of heterodox religious views or even to the public discussion of religion. His response was to adopt, as he put it, a policy of "total silence on the question of religion" (*Corr,*[3] 317). One of the consequences of Mill's strategic silence on religion has been to obscure the fact of his utter commitment to Comte's religious aim. That aim, as earlier said, was the aim of Bentham as well as of Saint-Simon—the eradication of theology and metaphysics and all that such transcendent orientations implied for human existence. In the case of Mill, Comte, and Saint-Simon, the realization of this aim involved the replacement of an allegedly obsolete theological orientation with a "positivist" equivalent defined in explicit opposition to the former. In short, the establishment of the positivist religion, like that of the Benthamite religion, required not only the replacement of theological morality with a militantly innerworldly substitute of human construction, but also the reorientation of religious aspirations and sentiments away from otherworldly concerns toward those "confined within the limits of the earth" ("UR," 421). The former was to be achieved, in Mill's case, by the establishment of nontheological utilitarianism and the latter by the social establishment of the Religion of Humanity.

Mill's comradeship with Comte in the endeavor to replace God with Humanity has been obscured not only by Mill's "total silence" on religion but by his eventual rejection of Comte's schemes of political and social reorganization. Mill's youthful attraction to Comte and Saint-Simon is well known.[4] The conventional view is that Mill's engagement with these quintessentially illiberal thinkers was a passing fancy, an expression of his youthful revolt against the narrowness of his inherited Benthamite creed. In this story, Mill is cast as the liberal hero. After a youthful flirtation with what he cryptically refers to in the *Autobiography* as a tendency toward "overgovernment," Mill returns in short order to the true liberal faith, famously renouncing Comte's schemes as "liberticide"[5] and "spiritual. . . despotism" (*OL,* 17). Such a view, however, is incomplete, if not misleading. Mill did eventually reject many aspects of Comte's "social doctrine" and his plans for social reorganization. His deep immersion in the classical-liberal tradition and his self-conscious "practical eclecticism" prevented him from swallowing whole the more egregiously illiberal aspects of his French compatriot's plans for the regeneration of society. Eventually, too, he would become embarrassed by Comte's sentimental and ritualistic "Catholicism without Christ."[6] Comte's plans to institutionalize the Religion of Humanity on the model of organized Catholicism could have little appeal for the Calvinist Mill. Nevertheless, while Mill may have rejected the form of Comte's new "religion without a God" he utterly embraced its substance and would do so until his death. What Mill wrote to his friend John Pringle Nichol in 1841 remained his settled view: "[There is every reason] for believing that the *culte de l'humanité* is capable of fully supplying the place of a religion, or rather (to say the truth) of *being* a religion—and this [Comte] has done, notwithstanding the ridiculousness which everybody must feel in his premature attempts to define in detail the *practices* of the *culte*."[7] As Mill put the same view in 1854: "The best . . . thing . . . in Comte's [*Système de politique positive*] is the thoroughness with which he has enforced and illustrated the possibility of making *le culte de l'humanité* perform the functions and supply the place of a religion."[8] In *Auguste Comte and Positivism* (1865), Mill publicly promoted Comte's new religion, suggesting to his readers that it may provide, "even to Christians, an instructive and profitable object of contemplation" (133). Mill never broke faith with Comte on this point. He would engage in vigorous missionary efforts on behalf of the new humanitarian faith all of his life.

Indeed, Mill's ultimate rejection of Comte's social doctrine and reorganizational schemes lends further support to the view that Mill's overriding purpose, the aim that governed his philosophic activity and collaborative engagements throughout his life, was the replacement of a theological with a purely human orientation. For, as we shall see, the principal bond that seems to have united these two thinkers, whose thought and outlook were in so many other respects antagonistic, was their mutual antitheological goal. Mill, in a less grandiose style, was as much a representative of nineteenth-century "secular messianism" as a Saint-Simon or a Comte. He, like his fellow social saviors, was furiously at work devising a purely human positivist or terrestrial morality to replace the theological morality bound up with mankind's now allegedly obsolete state of development. Mill, too, fully intended to reorient spiritual aspirations away from the traditional transcendent God and toward the Great Being of Humanity and to establish a new religion that embodied the intramundane spirituality (*ACP*, 132). Mill, like his mentors and comrades, preached a gospel of social and political salvation.

As said, Mill and Comte were far from alone in their attempts to create a secular, social, or political "religion." Like other nineteenth-century Continental thinkers, they were acutely aware of the spiritual vacuum produced by the "critical metaphysics"—the attack on revealed religion—of the eighteenth century, an attack aimed particularly at Christianity, but one that affected traditional Jewish faith as well. Comte and Mill, like others among their contemporaries, were searching for a new spiritual substance to fill the void created by the loss of belief in—the "death" or "murder" of, as Nietzsche would put it—the transcendent God of the Western tradition. D. G. Charlton classifies such efforts into two principal groups—what he calls the "metaphysical" religions of German inspiration and the "social and political" religions emanating mainly from France.[9] It is this latter strain of intramundane religiosity that Mill carried into the Anglo-American tradition. Moreover, it is significant that Mill rejected the new religiosity stemming from Germany as insufficiently dynamic. He complained to Comte of the "quietist tendencies in the metaphysics of Schelling and Hegel" (Corr, 278).

Both Mill and Comte were unquestionably impelled by a powerful quasi-religious impulse. Indeed, they both exhibited the driving will of the religious founder and regarded themselves as such. That will, moreover, was purposefully directed away from a transcendent God and toward the intramundane abstraction Humanity. In short, the character of their new religiosity was predominantly antitranscendent and anti-Christian and not skeptical, agnostic, or atheistic. Both Mill and Comte were at pains to emphasize the "religious" character of their "religion without a God." Comte was indignant at being categorized with the dogmatic atheists. Mill too would insist that the utilitarian ethic and the Religion of Humanity were "more profoundly religious" than anything previously called by that name. Mill, like Comte, was convinced that the "human" morality and religion he offered the world was vastly superior to any that had heretofore governed mankind. Mill was no more immune to the Promethean impulse of the age than was Karl Marx. Indeed, one may even suspect that Mill, that "wayward intellectual deity" in the words of Mrs. Grote,[10] regarded his role and contribution to be of such significance as to merit him a place among the other figures he identified as great utilitarians: Socrates, Aristotle, and Christ.[11]

The "Mental Crisis"

We have seen that the adolescent Mill underwent something like a conversion experience in the presence of Bentham's writings. He had found true religion in Bentham's nontheological utilitarianism, and it had given him, as he says in true Benthamite fashion, "an object in life; to be a reformer of the world." Mill tells us precisely how much that object meant to him:

> My conception of my own happiness was entirely identified with this object. The personal sympathies I wished for were those of fellow labourers in this enterprise. . . . [A]s a serious and permanent personal satisfaction to rest upon, my whole reliance was placed on this: and I was accustomed to felicitate myself on the certainty of a happy life which I enjoyed, through placing my happiness in something durable and distant, in which some progress might be always making, while it could never be exhausted by complete attainment.

For a few years, the feeling of being "engaged with others in struggling to promote . . . general improvement" brought satisfaction. But this was not to last.

> [T]he time came when I awakened from this as from a dream. It was in the autumn of 1826 [Mill was 20 years old]. I was in a dull state, . . . the state, I should think, in which converts to Methodism usually are, when smitten by their first "conviction of sin." In this frame of mind it occurred to me to put the question directly to myself, "Suppose that all your objects in life were realized; that all the changes in institutions and opinions which you are looking forward to, could be completely effected at this very instant: would this be a great joy and happiness to you?" And an irrepressible self-consciousness distinctly answered, "No!" At this my heart sank within me: the whole foundation on which my life was constructed fell down. All my happiness was to have been found in the continual pursuit of this end. The end had ceased to charm, and how could there ever again be any interest in the means? I seemed to have nothing left to live for. (*Auto,* 111–12)

The spiritual needs once met by the Benthamite "religion" did not of course disappear with Mill's fall from that faith. Mill would struggle with the problem of meaning and purpose for the rest of his life. He was subject to recurring bouts of depression, whose main antidote was intensive and concentrated work toward the "improvement of mankind." More important from the perspective of this study, Mill's intense need for spiritual fulfillment and purpose led him to the welcoming arms of kindred spirits across the Channel. His quest for a religion to replace the "obsolete" transcendent faith of Western Christendom and for a god who could meet his moral and intellectual criteria led him unerringly to France, the very home of secular, social, and political religion.[12] Mill's spiritual yearnings would reissue in the form of a lifelong susceptibility to the appeal of the new "social gospel" of political salvation preached by the French secular messiahs. After a brief flirtation with Saint-Simon, Mill found his spiritual home in Comte's Religion of Humanity, and there he remained until the end of his days.

I: Saint-Simon's Philosophy of History

A social system in its decline, a New System arrived at maturi-
ty—such is the fundamental character which the general
progress of Civilisation has assigned to the present epoch.

—*Auguste Comte*

As said, neither Mill's need to feel a sense of comradeship in pursuit of a
common cause nor his spiritual yearning for a "definite creed" and life-
purpose—for a religion—disappeared with his loss of faith in the creed of
his father.[13] It is significant that Mill's movement toward Saint-Simon and
Comte was bound up with his recovery from the severe mental depression
he describes in the *Autobiography*.[14] Mill's strong susceptibility to the Saint-
Simonian and Comtean philosophy evinces the yearnings of a young man
at spiritual sea. His state of mind at the time is poignantly captured in a
letter he wrote to his friend John Sterling in early 1829. Mill refers in the
letter to his political collaboration with the philosophic radicals, with
whom, he felt, he no longer shared common philosophic ground.

> At present I believe that my sympathies with society, which were never
> strong, are, on the whole, stronger than they ever were [during his crisis].
> By loneliness I mean the absence of that feeling which has accompanied me
> through the greater part of my life, that which one fellow traveller, or one
> fellow soldier has towards another—the feeling of being engaged in the
> pursuit of a common object, and of mutually cheering one another on, and
> helping one another in an arduous undertaking. This, which after all is one
> of the strongest ties of individual sympathy, is at present, so far as I am con-
> cerned, suspended at least, if not entirely broken off. There is not now a hu-
> man being . . . who acknowledges a common object with me, or with whom
> I can cooperate even in any practical undertaking without the feeling, that
> I am only using a man whose purposes are different, as an instrument for
> the furtherance of my own.[15]

This, then, was Mill's state of mind upon first encountering the disciples
who were preaching Saint-Simon's "new Christianity" or Religion of
Love, the immediate predecessor of Comte's and Mill's Religion of Humanity. Mill's engagement with the sect was conducted mainly through
his close relationship with Gustave d'Eichthal, Comte's first disciple and
a member of the inner circle of the Saint-Simonian sect. The two men met
in 1828 at a meeting of the London Debating Society and immediately established an intensive and ultimately lifelong correspondence.[16] Mill's
spiritual yearnings at the time were evidently apparent. D'Eichthal re-

counts how upon first meeting Mill he immediately recognized a fellow "apostle."[17] Convinced that "only the Saint-Simonians could lead the world to the millennium," d'Eichthal courted Mill as a potential convert, and, despite initial hesitancy on Mill's part, met with no little success.[18] It was through d'Eichthal that Mill became acquainted with the writings of Comte, especially the early version of the *Système de politique positive.*[19] Mill began to study the works of Saint-Simon and Comte in earnest in 1829. Although he thought Saint-Simon's writings somewhat shallow and superficial, he was immediately impressed by Comte's work.

Despite d'Eichthal's intense missionary efforts, Mill's aversion to hierarchical organization, as well as his newfound aversion to sectarianism, led him to resist any formal bond with the Saint-Simonians.[20] As he repeatedly assured d'Eichthal, however, he was a most sympathetic fellow-traveler: "[A]lthough I am not a Saint-Simonist nor at all likely to become one, *je tiens bureau de Saint-Simonisme chez moi.*"[21] D'Eichthal waited patiently for Mill to capitulate and regularly sent him copies of the Saint-Simonian *Globe* and *Le Producteur.* In 1831, Mill said he had derived "great advantage" from the material and that he had moved closer to the views expressed therein.[22] Mill suggested to d'Eichthal persons to whom he should send the *Globe* and introduced him and other Saint-Simonians to potential English converts. Such cooperation only increased d'Eichthal's desire to convert him, and Mill finally had to emphasize his conviction that "England [was] unprepared for the appearance of the messiah."[23] Despite the distance he maintained, Mill would become a chief carrier of the ideas of Saint-Simon into English society, a service he would also perform for the ideas of Comte.

The height of Mill's receptivity to Saint-Simonism was reached in 1830 and 1831. In the latter year, he published a series of articles titled "The Spirit of the Age," an interpretation of the contemporary state of English society wholly informed by Saint-Simon's philosophy of history and to which we will return below. The extent of Mill's embrace of Saint-Simonism may be gathered from the thoughts he expressed to d'Eichthal in 1831: "[T]he daily reading of the *Globe,* combined with various other causes, has brought me much nearer to many of your opinions than I was before, and I regard you as decidedly *a la tete de la civilisation.* I am now inclined to think that your social organisation, under some modification or other, which experience, no doubt, will one day suggest to yourselves, is likely to be *the final and permanent condition of the human race.*"[24] (emphasis added)

What was it that Mill found so attractive in the writings of the Saint-Simonians? Mill himself would say that upon absorbing these writings, including Comte's early version of the *Système de politique positive*, "I had much changed from what I was, before I read any of their publications; but it was their works which gave order and system to the ideas which I had already imbibed from intercourse with others, and derived from my own reflections." This is undoubtedly true. The Saint-Simonians held views and aspirations remarkably similar to Bentham's in certain crucial respects, which enabled Mill to make an easy transition from his old to his new faith. Saint-Simon's criterion of a "good" social organization was identical to Bentham's—"that it make the majority of men in society as happy as possible."[25] More important, however, Mill undoubtedly felt at home among Saint-Simonian apostles who believed that an utterly "terrestrial ethics" would inevitably replace the "celestial ethics" that had heretofore governed Western civilization. As Saint-Simon had said, "[T]he transition which is now taking place . . . consists in the passage from the theological system to the terrestrial and positive system."[26] The fundamental beliefs and aspirations of the Saint-Simonians were completely in accord with what we have characterized as the essence of Benthamite utilitarianism—its militant antitheological intent. As we have seen, Mill's own intent led him directly to the most intense of the new secular or social religionists of the period, with whom he would remain a fellow traveler until the end of his days.[27]

Mill shared further common ground with the Saint-Simonians in their mutual hatred of the ancien régime and especially of the aristocracy. As Mill put it in the *Autobiography*, he and his fellow Benthamites had long felt the "predominance of the aristocratic classes, the noble and the rich, in the English Constitution, an evil worth any struggle to get rid of"[28] (145). Mill also approved the Saint-Simonians' views on the equality of women and was sympathetic to their religious aspirations, although he was embarrassed by the notorious theatricality and extremism that marked the sect's decline.[29] Moreover, Mill, like his fellow traveler Thomas Carlyle, well understood the religious dimension of the Saint-Simonian movement. Carlyle's 1830 remarks to d'Eichthal could have been written by Mill: "[The Saint-Simonian opinions are] often such as I, in my own dialect, have been accustomed to cherish— . . . [t]hat the last century was a period of Denial of Irreligion and Destruction; to which a new period of Affirmation, of Religion, must succeed, if Society is to be reconstituted, or even to continue in existence."[30] Mill, like Carlyle, may have doubted the wisdom of establishing Saint-Simon himself as a god but he agreed with the Saint-Simonians that religion is the essential bond and animating force of a society. As discussed, Mill was not alone in believing that the success of the eighteenth-century "critical philosophy" in undermining Christianity, while necessary and on the whole salutary, had performed only half of the historical task. As Mill told Carlyle, "Christianity . . . is gone, never to return, only what was best in it to reappear in another, and still higher form."[31] The task that remained was the articulation and propagation of a new creed, a new faith, a new and "higher" religion to replace a Christianity perhaps suitable in former "age[s] of credulity"[32] but no longer in harmony with the more advanced state of the human mind.

Two chief elements of the Saint-Simonian doctrine were of fundamental importance for the development of Mill's thought: Saint-Simon's philosophy of history and his conception of a modern "spiritual power." The Saint-Simonian philosophy of history was actually something of a godsend for Mill. It provided him with both a rationale for and further impetus to his already well-formed intention to establish a new and purely human morality and orientation to replace their now-obsolete theological counterparts.

The deep impression that Saint-Simon's views made on the young Mill is most strikingly evinced in the series of articles he wrote for the radical journal *The Examiner,* published from January to May of 1831 under the title "The Spirit of the Age." Mill comments on the series in the *Autobiography:*

> I attempted, in the beginning of 1831, to embody in a series of articles, headed "The Spirit of the Age," some of my new opinions, and especially to point out in the character of the present *age,* the anomalies and evils characteristic of the transition from a system of opinions which had worn out, to another only in process of being formed. . . . [A]t that particular moment, [however,] when great political changes were impending, and engrossing all minds [agitation over the Reform Bill], these discussions were ill-timed, and missed fire altogether. The only effect which I know to have been produced by them, was that Carlyle, then living in a secluded part of Scotland, read them in his solitude, and saying to himself (as he afterwards told me) "Here is a new Mystic," inquired on coming to London that autumn respecting their authorship; an inquiry which was the immediate cause of our becoming personally acquainted. (147–48)

In "The Spirit of the Age," Mill applies the central ideas of the Saint-Simonian philosophy of history to the English political context. He argues, on its basis, for both the demise of the traditional aristocracy and the rise of a democracy governed by a new "Aristocracy of intellect"—the modern spiritual power as conceived by Saint-Simon. The articles were written during the period of Mill's youthful revolt against the narrowness of his inherited Benthamite creed and at the height of his receptivity to the

Saint-Simonians. As a result, F. A. Hayek has suggested, Mill "went much further than sober reflection would allow him to remain."[33] Although Mill did moderate his views over time, his thought and aspirations were deeply and permanently shaped by his French brethren.[34] This is particularly true in the case of the two leading ideas that Mill took from the Saint-Simonians; there is no reason to believe he ever fully disavowed either Saint-Simon's philosophy of history or his conception of a spiritual power. As we shall see, there are echoes of both ideas in *On Liberty*, published in 1859. Moreover, Mill advanced Comte's version of the Saint-Simonian philosophy of history in *Auguste Comte and Positivism* (1865) as well as in his last major essay, "Theism" (1868–1870).

What Mill chiefly took from the Comtean and Saint-Simonian philosophy of history was its central conception of his age as an "age of transition," which is the main theme of his "Spirit of the Age." We are concerned not only with the extent to which Mill accepted this philosophy of history but the way in which it shaped his understanding of political and religious developments and his own role in them. As Frank Manuel explains, Saint-Simon had conceived of human history as a more or less dialectical process characterized by alternating periods that he called at various times either "natural" and "transitional" periods or "organic" and "critical" periods. He further divided history into three great stages: ancient polytheism, monotheism/feudalism, and the final, positive stage. The maturation of each stage constitutes a natural, or organic, period (sometimes also termed a "synthetic" period). The movement from one stage to the next is punctuated by a transitional, or critical, period. The organic periods are the "good periods" of society.[35] These are characterized by the "integration" or harmonious organization of the various organs of the social system, itself conceived as a single living organism, as well as by harmony between its institutions and the state of civilization. Organic periods are also marked by the predominance of one ideal; a feeling of certainty; rulers who are recognized as the best or wisest men; and the subordination of temporal to spiritual authority. In short, a natural or organic period of society is one that has achieved a large measure of consensus on all important moral and spiritual concerns.[36]

A transitional or critical period, by contrast, is characterized by criticism, analysis, lack of organization and consensus, and lack of integration or harmony between institutions and the state of civilization (for instance, moral advances may call for a redefinition of property rights or the release of education from religious authority). It is a period of anarchy, of revolution, and of conflicting opinions, values, and beliefs, marked by bitter class struggles, war, and crisis. As Manuel puts it, during such periods "[s]piritual chaos reigned, as the dying and the newborn ideologies engaged in struggles for supremacy."[37] Such periods are necessary transitional evils between one social stage and another; they can be ameliorated but not eliminated. Indeed, it is the duty of the philosopher to assist the process by first grasping the necessary path of history and then doing what he can to ease the transition from the old to the new stage. Although the "law of alternativity" determines the dialectical movement from the organic through the critical to a new organic stage, Saint-Simon believed that the emergence of the aborning positive stage marked the culmination of the historical process—the "end of history." Unilinear progress assured that each successive stage was more highly developed than the last; and mankind was approaching a state of perfection, the final stage, a veritable heaven on earth.

Comte's "positive science" or philosophy of history, while somewhat different in detail and terminology, is similar in structure and substance to Saint-Simon's.[38] Mill's writings and correspondence reveal that he embraced both versions of the doctrine. Comte's view was that the necessary and inevitable movement of history was from the primitive "theological" state of the human mind (and society) through the intermediate "metaphysical" state toward the establishment of the final "positivist" state. Mill succinctly characterized Comte's view as the "natural law of the spontaneous decline in religious spirit" (*Corr*, 130). What Mill took from Comte's and Saint-Simon's theories more generally was, as he said, the "provisional character of all doctrines . . . which exclude the general movement of humanity" (*Corr*, 237). That is, Mill came to believe, with Comte and Saint-Simon, that all past and present social institutions, including religious institutions, must be regarded as provisional, relative to time and place, assuming as they do a "particular state of society without prejudging whether this state must or even can last indefinitely" (*Corr*, 228). He seems, moreover, to have anticipated, as did Saint-Simon and Comte, that the aborning positivist state was to be the final state of development of the human mind.[39] Mill completely embraced Comte's version of the movement of history through the three stages, which Comte called his theory of "social dynamics." Indeed, Mill regarded Comte's formulation of the "general laws of social dynamics and of the historical development of humanity, including the practical and ever so important corollaries derived therefrom," as perhaps Comte's most important and original contribution (*Corr*, 165). What differences the two men would eventually discover in their respective views centered on "social statics," or contemporary social doctrine. They would ultimately part company over their irreconcilable views on the role of women in society; the relative importance of physiology (Comte) and psychology (Mill) in determining human character and behavior; and on the independent value of the discipline of political economy. But Mill never disavowed the Comtean and Saint-Simonian philosophy of history or social dynamics. As noted, he was still employing the Comtean framework to explain the origin of the idea of god in his final major essay, "Theism" (see Chapter 5).

In light of what we have seen to be Mill's religious aspirations, it is not difficult to understand why he so eagerly and tenaciously embraced the Saint-Simonian / Comtean philosophy. First, it explained to his satisfaction the nature of his own historical era as, above all, a period of transition from one stage to the next—from the declining theological / metaphysical / feudal stage to the final nontheological or positive stage. It also assigned Mill an important task. As said, both Saint-Simon and Comte had declared it the duty of the philosopher to assist the processes of history by easing the transition from the old age to the new. As Mill himself explained to d'Eichthal:

[W]e ought to consider what is the stage through which, in the progress of civilisation, our country has next to pass, and to endeavour to facilitate the transition & render it safe & healthy. I am convinced that my own country & I suspect that France must pass through several states before it arrives at Saint-Simonism, even if that doctrine is true; and that although we ought to arrive if we can at a general system of social philosophy, and to keep it always in our own view, we ought not to address it to the public, who are by no means ripe for its reception, but to . . . educate their minds by accustoming them to think rightly on those subjects on which they already think, . . . and (in England at least where the *philosophie critique* has never yet got the better of the *doctrine theologique et feodale*) to endeavour to alter those parts of our social institutions and policy which at present oppose improvement . . . & by giving all the ascendancy to mere wealth, which the possession of political power confers, prevents the growth of a *pouvoir spirituel* capable of commanding the faith of the majority, who must and do believe on authority.[40]

Mill, like other of his contemporaries, was convinced that he and his generation were living on the borderline of a new and unprecedented epoch in world history, defined, as he believed, by its progression from the *doctrine théologique et féodale* toward the ascendancy of the positivist faith.

The second, and related, Saint-Simonian conception that significantly shaped Mill's thought—the notion of a modern spiritual power—will be discussed after an examination of Mill's correspondence with Comte.

We have emphasized that throughout his life Mill was, in some sense, a religious seeker. His search for a spiritual home took him from Benthamism to Saint-Simonism, with brief stops along the way at the thought of Wordsworth, Coleridge, and Carlyle, until he found a permanent home in Comtean positivism and the Religion of Humanity.[41] Positivism gave Mill a "definite creed" to live by and the Religion of Humanity gave him a "god"—an ultimate entity—to serve. The positivist religion thus served to channel Mill's deepest energies and satisfy his deepest needs. It provided the meaning and purpose he so urgently required while simultaneously providing free reign for the elaboration of his nontheological utilitarianism, which, indeed, he now understood to have been sanctioned by History itself. And, as we have seen, Mill's youthful training in and conversion to Benthamism meant that he was well prepared for the embrace of the Religion of Humanity. Bentham's nontheological utilitarianism was equivalent in all its essentials to Comte's "religion without a God." It was an easy path from serving humanity through the Benthamite program— selfless devotion to the greatest temporal happiness of the greatest number—to a similar altruistic service to the Great Being of Humanity as conceived by Comte. The "cause of humanity" surely found one of its ablest and strongest-willed advocates in the "Saint of Rationalism"[42] (*Corr*, 73). Through Mill's tireless devotion to the cause and his thoroughgoing familiarity with the symbols and resonances of the liberal tradition, the social ideals of the French "party of humanity," transmitted through its spiritual offshoot the Religion of Humanity, seeped into Anglo-American consciousness.[43]

II: The Correspondence of Mill and Comte

It is appropriate to preface a study of Mill's published writings on religion with an examination of selections from his private correspondence. For various reasons, Mill's published writings are not always a reliable guide to his genuine views, especially concerning religion. First, as briefly discussed, Mill engaged in severe self-censorship with respect to religion. Second, Mill's public writings were often shaped by polemical and rhetorical considerations. As Hamburger says, Mill was trained to "pursue the truth, not for its own sake, but as an instrument for the improvement of mankind."[44] As is not uncommon, the overriding value Mill invested in his ultimate end led him at times to attend less rigorously to the means than may have been appropriate. In his letters, however, Mill often expressed himself candidly. What he reveals is essential to an accurate understanding not only of his religious thought, but of the role religion played in shaping his philosophy and politics as well. Mill's correspondence and other private writings, such as his diary of 1854, reveal a person intensely preoccupied with religion and theology. More particularly, they reveal what we have called his deep antitheological animus as well as his personal commitment to the Religion of Humanity. Equally important, Mill's private writings reveal the extent to which he regarded his mission as bound up with the overthrow of Christianity and the propagation of the new humanitarian creed.

The correspondence between Mill and Comte is especially revealing of Mill's true religious thought and aims, for the two comrades-in-arms spoke fully and freely of their mutual antitheological views and goals. As earlier remarked, a close reading of the correspondence even suggests that hostility to traditional theology and religion may have been the principal bond that united these two thinkers, whose views, as is generally recognized, were incompatible in very many respects. What is certain is that the predominant theme of their five-year correspondence was the need to replace traditional religion, theology, and metaphysics with positivism, itself understood as the basis of a new religion.

Mill initiated the correspondence with Comte in December 1841, assuming the tone of earnest student to distinguished teacher, of neophyte to master.[45] He wrote to express "sympathy and support from abroad" and to acknowledge his "great intellectual debt ... to the one great mind of our time, whom I respect and admire most" (*Corr*, 35). Comte responded with warmth and encouragement and a call to comradeship, reassured that "methodical positivism will not be crushed in its decisive progress as long as its various promoters maintain with dignity such sentiments of mutual solidarity" (*Corr*, 308).

Mill's first letter points to the religious attraction that Comte's philosophy held for him. He intimates that he apprehended Comtism as a potential religious substitute for his lost Benthamite faith. He says that reading Comte's "short essay on Positive Polity [in 1828] ... was responsible for my definite leaving [of] the Bentham section of the revolutionary school in which I grew up."[46] He explains his attraction to the two schools of thought by their mutual "positivity" and explains what that concept means to him. Benthamism, he says, appears "even today the best preparation for true positivity, applied to social doctrines ... because it categorically refuses all attempts to explain any kind of phenomenon by ridiculous metaphysical entities [nature, natural rights, essences, etc.,] the essential worthlessness of which it taught me to feel from earliest youth"

(*Corr*, 35). Mill further explains that his studies in science and especially its methodology also prepared him to appreciate the importance of Comte's *Cours de philosophie positive*, which he began to read in 1837 (it was published in six volumes from 1830 to 1842).[47] Mill, then, seems to account for his initial attraction to Comte by the similarity in outlook and method between Benthamism and Comtism—their mutual "positivity."[48]

What should be emphasized at this point, however, is that both Mill and Comte conceived of positivism not only as the inevitable next step beyond traditional theology and metaphysics, but as itself akin to a religion. In this first letter, Mill immediately gets to the point—traditional religion must be replaced by "positive philosophy."

> You know, dear Sir, that religion has so far had deeper roots in our country than in the rest of Europe, even though it has lost, here as elsewhere, its traditional cultural value, and I consider it regrettable that the revolutionary philosophy, which a dozen or so years ago still was in full swing, today has fallen into neglect before completing its task [the destruction of the ancien régime along with its theological underpinnings]. It is all the more urgent that we replace it by embarking on the path of positive philosophy: and it is with great pleasure that I can tell you that, in spite of the openly antireligious spirit of your work, this great monument of the truly modern philosophy [Comte's *Cours*] begins to make headway here. (*Corr*, 36)

Comte responds to Mill's overture by acknowledging that Benthamism is indeed a "direct precursor of sociological positivism," as Mill had recognized. Comte also expresses his gratitude that "the most advanced minds vibrate in essential unison with mine," for this sustains him in his "necessary and permanent struggle with all the theological and, particularly, metaphysical thinkers [advocates of the Rights of Man]." Mill, he adds, is right to see that "the purely negative philosophy has been arrested ... before it could complete its task— ... to eradicate politically the last vestiges of the old regime, beginning with the theological establishment— ... [and that only] the rise of positivist philosophy ... [can] enable us [to achieve that end]." (*Corr*, 37–40)

It is apparent that Comte and Mill shared a desire to bring to fruition what they regarded as the aborted process of political and social revolution and to do so, to paraphrase Mill's disciple John Morley, by cutting at the theological roots of the old order.[49] For both thinkers, positivism was *defined* by its opposition to all theological and metaphysical approaches, systems, and theories, regarded by both as the relics of a bygone era. Its principal task was to eradicate the theological orientation of the West—as well as its offshoot, the metaphysics of natural rights and natural law— and all such an orientation implied for human existence. This, as discussed, was Bentham's end as well. In short, what Mill found attractive in both Benthamism and Comtism was their mutual endeavor to formulate a "positive"—that is, strictly human or nontheological—ethics and politics. For Mill, a positive ethics was in all essentials identical to nontheological utilitarianism.

Mill's Conversion to the Religion of Humanity

Mill's letter of December 15, 1842, provides the most overwhelming and explicit evidence of the religious nature of his commitment to Comtean positivism. Indeed, the letter recounts what can only be regarded as Mill's "conversion" to the full-bodied Religion of Humanity. All six volumes of the *Cours* had now appeared and Mill was able to consider the work in its entirety. He had been impressed with volume 4 for its "high scientific value" and volume 5 for the "historical conception presented." It was, however, volume 6 that made the greatest impression on him; this volume, he told Comte, "transcends . . . all you have written previously."[50] After reading the *Cours* several times, Mill came to feel that he had finally grasped Comte's system as a whole and understood its meaning, which, he now discovered, was "primarily of a moral nature." He explained to Comte: "I think that what is now taking shape in my mind is a first specific formulation of the grand general conclusion to your treatise: *my realization that positive philosophy, once it is conceived as a whole, is capable of fully assuming the high social function that so far only religions have fulfilled, and, quite imperfectly so*" (*Corr*, 118, emphasis added). Mill had recognized that phenomenological positivism could serve as the spiritual replacement for Christianity that his age so sorely needed. Indeed, it could perhaps serve mankind's spiritual and social needs more fully than any previous religion had done.

Mill's recognition, moreover, was not merely an intellectual comprehension. As upon his reading of Bentham's *Traités*, Mill seems to have been spiritually transformed through his meditation on Comte's magnum opus.[51] And, as said, the effect of that meditation was permanent and far-reaching—Mill's full-fledged conversion to the positivist Religion of Humanity. He explained:

> Having had the rather rare fate in my country of never having believed in God, even as a child, I always saw in the creation of a true social philosophy the only possible base for the general regeneration of human morality, and in the idea of Humanity the only one capable of replacing that of God. But there is still a long way from this speculation and belief to the manifest feeling I experience today—that it is fully valid and that the inevitable substitution is at hand.

Mill's profound experience seems to have generated a sense of personal crisis. He questioned his worthiness to participate in the great task of "political and especially moral regeneration" that Comte's vision had revealed to him.

> Even when one is relatively well prepared, compared to most thinking persons, to draw the intellectual consequences of this conviction [that the substitution of Humanity for God is at hand], this is impossible without some kind of crisis in the life of any man whose moral nature is not too unworthy of the obligations it imposes. [This is so] whether because it is not clearly evident that the direct task of political and especially moral regeneration (which one had always projected into some far-off future) has become truly possible in our day and that the time has come when individual dedication can actually create an appreciable benefit for so great a cause, or whether [because] by unleashing, by way of a necessary reaction, the bitter realization that our particular imperfections make us more or less unworthy of such a destiny. By the way, there is no reason to believe that in my case the outcome of this crisis be anything but favorable, either to my individual happiness or to the usefulness of my role in society. (*Corr*, 118–19)

Mill seems to have been quite overwhelmed by his experience. Comte's work, he said, is perfect—"capable of constituting a . . . final form of the new general philosophy (that means, a full and lasting systematic presentation of all the true concepts [of positive philosophy]." Indeed, not only the intellectual virtuosity he perceived in Comte's "immense system" but also the very person of Comte seems to have struck Mill with religious awe. He could not find the words to express his response:

> . . . I have long thought that a fully rational mind could exist only under the complete guidance of positive philosophy, [but] I had never anticipated that there could already exist . . . as complete an expression [as yours] of the eminent nature of the positive mind. You scare me by the unity and completeness of your convictions, which thus seem never to require confirmation by any other philosopher. I feel . . . the precious sympathy you show, . . . in that note you devote to me [in volume 6 of the *Cours*], proclaiming it with such noble confidence to all the philosophers of Europe; I have great need of it . . . today, lest I tremble before you. (*Corr*, 119)

Mill is at pains to emphasize that there may be some "secondary" differences between his and Comte's views, and perhaps even that some "real differences might subsist." He wishes to assert such differences as strongly as possible because he fears he is in danger of losing all objectivity and critical distance: "[T]oday I feel the need to defend myself against being carried away, always a greater danger for a man of my particular nature than an excess of critical spirit" (*Corr*, 120). It is noteworthy that sixteen years earlier, Mill had attributed his first "mental crisis" to a youthful training that developed the analytical spirit at the expense of the emotions. In response, he had initiated a program of personal improvement that specifically attended to the cultivation of the emotions. It seems to have had considerable success.

"Total Silence on the Question of Religion"

The correspondence reveals a little-known side of Mill, one rather at odds with the image of the disinterested sage he cultivated so carefully throughout his public career. Indeed, the light it sheds on Mill is not altogether flattering and even raises doubts about the integrity of his published philosophical writings, certainly with respect to religion. Mill wished to appear an impartial philosopher devoted to truth, above the fray of politics and passion, a self-characterization that was largely, although by no means completely, accepted by his contemporaries and by posterity.[52] In short, although his philosophy has often been criticized for its inconsistency and lack of originality, Mill nevertheless was in his day and is today widely acknowledged as a "great moral figure."[53] What has been obscured in this stylized portrait is Mill's shadow. The correspondence reveals that side of Mill that led Maurice Cowling to call him a "proselytizer of genius."[54] Mill was not only less than candid in expressing his own true views but, as he knew, and as Comte once angrily charged (*Corr*, 345), he was not above dissembling. Mill can be seen as a manipulative strategist who carefully crafted his arguments to obscure his genuine views while attempting to lead the unsuspecting reader closer to his own position. This pertains above all to the subject of religion. The correspondence brings to light a Mill who sought to undermine traditional religious belief surreptitiously while simultaneously inculcating the positivist worldview. Mill's published writings must therefore be interpreted with some care, that is, with an awareness of the subterranean current running throughout his corpus—its antitheological and especially its anti-Christian themes. Mill's own explicit statements are the best evidence of his strategy in this regard.

Mill's second letter to Comte exposes both the antitheological impetus driving his philosophic activity and his policy of strategic self-censorship with respect to religion. In the letter, Mill discusses his forthcoming book *A System of Logic: Ratiocinative and Inductive*. He warns Comte not to judge his approach to "philosophic issues" by this work, for this may lead Comte to assume a greater distance between their respective views than actually exists. More particularly, Mill is concerned that Comte "might not sufficiently consider the concessions I felt forced to make to the prevailing attitudes of my country." Mill had been taught by his father that he must avoid any public criticism of religion if he hoped to gain influence over the public mind, advice that he took to heart. As he explains:

> You are doubtless aware that here an author who should openly admit to antireligious or even antichristian opinions, would compromise not only his social position, which I feel myself capable of sacrificing to a sufficiently high objective, but also, and this would be more serious, his chance of being read. I am already assuming great risks when, from the start, I carefully put aside the religious perspective and abstained from rhetorical eulogies of the wisdom of Providence, customarily made even by unbelievers among the philosophers of my country. I rarely allude to such notions and, even as I try not to awaken any religious antipathy in the common reader, I believe I have written in such a way that no reader, be he Christian or an unbeliever, can mistake the true nature of my opinions.[55] (*Corr*, 42)

Comte completely understood Mill's need for caution. Mill can best assist the "free development of true philosophic action in England," he responded, if he is careful to "express [him]self in certain [discreet] terms: the style of French philosophers of the period of Louis XIV can give an idea of what these are." Comte adds encouragingly, "If this restriction was unable to hold back the growth of negative metaphysics, could it any more effectively contain the positive impetus?" Comte looks forward to reading the *Logic* "in spite of its metaphysical formulations and theological precautions." Mill can rest assured that Comte will not "suspect [him] of metaphysical tendencies." Moreover, Comte is glad that such precautions are unnecessary in France, where he is able to use his public lectures on astronomy as a vehicle "to eliminate completely all theological philosophy, even in its simple form of deism, and finally to reduce all moral and social doctrines to rational positivism" (*Corr*, 48–50). Mill was always envious of what he believed to be the complete freedom of discussion with respect to religion in France. His passionate and long-standing desire for the same freedom at home would finally find a voice in *On Liberty*.

Mill revealed his penchant for strategic planning in service of the positivist goal. The cause of positivism, he explained in 1845, would be "more hindered than helped by an attempt to publicly set up an antireligious school: it would frighten the public, broach premature discussions, at least in England, and would probably lend new strength to religious reaction." Mill frequently reminded Comte that the success of the positivist "philosophical revolution" depended upon the judicious exercise of self-restraint regarding religious questions and issues (*Corr*, 288–89). Criticizing religion within the English context was inexpedient and counterproductive to the positivist cause. In discussing whether a pamphlet condensing Comte's *Cours* (*Le Discours sur l'esprit positif*) would be suitable for the English public, Mill makes his strategy perfectly clear:

> The only characteristic feature of the new [positivist] philosophy of which one could gain sufficient knowledge from this essay [*Le Discours*] would be its radical incompatibility with any kind of theology, and this is precisely what should under no circumstances be known as yet, because this idea, were it to become widespread, would turn away a great number of minds from positivism. [It would] especially [alienate] the young who, if they were not frightened off in the beginning, would eventually become accustomed to all its consequences, even the antireligious ones. The time has not yet come when we in England shall be able to direct open attacks on theology, including Christian theology, without compromising our cause. *We can only evade the issue by simply eliminating it from all social and philosophical discussion, and by passing over all questions pertaining to it on our agenda.* (*Corr*, 227, emphasis added)

And in response to Comte's suggestion in 1845 that he and Mill establish a journal, *La revue positive*, devoted to the propagation of positivism, Mill explains that the time has not yet come

> when a frankly positivist journal would have the slightest chance of success. . . . [Nevertheless] things are not the same for letting the positive spirit penetrate into the mind of the public in a more gradual fashion, by means of journals already in existence.[56] . . . The favorable reception given to my *Logic* is one proof among many that there is a public able to appreciate discussions of a positive type, . . . as long as a few indispensable limitations, which are easy to follow, are kept in mind. (*Corr*, 304. The limitations Mill refers to involve "frontal attacks on religion" [304n1].)

Comte did not take Mill's lack of interest in *La revue positive* gracefully. He lashed back that Mill should "be eager to have a . . . mouthpiece published abroad which systematically expresses the philosophic orientation which [you] are forced to simulate every day [in England]" (*Corr*, 345).

Comte also approached Mill in 1845 with the idea of publishing in English his short essay "Sainte Clotilde." Mill's response was to reiterate his belief that the cause of positivism was best served by keeping a low profile regarding its antireligious intent:

> To place positivism in open opposition to religion in any form is, it seems to me, the only completely inappropriate way of employing it in England today. . . . *Today, I believe, one ought to keep total silence on the question of religion when writing for an English audience, though indirectly one may strike any blow one wishes at religious beliefs.* (emphasis added)

Mill further counseled Comte to write anything he intended for the English public "as if religion did not exist, . . . [for] if today you publish a pamphlet under your name in English in which every religious belief is openly rejected, you might well find every journal of this country closed to you. Anti-religious *language* is feared and rejected in England more than the lack of religion itself" (*Corr*, 317–18).

Aside from the explicit discussion of their mutual antitheological and antimetaphysical aims, the letters convey a strong impression of the close conspiratorial air that surrounded the relationship between Mill and Comte during the years of their most intense engagement. The two brothers-in-arms plot strategy and tactics for the positivist "philosophical revolution." They consider how best to combine their forces for the "systematic propagation of the new philosophy," which must succeed if they "preserve and vary [their] approaches" (*Corr*, 232). They provide mutual encouragement and inspiration to carry on the struggle. Even their disagreements are seen as useful, for controversy will draw other thinkers into their orbit (*Corr*, 125).

On numerous occasions Mill makes it clear that the triumph of positivism, as well as the degree of influence and reputation he himself may achieve, demands a strategic sensitivity to contemporary religious prejudices and a necessary, if regrettable, lack of candor. He is also proud of the courage he displays by what he conceives as his refusal to kowtow to religious prejudice. He tells Comte:

> All in all, the English public seems to me well enough prepared to accept . . . your principles of general philosophy, while however imposing the completely irrational proviso of a Providence manifest in general laws—a concept prepared and even belabored by the timid semiphilosophers who corresponded here during the eighteenth century to the strong negative school in France. But I do not find our public nearly so well prepared for your social philosophy, since one of the principal foundations of that philosophy is the natural law of the spontaneous decline in religious spirit— an idea that scares almost all the minds of England to such an extent that if I proclaimed it openly, no one would dare read me. I am already at some risk, asserting strongly all through my book [the *Logic*] how much I admire your great work without adding the slightest theological stricture, which no other Englishman in my place would, I believe, fail to do. (*Corr*, 129–30)

Mill, one suspects, was delighted to find in Comte someone with whom he could at last speak freely concerning religion. Mill's guardedness, what he called his "instinct for closeness" (*Auto*, 141), extended even to his friends, with a few exceptions. His continued repression on the subject of religion, as well as his growing confidence in the positivist perspective

and the growing reach of his reformist ambition, inspired a corresponding desire to disclose his genuine views to the public. Mill was in many
respects a conscientious person, and he did admire candor and the
courage of one's convictions. On some level, he undoubtedly experienced
his own studied silence on religion as cowardly and dishonest. One important result was the psychic outburst of *On Liberty* and its passionate
plea for freedom of discussion. A chief object of that essay was to promote
freedom of discussion concerning religion (see Chapter 6). Not only
was this Mill's own heartfelt desire, but he also believed such liberty to
be essential to the elimination of lingering theological and metaphysical
beliefs.

Advancing the Cause

Mill was proud to be almost single-handedly responsible for bringing
Comte's philosophy to the attention of the English public (*Corr*, 270). His
high praise of Comte in *A System of Logic* encouraged many thinkers, especially scientists, to read Comte's major work, the *Cours*. Mill was a tireless proselytizer in any area that engaged his interest, and one of his chief
interests was to encourage the widespread embrace of what he, with
Comte, sometimes called the "final philosophy" of positivism (*Corr*, 164).
Positivism, Mill said, meant primarily the "method by which human reason succeeded in discovering and demonstrating the laws of phenomena" (*Corr*, 228). Its "essential principle . . . [is] that of categorically rejecting all speculation on first causes and limiting oneself to seeking the
effective laws of phenomena" (*Corr*, 288). One suspects, however, that
Mill's public characterization of positivism as a mere method of inquiry
relating to phenomenological concerns, and his studied public silence on
its theological and ontological implications, were meant to veil the radical implications of positivism from an audience largely shaped by conventionally Christian presuppositions. As he told Comte, the best approach to insinuating positivism in the public mind was to ignore its
"incompatibility with any kind of theology" and to simply "evade the issue" of religion. For there can be no doubt that Mill comprehended perfectly the essence of Comtean positivism—its "radical opposition to both
the theological and the metaphysical schools" (*Corr*, 232). As he makes
clear in the correspondence, Mill was well aware, as he says, that the "central idea of [Comte's] work is replacing the religious with the scientific
point of view," an idea with which he was in complete accord (*Corr*, 351).

Comte was duly appreciative both of the positivist ideas that Mill expressed in the *Logic* and of Mill's public praise of his work. Mill, in turn,

was grateful for Comte's approval. He was reassured by their "agreement on all essential points" and buoyed by his anticipation of collaborating toward the "establishment of the final philosophy." As he told Comte:

> [Y]our view of my book [the *Logic*] is the only one that could have a marked influence on my own, which was and could be only provisional, as long as the truly positive and doctrinal part of the work was not sanctioned by the most competent judge, indeed the only one so far competent on any questions of systematic methodology. Now that it has acquired this precious approval, I can congratulate myself that I henceforth shall have the unshakable confidence of playing a role not only in the initial diffusion, but even in the establishment of the final philosophy, even though the role I play in this noble effort be a modest one. We can also rejoice together of the happy augury for this philosophy: such spontaneous agreement between two philosophers who so far were the only ones to devote themselves seriously to organizing a positive method . . . and even so find themselves now in agreement on all essential points. (*Corr*, 164–65)

Both Mill and Comte acknowledged Mill's responsibility for making Comte's views known in England, as well as the instrumental role this was to play in inaugurating the positive society. The elevation of Comte in the public eye was a deliberate strategy on Mill's part, designed to facilitate the "establishment of the positive school." In 1844, Comte wrote Mill that "my name and my work are increasingly known today in England. You can well imagine that I attribute to you most of this unforeseen fame, which certainly would not have come about, at least to this extent, without the noble and decisive tribute which you were brave enough to bestow on me in public. . . . [This] unexpected fame . . . can become useful for the growth and especially for the establishment of the positive school" (*Corr*, 224–25).

Comte always attached the greatest importance to Mill's public avowal of his ideas. In 1844, Comte's French disciple Maximilien Littre published a series of articles on Comte's philosophy, which Comte, in typically dramatic fashion, regarded as a "decisive event in the rising movement of systematic positivism." He reminded Mill of the assistance he had given Comte and positivism: "Reading [the Littre articles] must . . . have provided a more personal kind of satisfaction [to you, considering your] important role [in] indirectly . . . bringing about . . . [the favorable] appraisal. The noble tribute included in your precious work had prepared the essential ground and furnished the critical example for it" (*Corr*, 268–70). There is truth in Comte's assessment.[57]

Mill provided Comte with frequent progress reports on the "cause of positivism" in England and Scotland, underscoring its implicit opposition to theology. "Positive philosophy," Mill thought, "will find more apostles today in Scotland than in England" because the philosophic tradition of that country stands closer to the positivist spirit and the influence of the Church in Scotland is weaker than in England. The Scottish philosopher Alexander Bain was Mill's protégé and positivist disciple. Mill was proud that he and Comte could "take credit . . . for having determined [Bain's] direction. . . . He will accomplish great things and will worthily uphold the cause of positivism in our country" (*Corr,* 258–59). And in 1843, Mill was glad to relay Bain's observation that "even in [Scotland,] so religious in appearance, . . . minds are admirably prepared for the social triumph of positivism. . . . At a distance [Mill continues to quote Bain], one can hardly believe, how very few points of everyday human life are touched by theological views. Theology is descending rapidly to the mere aesthetic and to a bond of social agglomeration, the desire of which is its greatest hold" (*Corr,* 205).

Mill and Comte were greatly concerned with developing the strategy and tactics most appropriate for furthering the positivist cause. Mill counseled Comte on the best way to lead "suitable minds" to embrace positivism and especially its method. Mill also discussed the anticipated impact of Comte's *Cours* on traditional religious belief: "[T]hese very volumes should accustom their readers to rid themselves of the theological element altogether, just as it happened in the case of Bain" (*Corr,* 205). (Bain completely lost his religious belief through reading the *Cours.*)

The exchange between the two comrades-in-arms was also a major source of moral support and encouragement. Mill was grateful that "even today I feel that the difficulties of spreading positivism are beginning to ease because of what you have done" (*Corr,* 267–68). What Mill chiefly gained from Comte's approval, however, was the courage of his convictions. The two men often reiterated their peculiarly self-aggrandizing belief that, as Mill said, the "spontaneous . . . harmony" between their views "would in itself almost constitute sufficient proof of the truth and even of the timeliness of the new philosophy." Comte's approval of the *Logic* gave Mill complete assurance "as to questions of methodology—where I fear no further differences of opinion of any importance, be it on the general theory of positivism, or on its particular application to the social sciences— all I need still hope for is an equally perfect agreement with respect to social doctrine" (*Corr,* 164–65). This, however, was not to be. Mill and Comte would eventually part ways, for several reasons that are discussed below. Nevertheless, despite their disagreements, the two men never lost the conviction that their agreement on the positivist method was strong evidence of its truth and that their mutual public acknowledgment was of vital assistance to the positivist cause.

One consequence of the heightened confidence that Mill gained through his collaboration with Comte that is of special interest here was, as mentioned, Mill's growing desire to disclose his true views on religion publicly. In 1845 he wrote to Comte:

> I would be filled with hope if I believed the time had come when we could frankly hoist the flag of positivism and succeed, shake off every shred of the doctrines of the past (except for their historical value) and refuse all concessions, even tacit, to theories of the supernatural. I do not consider that this era is as distant as it appears to many others; all we need is a little daring, and I might not be averse to making the attempt myself. But I would do so in a book. As in every philosophical revolution, books must come before journals. (*Corr,* 288)

It would have assisted the interpretation of Mill's corpus if the imagined book had in fact materialized. All of his explicit writings on religion were published posthumously and, as we will see, it is difficult to decide whether even they provide an accurate account of Mill's true views.[58]

By 1844, Mill was advising Comte about how to respond to the attacks that would probably be provoked by the increasing influence of the positivist school. The "scientists and priests," that "powerful class" whose "social prestige" was threatened by the rise of positivism, might attempt to "silence" Comte or at least prevent him from earning a living.[59] Indeed, the increasing determination of Comte's enemies, Mill warned, raised the possibility of a "duel to the death." There was, however, some consolation—if Comte "submit[s] to the suffering of a martyr, [he] will . . . have the honors, and humanity will reap the benefits" (*Corr,* 277). Such symbolism speaks volumes about the quasi-religious nature of positivism in the minds of both Mill and Comte.

In 1846, the correspondence began to draw to a close. During its early years, years of high enthusiasm and mutual devotion to a common cause, Mill and Comte studiously ignored their differences. As time wore on, however, certain crucial differences in their views, especially regarding the relative importance of physiology (Comte) or psychology (Mill) in the determination of human character and behavior, proved irreconcilable. But the principal such issue was the diametrically opposed views that Mill and Comte held on the social role of women. Mill was the prototypical radical feminist; Comte the very type of the antifeminist. It is amusing to observe the head-to-head clash of these two gigantic egos, neither of whom would concede an inch to the other on this issue. There was absolutely no common ground in their views, and their letters became increasingly acerbic and even insulting. Mill concluded that since he and Comte could not both be right on this issue, "one of [them must] insufficiently understand ... the true theory of human nature" (*Corr,* 357). Comte was of course outraged at the implication. Both men perceived such issues as insurmountable obstacles to future collaboration, and the once-grand passion ended, as did most of Mill's other such attractions, in a quiet death.[60] Comte did not respond to Mill's final letter, and the five-and-a-half year correspondence came to a close. As Mill said, "I was the first to slacken correspondence; he was the first to drop it" (*Auto,* 162).

Oddly enough, in the end it was Comte and not Mill who argued that the establishment of positivism, at least during the "revolutionary transition," did not require complete conformity of opinion regarding "social statics" or the social doctrine for which Mill yearned. All that was required during this time, Comte said, is "that one accept in common its fundamental method and general theory of development, along with its law of social hierarchy." Mill, said Comte, was too inflexible; indeed, he is an old-style theologian: "Your all too rigorous standards here seem to me involuntarily drawn from the old style of thinking, when the theological nature of philosophy ... required a narrow accord on particulars without which the whole system of beliefs was constantly compromised." Comte argued for greater flexibility. Positivism's "conformity in methods," he told Mill, mitigated the need for total agreement on contemporary doctrine or policy (*Corr,* 357–58).

In one of his last letters (January 23, 1846), Comte reemphasized his conviction that the total agreement on social doctrine that Mill craved was impossible:

> A complete agreement in philosophic doctrine can never come to be. However great the intellectual normalization which humanity may eventually attain, differences in organization [that is, physiology], education and circumstance will always exert sufficient influence to determine a habitual diversity of opinion on many secondary questions. ... Still, once the revolutionary transition has come to an appropriate close, much more philosophic agreement than we find today on all ideas which truly matter in the final harmonization of modern society will certainly arise. ... [O]ne will then have to become more demanding concerning the normal conditions of philosophic cooperation since such cooperation will increasingly apply to the more specialized and immediate concerns. However, to prepare for this normal state, it would be unreasonable to prescribe the same degree of intellectual conformity as will eventually be realized. (*Corr,* 357)

In short, greater freedom and flexibility are needed during the "transition" from the present anarchy to the "final . . . intellectual normalization [and] harmonization of modern society." We will hear an echo of this long-standing Saint-Simonian and Comtean view in Mill's *On Liberty*.

Mill, however, had taken all he needed from Comte. With Comte's philosophy of history and Religion of Humanity firmly in tow, he moved on to greener pastures.

Atheism That Is Not Atheism

As may be expected, Mill's strategic silence on the religious question was not completely effective, and over the years he developed something of a reputation for holding irreligious if not atheistic views. For instance, William Ward, a Roman Catholic priest involved in the Oxford Movement, which sought to restore neglected church doctrines and rituals, drew public attention to Mill's "unbelief and the atheistic tendency of [his] writings by . . . cit[ing Mill] in every chapter" of his book, *The Ideal of a Christian Church* (1844). Mill was amused, indeed gleeful, to receive such "striking publicity" from such an unexpected source. Ward also drew attention to the close relation between Mill's and Comte's views, although, as Mill informed Comte, "it goes without saying that [Ward] censors you even more soundly than me for your lack of religion" (*Corr,* 296). Comte and Mill were beginning to be associated in the public mind, an association that gained considerable strength after the publication of Mill's widely influential *Auguste Comte and Positivism* in 1865.

The growing public association of Mill and Comte with atheism and irreligion led to an interesting exchange between the two men on the nature of positivist "religious" belief, one that points to the antitranscendent roots of its antireligious stance. In 1845, when Comte asked Mill for help in securing the publication of his essay "Sainte Clotilde" in English, he not only wanted to recognize Clotilde publicly, but also thought the pamphlet would facilitate the conversion of women to positivism. Mill, however, did not think it suitable for the English public, and his remarks provide a good glimpse into his view of traditional religion and his settled strategy with respect to its public discussion.

> Your [essay] is doubtless quite fit to soften the [religious] prejudices of men and women who, already half-detached from traditional notions, still strongly cling, in their imagination or emotions, to the satisfactions of the traditional system of beliefs, an organic system that provided solace to the moral and sympathetic part of our nature, or was supposed to do so; but for

these very reasons I consider it unsuited for an English audience. *To place positivism in open opposition to religion in any form is, it seems to me, the only completely inappropriate way of employing it in England today.*

Perhaps a time will come when giving publicity here to this little work will be very useful: that will be the moment, which may not be far distant, when you will be publicly attacked and denounced here as an atheist. Then it may be fitting to have the public see and understand what immense distance separates your atheism from the only one known here, that of the school of Diderot and d'Holbach. Today, I believe, one ought to keep total silence on the question of religion when writing for an English audience, though indirectly one may strike any blow one wishes at religious beliefs. This restraint is particularly necessary on the part of a writer already known for having openly professed antireligious opinions, for the editors of journals will examine such matters more closely than any other case.

But this is the only restraint you need observe. In every other respect, nothing in your writings would be an obstacle to their reception here. I do realize that in a systematic work, or even in one devoted to a single social issue of the first rank, leaving the religious question aside might be impossible, but as long as it is just a matter of book reviews or of secondary issues, *it is possible, it seems to me, to deal with the subject as if religion did not exist . . .* (*Corr*, 317–18, emphases added)

Although Comte said he understood Mill's reasons for rejecting publication of the pamphlet, he still thought it would provide a good opportunity for the advancement of positivism. Comte welcomed the prospect of being attacked publicly for his irreligion, he said, as this would permit him to clarify the nonatheistic nature of his and Mill's "atheism." Comte would respond to such charges by

writing a public letter concerning atheism. . . . [Then w]e shall finally have . . . it out concerning the absurd and malevolent insinuations [against atheists]. In reality, the appellation atheist fits us only if one restricts the term to the narrow etymological meaning, and this is almost always the wrong way of interpreting common terms, for *truly the only thing we have in common with those so designated is that we do not believe in God.* . . . If this purely negative coincidence should suffice to attach us logically to this type of mind [Holbachian atheism], it would be almost as correct to call us also Christians because we likewise do not believe in Minerva and Apollo. Thus, while historically one must consider persons called atheists to stand closest, among metaphysicians, to a truly positive spirit . . . we must . . . today attach great importance to jointly refuting this label: we must bring out on every suitable occasion in public and even in private, the radical differences which clearly separate any truly systematic positivism from [the] simple provisional negativism [of denying the existence of God].

As for me, I have already had occasion of privately convincing several persons of good will, and even ladies, that *it is possible today not to believe in God and still not be a real atheist.* (*Corr*, 319–20, emphases added)

Both Comte and Mill would strenuously assert the authentic and superior spirituality of their secular or social religiosity. Mill would claim that the Religion of Humanity, as well as the nontheological utilitarian ethics it embodied, was not only a "real" religion but better and "more profoundly religious" than anything that had heretofore gone by that name (*Util*, 423). Comte's remarks well indicate that positivism was not a variant of a more or less benign atheism or skeptical agnosticism. What they suggest is that the impulse behind the Comtean form of positivism that Mill embraced is better described as antitheistic or antitranscendent than as antireligious. Atheists and agnostics are typically indifferent to the religious question. Comte and Mill were obsessed with the religious question. Indeed, their hostility toward traditional religion resembles hostility toward a rival; traditional faith is apprehended as a competitor to the new faith they seek to inspire.[61] Moreover, their aim is not merely to ignore or even to eviscerate traditional religious belief. The express and self-avowed aim of both "secular positivists" is to found a new religion. It should be emphasized that both Comte and Mill regarded their new Religion of Humanity as an unqualified moral advance over traditional forms of transcendent faith. As Comte wrote to Mill:

> [M]y basic work [the *Cours*] has . . . established for all advanced minds the intellectual superiority of positive philosophy. . . . [T]he second essential work [*Système de politique positive*], with its purely social perspective from the outset, with all basic principles established in advance, will have the mission of lending this new philosophy the . . . distinction of moral superiority, which is no less indispensable for the final victory [of positivism] than the other. Besides, this moral superiority is from now on the only one still subject to serious debate. (*Corr*, 323)

Mill would categorically assert the superiority of his nontheological ethics and religion. In this, as in other respects, the two religious "founders" follow in the footsteps of their principal forebears. Like Diderot and other eighteenth-century philosophes, they "regarded it their sacred duty to show not only that their morality was just as good as religious ethics, but much better."[62] Mill and Comte took a backseat to no one in this regard. Comte was well aware of the importance of winning the moral high ground for the positivist religion, and Mill accepted the same challenge.

The Implicit Aim of the Logic and Political Economy

Mill's theoretical works, especially book 6 of *A System of Logic* ("On the Logic of the Moral Sciences") and *Principles of Political Economy* (1848), were thoroughly informed by various aspects of Comtean positivism as well as Saint-Simonian views.[63] His private correspondence makes it clear that Mill regarded these two works as instrumental to what we have seen to be his and Comte's mutual antitheological ends. As Mill explained, the *Logic* should prove "very appropriate for easing the transition of my country from the metaphysical to the positive spirit" (*Corr*, 120). Mill completed the *Logic* in 1841; two-thirds of it had been written before he read Comte's *Cours*.[64] Mill, at this time still assuming the character of neophyte to master, told Comte: "Had I known [the *Cours*] earlier, . . . I might perhaps have translated it instead of writing a new one; or had I written my own, I would probably have shaped the presentation of my ideas somewhat differently, . . . and given some parts a less metaphysical form"[65] (*Corr*, 82). As it was, however, Mill's absorption of the sixth volume of the *Cours* and his rereading of volumes 4 and 5 (the same volumes that effected his final "conversion" to the Religion of Humanity) led him to recast the *Logic* thoroughly before its publication in 1843, especially book 6, which is taken more or less directly from the *Cours*. As Mill said, his meditation on Comte led to a

> complete revision . . . in the last part, to bring it into greater harmony with my present mode of thinking. . . . I have given much more space to the new [positivist] doctrine, though I approach it from the point of view of my own work; I believe that in this respect, my book is now the most advanced that my country is yet capable of accepting. Moreover, I have the well-founded hope that anyone in our country capable of understanding your work will learn in my book where to find something better than what I have provided. (*Corr*, 130)

The "something better" no doubt alludes to Comte's overt hostility to Christianity and theology in general, as well as his philosophy of history—including the "natural law of the spontaneous decline in religious spirit," which relegated traditional faith to the dustbin of history.

Nevertheless, considering his audience and what they were "capable of accepting," Mill concluded that his work was still useful in the English context, inasmuch as it had accomplished "the most important thing"—striking "the first . . . forceful blow . . . to the ontological school in England." Mill is referring here to the Kantianism associated with Sir William Hamilton, which he would attack in *An Examination of Sir William Hamilton's Philosophy*, the work discussed in Chapter 4. For now, we are interested in the relation between Mill's attack on Hamilton and his own antitheological aims. On July 11, 1842, Mill wrote to Comte that if the *Logic* is read and well received, it will be the first somewhat forceful blow administered to the ontological school in England, at least in our day, and . . . sooner or later this blow will prove mortal to it. Now this was the most important thing to do, since this school alone is essentially theological and since its philosophy here presents itself as the national support of the old social order, and not only in terms of Christian, but even of Anglican ideas. Moreover, I think I did all I could to assure that only positivism benefit from this triumph, if triumph there will be. (*Corr*, 83)

Some months later, on March 13, 1843, Mill cast himself as the hero facing down the "enemy" ontological school through his *Logic* (*Corr*, 139). He again identified the implicit opponent of the *Logic* as the loosely Kantian or "intuitionist" school (associated with Hamilton), which he regarded as the last remnant of theologically oriented philosophy in England.

I begin to hope that this book will become a true philosophic rallying point for that part of our young English scientists who are not closely tied to religious ideas, and I believe that such an essential emancipation is less rare, even in our country, than it seems. Above all, the book appears to me eminently well suited to serve as a dike to halt the dangerous advance of German philosophy [that is, Hamiltonian Kantianism]. Up to now, this philosophy has been more useful than harmful to us. It has prompted a trend toward scientific generalization and a systematic approach to human knowledge. . . . *But, from a social point of view, this philosophy is clearly reactionary today, whatever its trend toward skepticism that it has been blamed for in its native land: there, indeed, it played precisely the role of undermining the traditional faith, but in England it is used to endow it with a philosophic hue.* . . . [Hamiltonian Kantianism] pretends to be superior to its predecessors, especially for taking into account all the phenomena of human sensibility and activity and analyzing them in its particular way; . . . and so far no one has appeared to stand up and face this enemy while properly fulfilling the same conditions. Henceforth we shall be able to choose: no longer will we have to go to the German camp to find a clearly developed philosophic system; positivism has now unfurled its flag in our country as well. (*Corr*, 138–39, emphasis added)

Mill had earlier written (December 15, 1842) that his *Logic*, "even in those portions that seem most metaphysical, . . . still appears to me very appropriate for easing the transition of my country from the metaphysical to the positive spirit" (*Corr*, 120).

As Comte further explained, the intuitionist or ontological school of Hamilton was singled out for attack because of its "religious spirit." On March 25, 1843, Comte wrote that he was "delighted" that Mill's *Logic*

is primarily directed against the social predominance, especially in England, of such a philosophy [the Kantian intuitionism identified with Hamilton] which is essentially outdated today. The principal schools of

modern metaphysics, diverse as they are (some openly critical,[66] others pre-
tending to adopt an organic approach), really constitute the only system of
thought today which we must confront head on. The theological spirit is all
too decadent, or all too neutralized to still remain a danger in any part of
Western Europe. From here on, it is the metaphysical spirit which constitutes the only antagonist that positivism must consider seriously. [German
metaphysics] alone still prolongs the influence of the religious spirit, too impotent to found new movements, yet still too effective to stamp out. It
would die of its own accord without this [metaphysical] transfusion. (*Corr,*
144–45)

Mill reminded Comte that his *Logic* "will not be without value in ad-
vertising yours. . . . [T]he important ideas I have derived from your great
work—and I acknowledge, as I must, the source whence they came—will
contribute, by the way I speak of your work, including its sociological aspects, to arousing the attention of some of the best prepared readers, and
to convincing them that today this is the only approach to the study of social phenomena worthy of the intellectual state of humanity"[67] (*Corr,* 68).

Mill also regarded his theoretical work in political economy, like his
work in logic, as a tool useful to the propagation of positivism. He anticipated that *Principles of Political Economy,* an enormously influential work
that went through seven printings in his lifetime, would "present powerful support to making the positive spirit penetrate into political discussion" (*Corr,* 228).

In 1844, Mill told Comte of his plans to write a treatise on political economy, one modeled upon the work of Adam Smith. "I believe that the plan,
if it could be properly executed, would have the advantage of preparing
the positive education of many thinkers who are more or less seriously
concerned with social questions. . . . [Such a work would provide] many
important opportunities of propagating some of the principles of the new
[positive] philosophy, just as Adam Smith did for most of the social applications of negative metaphysics, without arousing suspicious distrust by
unfurling a party flag" (*Corr,* 237). Mill further explained that a work such
as the one he envisioned, which would focus on concrete applications of
principle as opposed to abstract speculation or theory, was the most appropriate way to influence the English mind, which "rarely accept[s] generalization of any kind . . . on moral and social questions" (*Corr,* 60).

Comte never shared Mill's favorable opinion of the independent value
of economics apart from "sociology." He believed, on the contrary, that
"the overall interpretation of history assigns . . . Political Economy . . . only
a purely preliminary role and provisional function." Nevertheless, he
could agree that Mill's proposed work in political economy might help ad-

vance the positivist cause: "[There is] no doubt your treatise on political economy . . . will be very useful today, as you yourself think, in making the positive spirit prevail in many worthy minds who are not sufficiently imbued by it but who nonetheless are on the road to it" (*Corr*, 247, 232).

As mentioned, over the course of the five-year correspondence with Comte, Mill grew more confident of his role in the propagation and establishment of positive philosophy. In 1846, he again stated his belief that the great advances in positivism that were under way probably meant that adherents of the "metaphysical school" would soon attack his ideas, as had already occurred to Comte in France. Mill looked forward to the opportunity to defend positivism against its theological and metaphysical opponents and planned to enlist the *Political Economy* in the anticipated confrontation:

> I believe that this time [of being attacked] will soon approach for me as well. . . . I am trying to hasten the moment by the book I am presently writing, a book in greater accord than my first with the practical and political spirit of England, and where I shall refrain even less than in the previous one from battling the stock ideas handed down to us. I believe that our times are most favorable for any new doctrine capable of sustaining thorough discussion. All the traditional ideas have visibly declined under our very eyes and everyone is shouting high and low for new principles. If we had here . . . two or three men held in general high esteem, whose moral and intellectual stature measured up to the needs of our age, we could hope to conquer soon that freedom which France happily enjoys: the freedom of saying everything. This above all is what we lack at present, for the only questions that make no progress at all today are those where public opinion prevents any real discussion. (*Corr*, 376–77)

Freedom of Discussion

Mill's remarks suggest that he considered freedom of discussion to be an effective means by which to undermine traditional beliefs, especially theological and religious beliefs ("those where public opinion prevents any real discussion"). Such a view was a basic tenet of Saint-Simonism, which regarded liberty of discussion as an indispensable element of the transitional stage, essential for the destruction of old beliefs and the engendering of the new truths of the organic age aborning. That Mill was aware of this view is further indicated by Comte's remarks on the relation between "freedom of instruction" and the erosion of traditional belief. It would be "very desirable," he wrote to Mill in 1844, "that true freedom of instruction, though completely anarchic in itself, were now to come and hasten [the] inevitable demise [of the metaphysical school. This would] . . . make everyone feel the need to oppose more dynamic and logical doctrines to the reactionary ideas of the theological school" (*Corr*, 233–34). That is, with the elimination of the metaphysical or natural rights school, the battle line would be clearly drawn; a direct confrontation between the two chief rivals—theology and positivism—was long one of Comte's cherished dreams (*Corr*, 319).

The value of free discussion to the destruction of the old order may also have been driven home to Mill by Comte's repeated mention of the freedom to attack religion that he enjoyed in France. Comte used his public lectures on science as a pulpit for the propagation of positivism. In 1843 he crowed to Mill about his "little social experiment": "For three hours . . . I came right out and proclaimed before four hundred persons the moral superiority of positivism over theological doctrines . . . and demanded, in the very name of morality, the freedom for the new philosophy to compete with all forms of the old." This, of course, is the very theme of *On Liberty*. What Comte discovered by his daring was that "[t]oday the theological school is lacking all true strength against those who dare refuse its characteristic methodology and fundamental doctrine" (*Corr*, 134–35). Mill admitted to having been not only influenced but also encouraged by such stories.

> I am awaiting with intense interest to see what will result from your kind of *social experiment*—the opening of your annual course in astronomy which . . . will be of great importance in the free spread of an entirely positive philosophy. I would be happy if I thought that things could progress to such a point in this country while I was still alive! This freedom of speech you enjoy in France is compensation for many woes. We are still very far from such a state, but who knows? In a period of moral transition, things may move faster than they seem. (*Corr*, 130–31, emphasis added)

There can be little doubt that Mill regarded freedom of discussion as an indispensable means to facilitate the widespread embrace and ultimate triumph of the positive philosophy, that is, to eradicate the vestiges of the theological and metaphysical states of the human mind (see Chapter 6). There is just as little doubt that Comte's "social experiment"—publicly proclaiming the moral superiority of positivism over theological doctrines—was a forerunner of the "experiments in living" so eloquently championed in *On Liberty*. Indeed, the term *social experiment* was commonly used by the Saint-Simonians to refer to the expression of unorthodox religious views and practices based thereon.

In one of Mill's last letters to Comte, he revealed that, despite their differences on "social statics," he remained firmly in the positivist camp and felt increasingly confident of its future success. On August 13, 1846, he assured Comte that

> the principles of your great work have unquestionably taken their place in the European discussion: nothing shall henceforth be able to repress them. From the moment this point has been attained, all is done. This is all a philosopher can accomplish, or must accomplish, for the sake of his ideas. Once his ideas are being listened to, once the adherents of contrary ideas are forced to take cognizance of them and to take them into account, the cause has triumphed: thus ideas take on true social force, which will be more or less powerful depending on their share of truth and the real import that is theirs. (*Corr,* 376)

Mill's faith in positivism and its future, like his faith in its spiritual expression, the Religion of Humanity, never wavered.

III: Saint-Simon's "Spiritual Power"

Mill's correspondence with Comte is also instructive for the light it sheds on his understanding of his dual role as speculative philosopher and political activist, as well as on the height of his reformist ambitions. The relative importance and significance of speculative / philosophical activity versus practical / political activity was extensively discussed by Comte and Mill. Their intense interest in this topic derived, in part, from another of their strong mutual commitments: to what Mill called the "great principle . . . of the definitive separation of the temporal and the spiritual powers, . . . [which Comte] alone among our contemporary philosophers ha[s] enunciated" (*Corr,* 51). Mill's interest in this principle stemmed from his Saint-Simonian period. As said, the two elements of the Saint-Simonian doctrine that made the strongest impression on him were Saint-Simon's philosophy of history and his concept of the *pouvoir spirituel.* This latter concept resembled an idea to which Mill had been drawn in Coleridge's writings—his notion of the "clerisy"[68]—which Mill, however, seems to have shaped to suit his own purposes. As Mill explained the notion in his essay "Coleridge" (1840):

> The clerisy of the nation, or national church in its primary acceptation and original intention, comprehended the learned of all denominations, the sages and professors of the law and jurisprudence, of medicine and physiology, of music, of military and civic architecture, with the mathematical as the common organ of the preceding; in short, all the so-called liberal arts and sciences, the possession and application of which constitute the civilisation of a country, as well as the theological.

Mill continues, in effect identifying "theology" with his own concerns—
"logic, ethics, . . . the rights and duties of men, . . . and . . . philosophy"—
and curiously omitting any reference to God:

> [The theological] was, indeed, placed at the head of all; and of good right
> did it claim the precedence. But why? Because under the name of theology
> or divinity were contained . . . logic, ethics, and the determination of ethi-
> cal science, in application to the rights and duties of men in all their various
> relations, social and civil; and lastly, the ground-knowledge, the *prima sci-
> entia*, as it was named—philosophy, or the doctrine and discipline of ideas.
> (Mill, *Dissertations and Discussions*, 2:439–40)

This seems to be an example of Mill's strategy of "deal[ing] with [a] subject as if religion did not exist."

It is thus not surprising that Mill was immediately attracted to Comte's
version of the "spiritual power" doctrine, on which Comte himself placed
no small weight. Comte regarded the "systematic separation of the spiritual and temporal powers . . . [as] the most important argument of my political philosophy" (*Corr*, 54–55). The spiritual power as conceived by
Saint-Simon and Comte was a positivist variant of the traditional "two
powers" doctrine associated with medieval Christendom. H. B. Acton
summarizes the traditional doctrine as follows:

> [T]here are two principal powers or authorities in human society, the spiri-
> tual and the temporal, . . . [which] differ both in their spheres and in their
> modes of operation. The temporal power is concerned with . . . war and
> with work, with men's bodies and their welfare, with their happiness here
> on earth. . . . "Temporal" is interpreted as immediate, topical, ephemer-
> al. . . . Its sphere is that in which politics and business are pursued. In me-
> dieval times its authorities were feudal lords, kings and emperors, whose
> activities were regulated by custom and by law and supported by secular
> judges and, ultimately, by the sword of justice, the *judicium sanguinis*. . . .
> [The] spiritual power, on the other hand was . . . concerned with the salva-
> tion of men's souls. It was said to be the *causa temporalis*, that for which the
> temporal exists, just as the soul is that for which the body exists. . . . The
> spiritual power . . . is primarily concerned with that *totum simul* in which
> past, present and future are one, and in which the whole is in each of the
> parts. It is the sphere of cultural continuity and identity, of change that is
> premeditated and prepared, of eternal and immutable morality.[69]

This latter is akin to the sense in which Mill employs the concept. Mill's
ultimate concern is for the soul of man, to whom he will offer salvation
through enrollment in his Religion of Humanity or Duty.

In line with his philosophy of history, his law of the three stages,
Comte believed that the necessary and inevitable development of the hu-

man mind, and thus of society, had resulted in the replacement of the traditional feudal temporal authorities, whose essence was military strength, with the captains of industry, who organize men not for warfare or violence but for concerted control over nature in service of human purposes. Thus in the temporal sphere of the final positivist state, power and authority are replaced by the expertise and organizational skills wielded by industrial chieftains.

The necessities of history also dictated that the traditional spiritual authority wielded by the medieval papacy and Catholic clergy, like the traditional temporal authority, was destined to be replaced by its positivist equivalent. Thus Comte conceived the modern spiritual power, in Acton's words, as

> the authority exercised over opinion by men of science, literary men and artists [what Comte liked to call the "philosophic elite"]. He thought too it would eventually have to be organized in ways analogous to those of the medieval church, but with positive science replacing theology, and a philosophy of history, indeed a science of history, developed from sociology and philosophy, replacing revelation. Like the medieval Papacy and clergy . . . it would be independent of the temporal power. It would not endeavour to coerce belief and opinion, but would support and communicate its doctrines by proof and demonstration. . . . Its scientific demonstrations would make it difficult though not impossible for the temporal power to reject its advice, and it would play an essential part in maintaining that consonance of beliefs and feelings without which society would disintegrate into warring factions.[70]

As discussed, Comte and Mill, at least during the most intense years of their relationship, were responding to their mutual fear of "anarchy"—intellectual, moral, and social. Such anarchy, they believed, had ensued upon the destruction of traditional beliefs effected by the "negative" philosophy of the eighteenth century—the critical attacks on religion by the philosophes and their descendants. Indeed, the radical insufficiency of the merely critical or negative doctrines of the eighteenth century was one of the major topics of their correspondence. The philosophes, to their credit, had successfully undermined faith in the established verities of religion. But Comte and Mill, in common with many of their predecessors and contemporaries, were acutely aware that religion constituted the indispensable social bond. They believed that the anarchy that threatened to ensue upon the destruction of traditional belief must be met by the social establishment of an authoritative doctrine that would supply the necessary foundation of personal and social order. Thus the urgent call for a "positive" philosophy to fill the gap left by the decline in traditional belief. The need for such a unifying philosophy was felt by thinkers as diverse as Saint-Simon, Comte, Coleridge, Carlyle, Chateaubriand, de Maistre, Newman, and others, not to mention Mill himself. All, says Acton, were "dismayed by the mainly destructive criticism that so many eighteenth-century writers had indulged in, and thought that the liberal emphasis on individual freedom of thought was in need of correction."[71] As the putatively liberal Mill wrote to his friend John Sterling in 1831:

> [L]iberalism . . . is for making every man his own guide & sovereign master, & letting him think for himself & do exactly as he judges best for himself, giving other men leave to persuade him if they can by evidence, but forbidding him to give way to authority; and still less allowing them to constrain him more than the existence & tolerable security of every man's person and property renders indispensably necessary. *It is difficult to conceive a more thorough ignorance of man's nature, & of what is necessary for his happiness or what degree of happiness & virtue he is capable of attaining than this system implies.* But I cannot help regretting that the men who are best capable of struggling against these narrow views & mischievous heresies [men like Wordsworth and Coleridge] should chain themselves . . . to the inanimate corpses of dead political & religious systems, never more to be revived.[72] (emphasis added)

The solution offered by Saint-Simon, Comte, and Mill to the anarchy created by liberal freedom was the creation of a modern counterpart to the medieval "spiritual power." This was conceived as an autonomous organization or association composed of the philosophical, intellectual, and spiritual elite. Its task was the formulation of the systematic body of truth, intellectual and moral, that would henceforth guide practical affairs in the newly emerging positivist society. As Comte had told Mill:

> [W]e need to distinguish frankly and systematically between speculative and active life, between philosophical action and political action, like the former Catholic division between spiritual and temporal power. . . . [What is needed today is the] spontaneous rise . . . of philosophic action pointing directly to the reshaping of modern opinions and customs, which will not get involved in the struggles for possession of power, except insofar as to instill into them the reality of its general doctrine. . . . [P]hilosophical action must prevail today over political action as such throughout Western Europe.

In other words, the role of the new spiritual power, as Comte said, was to create and transmit the "new social doctrines" that alone could "direct the European revolution toward its necessary goal"—the positive society that must inevitably replace the obsolete theologically based societies of the past (*Corr*, 45).

Comte's views on the separation of spiritual and temporal power represented his special interpretation of the traditional "two powers" doctrine of Western Christendom.[73] He, like Saint-Simon, was at pains to emphasize the historical contribution made by medieval political and spiritual developments to the formation of Western society. He was especially impressed by the organizational achievements of medieval Catholicism, which he understood as the institutionalization of universal authority in matters spiritual and moral. A spiritual power so organized not only constituted a formidable restraint on the pretensions of temporal rulers but wielded an irresistible influence over the moral and spiritual formation of the populace. A spiritual power that could gain the unquestioning allegiance of the people, that could win their faith in its moral leadership, was, Comte argued, the ultimate power in any social order, particularly through the power it could wield over education. His avowed aim was to win for the new positivist elite—first understood as scientific authorities and later as a more heterogeneous group of positivist intellectuals and artists—the unquestioned authority in moral and political matters that he believed was once invested in institutionalized Catholicism. Comte regarded positivism as the legitimate—that is, historically determined—heir of the medieval spiritual power: "We systematic positivists are the true successors of the great men of the Middle Ages, taking up social studies at the point where Catholicism left off in order to consolidate and gradually bring to perfection the definitive active realization which can take place henceforth only under a new intellectual regime. I make a clear break with the entire system of the past but nevertheless . . . maintain that there is a true continuity in the succession of social philosophies" (*Corr*, 324).

Mill's conception of the "spiritual power," while somewhat less formalized than Saint-Simon's or Comte's, was, like theirs, concerned with ensuring the development and social predominance of authoritative knowledge in the sphere of morals and thus politics—a knowledge concerned with engendering the necessary "social unity" of the aborning positivist society. Mill condemned the hierarchical institutional means by which Comte aimed to establish a modern spiritual power, but he never disavowed the end. Mill's own view was that the spiritual power would emerge more or less spontaneously once the elite achieved unanimity with respect to moral and political truth. This latter depended, as we shall see, upon the prior formulation of the appropriate *method* by which such truth was to be established. As Mill put it in *Auguste Comte and Positivism*, "[I]n order that th[e] salutary ascendancy over opinion should be exercised by the most eminent thinkers, it is not necessary that they should be associated and organized. The ascendancy will come of itself when the unanimity is attained" (98).

Mill is generally remembered for his harsh condemnation of Comte's plans for social reconstruction and schemes for institutionalizing the spiritual power on the Catholic model, so it is instructive to learn that he had not always found Comte's views so repulsive. In 1842, Mill commended Comte for emphasizing not only the need to constitute but also to institutionalize a new spiritual power and even implied that the use of force in establishing the new positivist or nontheological morality may be justified: "You were . . . highly judicious in concentrating your efforts on describing the new spiritual power, whose very rise, and especially its incorporation into the social system, would . . . suffice to dissipate a great part of disorder, even material disorder, in any kind of temporal government. . . . *[e]ither by correcting and broadening the ideas of the governing classes, or by instilling in them, willingly or by force, a superior kind of morality"* (Corr, 110, emphasis added). Indeed, at this time, Mill even seems to have moved far toward the acceptance of Comte's schemes for organizing the temporal order. Comte, he says, has "establish[ed] the undeniable principle that the direction [of our development] is henceforth up to the leaders of industry." He is so far involved with Comte's plan for the reorganization of society that he wishes to discuss some of the many details that "positive sociology" will have to resolve upon the establishment of the new order. For instance, they will need to discuss "how to reduce the influence, inevitable up to a point but all too extensive today, of pure chance, especially of birth, in deciding who will hold the leading positions in industry" (Corr, 110). This certainly rings an ominous note to the traditional liberal ear.[74]

Although Mill would eventually condemn Comte's plan for institutionalizing the spiritual power as "spiritual domination" or "despotism" (OL, 17), it is clear that during the years of their correspondence both thinkers were profoundly convinced of the need to deny spiritual power or authority to temporal rulers. But what does that mean in the case of Mill? Mill's deep interest in the separation of the two powers is of course intimately related to the religious dimension of his thought under examination in this work. More particularly, it reflects not the desire for liberty of conscience traditionally characteristic of the liberal temper but the intensely antitheological nature of Mill's enterprise. Mill's interest in the separation of the two powers was not primarily derived from a classical-liberal concern to limit the temporal power to exclusively mundane matters. His principal interest was in wresting spiritual and moral authority from its traditional religious carriers and gaining "worldly power" for a new secular or positivist elite[75] (Spirit, 33). Mill was not at this time (nor, arguably, at any other) preoccupied with the issue of limited government.[76] What principally concerns Mill in his correspondence with Comte is the issue of authority, and, most especially, moral and spiritual authority.[77] The political establishment to which he wished to deny spiritual power was intimately bound up with the religious establishment and thus with traditional theological beliefs. It is such beliefs, as he says in the *Autobiography*, that are "the great intellectual support of false doctrines and bad institutions. By the[ir] aid, . . . every inveterate belief and every intense feeling . . . is enabled to dispense with the obligation of justifying itself by reason [by appealing to a divine origin], and is erected into its own all-sufficient voucher and justification. There never was such an instrument devised for consecrating all deep seated prejudices" (134). Mill's antitheological aim dovetailed with his political aim—to undermine the British aristocracy in service of democratization. This latter aim necessarily entailed the evisceration of the moral authority of the religious establishment that supported the traditional English constitution.

Mill's great desire for the establishment of a modern counterpart to the medieval spiritual power, while related to his political aims, was, however, chiefly derived from what we have characterized as his overriding aim—the replacement of a theological with a purely human orientation and morality. In order to facilitate the birth of the new world of positivist, humanitarian, or nontheological utilitarianism, the acquisition of moral authority—the creation of a new spiritual power—was essential. Mill set his mind to the task.[78] Needless to say, all of this is far removed from the conventional view of Mill as the champion of individuality and individual liberty—a view which is, in many respects, misleading (see Chapters 6 and 8). For the Mill of the correspondence with Comte, "spiritual power" is the power and the authority to form and mold the beliefs and opinions of the populace in line with the new and superior *human* morality he aimed to establish.[79]

Unanimity and Authority

[T]he first men of the age will one day join hands and be agreed: and then there is no power in itself, on earth or in hell, capable of withstanding them.

—*J. S. Mill*, The Spirit of the Age

It is necessary to explore one other aspect of Comte's understanding of the spiritual power before returning to Mill. Comte's model for the anticipated modern spiritual power was the contemporary authority of science.

According to Comte, scientific authority is principally based upon trust or "confidence." Because most people, both laymen and professionals in non-scientific fields, cannot themselves demonstrate or establish scientific theories, they inevitably take them upon trust from the scientific authorities. A mathematician, for instance, accepts physiological propositions on trust from physiologists, and vice versa; indeed, mathematicians accept theorems on trust from one another. In short, because no person can reinvent the wheel in every single department of life and thought, we of necessity accept many of our most important beliefs on trust. And the reason we can do so with confidence is that the authorities, the expert men of science, those who know, have *unanimously* accepted their truth. The unanimity that ensures the unchallenged authority of science is itself an outcome of the fact that scientific practitioners have achieved full confidence in the *methods* employed to arrive at results in their respective disciplines. The authority of science, then, is a result of professional scientists establishing or proving their theories in accordance with accepted methods.

This is the aspect of Comte's conception of the "spiritual power" that had the greatest significance for Mill. Comte and Mill were concerned with establishing the same unchallenged authority concerning moral and political truths that they believed had been gained by science. The lesson Comte and then Mill drew from the contemporary authority of science was the necessity of establishing a *method* by which philosophers can reach unanimity regarding moral and political truths. Once such a method has been devised and accepted, the results obtained by means of it must gain unanimous acceptance among the experts. Their unanimity, in turn, will ensure that the masses—unable in this area as in the area of physical science to themselves demonstrate the truth of the propositions—will place as unfailing a trust in the new spiritual power as they do in the scientific authorities. The spiritual power to which all defer as the ultimate authority on matters moral and political is thus triumphant. This, as said, is the prospect to which Mill was drawn. As Mill wrote to John Sterling in 1831: "I once heard [it said] that almost all differences of opinion when analysed, were differences of method. But if so, he who can throw most light upon the subject of method, will do most to forward that alliance among the most advanced intellects & characters of the age, which is the only definite object I ever have in literature or philosophy, so far as I have any general object at all."[80]

Mill was to devote the most intense efforts to devising the *method*—the "canons of induction"—by means of which unanimity in the "human sciences" could be achieved; the result of such efforts was *A System of Logic*. As Mill explained in the early draft of his *Autobiography:*

I no longer believed that the fate of mankind depended on the possibility of making all of them competent judges of questions of government and legislation [as his father and Bentham had taught]. From this time my hopes of improvement rested less on the reason of the multitude, than on the possibility of effecting such an improvement in the methods of political and social philosophy, as should enable all thinking and instructed persons who have no sinister interest to be so nearly of one mind on these subjects, as to carry the multitude with them by their united authority.[81]

One of the chief purposes of the *Logic,* then, and especially book 6 ("On the Logic of the Moral Sciences"), was to establish such methods as would lead to unanimity of opinion among the elite, a unanimity that would establish an authority in moral, spiritual, and political matters as unchallenged as the authority of science. As Acton understands it, the new spiritual authority of Mill and Comte was one "in which the natural and the social sciences replaced revelation."[82] Mill fully anticipated that the results of the new "positive" approach to moral truth would be in accord with nontheological utilitarianism. The spiritual power—especially concerned, as Comte had emphasized, with the education of the populace—would of course inculcate the new utilitarian morality directed toward service to humanity.

Mill adopted Comte's view that a modern spiritual power must be essentially concerned with the sciences of man and society, which, for Mill as for others of his era, included political philosophy and political economy, as well as the anticipated positivist development of the moral and political sciences. Mill's view, as he put it in his 1836 review of Tocqueville's *Democracy in America,* was: "The multitude will never believe these truths, until tendered to them from an authority in which they have as *unlimited confidence* as they have in the unanimous voice of astronomers on a question of astronomy." Indeed, as Acton observes, "although Mill uses the same word as Comte, 'confidence' (*confiance*) for the trust in superior intellectual authority, he goes further than his predecessor, who had qualified it by the adjective 'provisional,' in characterizing it as 'unlimited'. At this time, therefore, Mill was according even more to authority than Comte had done."[83] In criticizing the liberal political economist Charles Dunoyer in 1845, Mill provided a further glimpse into his own understanding of the spiritual power. What Mill found blameworthy in Dunoyer, he told Comte, was his "not having caught even a glimpse of the necessity . . . of a spiritual power. . . . He proposes a social system in which he necessarily expects that his own moral and political views are accepted, but does not pay the slightest attention to the conditions necessary for the existence of any system of common beliefs accepted as an authority. It is truly too naive to believe that today mere freedom of speech is sufficient for that" (*Corr,* 296).

As said, Mill's attraction to the Saint-Simonian conception of the spiritual power is a reflection of the concern he shared with that school regarding the necessary conditions of "social unity" in an "anarchical period of transition" (*Corr,* 341). Having discovered the importance of ideas and beliefs to the formation of human experience, Mill, like Saint-Simon and Comte, became concerned with ensuring unanimity of opinion among the elite that was to guide social development in the "normal" state that would follow the contemporary state of transition. The aim, as Comte put it, was to create "the continuing presence, in today's fluctuating milieu, of a constantly homogenous and decisive point of view in the sciences and philosophy, also in politics and ethics" (*Corr,* 284). As Mill himself put it in "The Spirit of the Age": "While . . . contending parties are measuring their sophistries against one another, the man who is capable of other ideas than those of his age, has an example in the present state of physical science, and in the manner in which men shape their thoughts and their actions within its sphere, of what is to be hoped for and laboured for in all other departments of human knowledge; and what, beyond all possibility of doubt, will one day be attained" (*Spirit,* 19).

Mill is well known for his early advocacy of the application of the methods of the natural sciences to the human or social sciences. Less widely understood, however, is how closely his advocacy of such methods in the exploration and discovery of moral and social truth was tied to his desire to create an unquestioned authority—a spiritual power or a "tribunal of the specially instructed"—capable of winning the trust and faith of the masses in its recommendations and theories. Mill had been greatly impressed by Comte's argument against "freedom of opinion" in science and why such freedom could no more be permitted in moral or social than in physical matters. *A System of Logic,* as we have seen, aimed to create the method whereby the intellectual elite would achieve unanimity, ensuring that its teachings gained ultimate ascendancy over public opinion. Mill, often praised as the great champion of liberty of thought and discussion, was, at least for a period of time, far more concerned with establishing unquestioned authority in moral matters than with celebrating the individual pursuit of truth. It is noteworthy that Mill's Benthamite friends wished to distance themselves from his new Saint-Simonian views. John Roebuck, for instance, protested against Mill's belief "in the advantages to be derived from an Aristocracy of intellect." Roebuck said he was "as opposed to that kind of aristocracy as to any other" nor were his "suspicions to be lulled asleep by ingenious plans for giving intellect her dominance."[84]

"The Spirit of the Age"

The extent of Mill's early illiberalism justifies a rather extensive quote from his "Spirit of the Age," published in early 1831 (when Mill was twenty-four years old):

> We never hear of the right of private judgment in physical science; yet it exists; for what is there to prevent any one from denying every proposition in natural philosophy, if he be so minded? The physical sciences however have been brought to so advanced a stage of improvement by a series of great men, and the methods by which they are cultivated so entirely preclude the possibility of material error when due pains are taken to arrive at the truth, that all persons who have studied those subjects have come to a nearly unanimous agreement upon them. Some minor differences . . . exist . . . [b]ut . . . it is seldom attempted to thrust them into undue importance, nor to remove them, by way of appeal from the tribunal of the specially instructed to that of the public at large. The compact mass of authority thus created overawes the minds of the uninformed. . . . [Thus] no one dares to stand up against the scientific world until he too has qualified himself to be named as a man of science; and no one does this without being forced, by irresistible evidence, to adopt the received opinion. The physical sciences, therefore, . . . are continually growing, but never changing: in every age they receive indeed mighty improvements, but for them the age of transition is past. (*Spirit*, 19–20)

The same methods followed in the moral sciences, Mill reasons, would create the same "compact mass of authority" to "overawe the minds of the uninformed" in moral and social matters as they do with respect to physical matters.

> It is almost unnecessary to remark in how very different a condition from this, are the sciences which are conversant with the moral nature and social condition of man. In those sciences, this imposing unanimity among all who have studied the subject does not exist; and every dabbler, consequently, thinks his opinion as good as another's. Any man who has eyes and ears shall be judge whether . . . a person who has never studied politics, for instance, or political economy systematically, regards himself as any-way precluded thereby from promulgating with the most unbounded assurance the crudest opinions, and taxing men who have made those sciences the occupation of a laborious life, with the most contemptible ignorance and imbecility. It is rather the person who *has* studied the subject systematically that is regarded as disqualified. He is a *theorist*: and the word which expresses

the highest and noblest effort of human intelligence is turned into a bye-word [*sic*] of derision. (21)

Mill continues to complain: Uneducated prejudice governs; no one defers to the authority of the instructed. Such, however, is the present state of affairs and the question is how to move beyond it. Mill does not wish unduly to denigrate the intelligence of the people; he says, "I yield to no one in the degree of intelligence of which I believe them to be capable." But most men will never have the requisite leisure to perform the intellectual labor necessary to establish moral truth or to examine the evidence whereby such truths are established. As a result, such inquiries must be conducted by the few who are able to make the "investigation and study of physical, moral, and social truths, . . . their peculiar calling. . . . *The remainder of mankind must, and except in periods of transition like the present, always do, take the far greater part of their opinions on all extensive subjects upon the authority of those who have studied them*" (24–27, emphasis added).

Mill, like Comte, does not advocate a slavish submission to authority. All men can inquire into and investigate the moral, social, and political truths formulated by the specialized experts; that is, they can "acquaint themselves with the evidence of the truths which are presented to them." Nevertheless, there are limits to their ability to know, and deference to the instructed remains essential. "Let him learn what he can, and as well as he can—still however bearing in mind, that there are others who probably know much with which he not only is unacquainted, but of the evidence of which, in the existing state of his knowledge, it is impossible that he should be a competent judge." In the final analysis, the educated layman must defer to expert knowledge. Mill admits that it will be to the good when the "proofs of the moral and social truths of greatest importance to mankind . . . shall begin to be circulated among the people." His aim is informed, not slavish, submission.

Nor will Mill allow common sense to count as authoritative knowledge:

It is easy to say that the truth of certain propositions is obvious to *common sense*. It may be so: but how am I assured that the conclusions of common sense are confirmed by accurate knowledge? Judging by common sense is merely another phrase for judging by first appearances; and every one who has mixed among mankind with any capacity for observing them knows that the men who place implicit faith in their own common sense are, without any exception, the most wrong-headed and impracticable persons with whom he has ever had to deal.[85]

Mill offers a ringing defense of the "authority of the best-instructed":

It is, therefore, one of the necessary conditions of humanity, that the majority must either have wrong opinions, or no fixed opinions, or must place the degree of reliance warranted by reason, in the authority of those who have made moral and social philosophy their peculiar study. . . . It is right that [every man] should follow his reason as far as his reason will carry him, and cultivate the faculty as highly as possible. But reason itself will teach most men that they must, in the last resort, fall back upon the authority of still more cultivated minds, as the ultimate sanction of the convictions of their reason itself. (26–31)

The "ultimate sanction" of moral truth is the "authority of . . . more cultivated minds," that is, a purely human and not a divine sanction. Mill's lifelong aim is by now familiar to readers of this work.

For the majority of his contemporaries, however, Mill's strong defense of the need for authority would point to traditional religious authority. Mill thus denies that the requisite authority in "moral and social philosophy" presently exists and explains its absence in terms of the Saint-Simonian philosophy of history. More particularly, he explains that the absence of such authority is characteristic of a period of anarchical transition such as his own:

But where is the authority which commands this confidence, or deserves it? Nowhere: and here we see the peculiar character, and . . . the . . . peculiar inconvenience, of a period of moral and social transition. At all other periods [the "organic" or "normal" periods] there exists a large body of received doctrine, covering the whole field of the moral relations of man, and which no one thinks of questioning, backed as it is by the authority of all, or nearly all, persons, supposed to possess knowledge enough to qualify them for giving an opinion on the subject. This state of things does not now exist in the civilised world—except . . . to a certain limited extent in the United States of America. The progress of inquiry has brought to light the insufficiency of the ancient doctrines; but those who have made the investigation of social truths their occupation, have not yet sanctioned any new body of doctrine with their unanimous, or nearly unanimous, consent. The true opinion is recommended to the public by no greater weight of authority than hundreds of false opinions; and, even at this day, to find any thing like a united body of grave and commanding authority, we must revert to the doctrines from which the progressiveness of the human mind, or, as it is more popularly called, the improvement of the age, has set us free. (32–33)

Mill is of course referring to traditional religious, Christian, views. The only "authority" that exists consists of the obsolete hand-me-downs of the theological and metaphysical states of the human mind—the "inanimate corpses of dead political & religious systems, never more to be revived."[86]

Mill closes with the suggestion that liberty of discussion and conscience is necessary, as Saint-Simon had taught, during the transitional period, along with the suggestion that it is necessary *only* during that transition:

> In the mean time, as the old doctrines have gone out, and the new ones have not yet come in, every one must judge for himself as he best may. Learn, and think for yourself, is reasonable advice for the day: but let not the business of the day be so done as to prejudice the work of the morrow. "Les superiorites morales . . . finiront par s'entendre;" *the first men of the age will one day join hands and be agreed: and then there is no power in itself, on earth or in hell, capable of withstanding them.* (emphasis added)

Mill curiously omits mention of a power in heaven. In any event, his reflections seem to have roused him to the very height of revolutionary fervor:

> But ere this can happen there must be a change in the whole framework of society, as at present constituted. Worldly power must pass from the hands of the stationary part of mankind into those of the progressive part. There must be a moral and social revolution, which shall . . . take away no men's lives or property, but which shall leave to no man one fraction of unearned distinction or unearned importance.[87]
> That man cannot achieve his destiny but through such a transformation, and that it will and *shall* be effected, is the conclusion of every man who can feel the wants of his own age, without hankering after past ages.[88] (33)

An earlier passage, replete with Saint-Simonian terminology, evinces the extent to which Mill had embraced Saint-Simon's philosophy of history in the early 1830s.

> Now, it is self-evident that no fixed opinions have yet generally established themselves in the place of those which we have abandoned; that no new doctrines, philosophical or social, as yet command . . . an assent at all comparable in unanimity to that which the ancient doctrines could boast of while they continued in vogue. So long as this intellectual anarchy shall endure . . . [w]e have not yet advanced beyond the unsettled state, in which the mind is, when it has recently found itself out in a grievous error, and has not yet satisfied itself of the truth. . . . This is not a state of health, but, at the best, of convalescence. It is a necessary stage in the progress of civilisation but it is attended with numerous evils; as one part of a road may be rougher or more dangerous than another, although every step brings the traveler nearer to his desired end. (13)

Thus the urgent need for a modern counterpart to the medieval spiritual power and for the methods of the *Logic*. As we shall see in our discussion of *On Liberty*, there is no reason to believe that Mill ever fully abandoned the youthful views that so significantly shaped his early philosophical endeavors.

Mill's correspondence is an indispensable guide to the interpretation of his published writings. It reveals both the seriousness of his intent to usher in the "positivist" age—defined in explicit opposition to the traditional theological orientation of the West—and the depth of his commitment to the "substitution" of Humanity for a transcendent God. We have seen that Mill's published writings must be interpreted with care because of his policy of "total silence on the question of religion" and in light of what we have seen to be his ulterior motive—to "indirectly . . . strike any blow one wishes at religious beliefs." Thus forearmed, we are better prepared to examine Mill's explicit writings on religion, a task to which we now turn.

3

"Nature" and "Utility of Religion"

> [T]he religions of the world will continue standing, if even as mere shells or husks, until high-minded devotion to the ideal of humanity shall have acquired the twofold character of a religion, viz., as the ultimate basis of thought and the animating and controlling power over action.
>
> —J. S. Mill, *diary*

The only of Mill's public writings explicitly to address the subject of religion is the small volume titled simply *Three Essays on Religion,* published posthumously in 1874. According to Mill's stepdaughter, Helen Taylor, who prepared the essays for publication, the first two, "Nature" and "Utility of Religion," were composed sometime between 1850 and 1858. The third essay, "Theism," was written at a later date, probably between 1868 and 1870, and is one of Mill's last major compositions (he died in 1873). In her introduction, Taylor warns the reader that the three pieces were not "intend[ed] to form a consecutive series . . . [and thus] must not . . . be regarded as a connected body of thought." Nevertheless, she is certain that Mill himself regarded the views expressed in the three essays as "fundamentally consistent." The evidence for this, she says, is that in 1873 Mill was making plans to publish "Nature" essentially as it stood, indicating, to her mind, that his views "had undergone no substantial change."[1] Taylor's remarks are of interest because the final essay, "Theism," written in the evening of Mill's life, seemed to his contemporaries to represent something of a departure not only from the views expressed in the two earlier essays but from Mill's own known views on religion. Certain of Mill's disciples were "painfully surprised," as one of them, John Morley, put it, by both the substance and the tone of Mill's final words on religion. Morley regarded "Theism" as not only internally inconsistent, but also inconsistent with the other two essays in the volume and with the views Mill had held throughout his life.[2] Others, especially certain Christian critics, were more pleasantly surprised—they thought they saw a positive development in Mill's religious thought, one that seemed to lead Mill closer to their own views.[3] We shall return to the issues of Mill's consistency and development after examining each of the three essays in some depth.

Despite Taylor's remarks, there are reasons to regard "Nature" and "Utility of Religion" as sufficiently distinct from "Theism" to justify a separate treatment. Mill's diary and correspondence reveal that during the 1850s he and his wife, Harriet Taylor Mill, were convinced they did not have long to live. Accordingly, they believed it imperative to record their most important thoughts for thinkers of the future. As Mill wrote to Harriet in 1853: "We must finish the best we have got to say, . . . [and] publish it while we are alive. I do not see what living depository there is likely to be of our thoughts, or who in this weak generation that is growing up will even be capable of thoroughly mastering & assimilating your ideas, much less of re-originating them—so we must write them & print them, & then they can wait until there are again thinkers."[4] A few months later, he continued with this theme:

> [I have] been feeling much . . . about the shortness & uncertainty of life & the wrongness of having so much of the best of what we have to say, so long unwritten & in the power of chance—& I am determined to make a better use of what time we have. Two years . . . would enable us I think to get the most of it into a state fit for printing—if not in the best form for popular effect, yet in the state of concentrated thought—a sort of mental pemican, which thinkers, when there are any after us, may nourish themselves with & then dilute for other people. The Logic & Political. Ec. may perhaps keep their buoyancy long enough to hold these other things above water till there are people capable of taking up the thread of thought & continuing it.[5]

In 1854, Mill and his wife each devised lists of subjects that they regarded as essential for the development of future thought and the eventual realization of their dreamed-of society. Mill's list included the following: "Differences of character (nation, race, age, sex, temperament). Love. Education of tastes. Religion de l'Avenir. Plato. Slander. Foundation of morals. Utility of religion. Socialism. Liberty. Doctrine that causation is will. . . . Family, & Conventional."[6] Harriet also made a list of topics she regarded as essential for this purpose, topics which included both nature and the utility of religion. And she sketched an essay that would "account for the existence nearly universal of some religion (superstition) by the instincts of fear, hope and mystery etc., and *throwing over all doctrines and theories, called religion.* . . . [and] how all this must be superseded by morality deriving its power from sympathies and benevolence and its reward from the approbation of those we respect" (emphasis added).[7] In the mid-1850s Mill wrote first drafts of several of these "mental pemicans," including the early draft of his *Autobiography,* as well as essays on justice, utilitarianism, nature, the utility of religion, and liberty. "Nature" and "Utility of Religion" were withheld from publication until after Mill's death. The essay on liberty was published as *On Liberty* (1859) and the two essays on justice and utilitarianism as *Utilitarianism* (1861). All of the essays were composed in close collaboration with Harriet Taylor. Although Mill's claim that Harriet was coauthor of most of his works may be an exaggeration, there is no question that both "Nature" and "Utility of Religion" and, to an even greater degree, *On Liberty,* bear her strong imprint, including direct quotations taken from letters she sent to Mill. The question of Harriet Taylor's influence on Mill's thought has been much debated, but there is no reason to doubt Mill's claim that she was a major contributor, in spirit and substance if not in form, to many of his works and especially those written before her death in 1857.[8]

This chapter examines the two contemporaneously composed "mental pemicans" on the subject of religion, "Nature" and "Utility of Religion." "Theism" will be examined in Chapter 5; the issues addressed in Mill's final essay on religion may be better appreciated after we have examined his participation in the Mansel controversy in Chapter 4.

I: "Nature"

[T]he duty of man is the same in respect to his own nature as in respect to the nature of all other things, namely not to follow but to amend it.

—*J. S. Mill, "Nature"*

The Refutation of Deism

When Mill analyzes or criticizes "religion" he generally has in mind a particular expression of Christianity that rose to prominence in the eighteenth century, which he variously refers to as "deism," "natural religion," or "natural theology." His *Three Essays on Religion* are thus striking, among other reasons, for the one-sided view of Christianity they explore. Mill's correspondence, however, provides insight into why he selected deism as the target of his criticism of religion. The refutation of deistic views, he believed, was essential to the realization of his aim: to eradicate the "poisonous root" of theology to prepare the ground for the growth of nontheological utilitarianism and its spiritual carrier, the Religion of Humanity. As Comte had emphasized, "[T]oday's rapid decay of theology ... [has left an] ordinary deism ... the last important phase of the theological state of mind. ... [It is this] Protestant or deistic metaphysics ... which, for the last century, has constituted ... the main support of the deplorable prolongation of the theological regime" (*Corr,* 301–2). Comte had identified two main camps of the deistic enemy: the "school of Voltaire" ("progressive" deism) and the "school of Rousseau" ("systematic" or "reactionary" deism) (*Corr,* 292, 309). In Mill's English context, deism was represented by such eighteenth-century lights as Bishop Joseph Butler and later by William Paley.

Mill believed that deism, or natural theology—and especially what he called its "irrational proviso of a Providence manifest in general laws"— was the last stronghold of theological belief in England (*Corr,* 129). In this, as in other respects, he was following Bentham. Natural religion, it may be recalled, was also the nominal target of Bentham/Grote's *Analysis of the Influence of Natural Religion on the Temporal Happiness of Mankind,* which so profoundly influenced Mill's development. Mill would carry on the battle against natural religion or deism throughout his life. In the *Autobiography* he is still complaining how "very little, with any claim to a philosophical character, has been written by sceptics against the usefulness of ... [deistic] belief" (71). Both "Nature" and "Theism" were intended to fill this gap in the skeptical literature. "Theism" refutes the principal deistic arguments for the existence of God, while "Nature" is a vehement attack on "optimistic Deism—a worship of the order of Nature and the supposed course of Providence."

The chief purpose of "Nature," then, is to refute the notion that nature is in any sense a proper guide and model for human behavior and to do so by dissevering the traditional association of nature with lawful order, with the right and the good, with God. As Mill put it, the essay shows that "it cannot be religious or moral in us to guide our actions by the analogy of the course of nature" ("Nat," 386). "Nature" is thus, among other things, an attack on natural law, a skirmish in the long-standing Benthamite and Comtean war against the "imaginary fictions" of traditional theology and metaphysics.[9] Mill also regarded the essay as a weapon in his ongoing and related battle against the "intuitionist" school of Sir William Hamilton and others, discussed in the following chapter. Mill's intuitionist enemies were a motley crew, united mainly by a belief that human beings possess an innate moral sense or other faculty that permits recognition of transcendent moral truth and of God's reality. Mill himself utterly denied the reality of innate faculties, senses, or ideas or of a capacity to apprehend moral truth intuitively. As he said, "[T]he great original error [is] thinking that an opinion deeply seated in the human mind proves itself. Until people can be untaught this cardinal error, they will never have any difficulty in persuading themselves of the truth of any doctrines which have long been part of the furniture of their mind. . . . [They will continue in the false belief] that *so* the thing must *be* because it is the nature . . . of the mind so to conceive it."[10] This was especially true of the allegedly implanted conviction of God and other religious prejudices. Mill's attack on nature—which, as he says, is sometimes used as a "general designation for those parts of our mental and moral constitution which are supposed to be innate, in contradistinction to those which are acquired"—was thus intended to slay not only the deistic conception of a providential governance of the universe, but the intuitionist and "moral sense" schools as well ("Nat," 399). Mill refutes the notion of an innate moral sense, faculty, or intuition by showing that what is good in human existence is exclusively the acquired product of training.

As said, however, his chief purpose is to show that the notion of a providential order that manifests itself through the universal governance of natural law is insupportable. He does so by showing that the course of nature cannot be a manifestation of God's purpose because nature is an utterly immoral realm of disorder, indeed of "perfect and absolute recklessness" ("Nat," 384). Mill's overriding purpose in this essay—to destroy the notion of providential order—leads him to sketch a view of nature remarkable not only for its wild hyperbole but also for what it reveals of the deep sense of cosmic disorder obviously experienced by both Mill and his wife.

Nature Defined

Mill identifies two definitions of *nature* in common usage, only one of which is the "correct" and "true scientific sense" of the term. The correct, scientific sense of *nature* is "the ensemble or aggregate of [a thing's] powers or properties." When used in this sense (as in "the nature of fire"), *nature* refers to

> the modes in which [a thing] acts on other things ([including] . . . the senses of the observer) and the modes in which other things act upon it, . . . [including] its own capacities of feeling, or being conscious. . . . The Nature of the thing means . . . its entire capacity of exhibiting phenomena. . . . [A]s the nature of any given thing is the aggregate of its powers and properties, so Nature in the abstract is the aggregate of the powers and properties of all things. Nature, [then,] means the sum of all phenomena, together with the causes which produce them.

The second sense of the ambiguous term *nature* is that suggested by the common opposition of nature to art, of natural to artificial. In the first and "correct" scientific sense of the term, "[a]rt is as much Nature as anything else, and everything which is artificial is natural. . . . Art is but the employment of the powers of Nature for an end" ("Nat," 374–75). Those who employ the term *nature* in the second sense are actually attempting to differentiate events that occur "spontaneously," that is, without the conscious intervention of human beings.

Mill, then, works with two distinct meanings of the term *nature*: 1) "all the powers existing in either the outer or the inner world and everything which takes place by means of those powers" (in this correct and scientific sense of the term, *nature* is a "collective name for everything which is"); and 2) "only what takes place without the agency, or without the voluntary and intentional agency, of man." Used in the latter sense, *nature* is a "name for everything which is of itself, without voluntary human intervention." It is this sense of the term that Mill characterizes as a wicked chaos. The attack on Providence simultaneously valorizes human agency and will. All that is good in existence is shown to be not the unfolding of God's plan but the work of man ("Nat," 375–77).

Having defined the term *nature* to his satisfaction, Mill hones in on the main object of the essay—to examine the validity of the long-standing association between nature and "ideas of commendation, approval, and even moral obligation." He briefly surveys the history of the various schools of thought that have employed the term *nature* to mean the "criterion" of morals and of law, from the Stoics and Epicureans, through the Roman jurists and international lawyers, to the "sentimental Deists." (It is worthy of remark that Mill omits any reference to the Greek conception of "right by nature.") These latter—the sentimental deists—are the chief object of his attack. Their views, Mill explains, rose to prominence in the eighteenth century in reaction to the Christian emphasis on the natural wickedness of man. It is this emphasis, "by the reaction which it provoked, [that] has made the deistical moralists almost unanimous in proclaiming the divinity of Nature, and setting up its fancied dictates as an authoritative rule of action." Such a view, of which Rousseau is the chief representative, has deeply influenced modern notions of morality, including the Christian. The "doctrines of Christianity have in every age been largely accommodated to the philosophy which happened to be prevalent, and the Christianity of our day has borrowed a considerable part of its colour and flavour from sentimental deism." Mill recognizes that the "so-called Law of Nature" is not, in his day, consistently regarded as the foundation of ethics or employed as the standard from which "to deduce rules of action with juridical precision," as had been attempted in former centuries. Nevertheless, the concept of nature and its "imaginary code" continues to influence moral philosophy and practice: "That any mode of thinking, feeling, or acting, is 'according to nature' is usually accepted as a strong argument for its goodness" ("Nat," 375–77).

Mill's aim, as emphasized, is to complete the work begun by Bentham—to demolish the concept of nature as a standard of moral obligation, rightness, or goodness, as well as the false and pernicious moralities and laws based upon it. This aim also dovetailed with that of Comte—to vanquish the last of the "metaphysical" enemies of positivism, which, in Mill's context, meant the deistical conception of a Providence manifested in the order of nature. To realize his purposes, Mill first identifies the sense in which those who refer morality and law to *nature* employ the term. All philosophical inquiries, he argues, concern either "what is" or "what ought to be." The domain of the former is science and history, of the latter, morals and politics. Both senses of the term *nature* identified by Mill—as a name for "everything which is" and as a name for "everything which is of itself, without voluntary human intervention"— refer exclusively to the scientific sense of nature: "what is." Obviously, however, those who employ *nature* as an ethical term intend to say something about what ought to be. What they mean to suggest, Mill recognizes, is that "what is, according to nature" provides some "external criterion" of how human beings should behave. "[T]hey think they are giving some information as to what the standard of action really is. . . . [T]hey have a notion . . . that 'what is,' constitutes the rule and standard of what ought to be." Such reflections lead Mill further to narrow the purpose of his essay: He will examine whether "what is"—that is, *nature* in its correct, scientific sense—can constitute the rule and standard of what ought to be. As he puts it, he will evaluate the truth of those doctrines "which make Nature a test of right and wrong, good and evil, or which in any mode or degree attach merit or approval to following, imitating, or obeying Nature" ("Nat," 377–78).

The Law of Nature

Such an inquiry necessarily entails the examination of the similarly ambiguous word *law*. This term, like *nature*, has two principal meanings, "one of which . . . denotes some definite portion of what is, [the] other, of what ought to be." An example of the former is the "law of gravitation"; of the latter, the "criminal or civil law," which Mill describes in Benthamite fashion as "somebody's suppositions, feelings, or commands respecting what ought to be." Only the first meaning of the term denotes the proper—scientific—sense of *law*—"observed uniformities in the occurrence of phenomena." This is "what is." The second sense refers to such entities as the "laws of the land, the law of nations, or moral laws; among which . . . is dragged in, by jurists and publicists, something which they think proper to call the Law of Nature." This sense refers to "what ought to be." The confounding of these two senses of the term *law,* like the two senses of *nature,* is a source of endless confusion in moral, political, and legal philosophy.[11] Mill pointedly ignores the question of whether there may not in fact be two distinct orders of law, what Ralph Waldo Emerson—and others among Mill's contemporaries[12]—called "Law for man, and law for thing." And, of course, the whole point of Mill's exercise is to deny that the moral law for man *is*—that is, immutably given to man by God. "What is" refers exclusively to phenomena; "what ought to be" is established by man.

For Mill, the term *law of nature* may only properly be used to refer to nature in the first, scientific, phenomenological sense—"observed uniformities in the occurrence of phenomena." These laws are "general propositions" that refer to the "conditions of the occurrence of . . . phenomena, . . . ascertained . . . either by direct observation or by reasoning processes grounded on it" ("Nat," 374). The proposition that air and food are necessary to animal life—universally true, so far as we know—is, Mill explains, a law of nature in the correct sense of the term.

Mill further elucidates the proper meaning of *law of nature.* He asks whether those who exhort their fellows to live in accord with nature use the term in the first or second sense he has identified. If *nature* is used in the first sense—"all which is," the powers and properties of all things— any such exhortation is meaningless. No one must be advised to follow nature in this sense because no one can avoid doing so. Whether one behaves well or ill, one necessarily acts in accord with nature understood as "all which is," for one necessarily employs the powers and properties of nature in all one's activities. While human beings necessarily obey the laws of nature in all they do, however, most of them do not consciously recognize this or consciously guide their actions by them. This observation leads Mill to acknowledge one meaningful sense of the generally "useless precept to follow nature." Bacon taught us that "we can obey nature in such a manner as to command it." This requires that we study nature to discover the properties of things in order consciously to utilize them to attain our purposes. Indeed, the study of nature in this sense is, for Mill, the "first principle of all intelligent action, or rather . . . the definition of intelligent action itself." Its fruit is a "rule of prudence" useful for permitting the judicious adaptation of means to the attainment of human ends. What Mill will not abide is the "unmeaning doctrine [of following nature] which superficially resembles the . . . rational precept *Naturam observare*." Those who uphold obedience or conformity to Nature as an ethical maxim or law imply that such "action must mean something more than merely intelligent action." (They imply, of course, that right behavior is that in conformity with a given moral law, although Mill strategically leaves this unstated, perhaps another illustration of his policy of dealing with questions of religion and God "as if [they] did not exist.") He will simply assert, on the contrary, that "no precept beyond this last [the prudential Baconian maxim], can be connected with the word Nature in the wider and more philosophical of its acceptations" ("Nat," 379–80).

Prometheus Unbound

Having declared that it is "unmeaning" to employ the term *nature* in the sense of "what is" as an ethical term, Mill next examines whether the exhortation to follow nature makes sense if we use the term in his second sense—that which occurs without human intervention, the "spontaneous course of things when left to themselves." The notion that nature in this sense is a helpful guide in the human endeavor to "adapt things to our use" is, Mill concludes, "palpably absurd and self-contradictory."

> For while human action cannot help conforming to Nature in the [first] meaning of the term ["all which is"], the very aim and object of action is to alter and improve Nature in the [second] meaning [the spontaneous course of events]. If the natural course of things were perfectly right and satisfactory, to act at all would be a gratuitous meddling. . . . [Indeed,] to do anything with forethought and purpose, would be a violation of that perfect order . . . of nature. . . . To dig, to plough, to build, to wear clothes, are direct infringements of the injunction to follow nature. ("Nat," 380–81)

Mill is of course aware that the proponents of natural law never enjoined the following of nature in the way he suggests. Nevertheless, as his aim is not to understand the traditional meaning of natural law but to press for the most far-flung exercise of human agency, such fine points of argument are more or less irrelevant. He continues by saying that all people implicitly recognize the absurdity of commending nature in the sense of spontaneously occurring events.

> Everybody professes to approve and admire many great triumphs of Art over Nature. . . . [But to approve the building of bridges and such is to] ac-

knowledge that the ways of Nature are to be conquered, not obeyed, . . . that her powers are often towards man in the position of enemies, from whom he must wrest by force and ingenuity, what little he can for his own use. . . . All praise of Civilisation, or Art, or Contrivance, is so much dispraise of Nature; an admission of imperfection, which it is man's business, and merit to be always endeavouring to correct or mitigate. ("Nat," 381)

The next move in Mill's attack on nature, understood as the standard of ordered and ethical life or as the expression of providential design, is to link the views he condemns, and especially the reluctance to intervene with the "spontaneous order of Nature," to religious superstition and priestcraft. Human beings, he says, are aware that their efforts to improve their condition are implicitly a "censure" of the natural order of existence. Thus, "in all ages," improving innovations have been "under a shade of religious suspicion. . . . [They have been regarded as being, if not] offensive [then at least] uncomplimentary . . . [to] the all-powerful beings . . . or Being supposed to govern the various phenomena of the universe, and of whose will the course of nature was conceived to be the expression. Any attempt to mould natural phenomena to the convenience of mankind might easily appear an interference with the government of those superior beings" ("Nat," 381). Undoubtedly most such attempts were first undertaken in "fear and trembling," only overcome after experience showed that human initiative did not in fact draw down divine vengeance. Priests, however, have always been skilled at devising plausible rationales for why certain innovations may be permitted, while preserving a "general dread of encroaching on the divine administration." Their usual device was to depict the main human inventions as the gifts of a god; oracles and revelation, however, served the same purpose, as did the Bible and the "infallible Church" of the Catholic religion. Whatever the particular device employed, each of these "expedients" enabled religious authority to "declare what exertions of human spontaneity were permitted or forbidden." Mill's point, in short, is that "any attempt to exercise power over nature, beyond a certain degree, and a certain admitted range, [was long regarded] as an impious effort to usurp divine power, and dare more than was permitted to man" ("Nat," 381–82). Mill was far from immune to the Promethean impulse that also carried various other nineteenth-century titans.[13]

Mill emphasizes that the religious prohibition against "prying into the secrets of the Almighty" is alive and well in his day. This manifests itself as the belief in providential design, or, as he puts it, a "vague notion" that the "general scheme of nature is a model for us to imitate, . . . that nature's . . . ways . . . are God's work, and as such perfect." The same religious prejudice sometimes leads not only natural scientists but, indeed, "anyone who makes [a] new exertion of human forethought and contrivance" to be charged with presumptuously attempting to "defeat the designs of Providence" or with "impiety . . . [for] disparag[ing] the works of the Creator's power" ("Nat," 382–83). Mill claims to find a "radical absurdity in all these attempts to discover . . . what are the designs of Providence, in order when they are discovered to help Providence in bringing them about" ("Nat," 397). He is oblivious to the parallel between the providentialist view he dismisses as absurd and his own efforts to "discover" the inevitable course of history and to "help bring about" the inevitable final positivist state.

Mill's Experience of Disorder

Mill next attempts to trace the origins of (to "deconstruct") man's "natural prejudices" against human control of the order of nature. In so doing, he provides a revealing glimpse into both his own experience of the cosmos and his rivalrous feelings toward its creator. Man's prejudices against such control, Mill argues, are perfectly understandable and natural, stemming as they do from the "awe" man feels when confronting the vastness of the universe and the "terror" elicited by the "enormous power [it] exemplif[ies]." Still, Mill wishes to emphasize, while such awe-inspiring feelings may "set . . . at defiance all idea of rivalry, . . . [they are] of a totally different character from admiration of excellence. Those in whom awe produces admiration may be aesthetically developed, but they are morally uncultivated." For Mill, the contemplation of the vastness and power of the universe produces not wonder or pleasure but a feeling akin to pain and terror. This feeling stems ultimately from fear of an enormous power which, for all we know, may be "maleficent" ("Nat," 384). The Greek experience of harmonious cosmic order remained beyond his reach.

Indeed, during the period when "Nature" was composed, Mill seems to have experienced the cosmos not merely as a realm of overawing power, but as a vast chaos: "[N]ext to the greatness of these cosmic forces, the quality which most forcibly strikes every one who does not avert his eyes from it, is *their perfect and absolute recklessness*" (emphasis added). Cosmic forces "go straight to their end, without regarding what or whom they crush on the road." Mill then indulges in an astonishing tirade against the evil and immoral ways of nature, wherein he anthropomorphizes what he earlier called the "general designation" or "collective name" of nature, personifying it, endowing its forces with conscious intent, thought, will, purpose. The passage must be quoted at length to appreciate the virulence and vehemence of his outburst:

> In sober truth, nearly all the things which men are hanged or imprisoned for doing to one another, are nature's every day performances. Killing . . . Nature does once to every being that lives, after protracted tortures such as only the greatest monsters whom we read of ever purposely inflicted on their living fellow-creatures. . . . [Even if we] arbitrar[ily] . . . refuse to account anything murder but what abridges a certain term supposed to be allotted to human life, nature also does this to all but a small percentage of lives, and does it in all the modes . . . in which the worst human beings take the lives of one another. Nature impales men, breaks them as if on the wheel, casts them to be devoured by wild beasts, burns them to death, crushes them with stones like the first christian [sic] martyr, starves them with hunger, freezes them with cold, poisons them by the quick or slow venom of her exhalations, . . . [along with] hundreds of other hideous deaths in reserve. . . . All this, Nature does with the most supercilious disregard both of mercy and of justice. . . . She mows down those on whose existence hangs the well-being of a whole people, perhaps the prospects of the human race for generations to come, with as little compunction as those whose death is a . . . blessing to those under their noxious influence. Such are Nature's dealings with life. Even when she does not intend to kill, she inflicts the same tortures in apparent wantonness. In the clumsy provision which she has made for that perpetual renewal of animal life . . . no human being ever comes into the world but another human being is literally stretched on the rack for hours or days.[14] . . . Next to taking life . . . is taking the means by which we live; and Nature does this too . . . with the most callous indifference. . . . [H]urricanes, . . . locusts, . . . the waves of the sea . . . wound . . . and kill [like] their human antitypes. . . . Even the love of "order" which is thought to be a following of the ways of Nature, is in fact a contradiction of them. All which people are accustomed to deprecate as "disorder" and its consequences, is precisely a counterpart of Nature's ways. Anarchy and the Reign of Terror are overmatched in injustice, ruin, and death, by a hurricane and pestilence. ("Nat," 384–86)

Mill never suggests that he is speaking metaphorically.

Mill rests his case on such evidence: "[I]t cannot be religious or moral in us to guide our actions by the analogy of the course of nature." And this, moreover, whether or not the seeming destructiveness of nature actually leads to the promotion of good in the long run, as maintained by traditional believers in a providential order. Such a consideration, Mill pronounces, is "altogether beside the point." Even if the "horrors" of nature do promote good ends, he explains, "still as no one believes that good ends would be promoted by our following the example, the course of Nature cannot be a proper model for us to imitate. Either it is right that we should kill because nature kills; torture because nature tortures; ruin and devastate because nature does the like; or we ought not to consider at all what nature does, but what it is good to do" ("Nat," 386). It does not seem to have occurred to Mill that the forces of nature, unlike human beings, are not conscious beings, endowed with minds and will. His attribution of purpose and intent to the impersonal forces of nature is not only peculiar but also especially strange from a philosopher such as Mill, one who accepted Comte's sociology of religion, which accounted for primitive man's belief in gods by his childish tendency to endow impersonal natural forces with will and personality. In any event, for the Mill of "Nature," the issue is closed; his pronouncement has the air of finality. Fifteen years later, as we shall see, he will speak in a somewhat more tentative voice.

The Attack on Providence

Mill's long-standing desire to expose the irrationality of the prevailing religious conception of divine Providence was finally satisfied with the publication of *Three Essays on Religion,* even if he himself was no longer available to meet the response of his public. In "Nature," Mill attacks this "misplaced feeling," this "powerful prepossession"—the notion that human beings should "imitat[e] the ways of Providence as manifested in Nature"—as one of the "great a priori fallacies" that stand in the way of progressive human control over nature, both physical and moral. He is unequivocal on this point:

> [H]owever offensive the proposition may appear to many religious persons, they should be willing to look in the face the undeniable fact, that the order of nature, in so far as unmodified by man, is such as no being, whose attributes are justice and benevolence, would have made, with the intention that his rational creatures should follow it as an example. . . . If made wholly by such a Being, and not partly by beings of very different qualities, it could only be as a designedly imperfect work, which man, in his limited sphere, is to exercise justice and benevolence in amending. The best persons have always held it to be the essence of religion, that the paramount duty of man upon earth is to amend himself: but all except monkish quietists have annexed to this in their inmost minds . . . the additional religious duty of amending the world and not solely the human part of it but the material; the order of physical nature.

For Mill, nature as given is not good. Indeed, nature is hardly an order at all but a realm of "perfect and absolute recklessness": "All which people are accustomed to deprecate as 'disorder' and its consequences, is precisely a counterpart of Nature's ways." Man's "religious duty" is to "amend" not only himself, but "the world," both materially and morally.

What goodness is to be realized in human existence must be achieved by human "exertion" ("Nat," 383–86).

> The scheme of Nature regarded in its whole extent, cannot have had, for its sole or even principal object, the good of human or other sentient beings. What good it brings to them, is mostly the result of their own exertions. Whatsoever, in nature, gives indication of beneficent design, proves . . . [that] the duty of man is to cooperate with the beneficent powers, not by imitating but by perpetually striving to amend the course of nature—and bringing that part of it over which we can exercise control, more nearly into conformity with a high standard of justice and goodness.

All justice and goodness, Mill suggests, are man-made (more particularly, he believed, they are the achievement of those few eminently wise and superior beings who appear from time to time in human history). There is no givenness to the order of being that can be relied upon to guide human action. Nature is above all to be amended: "[A]ll human action whatever, consists in altering, and all useful action in improving, the spontaneous course of nature" ("Nat," 402). Whatever order, whatever "justice and benevolence," are to be brought to this "clumsily made" world must be brought through human agency.

Even the most devout believers, Mill is anxious to point out, do not accept the notion of a providential order without qualification, but do so only selectively and arbitrarily. No one, he says,

> religious or irreligious, believes that the hurtful agencies of nature, considered as a whole, promote good purposes, in any other way than by inciting human rational creatures to rise up and struggle against them. If we believed that those agencies were appointed by a benevolent Providence as the means of accomplishing wise purposes which could not be compassed if they did not exist, then everything done by mankind which tends to chain up these natural agencies or to restrict their . . . operation, from draining a pestilential marsh down to . . . putting up an umbrella, ought to be accounted impious. ("Nat," 386)

Indeed, if human beings really believed that the forces of nature were the instrument of providential design, then they should cherish natural disasters "as medicines provided for our earthly state by infinite wisdom" ("Nat," 387). Moreover, the empirical evidence refutes the conventional religious belief in Providence. Each generation, Mill says, is more successful than its predecessors in averting "natural evil" through technological control of the forces of nature. Therefore, if natural disasters were actually agencies of long-term good, as the providentialists maintain, then the condition of later generations should be growing more and more calamitous in proportion to their aversion of such disasters. This, Mill suggests, is patently absurd. He will admit that good may sometimes come from evil. He points out, however, that evil often comes from good. Every unfortunate event later interpreted as providential can be matched by some seemingly beneficial event that ultimately produced pernicious consequences. Actually, he concludes, human events are so complicated and so dependent on particular circumstances that every event probably affects the individuals it touches both positively and negatively. These are no grounds for accepting the traditional conception of Providence.

Still, Mill does seem to admit that there is a natural order of a kind— good, he recognizes, tends to produce good, and evil, evil. But even this limited evidence of order is, to his mind, evidence of nature's maleficence: "[I]t is one of Nature's general rules, and part of her habitual injustice, that 'to him that hath shall be given, but from him that hath not, shall be taken even that which he hath' (Matthew, 25:29)." It is easier for the healthy to become wealthy; those who experience one kind of pain are more vulnerable to other kinds. Poverty produces "a thousand mental and moral evils." Lack of intelligence engenders moral defects, and moral defects impair the intellect, "and so on without end." Mill's point is to challenge those theologians who have attempted to justify the all-too-real suffering in the world with the weak argument that suffering exists to prevent even greater suffering. It is clear, in short, that Mill's attack on the prevailing religious conception of a providential order was not, as he himself suggests, primarily motivated by its "irrationality." Far more was it motivated by the intense moral revulsion engendered in Mill by the traditional equation of the natural order of things with providential design. "Not even on the most distorted and contracted theory of good which ever was framed by religious or philosophical fanaticism, can the government of Nature be made to resemble the work of a being at once good and omnipotent" ("Nat," 388–89). Mill, like Ivan Karamazov, cannot and will not accept a world in which such vast and seemingly unjustified suffering is permitted. Mill, like the Grand Inquisitor, will "correct" God's work. Not only the notion of Providence but also conventional Christianity and its God stood in the way of the massive reconstruction of society in service of temporal human happiness that Mill envisaged. The purpose of "Nature" was to destroy the former; the other two essays on religion targeted the latter. "Utility of Religion" attacks the social utility of conventional Christianity. "Theism" presents Mill's fullest elaboration of the god he offers in place of the orthodox Christian God, a "probable" god limited in power and possibly in wisdom, who therefore *requires* the active collaboration of human beings for the realization of his ends.

The Demand for a Desert-Based Justice

"Nature" is also of interest for the insight it yields into Mill's motivation for rejecting what he conceived to be the traditional Christian God, and especially into the relation between that rejection and his demand for justice. The failure of the world to measure up to Mill's personal standard of justice was one of the chief forces underlying both his rejection of the Christian God of his contemporaries and the development of his own special conception of god. Mill could not accept the lack of rational transparency of the existing world order nor reconcile the seeming injustice of that order with his conception of the Christian God. His solution to this intellectual and moral conundrum was to create a god who satisfied his personal standards of rationality and morality.

According to Mill, the theodicy proffered by the providentialists—that all the suffering in the world exists because it is the means whereby God prevents even greater suffering—makes no sense if the god in question is conceived to be the omnipotent and all-benevolent Creator of Christian theology. That notion, Mill insists, "could only avail to explain and justify the works of limited beings, compelled to labour under conditions independent of their own will; but can have no application to a Creator assumed to be omnipotent, who, if he bends to a supposed necessity, himself makes the necessity which he bends to. If the maker of the world *can* all that he will, he wills misery, and there is no escape from the conclusion" ("Nat," 388). Mill here introduces one of his central religious themes, one adopted from his father and which guided his religious thought throughout his life—the irrationality and immorality of the conventional Christian God. For Mill, the irreconcilability of omnipotence and absolute goodness was a self-evident proposition. We shall return to this central feature of Mill's thought in our examination of his other essays on religion.

For now we are mainly interested in the fact that the world as perceived by Mill is as full of injustice as of misery and in the seeming irreconcilability of such evils with an all-benevolent and omnipotent God. Mill can make no sense of the existing world. He can make no sense of it even if God's purpose is not what Mill thinks it should be—to will man's happiness—but to will man's virtue. As he says: "[I]f the Creator of mankind willed that they should all be virtuous, his designs are as completely baffled as if he had willed that they should all be happy: and the order of nature is constructed with even less regard to the requirements of justice than to those of benevolence." Mill, moreover, claims to know what the "requirements of justice" entail, and he is quite certain that the designer of "a world such as this" (as he was to call it in "Theism") has failed to realize them.

> If the law of all creation were justice and the Creator omnipotent, then, in whatever amount suffering and happiness might be dispensed to the world, each person's share of them would be exactly proportioned to that person's good or evil deeds; no human being would have a worse lot than another, without worse deserts; accident or favouritism would have no part in such a world, but every human life would be the playing out of a drama constructed like a perfect moral tale. ("Nat," 389, emphasis added)

One may wonder how Mill knows that this is what justice would entail. The only conception of justice worthy of the name, he suggests, is a perfect, merit-based, distributive justice—what Mill was one of the first to term "social justice"—where earthly rewards and punishments are meted out in exact equivalence to good or evil deeds, known and visible to the human eye. No appearance of chance or accident, no mystery or uncertainty, is compatible with Mill's rigid conception of a perfectly just world, one wherein moral desert is totally transparent to the conscious reasoning mind. Needless to say, such a static perfection is all the more strange in an ostensible philosopher of "experience," one who seems to champion a process of learning through trial and error. We will return to this issue in the discussion of *On Liberty* in Chapter 6.

By Mill's perfectionist standard, this world, wherein the wicked sometimes prosper and the saints sometimes starve, must be condemned as radically unjust, and Mill does so condemn it. He argues, moreover, that the radical injustice of this world has been generally recognized. This, he says, is evinced by the widespread belief in an afterlife, which "amounts to an admission that the order of things in this life is often an example of injustice, not justice" ("Nat," 389). Human beings believe in an afterlife—in an ultimate reconciliation and the administration of divine justice—*because* they experience this world as unjust. Mill does not seem to have allowed for the possibility that his own conception of justice may be flawed, based as it is upon a necessarily limited human perspective. As we shall see in our discussion of the Mansel controversy in the following chapter, Mill felt entirely qualified to judge God and the world he created. Both, not surprisingly, fell far short of Mill's impossible standard. Mill's response was not to question his own moral and intellectual presuppositions but to invent a new god compatible with them. Moreover, he would demand that prevailing injustice and misery be rectified by strictly human efforts. Mill was trained from birth to find quasi-religious fulfillment in the militant pursuit of intramundane social reform, and trained as well to consider a transcendent reconciliation—the selfish "posthumous religious sanction" that is divine justice—a mere chimera. Accordingly, Mill, like the more radical carriers of a similar impulse, the revolutionary communists and socialists, would demand justice—human and total—here and now.

Mill was obsessed with his idea that true justice must be a perfect desert-based justice, transparent to the reasoning mind and manifested in an equivalence between moral merit and temporal reward. It is this idea that fueled his hatred of aristocratic privilege, which, as he says in "The Spirit of the Age" and elsewhere, he regarded as unearned and unmerited, morally or otherwise. It is this obsession too that seems to have led Mill to embrace the Saint-Simonian restrictions on inheritance and eventually to announce his new "discovery" in political economy—that the allegedly natural economic "law of distribution" is in fact not a law at all. Distribution of the fruits of production, he declared, is both theoretically and practically separable from the "natural law of production" and thus totally under the control and direction of the will of "society." The moral demand underlying such economic demands was that earthly pleasures and pains must be "dispensed to all according to what they have done to deserve them [and not according to the] fatality of their birth, . . . the fault of their parents, of society, or of uncontrollable circumstances" ("Nat," 389). The pretense of knowledge implied in such a demand is staggering. Moreover, it ominously resembles the socialist demand for perfect "distributive" justice, whose realization would entail the death of the free or classical-liberal society as historically achieved in the West.[15]

The Concept of a Limited God

With respect to God, Mill's solution to the problem of suffering and evil in the world is to "save [God's] goodness at the expense of his power" and other attributes. The only way Mill can reconcile the existing world with absolute goodness is to posit a limited or finite god, one confronted by various insurmountable obstacles not of his own making. Mill's speculations issued in several variations on this theme over the years. In "Nature" he comes close to subscribing to the Manichaean view of dual contending forces or powers—principles of good and evil, darkness and light—struggling for ultimate mastery and victory. This was a conception, as Mill tells us, that his father had found eminently more plausible, and certainly more moral, than the traditional Christian conception of an all-good and omnipotent God.

[T]he only admissible moral theory of Creation is that the Principle of Good cannot at once and altogether subdue the powers of evil, either physical or moral; could not place mankind in a world free from the necessity of an incessant struggle with the maleficent powers, or make them always victorious in that struggle, but could and did make them capable of carrying on the fight with vigour and with progressively increasing success. Of all the religious explanations of the order of nature, this alone is neither contradictory to itself, nor to the facts for which it attempts to account. . . . According to it, man's duty would consist, not in simply taking care of his own interests by obeying irresistible power [as, Mill suggests, the Christians believe], but in standing forward a not ineffectual auxiliary to a Being of perfect beneficence, a faith . . . better adapted for nerving him to exertion than a[n] . . . inconsistent reliance on an Author of Good who is supposed to be also the author of evil. ("Nat," 389–90)

Mill expressed a similar Manichaean view in his diary entry of February 14, 1854, written during the same period as "Nature": "If human life is governed by superior beings, how greatly must the power of the evil intelligences surpass that of the good, when a soul and an intellect like hers [his wife's], such as the good principle perhaps never succeeded in creating before—one who seems intended for an inhabitant of some remote heaven, and who wants nothing but a position of power to make a heaven even of this stupid and wretched earth—when such a being must perish like all the rest of us in a few years."[16]

Mill's god, like Hegel's, "really needs" man ("The," 488). Accordingly, as Mill points out, faith in his god is "better adapted for nerving [men] to exertion" than faith in the traditional omnipotent God. It will be recalled that for Mill such human exertion is crucial because the vigorous exercise of human agency is essential to the realization of whatever goodness, justice, and order this reckless disorder of existence can hope to realize.

Mill further maintains that the faith of those who profess belief in a "superintending Providence" is, if perhaps only unconsciously, actually a faith in a limited god such as he has described. The vulgar may have a "base confidence" that they are "favourites of an omnipotent but capricious and despotic Deity" but Mill cannot believe that the truly good have ever really believed in an "omnipotent . . . Governor of the world." The truly good have, like Mill, "always saved [God's] goodness at the expense of his power." That is, they, like Mill, have believed in an all-beneficent god of limited power, one who would like to remove all obstacles in their paths but cannot do so without causing greater harm, without harming the general good. As Mill says, "They have believed that he could do any one thing, but not any combination of things: that his government, like human government, [is] a system of adjustments and compromises; that the world is inevitably imperfect, contrary to his intention." The god embraced by the truly good is one whose utmost exertion of power results only in a world as imperfect as this world—one, regretfully, "no better than it is." According to Mill, the experience of such an imperfect world inevitably suggests to the good, as to himself, that God's power is "not merely finite, but extremely limited" (although of course far greater than human power). For Mill, omnipotence implies perfection as he himself conceives it.

Mill illustrates his point. The traditional God is the kind of god who could do no better than make the vast majority of all men who have yet existed "been born Patagonians, or Esquimaux, or something nearly as brutal and degraded." He could do no better than to endow human beings with merely the *capacity* for development, a capacity, moreover, that after century upon century of struggle and suffering, as well as the sacrifice of "many of the best specimens" of the human race, has produced only a few specimens capable of "grow[ing] into something better, . . . of being improved in centuries more into something really good" ("Nat," 390–91). Mill had no great regard for the present stage of development of the mass of men, an issue to which we will return in our discussion of *On Liberty*.

Mill's concept of God, like his philosophy in general, was rather eclectic. He now suggests that the true god resembles the Demiurge of Plato, a view to which he will repeatedly return.

> It may be possible to believe with Plato that perfect goodness, limited and thwarted in every direction by the intractableness of the material, has done this because it could do no better. But that the same perfectly wise and good Being had absolute power over the material, and made it, by voluntary choice, what it is; to admit this might have been supposed impossible to any one who has the simplest notions of moral good and evil. Nor can any such person, whatever kind of religious phrases he may use, fail to believe, that if Nature and Man are both the works of a Being of perfect goodness, that Being intended Nature as a scheme to be amended, not imitated, by Man.

Only the morally uncultivated, by this argument, could possibly believe in the traditional Christian God or deny that man's task is to control and perfect the order of nature. Mill thus returns to the chief object of the essay: Man must renounce the idea that nature is intended to serve as a model or exemplar to guide human action. He acknowledges the strong human desire to discover a perfect model of "what ought to be" in some part of nature, the desire "for some . . . definite indication of the Creator's designs." Such a desire should be resisted, however, for it leads to pernicious consequences. That is, the particular aspect of the natural order chosen by various persons as the exemplar of divine goodness is inevitably arbitrary, depending more often than not merely upon the "practical conclusions" they desire to establish. Mill insists, however, that "it is impossible to decide that certain of the Creator's works are more truly expressions of his character than the rest." In the next breath, however, he tells us that he himself does in fact know something about which of God's works are truly expressive of his character: "[T]he only selection which does not lead to immoral results, is the selection of those which most conduce to the general good." (As it turns out, the "selection of those [actions] which most conduce to the general good" is precisely the function to be performed by Mill's own nontheological utilitarian standard.)[17] Mill concludes that the only moral maxim that can be drawn from the natural order is that God "intends all the good and none of the evil" ("Nat," 391). Precisely how this conclusion can be garnered from an examination of nature, characterized by Mill as a wicked chaos, is unclear.

Mill's dark picture of nature makes Tennyson's "red of tooth and claw" seem idyllic by comparison. Such darkness, however, is essential to Mill's purposes in this essay, among the most important of which, as we have seen, is to call into question the conventional view of divine Providence. Mill beats this drum vigorously and incessantly. Anyone, he says, who takes a hard look at nature and what evidences it provides for the existence of a Creator would draw very different conclusions from those of the Christian apologists for Providence:

> [T]hose who flatter themselves with the notion of reading the purposes of the Creator in his works, ought in consistency to have seen grounds for inferences from which they have shrunk. If there are any marks at all of special design in creation, one of the things most evidently designed is that a large proportion of all animals should pass their existence in tormenting and devouring other animals. . . . If a tenth part of the pains which have been expended in finding benevolent adaptations in all nature, had been employed in collecting evidence to blacken the character of the Creator, what scope for comment would not have been found in the entire existence of the lower animals, divided, with scarcely an exception, into devourers and devoured, and a prey to a thousand ills from which they are denied the faculties necessary for protecting themselves. If we are not obliged to believe the animal creation to be the work of a demon, it is because we need not suppose it to have been made by a Being of infinite power. . . . If we were looking to nature for a model upon which to imitate the Creator's will, all human enormities would be more than justified by the apparent intention of Providence that throughout all animated nature the strong should prey upon the weak. ("Nat," 398–99)

In short, the evidences of nature support not the Christian notion of an all-benevolent and omnipotent God but, as we shall see, Mill's own hypothesis of a god strictly limited in power and perhaps in wisdom as well.

On the Natural Goodness of Man

The Mill of "Nature" is as hostile as Burke to what Mill called the "untutored feelings of human nature." He utterly rejects the notion of man's "natural goodness" and the related view that his instincts or "active impulses" should be regarded as special indications implanted by God to lead him to the good. The discussion highlights Mill's long-standing opposition to the notions of innateness and intuitiveness. As said, his view was that the overwhelming majority of all human attributes, beliefs, sentiments, virtues, ideas, and so forth are acquired through experience over time.

Mill's target in this discussion is the Rousseauian (and deistic) conviction that man, being naturally good, has merely to honor and act upon his natural impulses to realize that goodness. Such a view was anathema to Mill. Such reasoning, to his mind, implies a divine sanction for doing whatever one is inclined to do. It implies that impulses are more reliable guides to God's intentions for man than the "artificial" rules of civilized society. Needless to say, both Mill and his father heartily believed in the necessity of strenuous and perpetual efforts toward self-improvement. The belief in man's natural goodness, however, sets up a pernicious "antithesis between man as God made him, and man as he has made himself." That is, Mill thought that such a belief—that man as God made him is good and not in need of radical emendation—denigrates human deliberation and forethought. Indeed, he thought, those who believe in man's natural goodness can even come to regard deliberation and forethought as contrary to God's intentions for man, thereby eviscerating one of the important means by which man makes himself. Not surprisingly, the Saint of Rationalism is utterly opposed to a view which, as he says, "exalts instinct at the expense of reason ... [and] consecrat[es] ... almost every variety of unreflecting and uncalculating impulse." Moreover, he points out, no one consistently acts upon such a view in practice. Life could not go on for one day if certain impulses were not kept under the strict control of reason.

In short, Mill is concerned to counter the "standing prejudice" of some of his contemporaries that "instinct [i]s ... a peculiar manifestation of the divine purposes," a view that can easily engender a deep hostility to reason and undermine its control over human impulse and instinct. This, for

Mill, would be disastrous, for he believes that "[n]early every respectable attribute of humanity is the result not of instinct, but of a victory over instinct. . . . [T]here is hardly anything valuable in the natural man except capacities—a whole world of possibilities, all of them dependent upon eminently artificial disciplines for being realised" ("Nat," 392–93). He points out that the contemporary belief in man's natural goodness could only have arisen because of the lengthy process of enculturation and habituation that civilized human beings have in fact undergone. Mill was of course appalled at praise of the "noble savage."[18] Indeed, he says, the feeling that is actually most natural in human beings is the far from admirable feeling of fear. Courage, the overcoming of such natural fear, is one of the most difficult human feats and is always acquired through effort. Consequently, all societies have attempted to encourage its cultivation by various means—through bestowing public honors on courageous persons as well as the creation of other appropriate customs. Mill takes this opportunity to dilate upon the origin of customs, betraying in the process the deep hold that Benthamite legal positivism and especially its conception of the Legislator held on his imagination. Customs, Mill says, "presuppose . . . that there must have been individuals better than the rest, who set the customs going." For example, the origin of customs that tend to cultivate courage is bound up with certain individuals superior in "strength and will." Those who first conquered their fears and acted with courage were hailed by the rest as heroes ("for that which is at once astonishing and obviously useful never fails to be admired"). The combination of admiration and fear they inspired in others permitted them to "obtain the power of legislators, and [thus they] could establish whatever customs they pleased" ("Nat," 394). We are left to conclude that customs originate through legislation initiated by the superior few.

Having discussed what he, with Bentham, refers to as the "self-regarding" virtues, Mill next turns to an examination of their opposite, the "social virtues." These, he maintains, are even more exclusively the product of artifice and cultivation, for "it . . is the verdict of all experience that selfishness is natural."[19] Mill does make one concession to innateness: "sympathy," he says, "is natural." This was essential to Mill's scheme of things. For it is this precious "germ" of human nature, when properly cultivated through education and socialization, that alone provides grounds for hope in the ultimate triumph of goodness in the world, a point to which we will return in later chapters. Nevertheless, the innate germ of sympathy requires artificial cultivation to issue in the proper "social feelings": "[Naturally] sympathetic characters, left uncultivated, and given up to their sympathetic instincts, are as selfish as others. The difference is in the *kind* of selfishness; theirs is not solitary but sympathetic selfishness; *l'ego-isme à deux, à trois,* or *à quatre;* and they may be very amiable and delight-ful to those with whom they sympathize, and grossly unjust and unfeel-ing to the rest of the world."[20] Mill here echoes Harriet Taylor's view that those with a "finer nervous organization" are most susceptible to sympa-thetic feelings because they have "so much stronger impulses of all sorts." Thus it is that these finer natures are also often the most selfish, although in a "less repulsive" way than those of "colder natures." Nevertheless, Mill doubts whether a person whose natural benevolence spontaneously triumphed over his or her natural selfishness ever existed. Even the finer natures require the benefit of teaching, whether from instructors, friends, books, or (Mill's personal favorite) from "intentional self-modelling ac-cording to an ideal"[21] ("Nat," 394–95).

Mill concedes in "Nature" that certain requisite capacities or potential-ities may exist in the natural man. As mentioned, this is essential within his framework in that it is the existence of such potentialities or "germs" that allows human beings to be improved morally through education and training. He is thus willing to admit that there may exist germs of all the virtues he has discussed. But such germs are fragile seeds indeed: "[T]he weeds that dispute the ground with these beneficent germs . . . are rankly luxurious growths . . . [which] would . . . entirely stifle and destroy the former, were it not so strongly the interest of mankind to cherish the good germs in one another, that they always do so, in as far as their . . . still very imperfect . . . degree of intelligence . . . allows." It is only through the en-couragement of the "good germs" in one another, begun in childhood, that a few "happily circumstanced specimens of the human race . . . [have managed to make] the most elevated sentiments of which humanity is ca-pable become a second nature." Some have even attained such excellence by self-culture, but even these owe it to a social cause, "for what self-cul-ture would be possible without aid from the general sentiment of mankind delivered through books, and from the contemplation of exalt-ed characters real or ideal?" Mill concludes that "this artificially created or at least artificially perfected nature of the best and noblest human be-ings, is *the only nature which it is ever commendable to follow*" ("Nat," 396–97, emphasis added). It is of interest that Mill omits any reference to the "perfected nature" that most of his readers would have had in mind and which he himself highlights in other contexts: that of Christ. Only the "best and noblest human beings" are to count as appropriate models.

There is one more false interpretation of nature that Mill must expose, one that concerns the notions of Providence and a limited god touched upon earlier in his essay. This is the Aristotelian notion that nature does nothing in vain. It has been said, Mill begins, that natural inclinations may be trusted up to a point, inasmuch as "all natural wishes . . . must have been implanted for a purpose." Some go even further, arguing that "every wish . . . must have a corresponding provision in the order of the universe for its gratification: insomuch (for instance) that the desire of an indefinite prolongation of existence, is believed by many to be in itself a sufficient proof of the reality of a future life." The Mill of "Nature" finds it impossible to trust such human desires. He believes we may have wishes destined to remain eternally unfulfilled. This is because he has no assurance that the only god he can accept—the limited god discussed above—is fully in control of the order of existence. As he says, "[L]imited as . . . the divine power must be, by inscrutable but insurmountable obstacles, who knows that man *could* have been created without desires which never are to be . . . fulfilled." There may be obstacles to the fulfillment of God's purposes that render an inevitable or assured harmony between intention and fulfillment questionable at best. Mill cannot trust that there is an order. Moreover, since the order of being cannot be trusted, even seemingly benign impulses may be "a trap laid by the enemy." The possibility of the existence of an evil principle or other unknown obstacles to the fulfillment of the good principle's purposes means that we can have no assurance that everything "infinite goodness can desire, actually comes to pass in this universe." Those who profess a trust in Providence do so only because their "slavish fears make them offer the homage of lies to a Being who, they profess to think, is incapable of being deceived and holds all falsehood in abomination" ("Nat," 397–98). Those who profess belief in an all-benevolent and omnipotent God, Mill says, are not only confused and irrational but also sycophantic liars.

Perhaps recognizing the extremity and irrationality of his vehement diatribe against nature and natural inclinations, Mill concludes the essay on a somewhat more moderate note. The majority of man's natural impulses, he now says, "must exist for good ends, and ought to be only regulated, not repressed." This should not, however, be taken as a concession to Aristotelian teleology; Mill does not mean that man's inclinations are in any sense meant to lead him to the realization of his potential excellences and certainly not toward any supranatural good. The "good end" to which Mill refers is survival. The species could not have survived unless "most of its inclinations had been directed to things . . . useful for its preservation." On the other hand, there are some human impulses that do deserve utter annihilation. There are certain "bad instincts which it should be the aim of education not simply to regulate but to extirpate, or rather . . . to starve them by disuse." Examples of these latter include the instinct to destroy for destruction's sake; the instinct of domination (delight in subjecting another to one's will);[22] and "natural cruelty"—the "pleasure [and even] voluptuous excitement [experienced] in inflicting . . . pain."[23] Although Mill will concede, then, that certain impulses of human nature may have "their good side" and thus, with proper training, may be made "more useful than hurtful," he nevertheless wishes to draw the most pointed attention to the necessity of such training. Without the strict training of natural impulses, "all of them, even those which are necessary to our preservation, would fill the world with misery, making human life an exaggerated likeness of the odious scene of violence and tyranny which is exhibited by the rest of the animal kingdom, except in so far as tamed and disciplined by man"[24] ("Nat," 398).

Let us conclude our discussion of "Nature" by recalling that this essay was composed more or less contemporaneously with *On Liberty*. It is difficult to reconcile the dire conception of nature, including human nature, presented in "Nature" with the celebration of a spontaneous and untrammeled freedom often thought to be the principal theme of *On Liberty*. Nor can it be reconciled with *On Liberty*'s putative plea for the self-cultivation of individuality. As Mill makes clear in "Nature," there are no internal or intuitive guidelines available to assist human beings in the actualization of potentiality, no inherent ordering principle, no possibility of natural movement toward the realization of excellence or virtue: "[T]here is hardly anything valuable in the natural man except capacities—a whole world of possibilities, all of them dependent upon eminently artificial disciplines for being realised" ("Nat," 393). There is no guarantee that natural inclinations are good or trustworthy (they may be promptings of the forces of evil). Neither human nature nor the physical order of nature can be trusted, only amended. All virtue is the result of "artificial discipline" or training, understood, moreover, to entail the strict application of Benthamite and associationist principles, of the proper administration of rewards and punishments. The puzzling inconsistency of the two essays is resolved, however, once one recognizes that Mill's intention in *On Liberty* was very far from the advocacy of spontaneous liberty and the self-cultivation of individuality, an issue to which we return in Chapter 6.

At this point, however, we turn to "Utility of Religion," the second of the *Three Essays on Religion* and one of the most important of the instruments that Mill designed to realize his religious goal—to replace theological with human morality and an otherworldly orientation with one "confined within the limits of the earth" ("UR," 421).

II: "Utility of Religion"

Religion has been powerful not by its intrinsic force, but because it has wielded th[e] additional and more mighty power [of human opinion].

—*J. S. Mill, "Utility of Religion"*

We have seen that "Utility of Religion" was one of the set of essays Mill wrote during the 1850s, when composing his "mental pemican" for thinkers of the future. The correspondence indicates that this topic, like that of "Nature," was urged upon him by Harriet Taylor, who regarded it as of utmost importance to the age.

"Utility of Religion" is perhaps Mill's strongest public expression of his intent to establish a new religion and it is not surprising that he withheld its publication during his lifetime. The essay represents Mill's synthesis of views concerning religion that he absorbed from Bentham, James Mill, Comte, and Harriet Taylor. Its general purpose is to show that, contrary to common belief, traditional religion (Christianity) is not in fact necessary for the achievement of either personal or social happiness and well-being. Mill claims that all the alleged benefits of traditional transcendent religion may be attained by widespread subscription to his proposed intramundane substitute—the Religion of Humanity—which, moreover, represents a significant moral advance over traditional Christianity. Finally, the essay shows not only that the new substitute for Christianity may achieve social effectiveness, but also *how* it may do so. All that is required is the ability to control the same social resources previously enjoyed by traditional religious authorities.

As we have seen, Mill had identified Grote's condensation of Bentham's views in *An Analysis of the Influence of Natural Religion on the Temporal Happiness of Mankind* as one of the books that profoundly influenced his mental development. "Utility of Religion," which in certain respects recapitulates the views expressed in the *Analysis* almost verbatim, testifies to the accuracy of Mill's statement. The chief argument of the essay is wholly Benthamite in both inspiration and substance: Virtue and morality do not require either religious belief or supernatural sanction to be socially and individually effective. Further, ethical life would be improved were the religious feelings traditionally directed toward supernatural objects and ends reoriented toward "[o]bjects . . . confined within the limits of the earth" ("UR," 421). The essay clearly evinces the extent to which Mill's mature views on religion remained true to those of the "mother church" of Benthamism. It also reveals the continuity of the Bentham-Comte-Mill endeavor to establish a wholly secular, positivist, or purely human ethics to replace what these compatriots all regarded as a moribund, immoral, and obsolete theological morality. As Mill put it in his diary entry of February 15, 1854: "All things, however effete, which have ever supplied, even imperfectly, any essential want of human nature or society, live on with a sort of life in death until they are replaced. So the religions of the world will continue standing, if even as mere shells or husks, until high-minded devotion to the ideal of humanity shall have acquired the twofold character of a religion, viz., as the ultimate basis of thought and the animating and controlling power over action."[25]

"Utility of Religion," written around the same time as this statement, is one of the instruments through which Mill hoped to achieve this "high-minded devotion to the ideal of humanity." It forcefully argues for both the need for and possibility of establishing a new and superior religion for mankind—the Religion of Humanity he intended as the replacement for the "mere shell or husk" that was Christianity.

The "Age of Weak Beliefs"

The essay begins by setting traditional believers at ease. Nothing, Mill concedes, is more important for human beings than to know the truth of the nature and government of the universe, and from the truth of such matters "follows . . . its usefulness without other proof." The problem, however, is that the present age is an "age of weak beliefs." Religious beliefs once accepted as facts have ceased to be so regarded by many people or are held half-heartedly, determined more by the will to believe than by respect for evidence. The result is a great display of public religiosity unmatched by genuine inner conviction. In short, says Mill, arguments for the truth of religion are no longer convincing to the majority and thus the greater and more intense focus on its utility. Mill is careful to note that arguments for the utility of religion are only necessary or indeed possible in an age of widespread unbelief ("UR," 403).

The situation as it stands—little genuine belief in traditional religion combined with a conviction that such belief is essential to personal and social well-being—has put conscientious thinkers in a difficult position, Mill says. They are torn between the commitment to truth and the commitment to the general good, the "two noblest of all objects of pursuit." The result of such a dilemma is indifference to one or both of these objects, paralysis of will, or pursuit of the trivial. Moreover, such a situation conduces to the suppression of the intellect and thus philosophy. Thinkers hesitate to examine religious beliefs critically because they fear that doubt will render mankind vicious and unhappy. They may also silence their intellects for fear that criticism and analysis will "dry up the fountain of . . . elevated feelings" within themselves or others, which they (wrongly) think requires the source-spring of religion.[26] Even worse, the decline of religious belief may lead men to embrace the false philosophy and theology of Mill's "intuitionist" opponents. As he says, doubt may lead them to "addict themselves with intolerant zeal to those forms of [philosophy] in which intuition usurps the place of evidence, and internal feeling is made the test of objective truth." (Note that for Mill as for Bentham, traditional religious feeling was *never* anything more than a perfectly arbitrary and subjective preference.) Mill sums up the situation: "[T]he whole of the prevalent metaphysics of the present century is one tissue of suborned evidence in favour of religion," and especially of deism or natural religion. His response is to show that all this effort to sustain moribund beliefs, although motivated in part by noble impulses, is a tremendous waste of human energy and ability, for traditional religion is unnecessary. The real question, as Mill sees it, is whether human well-being may not be better served by ceasing the agitation over supernatural religion and redirecting that energy toward the development of a naturalistic or intramundane substitute. As he puts the issue, the question is whether the present "straining to prop up" traditional religious beliefs "yield[s] . . . any sufficient return in human well-being; and whether that end would not be better served by a frank recognition that certain subjects are inaccessible to our faculties, and by the application of the same mental powers to the strengthening and enlargement of those other sources of virtue and happiness which stand in no need of the support or sanction of supernatural beliefs and inducements" ("UR," 404–5). "Other sources" refers to Mill's own solution to the problem of declining religious faith: nontheological utilitarianism embodied in the Religion of Humanity.

It may be of interest to supplement Mill's public statements about the wasted energy spent "propping up" the false beliefs of traditional religion with remarks he inscribed in his diary in February 1854, during the same period when he composed "Utility of Religion." There Mill says:

If it were possible to blot entirely out the whole of German metaphysics, the whole of Christian theology, and the whole of the Roman and English systems of technical jurisprudence, and to direct all the minds that expand their faculties in these three pursuits to useful speculation or practice, there would be talent enough set at liberty to change the face of the world. . . . [As it is, however, all the intellectual effort at present directed to these three] useless mental pursuits . . . is now far worse than wasted.[27]

The "Temporal Usefulness of Religion"

Mill explicitly acknowledges the connection between the argument of "Utility of Religion" and those of Bentham and Comte. These two thinkers, he says, are the only "sceptical writers . . . [who] have directly inquired into the temporal usefulness of religion" and he thus "shall use both of them freely in the . . . present discourse."[28] Mill begins with the same question that informs the *Analysis:* He inquires whether religious belief, "considered as a mere persuasion, apart from the question of its truth, is really indispensable to the temporal welfare of mankind." He is quick to acknowledge that it may be or, at least, may once have been indispensable: "[I]t is . . . perfectly conceivable that religion may be morally useful without being intellectually sustainable. . . . [Even] unbeliever[s] . . . [cannot] deny, that there have been ages, and that there are still both nations and individuals, with regard to whom this is actually the case" ("UR," 405–6). What Mill gives with one hand, however, he takes away with the other. For what needs to be examined, he continues, is whether beliefs that may have been beneficial in the past will continue to be so in the future and whether such benefits as have been obtained from traditional religion may be done so in the future at less cost.[29] Mill, following Saint-Simon and Comte, will argue that while traditional religious beliefs may have been useful during former and less advanced stages of mankind's development, they have outlived their usefulness and need to be supplanted by improved moral doctrine and aspirations.

Mill also develops the Saint-Simonian and Comtean theme of the inadequacy of the "negative" criticism of traditional religious belief of the eighteenth-century philosophes, a theme that Mill and Comte thoroughly explored during the years of their correspondence. The problem with that approach, Mill now says, is that the negative critique of religion merely informs us that "nothing can be known" and does not provide requisite moral and spiritual guidance. As we know, Mill and his cohort were deeply concerned with proffering a "positive" faith to replace the allegedly obsolete transcendent faith undermined so effectively by the "critical philosophy" of the previous century. Mill also follows Comte in acknowledging the relative value of the religious beliefs of former ages.[30] While untrue on the whole, such beliefs "may have pointed in the same direction with the best indications we have and . . . may have kept us right when [those indications] might have been overlooked." Nevertheless, the usefulness of earlier religious beliefs has been purchased at a high price—the many "positive evils" they have also always engendered. More than this, "mankind have been . . . unremittingly occupied in doing evil to one another in the name of religion" throughout the course of human history. Such evils, Mill admits, may not be the necessary consequence of all religion, but only of "particular forms of it." He also concedes that modern religion is much improved over older versions. The worst of its evils have been "extirpated" and those remaining will undoubtedly disappear as the "process of extirpation" continues into the future. What is especially heartening is that modern man has discovered how easy it is to separate the good from the ill in religious belief and practice. This is an important development because it shows that "some of the greatest improvements ever made in the moral sentiments of mankind have taken place without [religion] and in spite of it." It shows that human beings are capable of "improving religion itself" ("UR," 405–6). Mill expressed a similar, if less politic, view in a diary entry of February 1854: "Two of the most notable things in the history of mankind are, first, the grossly immoral pattern of morality which they have always set up for themselves in the person of their Gods, whether of revelation or of nature; and secondly, the pains they have taken, as soon as they began to improve, in explaining away the detestable conclusions from their premises, and extracting a more tolerable morality from this poisonous root."[31] Mill's discussion of the ongoing advance of religious thought is prelude to and preparation for the impending announcement of his own new religion.

Although there is no reason to assume that the ongoing process of the improvement of religion will cease, Mill continues, "for the sake of fairness it should be assumed to be complete. *We ought to suppose religion to have accepted the best human morality which reason and goodness can work out,* from philosophical, christian, or any other elements" (emphasis added). (This is a good illustration of Mill's characteristic procedure. He is not interested in "fairness" but in showing that the benefits of religion may be achieved without recourse to transcendent, otherworldly religion. He thus builds his argument upon the very point at issue—traditional Christians certainly did not suppose their religion "to have accepted the best human morality which reason and goodness can work out.") Upon this hypothetical assumption, however, Mill proceeds by saying that "the ground is now clear" for determining whether the useful properties of religion are inherent in religion per se or whether it is possible to obtain the benefits generally ascribed to religion in some other way ("UR," 406).

Mill's inquiry is divided into two parts. He first examines the useful-ness of religion for society—its benefit to "social interests"—and, second, and what is of greater importance, its benefit for the individual—its ca-pacity to improve and ennoble individual human nature.

Mill's general conclusion concerning the social utility of religion is straightforward and predictable. The inculcation of morality and virtue, essential of course to the well-being of society, is unfairly attributed to re-ligion when the truth of the matter is that "any system of moral duties in-culcated by education and enforced by opinion" would have the same beneficial effects. People are mistakenly inclined to attribute to religion per se what is actually the effect of habituation and training. They make this mistake because "almost all who are taught any morality whatever, have it taught to them *as* religion. . . . [Thus] the effect which the teaching produces as teaching, it is supposed to produce as religious teaching, and religion receives the credit of all the influence in human affairs which be-longs to any generally accepted system of rules for the guidance and gov-ernment of human life." The source of religion's apparent efficacy in in-culcating morality and virtue is that religious beliefs and habits are impressed as duty on the mind of the child. "[I]t is this which is the great moral power in human affairs, and . . . religion only seems so powerful because this mighty power has been under its command" ("UR," 407). So much for the allegedly indispensable role of religion in shaping private and public morality.

The Three Sources of Morality

Mill elaborates this main contention. There are, he claims, three princi-pal sources of morality in human existence—authority, education, and public opinion—none of which have any essential or necessary connec-tion to religion. Mill implicitly dismisses the great revelatory traditions of the West in one fell swoop.

He addresses *authority* first. As discussed, Mill exhibited the most in-tense interest in this subject at least from the time of his introduction to the Saint-Simonian conception of a spiritual power. In "Utility of Reli-gion," Mill reiterates many of the views expressed in "The Spirit of the Age," indicating that his attraction to the idea of establishing a modern spiritual power was not merely one of his youthful aberrations, as is sometimes suggested.[32] Mill begins by affirming his long-standing view that the great mass of men take their beliefs from authority. "[E]ven the wisest," he explains in the Comtean manner, inevitably accept the truths of science or history, for instance, on the evidence of authority, having not personally examined the evidence or proofs that support those truths. Thus it is not surprising that for the vast majority of human beings, "the general concurrence of mankind, in any matter of opinion, is all powerful," trumping even the "evidence of their senses" in certain cases. In short, the authority of public opinion is all but omnipotent: "[A]ny rule of life and duty . . . [which] has conspicuously received the general assent, . . . obtains a hold on the belief of every individual." The converse is true as well—the beliefs held by most men weaken in proportion to the decline of belief among their fellows. This, Mill points out, is evinced by the contemporary state of religious opinion, the state of "weak beliefs" to which he earlier alluded: "[F]or exactly in proportion as the received systems of belief have been contested, and it has become known that they have many dissentients, their hold on the general belief has been loosened, and their practical influence on conduct has declined and since this has happened to them notwithstanding the religious sanction which attached to them, there can be no stronger evidence that they were powerful not as religion, but as beliefs generally accepted by mankind"[33] ("UR," 407–8). The evidence proves Mill's point (his synthesis of Benthamite and Saint-Simonian views): It is authority—and especially an authority that has successfully shaped public opinion—and not religion that is the true governing power over human belief and conduct.

The second major source of human belief and thus practice is, for Mill as for his father and Helvetius, the "tremendous . . . power of *education*— . . . [the] unspeakable . . . effect of bringing people up from infancy in a belief, and in habits founded on it" (emphasis added). Consider, Mill says, that the vast majority of people in all ages have been reared since infancy on religious belief of one kind or another and on associated moral maxims taught as divine commandments. It is no wonder people think religion essential for moral government. But children, Mill continues, tend to regard the allegedly divine commands of religion as commands of their parents. From this fact, he concludes, "it is reasonable to think that any system of social duty which mankind might adopt, even though divorced from religion, would have the same advantage of being inculcated from childhood, and would have it hereafter much more perfectly than any doctrine has it at present." This latter point is due to the fact that society is now more directly concerned with universal education than in previous eras. Another reason why it is crucial to begin training children in their proper moral duties when they are very young is that "the impressions of early education . . . possess . . . [an enduring] command over the feelings even of those, who have given up the opinions which they were early taught." Mill had earlier pointed out that one important way in which authority shapes the human mind and thus behavior is through influencing what we would call the unconscious portion of the mind, or, as Mill put it, through its "involuntary influence [over] . . . men's conviction, . . . persuasion, [and] . . . involuntary sentiments" ("UR," 408–9). Only exceptional persons are capable of freeing themselves from the opinions and feelings acquired during their upbringing. Mill is almost Freudian in the determinative emphasis he places on early childhood experiences.

Mill's plans to institute a new social religion through the training and education of the young were, then, bound up with the passionate conviction he shared with James Mill and his predecessors of the "almost boundless . . . power of education." For universal education, "from infancy," as Mill will say in *Utilitarianism*, is to be the mechanism whereby the Religion of Humanity will achieve social effectiveness. As proof of the "almost boundless . . . power of education," Mill offers the example of Sparta—"the greatest recorded victory which education has ever achieved over a whole host of natural inclinations in an entire people—the maintenance through centuries of the institutions of Lycurgus." Moreover, and more directly to his point, Mill emphasizes that the Spartan success in molding its people in socially beneficial ways was achieved without the assistance of religion:

> [I]t was not religion which formed the strength of the Spartan institutions: the root of the system was devotion to Sparta, to the ideal of the country or State; which transformed into ideal devotion to a greater country, the world, would be equal to that and far nobler achievements. Among the Greeks generally, social morality was extremely independent of religion. The inverse relation was rather that which existed between them; the worship of the Gods was inculcated chiefly as a social duty. . . . Such moral teaching as existed in Greece had very little to do with religion. . . . For the enforcement of human moralities secular inducements were almost exclusively relied on. The case of Greece is . . . the only one in which any teaching, other than religious, has had the unspeakable advantage of forming the basis of education . . . The . . . power of education over conduct . . . afforded . . . by this . . . case . . . constitut[es] a strong presumption that in other cases, early religious teaching has owed its power over mankind rather to its being early than to its being religious. ("UR," 409–10)

Again, Mill's diary provides a helpful supplement to his published statements. That Mill intended duty or devotion to one's "country or mankind" to serve as a full-fledged religion is clear from remarks he inscribed in March 1854: "When we see and feel that human beings can take the deepest interest in what will befal [*sic*] their country or mankind long after they are dead, and in what they can themselves do while they are alive to influence that distant prospect which they are never destined to behold, we cannot doubt that if this and similar feelings were cultivated in the same manner and degree as religion they would become a religion."[34] Mill's investment of the "ideal of the country or State"—expanded, indeed, into "ideal devotion to a greater country, the world"—with quasi-religious or *ultimate* value rests in uneasy tension with his putative concern for the individual and his liberty. This is especially problematic in light of the fact that Mill is aiming for the elimination or at least the evisceration of any supranatural or world-transcendent allegiance which historically served (and existentially serves) as the basis of spiritual resistance to secular or political power. We will return to this issue in the concluding chapter.

Mill now turns to the third and last possible source of morality, the power of *public opinion*—"the praise and blame, the favour and disfavour, of [one's] fellow creatures." He begins by emphasizing that this power, like that of authority and education, is independent of religion; it strengthens "any system of moral belief which is generally adopted, whether connected with religion or not." There is, however, a difference between public opinion and the other two sources of morality. The former operate principally through men's "involuntary beliefs, feelings, and desires," while the power of public opinion "operates directly on [men's] actions, whether their involuntary sentiments are carried with it or not." (What such a view reveals of Mill's understanding of "education" is rather startling. Education, he suggests, is early training and instruction that is concerned with shaping the mind and conscience principally through influencing "involuntary beliefs, feelings, and desires" and not with the development of rationality.)

Most men are "generally quite unconscious" of how much of their behavior is "determined" by the force of public opinion. They "flatter themselves" that they are acting in obedience to their conscience, oblivious to the fact that much of what they regard as the promptings of conscience is nothing more than the internalized voice of the "received social morality," that is, of public opinion. Mill allows that some men do resist the dictates of public opinion in the name of conscience, but only rarely and with difficulty. More often, however, conscience and public opinion act in tandem and this because public opinion has usually "made the conscience in the first instance." The fact of this identity of conscience and public opinion means that for the great majority of mankind the "overpowering . . . motive" in the determination of their behavior is the pressure of public opinion.

In fact, Mill explains, most of the "strongest passions" are simply names for certain "motives" derived from public opinion: the love of glory, praise, admiration, respect and deference, "even the love of sympathy," and, more negatively, such motives as "vanity, . . . the fear of shame, the dread of ill repute, or of being disliked or hated."[35] But the power of public opinion extends much further than the simple desire to attract the favorable sentiments of our fellows and avoid their unfavorable sentiments. For these latter sentiments can elicit various and possibly severe "penalties": "exclusion from social intercourse and . . . the . . . good offices which human beings require from one another; the forfeiture of all that is called success in life; often the great diminution or total loss of means of subsistence . . . [Indeed, the disapprobation of our fellows can reach so] far as actual persecution to death." Public opinion shapes almost every aspect of human aspiration and behavior. Most of the time, people want the things they want only because of the "power" those things confer over the sentiments of their fellows. People are also dependent upon public opinion for the attainment of most of their ends, as this attainment requires other persons to be favorably disposed toward the seeker. Mill's attitude toward the alleged omnipotence of public opinion was ambivalent. On the one hand, his aim—to show that public opinion and not religious belief is the actual governor of human conduct—leads him to stress its all-encompassing power. On the other hand, the essay conveys the strong impression that Mill hated and feared the fact that human beings are inevitably "dependent on the opinion of others" almost as much as Rousseau.[36] Moreover, the exaggerated value he attached to public opinion explains in part both his own deep concern with shaping that opinion and his demand for freedom from conventional opinion in *On Liberty*. It is also related to his denial of any supranatural allegiance or accountability. The only opinion that matters is the opinion of other human beings.

But let us return to our main topic: the utility of religion for mankind's temporal happiness. Mill believes his analysis of the significance of public opinion clearly shows that there is no such utility. "Any one who fairly and impartially considers the subject, will see reason to believe that those great effects of human conduct, which are commonly ascribed to motives derived directly from religion, have mostly for their proximate cause the influence of human opinion. Religion has been powerful not by its intrinsic force, but because it has wielded that additional and more mighty power" ("UR," 410–11).

Mill concedes that religion has had an "immense" influence on the direction of public opinion; indeed, in many respects public opinion has been completely determined by religion. Nevertheless, he follows Bentham / Grote in insisting that, historically, religious sanctions were really effective only when supported by concurring public opinion, at least once men stopped believing that "divine agency . . . employ[s] temporal rewards and punishments." "[T]he spell was broken" when the first person who violated an allegedly divine command was not "struck dead on the spot" or severely injured. Mill asks us to consider the Jews: Despite their belief that violations of the divine law would be punished by temporal events, "their history was a mere succession of lapses into Paganism." The endless warnings of their prophets and historians went unheeded because the religious sanctions were not supported by widespread public concurrence. In any event, over time experience taught the great majority that temporal punishments for violating religious sanctions were not inevitably forthcoming. It was this experience and the knowledge it engendered that led to the decline of the "old religions" and the widespread adoption of one that relegated the "principal scene of divine retribution" to a world beyond time and space ("UR," 412). Christian belief is accounted for, again in the Comtean manner, by man's phenomenal experience over time and especially by his growing powers of observation and generalization.

The Inefficacy of the Religious Sanction

Mill now elaborates Bentham's and James Mill's view regarding the inefficacy of the "posthumous" religious sanction, which, we recall, was of central importance for the development of Bentham's nontheological utilitarianism. As Mill says, the remoteness and uncertainty of rewards and punishments, eminently characteristic of the religious sanction and especially of those thought to be effected posthumously, greatly detracts from their ability to govern human behavior. The uncertainty of the religious sanction is especially problematic. All religions assist the "self-delusion" that bad behavior in this life will in fact escape the divine punishment. This is because judgment is thought to be passed on one's life as a whole, and not on isolated acts; thus every person, even the worst criminal, is easily convinced that in the end the balance will be in his favor. Not only this, but

bad religions teach that divine vengeance may be bought off, by offerings, or personal abasement; the better religions, not to drive sinners to despair, dwell so much on the divine mercy, that hardly any one is compelled to think himself irrevocably condemned. . . . [Indeed, the enormity of eternal punishments is itself a reason] why nobody (except a hypochondriac here and there) ever really believes that he is in any very serious danger of in-

> curring them. Even the worst malefactor is hardly able to think that any
> crime he has had it in his power to commit . . . in this short space of exis-
> tence, can have deserved torture extending through an eternity. ("UR," 413)

Thus the endless complaints of religious thinkers and preachers about the weak influence of religious motives on men's actual conduct.

Mill next rehearses Bentham's examples of the inefficacy of the religious sanction when not supported by concurring public opinion. Oaths in courts of law are taken seriously, because their importance to society is widely recognized and public opinion genuinely condemns a violation of this norm. Violations of other kinds of oath-taking, by contrast, such as "university and custom-house oaths," although equally condemned from the point of view of religion, are in practice "utterly disregarded," even by honorable persons. The reason is that public opinion does not find these reprehensible, despite the religious prohibition against them. Duelling and the religious prohibition of "illicit sexual intercourse" offer similar examples of cases where public opinion trumps the religious sanction. Both of these activities are considered sins, yet even religious persons engage in such activities with little fear of their fellows' disapprobation. The double sexual standard is particularly illuminating in this regard. Although illicit sexual intercourse is regarded as a very great religious sin, most men, says Mill, feel "very little scruple in committing it; while in the case of women, though the religious obligation is not stronger, yet being backed in real ernest [sic] by public opinion, it is commonly effectual" ("UR," 413).

Mill recognizes that there are certain persons for whom the fear of religious punishment does indeed act as a powerful influence on behavior, for instance, hypochondriacs and the depressed. Moreover, if such states of mind are prolonged, they can permanently shape the mind and imagination, and in fact, says Mill, this is "the most common case of what, in sectarian phraseology, is called conversion." Religious conversion, then, is a mental disease. Mill also notes that while a person's depression often ceases upon conversion, this does not mean that the person is now more susceptible to religious motives than before. The impelling force of public opinion over human action remains determinative even in the case of religious conversion. What actually happens is that the convert now governs his life by the opinion of his new religious communicants, as before it was governed by the opinions of the profane world. Mill will not acknowledge the possibility of any influence beyond that of temporal and worldly public opinion.

Mill concludes that the evidence against the efficacy of the posthumous religious sanction is overwhelming:

At all events, there is one clear proof how little the generality of mankind, either religious or worldly, really dread eternal punishments: . . . [W]e see how, even at the approach of death, when the remoteness which took so much from their effect has been exchanged for the closest proximity, almost all persons who have not been guilty of some enormous crime (and many who have) are quite free from uneasiness as to their prospects in another world, and never for a moment seem to think themselves in any real danger of eternal punishment.

Mill does not wish to deprecate those persons who died as martyrs for the sake of religion; of course such actions were not undergone for the sake of the approval of their fellow-religionists. But such heroic valor is not unique to Christianity. It must be acknowledged that "human opinion" has been capable of producing similar strength of character in other persons, including some not generally regarded as moral exemplars—for instance, "the North American Indian at the stake." More important, however, Mill does not believe that the great religious martyrs were motivated by the possibility of heavenly pleasure or hellish torment. One hears the voice of personal experience: "Their impulse was a divine enthusiasm—a self-forgetting devotion to an idea: a state of exalted feeling, by no means peculiar to religion, but which it is the privilege of every great cause to inspire; a phenomenon belonging to the critical moments of existence, not to the ordinary play of human motives" ("UR," 414–15). Such cases do not therefore shed much light on the relative efficacy of religious or secular opinion in shaping the ordinary, day-to-day conduct of the average person.

The Ultimate Origin of Morality

Mill is now ready to conclude his discussion of the "vulgarest part" of his subject—the value of religion in its social aspect, or, as he puts it more colorfully, the value of the "coarse and selfish . . . social instrument [of] the fear of hell . . . as a supplement to human laws, . . . [as a] more cunning sort of police." For Mill, the very notion of ultimate divine justice is despicable, base, servile. Before concluding, however, he must examine the view, held by even the nobler sort, that religion is essential, if not to enforce, then to teach "social morality." This issue leads Mill to the question of the ultimate origin of morality. Is it true, he asks, that all the great morality recognized throughout human existence derived from religion, as is sometimes alleged? A related question is whether human beings can be induced to accept and enforce a morality understood to have originated with a strictly secular or human source or whether the majority of men will adopt a morality only if they believe it to be of divine origin.

This latter, Mill admits, seems to have been the case for ancient peoples. They generally regarded their morals and laws, as well as their intellectual beliefs and practical arts, as divine revelations. Mill explains this, however, on naturalistic, Comtean grounds. Ancient men had greater "hopes and fears" of those powers because they believed divine agency to operate in the daily course of events, having not yet discerned the universal reign of law—"the fixed laws according to which physical phenomena succeed one another." Moreover, such "rude minds . . . felt an involuntary deference . . . for power superior to their own." As these men, like the majority of men in all times, tended to associate this superior power with knowledge and wisdom, they formed a desire to act in conformity with what they took to be the preferences of more powerful beings ("UR," 415–16).

Mill's next step is to suggest that those who find it necessary to insist upon the supernatural origin of moral rules are "savages" or their equivalent. The topic leads him explicitly to reject the uniqueness of revealed Christian morality, as well as to deny the necessity of continuing belief in the Christian revelation. Whatever benefits the world has derived from Christianity have been gained, he says, "once for all." Mill also identifies those aspects of Christian morality that reasonable people can accept. As he says in his diary, the task of improving religion requires the "extract[ion of] . . . a more tolerable morality from th[e] poisonous root" of traditional religion, a task Mill assigns to the "best and foremost portion of our species." It is perhaps worth repeating that Mill's driving purpose from the time of his first "conversion" to Benthamism until his death was the replacement of "theological" with a "purely human" morality and orientation. "Utility of Religion" represents one of his most forceful and sinuous instruments toward that end.

[D]oes it follow that [modern men] would . . . give up moral truths any more than scientific, because they believed them to have no higher origin than wise and noble human hearts? Are not moral truths strong enough in their own evidence, at all events to retain the belief of mankind when once they have acquired it? I grant that some of the precepts of Christ as exhibited in the Gospels—rising far above the Paulism which is the foundation of ordinary Christianity—carry some kinds of moral goodness to a greater height than had ever been attained before, though much even of what is supposed to be peculiar to them is equalled in the *Meditations* of Marcus Antonius, which we have no ground for believing to have been in any way indebted to Christianity. But this benefit, whatever it amounts to, has been gained. Mankind have entered into the possession of it. It has become the property of humanity, and cannot now be lost by anything short of a return to primaeval barbarism. [Such moral conceptions as] the "new commandment to love one another"; the recognition that the greatest are those who serve . . . others; the reverence for the weak and humble; . . . the lesson of the parable of the Good Samaritan; that of "he that is without sin let him throw the first stone"; the precept of doing as we would be done by; and such other noble moralities as are to be found, mixed with some poetical exaggerations; . . . and some maxims . . . in the authentic sayings of Jesus of Nazareth; these are surely in sufficient harmony with the intellect and feelings of every good man or woman, to be in no danger of being let go, after having been once acknowledged as the creed of the best and foremost portion of our species. . . . [T]hat they should be forgotten, or cease to be operative on the human conscience, while human beings remain cultivated or civilised, may be pronounced, once for all, impossible. ("UR," 416–17)

Mill does not mention in this context the "poisonous root" from which he is trying to extract a "more tolerable morality."

He does, however, identify the moral perversions commonly associated with Christianity, although these, he admits, may not be "unequivocally deducible from the very words of Christ." Such perversions include the notions of "atonement and redemption, original sin and vicarious punishment" and, indeed, the "doctrine that belief in the divine mission of Christ [is] a necessary condition of salvation." Mill explains: "It is nowhere represented that Christ himself made this statement, except in the huddled-up account of the Resurrection . . . in the concluding verses of St. Mark, which some critics (I believe the best) consider to be an interpolation" ("UR," 424). Finally, the invidious notion that "'the powers that be are ordained of God' and . . . [its] corollaries . . . in the Epistles, belong to St. Paul, and must stand or fall with Paulism, not with Christianity." Here Mill loosely follows the argument of Bentham's *Not Paul, But Jesus* (1823), wherein Bentham blamed Paul for everything he found distasteful in Christianity.[37] Mill, however, sees one "moral contradiction" embodied in Christianity in all its forms that cannot be assigned to Paul's pernicious influence and that cannot be explained away: it is that such a precious gift should have been bestowed merely on a few and withheld from the many, and this when it would have cost the "Divine Giver" nothing to have given it to all ("UR," 424).

Having pronounced historical Christianity to be no longer necessary and having identified which of its precepts and doctrines may safely be carried forth into the Religion of the Future, Mill points out the "evil consequence" of clinging to its notion of the supernatural origin of morality. Such a notion not only impedes intellectual development in general but, more particularly, it inhibits the indispensable criticism, correction, and reconstruction of inherited moral rules.

[T]here is a very real evil consequent on ascribing a supernatural origin to the received maxims of morality. That origin consecrates the whole of them, and protects them from being discussed or criticized. . . . [Thus, if there are certain] imperfect . . . moral doctrines received as a part of religion . . . which were either erroneous from the first . . . or which . . . are no longer suited to the changes that have taken place in human relations (and it is my firm belief that in so-called christian morality, instances of all these kinds are to be found), . . . [these imperfect doctrines are held to be as obligatory] as the noblest, most permanent and most universal precepts of Christ. Wherever morality is supposed to be of supernatural origin, morality is stereotyped; as law is, for the same reason, among believers in the Koran.

Mill will decide which of the Christian precepts should be maintained and which will have to be jettisoned in the interests of moral advance. He concludes by announcing the imminent, if peaceful, demise of supernatural religion: "[B]elief . . . in the supernatural, great as are the services which it rendered in the early stages of human development, cannot be considered to be any longer required, either for enabling us to know what is right and wrong in social morality, or for supplying us with motives to do right and to abstain from wrong" ("UR," 416–17).

The Nature of Religion

Having demonstrated to his satisfaction that supernatural beliefs are no longer essential for social purposes, Mill now examines the second aspect of the problem of the utility of religion—its alleged necessity with respect to the "perfection of the individual character." This of course is the higher aspect of the subject; it goes without saying that the perfection of the individual is prerequisite to the achievement of the greatest excellence in "social conduct." Mill approaches the problem by first determining what it is in human nature that has generated the need for religion, what desires of the human mind religion satisfies, and what human qualities it cultivates. This is essential to Mill's purpose, for only after such issues are resolved is it possible to determine how those human desires might be satisfied and how those qualities ("or qualities equivalent to them") can be "unfolded" and perfected "by other means" ("UR," 417–18). "Other means" implicitly refers to the Religion of Humanity and nontheological utilitarianism.

In the foregoing passage Mill seems to assume an unfolding nature, which is difficult to reconcile with the general tenor of his essay "Nature" and its unremitting hostility to such a concept. There, it will be recalled, Mill vehemently insisted that man's principal duty is *not* to follow or unfold, but to amend, discipline, and regulate his nature. He also implicitly repudiated Aristotelian teleology in that essay. The explanation of the apparent contradiction, we may suggest, is bound up with Mill's different polemical purposes and rhetorical strategies in the two essays. "Nature" was intended to undermine the deistic understanding of providential government as well as the intuitionist conception of an innate moral sense and metaphysical conceptions of natural right and natural law. Thus Mill could not concede the slightest ground to the beneficence or goodness of nature, human or physical. In "Utility of Religion," on the other hand, Mill wants to persuade his readers that his own purely human morality can serve every bit as well as traditional theological morality to bring to perfection the very best of human potentiality. Thus the strategic appeal to the "unfolding" of nature (which he will also employ in *On Liberty*). Which was his true view? Opinions may differ, but one might suggest that the ineradicable impact of James Mill's associationism and Benthamite schemes of behavioral modification on Mill's psyche made him permanently leery of the notion of spontaneous unfolding. Mill had no trust in the natural, or in any other, order. For him, goodness and excellence were inevitably the products of prolonged struggle and conscious effort, with a great deal of the "external inducement" of punishment thrown in for good measure.

Let us return to the topic at hand: the alleged necessity of religion for the perfection of individual character. This problem first leads Mill to explore the "natural history" of religion—the origin of man's belief in gods. He employs his invariable principle of explanation: No cautious thinker can accept any positive belief, conviction, or concept, including and especially religious belief, "unless he is able to account for the existence of the opposite opinion." The converse, he implies, is also true: If it is possible to account for a belief on other grounds than those held by the believer, that is sufficient to cast doubt on the believer's explanation. This applies as much to the question of religious truth as to any other. Mill acknowledges elsewhere that there is a "certain presumption of the truth of any opinion held by many human minds [such as the belief in God, a presumption] requiring to be rebutted by assigning some other real or possible cause for its prevalence" ("The," 430). In short, if there is a plausible naturalistic account of the origin of a given phenomenon, belief, or concept, we have no right to assume a supernatural or divine origin.

Mill rejects Hume's view that the origin of the belief in gods was fear. As earlier mentioned, he prefers the Comtean explanation:

[The] universality [of the belief in gods] has been very rationally explained [by Comte] from the spontaneous tendency of the mind to attribute life and volition, similar to what it feels in itself, to all natural objects and phenomena which appear to be self-moving. . . . [Early man thought such objects were alive and] naturally persisted [in this belief] so long as the motions and operations of these objects seemed to be arbitrary, and incapable of being accounted for but by the free choice of the Power itself. . . . But as it must soon have appeared absurd that things which could do so much more than man, could not or would not do what man does, as for example to speak, the transition was made to supposing that the object present to the senses was inanimate, but was the creature and instrument of an invisible being with a form and organs similar to the human. ("UR," 418)

Following Comte, Mill believed that the origin of man's changing conception of god—from primitive fetishism through polytheism and monotheism to the ultimate positivist understanding of the law-governed nature of phenomena—can be traced to the development of the human mind. More particularly, man's changing conception of god reflects the growth in scientific knowledge which itself is the product of the growth of man's powers of observation and abstraction (or generalization).

Mill admits that the development of religion was very much related to fear but, contrary to Hume, he denies that fear was the original cause of man's belief in gods. That belief did not arise from fear, but preceded it. Once man came to believe in such beings, however, "fear of them necessarily followed." For they seemed able to inflict "great evils" on human beings at will, and the only way men felt able to avert such evils was through "solicitations" addressed to the deities. Fear in the face of the gods was perfectly understandable, since doubt of their existence was thought to be one of the gravest possible offenses. But the issue that requires explanation is not the origin of the belief in gods in primitive minds, but the reason such a belief persists among the "cultivated." Mill finds a sufficient explanation for this persisting belief in the limits of man's knowledge and in the "boundlessness of his desire to know." Although human existence is full of mystery ("we neither know the origin of anything which is, nor its final destination"), man has an insatiable desire to speculate on the nature of the universe, including the world he inhabits. He has an unquenchable desire to know the "cause" or "agency" that made the world what it is as well as the "powers" on which its "future fate" depends. Mill's anxieties are on the surface:

Who would not desire this more ardently than any other conceivable knowledge, so long as there appeared the slightest hope of attaining it? What would not one give for any credible tidings from that mysterious region, . . . especially any theory of it which we could believe, and which represented it as tenanted by a benignant and not a hostile influence? But since we are able to penetrate into that region with the imagination only, assisted by specious but inconclusive analogies derived from human agency and design, imagination is free to fill up the vacancy with the imagery most congenial to itself; sublime and elevating if it be a lofty imagination, low and mean if it be a grovelling one. ("UR," 418–19)

Nature cannot not be trusted; we have longings to know that may never be fulfilled. There is no possibility of possessing knowledge of the mysterious beyond. The response of the cultivated to such a predicament is the imaginative creation of a god, the endless delight in speculating on the nature of the universe. A more appropriate response, Mill suggests, is to do without supernatural belief, turning those wasted energies toward the creation of spiritual perfection in temporal existence.

Mill next turns to two of his and Harriet's favorite themes—the equivalency of religion and poetry and the human need for ideals. Having found spiritual sustenance in the works of Wordsworth in the period immediately following his youthful "mental crisis," Mill, in line with the general Romantic understanding of the age, developed a great appreciation for the capacity of poetry to provide, as he says in the *Autobiography*, a permanent "source of inward joy"[38] (121). For Mill, the major benefit of poetry and religion is their mutual capacity to generate elevated and intense feeling through the evocation of an ideal. Both "religion and poetry address themselves, . . . to the same part of the human constitution: they both supply the same want, that of ideal conceptions grander and more beautiful than we see realised in the prose of human life." What differentiates religion from poetry is that the former "is the product of the craving to know whether these imaginative conceptions have realities answering to them in some other world than ours." In the religious state, Mill explains,

the mind eagerly catches at any rumours respecting other worlds, especially when delivered by persons whom it deems wiser than itself. To the poetry of the supernatural, comes to be thus added a positive belief and expectation . . . in a God or Gods, and in a life after death, [which] becomes the canvas which every mind . . . covers with such ideal pictures as it can either invent or copy. In that other life each hopes to find the good which he has failed to find on earth, or the better which is suggested to him by the good which on earth he has partially seen and known. . . . *So long as human life is insufficient to satisfy human aspirations, so long there will be a craving for higher things, which finds its most obvious satisfaction in religion.* So long as earthly life is full of sufferings, so long there will be need of consolations, which the hope of heaven affords to the selfish, the love of God to the tender and grateful.[39] (emphasis added)

Mill suggests, in short, that so long as human beings suffer or experience unfulfilled aspirations—and no longer—will man cling to the "baseless fancies" that constitute supernatural religious belief ("UR," 419–20). Religion, he seems to agree with Marx, is the opium of the people.

Mill does not question the historical value of religion as a source of personal fulfillment and high feeling. As we have seen, he had learned from the Saint-Simonians and Comte that religion had played a largely beneficent role in mankind's progress through history, one, however, destined to disappear as the human mind moved inevitably and necessarily toward the final positivist or nontheological state. What he does question is whether the benefits derived from religion—"personal satisfaction and elevated feeling"—require belief in "the unseen powers" thought to exist in a world beyond time and space. Mill will accept "religion," so long as it is exclusively intramundane; what must be abandoned is an orientation toward the transcendent dimension of reality. As Mill puts it, the question is whether, in order to obtain the benefits of religion,

> it is necessary to travel beyond the boundaries of the world which we inhabit; or whether the idealization of our earthly life, the cultivation of a high conception of what *it* may be made, is not capable of supplying a poetry, and in the best sense of the word, a religion, equally fitted to exalt the feelings, and (with the same aid from education) still better calculated to ennoble the conduct, than any belief respecting the unseen powers. ("UR," 420)

The Religion of Humanity

[There] is a radical inferiority of the best supernatural religions, compared with the Religion of Humanity . . .

—*J. S. Mill, "Utility of Religion"*

Having shown that religion possesses no unique social utility, that what is of value in historical Christianity is separable from its pernicious supernatural orientation and easily incorporated into a new purely human morality, and that the origin of the belief in gods and ultimate divine justice is explainable on naturalistic grounds, Mill is now ready to introduce the capstone of his argument—the Religion of Humanity.

Mill is aware that to many minds an exclusively intramundane religion—a "religion without a God"—such as he has proposed will seem little more than a vulgar Epicureanism. If there is no afterlife, "[l]et us eat and drink, for to-morrow we die." He responds to such potential critics by pointing out first that the Epicurean outlook embodies a certain degree of wisdom, provided it remains balanced by longer-term considerations. For instance, it is right that we attempt to find pleasure in our pursuits in order to "control those mental dispositions which lead to undue sacrifice of present good for a future which may never arrive." One again hears the voice of personal experience in such counsel. But there are limits to the pursuit of present enjoyment. "The 'carpe diem' doctrine . . . is a rational and legitimate corollary from the shortness of life. But that because life is short we should care for nothing beyond it, is not a legitimate conclusion." Needless to say, Mill does not mean "beyond" the terrestrial, but merely beyond the present age. Human beings are to live for the future of the "human species." They are, Mill insists, quite capable of caring for

> things which they will never live to see. . . . [For] if individual life is short, the life of the human species is not short; its indefinite duration is practically equivalent to endlessness [to the eternity of God]; and being combined with indefinite capability of improvement, it offers to the imagination and sympathies a large enough object to satisfy any reasonable demand for grandeur of aspiration. If such an object appears small to a mind accustomed to dream of infinite and eternal beatitudes, it will expand into far other dimensions when those baseless fancies shall have receded into the past. ("UR," 420)

One of Mill's missions is to assist in the deflation of those "baseless fancies." Once human beings abandon such silliness, they will come to see that the grand dream of the indefinite improvement of the human race is more than equivalent to their former "dream[s] of infinite and eternal beatitudes." Their previously wasted energies can be put to social use, to create the "hoped-for heaven" here and now.[40]

Mill takes into account another possible objection to his new social religion—that its noble morality may be too difficult for the masses. It is not, he responds, only the superior human beings who can find spiritual sustenance and fulfillment in the Religion of Humanity or who are capable of realizing its motivational essence—"identifying their feelings with the entire life of the human race." The ability to so empathize "certainly will be if human improvement continues, the lot of all. Objects far smaller than this, and equally confined within the limits of the earth (though not within those of a single human life), have been found sufficient to inspire large masses and long successions of mankind with an enthusiasm capable of ruling the conduct, and colouring the whole." Service to humanity, "confined within the limits of the earth," can become a "real religion." Mill appeals to both history and experience in support of his argument: "Rome was to the entire Roman people, for many generations as much a religion as Jehovah was to the Jews; nay, much more, for they never fell off from their worship as the Jews did from theirs." If the Romans, no better than other people, indeed an essentially selfish and practical people, were able to derive a "certain greatness of soul" from such an idea, there is no reason other peoples cannot do the same ("UR," 420–21). We may note how Mill's Religion of Humanity shades off into the sacralization of the state and thus to the establishment of a full-fledged political religion.

Mill is certain that it is possible to ground morality on the good of the intramundane whole—on the good of humanity—without either sacrificing the individual to the social aggregate or unduly inhibiting individual freedom and spontaneity. Nor would a morality grounded in humanity lack the requisite motivation to successful practice. The superior natures would embrace such an "exalted morality" from motives of "sympathy and benevolence and the passion for ideal excellence"; "the inferior, from the same feelings cultivated up to the measure of their capacity" plus, when necessary, "the superadded force of shame." As discussed, Mill regarded his new social religion as a marked advance in the development of religious and moral thought. In particular, the "exalted morality" embodied in the Religion of Humanity would not, unlike the selfish and self-interested Christian morality, "depend for its ascendancy on any hope of [posthumous] reward" or be narrowly preoccupied with merely personal salvation. There would, however, be a certain gratification to be gained through serving humanity, one, moreover, as capable as transcendent religion of providing consolation in suffering and support in moments of weakness. Furthermore, the rewards of the Religion of Humanity are not, like those alleged by Christianity, relegated to a "problematical future existence" but are to be realized in the present. Such rewards, Mill says in the Comtean manner, would consist of "the approbation, in this [existence], of those whom we respect, and ideally of all those, dead or living, whom we admire or venerate." The thought that "Socrates, or Howard, or Washington, or Antoninus, or Christ, would have sympathized with us, . . . has operated on the very best minds, as a strong incentive to act up to their highest feelings and convictions." The "very best minds" require no more transcendent motivation than the imaginative approval of the great moral figures of humanity's historical past. A "Howard" or a Christ would serve equally well for such a purpose.

As noted, Mill took this latter conception from Comte, who himself absorbed it from the tradition that stems from Diderot. Mill, like Comte, finds it necessary to purify the ideal of Humanity by "dismissing" its less worthy members. As he says in *Auguste Comte and Positivism*: "That the ennobling power of this grand conception [of serving Humanity instead of God] may have its full efficacy, we should, with M. Comte, regard the

Grand Etre, Humanity, or Mankind, as composed, in the past, solely of those who, in every age and variety of position, have played their part worthily in life. It is only as thus restricted that the aggregate of our species becomes an object deserving our veneration. The unworthy members of it are best dismissed from our habitual thoughts" (136–37).

As "Utility of Religion" proceeds, Mill approaches ever more exalted heights of passion and fervor. The new human morality he proposes is not only equivalent in all respects to the moralities derived from transcendent religion, but is justly entitled to claim itself a true religion in every sense of the word: "To call the . . . sentiments [associated with the Religion of Humanity] by the name morality . . . is claiming too little for them. They are *a real religion*" (emphasis added). An internal adhesion to the dictates of the Religion of Humanity generates, like traditional religion, "outward good works." More important, however, the new religion fully embodies the very "essence" of religion. This, Mill says, "consists of . . . the strong and earnest direction of the emotions and desires toward an ideal object, recognised as of the highest excellence, and as rightfully paramount over all selfish objects of desire" ("UR," 421–22). This "ideal object" is of course the Great Being of Humanity, "whose service," Mill proposes elsewhere, "is to be the law of our life" (*ACP,* 137). Mill's characteristic reticence, and indeed, caginess, are now thrown to the winds; transported by his moral fervor, he pulls out all the stops. The Religion of Humanity is not only entitled to be regarded as a real religion; it is in fact, a "better religion than any . . . ordinarily called by that title":

> This condition [the embodiment of the essence of religion] is fulfilled by the Religion of Humanity in as eminent a degree, and in as high a sense, as by the supernatural religions even in their best manifestations, and far more so than in any of their others. . . . [A]ny one, who can distinguish between the intrinsic capacities of human nature and the forms in which those capacities happen to have been historically developed [can see] that the sense of unity with mankind, and a deep feeling for the general good, may be cultivated into a sentiment and a principle capable of fulfilling every important function of religion and itself justly entitled to the name. I will now further maintain, that it is not only capable of fulfilling these functions, but would fulfil them better than any form whatever of supernaturalism. It is not only entitled to be called a religion: it is a better religion than any of those which are ordinarily called by that title.

Mill explains why the Religion of Humanity represents a moral advance over traditional religion. First, unlike Christian ethics, whose conception of divinely administered rewards and punishments, as well as its emphasis on personal salvation, taints moral action by encouraging self-interested behavior or outright selfishness, the Religion of Humanity is disinterested, that is, "unselfish":

> It carries the thoughts and feelings out of self, and fixes them on an unselfish object, loved and pursued as an end for its own sake. The religions which deal in promises and threats regarding a future life, [by contrast,] fasten down the thoughts to the person's own posthumous interests; they tempt him to regard the performance of his duties to others mainly as a means to his own personal salvation; and are one of the most serious obstacles to the great purpose of moral culture, the strengthening of the unselfish and weakening of the selfish element in our nature. ("UR," 422)

The selfish desire for personal salvation poses such an obstacle to genuine virtue because the "tremendous magnitude" of the rewards and punishments anticipated by supernatural religion makes it difficult for believers to maintain any reserve of feeling for or interest in other "distant" and "ideal" objects. Mill here echoes Rousseau's complaint against Christianity: it diverts energy and attention from temporal and social ends. This of course is not coincidental. As discussed, the notion of a secular, social, or civil religion is peculiarly French; Mill's thought, as Bentham's, was significantly shaped, if not dominated, by influences emanating from France.[41]

Mill seems to recognize that he has perhaps gone too far. He concedes that many of mankind's great "unselfish" benefactors have believed in "supernaturalism." But this too can be explained away. Those believers in supernaturalism who managed to remain disinterested did so because they did not concentrate on the "threats and promises" of their religion, but on their conception of a loving and trustworthy God. For the "common minds," however—the great majority of men—traditional religion operates primarily through the base motive of self-interest. Christ himself is implicated in this defilement of the moral life. "Even the Christ of the Gospels holds out the direct promise of reward from heaven as a primary inducement to the noble and beautiful beneficence towards our fellow-creatures which he so impressively inculcates. This is a radical inferiority of the best supernatural religions, compared with the Religion of Humanity. . . ."

Mill's Religion of Humanity incorporated not only Comte's Great Being of Humanity but also his well-known ethical distinction between selfish "egoism" and selfless "altruism."[42] The main purpose of morality, Mill tells us, is to "cultivate the unselfish feelings" through habitual exercise. Selfishness, Mill reiterates, is woven into the very fabric of Christianity, for "the habit of expecting to be rewarded in another life for our conduct in this, makes even virtue itself no longer an exercise of the unselfish feelings" ("UR," 423). Although all of this sounds very high-minded, Mill himself, as we shall see, had not the least aversion to employing, and quite extensively, the allegedly selfish "inducement" of "rewards and punishments," so long as these are distributed and administered by strictly *human* "preceptors" or judges. It is the traditional notion of *divine* judgment—of man's accountability to God—that Mill is concerned to undermine and certainly not human judgment, justice, retribution, reward, or punishment in general.

In addition to the cultivation of selfishness, the "old religions" (Mill means Christianity), and especially their peculiar conception of God, have a second pernicious effect on human beings, to which we have earlier alluded: they degrade the human intellect and thus character. (We hear the echo of James Mill.) This is because it is all but impossible for such religions to work their moral effects without engendering intellectual torpidity, not to say a "positive twist" in the mental faculties. "For it is impossible that any one who habitually thinks, and who is unable to blunt his inquiring intellect by sophistry, should be able without misgiving to go on ascribing absolute perfection to the author and ruler of so clumsily made and capriciously governed a creation as this planet and the life of its inhabitants." Mill returns to the theme of "Nature." Only a "sophisticated . . . heart," he thunders, can adore the creator of such a planet, with its "blind partiality, atrocious cruelty, and reckless injustice." Mill recognizes that the God worshipped by the old religions is not in general "the God of Nature only, but also the God of some revelation," whose character may mitigate the bad moral influences of the religion in question. "This is emphatically true of Christianity; since the Author of the Sermon on the Mount is assuredly a far more benignant Being than the Author of Nature." Unfortunately, however, the Christian is required to believe his God the author of both—to Mill's mind, a logically impossible proposition. He concludes that such an attempt must involve the Christian believer "in moral perplexities without end; since the ways of his Deity in nature are on many occasions totally at variance with the precepts . . . of the same Deity in the Gospel." The Christian solution to this conundrum, Mill suggests, is to forego the attempt to reconcile the two standards, to "confess . . . that the purposes of Providence are mysterious, that its ways are not our ways, that its justice and goodness are not the justice and goodness which we can conceive." As we shall see in our discussion of Mill's participation in the Mansel controversy, such a solution is anathema to Mill. The only solution, he insists, is to recognize the untenability of the Christian conception of God. Those who attempt to finesse this obvious fact by the above strategy—those, like Mansel, who acknowledge the mystery of Providence and employ the terms *justice* and *goodness* in an equivocal sense with respect to man and God—seem to know not what they do. For those who adopt such a strategy, "the worship of the Deity ceases to be the adoration of abstract moral perfection. It becomes the bowing down to a gigantic image of something not fit for us to imitate. It is the worship of power only."

Furthermore, it is not only its conception of God and its selfish ethics that make Christianity so inferior to the Religion of Humanity. There is also the problem of the

> moral difficulties and perversions involved in revelation itself. . . . [E]ven in the Christianity of the Gospels, . . . there are some of so flagrant a character as almost to outweigh all the beauty and benignity and moral greatness which so eminently distinguish the sayings and character of Christ. The recognition, for example, of the object of highest worship, in a being who could make a Hell; and who could create countless generations of human beings with the certain foreknowledge that he was creating them for this fate. Is there any moral enormity which might not be justified by imitation of such a Deity? And is it possible to adore such a . . . dreadful idealization of wickedness . . . without a frightful distortion of the standard of right and wrong? ("UR," 423–24)

As we know, Mill is here parroting the views of his father. As said, John Mill was surely involved in the most profound self-deception in his repeated insistence that he grew up "without any religious belief." In fact, the narrow conceptions of god and religion that he absorbed from James Mill would shape his own religious views until the end of his life. Despite a certain amount of struggle, Mill never fully overcame the views in which he had been indoctrinated, whether concerning religion, ethics, psychology, or other areas of belief.

The Limited God Revisited

Mill begins the last part of "Utility of Religion" with an impassioned presentation of his own preferred conception of god, to which we were briefly introduced in "Nature." Mill's new god is a hypothetical or probable god, limited on the model of either the Platonic Demiurge or Manichaean dualism, and developed in accordance with the religious convictions he acquired during his unusual upbringing. Mill assumes a tone of high authority:

One only form of belief in the supernatural—one only theory respecting the origin and government of the universe—stands wholly clear both of intellectual contradiction and moral obliquity. It is that which, resigning irrevocably the idea of an omnipotent creator, regards Nature and Life not as the expression throughout of the moral character and purpose of the Deity, but as the product of a struggle between contriving goodness and an intractable material, as was believed by Plato, or a Principle of Evil, as was the doctrine of the Manichaeans. A creed like this, which I have known to be devoutly held by at least one cultivated and conscientious person of our own day [that is, James Mill], allows it to be believed that all the mass of evil which exists was undesigned by, and exists . . . in spite of the Being whom we are called upon to worship. A virtuous human being assumes in this theory the exalted character of a fellow-labourer with the Highest, a fellow-combatant in the great strife; contributing his little, which by the aggregation of many like himself becomes much, towards that progressive ascendancy, and ultimately complete triumph of good over evil, which history points to, and which this doctrine teaches us to regard as planned by the Being to whom we owe all the benevolent contrivance we behold in Nature.

Mill, then, appears to advocate a qualified form of supernatural or transcendent belief. This appearance is misleading. For he immediately points out the difficulties involved in believing in a god such as he has described, difficulties that can only be overcome by the adoption of the Religion of Humanity. The problem, Mill says, is that the evidence that would justify belief in a limited transcendent god is "too shady and unsubstantial, and the promises it holds out too distant and uncertain, to admit of its being a permanent substitute for the religion of humanity." But all is not lost. Those who prefer to maintain belief in a transcendent deity even though such a belief is not "grounded on evidence" may feel free to do so, provided they also and simultaneously adopt Mill's Religion of Humanity. "[B]ut the two may be held in conjunction; and he to whom ideal good, and the progress of the world towards it, are already a religion, even though that other creed may seem to him a belief not grounded on evidence, is at liberty to indulge the pleasing and encouraging thought, that its truth is possible" ("UR," 425–26).

Provided, then, that one subscribes to Mill's religion of "the progress of the world towards . . . ideal good," one may continue to "indulge the pleasing and encouraging thought" that there may actually exist a god something like the transcendent God of traditional Christianity. Moreover, Mill says, the future triumph of good over evil, to which history points and which involves the triumph of the ideal embodied in his Religion of Humanity, may actually be part of the divine design—that is, it may be "regard[ed] as planned by the Being to whom we owe all the benevolent contrivance we behold in Nature" ("UR," 425). Mill regarded this being as his probable Demiurge or the good principle of the Manichaeans. His Christian readers would of course regard him as the traditional God. Whatever conception of God one holds, Mill suggests, his will is for the realization of Mill's humanitarian ideals. Mill seems to know God's plan.

James Collins has called Mill's strategy here and elsewhere (for example, in "Theism") the introduction of an "Interim God."[43] Mill's limited Demiurge seems destined ultimately to disappear as humanity progresses from the worship of an otherworldly, supernatural, transcendent deity to a service to humanity, "confined within the limits of the earth." As Mill had explained: "So long as human life is insufficient to satisfy human aspirations, so long there will be a craving for higher things, which finds its most obvious satisfaction in religion. So long as earthly life is full of sufferings, so long there will be need of consolations, which the hope of heaven affords to the selfish, the love of God to the tender and grateful." The widespread embrace of the Religion of Humanity, destined to bring the greatest temporal happiness to the greatest number and to satisfy humanity's religious and spiritual needs much more perfectly than any previous religion has ever done, will eliminate not only the sufferings of earthly life but the compensatory need for "baseless" supernatural "fancies" as well.

God as Hypothesis

Mill had long considered the existence of God a hypothesis, that is, "a proposition to be proved by evidence." As he said to Carlyle in 1833 in explaining the divergence between their respective views:

> The first and principal of these differences is, that I have only, what appears to you much the same thing as, or even worse than, no God at all; namely, a merely probable God. By *probable* . . . I mean that the existence of a Creator is not to me a matter of faith, or of intuition; & as a proposition to be proved by evidence, it is but a hypothesis, the proofs of which as you I know agree with me, do not amount to absolute certainty. As this is my condition in spite of the strongest wish to believe, I fear it is hopeless; the unspeakable good it would be to me to have a faith like yours, I mean as firm as yours, on that, to you, fundamental point, I *am* as strongly conscious of when life is a happiness to me, as when it is, what it *has* been for long periods now past by, a burthen. . . . The reason why I think I shall never alter on this matter is, that none of the ordinary *difficulties* as they are called, as the origin of evil, & such like, are any serious obstacles to me; it is not that the logical understanding, invading the province of another faculty, will not *let* that other higher faculty do its office; there is wanting something positive in me, which exists in

others; whether that something be, as sceptics say, an acquired association, or as you say, a natural faculty.[44]

Whether or not one accepts Mill's self-interpretation (his cavalier dismissal of the problem of evil—as well as of the demands of his "logical understanding"—does not ring true), he was right when he said he "shall never alter on this matter." Mill restated the same view over thirty years later in *An Examination of Sir William Hamilton's Philosophy*: "[T]he Divine Intelligence is but an assumption, to account for the phaenomena of the universe; and . . . we can only be warranted in referring the origin of those phaenomena to an Intelligence, by analogy to the effects of human intellect" (440). Mill was referring to the Argument from Design, which he would develop and defend at great length in "Theism."

As a hypothesis, Mill believed, the question of God's existence is to be subjected to the same canons of scientific induction applicable to the investigation of all other phenomena. One of the chief tasks of "Theism" is to conduct precisely such a "scientific" investigation of this question. As we will discuss more thoroughly in Chapter 5, Mill concludes that while the hypothesis of God cannot be proven false, it also cannot be proven true. The evidences with respect to the hypothesis of God are inconclusive; accordingly, God is best conceived as "probable." There are insufficient grounds for a full-fledged belief in God, but sufficient grounds for what Mill conceives as an imaginative and sentimental "hope." As Mill puts it in "Utility of Religion": "[T]hough the scepticism of the understanding does not necessarily exclude the Theism of the imagination and feelings, . . . [such] vague possibility must ever stop far short of a conviction" (425).

Mill thus lays down the permissible realm of belief in God. First, he pronounces, "all dogmatic belief" is disallowed. Second, "those who need it" may indulge in the "imaginative hope" that God and personal immortality are "possibilities." Such hope is unobjectionable because it may "feed . . . and animat[e] the tendency of the feelings and impulses towards good" ("UR," 426). What deserves emphasis in this regard is that Mill was greatly concerned with the problem of motivation. For Mill, the pursuit of good required the intense *desire* for good. As a result, he was most interested in mustering all possible sources of that desire in service of the ultimate good embodied in his new Religion of Humanity. One of the most important of such sources was the traditional religious aspirations and sentiments of Mill's Christian or Christianized contemporaries. Mill is greatly interested in tapping this source of the desire for good. For, as he will say in "Theism," the supernatural aspirations of Christians are so "excellently fitted to aid and fortify that real, though purely human religion, which sometimes calls itself the Religion of Humanity and sometimes that of Duty" (488). His strategy seems to have been to appeal to the traditional religious feelings and aspirations of his contemporaries in such a way as would lead to a more or less unconscious reorientation away from supernatural objects and toward his own innerworldly end—a service to humanity "confined within the limits of the earth." We will discuss this issue more extensively after examining "Theism," where Mill employs the same strategy.

Immortality

In order to establish the superiority of the Religion of Humanity over all forms of supernatural religion, Mill finds it necessary to address the one undeniable "advantage" the latter have over the Religion of Humanity—the promise of immortal life ("the prospect they hold out to the individual of a life after death"). As said, Mill allows that there are sufficient grounds for "hoping" and "feeling" that the supernatural religions represent the truth, but insufficient grounds for belief and conviction. It thus becomes necessary to "estimate the value of this element—the prospect of a world to come—as a constituent of earthly happiness" ("UR," 426). That is, Mill will conduct something like a utilitarian cost-benefit analysis with respect to the replacement of transcendent religion by the Religion of Humanity. Are the costs entailed by the absence of full assurance of personal immortality greater than the benefits obtained in moral advance by subscription to the new humanitarian religion? Mill concludes, not surprisingly, that the benefits of the belief in personal immortality have been generally overrated; on balance, the gains to humanity from embracing his new religion far outweigh what must be sacrificed.

Mill's chief argument is that the appeal of personal immortality, like other aspects of Christian belief and ethics, is essentially an appeal to the selfish, the unhappy, and the morally uncultivated. As such, the "flattering expectation" of personal immortality can be expected to diminish over time with the more widespread embrace of the superior, unselfish morality and spiritual aspirations embodied in the Religion of Humanity and the increasing happiness effected by such embrace. Mill suggests, then, that the belief in personal immortality, like the belief in the transcendent God of traditional Christianity, may be held as an interim belief, one useful during the transition from transcendent to intramundane religion.

> I cannot but think that as the condition of mankind becomes improved, as they grow happier in their lives, and more capable of deriving happiness

from unselfish sources, they will care less and less for this flattering expectation [personal immortality]. It is not, naturally or generally, the happy who are the most anxious either for a prolongation of the present life, or for a life hereafter; it is those who never have been happy.[45] They who have had their happiness can bear to part with existence: but it is hard to die without ever having lived. When mankind cease to need a future existence as a consolation for the sufferings of the present, it will have lost its chief value to them, for themselves. I am now speaking of the unselfish. Those who are so wrapped up in self that they are unable to identify their feelings with anything which will survive them, or to feel their life prolonged in their younger contemporaries[46] and in all who help to carry on the progressive movement of human affairs, require the notion of another selfish life beyond the grave, to enable them to keep up any interest in existence. . . . But if the Religion of Humanity were as sedulously cultivated as the supernatural religions are (and there is no difficulty in conceiving that it might be much more so), all who had received the customary amount of moral cultivation would up to the hour of death live ideally in the life of those who are to follow them. . . . [I]t appears to me probable that after a length of time different in different persons, they would have had enough of existence, and would gladly lie down and take their eternal rest. . . . The mere cessation of existence is no evil to any one; . . . only . . . the illusion of imagination [makes it seem so. The only thing the] sceptic loses by his scepticism is . . . the hope of reunion [with deceased loved ones, a] loss [which] . . . is neither to be denied nor extenuated. . . . [It is this] which will always suffice to keep alive . . . the imaginative hope of a futurity which, if there is nothing to prove, there is as little in our knowledge and experience, to contradict. ("UR," 426–27)

It may again be of interest to supplement Mill's published remarks with the thoughts inscribed in his diary during the same period. In his entry of March 19, 1854, Mill also discussed the prospect of immortality and its relation to Christian belief:

The belief in a life after death, without any probable surmise as to what it is to be, would be no consolation, but the very king of terrors. A journey into the entirely unknown—the thought is sufficient to strike with alarm the firmest heart. It may be otherwise with those who believe that they will be under the care of an Omnipotent Protector. But seeing how this world is made, the only one of the works of this supposed power by which we can know it, such a confidence can only belong to those who are senseless enough and low-minded enough to think themselves in particular special favourites of the Supreme Power. It is well, therefore, that all appearances and probabilities are in favour of the cessation of our consciousness when our earthly mechanism ceases to work.[47]

Mill concludes "Utility of Religion" with a final observation concerning the necessity of the "belief in a heaven." History, he says, shows the dispensability of that belief. Peoples of many cultures and ages have lived perfectly satisfactory lives without it, and certainly neither the Greeks nor the Romans had a "tempting idea of a future state." The Buddhist religion provides an even more telling example. It holds out as its ultimate reward not eternal existence, in heaven or elsewhere, but "annihilation; the cessation, at least of all conscious or separate existence." The embrace of this religion by millions of ordinary people shows, to Mill's mind, that the belief in personal immortality is far from indispensable to happiness and fulfillment. It is entirely possible, he asserts, that a truly happy and fulfilled person would be perfectly willing to leave existence

> after the best that it can give has been fully enjoyed through a long lapse of time; when all its pleasures, even those of benevolence, are familiar, and nothing untasted and unknown is left to simulate curiosity and keep up the desire of prolonged existence. . . . [It seems to me] probable, that in a higher, and above all, a happier condition of human life, not annihilation but immortality may be the burdensome idea; and that human nature, though pleased with the present, and by no means impatient to quit it, would find comfort and not sadness in the thought that it is not chained through eternity to a conscious existence which it cannot be assured that it will always wish to preserve. ("UR," 427–28)

Perhaps it is not irrelevant that Mill wrote this passage during a time when he believed that both he and his wife were in imminent danger of death; much of it has the air of "whistling past the graveyard." Moreover, Mill's estimate of the value of personal immortality would undergo substantial revision in following years largely as a result of the enduring grief he experienced in response to the untimely death of his wife in 1857. Mill always regarded the hope of reunion with loved ones as the main benefit of the belief in personal immortality. As we shall see, in "Theism," written in the evening of his life, Mill is less cavalier about the prospect of abandoning belief in one's own immortality or that of one's loved ones. He will thus allow and even encourage "imaginative hope" in personal immortality of a kind.

Before examining Mill's final essay on religion, "Theism," we first turn to his participation in the Mansel controversy of the mid-1860s. Not only will this provide a more concrete sense of the temporal divide between the first two essays and the third, but the issues brought to the surface by this controversy are also most relevant to our discussion. Mill's moral outrage over the suggestion that human beings are unfit to judge God and his creation would provoke a defiant outburst that would make the rejection of the conventional Christian God a matter not only of moral superiority but of moral necessity.

Sir William Hamilton
and the Mansel Controversy

Two of the most notable things in the history of mankind are, first, the grossly immoral pattern of morality which they have always set up for themselves in the person of their Gods, whether of revelation or of nature; and secondly, the pains they have taken, as soon as they began to improve, in explaining away the detestable conclusions from their premises, and extracting a more tolerable morality from this poisonous root.

—*J. S. Mill, diary*

Although the fame of Sir William Hamilton suffered a substantial eclipse in the twentieth century, in the first half of the nineteenth century his influence ranked with Mill's. The two thinkers were widely regarded as the most important philosophical influences emanating from Britain. Accordingly, Mill's critique, *An Examination of Sir William Hamilton's Philosophy* (1865), attracted significant attention and went through three printings in the same number of years. The *Examination* is a lengthy and sometimes tedious refutation of Hamilton's "philosophy of the conditioned," which is described by James Collins as "a strange melange of Scottish common sense, Kantian criticism, and German idealism."[1] Hamilton's philosophy, while today of little more than historical interest, was, like its creator, highly influential in its day.

The chief interest of Mill's critique from the perspective of this work is its attack on "intuitionism" and its relation to Mill's overriding religious aim—the replacement of a theological with a purely human orientation. The heart of Mill's dispute with Hamilton was, on its face, epistemological: he took issue with Hamilton's version of the Kantian doctrine of the relativity of all knowledge. Mill seems to have been initially well disposed toward Hamilton and, indeed, to have regarded him as something of an ally in the fight to establish the positive philosophy. Mill's positivism, like Saint-Simon's and Comte's, rejected the possibility of absolute knowledge; all human knowledge was seen as conditional, relative to the thinker or perceiver as well as to his time and place in history. Mill initially understood Hamilton's conception of the relativity of knowledge to be in substantial agreement with his own. Hamilton, like Mill, insisted on the radical inaccessibility to the human mind of any speculative knowledge of the "unconditioned"—whether conceived as the traditional transcendent God of Christianity, the noumenal realm of Kant, or the "absolute" and "infinite" of German idealism. Human knowledge, agreed Hamilton, Kant, Mill, and Comte, was confined to the realm of phenomena.

Mill, then, had hoped to enlist Hamilton's prestige in his fight to establish the positivist worldview, central to which were the relativity of knowledge and its restriction to phenomena. He intended to do so by reviewing Hamilton's *Lectures on Metaphysics and Logic* (1860–1861) in a short article. During the course of his reading of Hamilton,[2] however, Mill decided to turn the anticipated review into a full-length book, and this for two reasons. First, he decided a critique of Hamilton would serve as a useful vehicle through which to propound his own views on "metaphysics" (that is, psychology) and especially on the associationist psychology he had absorbed from his father and to which he was utterly committed. Second, and more important, Mill's reading of Hamilton forced upon him the realization that he had radically misconceived the nature and import of Hamilton's philosophy. Far from being an epistemological ally in the positivist cause, Mill discovered to his horror that Hamilton, despite his use of the language of the relativity of knowledge, was in fact one of the leaders of the camp of Mill's "most resolute enemies," whom Mill somewhat loosely called the "Intuitionists."[3] What Mill discovered was that Hamilton, while professing to restrict all knowledge to knowledge of phenomena, in truth completely undermined that doctrine by claiming that authentic knowledge of the unconditioned was available to human beings in the form of "Belief" (or faith).[4]

I: The Attack on "Intuitionism"

Nor was this the worst offense in Mill's eyes. Part of Mill's self-appointed mission was to eradicate the belief in a priori knowledge of any sort, that is, knowledge thought to be *given* or intuited or acquired in any other manner than through phenomenal experience in time.[5] After recovering from his youthful Romanticism, Mill would strenuously deny the validity of intuitive or innate knowledge of any sort, whether respecting God, morals, politics, cosmology, mathematics, science, or any other area of human speculation. The *Examination* must be understood in light of Mill's campaign against such knowledge, for, as Mary Warnock observes, its "main aim" was "to reject th[e] very idea . . . of 'intuitionism' . . . in all its forms."[6] When Mill discovered that Hamilton, the ostensible phenomenological relativist, was not only providing aid and comfort to the enemy "Intuitive school" but, indeed, as Alan Ryan puts it, was "a much more committed and unrestrained intuitionist than [Mill] had previously supposed," his task was clear.[7] The *Examination* would destroy the school of intuitionism and Hamilton's reputation in one blow. Not only would Mill expose the false philosophy of the intuitionists but the intellectual weakness of its chief expounder as well. Hamilton's reputation would never recover from Mill's exposure of the numerous inconsistencies, confusions, and general unintelligibility of his philosophy.

We may observe, however, that Mill's seemingly categorical rejection of intuitive knowledge was in fact selective. He condemned such knowledge when used to support traditional religious belief, as in the case of Hamilton, but not when it supported his own convictions or emanated from his own favored sources. For instance, despite his attack on intuitionism in all his philosophical writings, he at times affirmed the superiority of intuitive knowledge to any other kind of knowledge. In 1833 he wrote to Carlyle: "I conceive that most of the highest truths, are . . . intuitive; that is, they need neither explanation nor proof, but if not known before, are assented to as soon as stated."[8] Further, Mill praised his wife's superior "intuition" with respect to moral knowledge. In discussing Harriet Taylor's character in the *Autobiography,* he says: "The benefit I received [from her] was far greater than any which I could hope to give; though to her, who had *at first reached her opinions by the moral intuition of a character of strong feeling,* there was doubtless help . . . to be derived from one who had arrived at many of the same results by study and reasoning [that is, Mill]" (148, emphasis added). While Mill's inconsistency is well established, his remarks to Carlyle and his appeal to Taylor's "moral intuition" are remarkable for their contradiction of his utter condemnation of "intuitive" knowledge in all his major published works. It is difficult to reconcile the conflicting views except to suggest, as stated, that Mill's public hostility to intuitionism derived from the sustenance that intuitionism provided to a theologically based ethic.

Mill's strategy in the *Examination* was to set his own school of thought—the inductive philosophy of "Experience and Association"—in stark opposition to the school of intuitionism.[9] The "Intuitive school," as mentioned, consisted of a rather motley group of thinkers, united only by a common refusal to limit knowledge exclusively to that gained by sense experience in time. Mill was hostile to any thinker or school that assumed givenness or "innateness," whether of ideas, faculties, a moral sense, or the structure of human consciousness. This included those who believed man to possess a capacity of intuition, either sensual or intellectual, that provided access to suprasensible knowledge.[10] For Mill, the intuitionists were guilty of the very worst sin: belief without evidence. In all forms of intuitionist philosophy, he said, "intuition usurps the place of evidence, and internal feeling is made the test of objective truth" ("UR," 404). Mill is implicitly referring to traditional religious feelings, which he, with Bentham, always believed were nothing but unfounded and subjective preferences masquerading as truth. Mill's hostility to the intuitionist camp was bound up with the fact that the vast majority of religious thinkers of his era defended theological morality on the grounds of intuition. They believed that man possesses some sort of innate moral sense or faculty by which he can apprehend moral truth and that the human mind has an intuitive conviction of God. Kantians of every variety, from Hamilton to Coleridge, were also consigned to the enemy intuitionist camp. Mill completely rejected the a priori Kantian categories. He strenuously defended the notion that the concepts of time and space and the structure of human consciousness, as well as the beliefs held by human beings, are products of phenomenal experience, organized by the psychological Laws of Association. As said, Mill denied an intuitive capacity to man, whether of sense or intellect. He also denied the notion of "necessary truth"; even the axioms of mathematics and geometry were, for Mill, products of human experience in time.[11]

Both *A System of Logic* and the *Examination*, then, were devoted to destroying the intuitionism that Mill regarded as the chief opponent of his own inductive or positivist epistemology. As Bernard Lightman explains, one of the main aims of the *Logic* had been to demonstrate conclusively that the only valid type of knowledge was that gained through the process of induction, or generalization from experience. As late as 1854, Mill was congratulating himself that the *Logic* was "taking its place as the standard philosophical representative in English . . . of the anti-innate principle & anti-natural-theology doctrines."[12] The attack on intuitionism, as discussed, was closely related to Mill's antitheological aims, for Mill regarded the loosely Kantian or intuitionist school, associated with Hamilton, as the bastion of theologically oriented philosophy in England. In his correspondence with Comte, Mill shed light on the relation between his later attack on Hamilton and his attack on theology or "ontology." As we saw in Chapter 2, he discussed the anticipated impact of the *Logic*:

[I]f my book is read and well received, it will be the first somewhat forceful blow administered to the ontological school in England [represented by Hamilton], at least in our day, and . . . sooner or later this blow will prove mortal to it. Now this was the most important thing to do, since this school alone is essentially theological and since its philosophy here presents itself as the national support of the old social order, and not only in terms of Christian, but even of Anglican ideas. (*Corr,* 83)

Above all, the [*Logic*] appears to me eminently well suited to serve as a dike to halt the dangerous advance of German philosophy [represented by Hamilton's "Kantianism"]. Up to now, this philosophy has been more useful than harmful to us. It has prompted a trend toward scientific generalization and a systematic approach to human knowledge. . . . But, from a social point of view, this philosophy is clearly reactionary today, whatever its trend toward skepticism that it has been blamed for in its native land: there, indeed, it played precisely the role of undermining the traditional faith, but in England it is used to endow it with a philosophic hue. (*Corr,* 138)

With respect to ethical theory, the most important aspect of Mill's attack on intuitionism concerned its opposition to nontheological utilitarianism. As Mill conceived it, the battle was between a purely human utilitarian consequentialism and the traditional "in-itself" or "transcendental" morality of the intuitionists.[13] The nontheological utilitarians believed, of course, that "the right and wrong of actions depends on the [temporal] consequences they tend to produce" while the "anti-utilitarians" (intuitionists such as Hamilton) believed the "right and wrong of actions depends . . . on an inherent quality of the actions themselves." As Mill put it, the question was whether "right means productive of happiness and wrong productive of misery, or right and wrong are intrinsic qualities of the actions themselves," as traditionally conceived (*Ham,* 454–56). We may recall in this context that Mill, with Bentham, truncated Christian utilitarianism by discountenancing the significance of "posthumous" consequences—divine justice or man's ultimate accountability to God—and limiting the utilitarian calculus to consequences "confined within the limits of the earth." The crucial ethical dichotomy he thus established is between, on the one hand, a strictly human consequentialism that evaluates the morality of an action by the beneficial intramundane or "social" consequences it tends to produce and, on the other, a theologically oriented "in-itself" morality that conceives moral action as action that is right-in-itself, and this regardless of apparent temporal consequences. This latter view points of course to a transcendent source of moral law; it views man's task as aligning himself with a given moral order and not as constructing a moral order. The outcome of the contest between the two conceptions would have important repercussions, personally, socially, and politically.[14]

Mill was at pains to point out the pernicious "practical consequences" of the intuitionist philosophy. As he said in the *Autobiography*, he wrote *A System of Logic* to counter the numerous "mischiefs" caused by the false philosophy that human beings have intuitive knowledge of the principles governing either themselves or the external world. Such a philosophy, he said, was "the great intellectual support of false doctrines and bad institutions. By the aid of this theory, every inveterate belief and every intense feeling, of which the origin is not remembered, is enabled to dispense with the obligation of justifying itself by reason, and is erected into its own all-sufficient voucher and justification. There never was such an instrument devised for consecrating all deep seated prejudices" (*Auto*, 134). Mill is referring to the traditional religious prejudices that sustained the British constitution. He further explains why the dispute between the intuitionists and the inductivists is of fundamental importance for the "practical reformer":

> [This dispute] is not a mere matter of abstract speculation; it is full of practical consequences, and lies at the foundation of all the greatest differences of practical opinion in an age of progress. The practical reformer has continually to demand that changes be made in things which are supported by powerful and widely spread feelings, or to question the apparent necessity and indefeasibleness of established facts; and it is often an indispensable part of his argument to shew, how those powerful feelings had their origin, and how those facts came to seem necessary and indefeasible. (*Auto*, 162)

These remarks provide a concise statement of Mill's approach to the undermining of traditional religious belief. If one can show how such beliefs and/or feelings might have come into existence, in some manner distinct from the traditional religious explanation, that is sufficient to at least call them into question if not to refute them. It is certainly sufficient to cast doubt on their supernatural origin.

The Obliteration of Givenness

It is clear, then, that the contest between an intramundane consequentialist morality and traditional "in-itself" morality was crucially bound up with Mill's purpose of replacing a theological with a purely human orientation. The realization of his end demanded above all the obliteration of the notion of givenness implicit in the "transcendental" morality of his opponents. Indeed, it demanded the destruction of givenness in all forms, whether of a given moral law; of given ideas, intuitions, or beliefs; of a given moral sense; indeed, even of the notion of "necessary truth" or self-evident mathematical axioms. Ryan seems perplexed by Mill's "unusual emotional intensity" in defending his view of the experiential source of mathematical axioms. Karl Britton also draws attention to the "crusading spirit" in which Mill conducted his attack on the notions of necessary, a priori, or intuitive truth.[15] The perplexity of such critics stems from their failure to attend to Mill's antitheological "religious" mission.

For Mill's passionate hostility to the notion of innateness or intuitiveness (that is, the ability to *recognize* moral or other truth), extending even to the rejection of the notion of necessary truth and the givenness of mathematical axioms, makes perfect sense in light of the seriousness of his intent to establish a purely human ethical order. In his *Autobiography*, Mill clarified the relation between his attack on the self-evidence of mathematical reasoning and his antitheological purposes: "[T]he chief strength of this false [a priori or intuitionist] philosophy in morals, politics, and religion, lies in the appeal which it is accustomed to make to the evidence of mathematics and of the cognate branches of physical science. [Thus t]o expel it from these is to drive it from its stronghold" (226). Once Mill's overriding aim—to replace the traditional theological orientation and morality of the West with a strictly human equivalent—is recognized, his curious "intensity" and "crusading spirit" with respect to intuited or a priori knowledge, extending even to the nature of mathematical axioms, is readily explained. For, as Mill says, to deny the necessary truth or self-evidence of such axioms is to strike a blow at the "chief strength" of the intuitionist philosophy, that is, at one of the last remaining "stronghold[s]" of theological morality. In short, Mill's vehemence regarding the philosophy of mathematics stemmed from that philosophy's relation to his moral and political mission: to "expel" a theologically oriented philosophy that sustained beliefs very inconvenient for the would-be founder of a new secular society and a new intramundane religion. For the givenness implicit in intuitive and a priori knowledge, as well as in the notion of an innate moral sense, points directly to a Giver, and, for most of Mill's contemporaries, to the orthodox Christian God. Mill's ambition to replace a theological with a nontheological orientation and ethic was ill-served by such indices of transcendent reality. And it is this threat that accounts for the "crusading spirit" with which he attacked a priori or intuitive knowledge. Thus his insistence that even mathematical axioms and the categories of time and space are contingent upon human experience in time. Thus, as Ryan observes, the "struggle between the intuitionists and the school of 'Experience and Association' was, [for Mill,] much more than an academic argument over the first principles of the moral sciences."[16] Indeed it was. For the obliteration of the notion of Givenness in any and all forms was essential to the accomplishment of Mill's religious mission.

Accordingly, Mill's denial of givenness extended to the givenness of human identity and purpose. To form the new men of the future, men governed by a purely human morality oriented exclusively toward an intramundane "service to Humanity," all human attributes must be conceived as acquired in time. As mentioned, despite certain convoluted efforts to retain some sense of human freedom, of free will and free choice, Mill never really overcame the determinist views upon which he had been reared. As he said, the "doctrine of circumstances"—that is, "the formation of character by circumstances" (*Auto*, 135)—was the strongest article of James Mill's faith; the son would remain something of an environmental determinist to the end.[17] Thus Mill, like his father, was committed to the view that all manifested differences among persons are the result not of natural or given abilities or characteristics but of (humanly manipulable) "circumstances." The pernicious notion of innate abilities must be undermined.

> I have long felt that the prevailing tendency to regard all the marked distinctions of human character as innate, and in the main indelible, and to ignore the irresistible proofs that by far the greater part of those differences, whether between individuals, races, or sexes, are such as not only might but naturally would be produced by differences in circumstances, is one of the great hindrances to the rational treatment of great social questions, and one of the greatest stumbling blocks to human improvement. (*Auto*, 162)

Mill posits a highly malleable human nature, one that can be shaped by an intense process of socialization in the direction of his nontheological and humanitarian ideals. This is especially the case with the substance of human conscience, which has heretofore been egregiously misformed by the "absurd" and "mischievous" impressions inculcated by traditional (religious) authorities.

> [The moral faculty] is . . . susceptible, by a sufficient use of the external sanctions and of the force of early impressions, of being cultivated in almost any direction; so that there is hardly anything so absurd or so mischievous that it may not, by means of these influences, be made to act on the human mind with all the authority of conscience. To doubt that the same potency might be given by the same means to the principle of utility, even if it had no foundation in human nature, would be flying in the face of all experience. (*Util*, 434)

The point that requires emphasis is that Mill's impassioned defense of the logic and philosophy of experience was inseparable from his entwined religious and political purposes. He found it essential to undermine the belief in intuitive knowledge because such belief sustained both the traditional theology he aimed to replace and the political and social order he sought to transform. And it goes without saying that innateness and intuitionism, "in-itself" and "transcendental" morality, even the self-evidence of mathematical axioms, point all too clearly to a world-transcendent source, which Mill is concerned to obscure. Mill's attack on the intuitionist "enemy" was well aimed.

II: The Mansel Controversy

Mill had little trouble demolishing Hamilton's arguments and, in short order, his reputation as well, which never recovered from Mill's attack. But Hamilton and the intuitionist philosophy he espoused were not the only victims of Mill's ire. Even more significant for the purposes of this work, Mill took the occasion of his critique of Hamilton to attack Henry Longueville Mansel, the Oxford don and Anglican priest who was Hamilton's foremost disciple in England. One of Mill's motives in attacking Hamilton had been his outrage over the way Mansel had applied Hamilton's "philosophy of the conditioned" to theology.

Mansel was a chief defender of an extreme Anglican orthodoxy in the face of the various contemporary threats to traditional religious belief. Between 1830 and 1870, established churches in England were confronted by a rising tide of religious doubt and unbelief emanating from diverse forces, including the growth of scientific knowledge, German biblical criticism and pantheism, and the Comtean philosophy of history, which relegated theology to the realm of childish superstition. Mansel, thoroughly schooled in German theology and Kantian philosophy, undertook the task of defending faith against the pretensions of reason. In the context of his times, this meant defending Anglican orthodoxy against German speculative philosophy and especially its claim to direct, intuitive insight into the nature of God. This Mansel accomplished in the series of Bampton Lectures he delivered in 1858. The lectures, despite their abstruse topic—German metaphysics—created "a sensation"; unprecedented crowds of listeners thronged to St. Mary's to hear Mansel discourse on "The Limits of Religious Thought."[18]

Mansel's chief argument was that irremediable epistemological limitations precluded human beings from criticizing revelation. Because man is a finite being with a conditioned consciousness, he is unable to know the transcendental world. Man has no immediate intuition of God and thus cannot know God's essence and attributes. Mansel also defended the literal truth of the Scriptures, which he regarded as infallible in all matters and beyond criticism or evaluation. For the finite being man is in no position to criticize or evaluate a communication from an infinite Being; those who do so are implicitly claiming their own infinitude. Mansel, in short, embraced an utterly uncompromising and extreme Anglican orthodoxy, refusing to concede any ground to the various contemporary forces pressing on traditional religious faith.

By the time of the Mill–Mansel controversy, theology had become inseparably entwined with epistemology. As Mansel put it, the "theological struggle of this age . . . turns upon the philosophical problem of the limits of knowledge and the true theory of human ignorance."[19] Thus, as Mill correctly apprehended, Mansel's motives for appealing to the epistemology articulated in Hamilton's philosophy of the conditioned were religious. As a contemporary critic put it, "Mansel was responding to intellectual developments which he felt threatened the Christian position, [and thus] his whole thought stressed the importance of epistemology in the religious situation of the time."[20] Mansel was also motivated by personal religious considerations. As Ryan says, he "genuinely seems to have thought that an acknowledgment of the limitations of human reason was a more reverent attitude towards the unknowable God than any attempt to look further into His nature, and he seems to have been impressed by a similar outlook in Hamilton."[21] As Hamilton had expressed their mutual view: "True, therefore, are the declarations of a pious philosophy:— 'A God understood would be no God at all;'—'To think that God is, as we can think him to be, is blasphemy.'—The Divinity, in a certain sense, is revealed; in a certain sense is concealed: He is at once known and unknown. But the last and highest consecration of all true religion, must be an altar—'To the unknown and unknowable God'."[22]

Mansel did take an extreme position. Aiming to refute the rationalists' claims to have identified God's nature, he categorically denied that either human intuition or human reason, whether speculative or practical, had access of any sort to the nature or attributes of the Unknowable God.[23] Reason is restricted to knowledge of the phenomenal world. It is therefore necessary to be content with the regulative or practical knowledge provided by revelation and to live without speculative knowledge of God— the Unknowable. Mansel, as said, also defended the infallibility of Scripture. Although such a belief was widespread among nineteenth-century Protestants, Mansel's absolute pronouncements were regarded as extreme by most participants in the controversy. The metaphysical and religious system he developed was markedly different from the views of most of his fellow English thinkers. Most important, Mansel's Victorian contemporaries had difficulty accepting his view that man has *no* knowledge of God. Although they could agree with Mansel that only "German transcendentalist[s] suppose . . . that we know the essence of Deity, what is His nature, and how He subsists," most English theologians thought man could gain at least a partial knowledge of God.[24]

Although Mansel denied that man had direct intuitive knowledge of God, both he and Hamilton did conceive a significant role for intuition in human existence. They argued that human beings have immediate intuitive knowledge received from sources other than the physical senses. As Mansel said, "It cannot . . . be maintained that the senses are the sole criteria of truth and of reality, unless we assume, in defiance of all consciousness, that there exist no immediate mental phenomena, but those communicated by sensation." Mansel also argued, with the Scottish moral sense and common sense schools, for the existence of various innate faculties, such as a "moral faculty" that provides individuals with intuitions of right and wrong and an a priori faculty of "religious intuition."[25] Mansel denied, however, that human beings possess any "direct faculty of religious knowledge, . . . by which, in its speculative exercise, we are enabled to decide, independently of all external Revelation, what is the true nature of God, and the manner in which He must manifest Himself to the world."[26] As a result, he argued, natural theology is incapable of establishing limits to the nature and attributes of God, a conclusion Mill would strenuously resist.

Finally, Mansel was also concerned to address the age-old problem of evil: how to reconcile the omnipotent and all-benevolent Christian God with a world in which the saints starve and the wicked prosper. His response was consistent with his epistemology: to insist upon the sheer inscrutability of God's ways.

The Human Ability to Judge God

As we have seen, Mill was drawn to do battle with Mansel because Mansel had applied Hamilton's philosophy of the conditioned to, as Mill put it, "the theological department of thought; the deduction of such corollaries and consequences [of Hamilton's philosophy] as directly concern religion" (*Ham*, 89). Mill's response was the notoriously intemperate polemic against Mansel that constitutes Chapter 7 of the *Examination*— "The Philosophy of the Conditioned, as Applied by Mr. Mansel to the

Limits of Religious Thought." What incensed Mill was Mansel's claim that human nescience forbids human judgment of God and his ways. As Collins explains, Mill was scandalized by "the sheerly equivocal way in which Hamilton and Mansel predicated the moral attribute of goodness to the absolute. They characterized the absolute as the infinite point of co-incidence for all attributes and antinomies and claimed that the goodness of this absolute was utterly different from, and contradictory of, our experiential notion of moral good."[27] In other words, Hamilton and Mansel denied that human moral conceptions could shed any light on the moral nature or attributes of God. Human conceptions of goodness and justice, held by necessarily finite and limited minds, were utterly inapplicable to the divine goodness and justice; thus the latter could not be judged by human standards. Human beings were obliged as a matter of faith to believe that God was everything that was good, but "good" as applied to the Almighty was at best related only analogically to "good" as applied to a human being. Because God's ways were mysterious to man and would ever remain so, biblical faith was the only adequate response to the human predicament. Mill utterly rejected Mansel's reasoning. To his mind, Mansel had used the legitimate doctrine of the relativity of all knowledge for an illegitimate—indeed, wicked—end: to justify a *view of religion which [Mill held] to be profoundly immoral*—that it is our duty to bow down in worship before a Being whose moral attributes are affirmed to be unknowable by us, and to be perhaps extremely different from those which, when we are speaking of our fellow-creatures, we call by the same names" (*Ham*, 163, emphasis added). In short, Mill's assault on Mansel was chiefly inspired by Mill's conviction, as Ryan puts it, of the "immorality of Mansel's doctrine of the unknowability of the moral attributes of God."[28] Perhaps even more to the point, what Mill could not abide was Mansel's insistence that human beings are in no position to judge God.

Mill begins his response to Mansel by restating the view he will refute. Mansel, with Hamilton, "maintains the necessary relativity of all our knowledge. He holds that . . . [while] an Absolute and an Infinite Being, are inconceivable by us . . . we are, nevertheless . . . bound to believe, the real existence of an absolute and infinite being, and that this being is God." Mill immediately gets to the point from which stems his violent disagreement with Mansel. Mansel, he says, contends that

> [t]hrough this inherent impossibility of our conceiving or knowing God's essential attributes, we are disqualified from judging what is or is not consistent with them. If, then, a religion is presented to us, containing any particular doctrine, respecting the Deity, our belief or rejection of the doctrine ought to depend

exclusively upon the evidences which can be produced for the divine origin of the religion; and no argument grounded on the incredibility of the doctrine, as involving an intellectual absurdity, or on its moral badness as unworthy of a good or wise being, ought to have any weight, since of these things we are incompetent to judge.

. . . There is nothing new in this line of argument as applied to theology. That we cannot understand God; that his ways are not our ways; that we cannot scrutinize or judge his counsels—propositions which, in a reasonable sense of the terms, could not be denied by any Theist—have often before been tendered as reasons why we may assert any absurdities and any moral monstrosities concerning God, and miscall them Goodness and Wisdom. The novelty is in presenting this conclusion as a corollary from the most advanced doctrines of modern philosophy—from the true theory of the powers and limitations of the human mind [the relativity of all knowledge], on religious and on all other subjects.

My opinion of this doctrine, in whatever way presented, is, that it is simply the most morally pernicious doctrine now current; and that the question it involves is, beyond all others which now engage speculative minds, the decisive one between moral good and evil for the Christian world. It is a momentous matter. (Ham, 89–90, emphases added)

The issue of mankind's ability to judge God and his ways is for Mill nothing less than "the decisive one between moral good and evil for the Christian world." The passionate moral intensity embodied in Mill's ostensible critique of Mansel's false epistemological inferences undoubtedly stems from this apocalyptic sense of urgency. (Moreover, it suggests that Ryan's remark that what separated Mill and Mansel "was the gulf between Mill's utterly secular, this-worldly temperament and [Mansel's] sense of the final mysteriousness of the world" is rather wide of the mark.[29] Mill, as this work aims to show, was driven throughout his life by the most intense, if misdirected, religious impulses. There is nothing remotely "secular" or areligious in his thought or being.)

Mill's general line of attack is to take the nominalist position that terms without a concrete referent, such as "the Absolute," are in themselves meaningless abstractions. Their meaning is to be identified only through the examination of particular entities:

[T]he words Absolute and Infinite have no real meaning, unless we understand by them that which is absolute or infinite in some given attribute; as space is called infinite, meaning that it is infinite in extension; and as God is termed infinite in the sense of possessing infinite power, and absolute in the sense of absolute goodness, or knowledge. . . . Hamilton's arguments for the unknowableness of the Unconditioned, do not prove that we cannot know an object which is absolute or infinite in some specific attribute, but only that we cannot know an abstraction called "The Absolute" or "The Infinite," which is supposed to have all attributes at once. (*Ham*, 94)

Mill is alluding in the last statement to German metaphysics and especially its suspension of the Law of Contradiction—a suspension that Hamilton and Mansel, following Hegel, seem to accept. Mill has little patience with what to him is the patent absurdity of such a notion. Mansel, Mill says, claims

> that the Absolute and Finite can be "nothing less than the sum of all reality," the complex of all positive predicates, even those which are exclusive of one another: and expressly identifies it with Hegel's Absolute Being, which contains in itself "all that is actual, even evil included. That which is conceived as absolute and infinite . . . must be conceived as containing within itself the sum not only of all actual, but of all possible modes of being." . . . If, therefore, Mr. Mansel would escape from the conclusion that an Infinite and Absolute Being is intrinsically impossible, it must be by affirming, with Hegel, that the law of Contradiction does not apply to the Absolute; that, respecting the Absolute, contradictory propositions may both be true.

For Mill such views are beyond the pale of reasonableness. He concludes: "One may well agree with Mr. Mansel that this farrago of contradictory attributes cannot be conceived: but what shall we say of his equally positive averment that it must be believed? . . . [M]y admission of the believability of what is inconceivable, stops at the self-contradictory." For Mill, then, a notion of God as Absolute and Infinite, a God who "possesses absolutely and infinitely all . . . conflicting attributes . . . and not solely . . . those which it would be thought decent to predicate of God" is nothing more than a "chimerical abstraction" (*Ham*, 95–98). Nor could such a fantastic being be of any concern to mankind, knowable or not.

As said, what disturbs Mill are the moral implications of Mansel's views. To Mill's mind, utter nescience requires man to worship a moral blank whose goodness, such as it is, may be entirely unrelated to any goodness man may know—an utter impossibility for Mill. Nor did he regard it as necessary, for Mill believed that man does have some—relative and phenomenal—knowledge of God and the nature of his goodness. In place of Hamilton and Mansel's nescience, Mill defends what he calls the "true view" of the nature of human knowledge. He agrees with Hamilton/Mansel that man can know nothing of the Unconditioned, of things-in-themselves, such as the essential nature of God. But, he argues, that does not mean that human beings can know nothing about God or that they are unable to "reject any statement as inconsistent with the character of God," as Mansel claims. As Mill says:

> We cannot know God as he is in himself; . . . granted: and what then? Can we know man as he is in himself, or matter as it is in itself? We do not claim

any other knowledge of God than such as we have of man or of matter. . . . I know something of Man and Nature, not as they are in themselves, but as they are relatively to us; and it is as relative to us, and not as he is in himself, that I suppose myself to know anything of God. The attributes which I ascribe to him, as goodness, knowledge, power, are all relative. They are attributes . . . which my experience enables me to conceive, and which I consider as proved, not absolutely, by an intuition of God, but phaenomenally, by his action on the creation, as known through my senses and my rational faculty. These relative attributes, each of them in an infinite degree, are all I pretend to predicate of God. When I reject a doctrine as inconsistent with God's nature, it is not as being inconsistent with what God is in himself, but with what he is as manifested to us. If my knowledge of him is only phaenomenal, the assertions which I reject are phaenomenal too. If those assertions are inconsistent with my relative knowledge of him, it is no answer to say that all my knowledge of him is relative. That is no more a reason against disbelieving an alleged fact as unworthy of God, than against disbelieving another alleged fact as unworthy of Turgot, or of Washington, whom also I do not know as Noumena, but only as Phaenomena. (*Ham*, 100)

Mill sums up his critique of Mansel's position:

Mr. Mansel has not made out any connexion between his philosophical premises and his theological conclusion. The relativity of human knowledge, the uncognoscibility of the Absolute, and the contradictions which follow the attempt to conceive a Being with all or without any attributes, are no obstacles to our having the same kind of knowledge of God which we have of other things, namely not as they exist absolutely, but relatively. The proposition, that we cannot conceive the moral attributes of God in such a manner as to be able to affirm of any doctrine or assertion that it is inconsistent with them, has no foundation in the laws of the human mind: while, if admitted, it would not prove that we should ascribe to God attributes bearing the same name as human qualities, but not to be understood in the same sense; it would prove that we ought not to ascribe any moral attributes to God at all, inasmuch as no moral attributes known or conceivable by us are true of him, and we are condemned to absolute ignorance of him as a moral being. (*Ham*, 107–8)

Mill points out that Mansel has only one possible way to meet his objections: He must insist not only on the unknowability of the absolute-infinite being in and of himself, but also on the unknowability of his relative attributes. "He must say that we do not know what Wisdom, Justice, Benevolence, Mercy, are, as they exist in God" (*Ham*, 100–101). This, as Mill acknowledges, is precisely Mansel's position. He quotes Mansel:

The representation of God after the model of the highest human morality which we are capable of conceiving, is not sufficient to account for all the phenomena exhibited by the course of his natural providence. The infliction of physical suffering, the permission of moral evil, the adversity of the good, the prosperity of the wicked, the crimes of the guilty involving the misery of the innocent, the tardy appearance and partial distribution of moral and religious knowledge in the world—these are facts which no doubt are reconcilable, we know not how, with the Infinite Goodness of God, but which certainly are not to be explained on the supposition that its sole and sufficient type is to be found in the finite goodness of man.[30]

We here approach the heart of the matter—the age-old problem of evil—translated into the terms of an epistemological argument concerning the limits of human knowledge.[31] For Mansel, the claim to knowledge of God's essence and attributes is nothing more than a "vulgar Rationalism which regards the reason of man, in its ordinary and normal operation, as the supreme criterion of religious truth."[32] What Mansel rejects is precisely the view Mill will defend: that "all the excellences of which we are conscious in the creature, must necessarily exist in the same manner, though in a higher degree, in the Creator. God is indeed more wise, more just, more merciful, than man; but for that very reason, his wisdom and justice and mercy must contain nothing that is incompatible with the corresponding attributes in their human character."[33]

This is *the* point of conflict between Mill and Mansel. Mill will fight to the death for the view that God's goodness cannot be different in kind from human goodness. As Mill says:

I will take my stand on the acknowledged principle of logic and of morality, that when we mean different things we have no right to call them by the same name. . . . Language has no meaning for the words Just, Merciful, Benevolent, save that in which we predicate them of our fellow-creatures; If in affirming [such words] of God we do not mean to affirm these very qualities, differing only as greater in degree, we are neither philosophically nor morally entitled to affirm them at all. [Although we may not be able to] conceive [such qualities] . . . as they are when raised to the infinite, . . . we can conceive them in their other elements, which are the very same in the infinite as in the finite development. Anything carried to the infinite must have all the properties of the same thing as finite, except those which depend upon the finiteness. Among the many who have said that we cannot conceive infinite space, did any one ever suppose that it is *not* space? . . . The parallel assertion may be made respecting infinite goodness. What belongs to it either as Infinite or as Absolute I do not pretend to know; but I know that infinite goodness must be goodness, and that what is not consistent with goodness, is not consistent with infinite goodness. . . . If in ascribing goodness to God I do not mean what I mean by goodness, . . . what reason have I for venerating it? If I know nothing about what the attribute is, I cannot tell that it is a proper object of veneration. To say that God's goodness may be different in kind from man's goodness, what is it but saying, with a slight change of phraseology, that God may possibly not be good? (*Ham*, 102)

Mill will save God's absolute goodness at all costs. It is possible, he says, to conceive a God, who, unlike Mansel's "impossible fiction, . . . is neither supposed to have no attributes nor to have all attributes, but to have good attributes. . . . [There is no] hindrance to our being able to conceive a Being absolutely just, for example, or absolutely wise" (*Ham*, 96). A god of perfect goodness and justice, however limited in other attributes, is the only god Mill will have.

Curiously, Mill, the self-styled nominalist, finally rests his argument for the human ability to know the nature of God and especially of his goodness on the "essence" of goodness:

> The Divine goodness, which is said to be a different thing from human goodness, but of which the human conception of goodness is some imperfect reflexion or resemblance, does it agree with what men call goodness in the *essence* of the quality—in what *constitutes* its goodness? If it does, the "Rationalists" [that is, Mill and his fellow travelers] are right; it is not illicit to reason from the one to the other. If not, the divine attribute, whatever else it may be, is not goodness, and ought not to be called by the name. Unless there be some human conception which agrees with it, no human name can properly be applied to it; it is simply the unknown attribute of a thing unknown; it has no existence in relation to us, we can affirm nothing of it, and owe it no worship. Such is the inevitable alternative. (*Ham*, 106–7)

Mill also defends against Mansel the right to criticize and evaluate the validity of alleged revelation. He rejects Mansel's view that the impotence of reason and natural theology necessarily limit man's knowledge of God to that found in the Scriptures. For Mill, revealed knowledge is to be judged by the same methods and on the same basis as all other phenomena, that is, in accordance with the canons of induction and in light of the "external evidences." Nor will Mill yield his right to judge the content of revelation by his personal moral standard. As he explains:

> No Rationalists . . . believe that what they reject as inconsistent with the Divine Goodness was really revealed by God. They do not both admit it to be revealed and believe it to be false. They believe that it is either a mistaken interpretation, or found its way by human means into documents which they may nevertheless consider as the records of a Revelation. They concede, therefore, to Mr. Mansel (and unless the hypothesis were admitted of a God who is not good, they cannot help conceding) that the moral objections to a religious doctrine are only valid against its truth if they are strong enough to outweigh whatever external evidences there may be of its having been divinely revealed. But when the question is, *how much* weight is to be allowed to moral objections, the difference will be radical between those who think that the Divine Goodness is the same thing with human goodness carried to the infinite, and Mr. Mansel, who thinks that it is a different quality, only having some analogy to the human. Indeed it is hard to see

how any one, who holds the latter opinion, can give more than a nominal weight to any such argument against a religious doctrine. For, if things may be right according to divine goodness which would be wrong according to even an infinite degree of the human, and if all that is known is that there is some analogy between the two, . . . it is impossible to assign any determinate weight to an argument grounded on contradiction of such an analogy. (*Ham*, 107–8n)

As said, it is obvious that, despite all the convoluted intellectual maneuvering, the real point at issue for Mill was not epistemological, but moral: whether or not human beings are capable of judging God. Mill himself felt perfectly entitled to do so. And his moral outrage at Mansel's suggestion that such judgment was beyond the pale of human ability or authority explains why Mill found Mansel's *Limits of Religious Thought* a "detestable" and "absolutely loathsome" book.[34] It also explains why, as Ryan observes, "[n]either Mill's attack nor Mansel's response stands out as a model of dispassionate and impersonal inquiry." This is something of an understatement. A better sense of the moral intensity impelling Mill's attack on Mansel is conveyed by Mill's "famous outburst"[35] that not only startled his contemporaries but impressed his descendants as well:

> If, instead of the "glad tidings" that there exists a Being in whom all the excellences which the highest human mind can conceive, exist in a degree inconceivable to us, I am informed that the world is ruled by a being whose attributes are infinite, but what they are we cannot learn, nor what are the principles of his government, except that "the highest human morality which we are capable of conceiving" does not sanction them; convince me of it, and I will bear my fate as I may. But when I am told that I must believe this, and at the same time call this being by the names which express and affirm the highest human morality, I say in plain terms that I will not. *Whatever power such a being may have over me, there is one thing which he shall not do: he shall not compel me to worship him. I will call no being good, who is not what I mean when I apply that epithet to my fellow-creatures; and if such a being can sentence me to hell for not so calling him, to hell I will go.* (*Ham*, 103, emphasis added)

Mill, an extremely self-controlled person deeply concerned with cultivating a public image of disinterestedness and impartiality, was provoked into an uncharacteristic show of his hand. This "emotional tirade"[36] may have been uncharacteristic and, as Mansel said, little more than "an extraordinary outburst of rhetoric,"[37] but the intensity of feeling it evinces nevertheless yields significant insight into the motivations that led Mill to develop his peculiar conception of god. It should also be mentioned that Mill's notorious show of defiance would have significant consequences for the later development of religious thought. As David Berman says, what Mill did was to make the rejection of the Christian God a matter of "moral superiority" and even necessity: "Mill's moral victory [over Mansel was] directly relevant to the history of British atheism. . . . [What was significant about Mill's] impassioned declaration against Mansel . . . [was] the moral superiority [it] evinced. As righteousness was perceived to pass from the champions of belief [such as Mansel] to the critics [such as] Mill, so . . . the onus of proof passed from unbelievers to the believers. . . ."[38] Mill's triumph was in turn related to the partial realization of his more general goal as characterized throughout this study—the replacement of a theological with a purely human orientation. Mill was an important figure in the development of what is today called secular humanism. William James suggested that Mill was almost single-handedly responsible for making nontheological humanism socially respectable.[39] In any event, the clear implication of Mill's outburst was that only the morally uncultivated, the base and servile, would worship a God such as conceived by Mansel.

It may be observed that Mill was rejecting what he conceived to be a vulgar God of Will and Power—the "Almighty" of the popular Victorian conception. Mill seems never seriously to have considered conceptions of the divine nature other than those he absorbed from his Calvinist father. Curiously, however, he does at times approach something like the conception of God articulated in Scholastic and Catholic philosophy, of God *as* Being, *as* Law, *as* Goodness, *as* Reason. For instance, as he speculates in the *Examination*, "if the necessity predicated of human actions is not a material, but a spiritual necessity; if the assertion that the virtuous man is virtuous necessarily, only means that he is so because he dreads a departure from virtue more than he dreads any personal consequence; there is nothing absurd or invidious in taking a similar view of the Deity, and believing that he is necessitated to will what is good, by the love of good and detestation of evil which are in his own nature" (440). Mill seems to suggest that God must *be* Goodness, which is thus not the product of his will but the expression of his being. Here as in various other remarks Mill reveals that the conception of God he condemns and rejects is the idea of a God of arbitrary will and omnipotence, a God that derives from the nominalist tradition in which he was bred.[40]

Moreover, as certain of Mill's critics—including his close associate, Alexander Bain—pointed out, Mill was not well read in theology or metaphysics and seems to have had a merely general acquaintance with the Scriptures.[41] He seems to have learned all he needed to know about God from his father and the popular conceptions of his contemporaries. Accordingly, the seriousness of Mill's theological investigations is called into question. Mill's critique of Mansel's theology was, in great measure, an emotional and polemical display, a reaction inspired by the narrow view of God he inherited from James Mill and by his own Promethean reach. It was also, of course, an instrument toward the fulfillment of his religious purposes as characterized in this study.

The Pretense of Knowledge

If we reason directly from God's goodness to positive facts, no misery, nor vice nor crime ought to exist in the world.

—*J. S. Mill, "Theism"*

Although Mill was at pains to defend himself against the suggestion that he was trying "to set up [his] own limited intellect as a criterion of divine or of any other wisdom," there can be little doubt that he believed he himself *knew* in what goodness and justice consist. Throughout his adult life, Mill was convinced of the utter superiority of his purely human morality and seems never to have feared that his own moral conceptions might be incomplete or erroneous. Nor would he entertain the possibility that the seeming injustice and evil within the world may in fact be reconcilable with the absolute goodness of an omnipotent God in a manner, as Mansel suggested, inaccessible to human beings. A serious engagement with Mill's corpus leaves one with the unmistakable impression that Mill believed he knew precisely the essence of goodness and justice and the manner in which they must manifest themselves in the phenomenal world. Indeed, as he tells us, the only authority to whom he might defer in questions of moral truth would be one who shares his own fundamental "standard of truth and rule of right. . . . [I]f I thought it not improbable that [another person's] notion of right might be my notion of wrong, I should not defer to his judgment" (*Ham*, 103). It is this strong conviction of the superiority and even infallibility of his personal standard of justice and conception of goodness that underlies Mill's sense of entitlement to judge God and the created order and that accounts for his loathing of a Mansel, who challenged that sense.

Indeed, Mill's blind rage at Mansel's denial of human authority to judge God's goodness and his ways led him to willfully distort his opponent's position in various ways. First, Mill knew that Mansel—despite certain extreme statements concerning the possible divergence of human and divine standards of morality—allowed that the human conception of goodness had some relation, if only analogically, to divine goodness. As Mill said:

I am anxious to say once more, that Mr. Mansel's conclusions do not go the whole length of his argument, and that he disavows the doctrine that God's justice and goodness are *wholly* different from what human beings understand by the terms. He would, and does, admit that the qualities as conceived by us bear *some likeness* to the justice and goodness which belong to God, since man was made in God's image. . . . [S]uch a semi-concession [is one] which no Christian could avoid making, since without it the whole Christian scheme would be subverted. (*Ham,* 106)

Yet Mill ignored Mansel's important "semi-concession" and proceeded to attack Mansel as if he himself had never written the passage quoted above.

Second, Mill's emotional resistance to Mansel's contention that the goodness and justice of God and man should be understood in an equivocal sense prevented him from recognizing the actual import of Mansel's arguments. For, as Ryan observes, "[I]t is not clear that Mansel intends to show that God's *goodness* is not ours; mostly, he argues that how God is working out an overall plan for His universe, a plan which is good in the same sense as a human plan would be good, simply remains unknowable. . . . [I]t is less a matter of the imperfect analogy between human and divine attributes (which is the object of Mill's complaint) than of the imperfection of our knowledge of the Almighty's programme."[42] That is, Mansel's principal purpose was not to distinguish between human and divine goodness and justice but to emphasize the limits to human knowledge, to present what he called the "true lesson of philosophy—a knowledge of the limits of human reason,"[43] especially as such limits apply to knowledge of the transcendent God. It is worth repeating that Mill, whose attack on Hamilton was motivated (or so he claimed) by epistemological considerations, seems to have been far less concerned with the epistemological aspects of Mansel's argument—the extent of the limits to human knowledge of the divine nature or the divine plan—than with its moral implications. Mill's moral outrage seems to have so overwhelmed his critical faculties that he all but ignored Mansel's main point—"the imperfection of our knowledge of the Almighty's programme." Mill, as we know, thought the prevailing conception of a providential order "completely irrational" (*Corr,* 129). Perhaps this accounts for his failure to address Mansel's concern with the limits to human knowledge of God's comprehensive plan. In any event, it seems clear that Mill's own chief concern was not epistemology but the judgment of God and the reckless disorder that is existence. Be that as it may, the full import of Mill's attack on Mansel was not lost on Mill's disciples. They had no difficulty recognizing it as what John Morley called a "rebellion against all [Christian] theories of the cosmic plan."[44]

Throughout his life, Mill would vehemently reject a priori or intuitive knowledge and insist that all valid belief must be founded on phenomenal evidence. Nevertheless, one may safely surmise that Mill's conviction of the truth—one is tempted to say the necessary truth—of God's absolute goodness was not derived from his own experience of the world. It was precisely because Mill found it impossible to reconcile his conception of absolute goodness with his perception of the actual order of existence—imperfect, indeed, recklessly disordered, devoid of inherent goodness or justice—that he was led to develop his unusual conception of god, which we have briefly discussed and which we will now examine more fully. Mill could not or would not reconcile the world-as-it-is with the Christian conception of an omnipotent and absolutely good God. To satisfy the demands of his intellectual and moral preconceptions, and to provide free reign for his own towering ambitions, Mill created a new god. His god may be probable, limited, possibly inept, and very much in need of man's assistance, but he is pure. That is, he is untainted by the "moral objections" necessarily raised by the Christian God—that wicked "Omnipotent Author of Hell"—whom, he had learned from his father, could not possibly be reconciled with the principle of goodness (*Ham*, 108n).

"Theism"

Though conscious of being in an extremely small minority, we venture to think that a religion may exist without belief in a God, and that a religion without a God may be, even to Christians, an instructive and profitable object of contemplation.

—*J. S. Mill,* Auguste Comte and Positivism

The seriousness of Mill's lifelong engagement with religion is further evinced by the fact that the last major essay he wrote before his death in 1873 was also his most thoughtful and theoretical consideration of the problem of God. As we recall, "Theism" was composed between 1868 and 1870, about fifteen years later than the other essays that appear in *Three Essays on Religion.* While much of "Theism" is anticipated in the earlier essays and especially in "Utility of Religion," there are also substantial changes in the final essay and, most prominently, a marked change of tone. John Morley, one of Mill's disciples, characterized "Theism" as a soliloquy, and certain passages do convey the tone of a personal musing not intended for public consumption.[1] Many of Mill's other published writings, by contrast, are highly if not disturbingly polemical, written with the express intent of shaping public opinion. There are passages in "Theism" that seem by comparison heartfelt and genuine. Nevertheless, given Mill's genius for proselytizing and the single-mindedness with which he pursued his religious goals, one can never be certain whether he is sincere or adopting a rhetorical pose.

Mill opens the discussion by drawing attention to the notably different tone of the essay. The fury of the age-old conflict between believers and unbelievers in religion has diminished, he says, and this because the "intolerance" of believers and the "reactionary violence" it provoked have diminished. Mill offers several more particular reasons for the "more softened temper" of the debate, reasons that will be familiar to those acquainted with his correspondence with Comte.[2] First, experience has chastened once "ardent hopes . . . in the regeneration of the human race by merely negative doctrine—by the destruction of superstition." The criticism of Christianity led by the eighteenth-century philosophes, however, has accomplished its task. Christianity is on the defensive; its opponents no longer need to adopt a militant stance. The second reason for the decrease in religious controversy relates to recent developments in the "philosophical study of history." As Mill says, these developments have "rendered possible an impartial estimate of the doctrines and institutions of the past, from a relative instead of an absolute point of view—as incidents of human development at which it is useless to grumble. . . . And the position assigned to Christianity or Theism by the more instructed of those who reject the supernatural, is that of things once of great value but which can now be done without; rather than, as formerly, of things misleading and noxious *ab initio*" ("The," 429). Both aspects of Mill's interpretation are of Saint-Simonian and Comtean inspiration.

In addition to these factors, scientific advance had contributed to the diminution of controversy over the question of the truth of religion. As Mill says, the ground upon which the "war against religious beliefs" was formerly conducted—"common sense" or "logic"—had shifted in the nineteenth century to that of science, both physical and social. The physical sciences were widely thought to have conclusively established certain facts irreconcilable with traditional religion. Furthermore, "the science of human nature and history is considered to show that the creeds of the past are natural growths of the human mind, in particular stages of its career, destined to disappear and give place to other convictions in a more advanced stage." This too is pure Comtism, although Mill does not identify its source by name. He concludes his explanation for the less hostile tone of contemporary religious controversy with a statement that is interesting for its curious blend of positivist philosophy of history and scientific evolutionism. Historical relativism, he says, has diminished such controversy insofar as religious beliefs have come to be regarded as "products thrown up by certain states of civilisation . . . which, like the animal and vegetable productions of a geological period perish in those which succeed it from the cessation of the conditions necessary to their continued existence."

Although Mill never expressly identifies his own views with those of the new historicists and scientists, he does express his approval of the new outlook—the tendency "to look upon human opinions preeminently . . . as facts obeying laws of their own, and requiring, like other observed facts, an historical or a scientific explanation." Such an approach, moreover, has an important bearing on the truth of religious beliefs, inasmuch as no cautious thinker can accept any positive belief, including and especially religious belief, "unless he is able to account for the existence of the opposite opinion." Mill reiterates his invariable method of procedure: The proper and sufficient way to "rebut . . . the . . . presumption of the truth of an . . . opinion held by many human minds [is] by assigning some other real or possible cause for its prevalence." Such an approach is especially important for the present subject—the "foundations of theism"—because the most commonly invoked argument for the truth of theism is "the general assent of mankind."

It is important to note that Mill was very far from embracing a thoroughgoing historicism. In line with his "practical eclecticism," Mill always picked and chose what served his purposes and discarded what did not. This was the case with Saint-Simonism and Comtism as with other schools of thought. Moreover, Mill's emotional and intellectual commitments, while fluid, were firmly rooted in certain of his father's assumptions, especially in his absolute conviction that any and all legitimate beliefs must be grounded on evidence. As we know, James Mill had impressed upon his son the idea that "belief without evidence" was the most unpardonable sin. Thus, says John Mill, relativism or no, "the most important quality of an opinion . . . is its truth or falsity, which to us resolves itself into the sufficiency of the evidence on which it rests." Accordingly, the chief purpose of "Theism" will be to examine the evidences upon which the truth or falsity of the hypothesis of God must stand or fall—and to test them, moreover, by the same scientific methods by which all other phenomenal hypotheses are tested. As Mill says, it is essential that

> religion should from time to time be reviewed as a strictly scientific question, and that its evidences should be tested by the same scientific methods, and on the same principles as those of any of the speculative conclusions drawn by physical science. It being granted then that the legitimate conclusions of science are entitled to prevail over all opinions . . . which conflict with them, and that the canons of scientific evidence which the successes and failures of two thousand years have established [canons, we again note, formulated by Mill himself] are applicable to all subjects on which knowledge is attainable . . . [we can] consider what place there is for religious beliefs on the platform of science; what evidences they can appeal to, such as science can recognise, and what foundation there is for the doctrines of religion, considered as scientific theorems.

Mill's "Theism" falls largely within the tradition of natural theology generally associated with the speculations of eighteenth-century English deism. As discussed, the deists were concerned to explore what man can know about God in the absence of express revelation, that is, what could be established by the rational examination of the evidences provided by nature. Thus, Mill says, his first area of inquiry will be "the problem of Natural Religion, that of the existence of God" ("The," 430–31).

The Law of the Three Stages

Mill begins by elaborating a variant of the naturalistic Comtean explanation of the origin of man's belief in gods, briefly discussed in "Utility of Religion." He follows Comte in describing the path by which men progressed from primitive polytheism to the more advanced conception of monotheism as a path of intellectual growth. For "untaught [and] prescientific . . . minds" it is entirely natural to attribute "conscious wills" to the diverse forces and phenomena of nature:[3] "[T]he natural tendency is to suppose as many such independent wills as there are distinguishable forces of sufficient importance and interest to have been remarked and named." Polytheistic systems tend to regard one deity as the chief god with sufficient power to control the other gods; that is, the minor gods rule the various departments of human existence, subject to the power and control of the principal god. Nevertheless, within such systems there is no "real acknowledgment of one Governor," which, Mill says, is the essence of genuine monotheism. This is because the belief in monotheism awaited the discovery of the "absolute unity of the Godhead," of universal law established by a "single will": "There could be no real belief in one Creator and Governor until mankind had begun to see in the apparently confused phenomena which surrounded them, a system capable of being viewed as the possible working out of a single plan." This required the gradual development of scientific thinking. Monotheism thus represents a significant intellectual advance over the "more natural" polytheistic conceptions of the earliest peoples. Monotheism is an "artificial product" dependent upon the growth of intellectual culture because "for a long time, the supposition appeared forced and unnatural that the diversity we see in the operations of nature can all be the work of a single will." In short, Mill, like Comte, explains the advance from polytheism to monotheism on mental grounds, as an intellectual and indeed scientific advance achieved through the growth of the human mind and especially of its powers of generalization and abstraction.

Even more particularly, Mill explains, the advance from polytheism to monotheism depended upon the discovery that the order of nature is governed by law and not by will. This required two distinct insights, derived from observation: first, that every event has a cause, that is, that it "depends for its existence on some antecedent, some fact or facts which preceded it"; and second, that all phenomena are interdependent, which means that all such antecedents / facts / causes are so inescapably entangled that every particular effect is the result of "the aggregate of all causes in existence" and not of one cause or antecedent only.[4] Once this "double conviction" had been attained, the way was clear toward the conception of monotheism, that is, the conception of the "absolute unity of the Godhead." This conception is based on the recognition that "no one event, certainly no one kind of events, can be absolutely preordained or governed by any Being but one who holds in his hand the reins of all Nature and not of some department only." Mill's main concern in this section is to show that monotheism is the "only Theism" capable of being supported by the scientific evidence.[5] For every other theory of supernatural government is inconsistent with the facts that science has established—that the universe is governed "through a continual series of natural antecedents according to fixed laws" and the "interdependence of each of these series upon all the rest" ("The," 431–32).

Although Mill does not mention it in "Theism," he believed, as we have seen, that beyond the primitive polytheistic and the more advanced monotheistic states of the human mind necessarily and inevitably lies its most advanced and final state: the positive state, which fully understands that all phenomena are strictly and universally governed by natural law and which has learned not to seek for causes beyond the phenomenal realm. It may be noted, however, that neither Mill's ultimate rejection of the notion of a first cause nor his reduction of the notion of cause to a "natural antecedent" is accompanied by the more radical closure to dimensions of reality beyond the phenomenal as is found, for instance, in Comte or Marx, or, indeed, in James Mill. That is, John Mill's positivism does not entail the prohibition of the quest for the source of human existence that is found in his compatriots. Although his speculations so eviscerate God as to make him, for all practical purposes, a nullity who may safely be ignored in the long run, Mill still allows that the desire to search for the origin of existence is "natural. . . . [I]t must be acknowledged that the question, to which Theism is an answer, is at least a very natural one, and issues from an obvious want of the human mind." In "Utility of Religion" he had ascribed the cause of the belief in God, at least among "cultivated minds," to the burning desire to know the source and nature of the universe. In "Theism" he suggests that the origin of that belief can be traced to man's phenomenal experience of the fact of universal causation:

Accustomed as we are to find, in proportion to our means of observation, a definite beginning to each individual fact, and since wherever there is a beginning we find that there was an antecedent fact (called by us a cause), . . .

but for which, the phenomenon which thus commences would not have been; it was impossible that the human mind should not ask itself whether the whole, of which these particular phenomena are a part, had not also a beginning, and if so, whether that beginning was not an origin; whether there was not something antecedent to the whole series of causes and effects that we term Nature, and but for which Nature itself would not have been. From the first recorded speculation this question has never remained without an hypothetical answer. The only answer which has long continued to afford satisfaction is Theism.

Mill's business, however, is to examine this problem of the "origin of all the phenomena of nature . . . merely as a scientific inquiry." This entails two specific questions: first, whether the theory which ascribes that origin to "the will of a Creator" is consistent with the scientific evidence; and second, assuming it is consistent, whether the conventional proofs of God's existence can withstand testing by modern scientific methods ("The," 432–33).

The short answer to Mill's two questions is that one and only one prevailing conception of theism is consistent with the truths of science—that which conceives a God who governs the world by invariable laws. A second prevailing conception—that of "a God governing the world by acts of variable will"—is radically untenable by scientific standards, radically inconsistent with the scientific evidence. The God of Mill's contemporaries—the "primitive" and "vulgar" God of Will and Power, a God who governs the world by "special decrees"—must be rejected, Mill believed. Such a conception of God is, to Mill's mind, incoherent. Conceived to be both omniscient and omnipotent, he is nevertheless "thought not to make up his mind until the moment of action; or at least not so conclusively, but that his intentions may be altered up to the very last moment by appropriate solicitation." We are reminded of James Mill's condemnation of prayer. John Mill refuses even to attempt to reconcile such a vulgar view of divine government with the perfect knowledge and wisdom also ascribed to the Deity. He rests his case on the fact that such a conception contradicts our experience of how things actually occur, on our universal experience that the phenomena of nature occur in accordance with general laws and originate from definite natural/phenomenal antecedents. Such, he recognizes, does not preclude the possibility that the laws that govern the universe are themselves the product of the divine will. But this in no way affects the universal reign of law. For, if God willed the universe, "that will must have established the general laws and willed the antecedents. If there be a Creator, his intention must have been that events should depend upon antecedents and be produced according to fixed, . . . general laws. But this being conceded, there is nothing in scientific experience inconsistent with the belief that those laws and sequences are themselves due to a divine will" ("The," 433–34).

Mill can accept a God such as that accepted by the "spiritual necessitarians"—Luther, Calvin, and their descendants—one, that is, whose will for man is realized through a determined course of natural events.[6] Moreover, he does not think it necessary to believe in the "watchmaker god" of the deists, one, that is, thought to have exerted his will "once for all, and after putting a power into the system which enabled it to go on of itself, has ever since let it alone." Mill allows that science does not preclude the possibility that all events on earth are the result of a "specific volition of the presiding Power, provided that this Power adheres in its particular volitions to general laws laid down by itself." A God of Will, to be scientifically acceptable, must realize his will through universal law. Mill thus rules out only what contemporary theologians called "special Providence," or a providence operating through particular acts of will; a "general Providence," one that operates through general laws, he suggests at this point, may be a possibility. This is a good example of the "softened temper" that characterizes Mill's final thoughts on religion. It is also an example of the changed outlook in "Theism" that so shocked Mill's intimates. Their shock is easy to understand when, for instance, one compares his concession to the possibility of providential governance in "Theism" to the ridicule he showered on that "completely irrational" notion in his correspondence with Comte. An even wider gulf appears when one compares the views in "Theism" to Mill's vehement attack on the notion of a providential order in "Nature."

Mill concludes his introduction by conceding that "[t]here is nothing to disprove the creation and government of Nature by a sovereign will." Nevertheless, we have yet to examine whether there is anything to prove it. (Mill, unlike modern social scientists, believed in the possibility of proof.) This requires a thorough examination and evaluation of the evidence, which Mill will "weigh in the scientific balance" ("The," 434).

I: The Evidences of Theism

There are two distinct kinds of evidences of a Creator, generally termed *a priori* and *a posteriori* proofs. Religious thinkers or "unthoughtful believers[s] whose creed really rests on authority" look with favor upon the former method or, indeed, upon any kind of proof that supports their pre-existing belief.[7] Philosophers, Mill says, have a duty to remain impartial between these two different methods in science and he will thus fairly examine both. He confesses, however, that he himself regards only one method as genuinely scientific: "The scientific argument is that which reasons from the facts and analogies of human experience—the *a posteriori* or inductive method." Unscientific reasoning, on the other hand, "is that which infers external objective facts from ideas or convictions of our minds." That is, the reasoning condemned by science is the a priorism employed by Mill's ancient foe, the theologically oriented school of "intuitionism" or "innatism." Of special concern with respect to the issue of theism, the intuitionists maintain that human beings possess an innate idea of God, an idea that points to his reality. Mill argues, against this view, that such an idea can be shown to have been acquired, to have "grown up from the impressions of experience." Further, even if it were impossible to trace the origin of the idea of God, the mere fact that someone holds such an idea does not prove the reality of the corresponding object: "The supposition that an idea, or a wish, or a need, even if native to the mind proves the reality of a corresponding object, derives all its plausibility from the belief already in our minds that we were made by a benignant Being who would not have implanted in us a groundless belief, or a want which he did not afford us the means of satisfying; and is therefore a palpable *petitio principii* if adduced as an argument to support the very belief which it presupposes." Mill here restates his conviction, elaborated in "Nature" fifteen years earlier, that his limited probable god is unable to guarantee that nature does nothing in vain.

A priori systems do have some claim to our consideration insofar as they start from "the facts of experience." This, Mill says, is true of the first argument for theism that he will examine—the alleged necessity of a first cause. This argument does have a basis in experience: the relations of cause and effect universally exhibited by the phenomena of nature. "[T]heological philosophers," however, not satisfied with such inductive evidence, "have affirmed Causation as a truth of reason apprehended intuitively by its own light" ("The," 434–35). Mill cannot let such a serious error pass unchallenged.

The Argument for a First Cause

Although the tone of Mill's religious writings may have become less militant over the years, neither his major opponents in moral philosophy—the intuitionists or innatists—nor his attitude toward them underwent any substantial change. Mill's refutation of the argument for the necessity of a first cause is implicitly directed against the intuitionist theologians and philosophers and should be understood in light of Mill's lifelong campaign against that school (which, as we recall, he regarded as one of the last strongholds of theological belief in England). The intuitionists attacked in "Theism" are the same "free-will theologians and philosophers" that Mill aimed to refute in the *Examination* (*Ham*, 438). One of Mill's concerns in "Theism" is to refute the notion of will, divine or human, as a causal agent in experience; its argument is of a piece with his refutation of the religious understanding of free will in the *Examination*. The intuitionists not only "consider[ed] the necessity of a first cause as a matter of intuition" but they conceived the first cause in the Christian-voluntarist manner, as a God of will or volition. Mill contests his opponents' two-part premise—the existence and necessity of a first cause, apprehended by intuition and conceived as divine volition. He aims to refute the notion of will as a cause of phenomenal experience by demonstrating that "several other agencies than Will can lay equal claim to that character" ("The," 439). His purpose—to defeat the Christian voluntarists—leads him to deny the reality not only of free will, divine or human, but also of the traditional Christian conception of a Creator God. He is also led to reassert the pagan conception of an uncreated and eternal primal "matter" (to which he adds a primal "force") as well as to reintroduce his conception of a Platonic-like Demiurge who imposes the form of order on a recalcitrant matter he did not create. Mill's argument reveals the deterministic and even materialistic character of his outlook; he comes close to suggesting that consciousness, mind, or will are mere by-products of biological or chemical forces. The pronounced determinism of the essay rests in uneasy tension with Mill's putative defense of human liberty.

The argument for the necessity of a first cause, Mill begins, is one that professes, not implausibly, to derive from human experience. The experience of universal causation within the world, it is argued, points to a cause of the world beyond that world to which it owes its existence. Mill's challenge to this argument is to clarify the actual "fact of experience." That fact, he says, is *not* that everything is dependent for its existence upon a cause; all we actually know from experience is that "every event or change" is so dependent. As Mill says, "There is in Nature a permanent element, and also a changeable; the changes are always the effects of previous changes; the permanent existences, so far as we know, are not effects at all." All beginnings in time, even those of "objects," are, in actuality, "events," that is, "changes" of the component parts—the specific elementary substance or substances, and their inherent properties, of which a thing consists.

These [permanent component parts] are not known to us as beginning to exist: within the range of human knowledge they had no beginning, consequently no cause; though they themselves are causes or con-causes of everything that takes place. Experience therefore, affords no evidences, not even analogies, to justify our extending to the apparently immutable, a generalization grounded only on our observation of the changeable. As a fact of experience, then, causation cannot legitimately be extended to the material universe itself, but only to its changeable phenomena.

It is thus a necessary part of the fact of causation, within the sphere of our experience, that the causes as well as the effects had a beginning in time, and were themselves caused. It would seem therefore that our experience, instead of furnishing an argument for a first cause, is repugnant to it; and that the very essence of causation as it exists within the limits of our knowledge, is incompatible with a First Cause. ("The," 436)

This is surely twisted reasoning. It may be objected that, on Mill's grounds, this argument would lead precisely to the inference of a first cause. Mill says that "the cause of every change is a prior change, and such it cannot but be; for if there were no new antecedent, there would not be a new consequent. If the state of facts which brings the phenomenon into existence, had existed always or for an indefinite duration, the effect also would have existed always or been produced an indefinite time ago" ("The," 436).

If, as Mill says, "the state of facts which brings the phenomenon into existence, had existed *always*" (which is what the understanding of God as a first cause means, among other things), "the effect also would have existed *always*" (which is what Mill claims for the so-called primal elements of the world, force and matter). Thus, if one accepts Mill's notion of the eternity of force and matter and his reasoning on the relation of cause to effect, why would one not infer that a first cause or a God exists? An "eternal" matter infers an equally eternal "state of facts which brings the phenomenon into existence"—a first cause or God. This may merely constitute one of Mill's weak inferences or even analogies, but Mill relies on no more substantial evidence in making his inferences concerning a cosmic Designer. Moreover, if the notion of a first cause must be ruled out of bounds because we have no experience of the beginning of the primal elements of force and matter in time, may not the notion of the eternity of force and matter be ruled out on similar grounds? All the energy and matter within our own highly limited experience is fleeting and changeable. No one has actually experienced the "eternity" of force or matter; these are merely hypotheses proffered to account for existing phenomena.

As mentioned, Mill's response to the argument for a first cause—that the fact of universal causation within the world points to a cause of that world beyond the world itself—is to reassert the pagan conception of an uncreated and eternal primal "matter," to which he adds a primal "force."[8] Mill believes he has discovered in experience "permanent element[s] which had no beginning" in time—eternal matter and force—and it is these, or, more precisely, the latter, which should in justice be regarded as the first or universal cause. "[A]s the primaeval and universal element in all causes, the First Cause can be no other than Force." Mill believes his refutation of the argument for a First Cause beyond the world is grounded in the most recent findings of science and especially its "last great generalization . . . the Conservation of Force":

> Whenever a physical phenomenon is traced to its cause, that cause when analysed is found to be a certain quantum of Force, combined with certain collocations [arrangements of matter]. And the last great generalization of science, the Conservation of Force, teaches us that the variety in the effects depends partly upon the *amount* of the force, and partly upon the diversity of the collocations. The force itself is essentially one and the same; and there exists of it in nature a fixed quantity, which (if the theory be true) is never increased or diminished. Here then we find . . . a permanent element; to all appearances the very one of which we were in quest. This it is apparently to which if to anything we must assign the character of First Cause, the cause of the material universe. For all effects may be traced up to it, while it cannot be traced up by our experience, to anything beyond: its transformations alone can be so traced, and of them the cause always includes the force itself: the same quantity of force, in some previous form. It would seem then that in the only sense in which experience supports in any shape the doctrine of a First Cause, viz., as the primaeval and universal element in all causes, the First Cause can be no other than Force.

It is noteworthy that Mill finds it necessary to revise the notion of a first cause to mean one that though "not sufficient of itself to cause anything, . . . enters as a con-cause into all causation" ("The," 436–37). This is not the traditional understanding of a first cause or the understanding of Mill's opponents.

Mill realizes that such considerations do not close the discussion. He recognizes that his account is far from satisfactory or final, that the inevitable response is to press for the origin of this allegedly primal force. More particularly, he must answer those who conceive God or the divine mind and will to be the origin of all that is, or, as Mill puts it, those who contend that "Mind is the only possible cause of Force or . . . that Mind is a Force, and that all other force must be derived from it inasmuch as mind is the only thing which is capable of originating change." The proponents of an originating or divine mind claim their view to be the "lesson of experience." Experience, however, Mill responds, discloses that force within inanimate nature is never an originating but merely a transferred force; "one physical object moves another by giving out to it the force by which it has first been itself moved." The wind communicates to the waves merely part of the motion that has been given to itself by some other agent.

Those who argue for the existence of an originating or divine mind argue that all "commencement" or "origination of motion" in our experience can be traced to "voluntary action. . . . [A]ll other causes appear incapable of this origination experience. . . . [They conclude therefore] that all the motion in existence owed its beginning to this one cause, voluntary agency, if not that of man, then of a more powerful Being" ("The," 437). Mill does not explicitly identify this "powerful Being," who is of course the God of Will and Power of his Christian-voluntarist opponents.

Mill acknowledges that this is not only an old argument, found in fact in Plato's *Laws*, but "is still one of the most telling arguments with the more metaphysical class of defenders of Natural Theology." He contends, however, that if the theory of the conservation of force is true, that is, if there is a constant total amount of force in existence, then "voluntary agency" or will "does not any more than other causes, create Force." The will, like other agencies, has no other means of originating motion than by "converting into that particular manifestation a portion of Force which already existed in other forms."

Mill, moreover, seems to suggest that mind, or at least thought, is itself a by-product of physical processes. The status of will is unclear:

> [I]t is known that the source from which this portion of Force is derived, is chiefly, or entirely, the Force evolved in the processes of chemical composition and decomposition which constitute the body of nutrition: the force so liberated becomes a fund upon which every muscular and even every merely nervous action, as of the brain in thought, is a draft. It is in this sense only that . . . volition is an originating cause. Volition, therefore, does not answer to the idea of a First Cause; since Force must in every instance be assumed as prior to it; and there is not the slightest colour, derived from experience, for supposing Force itself to have been created by a volition. As far as anything can be concluded from human experience Force has all the attributes of a thing eternal and uncreated.

Mill now backtracks somewhat from his implicit physical determinism. Even if it is granted that will does not create force, such determinism would require the demonstration that force originates will. If such cannot be shown, then will "must be held to be an agency, if not prior to Force yet coeternal with it." Moreover, if it is true that will can originate not force itself but the transformation of force from one of its manifestations into that of mechanical motion and that, within human experience, there is no other agency capable of so doing, then, Mill concedes, it may be possible to argue for the notion of will as the originator not of the universe itself but of the cosmos or order of the universe ("The," 437–38). Mill here paves the way for his conception of god as Demiurge, the Limited Maker of the cosmos who imposes order on a preexisting and somewhat recalcitrant primeval matter, a conception that we have encountered in "Utility of Religion" and to which we will return below.

As said, the Mill of "Theism" is still fighting his old battle against the "free-will theologians and philosophers" and in the process revealing the deeply deterministic strand of his outlook. He concedes the possibility of regarding will as the originating cause *of* the cosmos but immediately rejects will as the cause of motion *within* the cosmos. This latter notion contradicts the facts:

> Whatever volition can do in the way of creating motion out of other forms of force, and generally of evolving force from a latent into a visible state, can be done by many other causes, [including, for instance,] chemical action, electricity, heat, and gravitation. . . . [A]ll these are causes of mechanical motion on a far larger scale than any volitions which experience presents to us. . . . [Indeed, such causes do not merely] pass on mechanical motion, but . . . creat[e] it out of a force previously latent or manifesting itself in some other form. Volition, therefore, regarded as an agent in the material universe, has no exclusive privilege of origination; all that it can originate is also originated by other transforming agents.

All these kinds of "transforming agents" or forces, including the force of volition, are not self-originating causes but, on the contrary, "have all had the force they give out put into them from elsewhere." But this "elsewhere" is again reduced by Mill to an intramundane physical entity: "the chemical action of the food and air":

> The force by which the phenomena of the material world are produced, circulates through all physical agencies in a never ending . . . stream. We have nothing to do here with the freedom of the will itself as a mental phenomenon—with the *vexata question* whether volition is self-determining or determined by causes. [Mill believes all volitions are "caused" or determined by prior phenomenal antecedents, and not "spontaneous," "self-originating" or "self-determining."][9] To the question now in hand it is only the effects of volition that are relevant, not its origin. The assertion is that physical nature must have been produced by a Will, because nothing but Will is known to us as having the powers of originating the production of phenomena.

Mill is certain that he has shown, on the contrary, that "all the power that Will possesses over phenomena is shared . . . by other and much more powerful agents, and that in the only sense in which those agents do not originate, neither does Will originate." Remaining within the limits of experience, then, no privileged position can be assigned to volition over other "natural agents" with respect to the production or causation of phenomena. Mill rejects both the notion of first cause as will and the correlative notion of human will as an originating force or cause of experience: "All that can be affirmed by the strongest assertor of the Freedom of the Will, is that volitions are themselves uncaused and are therefore alone fit to be the first or universal Cause. But, even assuming volitions to be uncaused, the properties of matter, so far as experience discloses, are uncaused also, and have the advantage over any particular volition, in being so far as experience can show, eternal."

The master conclusion of Mill's argument, then, is that "[t]heism . . . in so far as it rests on the necessity of a First Cause, has no support from experience" ("The," 438–39).

Before closing his attack on the voluntarist intuitionists, Mill clears up one final and related matter: the question of whether mind can have been produced only by mind, alleged by the intuitionists to be a self-evident proposition. Mill admits that there exist certain "indications" in nature that point to "intelligent contrivance by Mind." For now, he merely wishes to examine whether the "mere existence of Mind . . . require[s], as a necessary antecedent, another Mind greater and more powerful." He reiterates James Mill's view that the question of the origin of human beings is not satisfactorily answered by the mere attribution of that origin to God, because such an attribution immediately raises the unanswerable question "Who created God?" As John Mill puts it: "[T]he difficulty is not removed by going one step back: the creating mind stands as much in need of another mind to be the source of its existence, as the created mind." (This of course is precisely the point at issue—whether there exists a God that can be understood as the first or uncaused cause, the uncreated Source of all that is.) Mill emphasizes, however, that human beings "have no direct knowledge (at least apart from Revelation) of a Mind which is even apparently eternal, as Force and Matter are: an eternal mind is . . . a simple hypothesis to account for the minds which we know to exist." The obvious response is that human beings also "have no direct knowledge" of "eternal . . . Force and Matter," that these are merely hypotheses to account for existing phenomena. An adequate hypothesis must at least "account for the facts" but, says Mill, mind is not accounted for merely by referring its origin to a prior mind. "The problem remains unsolved, the difficulty undiminished, nay, rather increased" ("The," 439–40). (An uncaused cause, a divine creative mind—God—would undoubtedly "account for the facts," but this Mill is unwilling to acknowledge.)

Mill anticipates the intuitionists' response: The causation of every human mind is a matter of fact, since we know each had a beginning in time. We even have grounds for believing that the human species itself had a beginning in time, and thus a cause in Mill's phenomenalist sense of the term. There is a wealth of evidence that animal and human life are relatively late developments in the history of the planet. Nevertheless, although it is clear that there must have been a cause that "called the first human mind, nay the very first germ of organic life, into existence," this, Mill answers, does not necessarily imply the existence of an Eternal Mind. "If we did not know that Mind on our earth began to exist, we might suppose it to be uncaused [eternal]; and we may still suppose this of the mind to which we ascribe its existence" ("The," 440). One might think Mill is conceding the position of his antagonists. He is not.

Mill has shown that in discussing human minds, we are discussing minds known to have come into existence in time. We are thus bound up in the field of human experience and subject to its canons—Mill's canons of induction. Therefore, "we are . . . entitled to ask where is the proof that nothing can have caused a mind except another mind." The only way human beings can discover what is able to produce what—what causes are adequate to what effects—is through experience. Mill is leading up to his view that mind may have been produced as an "unconscious" product of physical forces.

> That nothing can *consciously* produce Mind but Mind, is self-evident, being involved in the meaning of the words; but that there cannot be unconscious production must not be assumed, for it is the very point to be proved. Apart from experience, and arguing on what is called reason, that is on supposed self-evidence, the notion seems to be, that no causes can give rise to products of a more precious or elevated kind than themselves. But this is at variance with the known analogies of Nature. How vastly nobler and more precious, for instance, are the higher vegetables and animals than the soil and manure out of which, and by the properties of which, they are raised up! [One may object, of course, that soil and manure do not "cause" or create vegetables, but are merely the conditions of their growth.] The tendency of all recent speculation is towards the opinion that the development of inferior orders of existence into superior, the substitution of greater elaboration and higher organization for lower, is the general rule of Nature. Whether it is so or not, there are at least in Nature a multitude of facts bearing that character, and this is sufficient for the argument.

Biological evolution, then, may have produced human consciousness.

Mill concludes that the argument for a first cause "is in itself of no value for the establishment of Theism. . . . The world does not, by its mere existence, bear witness to a God" ("The," 440).

The Argument from the General Consent of Mankind

The second argument Mill will refute—the argument for the existence of God based on the general consent of mankind—is a sweeping attack on the intuitionist or innatist position that human beings possess a native, intuitive sense or faculty that points toward the existence of God. Mill will refute the notion of an innate idea of God by offering the naturalistic Comtean explanation for the origin of man's conceptions of God.

Although the general-consent argument carries little scientific weight, Mill says, it has had an altogether unjustified influence over human opinion. He attributes this influence to the fact that the argument is, at bottom, an appeal to authority—the general authority of mankind and some of its "wisest men." He singles out Socrates and Plato, Bacon, Locke, Newton, Descartes, and Leibnitz. Mill is careful to note, however, that such wise men, although influential in promoting a belief in the existence of God, have been in other respects "conspicuous examples of breaking loose from received prejudices" ("The," 441). That said, he restates his long-standing view that "it is by authority that the opinions of the bulk of mankind are principally and not unnaturally governed."

Mill has a difficult time developing his argument because, as discussed, he is generally quite concerned to persuade his readers that the less knowledgeable and cultivated are best served by deferring to authority. In this case, however, he must challenge authority, for the existence of God is supported by the widely received, and thus authoritative, opinion of mankind. He therefore begins by distinguishing between the mass of mankind, which does and should defer to authority, and "thinkers," for whom the argument from other people's opinions has little weight, being, as it is, mere "second-hand evidence." The thinkers' task is not to embrace received opinion uncritically but to discover and weigh "the reasons on which this conviction of mankind or of wise men was founded."

As said, this argument, like the argument against a first cause, is designed to challenge the enemy of intuitionism. Mill is especially disturbed by the fact that the general-consent argument is chiefly used as "evidence that there is in the mind of man an intuitive perception, or an instinctive sense, of Deity." The moral intuitionists infer from the generality of the belief in God that such a belief is inherent to the human constitution and, from this, that such a belief must be true. Such a mode of reasoning, Mill argues, merely begs the question, "since it has . . . nothing to rest upon but the belief that the human mind was made by a God, who would not deceive his creatures." Mill has not Locke's faith.

For Mill, as we have seen, all knowledge, beliefs, and convictions are the acquired result of experience over time. One of his fundamental assumptions is the rejection of innate beliefs or innate knowledge of any kind. Thus the mere existence of a belief or conviction, in a god or anything else, no matter how widespread, does not provide for Mill a sufficient ground for inferring that the belief is innate or valid, independently of evidence. Although Mill rejects the innate idea of God, he does believe there may be evidence to support the belief in a Deity. For now, however, he wishes to make the point that valid belief in God must be based not on intuition but on evidence and, more particularly, on the specific evidence that Mill himself finds most persuasive:

> [I]f there are external evidences of theism, even if not perfectly conclusive, why need we suppose that the belief of its truth was the result of anything else? The superior minds to whom an appeal is made, from Socrates downwards, when they professed to give the grounds of their opinion, did not say that they found the belief in themselves without knowing from whence it came, but ascribed it, if not to revelation, either to some metaphysical argument, or to those very external evidences which are the basis of the argument from Design.[10] ("The," 441–42)

As we shall see, Mill is eager to defend the argument from design as this, he believes, lends support to his own conception of a limited god.

The Origin of Belief in Gods

As we recall, Mill introduced "Theism" with a brief elaboration of Comte's law of the three stages. He again draws upon Comte in refuting the argument from general consent; he explains man's seemingly innate or intuitive knowledge of God by employing Comte's account of the origin of man's changing conceptions of God.

To those who would argue that savages and barbarians, who generally believe in a deity or deities, did not derive such belief from observing the "marvellous adaptations of Nature," Mill answers that all such peoples, as well as "the ignorant" in developed countries, "take their opinions from the educated" who, in turn, tend to base their belief in God on the evidences of design in nature. Furthermore, "savages" do not believe in the "God of Natural Theology," but in a crude anthropomorphism. Mill restates the Comtean interpretation of the development of religious belief from fetishism through polytheism to monotheism, explaining it, as Comte did, by the progressive development of the mind's ability to abstract, generalize, and classify. Note that Mill is propounding the Comtean philosophy of history around 1870, in the evening of his life. As previously remarked, Mill's commentators have often taken his dismissal of Comte's plans for social and religious reconstruction for more than it is worth. Mill did reject Comte's schemes for institutionalizing his new religion and many of his illiberal political prescriptions. But Mill's views were fundamentally shaped by Comte's philosophy of history and especially its law of the three stages of the human mind and society. Mill believed to the end that the final state of human mental development was positivistic in the Comtean sense. Moreover, one reason Mill clung to Comte's view was that it provided him with a convincing naturalistic explanation for the origin of mankind's religious convictions—an explanation, he believed, that was sufficient to cast doubt on the notion that such convictions were innate, that is, implanted by a supernatural Source. As "Theism" makes clear, Mill pursued his positivist, antitheological mission until the end of his days.

But to return to the argument of "Theism": In the primitive "theological" state of the human mind, the conception of a god or gods is nothing more than a crude anthropomorphism, that is, a

> crude generalization which ascribes life, consciousness and will to all natural powers of which [man] cannot perceive the source or control the operation. And the divinities believed in are as numerous as those powers. Each river, fountain or tree has a divinity of its own. To see in this blunder of primitive ignorance the hand of the Supreme Being implanting in his creatures an instinctive knowledge of his existence, is a poor compliment to the Deity. The religion of savages is Fetichism [sic] of the grossest kind, ascribing animation and will to individual objects, and seeking to propitiate them by prayer and sacrifice.

This is not surprising when one considers that for the primitive mind there is no definite boundary that clearly distinguishes the class of conscious human beings from that of inanimate objects and this because the "brute animals" form an intermediate class between the other two. Over time, as the mind and its capacity for generalization develop, primitives begin to advance from their fetishism toward polytheism and eventually monotheism. "As observation advances, it is perceived that the majority of outward objects have all their important qualities in common with entire classes or groups of objects which comport themselves exactly alike in the same circumstances, and in these cases the worship of visible objects is exchanged for that of an invisible Being supposed to preside over the whole class." Thus emerge the various gods of the sky, the ocean, the forest, and so on. The movement from fetishism through polytheism to monotheism is, as stated, a result of man's increasing ability to generalize from experience.

This step, however, is made in hesitation, fear, "and even terror"; primitive men cling to the belief in supernatural powers because they worry over the "terrible resentment of a particular idol." Such terror maintains the religious beliefs of barbarians until the "Theism of cultivated minds" is ready to take their place. And such a theism, Mill says, if we trust the views of its advocates, "is always a conclusion either from arguments called rational, or from the appearances in Nature" ("The," 442–43). Mill is referring to the rational religion of the eighteenth-century deists.[11]

Some of the intuitionists, we recall, claimed that human beings possess an instinctive belief in a deity that results from a universal "natural faculty." Mill finds this contention absurd. He cannot believe that even the "strongest Intuitionist will . . . maintain that a belief should be held for instinctive when evidence (real or apparent), sufficient to engender it, is universally admitted to exist." He points out that, in addition to the evidence that leads men to believe in the existence of a god, there are numerous other causes—emotional and moral—of such a belief, which, moreover, account for it far more plausibly than an innate sense or faculty. Among such causes are the satisfaction a belief in God gives to "obstinate questionings with which men torment themselves respecting the past; the hopes which it opens for the future; the fears also, since fear as well as hope predisposes to belief; . . . [and the] power which belief in the supernatural affords for governing mankind, either for their own good, or for the selfish purposes of the governors." Mill never abandoned the hatred of priestcraft he acquired from his father and Bentham.

Mill concludes with a sweeping dismissal of the intuitionist or innatist point of view: "[T]he general consent of mankind does not . . . afford ground for admitting, even as an hypothesis, the origin in an inherent law of the human mind, of a fact otherwise so more than sufficiently, so amply, accounted for" ("The," 443).

The Argument from Consciousness

The third class of argument for the existence of God was yet another stronghold of intuitionist metaphysics, especially, says Mill, of the variant that derives ultimately from Descartes. The aim of the Cartesian intuitionists is "to prove the existence and attributes of God from what are called truths of reason, supposed to be independent of experience." Their principal argument, the argument from consciousness, derives from Descartes's well-known "assumption that whatever he could very clearly and distinctly apprehend, must be true." The result, according to Mill, is to make the illegitimate leap from a merely "subjective notion of god to its objective reality." Mill summarizes Descartes's view as follows: "The idea of a God, perfect in power, wisdom, and goodness, is a clear and distinct idea, and must therefore, on this principle correspond to a real object. This bold generalization, however, that a conception of the human mind proves its own objective reality, [Descartes qualified by the addition] 'if the idea includes existence.' Now the idea of God implying the union of all perfections, and existence being a perfection, the idea of God proves his existence." Mill rejects such a conception on the ground that it overlooks one of man's most "precious attributes"—the capacity of imaginative idealization. As Mill says, it "denies to man one of his most familiar and most precious attributes, that of idealizing as it is called—of constructing from the materials of experience a conception more perfect than experience itself affords."[12] What Mill suggests is that the widespread embrace of the Romantic outlook means that a view such as Descartes's is no longer convincing to the contemporary mind. As a result, Mill explains, Descartes's successors have tried to ascribe intuitive knowledge of God to an "inward light"—"to make it a truth not dependent on external evidence, a fact of direct perception, or [as they call it] of consciousness." The chief problem with this view, Mill argues, is that it is impossible to convince someone who has not experienced an inner light—and the inner perception it is said to provide—of its reality. As Mill puts it, merely "proclaiming with ever so much confidence that *he* perceives an object, [does not] convince other people that they see it too." The "prophet" of the inner light, Mill says, insists that everyone is capable of seeing and feeling as he does, "nay, that we actually do so, and when the utmost effort of which we are capable fails to make us aware of what we are told we perceive, this supposed universal faculty of intuition is but . . . a lantern . . . which none see by but those who bear it." Try as he might, Mill could find no such inner light within himself. "And the bearers [of such a light] may fairly be asked to consider whether it is not more likely that they are mistaken as to the origin of an impression in their minds, than that others are ignorant of the very existence of an impression in theirs" ("The," 444–45). His argument could of course be turned on its head.

Kant and the Nature of Law

Mill next takes up the philosophy of Kant. Mill understood Kant to have regarded the idea of God as native to the mind, meaning that it is constructed by the laws of the mind and not derived from external sources. Further, says Mill, Kant did not think it possible to show, either logically or through the medium of direct perception, that this "idea of speculative reason" has a corresponding objective reality external to the human mind.[13] In Kant's view, Mill says, God is "neither an object of direct consciousness nor a conclusion of reasoning, but a Necessary Assumption," necessary not logically but practically, imposed by the reality of the "moral law." According to Mill, Kant regarded duty as a "fact of consciousness: 'Thou Shalt' is a command issuing from the recesses of our being, and not to be accounted for by any impressions derived from experience; and this command requires a commander, . . . though it is not clear whether Kant means that conviction of a law includes conviction of a lawgiver, or only that a Being of whose will the law is an expression, is eminently desirable."

Mill's speculation on Kant provides an interesting glimpse into the reasons for his rejection of the conventional God of his English contemporaries—the God of Will and Power we have heard him repeatedly condemn. If Kant's meaning is that the conviction of a law, of a moral command, requires a commander, says Mill, then Kant's argument is based on an ambiguous meaning of the word *law*: "A rule to which we feel it a duty to conform has in common with laws commonly so called, the fact of claiming our obedience; but *it does not follow that the rule must originate, like the laws of the land, in the will of a legislator*" (emphasis added). Mill here reveals the extent to which his understanding of "law" had been shaped by Benthamite and Austinian legal positivism. He also reveals, however implicitly, his intuitive sense of the moral baseness of that positivism. He continues: "We may even say that a feeling of obligation which is merely the result of a command is not what is meant by moral obligation, which, on the contrary, supposes something that the internal conscience bears witness to as binding in its own nature" ("The," 445–46). Mill is suggesting that true law, as opposed to mere command, whether of God or the Legislator, is something that is "binding in its own nature." This of course is one of the traditional meanings of *natural law*, which Mill, with Bentham, never tired of castigating in the most vehement terms. Mill's abhorrence for what he took to be the vulgar God of Will and Power worshipped by the English was unbounded. Mill would obey no law issuing from, let alone worship, any god who claimed to rule by divine fiat. He is here but a short step away from the comprehension of God not as Will and Power but *as* Being, *as* Goodness, *as* Law, *as* Justice. It seems strange that such intimations never led Mill to seek an understanding of either the nature of God or the nature of law that was deeper than the vulgar conceptions he acquired from Bentham and Austin or the popular English mind. His intimations seem to have pointed in the right direction; he recognized that the notion of law as command, as the product of will, was, like the vulgar God of Will and Power, morally suspect. In neither area, however, did Mill pursue such intimations. He instead foreclosed his internal movement with a positivistic search for external "evidences" and the militant assertion of the superiority of his new secular or human ethic. To know the reason for this would be to know the reason for Mill's violent hostility to transcendent religion and all it implies. One suspects that these intimations of truth, while genuine, were ignored or left fallow because, ultimately, Mill's predominant motive was not to apprehend the truth but to build a new world in accord with his vision. As we have said, Mill's predominant impulse, like that of other nineteenth-century titans, was Promethean. He did not seek out a God and a law of Being because such would have required an alignment with *what is* in a way that would have dramatically dampened his reformist aspirations to usher in a new moral world of entirely human construction.

Mill, moreover, immediately turns aside from such intimations and toward his more usual self-assertion. He uses the occasion of his reflection on Kant to claim for the "godless" the capacity to adhere to the very highest moral standards. Contrary to those, like Kant, who think that a highly developed sense of duty necessarily points to God or a given moral law, Mill declares that "as a matter of fact, the obligation of duty is both theoretically acknowledged and practically felt in the fullest manner by many who have no positive belief in God, though seldom, probably, without habituation and familiar reference to him as an ideal conception [one of Mill's own preferred conceptions of God]."

Mill will accept Kant's contention that the intense inner conviction of the reality of the moral law points to a God, but only if it is understood in what Mill identifies as its second possible meaning: that the inner conviction of a moral law means "only that a Being of whose will the law is an expression, is eminently desirable." Mill employs this meaning to explain why "good men and women cling to the belief" in God as well as to support his own argument for the necessity of conceiving god as limited:

> But if the existence of God as a wise and just lawgiver, is not a necessary part of the feelings of morality, it may still be maintained that those feelings make his existence . . . desirable, as Kant thought. No doubt they do, and that is the great reason why we find that good men and women cling to the belief, and are pained by its being questioned. But surely it is not legitimate to assume that in the order of the Universe, whatever is desirable is true. . . . Optimism . . . is a thorny doctrine to maintain and had to be taken by Leibnitz in the limited sense, that the universe being made by a good being, is the best universe possible, not the best absolutely: that the Divine power, in short, was not equal to making it more free from imperfections than it is. [Leibnitz believed what Mill himself believes.] But optimism prior to belief

in a god and as the ground of that belief sees a speculative delusion. Nothing . . . contributes more to keep up the belief in the general mind of humanity than this feeling of its desirableness, which . . . is a *naïf* expression of the tendency of the human mind to believe what is agreeable to it. Positive value the argument of course has none. ("The," 446)

The Argument from Marks of Design in Nature

Mill always regarded the argument from design as by far the most important argument for the existence of God. In "Utility of Religion" he had advanced his view that the "analogies of Nature with the effects of human contrivance" bear enough evidence of the existence of an intelligent designer to allow for hope in a "probable" god (426). Mill's acceptance of the design argument in "Utility" predates by at least ten years his lengthy development of the same theme in "Theism." This is significant because, as said, some of Mill's intimates and disciples felt betrayed by the views expressed in "Theism," which they regarded as a departure from his known views on religion.

The argument from design appeals to him, Mill says in "Theism," because it can claim to be a genuinely scientific argument, one grounded in experience, and thus amenable to judgment by "the established canons of Induction." Mill is now on his own territory, and he discusses the argument with characteristic confidence. He claims that the order of nature does in fact evince purposiveness—a "final cause"—that points to the existence of an intelligent mind conspiring to an end, to a God. As mentioned, Mill's interest in advancing this argument for the existence of God is related to his belief that the kind of god evinced by the marks of design in nature is *exactly* the kind of probable limited god he described in "Nature." In short, Mill was particularly devoted to this "proof" of God's existence because he believed it provided conclusive evidence to support his own hypothesis of a limited or finite god.

Mill first states the argument he will examine: that "the order of Nature, or some considerable parts of it . . . exhibit . . . certain qualities found to be characteristic of such things as are made by an intelligent mind for a purpose." The reason that this hypothesis, if true, would serve as good evidence for the existence of a God is that it accords with one of the established canons of scientific induction: "[W]e are entitled, from . . . great similarity in the effects, to infer similarity in the cause, and to believe that things which it is beyond the power of man to make, but which resemble the works of man in all but power, must also have been made by Intelligence, armed with a power greater than human." Mill cautions, however, that while the argument as just stated has validity, it should not be overrated.[14] The evidence of design in creation satisfies only the weak standard of analogy and not the firmer standard of direct induction. Nevertheless, observation reveals that there are "considerable . . . resemblances between some of the arrangements in nature and some of those made by man . . . [which] afford a certain presumption of similarity of cause; but how great that presumption is, it is hard to say. All that can be said with certainty is that these likenesses make creation by intelligence considerably more probable than if the likenesses had been less, or than if there had been no likenesses at all." Analogy suffices only for probability statements, whereas genuine induction, Mill thinks, ensures certainty.[15]

As usual, however, what Mill takes away with one hand he gives back with the other. There is more evidence of theism than the above arguments would suggest. For the slender analogical evidence afforded by the "resemblances" between intelligent design in nature and human design is considerably strengthened by the special character of those resemblances—their teleological character: "The circumstances in which it is alleged that the world resembles the works of man are not circumstances taken at random, but are particular instances of a circumstance which experience shows to have a real connection with an intelligent origin, the fact of conspiring to an end." Thus the design argument, properly understood, is more than mere analogy; it is a real inductive argument ("The," 446–47). For Mill there is no higher praise.

Mill proceeds to analyze the argument, using as his example of intelligent design in nature the structure of the eye. The parts that compose an eye, and the "collocations" or particular arrangement of those parts, are similar to one another in that all of them serve the same end: to enable sight. Moreover, "the particular combination of organic elements called an eye had, in every instance, a beginning in time and must therefore have been brought together by a cause or causes." We also have innumerable examples of eyes, many more than necessary to eliminate randomness or chance. What all of this points to is the existence of purposive design in nature and thus to a designing "intelligent will":

> We are therefore warranted by the canons of induction in concluding that what brought all these elements together was some cause common to them all; and inasmuch as the elements agree in the single circumstance of conspiring to produce sight, there must be some connection by way of causation between the cause which brought those elements together—the final cause—and the fact of sight. [That is, s]ight, being a fact not precedent but subsequent to the putting together of the organic structure of the eye, can only be connected with the production of that structure in the character of a final, not an efficient cause; that is, it is not Sight itself but an antecedent

Idea of it, that must be the efficient cause. But this at once marks the origin as proceeding from an intelligent will.

This, Mill concludes, is the "sum and substance of what Induction can do for Theism" ("The," 448).

Once again, however, what Mill gives he immediately takes away. For he immediately points out that the evidences of design in nature, while they may point to a God, to an intelligent designing will, may, on the other hand, be the product of naturalistic evolutionary forces: "Creative forethought is not absolutely the only link by which the origin of the wonderful mechanism of the eye may be connected with the fact of sight." If the newly emerging theory of evolution—"the principle of 'the survival of the fittest'"—should prove in time to be valid, Mill says, the above conclusions will have considerably less force. If that theory, though "startling, and *prima facie* improbable," should in fact prove to be correct, it would weaken the evidence for creation while nevertheless remaining consistent with it, a point that seems to have been lost among many of Mill's descendants.

In any event, whatever the progress of science may ultimately reveal about the validity of the theory of evolution, Mill concludes that, "in the present state of our knowledge, the adaptations in Nature afford a large balance of probability in favour of creation by intelligence." He emphasizes, however, that such a conclusion is merely a probability unsupported by the other arguments of natural theology. To concede the validity of these other arguments would be to open the door to his intuitionist opponents and their conventionally Christian God, while the design argument, Mill contends, points directly to his own conception of a limited god. Thus he must emphasize that "[w]hatever ground there is, revelation apart, to believe in an Author of Nature, is derived [solely] from the appearances in the universe" ("The," 449–50). Mill will discuss and dismiss revelation later in the essay.

II: Attributes of God

Having shown to his satisfaction that nature does offer "indications" of the existence of a deity, Mill next turns to explore which, if any, attributes of that deity may also be inferred from the evidence provided by nature. Mill's first concern, as always, is to establish his limited god in opposition to what he conceives to be the God of his Christian-voluntarist contemporaries, a God whose essence is will and power, an omnipotent, omniscient, yet capricious and arbitrary God who governs the universe by divine fiat. He begins the discussion by acknowledging that "the power if not the intelligence" of the God evident in nature is undoubtedly far greater than human power. "But from this to Omnipotence and Omniscience there is a wide interval." Here in a nutshell is the conception of God that Mill propounds throughout his explicit writings on religion and that implicitly informs all his work, including his practical political and social prescriptions. As he was at pains to emphasize, the conception of God he sought to establish "is of *immense practical importance*" (emphasis added).

Mill now indicates the reason for his enthusiastic promotion of the argument from design. As said, he is convinced it provides substantial support for his concept of a limited god, which he seems to have regarded as his most important contribution in the area of religious thought. As James Collins adds, "This recognition of a finite God, on an interim basis, constituted [Mill's] chief amendment of the Comtean religion of humanity."[16] Mill says:

> It is not too much to say that every indication of Design in the Kosmos is so much evidence against the Omnipotence of the Designer. For what is meant by Design? Contrivance: the adaptation of means to an end. But the necessity for contrivance—the need of employing means—is a consequence of the limitation of power. Who would have recourse to means if to attain his end his mere word was sufficient? The very idea of means implies that the means have an efficacy which the direct action of the being who employs them has not. Otherwise they are not means, but an incumbrance. A man does not use machinery to move his arms. . . . But if the employment of contrivance is in itself a sign of limited power, how much more so is the careful and skilful choice of contrivances? Can any wisdom be shown in the selection of means, when the means have no efficacy but what is given them by the will of him who employs them, and when his will could have bestowed the same efficacy on any other means? Wisdom and contrivance are shown in overcoming difficulties, and there is no room for them in a Being for whom no difficulties exist. The evidences, therefore, of Natural Theology distinctly imply that the author of the Kosmos worked under limitations; that he was obliged to adapt himself to conditions independent of his will, and to attain his ends by such arrangements as those conditions admitted of. ("The," 451)

The evidences of design in nature, far from pointing to the Christian God of Will and Power, point to a being of a very different sort. Or, as Mill expressed the same idea in his diary in 1854:

> When the advocates of theism urge the universal belief of mankind as an argument of its own correctness, they should accept the whole of that belief instead of picking and choosing out of it. The appearances in nature forcibly

suggest the idea of a maker (or makers), and therefore all mankind have believed in gods. The same appearances not only do not suggest, but absolutely contradict, the idea of a perfectly good maker; and accordingly
mankind have never made their gods good, though they have always flat-
tered them by calling them so.[17]

The evidence of design, Mill emphasizes, coheres with that yielded by
his analysis of the other traditional arguments for the existence of God,
discussed in the preceding section. All the evidences of natural theology
point precisely to Mill's own conception of a Demiurge limited in power
and perhaps in wisdom.

[W]e found that the appearances in Nature point indeed to an origin of the
Kosmos, or order in Nature, and indicate that origin to be Design but do not
point to any commencement, still less, creation, of the two great elements of
the Universe, the passive element and the active element, Matter and Force.
There is in Nature no reason whatever to suppose that either Matter or
Force, or any of their properties, were made by the Being who was the author of the collocations by which the world is adapted to what we consider
as its purposes; or that he has power to alter any of those properties. It is
only when we consent to entertain this negative supposition that there aris-
es a need for wisdom and contrivance in the order of the universe. The Deity had on this hypothesis to work out his ends by combining materials of
a given nature and properties. Out of these materials he had to construct a
world in which his designs should be carried into effect through given
properties of Matter and Force. . . . This did require skill and contrivance,
and the means by which it is effected are often such as justly excite our wonder and admiration:[18] but exactly because it requires wisdom, it implies limitation of power, or rather the two phrases express different sides of the
same fact.

In short, the type of god evinced by an "impartial" and "scientific" examination of the order of nature is not the Christian God who created the
world, but Mill's own god, one that resembles the Platonic Demiurge.

Mill anticipates and responds to various possible objections to his conception of God. For instance, it might be thought that the evidences of
God's existence in nature, meager as they are, are purposive. This may
suggest that the Creator, though under no obligation or necessity to do so,
desired to leave "traces by which man might recognise his creative hand."
Mill's answer is that this too implies "a limit to his omnipotence. For if it
was his will that men should know that they themselves and the world
are his work, he, being omnipotent, had only to will that they should be
aware of it." Mill rejects in advance the possibility that there may be an
explanation, unknown to man, for God's mysterious ways. He is aware
that "ingenious men" have invented various reasons to explain why God

did not make the knowledge of his existence a matter of "absolute necessity," but these he dismisses as "unfortunate specimens of casuistry . . . [which] are of no avail on the supposition of omnipotence." For Mill, omnipotence *means* perfection as he himself conceives perfection. He also knows that believers will dismiss his arguments with the "easy answer" that man does not have full knowledge of God's ways or, as he says,

> that we do not know what wise reasons the Omniscient may have had for leaving undone things which he had the power to do. [But] it is not perceived that this plea itself implies a limit to Omnipotence. When a thing is obviously good [that is, good as Mill conceives it] and obviously in accordance with what all the evidences of creation imply to have been the Creator's design, and we say we do not know what good reason he may have had for not doing it, we mean that we do not know to what other, still better object—to what object still more completely in the line of his purposes, he may have seen fit to postpone it. But the necessity of postponing one thing to another belongs only to limited power. Omnipotence could have made the objects compatible.

Mill is deeply impressed by the notion of omnipotence, which, to his mind, seems to necessitate the creation of a visible and rationally transparent perfection, modeled on his own personal standard. As with his insistence that true justice must entail the distribution of temporal pleasures and pains in exact correspondence to transparent moral goodness or obliquity, Mill simply cannot reconcile the halting imperfection of actual human existence with the notion of omnipotent goodness. He refuses to entertain the possibility that there may be a reason why the world falls so far short of his own static and narrow conception of perfection.

Mill's insistence on a limited god, as well as his conception of god as Demiurge, does have a saving grace: As earlier discussed, both are meant to save God's goodness at the expense of his power:

> If the Creator, like a human ruler, had to adapt himself to a set of conditions which he did not make, it is as unphilosophical as presumptuous in us to call him to account for any imperfections in his work; to complain that he left anything in it contrary to what, if the indications of design prove anything, he must have intended. . . . [I admit that the Creator] must at least know more than we know, and we cannot judge what greater good would have had to be sacrificed, or what greater evil incurred, if he had decided to remove this particular blot. Not so if he be omnipotent. If he be that, he must himself have willed that the two desirable objects should be incompatible; he must himself have willed that the obstacle to his supposed design should be insuperable. It cannot therefore *be* his design. It will not do to say that it was, but that he had other designs which interfered with it; for no one purpose imposes necessary limitations on another in the case of a Being not restricted by conditions of possibility.[19] ("The," 452–53)

Mill thinks that his notion of a limited god can save a kind of Christianity as well as God's goodness. As he says,

> what is morally objectionable in the Christian theory of the world, is objectionable only when taken in conjunction with the doctrine of an omnipotent God, and . . . by no means imports any moral obliquity in a Being whose power is supposed to be restricted by real, though unknown obstacles, which prevented him from fully carrying out his design. . . . The belief of Christians is neither more absurd nor more immoral than the belief of Deists who acknowledge an Omnipotent Creator. . . . [L]et us cut down our belief of either to what does not involve absurdity or immorality; to what is neither intellectually self-contradictory nor morally perverted. ("The," 469)

Mill will purify Christianity of its immoral accretions, including, as he said in "Utility of Religion," the notion that salvation requires a belief in Christ as God.

Mill now makes his final pronouncement: "Omnipotence, therefore, cannot be predicated of the Creator on grounds of natural theology. The fundamental principles of natural religion as deduced from the facts of the universe, negative his omnipotence." But what has he to say of God's alleged omniscience? For Mill, the notion of limited power may save this attribute of God as well as his goodness: If and only if "we suppose limitation of power, there is nothing to contradict the supposition of perfect knowledge and absolute wisdom." Having made this concession, however, Mill quickly adds, "neither is there anything to prove it." He himself is not inclined to regard God's knowledge or skill as infinite, for his workmanship exhibits far too many "defects." The knowledge required by a Demiurge "to plan and execute the arrangements of the Kosmos" as well as the skill and ingenuity evinced thereby are of course far greater than their human equivalents, as the power evinced in design is far greater than human power. This does not mean, however, that we are required to believe that either the Deity's knowledge or skill is infinite or "even the best possible. [Indeed,] if we venture to judge them as we judge the works of human artificers, we find abundant defects."

Mill here returns to one of the main themes of "Nature": the all-too-abundant disorder or defects of this world. He catalogs the defects of the Demiurge's workmanship. First is the human body. Although it is an "artful and ingenious contrivance," one would expect "so complicated a machine" to last longer and not break down as often as it does. Moreover, recapitulating his remarks about the Patagonians and Eskimos in "Nature," Mill wonders why God was unable to create a better race than one "so constituted as to grovel in wretchedness and degradation for countless ages before a small portion of it was enabled to lift itself into the very imperfect state of intelligence, goodness and happiness which we enjoy." It may be that "the divine power [was] not equal to doing more; the obstacles to a better arrangement of things may have been insuperable. But it is also possible that they were not." It may be that the Deity did not care or it may be that he is merely a blunderer. We do not know whether the skill of the "Demiourgos reached the extreme limit of perfection compatible with the material it employed and the forces it had to work with." Mill is not even sure how, on grounds of natural theology, we can assure ourselves of the Creator's foresight; he may not in fact "foreknow . . . all the effects that will issue from his own contrivances."

Indeed, what this suggests to Mill is that the skill and power of man may one day equal that of the Demiurge, that is, man himself may eventually be able to create a human being, to make a man. Mill perceives an analogy between the workmanship of the Demiurge and that of human beings. For both, their knowledge of the properties of things enables them to make things fitted to produce a given result. Neither man nor the Demiurge, however, has the power to foresee what other agencies may counteract the operation of the "machinery" they have made. This leads Mill to speculate on the possibility that human beings may one day succeed in creating life: "Perhaps a knowledge of the laws of nature upon which organic life depends, not much more perfect than the knowledge which man even now possesses of some other natural laws, would enable man, if he had the same power over the materials and the forces concerned which he has over some of those of inanimate nature, to create organized beings [that is, human beings] not less wonderful nor less adapted to their conditions of existence than those in Nature"[20] ("The," 453–54).

Mill will next examine more closely the nature of the limits to the Creator's power, as indicated by the evidences of natural religion. There are three possibilities: another "Intelligent Being"; the "insufficiency and refractoriness of the material"; or simple incompetence. If the first two possible obstacles are rejected, then we may have to admit "that the author of the Kosmos, though wise and knowing, was not all-wise and all-knowing, and may not always have done the best that was possible under the conditions of the problem."

The first of these hypotheses—another intelligent being—was for a long time and is still in certain places

the prevalent theory even of Christianity. Though attributing, and in a certain sense sincerely, omnipotence to the Creator, the received religion represents him as for some inscrutable reason tolerating the perpetual coun-teraction of his purposes by the will of another Being of opposite character and of great though inferior power, the Devil. The only difference on this matter between popular Christianity and the religion of Ormuzd and Ahri-man, is that the former pays its good Creator the bad compliment of having been the maker of the Devil and of being at all times able to crush and an-nihilate him and his evil deeds and counsels, which nevertheless he does not do.

Mill now observes, however, that the hypothesis of two contending pow-ers contradicts the evidence of natural theology, and especially its dis-covery of the law-governed character of existence. For "all forms of poly-theism, and this among the rest, are with difficulty reconcilable with a universe governed by general laws. Obedience to law is the note of a set-tled government, and not of a conflict always going on." As we know, for Mill, as for many of his contemporaries, nothing had been more firmly es-tablished by science than the universal government of law. Mill explains more fully why the hypothesis of dual powers must be ruled out under the fact of the universal reign of law:[21]

> When powers are at war with one another for the rule of the world, the boundary between them is not fixed but constantly fluctuating. This may seem to be the case on our planet as between the powers of good and evil when we look only at the results; but when we consider the inner springs, we find that both the good and the evil take place in the common course of nature, by virtue of the same general laws originally impressed—the same machinery turning out now good, now evil things, and oftener still, the two combined. The division of power is only apparently variable, but really so regular that, were we speaking of human potentates, we should declare without hesitation that the share of each must have been fixed by previous consent. Upon that supposition indeed, the result of the combination of an-tagonist forces might be much the same as on that of a single creator with divided purposes.[22] ("The," 454)

What the evidences of natural religion point to, however, is something quite different from the picture of antagonistic powers fighting for rule of the world. Mill for the first time identifies the end or intention of the Demi-urge's bungling attempt at cosmic design: "The indications of design point strongly in one direction, the preservation of the creatures in whose structure the indications are found." Mill now recognizes, as he did not in "Nature," that "the destructive elements of nature, . . . have a generally beneficent purpose, that is, they are the means of preserving life. . . . [T]he destroying agencies are a necessary part of the preserving agencies." Thus it makes no sense to assume that "the preserving agencies are wielded by one Being, the destroying agencies by another," for the maintenance of life in our world is dependent upon both kinds of processes. As noted, this is a very different attitude than Mill assumed in "Nature," where nature is portrayed as a purposefully malevolent force, akin to the "evil principle" of the Manichaeans, bent on destruction and injustice. Now, however, perhaps having further developed the implications of his idea of God, Mill thinks he can explain the destructive forces of nature in another way: the ineptness of his limited, bungling god.

> [T]he imperfections in the attainment of the purposes which the appearances indicate [that is, preservation of life] . . . have not the air of having been designed. They are like the unintended results of accidents insufficiently guarded against . . . or else they are the consequences of the wearing out of a machinery not made to last for ever: they point either to shortcomings in the workmanship as regards its intended purpose, or to external forces not under the control of the workman, but which forces bear no mark of being wielded and aimed by any other and rival Intelligence.

Mill's speculations on the implications of a limited, and possibly inept, god thus seem to have ultimately led him to reject the Manichaeism of his father that sometimes informed his own earlier speculations (although, curiously, at the end of "Theism," he reverts to the Manichaean view he rejects in this passage; see page 231). His "final" conclusion is that "there is no ground in Natural Theology for attributing intelligence or personality to the obstacles which partially thwart what seem the purposes of the Creator. The limitation of his power more probably results either from the qualities of the material—the substances and forces of which the universe is composed not admitting of any arrangements by which his purposes could be more completely fulfilled; or else, the purposes might have been more fully attained, but the Creator did not know how to do it" ("The," 455). A god limited in knowledge or by conditions outside his control may be exempted from the moral condemnation his defective design would otherwise deserve. And, perhaps more important, such a god, shorn of omnipotence, provides the most extensive canvas for the far-flung exercise of human agency. Having defeated omnipotence, Mill rises to meet the challenge. What goodness and justice this poorly constructed world are to achieve must be achieved through the efforts of wise and good human beings. He himself has a plan.

III: Moral Attributes of the Deity

The next topic to be examined concerns the moral attributes and moral purposes of the Deity, as disclosed by the evidence found in nature. Mill feels free to examine such evidence impartially, as he, unlike the natural theologians, is not burdened with the necessity of conceiving the Creator as omnipotent. As he puts it, he does "not have to attempt the impossible problem of reconciling infinite benevolence and justice with infinite power in the Creator of such a world as this. The attempt to do so not only involves absolute contradiction in an intellectual point of view but exhibits to excess the revolting spectacle of a jesuitical defence of moral enormities." One is struck by the palpable contempt for this world and the tone of moral superiority conveyed by such remarks.

At this point Mill refers the reader to his essay on "Nature," thus indicating, as Helen Taylor said, that he did not regard the views expressed in "Theism" as inconsistent with those expressed in the former essay. The reason may be that, having managed to his satisfaction to eliminate the omnipotence of God, he could similarly eliminate the "moral perplexity," not to say moral outrage, so dramatically expressed in "Nature." Mill's tone in "Theism" is far more conciliatory. "Grant that creative power was limited by conditions the nature and extent of which are wholly unknown to us, and the goodness and justice of the creator may be all that the most pious believe; and all in the work that conflicts with those moral attributes may be the fault of the conditions which left to the Creator only a choice of evils" ("The," 456). In other words, Christians may continue to believe in their God so long as they are willing to accept Mill's qualifications.

Mill will now attempt to infer from the evidences of design in nature "what that design was," that is, what were the Deity's probable purposes. The best way to do this, he explains, is to examine those aspects of nature that display the most "conspicuous traces" of purposeful design, such as the "construction of animals and vegetables," and to ask their purpose. As in "Nature," Mill can find no evidence of moral purpose in the order of nature. "There is no blinking the fact that [the traces of design] tend principally to no more exalted object than to make the structure remain in life and in working order for a certain time, the individual for a few years, the species or race for a longer but still a limited time." The same holds for the "less conspicuous marks of creation" in inorganic nature, such as the solar system. This too seems to have been designed for no other purpose than the maintenance and stability of the system itself, that is, "to keep the machine going," and that only for a limited time.

> The greater part, therefore, of the design of which there is indication in Nature . . . is no evidence of any moral attributes, because the end to which it is directed, and its adaptation to which end is the evidence of its being directed to an end at all, is not a moral end: it is not the good of any sentient creature, it is but the qualified permanence, for a limited period of the work

itself, whether animate or inanimate. The only inference that can be drawn from most of it, respecting the character of the Creator, is that he does not wish his works to perish as soon as created; he wills them to have a certain duration. From this alone nothing can be justly inferred as to the manner in which he is affected towards his animate or rational creatures. ("The," 456–57)

Not only is there no evidence of any "moral attributes" or "moral end" in nature, but the Designer appears not even to have aimed, or at least not exclusively, for the "good of any sentient creature." As said, the absence of any moral order in nature means, for Mill, that what moral order is to be achieved in human existence must be achieved by human agency, especially that of the best and wisest among men—the men he once hoped would constitute the modern "spiritual power."

Having denied that the design of nature evinces a moral end, Mill concedes that the Designer seems to have had certain moral—that is, utilitarian—leanings. The Demiurge seems to have inserted various "provisions" within his design for human pleasure (and pain). These, however, seem to have a merely preservative function; pleasure is related to that which helps the individual and the species survive and pain to that which inhibits survival. While it is difficult to find evidence of unadulterated "benevolent purpose" in the order of nature, Mill concedes that, in the end, God appears to be something like a benevolent utilitarian:

> [I]t does appear that granting the existence of design, there is a preponderance of evidence that the Creator desired the pleasure of his creatures. This is indicated by the fact that pleasure of one description or another is afforded by almost everything, the mere play of the faculties, physical and mental, being a never-ending source of pleasure, and even painful things giving pleasure by the satisfaction of curiosity and the agreeable sense of acquiring knowledge; and also that pleasure, when experienced, seems to result from the normal working of the machinery, while pain usually arises from some external interference with it, and resembles in each particular case the result of an accident.[23]

Mill's notion of a limited god also enables him to justify the presence of pain in the world, insupportable under the Christian conception of God. Pain, he thinks, unlike pleasure, does not seem to have been purposefully contrived, but seems rather a "clumsiness in the contrivance employed for some other purpose." The "author of the machinery" did no doubt devise the painful aspects of existence, but various insuperable limitations, and not any malevolence on his part, may have made these necessary, that is, "they may have been a necessary condition of [the] susceptibility to pleasure." Such a supposition is inconsistent with the traditional notion of an omnipotent Creator, but perfectly consistent with a God understood to be limited in the sense for which Mill contends—"a contriver working under the limitation of inexorable laws and indestructible properties of matter." Pain, in short, is probably not part of God's intention. It "usually seems like a thing undesigned; a casual result of the collision of the organism with some outward force to which it was not intended to be exposed." The evidence, Mill concludes, suggests that God, like the utilitarians, finds pleasure, but not pain, agreeable: "[T]here is a certain amount of justification for inferring, on grounds of Natural Theology alone, that benevolence is one of the attributes of the Creator" ("The," 458).

Mill's God may express certain utilitarian leanings but he does not quite measure up to the standards of the best human morality—nontheological utilitarianism. This, as we know, is *exclusively* concerned with realizing the greatest possible happiness for the greatest number of human beings. The God evinced by nature, however, does not appear to have been devoted exclusively to ensuring the happiness of his creatures. As Mill says, "it is not credible" that their happiness was God's sole motive in their creation.

> But to jump from this [God's limited benevolence] to the inference that his sole or chief purposes are those of benevolence, and that the single end and aim of Creation was the happiness of his creatures, is not only not justified by any evidence but is a conclusion in opposition to such evidence as we have. . . . Certainly if the Deity's motive in creating sentient beings was their happiness, his purposes, in our corner of the universe at least, must be pronounced . . . to have been thus far an ignominious failure; and if God had no purpose but our happiness and that of other living creatures it is not credible that he would have called them into existence with the prospect of being so completely baffled.

It goes without saying that Mill offers his nontheological utilitarianism as a decided advance in this regard. The utilitarians, as well as the future ministers and acolytes of the Religion of Humanity, unlike the bungling Demiurge, not only care for the good of sentient creatures but have as their "single end and aim" the greatest happiness for the greatest number of them. Mill and his disciples will rectify the Deity's "ignominious failure," at least "in our corner of the universe." Mill's reflections on the enormity of the Deity's failure seem to have roused him to the depths of his being:

> If man had not the power by the exercise of his own energies for the improvement both of himself and of his outward circumstances, to do for himself and other creatures vastly more than God had in the first instance done, the Being who called him into existence would deserve something very different from thanks at his hands. Of course it may be said that this very capacity of improving himself and the world was given to him by God, and

that the change which he will be thereby enabled ultimately to effect in human existence will be worth purchasing by the sufferings and wasted lives of entire geological periods. This may be so; but to suppose that God could not have given him these blessings at a less frightful cost, is to make a very strange supposition concerning the Deity. It is to suppose God could not, in the first instance, create anything better than a Bosjesman or an Andaman islander, or something still lower; and yet was able to endow the Bosjesman . . . with the power of raising himself into a Newton or a Fenelon. We certainly do not know the nature of the barriers which limited the divine omnipotence; but it is a very odd notion of them that they enable the Deity to confer on an almost bestial creature the power of producing by a succession of efforts what God himself had no other means of creating. ("The," 458–59)

Thank goodness man has the power generated by "his own energies . . . to do for himself and other creatures vastly more than God had in the first instance done." Thank goodness man can make himself. And thank goodness he has the power and ability to insert some morality and justice into "such a world as this."

For, according to Mill, the *only* morality on the part of the Creator evinced by the order of nature is the limited benevolence described above.

> [I]f we look for any other of the moral attributes . . . as, for example Justice, we find a *total blank*. There is no evidence whatever in Nature for divine justice, whatever standard of justice our ethical opinions may lead us to recognise. *There is no shadow of justice in the general arrangements of Nature; and what imperfect realisation it obtains in any human society (a most imperfect realisation as yet) is the work of man himself,* struggling upwards against immense natural difficulties, into civilisation, and making to himself a second nature, far better and more unselfish than he was created with. But on this point enough has been said in another Essay, already referred to, on Nature. (emphases added)

Justice, for Mill, is a wholly human construction and achievement. The order of nature is devoid of justice. We have discussed at length how Mill, with Bentham, was concerned to defeat the notion of ultimate divine justice—the selfish notion of the posthumous religious sanction. Mill also followed Bentham in attacking the "metaphysical" fictions of natural law and natural rights and in embracing the positivistic view of law as a product of the human will or Legislator. And, with Comte, he was concerned to eradicate once and for all any notion of justice related to traditional theological conceptions. There is no higher law and no higher justice, he believed. Human beings must create whatever justice is to be achieved, and it must be achieved in present existence.

To sum up the results of Mill's "scientific" investigation into the nature of the divine attributes: What he finds is a Being of great power, but one limited by obstacles beyond the possibility of human knowledge, and limited possibly in intelligence as well. This Being appears to be concerned with the happiness of his creatures, at least to some extent, but there seem to be other things for which he cares even more. Thus he certainly cannot be thought to have created the universe for the sole purpose of the happiness of his creatures, as the utilitarian Mill would have done. This is all we can know of the Deity on the basis of natural religion. "Any idea of God more captivating than this comes only from human wishes, or from the teaching of either real or imaginary Revelation" ("The," 459). Mill leaves the reader to decide for himself whether or not this limited, partially benevolent God is preferable to the nontheological utilitarian dispensation, which is *exclusively* concerned with the happiness of its creatures.

IV: Immortality

Mill next explores whether the signs of nature throw any light on the question of the immortality of the soul and a future life. The "indications" of immortality fall into two classes: those dependent upon and those independent of some particular "theory respecting the Creator and his intentions." The arguments set forth in Plato's *Phaedon* are representative of the latter type. Like such arguments in general, Mill says, it depends not upon a theory of God but upon "preconceived theories respecting death and . . . the nature of the thinking principle in man, considered as distinct and separable from the body." Mill also notes that the modern objection to such a view of the "thinking principle" is anticipated in that dialogue, namely, "that thought and consciousness, though mentally distinguishable from the body, may not be a substance separable from it, but a result of it." Mill once again toys with the idea that human consciousness or the "soul" is a by-product of physical forces. He first clarifies the modern conception of the soul. Those moderns who deny its immortality generally do not regard the soul as a substance per se, but as "the name of a bundle of attributes . . . (of feeling, thinking, reasoning, believing, willing, etc.)" which they believe to be a product of the "bodily organization" and dependent upon it.[24] When that organization is dispersed, the attributes cease to exist as well. This new conception of the soul means that "those . . . who would deduce the immortality of the soul from its own nature have first to prove that the attributes in question are not attributes of the body but of a separate substance."[25] Mill himself takes no firm position on this matter. The "verdict of science" on this point, he says, is not yet conclusive; it has not yet proved experimentally that the bodily organization is capable of producing thought or feeling. Nor can science produce an organism of any kind; these "can only be developed out of a previous organism." On the other hand, "the evidence is well nigh complete" that thought and feeling are always preceded or accompanied by some bodily state or action, and we know that brain disease can affect mental functions. In short, "we have . . . sufficient evidence that cerebral action is, if not the cause, at least, in our present state of existence, a condition *sine qua non* of mental operations." Experience has given us no reason to believe that the mind survives death. Nevertheless, Mill points out, such considerations only amount to a lack of evidence *for* immortality but provide no "positive arguments" against it ("The," 460–61).

Mill's discussion of the "proofs" of immortality in "Theism" may be compared with remarks that he inscribed in his diary in 1854: "A person longing to be convinced of a future state, if at all particular about evidence, would turn with bitter disappointment from all the so-called proof of it. On such evidence no one would believe the most commonplace matters of fact. The pretended philosophical proofs all rest on the assumption that the facts of the universe bear some necessary relation to the fancies of our own minds."[26]

At this later stage of his life, however, Mill *wants* to believe in immortality and is critical of those who would reject its possibility a priori. He thus insists that, although we always associate "the phenomena of life and consciousness" with the action of a physical organism, this does not mean it is absurd per se to think these phenomena can exist under other conditions.

> [T]he uniform coexistence of one fact with another does not make the one fact a part of the other, or the same with it. The relation of thought to a material brain is no metaphysical necessity; but simply a constant coexistence within the limits of observation. . . . [T]he brain, . . . on the principles of the Associative Psychology, . . . is, like matter itself, merely a set of human sensations either actual or inferred as possible, namely, those which the anatomist has when he opens the skull, and the impressions which we suppose we should receive of molecular or some other movements when the cerebral action was going on, if there were no bony envelope and our senses or our instruments were sufficiently delicate. Experience furnishes us with no example of any series of states of consciousness, without this group of contingent sensations attached to it; but it is as easy to imagine such a series of states without, as with, this accompaniment, and we know of no reason in the nature of things against the possibility of its being thus disjoined. We may suppose that the same thoughts, emotions, volitions, and even sensations which we have here, may persist or recommence somewhere else

under other conditions, just as we may suppose that other thoughts and sensations may exist under other conditions in other parts of the universe.

Mill suggests, then, that we are entitled to believe in the reality of immortality because we have no evidence to the contrary. In short, "[t]here is . . . in science, no evidence against the immortality of the soul but that negative evidence, which consists in the absence of evidence in its favour." And even this "negative evidence" is of a relatively weak kind. We know of course that the soul does not remain on earth and visibly interfere in the events of life, for if it did we would have positive evidence for this. But "there is absolutely no proof . . . that [the soul] does not exist elsewhere. . . . A very faint, if any, presumption, is all that is afforded by its disappearance from the surface of this planet" ("The," 462).

Mill realizes, however, that one of the most striking evidences of nature may provide a "very strong presumption against the immortality of the thinking and conscious principle." This is the universal fact that all things perish, the most beautiful and precious along with the ugly and the cheap. One would think the universality of this experience would lead Mill to exclude the hypothesis of immortality on the same grounds by which he excluded the necessity of a first cause. (That is, the universality of the experience that every existent in our world is preceded by a phenomenal antecedent or cause. In the same manner, our universal experience is that every existent in our world perishes.)[27] Mill, however, approaching the end of his worldly existence and longing for the possibility of reunion with his beloved Harriet, seems eager to prove the possibility of immortality. He will thus find a way around the universal fact of experience that all things perish. Indeed, he is suddenly willing to treat human consciousness as somehow qualitatively different from inanimate nature, contrary to his usual insistence that the canons of induction apply alike to all phenomenal experience, within which he includes even the existence of God. Mill now reveals that, far from being a sensationalist or materialist, as one would think from his earlier discussion of the primacy of matter and force and his lifelong insistence that all knowledge must be based on sensory experience, he is in fact a Berkeleian idealist.

Mill recognizes that the universal experience that all things perish may lead some persons to wonder why this should not apply to man as well.

Why indeed. But why, also, should it *not* be otherwise? Feeling and thought are not merely different from what we call inanimate matter, but are at the opposite pole of existence, and analogical inference has little or no validity from the one to the other. *Feeling and thought are much more real than anything else; they are the only things which we directly know to be real,* all things else being merely the unknown conditions on which these, in our present state of existence or in some other, depend. *All matter apart from the feelings of sentient being has but an hypothetical and unsubstantial existence: it is a mere assumption to account for our sensations;* itself we do not perceive, we are not conscious of it, but only of the sensations which we are said to receive from it: *in reality it is a mere name for our expectation of sensations, or for our belief that we can have certain sensations* when certain other sensations give indication of them. ("The," 462–63, emphases added)

Mill here espouses a full-fledged idealist position. Only mind is known to be real: "Mind . . . is in a philosophical point of view the only reality of which we have any evidence." Matter has only a "hypothetical and unsubstantial existence." Matter is a "mere assumption," a "mere name for our . . . belief" in the possibility of sensation or, as Mill elsewhere defined it, only a "permanent possibility of sensation" (*Ham*, 184). Mill's views on mind and matter and their relationship are difficult to disentangle. It is unclear how a "permanent possibility" with a merely "hypothetical and unsubstantial existence" can not only constitute one of the primordial elements of existence but do so in such a manner as to create an intractable problem for the Demiurge, as Mill insists. Moreover, if Mind is the ultimate reality, is not a mind necessary to call those "contingent possibilities of sensation" into actuality? Mill sometimes seems to regard matter as something like an electromagnetic energy field that becomes substantial only when called into actuality by a perceiving mind. He seems to acknowledge that only the presence of minds permits the perception of matter, which, as he says, cannot be perceived directly. One would thus think he would have conceived Mind, which he calls "the only substantive reality," as the primordial substance and not the "mere assumption" of matter, "something," he says, "which has no reality except in reference to something else." How something with only a "hypothetical and unsubstantial existence," something that "has no reality except in reference to something else," can prohibit God from realizing his plans is a mystery.

But to return to Mill's argument for immortality:

Because these contingent possibilities of sensation [matter] sooner or later come to an end and give place to others, is it implied in this, that the series of our feelings must itself be broken off? This would not be to reason from one kind of substantive reality to another, but to draw from something which has no reality except in reference to something else, conclusions applicable to that which is the only substantive reality. Mind, (or whatever name we give to what is implied in consciousness of a continued series of feelings) is in a philosophical point of view the only reality of which we have any evidence; and no analogy can be recognised or comparison made between it and other realities because there are no other known realities to compare it with. That is quite consistent with its being perishable; but the question whether it is so or not is *res integra*, untouched by any of the results of human knowledge and experience. The case is one of those very rare cases in which there is really a total absence of evidence on either side, and in which the absence of evidence for the affirmative does not . . . create a strong presumption in favour of the negative. ("The," 462–63)

Having established that the belief in immortality is not to be ruled out of court, Mill admits that most human beings do not ground their belief in it on scientific arguments (as he thinks he does) but on the unpleasantness of the thought of ceasing to exist and on the "general traditions of mankind." This "natural tendency" of men's belief to follow their "wishes" and the general opinion is, moreover, reinforced by "rulers and instructors" who seek to manipulate men's beliefs for their own sinister purposes of control and manipulation. As Mill puts it, man's tendency toward wishful thinking is

reinforced by the utmost exertion of the power of public and private teaching; rulers and instructors having at all times, with the view of giving greater effect to their mandates whether from selfish or from public motives, encouraged to the utmost of their power the belief that there is a life after death, in which pleasures and sufferings far greater than on earth, depend on our doing or leaving undone while alive, what we are commanded to do in the name of the unseen powers.

Mill remained a Benthamite to the end. The above "circumstances," he says, may be "powerful . . . causes of belief. As rational grounds of it they carry no weight at all" ("The," 463).

As may be expected, Mill rejects the argument from tradition or the general belief of mankind in personal immortality. If one accepts traditional or general opinion as a guide, he says, one has no choice but to accept it in its entirety. With respect to the issue of immortality, this means that one must accept not only the belief in the soul's existence after death but also in ghosts—dead souls who show themselves to the living—inasmuch as these two beliefs have always coexisted traditionally. In fact, Mill thinks, the belief in the afterlife was predicated upon the belief in ghosts. "Primitive men would never have supposed that the soul did not die with the body if they had not fancied that it visited them after death." Men such as those in the age of Homer believed their dreams were "real apparitions." "Waking hallucinations [and] delusions . . . of sight and hearing" were also common, supplying material for the play of imagination and for the investment of such delusions with reality. Mill is forgiving of such delusions, for early men did not have the benefit of scientific knowledge. They

are "not to be judged of by a modern standard: in early times the line between imagination and perception was by no means clearly definite; there
was little or none of the knowledge we now possess of the actual course
of nature, which makes us distrust or disbelieve any appearance which is
at variance with known laws." Nevertheless, rejecting the legends and
stories of the phenomenal appearance of disembodied spirits, Mill thinks,
is equivalent to removing the principal ground of the general belief in life
after death. Moreover, what really requires an explanation is why people
still accept these traditional beliefs, even in the modern civilized age
which has rejected "superstitions." Mill's explanation for the prevalence
of these beliefs is the dominance of the socialization process, that is, of the
fact that the "reigning opinion, whatever it may be, is the most sedulously inculcated upon all who are born into the world." On the other hand,
progress has been made; the related beliefs in ghosts and the afterlife are
increasingly being challenged, "especially among cultivated minds." Finally, those cultivated minds who continue to adhere to the belief in immortality ground their belief not on the opinion of others but, like Mill, on
"arguments and evidences." And it is these which it is Mill's concern to
"estimate and judge" ("The," 464–65). Mill cannot concede any validity
to the received opinion of mankind, to traditional belief and custom,
bound up as it is with theological conceptions, and this even when it supports the conclusions he wishes to establish.

Finally, Mill will examine arguments for a future life based upon the evidences of the existence and attributes of the Deity that he has established
earlier in the essay. He recapitulates his findings: a "preponderance of
probability" of the existence of a Deity and a "considerably less prepon-
deran[t] probability" of his benevolence. The God that Mill thinks is
evinced by nature is one whose intelligence is high and of course greater
than that of human beings; one, that is, "adequate to the contrivances apparent in the universe," but not necessarily more than this. And of course
the power of this God has been "not only not proved to be infinite" but
shown to be limited, "contrivance being a mode of overcoming difficulties, and always supposing difficulties to be overcome."

Mill does not think the evidences of natural theology, "apart from express revelation," support the belief in immortality and a future life. The
chief reason is one we have met with before: The limited god of Mill's conception cannot ensure that all the good he may intend will actually be realized. Mill points out that the most common argument for personal immortality is based on the conviction of God's absolute goodness. Such a
view makes it extremely improbable that "he would ordain the annihila-

tion of his noblest and richest work, after the greater part of its few years of life had been spent in the acquisition of faculties which time is not allowed him to turn to fruit; and the special improbability that he would have implanted in us an instinctive desire of eternal life, and doomed the desire to complete disappointment" ("The," 465). For Mill, as we know, there is no reason why our desires, however natural or universal, must be realized, for the limitations imposed on absolute goodness may pose insurmountable obstacles to their fulfillment.

In short, the argument from God's absolute goodness might hold for "a world the constitution of which made it possible without contradiction to hold it for the work of a Being at once omnipotent and benevolent." But that is not the kind of world in which we live or the kind of god that Mill thinks is evinced by observation of that world. God's goodness may be perfect but the limits to his power may preclude the realization of his benevolent intentions for man. "The benevolence of the divine Being may be perfect, but his power being subject to unknown limitations, we know not that he could have given us what we so confidently assert that he must have given; *could* (that is) without sacrificing something more important." All good things are not necessarily compatible or attainable. Moreover, as we have seen, while Mill's god does desire human happiness, such is far from being his "sole or chief purpose." Nor do we know what other purposes may have interfered with the exercise of his benevolence: "[W]e know not that he *would*, even if he could have granted us eternal life." The same answer may be given to those who argue that God would not have given us a desire for immortality if such was impossible to fulfill. "The scheme which either limitation of power, or conflict of purposes, compelled him to adopt, may have required that we should have the wish although it were not destined to be gratified." The existence of a limited god means that we cannot trust the comprehensiveness of order. Even if such order was intended by God, its realization may have been beyond his reach.

The only thing of which Mill is absolutely certain with respect to the divine government of the world is that God "either could not, or would not, grant to us every thing we wish." Thus it would not be exceptional if our wish for immortality were not granted, for many of our wishes are not granted. "Many a man would like to be an . . . Augustus Caesar, but has his wish gratified only to the moderate extent of a . . . Secretaryship of his Trades Union." Mill will have us face the facts.

Mill has reached his final conclusion with respect to the question of immortality: "[T]here is . . . no assurance whatever of a life after death, on grounds of natural religion." All, however, is not lost. As we recall, in

"Utility of Religion" Mill allowed not for the *belief* in a supernatural God and a future life but for "imaginative hope." At the end of his life his position was unchanged. Mill now says that while *belief* in personal immortality must be ruled out on the grounds of insufficient evidence, there is no harm in indulging the *hope* for such.

> But to any one who feels it conducive either to his satisfaction or to his usefulness to hope for a future state as a possibility, there is no hindrance to his indulging that hope. Appearances point to the existence of a Being who has great power over us—all the power implied in the creation of the Kosmos, or of its organized beings at least—and of whose goodness we have evidence though not of its being his predominant attribute: as we do not know the limits either of his power or of his goodness there is room to hope that both the one and the other may extend to granting us this gift provided that it would really be beneficial to us. The same ground which permits the hope warrants us in expecting that if there be a future life it will be at least as good as the present, and will not be wanting in the best feature of the present life, improvability by our own efforts. ("The," 466)

Mill's concession to the possibility of a future life, however, is tempered by the crucial qualification that such should *not* be understood to entail the future administration of rewards and punishments—divine justice. It is critical to an understanding of Mill's mission to recognize why, even at the very end of his life, he will not concede the possibility of divine justice. We know that the denial of the efficacy of the posthumous sanction was *the* essential tenet of the Benthamite "religion," its defining attribute and the linchpin of its attempt to found an exclusively intramundane ethic and orientation. For all of Mill's willingness to allow an "imaginative hope" in personal immortality and a limited supernatural Demiurge, he never abandoned his goal to replace a theological with a purely human orientation nor his commitment to the establishment of an intramundane social religion. To realize these ends, the evisceration, if not obliteration, of the notion of man's accountability to God was essential.

> Nothing can be more opposed to every estimate we can form of probability, than the common idea of the future life as a state of rewards and punishments in any other sense than that the consequences of our actions upon our own character and susceptibilities will follow us in the future as they have done in the past and present. Whatever be the probabilities *of* a future life, all the probabilities *in case of* a future life are that such as we have been made or have made ourselves before the change, such we shall enter into the life hereafter; and that the fact of death will make no sudden break in our spiritual life, nor influence our character any otherwise than as any important change in our mode of existence may always be expected to modify it. Our thinking principle has its laws which in this life are invariable, and

any analogies drawn from this life must assume that the same laws will continue.[28] To imagine that a miracle will be wrought at death by an act of God making perfect every one whom it is his will to include among his elect, might be justified by an express revelation duly authenticated, but is utterly opposed to every presumption that can be deduced from the light of Nature. ("The," 466–67)

It is not clear what all of this has to do with the evidences of nature. It seems no more absurd to hope for such a miracle after death than to hope for immortality, which Mill has expressly permitted. We have and can have no evidence to sustain or deflate the former hope, which, according to Mill, is exactly our situation with respect to the latter. Moreover, the final judgment and expectation of transfiguration of Christian belief, like the immortality of the "thinking principle," is thought to occur outside this world and thus, according to Mill, outside the realm subject to the canons of induction. In short, it is not clear why, on Mill's grounds, the Christian expectation of a final judgment and transfiguration is any more absurd than a belief in personal immortality. One is tempted to conclude that it was Mill's lifelong drive to eviscerate the belief in ultimate, transcendent justice, as well as his related abhorrence, inherited from his father, of the conception of the Christian God, that engendered such speculation and not any rigorous adherence to scientific method.

V: Revelation

Mill also examines the evidences for revelation—claims to have established "direct communication with the Supreme Being." He will not, he says, limit his focus exclusively to the Christian Revelation or attempt to judge whether its "special evidences . . . do or do not come up to the mark."[29] His subject will be "Revelation generally" because, as he cryptically remarks, this is "necessary to give a sufficiently practical bearing to the results of the preceding investigation."

Mill first points out that the results of his earlier investigation—the evidence he has found, however "slight . . . and [in]conclusive," for the existence of a Creator—make it easier to believe in the authenticity of revelation. The evidences of nature point toward a God, thus "the alleged Revelation" does not first have to prove the very existence of the Being from whom it professes to come. As Mill has shown, the evidences of nature point toward the existence of a Being of power, wisdom, and goodness, limited in varying degrees. Consequently, it is clear that the "sender of the alleged message is not a sheer invention; there are grounds independent of the message itself for belief in his reality, grounds which, though insufficient for proof, are sufficient to take away all antecedent improbability from the supposition that a message may really have been received from him. . . ."

Moreover, Mill believes the evidence yielded by natural theology increases the probability of revelation in another important way. As we have said, the evidence is all in favor of a God limited by unknown obstacles, a discovery, Mill thinks, that sheds new light on the notorious "imperfections in the Revelation itself." That is, the questionable or inconclusive character of the revelation can be accounted for by the fact that the limited god was unable to provide something better. He obviously must have encountered obstacles that prevented him from proving the authenticity of the revelation or from providing more certain or definitive information. The limited god disclosed by nature

> removes some of the chief stumbling blocks to the belief of a Revelation, since the objections grounded on imperfections in the Revelation itself, however conclusive against it if it is considered as a record of the acts or an expression of the wisdom of a Being of infinite power combined with infinite wisdom and goodness, are no reason whatever against its having come from a Being such as the course of nature points to, whose wisdom is possibly, his power certainly, limited, and whose goodness, though real, is not likely to have been the only motive which actuated him in the work of Creation. ("The," 468–69)

The concept of a limited god makes everything more clear.

On the hypothesis of such a god as Mill conceives to be evinced by the order of nature, then, it is not prima facie improbable that God, desiring to some extent the happiness of his creatures, would have given proof of his existence by providing knowledge of himself beyond that which human beings can glean through their "unassisted faculties," as well as some practical knowledge intended for moral guidance. Mill's Christian readers should feel less uneasy about Mill's new god. Furthermore, on "the only tenable hypothesis, that of limited power," there is no reason to complain that the help given should have been greater or in any way different from what was given. A limited god may have been unable to provide a better revelation, even if willing.

As always for Mill, the fundamental question is *evidence*. He will first determine if any evidence would be sufficient to prove a divine revelation and, if so, what that evidence must be. This leads him to an examination of the evidence for the authenticity of the alleged miracles that accompanied the Christian and other revelations. The two questions—the authenticity of revelation and of miracles—are more or less inseparable.

Mill identifies two classes of evidences of revelation: external and internal. External evidences consist of testimony, either of eyewitnesses or one's own senses. Internal evidences are the indications that point to a divine origin, especially the "excellence of its precepts, and its general suitability to the circumstances and needs of human nature." Mill's latter remark seems to suggest that recognition may count as internal evidence, although he never explicitly says as much. His gloss on the value of internal evidences or recognition of the moral propriety of the revelation is also instructive in light of his aim to replace theological with human morality. Mill insists that the "excellence" of moral rules in an alleged revelation does not necessarily point to a supernatural origin. He says that internal evidences are chiefly of negative value, that they

> may be conclusive grounds for rejecting a Revelation, but cannot of themselves warrant the acceptance of it as divine. If the moral character of the doctrines of an alleged Revelation is bad and perverting, we ought to reject it from whomsoever it comes; for it cannot come from a good and wise Being. But the excellence of their morality can never entitle us to ascribe to them a supernatural origin: for we cannot have conclusive reason for believing that the human faculties were incompetent to find out moral doctrines of which the human faculties can perceive and recognise the excellence. ("The," 469–70)

This is a good example of Mill's maddening and perhaps strategic ambiguity. The human ability to "recognize" moral excellence, he suggests, does not negate the possibility that men themselves may also be able to "find out moral doctrines." *Recognition* of course implies the existence of something objectively present that may be recognized. *Find out* may also mean this, or it may, as Mill has elsewhere suggested, mean that man can invent, construct, formulate, or devise moral rules. Mill's meaning in the above passage is unclear, and perhaps designedly so. His actual view was that the most excellent morality was the product of the "best" and the "wisest" human beings. Indeed, as we have seen, his whole life was spent in the effort to defeat the concept of a *given* transcendent or theological morality and to establish a purely human nontheological or secular substitute in its place. To expressly acknowledge this would have alienated many of his readers. Mill's willful ambiguity enabled him to skirt around the all-important issue of whether morality is given, to be discovered or found, or whether it is the product of human construction.

The kind of evidence that would be sufficient to prove the authenticity of a "supernatural fact" such as revelation, Mill suggests, is external evidence and especially "the evidence of our senses." If he actually saw a Being "commanding a world to exist, and a new world actually starting into existence," this would undoubtedly transform the possibility of creating worlds from speculation to a fact of experience. Mill had a strong propensity for literalism; he could never quite free himself from the tyranny of fact, understood to entail sensory evidence. Symbolic or metaphorical thought he distrusted; what Mill craved was *physical proof*. He was also aware of the problem created by the Romantic discovery of the power of the imagination: how to discriminate between the imagined and the real. This is a problem, he says, in evaluating the authenticity of alleged miracles. How does one determine whether or not a witness is hallucinating or whether his senses have been deceived in some way? All physical research, Mill points out, must address this problem and it does so through several means: experimental repetition; ensuring the normalcy of the witnesses' senses; and, most important, confirming the testimony of one's own senses by comparing it with that of other persons. All such means serve to assure the trustworthiness of the senses, absolutely crucial for someone like Mill who believes, as he says, that "our senses are all that we have to trust to" ("The," 470–71).

The belief that all knowledge is derived from the senses was another of Mill's foundational assumptions. He held it tenaciously throughout his life, for it was essential to the realization of one of his chief purposes: the destruction of the school of intuitionist philosophy, which, as discussed, assumed that human beings have access to knowledge independently of the senses, whether through a faculty of "moral sense," intellectual or moral intuition, or speculative reason. The antitheological import of Mill's sensationalism seems to have been well understood by his contemporaries. As Henry Reeve said of Mill's teaching: "[W]e deplore the influence of Mill on philosophy, . . . for it has contributed to the reaction against all we hold to be spiritual truth, and to the strong materialist tendency of modern science, by teaching that all knowledge is derived exclusively from the senses, and that all character is formed by circumstances."[30]

What should also be highlighted is the confusion involved in such an emphasis on sensory evidence by a thinker who has called matter "hypothetical and unsubstantial," merely a "permanent possibility of sensation," and mind the "only substantive reality." On Mill's expressed view of the relation between matter and mind, it would seem that mind—"the only reality of which we have any evidence"—must inevitably produce the alleged evidence of the senses ("The," 463). Mill often suggests, however, that sensory evidence is fundamental, that such evidence is an objective fact that exists independently of a perceiving agent. He repeatedly refers to physical or sensory "facts" as if they exist independently of theory, belief, or a perceiving human mind, and this while simultaneously denying the substantive reality of matter.

To return to the proof of revelation: Such proof of its validity as would be provided by the testimony of the senses is of course unavailable at present, Mill says. The evidence relied on by "Protestant Christians . . . is not the evidence of our senses, but of witnesses, and even this not at first hand, but resting on the attestation of books and traditions." Moreover, such miracles as are recorded are of a type that would have been very difficult to verify even under the best of circumstances, and involve the kind of events that could have been brought about by the normal action of human beings or nature.

Mill appeals to the authority of David Hume, the "only thinker . . . on the sceptical side" who has addressed the question of the authenticity of miracles. He summarizes Hume's argument against miracles, which, with certain qualifications, he accepts: The evidence for miracles consists principally of the testimony of witnesses. The reason we generally rely on such testimony is our experience that, assuming "certain conditions," it is usually truthful. Experience also shows, however, that the testimony of witnesses is often false, either intentionally or unintentionally. Thus, when the fact allegedly testified to is of a kind which is at greater variance with experience than the known fact that testimony is often false, we should not believe the former fact. This, moreover, is the procedure "all prudent persons" actually employ in life. A miracle, of course, is almost by definition an event that contradicts experience; it is "a breach of a law of nature, that is, of an otherwise invariable and inviolable uniformity in the succession of natural events." Human beings therefore have the most compelling reason for disbelieving in alleged miracles. On the other hand, most people have encountered a witness who lies or errs; the experience is common. In the case of the testimony of witnesses to miracles, therefore, the latter explanation is to be preferred ("The," 470–72).

Mill faults Hume, however, for having failed to see that there is another side to the issue: the positive testimony of those who have claimed to witness miracles. The "testimony of experience" is not wholly negative. One must weigh the existing positive evidence against the general presumption against miracles suggested by the normal course of human experience. Nevertheless, Mill emphasizes, Hume is on solid ground inasmuch as the "negative presumption" against miracles is very strong indeed. The reason Mill emphasizes this is that miracles violate one of his absolute convictions: that "all phenomena have been shown, by indisputable evidence, to be amenable to law. . . . But a miracle, in the very fact of being a miracle, declares itself to be a supersession not [merely] of one natural law by another [as is the case in the discovery of new natural laws], but of the law which includes all others, which experience shows to be universal for all phenomena, viz., that they depend on some law; that they are always the same when there are the same phenomenal antecedents, and neither take place in the absence of their phenomenal causes, nor ever fail to take place when the phenomenal conditions are all present." Mill admits that former generations did not have the benefit of knowledge of the law-governed character of the universe; even the instructed could not have regarded known laws as scientifically established truth. Men always recognized a certain regularity in the occurrence of the most familiar phenomena, such as the heavenly bodies. But it is instructive that comets, eclipses, and the like—phenomena which were only with difficulty and over time reconciled with a general rule and were thus thought to occur in violation of law—were typically regarded as "signs and omens of human fortunes." The conclusive arguments against miracles had to wait until the modern stage of the progress of science.

The modern defenders of miracles, however, are also aware of the universal reign of law and have thus adapted their defense to incorporate that knowledge. They now maintain that miracles may in fact be law-governed, that is, governed by an as-yet-undiscovered law. There are two senses in which this may be understood, one objectionable, the other not. As previously noted, Mill does not at this point object to the notion of "general Providence," that is, to the notion that God, in performing miracles—"in the exercise of his power of interfering with and suspending his own laws—guides himself by some general principle or rule of action." Mill regards this view as the most probable because it maintains the integrity of the universal reign of law.

Mill explains what a miracle is and the manner in which an alleged miracle may be verified or refuted:

> To constitute a miracle a phenomenon must take place without having been preceded by any antecedent phenomenal conditions sufficient again to reproduce it; or a phenomenon for the production of which the antecedent conditions existed, must be arrested or prevented without the intervention of any phenomenal antecedents which would arrest or prevent it in a future case. The test of a miracle is: Were there present in the case such external conditions, such second causes we may call them, that whenever these conditions or causes reappear the event will be reproduced? If there were, it is not a miracle; if there were not, it is a miracle, but it is not according to law: it is an event produced, without, or in spite of law. ("The," 472–73)

Mill also clears up what it means to say a miracle was caused by "second causes." For instance, if God willed to create a thunderstorm by miracle, he might do it by means of winds and clouds. A miracle would occur only if winds and clouds insufficient to raise a storm nevertheless did so (or if winds and clouds sufficient to raise one did not). The miracle in this case is not the creation of the thunderstorm, but the alteration of the second causes—the "means"—the winds and clouds, the "physical antecedents" of the storm. If the physical antecedents were not deliberately altered in some way, "but the event called miraculous was produced by natural means, and those again by others, and so on from the beginning of things; if the event is no otherwise the act of God than in having been foreseen and ordained by him as the consequence of the forces put in action at the creation; then there is no miracle at all, nor anything different from the ordinary working of God's providence" ("The," 474). Mill of course does not believe in God's providence in any traditional sense. He is here employing the term rhetorically or identifying it with his own "necessitarian" or deterministic understanding of the course of human events.

Finally, Mill suggests various alternative explanations for the occurrence of what appear to certain minds as miracles. First, and most obviously, the event may have been the effect of natural physical causes, in some manner unknown to the persons present or even to contemporary science (perhaps the governing law has not yet been discovered). Mill would not even trust the evidence of his own senses if he himself were to witness a miracle, he says, for even if we have the

> direct evidence of our own senses; even then so long as there is no direct evidence of its production by a divine volition, like that we have for the production of bodily movements by human volitions, so long will the hypothesis of a natural origin for the phenomenon be entitled to preference over that of a supernatural one. The commonest principles of sound judgment forbid us to suppose for any effect a cause of which we have absolutely no experience, unless all those of which we have experience are ascertained to be absent.

Human beings have many experiences for which they cannot account, and this because those experiences depend on laws that scientific observation has not yet brought to light or on unsuspected facts of which we have no knowledge. Thus, when modern people encounter an unusual event—for instance, a child prodigy—they do not consider it the work of a god or a demon, but as the effect of "some unknown natural law or of some hidden fact" ("The," 476). Nor can Mill give credence to so-called miracles that seem to depend on the will of a human being. It is always possible that the alleged "wonder-worker" may have acquired, knowingly or not, the power to utilize some law of nature, or he may be a "mere juggler" utilizing ordinary known laws (such as commanding an eclipse to appear when one knows in advance one is about to occur). Or else the so-called miracle may merely be a fortuitous event, an accident, a lucky coincidence.

Mill is deeply suspicious of the very notion of miracle. There certainly are many possible and much more plausible reasons for alleged miracles than divine intervention. The best way to test such alleged miracles would be to ask for a repetition. Indeed, "[i]t is worthy of remark, that recorded miracles were seldom or never put to this test. . . . No miracle-worker seems ever to have made a *practice* of raising the dead" ("The," 477–78). The few recorded miracles could have been "cunningly selected" cases or coincidences. In short, there is nothing to rule out the possibility that "every alleged miracle was due to natural causes." So long as this is a possibility, no "scientific observer" or even any person of normally sound judgment would consider an event a miracle. Indeed, "anyone . . who set down as one of the alternative suppositions that there is no other cause for [an event] than the will of God . . . would be laughed at."

Nevertheless, in this case as in others, Mill immediately gives back what he has taken: "[W]e cannot . . . conclude absolutely that the miraculous theory of the production of a phenomenon ought to be at once rejected." This is only possible for those who do not believe in the existence of God. Mill does want to point out, however, that the existence of God cannot itself be proved by miracles.

> [F]or unless a God is already recognised, the apparent miracle can always be accounted for on a more probable hypothesis than that of the interference of a Being of whose very existence it is supposed to be the sole evidence. . . . Once admit a God, [however,] and the production by his direct volition of an effect which in any case owed its origin to his creative will, is no longer a purely arbitrary hypothesis to account for the fact, but must be reckoned with as a serious possibility. The question then changes its character, and the decision of it must now rest upon what is known or reasonably surmised as to the manner of God's government of the universe: whether this knowledge or surmise makes it the more probable supposition that the event was brought about by the agencies by which his government is ordinarily carried on, or that it is the result of a special and extraordinary interposition of his will in supersession of those ordinary agencies. ("The," 477–78)

Mill is again alluding to what theologians traditionally termed a general and a special providence. General providence, he again seems to admit, may be a reality, but the evidences of nature suggest that a special providence is highly improbable.

Mill recapitulates his conviction that the "positive evidence of miracles" is entitled to carry some weight, even though it is necessarily a matter of mere inference and speculation, and not of the more compelling direct evidence of the senses. The fact that there is always the possibility of a natural explanation for alleged miracles greatly reduces their probability. The only evidence, Mill thinks, that would serve as a counterweight to the improbability of miracles is "if the miracle . . . [was] congruous with what we think we know of the divine attributes." Such congruity might exist, for instance, between a miracle that serves a highly beneficial purpose (such as accrediting some important belief) and the goodness of God. Mill counsels caution. He believes he has shown that it is highly "precarious" to draw any inference from the "goodness of God to what he has or has not actually done. . . . *If we reason directly from God's goodness to positive facts, no misery, nor vice nor crime ought to exist in the world*" (emphasis added). We again see the tenacity with which Mill clung to his rigid conception of what a world governed by absolute goodness *must* look like—a state of static perfection—all the more strange in a philosopher of "experience" who touted the benefits of trial-and-error experimentation and human freedom. At the end of his days, Mill was no more willing to reconcile God's absolute goodness with the relative scarcity of miracles than with the imperfection of this world. Because Mill cannot understand God's ways, he insists that the conception of God must be revised to cohere with his own conception of a truly good divine government.

If God is good, Mill wants to know, then why does he not do more good for man?

> [If God once] deviated from the ordinary system of his government in order to do good to man, [why] should . . . he . . . not have done so on a hundred other occasions; nor why, if the benefit aimed at by some given deviation, such as the revelation of Christianity, was transcendent and unique, that precious gift should only have been vouchsafed after the lapse of many ages, or why, when it was at last given, the evidence of it should have been left open to so much doubt and difficulty. Let it be remembered also that the goodness of God affords no presumption in favour of a deviation from his general system of government unless the good purpose could not have been attained without deviation. If God intended that mankind should receive Christianity or any other gift, it would have agreed better with all that we know of his government to have made provision in the scheme of creation for its arising at the appointed time by natural development; which . . . all the knowledge we now possess concerning the history of the human mind, tends to the conclusion that it actually did.

Mill is attributing to God his own understanding of causation in history, a curious blend of necessitarianism or determinism and Comtism.

To return to the evidence for miracles and thus for revelation: In addition to all the difficulties that arise from the impossibility of reconciling

God's goodness with the facts of existence, there is the difficulty of the very inadequate testimony that exists for the miracles that allegedly accompanied the foundation of Christianity and of every other revealed religion. At its best, it is "the uncross-examined testimony of extremely ignorant people, credulous as such usually are, . . . unaccustomed to draw the line between the perceptions of sense, and what is superinduced upon them by the suggestions of a lively imagination; unversed in the difficult art of deciding between appearance and reality, and between the natural and the supernatural." Moreover, the people of those times believed miracles could be the work not only of the "spirit of God" but of a "lying spirit" as well. Nor do we even have the direct testimony of the "supposed eye-witnesses," who are often unnamed in the extant documents or cast as traditional figures familiar to the popular mind of the time. In short, the so-called witnesses are of extremely poor quality and there is little reason to give credence to their testimony. Interestingly, Mill also claims that "stories of miracles only grow up among the ignorant and are adopted, if ever, by the educated when they have already become the belief of multitudes." This is in rather obvious contradiction to his generally settled conviction that the ignorant take their views from the wise and cultivated. Mill summarizes his findings: "The conclusion I draw is that *miracles have no claim whatever to the character of historical facts and are wholly invalid as evidences of any revelation*" ("The," 479–81, emphasis added).

Having made this pronouncement, however, Mill cannot leave the subject alone. As there was insufficient evidence to allow for *belief* in a supernatural God or in personal immortality and a future life, so there is insufficient evidence to allow for *belief* in miracles and thus for the revelation to which they attest. Nevertheless, Mill sees no harm in indulging in the hope that all of it may be true:

> Considering that the order of nature affords some evidence of the reality of a Creator, and of his bearing good will to his creatures though not of its being the sole prompter of his conduct towards them: considering, again, that all the evidence of his existence is evidence also that he is not all-powerful, and considering that in our ignorance of the limits of his power we cannot positively decide that he was able to provide for us by the original plan of Creation all the good which it entered into his intentions to bestow upon us, or even to bestow any part of it at any earlier period than that at which we actually received it—considering these things, when we consider further that a gift, extremely precious, came to us which though facilitated was not apparently necessitated by what had gone before, but was due, as far as appearances go, to the peculiar mental and moral endowments of one man [Christ], and that man openly proclaimed that it did not come from himself but from God through him, then we are entitled to say that there is nothing so inherently impossible or absolutely incredible in this supposition as to

preclude any one from hoping that it may perhaps be true. I say from hoping; I go no further; for I cannot attach any evidentiary value to the testimony even of Christ on such a subject, since he is never said to have declared any evidence of his mission (unless his own interpretations of the Prophecies be so considered) except internal conviction; and everybody knows that in prescientific times men always supposed that any unusual faculties which came to them they knew not how, were an inspiration from God; the best men always being the readiest to ascribe any honourable peculiarity in themselves to that higher source, rather than to their own merits. ("The," 481)

It was this passage, and especially the reference to the "extremely precious" gift of Christianity, that encouraged some of Mill's Christian readers to think that he might be moving closer toward their own views.[31] Such, however, was wishful thinking. The views expressed in the above passage do not represent a dramatic departure from either Mill's long-standing hostility to Christianity or his long-standing respect for the *man* Christ. Mill, with Bentham, always separated the person of Christ from institutional Christianity, which they associated with Paul. Mill had long believed, as he says in the above passage, that Christ was one of the "best men," perhaps even sent on a special mission by God. But Mill, like various of his contemporaries, did not regard Christ as God, nor did he think Christ ever so regarded himself. He did believe there was much of value in Christianity and especially in certain elements of Christian ethics. One of his efforts, as we have seen, was to "purify" Christianity of its "immoral" accretions, to separate the gold from the dross, and to incorporate the good elements of historical Christianity into the intramundane Religion of the Future (see Chapter 6). Mill also believed that what was of benefit in Christian ethics had become the permanent possession of the human race and would endure once institutional Christianity had passed into the oblivion that was its historical fate. As we know, Mill, with Saint-Simon and Comte, had long viewed Christianity as a necessary but now obsolete stage in the development of the human mind. As he said in a letter to Carlyle in 1833, he looked forward to the time when he could "speak of Christianity as it may be spoken of in France; as by far the greatest and best thing which has existed on this globe, but which is *gone, never to return, only what was best in it to reappear in another and still higher form, some time* (heaven knows when) [emphasis added]. . . . One could not, *now,* say this openly in England and be read—at least by the many; yet it is perhaps worth trying." Mill's self-selected task, as has been emphasized, was to elaborate that "higher form"—the new nontheological or secular ethics and its spiritual carrier, the Religion of Humanity—destined to replace a moribund Christianity that has outlived its usefulness.

We might also note that Mill's characterization of Christianity in this letter, as "by far the greatest and best thing which has existed on this globe," should not be taken at face value; as we have seen, this was far from his considered view. Mill, as he himself acknowledged, was something of a chameleon, adopting both the views and emotional coloration of the persons with whom he collaborated at various periods. The foregoing remarks were written in the context of Mill's attempt to remain in Carlyle's good graces after acknowledging that he (Mill) has not been quite truthful with respect to his genuine religious views. He cajoles Carlyle by assuring him that their views are not that far apart: "[A]s far as I know *your* impressions about Christ, [and] *mine* . . . are exactly the same."[32]

Skepticism: The Only Rational Attitude

After weighing in the balance all the evidence for and against theism, Mill pronounces his final judgment: "[T]he rational attitude of a thinking mind towards the supernatural, whether in natural or in revealed religion, is that of scepticism as distinguished from belief on the one hand, and from atheism on the other." Mill, like Comte, is especially careful to reject atheism in both its possible forms: a "negative" atheism that dogmatically denies the existence of a deity and a "positive" atheism that denies there is any evidence on either side of the argument. Mill summarizes his conclusions: "[T]here is evidence [for a god], but insufficient for proof, and amounting only to one of the lower degrees of probability. The indication given by such evidence as there is, points to the creation, not indeed of the universe, but of the present order of it by an Intelligent Mind, whose power over the materials was not absolute, whose love for his creatures was not his sole actuating inducement, but who nevertheless desired their good." In other words, as previously noted, the evidence points precisely to the limited god of Mill's conception, a god limited in power, and possibly in knowledge, foresight, skill, and benevolence as well.

Mill also makes his final judgment on the validity of the traditional conception of Providence: "*The notion of a providential government by an omnipotent Being for the good of his creatures must be entirely dismissed*" (emphasis added). The reasons for this sweeping dismissal are unclear inasmuch as earlier in the essay Mill had seemingly acknowledged that a general providence was compatible with the universal government of law established by science. One suspects that Mill's conviction that absolute goodness was utterly irreconcilable with the gross injustice and evil in the world overcame his more balanced assessment of this issue. Mill could never trust that, despite appearances, all may in fact be working toward the good. Indeed, he now says, one cannot even trust that God, that is, the limited Demiurge of his conception, still exists: "Even of the continued existence of the Creator we have no other guarantee than that he cannot be subject to the law of death which affects terrestrial beings, since the conditions that produce this liability wherever it is known to exist are of his creating." And, as said, Mill concedes that miracles remain a possibility. Although there is no proof of this, Mill will allow hope for those who need that sort of consolation:

> That this Being, not being omnipotent, may have produced a machinery falling short of his intentions, and which may require the occasional interposition of the Maker's hand, is a supposition not in itself absurd nor impossible [it seems Leibnitz was wrong]; it remains a simple possibility, which those may dwell on to whom it yields comfort to suppose that blessings which ordinary human power is inadequate to attain, may come not from extraordinary human power, but from the bounty of an intelligence beyond the human, and which continuously cares for man.

With respect to immortality, Mill again allows for the possibility of continued existence, but he demotes the idea, like that of the existence of God, from the level of "Belief" to that of imaginative "hope."

> The possibility of a life after death rests on the same footing—of a boon which this powerful Being who wishes well to man, may have the power to grant, and which if the message alleged to have been sent by him was really sent, he has actually promised. The whole domain of the supernatural is thus removed from the region of Belief into that of simple Hope; and in that, for anything we can see, it is likely always to remain; for we can hardly anticipate either that any positive evidence will be acquired of the direct agency of Divine Benevolence in human destiny, or that any reason will be discovered for considering the realisation of human hopes on that subject as beyond the pale of possibility. ("The," 482–83)

The Role of Imaginative Hope

Mill, then, has found a way out of his old conundrum—how to reconcile the desire to believe in a deity of some sort, or at least in a Good Principle, while avoiding the sin of believing without evidence. His solution is the replacement of belief with "imaginative hope." His first step is to exorcise the demon of James Mill. He will consider whether or not the "indulgence of hope, in a region of imagination merely, in which there is no prospect that any probable grounds of expectation will ever be obtained, is irrational, and ought to be discouraged as a departure from the rational principle of regulating our feelings as well as opinions strictly by evidence." Such a consideration leads him to explore the role of imagination in practical experience, a subject, he complains, heretofore neglected by philosophers but one that will assume increasing prominence in the future. This is because the problem of establishing "the principles which ought to govern the cultivation and regulation of the imagination" will become more urgent as traditional religious belief and dogma, which long served to regulate man's imaginative speculation, further decline. That is, the inevitable erosion of the traditional Christian worldview must be met by something that can serve to keep the religious imagination within the bounds of rationality and reality. On the one hand, a sound imagination grounded in reason is essential to "prevent . . . [the imagination] from disturbing the rectitude of the intellect and the right direction of the actions and will." On the other, moralists and others will wish, and rightly so, to employ the imagination as a "power" to increase human happiness and elevate human character. The problem of the imagination has "never yet engaged the serious consideration of philosophers. . . . I expect, [however,] that this will hereafter be regarded as a very important branch of study for practical purposes, and the more, in proportion as the weakening of positive beliefs respecting states of existence superior to the human, leaves the imagination of higher things less provided with material from the domain of supposed reality." Mill is particularly aware of the great potential power of the imagination to generate and sustain religious enthusiasm and especially the pursuit of religious and spiritual ideals.

> To me it seems that human life, small and confined as it is, and as, considered merely in the present, it is likely to remain even when that progress of material and moral improvement may have freed it from the greater part of its present calamities, stands greatly in need of any wider range and greater height of aspiration for itself and its destination, which the exercise of imagination can yield to it without running counter to the evidence of fact. . . . [I]t is a part of wisdom to make the most of any . . . probabilities on this subject, which furnish imagination with any footing to support itself upon. And I am satisfied that the cultivation of such a tendency in the imagination, provided it goes on pari passu with the cultivation of severe reason, has no necessary tendency to pervert the judgment; but that it is possible to form a perfectly sober estimate of the evidences on both sides of a question and yet to let the imagination dwell by preference on those possibilities which are at once the most comforting and the most improving, without in the least degree overrating the solidity of the grounds for expecting that these rather than any others will be the possibilities actually realised. ("The," 483)

Mill will have it both ways. He will allow his imagination and emotions free reign, provided he continues to cultivate a "severe reason." And, moreover, he sees no reason not "to make the most of any . . . probabilities" on the subject of God and the afterlife in order to increase the "range and . . . height of aspiration" concerning "human life . . . and its destination," "small and confined as it [presently] is." As we shall see, what Mill suggests is that imaginative hope in God and immortality can serve to generate emotion and motivation sufficient to rally the masses behind his new Religion of Humanity.

Although traditional wisdom has neglected this area of experience, Mill continues, human happiness is greatly dependent upon the imagination. For instance, the balanced employment of the imagination underlies a "cheerful disposition," that is, the tendency to dwell on the bright side of life, present and future. Mill argues (against his inner demon) that it is not the case that "every aspect, whether agreeable or odious of every thing, ought to occupy exactly the same place in our imagination which it fills in fact, and therefore ought to fill in our deliberate reason." If this were true it would be as foolish to be cheerful as to be perpetually gloomy and morose. Moreover, observation shows that the cheerful are no less sensitive to evil than others and no less careful of practical necessities and their provision. Actually, the cheerful are better able to do all things well, moral and practical, for "a hopeful disposition gives a spur to the faculties and keeps all the active energies in good working order." Nor are the imagination and reason necessarily in conflict; what is required is a balanced and judicious employment of both, to be achieved through "appropriate culture, . . . [so that] they do not succeed in usurping each other's prerogatives." Dwelling on gloomy prospects is neither necessary nor virtuous. "The true rule of practical wisdom is . . . giving the greatest prominence to those of their aspects which depend on, or can be modified by, our own conduct. In things which do not depend on us," Mill says, it is better to look at the pleasant side of things and of mankind. Such an approach not only makes this life more enjoyable, but it is also practical. It enables us to "love [men] better and work with more heart for their improvement." Mill in the evening of his life was at his most endearing and most sincere. The final passages of "Theism" provide a rare unposed expression of the idealism he maintained until the end of his days:

> To what purpose, indeed, should we feed our imagination with the unlovely aspect of persons and things? All *unnecessary* dwelling upon the evils of life is at best a useless expenditure of nervous force. But if it is often a waste of strength to dwell on the evils of life; it is worse than waste to dwell habitually on its meannesses and basenesses. It is necessary to be aware of them; but to live in their contemplation makes it scarcely possible to keep up in oneself a high tone of mind. The imagination and feelings become

tuned to a lower pitch; degrading instead of elevating associations become connected with the daily objects and incidents of life, and give their colour to the thoughts, just as associations of sensuality do in those who indulge freely in that sort of contemplations. Men have often felt what it is to have had their imaginations corrupted by one class of ideas, and I think they must have felt with the same kind of pain how the poetry is taken out of the things fullest of it, by mean associations, as when a beautiful air that had been associated with highly poetical words is heard sung with trivial and vulgar ones.[33]

Another indication of Mill's growth is the tentative step he seems to have taken toward freeing himself from his ingrained literalism, from the tyranny of fact. What his discussion of the imagination is meant to show, he says, is that "in the regulation of the imagination literal truth of facts is not the only thing to be considered." His usual preaching turns to soliloquy:

Truth is the province of reason, and it is by the cultivation of the rational faculty that provision is made for its being known always, and thought of as often as is required by duty and the circumstances of human life. But when the reason is strongly cultivated, the imagination may safely follow its own end, and do its best to make life pleasant and lovely inside the castle, in reliance on the fortifications raised and maintained by Reason round the outward bounds. ("The," 484–85)

It would take a very hard heart not to feel the pathos of such remarks. They are almost sufficient to counterbalance those many, many passages in which Mill's breathtaking arrogance wins the upper hand.

Mill soon reverts to his old self, however, as well as to his main topic: the rationality of the indulgence of imaginative hope with respect to the existence of God and immortality. Once again, he emphasizes, while there are no grounds for belief in either area, hope is "legitimate and philosophically defensible." The pathos of Mill's impoverished rationality speaks for itself—he requires a utilitarian justification even for mere hope:

The beneficial effect of such a hope is far from trifling. It makes life and human nature a far greater thing to the feelings, and gives greater strength as well as greater solemnity to all the sentiments which are awakened in us by our fellow-creatures and by mankind at large. [This is essential, for such sentiments of fraternity with mankind are to replace traditional religious sentiments oriented toward God in the society of the future.] It allays the sense of that irony of Nature which is so painfully felt when we see the exertions and sacrifices of a life culminating in the formation of a wise and noble mind, only to disappear from the world when the time has just arrived at which the world seems about to begin reaping the benefit of it. The truth that life is short and art is long is . . . one of the most discouraging parts of our condition; this hope admits the possibility that the art employed in improving and beautifying the soul itself may avail for good in some other life, even when seemingly useless for this. But the benefit consists less in the presence of any specific hope; than in the enlargement of the general scale of the feelings; the loftier aspirations being no longer in the same degree checked and kept down by a sense of the insignificance of human life—by the disastrous feeling of "not worth while." The gain obtained in the increased inducement to cultivate the improvement of character up to the end of life, is obvious without being specified. ("The," 485)

The Model of Christ

Such meditations lead Mill to expound upon another of his lifelong convictions: the human need for a concrete model of perfection. This, in turn, leads to his most extended discussion of Christ as well as to his final thoughts on the value of establishing the Religion of Humanity, which he has not yet explicitly discussed in this final essay on religion. He begins by pointing out that one of the main benefits achieved by traditional religion has been the model of ideal moral perfection it has held up to mankind in the person of Christ.

There is another and a most important exercise of imagination which, in the past and present, has been kept up principally by means of religious belief and which is infinitely precious to mankind, so much so that human excellence greatly depends upon the sufficiency of the provision made for it. This consists of the familiarity of the imagination with the conception of a morally perfect being, and the habit of taking the approbation of such a Being as the *norma* or standard to which to refer and by which to regulate our own characters and lives. [Mill took for his own model his wife, Harriet.][34] This idealization of our standard of excellence in a Person is quite possible, even when that Person is conceived as merely imaginary. But religion, since the birth of Christianity, has inculcated the belief that our highest conceptions of combined wisdom and goodness exist in the concrete in a living Being who has his eyes on us and cares for our good. Through the darkest and most corrupt periods Christianity has raised this torch on high—has kept this object of veneration and imitation before the eyes of man. ("The," 485–86)

Lest one be tempted to mistake Mill's implicit praise of Christianity for approbation, however, one is quickly set straight: "True, the image of perfection has been a most imperfect, and in many respects a perverting and corrupting one, not only from the low moral ideas of the times, but from the mass of moral contradictions which the deluded worshipper was compelled to swallow by the supposed necessary of complimenting the Good Principle with the possession of infinite power." Such delusion, however, is only to be expected, considering the "low stage" of present human development: "But it is one of the most universal as well as of the most surprising characteristics of human nature, and one of the most speaking proofs of the low stage to which the reason of mankind at large has ever yet advanced, that they are capable of overlooking any amount of either moral or intellectual contradictions and receiving into the minds propositions utterly inconsistent with one another, not only without being shocked by the contradiction, but without preventing both the contradictory beliefs from producing a part at least of their natural consequences in the mind"[35] ("The," 486).

The Christian religion, however, while morally perverse beyond measure in Mill's view, still has one advantage that any competitor must at least meet, if not overcome—the undoubted advantage of positing a *real* God.[36]

> Pious men and woman have gone on ascribing to God particular acts and a general course of will and conduct incompatible with even the most ordinary and limited conception of moral goodness, and have had their own ideas of morality . . . totally warped and distorted, and notwithstanding this have continued to conceive their God as clothed with all the attributes of the highest ideal goodness which their state of mind enabled them to conceive, and have had their aspirations towards goodness stimulated and encouraged by that conception. And, it cannot be questioned that the undoubting belief of the real existence of a Being who realises our own best ideas of perfection, and of our being in the hands of that Being as the ruler of the universe, gives an increase of force to these feelings beyond what they can receive from reference to a merely ideal conception.

Mill weighs the pros and cons of traditional Christianity against the skeptical religion of hope he wishes to promote. He concludes that the Religion of Humanity, despite the "advantages" enjoyed by Christianity, is the decided winner of the contest, and this because it represents a definite moral advance:

> This particular advantage [of a real God] it is not possible for those to enjoy, who take a rational view of the nature and amount of the evidence for the existence and attributes of the Creator. On the other hand, they are not encumbered with the moral contradictions which beset every form of religion which aims at justifying in a moral point of view the whole government of the world. They are, therefore, enabled to form a far truer and more consistent conception of Ideal goodness, than is possible to any one who thinks it necessary to find ideal goodness in an omnipotent ruler of the world. The power of the Creator once recognised as limited, there is nothing to disprove the supposition that his goodness is complete and that the ideally perfect character in whose likeness we should wish to form ourselves and to whose supposed approbation we refer our actions, may have a real existence in a Being to whom we owe all such good as we enjoy. ("The," 486–87)

Such reflections lead Mill to Christ. Although the general tendency of Christianity has been to "warp and distort" morality, as Mill has said, it has also managed to have some positive effect on the formation of character and this is largely due to Christ. Such limited beneficial effects as Christianity has achieved have resulted from its "holding up in a Divine Person a standard of excellence and a model for imitation." Mill emphasizes that such a standard and model "is available even to the absolute unbeliever and can never more be lost to humanity."

> For it is Christ, rather than God, whom Christianity has held up to believers as the pattern of perfection for humanity. It is the God incarnate, more than the God of the Jews or of Nature, who being idealized has taken so great and salutary a hold on the modern mind. And whatever else may be taken away from us by rational criticism, Christ is still left: a unique figure not more unlike all his precursors than all his followers, even those who had the direct benefit of his personal teaching.

Even the newly emerging biblical criticism cannot destroy the value of Christ's example.

> It is of no use to say that Christ as exhibited in the Gospels is not historical and that we know not how much of what is admirable has been superadded by the tradition of his followers. The tradition of followers suffices to insert any number of marvels, and may have inserted all the miracles which he is reputed to have wrought. But who among his disciples or among their proselytes was capable of inventing the sayings ascribed to Jesus or of imagining the life and character revealed in the Gospels? Certainly not the fishermen of Galilee; as certainly not St. Paul, whose character and idiosyncrasies were of a totally different sort; still less the early Christian writers in whom nothing is more evident than that the good which was in them was all derived, as they always professed that it was derived, from the higher source. What *could* be added and interpolated by a disciple we may see in the mystical parts of the Gospel of St. John, matter imported from Philo and the Alexandrian Platonists and put into the mouth of the Saviour in long speeches about himself such as the other Gospels contain not the slightest vestige of, though pretended to have been delivered on occasions of the deepest interest and when his principal followers were all present; most prominently at the last supper. The East was full of men who could have stolen any quantity of this poor stuff, as the multitudinous Oriental sects of Gnostics afterwards did.

Mill extols the "sublime genius" of the "man" Christ:

> But about the life and sayings of Jesus there is a stamp of personal originality combined with profundity of insight, which if we abandon the ideal expectation of finding scientific precision where something very different was aimed at, must place the Prophet of Nazareth, even in the estimation of

those who have no belief in his inspiration, in the very first rank of the men of sublime genius of whom our species can boast. When this pre-eminent genius is combined with the qualities of probably the greatest moral reformer, and martyr to that mission, who ever existed upon earth, religion cannot be said to have made a bad choice in pitching on this man as the ideal representative and guide of humanity; nor, even now, would it be easy, even for an unbeliever, to find a better translation of the rule of virtue from the abstract into the concrete, than to endeavor so to live that Christ would approve our life.

Mill is careful to add, however, that this great genius and moral reformer was not God, nor did Christ ever claim to be God.

When to this we add that, to the conception of the rational sceptic, it remains a possibility that Christ actually was what he supposed himself to be—not God, for he never made the smallest pretension to that character and would probably have thought such a pretension as blasphemous as it seemed to the men who condemned him—but a man charged with a special, express and unique commission from God to lead mankind to truth and virtue; we may well conclude that the influences of religion on the character which will remain after rational criticism has done its utmost against the evidences of religion, are well worth preserving, and that what they lack in direct strength as compared with those of a firmer belief, is more than compensated by the greater truth and rectitude of the morality they sanction. ("The," 487–88)

The result of such "rational criticism" will be a purified Christianity suitable for incorporation into the Religion of Humanity.

The Religion of Humanity

Mill admits that Christianity has produced certain beneficial influences on individual character and these, he says, are not only "well worth preserving" but will blossom even more profusely as people come to embrace the "greater truth and rectitude of the morality" that he hopes will supersede Christian morality. He is now ready to introduce the topic for which all of the above has been prologue: the Religion of Humanity. Having acknowledged the moral greatness of Christ and the value of the influence he has wrought on human character, Mill suggests that the beneficial influences permanently effected by Christianity can be harnessed in support of the new religion he hopes to establish in its place.

Impressions such as these, though not in themselves amounting to what can properly be called a religion, seem to me excellently fitted to aid and fortify that real, though purely human religion, which sometimes calls itself the Religion of Humanity and sometimes that of Duty. To the other inducements for cultivating a religious devotion to the welfare of our fellow-creatures as an obligatory limit to every selfish aim, and an end for the direct promotion of which no sacrifice can be too great, it superadds the feeling that in making this the rule of our life, we may be cooperating with the unseen Being to whom we owe all that is enjoyable in life.

Mill will meet the undoubted advantage enjoyed by the rival Christianity—its positing of a *real God*—by proposing one of his own and implicitly associating him with Christ. The "unseen Being" to whom Mill refers is undoubtedly the probable limited god we have discussed at length, although most of his readers would probably have thought of Christ. Mill's laudatory remarks about Christ and Christianity in the foregoing passages should be understood in light of his unwavering purpose—to promote his new intramundane Religion of Humanity. His strategy seems to have been to capture both the sentiments and transcendent aspirations of his Christian readers by creating an association in their minds between his new god and Christ and between his own humanitarian aspirations and traditional Christian aspirations. As he will say later in the essay, "supernatural hopes . . . may . . . contribute not a little to give to [the Religion of Humanity] its due ascendancy over the human mind" ("The," 488–89). And, as he remarked in the foregoing passage, "impressions" such as he has expressed, including his praise of the "man" Christ and his assurance that the beneficial influences of Christianity "will remain after rational criticism has done its utmost," are "excellently fitted to aid and fortify that real, though purely human religion, . . . the Religion of Humanity . . . "

Mill further elaborates the benefits to be derived from adopting his new religion, as well as its advantages over Christianity, curiously reverting, along the way, to the Manichaeism he had explicitly rejected earlier in the essay (when he said that the notion of dual powers is incompatible with the scientific discovery of the universal reign of law; see page 198). One of the chief benefits of the Religion of Humanity, Mill says, is the impetus it gives to human will and agency, for, as said, such a god as Mill conceives is so limited and ineffective on his own that he "really needs" man's help.[37] Also note Mill's expectation of the "not uncertain final victory of Good":

One elevated feeling this form of religious idea admits of, which is not open to those who believe in the omnipotence of the good principle in the universe, [is] the feeling of helping God—of requiting the good he has given by a voluntary cooperation which he, not being omnipotent, really needs, and by which a somewhat nearer approach may be made to the fulfillment of his purposes. The conditions of human existence are highly favourable to the growth of such a feeling inasmuch as a battle is constantly going on in which the humblest human creature is not incapable of taking some part, between the powers of good and those of evil, and in which every event, even the smallest help to the right side, has its value in promoting the very slow and often almost insensible progress by which good is gradually gaining ground from evil, yet gaining it so visibly at considerable intervals as to promise the very distant but not uncertain final victory of Good. To do something during life, on even the humblest scale if nothing more is within reach, toward bringing this consummation ever so little nearer, is the most animating and invigorating thought which can inspire a human creature; and *that it is destined, with or without supernatural sanctions, to be the Religion of the Future I cannot entertain a doubt. But it appears to me that supernatural hopes, in the degree and kind in which what I have called rational scepticism does not refuse to sanction them, may still contribute not a little to give to this religion its due ascendancy over the human mind*. ("The," 488–89, emphasis added)

To the end, then, what Mill gives with one hand he takes away with the other. He gives the gift of hope in things supernatural, but takes it back by attempting to enlist such hope in the intramundane service to humanity, for which, ominously, "no sacrifice can be too great." From all we know of Mill's strategy regarding religion, of his deep animus toward Christianity, of his rejection of the traditional Christian God as the very perfection of immorality, of his utter conviction of the superiority of the new purely human or nontheological utilitarian ethics he championed, and of the seriousness of his intent to found an exclusively intramundane Religion of Humanity, one is led to conclude that Mill's final remarks on religion were intended not as praise of Christianity or Christ but to convert his readers to his new religion. His argument seems designed to enlist the religious aspirations and feelings of his contemporaries—who were of course shaped to varying degrees by Christian aspirations and values, and committed to that religion in varying degrees as well—in service of the Religion of Humanity. As we have seen, Mill expressly stated his intention and strategy: surreptitiously to lead his readers away from a theological and toward a positivist orientation and to establish socially the Religion of Humanity. There are compelling reasons to believe that his final words on religion were designed to bring Christian believers into the fold of the new humanitarian church.

Nor can there be any doubt that Mill is constructing the "Interim God" that Collins mentions. Mill's probable limited god is destined to disappear over time as mankind embraces more and more fully the inevitable Religion of the Future. As Mill said in "Utility of Religion," when human beings learn to achieve complete happiness in this life—which the widespread embrace of the Religion of Humanity will undoubtedly bring about, if not tomorrow then someday—they will no longer require the consolation of otherworldly hopes and aspirations. In the meantime, the supernatural hopes and religious ideals of Christian believers, as well as reverence for the great man Christ, "may still contribute not a little to give to [the Religion of Humanity] its due ascendancy over the human mind." Be that as it may, Mill was convinced that this religion, "with or without supernatural sanctions," is destined to be the Religion of the Future. Mill was prophetic.

On Liberty

In the present age of transition, everything must be subordinate to freedom of inquiry: if your opinions, or mine, are right, they will in time be unanimously adopted by the instructed classes, and then it will be time to found the national creed upon the assumption of their truth.

—*J. S. Mill to John Sterling*

Mill's *On Liberty* (1859) is widely regarded as a classic if not "sacred" evocation of the liberal conception of liberty.[1] The essay, however, like the term *liberty*, has been the subject of a confusing and contentious array of divergent interpretations. Classical and modern liberals, socialists, libertarians, historicists, positivists, and others have read it as an endorsement of their particular notion of liberty—negative, positive, individual, social, inner, political, and so on. Although its internal coherence as well as its consistency with Mill's corpus have at times been challenged, the ideas and practices championed in *On Liberty* are widely thought to constitute one of the most complete expressions of the modern conception of liberty. However accurate such a view may be, one thing does seem clear: The majority of Mill's commentators share his assumptions to such a degree that they have failed to perceive or attend to what is arguably the most significant aspect of the essay—what we have called Mill's antitheological intent and what Joseph Hamburger has identified as its "anti-Christian theme."[2] As this work has attempted to show, Mill's corpus cannot adequately be comprehended without taking account of the antitheological impetus that informed all his philosophic activity. This is true, above all, of *On Liberty*. Few Mill scholars, however, have explored the significance of Mill's religious views and aspirations, and especially of his profound commitment to the Religion of Humanity, for the development of his thought.[3] What needs to be emphasized is the astonishing reach of Mill's ambition and the seriousness of his intent to found a new religion.

What follows is intended as a supplement to the conventional interpretations of *On Liberty* and not as a definitive or comprehensive treatment. Although Mill's plea for freedom from conventional opinion and practice may of course be evaluated on its merits—that is, apart from Mill's own intent and purposes—a proper interpretation of the essay requires a recognition of that intent. In particular, we are interested in the role that Mill conceived *On Liberty* to play in furthering his dual purpose—to eradicate the "poisonous root" of theological belief and so prepare for the growth and establishment of the Religion of Humanity and the new moral order it embodied. In elaborating that role, we draw upon Hamburger's important article "Religion and *On Liberty*." The reason for highlighting Hamburger's work is that he is one of the few scholars to have recognized both the nature and significance of Mill's engagement with religion. According to Hamburger, *On Liberty* was an integral component of a comprehensive plan designed by Mill and his wife in the 1850s, a two-part plan that aimed to realize what we have identified as Mill's dual goal—to undermine Christianity and institute a new social religion. Whether or not the Mills consciously devised such a plan is uncertain; the evidence is inconclusive. Hamburger's suggestion is entirely plausible and consistent with all of Mill's writings and intentions, but we have not found such a plan expressly discussed in his writings. Nevertheless, even if Mill did not actually devise a concrete plan, he certainly did aim precisely for the two goals we have identified and he certainly did consider his writings instrumental to their realization.

The Provisional Value of Freedom

On Liberty, then, was intended to play a crucial role in the fulfillment of Mill's dual purpose and, more particularly, in the achievement of the first stage of his two-part plan—the undermining of Christian belief. As we recall, Mill believed that one of the chief props sustaining the moribund and obsolete Christianity of his day was the absence of free discussion, perpetuated by the long-standing taboo within English society against religious criticism. The most effective way to assist the further corrosion of the decrepit foundation of Christian belief was to subject such belief to the acid of free and untrammeled criticism. As Mill put it to Comte, what England needs is "that freedom which France happily enjoys: the freedom of saying everything. *This above all is what we lack at present, for the only questions that make no progress at all today are those where public opinion prevents any real discussion*" (*Corr*, 377, emphasis added). Mill is referring to the only freedom available in post-Revolutionary France unavailable in the liberal heyday that was Victorian society—the freedom to criticize religion. For Mill, as for Saint-Simon and Comte, the inevitable "progress" of thought from theology to positivism demanded an interim period of destructive criticism of received views. In Mill's case, such criticism was intended to serve a demolition function essential to preparing for the growth of the Religion of the Future—the Religion of Humanity.

We have seen that the youthful Mill had thoroughly embraced the Saint-Simonian philosophy of history. According to this philosophy, history is characterized by alternating "critical" and "organic" periods. The critical periods are transitional phases during which the passing beliefs of the old order gradually give way to the new stable belief system that characterizes an organic or "normal" state of mind and society. We have also seen that Mill's "Spirit of the Age" was entirely modeled on the Saint-Simonian philosophy of history and especially on its conception of the present age as an "age of transition." The Mill of *On Liberty* bears a marked resemblance to the Mill of "The Spirit of the Age." In both works his thought seems to be structured by the Saint-Simonian conception of organic periods punctuated by periods of transition. First, although he does not mention it in *On Liberty*, we know from contemporaneous writings that at the time he was writing that essay Mill was dreaming of a final future state unified emotionally, morally, and intellectually by its commitment to the Religion of Humanity.[4] Such a state clearly corresponds to the organic or "normal" state as characterized by Saint-Simon and Comte, and even to their conception of the final positive stage that is the "end of history." Even more transparently, Mill's defense of freedom of discussion in *On Liberty* is entirely in keeping with the Saint-Simonian conception of a "transitional" period in human thought and society, such as Mill conceived his own period to be. Mill alludes to this fact in his diary entry of January 22, 1854, during the period in which *On Liberty* was composed:

> In this age a far better ideal of human society can be formed, and by some persons both here and in France has been formed, than at any former time. But to discern the road to it—the series of transitions by which it must be reached, and what can be done, either under existing institutions or by a wise modification of them, to bring it nearer—is a problem no nearer being resolved than formerly. The only means of which the efficacy and the necessity are evident, is universal Education: and who will educate the educators?[5]

The Saint-Simonians had a clear view of the role that freedom of discussion was to play in the movement of history. Its task was to serve as something like a midwife, assisting the transition from the unsettled critical state to the stable organic state. As Richard Pankhurst describes the Saint-Simonian view: "Freedom as found in the Anglo-Saxon world led to anarchy and a confusion of opposing beliefs which could not be viewed as the final end of humanity; it was, however, a necessary transitional phase offering free scope to the idea which could rally all its rivals to it and thus conduct humanity to the great unity desired of God."[6] In the Saint-Simonian view, in short, freedom of discussion was not only essential to the final destruction of the outworn beliefs of the past "organic" state, but also to permit the emergence of the new ideas henceforth destined authoritatively to govern human society. Comte had embraced a similar understanding of the temporary, provisional, or instrumental value of freedom of discussion in an age of transition. As Mill put their mutual idea in "The Spirit of the Age," the majority of "mankind must, and *except in periods of transition like the present,* always do, take the far greater part of their opinions on all extensive subjects upon the authority of those who have studied them" (emphasis added). As we shall see, certain curious remarks in *On Liberty* suggest that Mill's understanding of the value of freedom of discussion remained very much in accord with that of his French brethren and his own earlier view. That is, there are indications in that work that Mill conceived of freedom of discussion as one of those provisional institutions essential to certain stages of society, such as the present age of transition, but destined to become less necessary as mankind advanced to the final organic or "normal" stage.

As we recall, one of Mill's purposes in writing the *System of Logic* was to establish the *method* by which thinkers would arrive at the unanimity of opinion that, in turn, would assure the ascendancy of the modern spiritual power. In *On Liberty,* by contrast, Mill presses for the greatest possible diversity of belief on the grounds that the perpetual antagonism of conflicting opinion, an "active controversy with opponents," is essential to the discovery of complete and not merely partial truth. What should be emphasized, however, is that Mill conceived such controversy as issuing ultimately in a "consolidation of opinion"—"a consolidation," he says, that is "as salutary in the case of true opinions, as it is dangerous and noxious when the opinions are erroneous." The Mill of *On Liberty* continued to believe that the unanimity of opinion for which he had yearned throughout the 1830s and 1840s—the "gradual narrowing of the bounds of diversity of opinion"—was both "inevitable and indispensable." Indeed, he was so convinced that such a unanimity would be the ultimate outcome of freedom of discussion that he makes express provision for it in *On Liberty.* The context is Mill's argument that an ongoing struggle of conflicting opinions is essential to the vital apprehension of truth, to the maintenance of a living belief that shapes soul and character. This argument leads Mill to a peculiar conundrum. Convinced that the dialectical confrontation of opposing views for which he contends will ultimately result in unanimity of opinion, his old desiderata, he asks whether the struggle of contending opinions—that is, "the absence of unanimity"—is in fact "an indispensable condition of true knowledge." His answer is straightforward: "I affirm no such thing. As mankind improve, the number of doctrines which are no longer disputed or doubted will be constantly on the increase; and the well-being of mankind may almost be measured by the number and gravity of the truths which have reached the point of being uncontested. . . . [Such a] narrowing of the bounds of diversity of opinion is necessary in both senses of the term, being at once inevitable and indispensable" (OL, 44–46).

Mill is perfectly clear that we may expect to reach an ever greater—and utterly desirable—unanimity of opinion in the future, although he is also concerned with the inevitable problems that will accompany that achievement. For as truth is discovered, accepted first by the elite and then by the masses, there will no longer exist the antagonism of opinion that is essential, he believes, for holding truth as "living truth" and not mere "torpid assent." As said, Mill is so convinced that unanimity will be the outcome of freedom of discussion that he proposes a solution to the attendant problem of maintaining the existential significance of truth in the absence of antagonism and controversy:

> [I]f opponents of all important truths do not exist, it is indispensable to imagine them, and supply them with the strongest arguments which the most skilful devil's advocate can conjure up. . . .
> . . . [T]he teachers of mankind [must] endeavour . . . to provide a substitute for [the lack of real controversy]; some contrivance for making the difficulties of the question as present to the learner's consciousness, as if they were pressed upon him by a dissenting champion, eager for his conversion. (OL, 39, 45)

Mill singles out the Socratic dialectic and the method of disputation of medieval scholasticism as models of such "contrivances."

In his discussion of the value of diverse "experiments in living" in Chapter III of On Liberty, Mill further indicates his belief that the freedom he advocates may be a merely provisional necessity in the present transitional state.[7] In a passage championing the need for such experiments, he says:

That mankind are not infallible; that their truths, for the most part, are only half-truths; that unity of opinion, *unless* resulting from the fullest and freest comparison of opposite opinions, is not desirable, and diversity not an evil, but a good, *until* mankind are much more capable than at present of recognising all sides of the truth, are principles applicable to men's modes of action, not less than in their opinions. . . . As it is useful that *while mankind are imperfect* there should be different opinions, so it is that there should be different experiments of living. (*OL*, 57, emphases added)

Commentators have long been perplexed by this strange implication of Mill's argument for liberty—as more and more truths are discovered, there seems to be less and less need for freedom. On its face, such an implication appears irreconcilable with Mill's trial-and-error philosophy of experience, of perpetual experimentation and progressive movement toward truth. Mill's model, however, while seemingly championing a creative fluidity and openness, actually moves toward closure and stationariness (toward the "end of history"?). Mill was not a modern evolutionary epistemologist; he firmly believed that truth, in morals and politics as in science, could be discovered once and for all.[8] Mill, the passionate proponent of progress—the "Movement-man," as he once characterized himself[9]—had a peculiar and simultaneous yearning for stationariness, which he also feared and dreaded. Such a yearning was evinced, for instance, in his portrayal of the "stationary state" of classical economics in a flattering light. In contrast to the general uneasiness and even gloom this anticipated end state induced among his fellow economists, Mill emphasized the possibilities for moral and cultural development available to those who had moved beyond the pursuit of mere commercial values.[10] Even as a young man Mill seemed to dread the possibility of closure, of stationariness, of lack of movement and creativity. There is a pathetic passage in the *Autobiography* in which he expresses his fear that all the possible combinations of musical notes may have been or may soon be exhausted. This apprehension of the end of novelty, growth, and creativity casts a curious light on the ostensible philosopher of progress. And, as we have seen, Mill's conception of justice was profoundly static: a state of lifeless and immobile perfection wherein each person receives the precise temporal reward or punishment justly deserved by his moral behavior and character. Mill had many demons.

Silence on Religion Revisited

We know that throughout his life Mill engaged in a meticulous and conscious self-censorship with respect to the subject of religion. Although we have emphasized the strategic aspects of Mill's policy of "total silence," other factors shaped his approach to the religious question as well. More particularly, there were potential penalties for religious criticism beyond the alienation of the reading public, especially the possibility of facing legal prosecution for blasphemous libel. As Hamburger explains, "blasphemous libel" had been

> defined by Blackstone as an offense "against God and religion." It included denying the being or providence of the Almighty, contumelious reproaches of Christ, and all profane scoffing at the holy scripture or exposing it to contempt and ridicule. Its status was reinforced by the doctrine, traced back to Hale, that Christianity was part and parcel of the laws of England, and therefore, "to reproach the Christian religion is to speak in subversion of the law." ... Blasphemous libel was a political offense, for its rationale depended on the belief that public hostility to Christianity damaged the regime. Thus while blasphemous libel, as hostility to the Almighty, could be regarded spiritually, it could also be regarded temporally as affecting the peace and good order of society. This latter prospective was legally the most significant.[11]

Prosecutions under these laws were frequent up to the early 1830s and continued sporadically into the twentieth century. Mill was not only well aware of such prosecutions but at times came to the active defense of individuals prosecuted for expressing anti-Christian views.[12] Mill's writings, including *On Liberty*, are replete with references to various such prosecutions that occurred throughout the century. In short, the climate of the time made the expression of anti-Christian views potentially dangerous, with penalties and costs severe enough to have served as a deterrence. The chief result of the libel laws was to drive criticism of Christianity underground. James Fitzjames Stephen, arguing against the laws on blasphemous libel in 1875, said that "they forced serious and quiet unbelievers to take up a line of covert hostility to Christianity," an implicit reference to John Mill.[13] Mill's "policy of prudent concealment" was partly founded upon correct assumptions. There were real, legal dangers attached to the public expression of religious criticism, although such dangers were more pronounced in the early decades of the century than the later.

Nevertheless, such dangers do not fully account for Mill's strategic silence on the question of religion and God. In the *Autobiography*, Mill tells us that one consequence of his unusual upbringing was the early development of what he called his "instinct for closeness," a habitual reserve and even guardedness that would remain with him throughout his life. As we have seen, Mill's secretiveness was reinforced by another of his father's lessons. His father's unconventional views on religion had "one bad consequence deserving notice. In giving me an opinion contrary to that of the world my father thought it necessary to give it as one which could not prudently be avowed to the world" (52). In this as in other respects Mill remained true to his father's teachings.

The result of these influences was that Mill early developed what Hamburger calls his "habit of prudently dissembling."[14] This habit derived from his lifelong fear of alienating potential converts by an untimely expression of his own unorthodox religious views. As Mill put it, he feared that his true religious views, "if unseasonably declared, might deprive [him] of a hearing altogether."[15] Mill did share his genuine views with members of his intimate circle, which at various times included Alexander Bain; John and Sarah Austin; Thomas Carlyle; some of the Benthamite radicals such as George Grote; certain of his French correspondents, especially d'Eichthal and Comte; other friends and disciples such as John Sterling and John Morley; and, of course, Harriet Taylor. According to Henry Reeve, the editor of the *Edinburgh Review* who knew the Mill family for more than fifty years, Mill and the other Benthamites held "certain esoteric doctrines on the relation of man to God and to a future state, which they did not willingly make known." Reeve also believed that Mill and his friends behaved sensibly in withholding their true views from the public: "They judged rightly—that if they disclosed to its full extent their absolute rejection of the principles of religious faith and of the accountability of man to God . . . they would stand but little chance of obtaining a hearing on any other subject."[16]

Other of Mill's close acquaintances, however, believed that he prolonged his silence on religion far longer than was necessary under the changed circumstances of English public opinion, that is, the growing liberality throughout the nineteenth century with respect to that topic. Mill himself comments on the wisdom of his policy of self-censorship and the changed requirements of his time in the *Autobiography*. He also uses the occasion to interject a little moral lesson regarding the righteousness of unbelief:

> This great advance in liberty of discussion, which is one of the most important differences between the present time [1873] and that of my childhood, has greatly altered the moralities of this question . . . . [I feel that] few men, holding with such intensity of moral conviction as [my father] did, unpopular opinions on religion, . . . would now either practice or inculcate the withholding of them from the world. . . . On religion in particular the time appears to me to have come, when it is the duty of all who being qualified in point of knowledge, have on mature consideration satisfied themselves

that the current opinions are not only false but hurtful, to make their dissent known. . . . Such an avowal would put an end, at once and for ever, to the vulgar prejudice, that what is called, very improperly, unbelief, is connected with any bad qualities either of mind or heart. The world would be astonished if it knew how great a proportion of its brightest ornaments—of those most distinguished even in popular estimation for wisdom and virtue—are complete skeptics in religion. (53)

Such was the background to and the social environment in which Mill prepared *On Liberty,* a knowledge of which is essential to an adequate comprehension of that essay.

Before exploring what Mill intended to achieve through the publication of *On Liberty,* however, we should briefly consider one other issue that has a bearing on its interpretation. Mill, while shrewd and deliberate, was of a less cunning nature than his father and of a less cavalier one than Bentham. As a result, he was not altogether at ease with the prudent policy that he had chosen to follow with respect to religion. Moreover, Mill had the sternest of Calvinist consciences and an image of himself as a devoted pursuer and proponent of truth. He also greatly admired people who exhibited forthrightness and the courage of their convictions, as well as the Romantic commitment to authenticity and self-expression. In short, Mill's moral seriousness, his yearning for Romantic freedom, and his pronounced self-assertiveness sat ill with his lack of candor in expressing his true views on religion. The pain and pressure of living a lie weighed on him heavily, as did the need to suppress what he regarded as the superior truth and morality of his convictions. Hamburger observes that "there are indications [Mill] personally felt inhibited by an environment that generated, if not fear, at least apprehension about the publication of unpopular religious opinions."[17] We may recall that Mill's letters to Comte often expressed a yearning envy for what he regarded as the true freedom that prevailed in France—"the freedom of saying everything"—that is, the freedom to criticize religion, even to the point of proclaiming one's atheism if one pleased.

Mill's *Autobiography* provides additional insight into the existential motivation that inspired his defense of absolute freedom of discussion in *On Liberty.* His father's counsel of concealment, he observes, was "attended with some moral disadvantages" (*Auto,* 52). The choice, as it seemed to John Mill, was between a dangerous "avowal" of unpopular opinions or "hypocrisy." The dilemma created by Mill's conflicting desires—the desire for candor and self-assertion on the one hand and his equally weighty desire for influence and reputation on the other—engendered a powerful psychic tension that would find release in the passionate rhetoric of *On Liberty*. The years of painful repression issued in the highly charged emotion that makes that essay such an enduringly powerful evocation of the urgent moral necessity of free thought and expression.

There is a passage from *On Liberty* that is utterly expressive of the personal inhibition and pain Mill obviously experienced as a result of his decision to suppress his heterodox religious views. Mill is lamenting the oppressive mental environment he experiences around him, the fact that his "country is not a place of mental freedom." The reason for this, he says, is the "social stigma" attached to the expression of nonconventional religious belief. This stigma

> induces men to disguise [their] . . . heretical . . . opinions . . . [and the] price [they pay] for this sort of intellectual pacification, is the sacrifice of the entire moral courage of the human mind. A state of things in which a large portion of the most active and inquiring intellects find it advisable to keep the general principles and grounds of their convictions within their own breasts, and attempt, in what they address to the public, to fit as much as they can of their own conclusions to premises which they have internally renounced, cannot send forth the open, fearless characters, and logical, consistent intellects who once adorned the thinking world. (34–35)

Mill, indeed, claims to have experienced Victorian society in the fullness of classical-liberal freedom as unfree, a place where everyone "live[s] under the eye of hostile censorship" (*OL*, 61). His contemporaries were astonished by this outburst and could not find a basis for Mill's complaint. This is not surprising inasmuch as Mill's feeling of oppression seems to have been the result not of social or political conditions but of his own long-standing repression of powerfully held unorthodox religious views. As said, what Mill longed for was the French "freedom of saying everything." He longed above all to speak his mind fully and freely with respect to his passionate religious convictions, convictions he regarded as not only vastly superior to the still-regnant theological morality but indispensable to the moral and intellectual improvement of mankind. It is this existential urgency to proclaim his own new faith and lead others to the light that rings out in every line of *On Liberty*.

The Philosopher as Politician

To properly appreciate *On Liberty* it is also helpful to situate that work in the context of Mill's shifting philosophical and political activities. From Mill's first appearance on the scene in the early 1820s until the end of the 1830s, his major reform efforts were political in a narrow sense, that is, concerned with institutional reform. His main ambition during these early years, like that of the philosophical radicals in Parliament whom he helped to organize and lead, was to reform the British constitution. As Hamburger summarizes it, Mill's aim in his first incarnation as political activist was "to provoke nothing less than a realignment of political parties in order to establish an independent Radical party led by his close associates. Realigned parties would reflect, respectively, the popular and the aristocratic interests in society, and ultimately their antagonism would lead to the democratization of the constitution. This scheme occupied Mill during the 1830s." Although Mill's "greatest wish" during these years was to be a member of Parliament, his position at India House precluded its fulfillment.[18] He thus turned to journalism as the main vehicle through which to influence the activities of the radicals in Parliament.[19] It is greatly to the point of this study that, during those years, as Mill acknowledged in the *Autobiography,* his politics were almost fanatically ideological and doctrinaire. As Hamburger explains, Mill

> was insistent that reform be fundamental, thorough, *total,* and he was entirely opposed to half-measures. The Radical party and no other was the agent by which reform was to be achieved. . . . [H]e was contemptuous of the moderate Left . . . and . . . anxious to . . . separate Radicals even from liberal Whigs. There was a willingness to be alone in virtuous isolation rather than compromise. . . . Mill, like the other Philosophic Radicals, was convinced that an independent Radical party could be established and realignment could be effected. Believing that there was an underlying reality of class conflict and a latent radicalism in the populace that could be brought to the surface, he thought there was no great difficulty in transforming institutions and redefining party boundaries. The expectation that great changes could be quickly accomplished seemed reasonable because he thought his tactics were grounded in reality. Thus Mill could believe in what he called "the practicability of Utopianism."[20]

Mill's hopes for a Radical party were to be disappointed. The English people, as he complained, proved far too wedded to the flexible and compromising spirit of Whiggism to throw themselves wholeheartedly behind the doctrinaire democratism of the Millian "irreconcilables."[21] The most important result of the disappointment of Mill's hopes for thoroughgoing and even total institutional reform was to turn his ambition from direct political engagement toward more theoretical activities—what Comte liked to call "philosophical action." Marx, in this respect as in others, was something of a latecomer: His famous assertion that the point of philosophy is not to understand the world but to change it had also been the conviction of post-Revolutionary French thinkers such as Comte. Mill was utterly in sympathy with such an outlook.

The failure of the philosophical radicals to achieve reform through the parliamentary process led Mill to abandon his hopes and efforts to achieve reform through such means. He came to realize, with Comte and others, that true reform could be achieved only by first transforming the opinions and beliefs of the populace. As a result, Mill redirected his focus after 1840. He decided, as he wrote to a friend, that "the progress of liberal opinions will again . . . depend upon what is *said & written*, & no longer upon what is *done*."[22] This is the point at which Mill wholeheartedly embraced his role as philosopher. Or, as Hamburger puts it, Mill now "undertook to develop the ideas and beliefs that would shape the politics of a future generation. . . . [He] became the architect of a new world, as he sought to visualize the kinds of institutions that would be suitable for mankind once it entered a new historical era in which the prevailing, established authorities and traditions would be without force."[23]

Hamburger's remarks are coherent with Mill's embrace of the Saint-Simonian philosophy of history and his lifelong effort to replace traditional religious authority and religion-infected custom with a nontheological or purely human equivalent. The first fruit of Mill's newly focused efforts was his *System of Logic* (1843), written sporadically during the 1830s and rapidly brought to completion upon Mill's retirement from politics at the end of the decade. The second such fruit was *Principles of Political Economy*, brought to market in 1848. As discussed earlier, both of these works served Mill's purpose—implicitly to inculcate the positivist worldview that he intended as a replacement for the historically obsolete theological state of mind. As Mill put it, the aim of these works was to "make new trains of thought intelligible" in order to facilitate the "mental regeneration" of Europe that he now believed prerequisite to the realization of the dreamed-of future society.[24]

"The Reconstruction of the Human Intellect"

By the 1850s, as Hamburger observed and Mill himself acknowledged, substantial political, legal, and economic reform had been achieved in the direction Mill desired. Nevertheless, he remained dissatisfied and explained why in the early draft of what eventually was published as his *Autobiography*.[25]

> In England, I had seen and continued to see many of the opinions of my youth obtain general recognition, and many of the reforms in institutions, for which I had through life contended, either effected or in course of being so. But these changes had been attended with much less benefit to human well being than I should formerly have anticipated, because they have pro-

duced very little improvement in that on which depends all real amelioration in the lot of mankind, their intellectual and moral state. . . .

. . . I had learnt from experience that many false opinions may be exchanged for true ones, without in the least altering the habits of mind of
which false opinions are the result. The English public . . . have thrown off
certain errors [but] the general discipline of their minds, intellectually and
morally, is not altered. *I am now convinced, that no great improvements in the
lot of mankind are possible until a great change takes place in the fundamental constitution of their modes of thought.* . . . [What is needed is] a renovation . . . in
the bases of belief.[26] (emphasis added)

In his diary entry of February 18, 1854, Mill reiterated this belief and again
revealed the astonishing sweep of his reformist ambition:

Nine-tenths of all the true opinions which are held by mankind are held for
wrong reasons. And this is one cause why the removal, now so constantly
going on, of particular errors and prejudices does not much improve the
general understanding. The newly admitted tenth commonly rests on as
mistaken principles as the old error. *What is the remedy? There can be none
short of the reconstruction of the human intellect ab imo* [from the bottom up].[27]
(emphasis added)

All of this is of importance for an adequate interpretation of *On Liberty*,
for that essay was one of the instruments by which Mill sought to realize
this goal—the "reconstruction of the human intellect *ab imo.*"

As this work has attempted to show, Mill's purpose from the time of his
first conversion to Benthamism until his death was to replace a "theological" orientation with a "purely human" equivalent (*OL*, 50–51). Thus it
is not surprising that by the 1850s Mill, in collaboration with his wife, had
developed a more or less conscious strategy toward that end. Their plan
to create a new moral and social world depended crucially upon the destruction or transformation of traditional religious beliefs and values. For
it was such beliefs and values that not only had generated and sustained
the traditional political order Mill sought to re-form but were also largely responsible for the "habits of mind" that prevented the improvement
of "the general understanding." In the language of this study, lingering
traditional religious beliefs prevented the widespread embrace and social
establishment of nontheological utilitarianism and the substitution of Humanity for God.

As we recall, in the 1850s Mill had written a set of essays designed to
constitute a concentrated expression or "mental pemican" of his principal
views: the essays on justice and utility eventually published as *Utilitarianism*, the essay eventually published as *On Liberty*, and the posthumously published essays "Nature" and "Utility of Religion." According

to Hamburger, each of these works was designed as a facet of Mill's comprehensive plan. The plan, Hamburger explains,

> was to complete the undermining of crumbling Christianity and to prepare for the acceptance of his version of utilitarian morality, which was to be incorporated into and be reinforced by the "Religion de l'Avenir," for which [Mill] adopted the phrase "Religion of Humanity." . . . Arguments in each [of the essays that constitute the "mental pemican"] were intertwined with and complemented one another, and all of them, including *On Liberty*, were written to implement the plan. Therefore each should be interpreted in tandem with the other writings of the 1850s and in light of Mill's ambitious proposal to reconstruct the human intellect.

Hamburger summarizes Mill's plan:

> First, it was necessary to clear away the false notions and bad mental habits that prevented the growth of something better. These bad mental habits were closely linked to morality and religion. Mankind, [Mill] said, possessed a "grossly immoral pattern of morality which they have always set up for themselves in the person of their gods, whether of revelation or of nature." This was a "poisonous root" that had to be extirpated. Among advanced thinkers this had been achieved, but not with the mass of mankind. [As Mill said,] "The old opinions in religion, morals, and politics . . . have still vitality enough left to be an effectual obstacle to the rising up of better opinions on the same subjects." This undergrowth—and [Mill] had in mind, mainly, Christianity-infested custom—had to be cleared away in order to accomplish a renovation in the basis of belief, "leading to the evolution of another faith, whether religious or not."

Mill's plan is undoubtedly familiar to readers of this work, as is Hamburger's conclusion: For Mill, "[t]he elimination of Christianity . . . was a matter of policy." *On Liberty* was intended as an essential instrument in the execution of that policy. One of its chief purposes was to engender the absolute freedom of discussion that, Mill believed, would prove fatal to the preservation of traditional religious belief. With the ground thus cleared of this "poisonous root," the way was open toward the establishment of the new purely human moral and social world. The celebrated essay was an integral component of Mill's "grandiose plan for human improvement," a plan that *essentially* involved religion and especially Christianity.[28]

Christianity and Christ

As has been emphasized, the fact that Mill engaged in rigorous self-censorship with respect to the subject of religion means that one must interpret his published work with care. Yet a close reading of *On Liberty* in the light of Mill's avowed antitheological aims and intent makes the anti-Christian theme of the essay not merely discernible but obvious. The aim of the essay, and especially Chapter II, is to justify an extension of freedom of discussion to include all "received opinion" (*OL,* 26). The received opinion to which Mill most often points is Christianity, while the view said to challenge that opinion is religious heterodoxy or skepticism. We know that Mill, like Saint-Simon and Comte, believed liberty of discussion to be one of the most effective ways, if not *the* most effective way, to erode traditional religious belief. In "Utility of Religion" Mill draws a straightforward relation between such liberty and the erosion of traditional belief: "[F]or exactly in proportion as the received systems of belief have been contested, and it has become known that they have many dissentients, their hold on the general belief has been loosened, and their practical influence on conduct has declined" (408).

As Hamburger points out, the fact that Mill perceived a relation between freedom of discussion and the evisceration of Christian belief may also be inferred from the way he constructs the argument in *On Liberty* and especially in Chapter II.[29] One of Mill's arguments for liberty of discussion concerns its value as a means to sift truth from error. Mill posits three possible effects from such liberty: Either the heretical opinion would be shown to be true, shown to be false, or shown to contain a portion of the truth. The way Mill presents the argument, however, Christianity would be undermined regardless of which of the three possible outcomes prevailed, that is, even if Christianity were shown to be true. Obviously, if the skeptical or heretical opinion were found to be true, Christianity would be undermined. Even, however, if the received doctrine (Christianity) were shown to be true, Mill suggests, it would probably not survive vigorous and free discussion. This is because the history of suppression of spirited critical and heretical views has reduced Christian belief to little more than "dead dogma, not a living truth."[30] Mill had long believed that his contemporaries gave to Christian belief a merely "dull and torpid assent"; it was a creed that "remain[ed] as it were outside the mind" (*OL,* 26, 33). As he put it in 1832, "Christianity, instead of a spirit pervading the mind, becomes a crust encircling it, nowise penetrating the obdurate mass within, but only keeping out such rays of precious light or genial heat as might haply have come from elsewhere."[31] Mill argued that most ethical doctrines and religious creeds were vulnerable to such a deadening of once vital belief, but he regarded this as especially true of contemporary Christianity. He thus expected that the lukewarm and poorly understood beliefs of his Christian contemporaries would crumble upon their exposure to "free and vigorous discussion" conducted among contestants who included such formidable and experienced advocates as himself. As Mill said, in a social environment characterized by such discussion, "beliefs not grounded on conviction are apt to give way before the slightest semblance of an argument" (*OL*, 27).

From Mill's point of view, moreover, the third possible outcome of freedom of discussion—that both the received and the heretical opinion may be shown to contain a portion of the truth—would also serve to undermine traditional Christianity. Mill did believe that Christianity, like other philosophical and religious systems, contained "a portion of truth." This notion of the "many-sidedness" of truth had been one of Mill's cherished convictions since the time of his rebellion against doctrinaire Benthamism. As we have seen in our discussion of his religious writings, Mill thought that what was of value in Christianity could be separated from its morally and intellectually pernicious elements.

The "part" of Christianity that Mill thought would be exposed for the falsehood it is and that would ultimately succumb to free inquiry was what he called theological morality or the "system of ethics erected on the basis of [Christ's deliverances] by the Christian Church" (*OL*, 50). Moreover, we know that Mill was concerned to eviscerate not merely theological or transcendental morality, but the traditional Christian conception of an omnipotent and all-benevolent God as well (see Chapter 7). It is worthy of note that Mill does not broach the subject of his new probable limited god in *On Liberty*, as he does in the simultaneously composed "Nature" and "Utility of Religion." This makes sense; if *On Liberty* was carefully crafted to engender freedom of discussion in service of undermining traditional religious views, it is not likely that Mill would wish to alarm his readers by introducing his controversial conception of a new God in that essay.

The part of Christianity, on the other hand, that may contain a portion of the truth and that may survive the critical attack on received opinion certain to be engendered by freedom of discussion is, Mill suggests, the ethical ideal embodied in the historical Christ. Indeed, Christ is the only aspect of Christianity that escapes Mill's condemnation in *On Liberty*, as well as in "Theism." In those works Christ is represented as a "sublime genius," "the ideal representative and guide of humanity," a "standard of excellence and a model for imitation." The ideal of Christ, as well as certain of his doctrines and precepts, if separated from the rest of Christianity, might continue to serve humanity after its incorporation into non-theological or humanitarian utilitarianism. Although Christ never intended to provide a "complete rule for our guidance, . . . the sayings of

Christ . . . are irreconcilable with nothing which a comprehensive morality requires. . . . [T]hey contain, [however,] and were meant to contain, only a part of the truth. . . . [M]any essential elements of the highest morality are among the things which are not provided for [in the recorded words of Christ]." The point Mill wished to emphasize was that "other ethics must exist side by side with Christian ethics to produce the moral regeneration of mankind" (*OL*, 51). "Other ethics" refers to his own non-theological utilitarianism and various elements of pagan ethics.

Mill's belief that the gold could be sifted from the dross of Christian belief and practice should be kept in mind in interpreting his often laudatory and even reverential statements about Christ. His praise of Christ as a model for imitation in *On Liberty* did not affect his fundamental judgment of Christianity in that work any more than it had in "Theism." For Mill, as Hamburger says, "evaluated Jesus in a fundamentally different way from the theological and institutional development of Christianity since its founding."[32] This is something of an understatement. As we know, Mill specifically rejected the divinity of Christ and claimed that Christ had never regarded himself as God. It is perhaps unnecessary to note that, however one may wish to "purify" or improve Christianity or even to replace its dogma with existential apprehension, one surely cannot remove the dogmatic notion that Christ is God and claim to have preserved Christianity. Nor, needless to say, is the substitution of Humanity for the transcendent Christian God compatible with Christianity.

We have seen that the new de-divinized Christ was very useful to Mill. He could be regarded as an exemplar of virtue by everyone, believers and unbelievers alike, including, as Hamburger emphasizes, those "who rejected Christianity and accepted the Religion of Humanity as a substitute."[33] For, as Mill explained in "Theism": "[R]ather than God, [it is Christ] Whom Christianity has held up to believers as the pattern of perfection for humanity . . . [and, as such,] is available even to the absolute unbeliever." Mill carefully consoled his audience, most of whom had been shaped by the Christian tradition to one degree or another, that "whatever else may be taken away from us by rational criticism [that is, the theological foundation for belief], Christ is still left." Mill speaks as reverentially of Christ in *On Liberty* as in "Theism." As suggested, however, this seems to have been an aspect of his conversion strategy; an appeal to Christ could be instrumental to the realization of Mill's ends. The reorientation of traditional religious emotion attached to the historical Christ, like that of inherited supernatural hopes, toward Mill's proposed substitute could greatly assist the "due ascendancy" of the latter. As Mill suggested, the traditional Christian inducements to good are "excellently fitted to aid and fortify that real, though purely human religion, ... the Religion of Humanity" ("The," 487–88). Mill goes so far as to suggest that Christ intended mankind to adopt the Religion of Humanity. He also aggressively refashions Christ in his own utilitarian image: "[I]n the golden rule of Jesus of Nazareth, we read the complete spirit of the ethics of utility. To do as one would be done by, and to love one's neighbour as oneself, constitute the ideal perfection of utilitarian morality"[34] (*Util*, 418). Mill seems to have conceived Christ, like Socrates, as something like a prophet or messenger from God sent to preach the utilitarian gospel.[35] In short, Mill's promotion of a de-divinized Christ did not represent a departure from his lifelong animus toward Christianity and his goal of instituting the Religion of Humanity.[36] As suggested, his aim seems to have been to enlist the supernatural hopes engendered by Christian faith, as well as feelings of reverence for Christ, to further the "due ascendancy" of the Religion of Humanity by creating an association between them in his readers' minds. Hamburger, like Collins and the author of this work, perceives a conscious strategy behind Mill's effort to "combine ... Christianity, in a special sense of the word, ... with the Religion of Humanity." Such an approach, he thinks, permitted Mill "to appear conciliatory, and it reduced the appearance of hostility to Christianity without requiring that he modify his religious skepticism or his harsh judgment of the ethical and political consequences of Christianity."[37] Hamburger's statement is consistent with all we know of Mill's aims, but it is incomplete. There seems to have been more to Mill's strategy than an attempt to appear conciliatory.

The Establishment of the Religion of Humanity

Such was the role Mill intended *On Liberty* to play in implementing the first stage of his plan—the "dismantling of Christianity."[38] The second stage involved the establishment of the Religion of the Future, the Religion of Humanity or Duty. As we have seen, Mill's commitment to the social institution of a Religion of Humanity, in one form or another, was long-standing, manifesting itself at least as far back as his 1821 conversion to Benthamism. The greatest (temporal) happiness principle, combined with the evisceration of transcendent justice and man's accountability to God, is equivalent to the investment of ultimate value in a "service to Humanity" understood in nontheological utilitarian terms. We also know that under the influence of Comte and his second conversion experience in 1841, Mill came to believe that the "inevitable substitution" of Humanity for God may be at hand, that the imminent establishment of a full-fledged Religion of Humanity was possible and even probable. In short, Mill's commitment to the establishment of an intramundane substitute for theological religion was unwavering. From first to last he was utterly devoted to founding a new moral order and society oriented exclusively and ultimately toward the Great Being of Humanity. Mill's last words on religion were a passionate attempt to bring his Christianized fellows into the fold, and they constitute as strong an appeal for the acceptance of the Religion of Humanity as anything he ever wrote.

As discussed, Mill had long subscribed to the Saint-Simonian and Comtean view that the critical philosophy or negative theology of the eighteenth-century philosophes was insufficient to accomplish the most pressing task of the era—moral and social regeneration. Mill, like various other reformers of his era, experienced the loss of traditional religious belief as a spiritual void and saw the insertion of a new spiritual substance as an urgent necessity. As he had written in his diary on January 23, 1854: "There is no doctrine really worth labouring at, either to construct or to inculcate, except the Philosophy of Life. A Philosophy of Life, in harmony with the noblest feelings and cleared of superstition [that is, traditional religion] is the great want of these times."[39] What was needed was a "positive" substitute for the feeble if not "dead beliefs" of Christianity, and Mill set himself diligently to this task. Comte's Religion of Humanity provided the framework for his efforts. Although the majority of modern commentators seem to take Mill's rejection of Comte's "despotic" social system in *On Liberty* as evidence that Mill came to reject Comtean philosophy *in toto*, this is far from true.[40] Mill *was* hostile to the institutional and ritualistic aspects of Comte's version of the Religion of Humanity, as well as to various illiberal aspects of Comte's social doctrine, but he championed the substance of Comte's humanitarian religion until the end of his days. The thoughts inscribed in Mill's diary on January 24, 1854, at the time he was drafting *On Liberty* and the other essays intended to constitute his "mental pemican," remained his settled view until the end:

> The best . . . thing in Comte's second treatise [*Système de politique positive*] is the thoroughness with which he has enforced and illustrated the possibility of making *le culte de l'humanité* perform the functions and supply the place of a religion. If we suppose cultivated to the highest point the sentiments of fraternity with all our fellow beings, past, present, and to come, of veneration for those past and present who have deserved it, and devotion to the good of those to come; universal moral education making the happiness and dignity of this collective body the central point to which all things are to tend and by which all are to be estimated, instead of the pleasure of an unseen and merely imaginary Power; the imagination at the same time being fed from youth with representations of all noble things felt and acted

heretofore, and with ideal conceptions of still greater to come: there is no worthy office of a religion which this system of cultivation does not seem adequate to fulfil. It would suffice both to alleviate and to guide human life. Now this is merely supposing that the religion of humanity obtained as firm a hold on mankind, and as great a power of shaping their usages, their institutions, and their education, as other religions have in many cases possessed.[41]

This latter task was to be assigned to the modern "spiritual power"—unorganized, it is true, but performing the same substantive function envisioned by Comte. As we have seen, Mill anticipated the problems that would inevitably arise once unanimity of opinion among the elite secured the ascendancy of truth and the "national creed" to be founded upon it. We have also seen that "Utility of Religion" was written to show not only *that* but also *how* the new replacement for Christianity could achieve social effectiveness after the freedom of discussion championed in *On Liberty* had done its work. All that was required was control of the same resources "as other religions have in many cases possessed."

Mill made extraordinary claims for his new religion. It would constitute a "real religion" that fully embodied the "essence of religion—the strong and earnest direction of the emotions and desires towards an ideal objected, recognised as of the highest excellence, and as rightfully paramount over all selfish objects of desire" ("UR," 422, 410). Indeed, the Religion of Humanity would serve humanity's religious needs much more effectively and fully than had the supernatural religions concerned with "the pleasure of an unseen and merely imaginary Power." As Mill puts it in "Utility of Religion," the Religion of Humanity "is not only capable of fulfilling [the] functions [traditionally performed by transcendent religion], but would fulfil them better than any form whatever of supernaturalism. It is not only entitled to be called a religion: it is a better religion than any of those which are ordinarily called by that title" (422). Mill was utterly convinced of the superiority of his own spiritual and moral conceptions and aspirations to those of his contemporaries, a conviction which permitted him to say that the best of the unbelievers "are more genuinely religious, in the best sense of the word religion, than those who exclusively arrogate to themselves the title"[42] (*Auto,* 54). In *Auguste Comte and Positivism,* Mill not only defends Comte's Religion of Humanity but holds it up as the very model of religion: "We . . . not only hold that M. Comte was justified in the attempt to develope [*sic*] his philosophy into a religion, and had realised the essential conditions of one, but that all other religions are made better in proportion as, in their practical result, they are brought to coincide with that which he aimed at constructing" (137).

Mill's diary and contemporaneous works such as "Utility of Religion" clearly reveal Mill's full commitment to the Religion of Humanity during the years he was planning and writing *On Liberty*. This is of interest in light of the fact that Mill did not explicitly identify the Religion of Humanity in *On Liberty* or in any other works published in his lifetime—with the exception of *Auguste Comte and Positivism* (138). As we know, the reason for such an omission was not lack of commitment, but the prudent and strategic policy of "total silence" on religion that Mill had consciously adopted at least as early as the 1840s. Mill implicitly points to his policy of silence in further remarks in *Auguste Comte and Positivism*: "[Comte's] religion is without a God. In saying this, we have done enough to induce nine-tenths of all readers, at least in our own country, to avert their faces and close their ears. To have no religion, though scandalous enough, is an idea they are partly used to; but to have no God, and to talk of religion, is to their feelings at once an absurdity and an impiety" (132). Mill's implicit acknowledgment of his lack of candor with respect to his true religious convictions and aspirations is supported by the wealth of material in his private correspondence that documents not only his prudence but the strategic considerations that shaped his policy of "total silence" as well.

Liberty and the Social Sanction

On Liberty significantly departs from Mill's other writings of the period in a manner that bears on our subject. We have seen that Mill's habitual strategic prudence with respect to religion accounts for his failure to make any explicit reference to the Religion of Humanity in *On Liberty*. Mill, however, not only fails to mention the Religion of Humanity explicitly in that work, but in contrast to his other contemporary writings such as "Utility of Religion" and *Utilitarianism*, he also scarcely alludes to the ethical ideals it embodies. The reason for this omission is of significance for a proper reading of the work, and especially for an adequate interpretation of the role that liberty played in Mill's thought. It also sheds light on Mill's *modus operandi* as a philosopher-reformer, and, more particularly, on the tension produced in his philosophical works by the overwhelming importance he attributed to his practical agendas. Mill's penchant for polemics and the strength of his desire for both practical and religious reform often meant that his ostensibly theoretical reflections were actually driven by less than disinterested purposes. In short, in many of Mill's works, and certainly in *On Liberty*, "rhetorical considerations prevailed."[43] Mill, as suggested, was very far from the disinterested observer and thinker he imagined himself to be.

Hamburger's explanation of Mill's failure to mention his religious and ethical aspirations or ideals in *On Liberty* is persuasive:

> The distinguishing features of the Religion of Humanity were its ideal of unity and fraternity with others, altruism, and condemnation of selfishness and hedonism—that is, motivations and interests which, in the language of *On Liberty*, are other-regarding. Yet in *On Liberty*, obviously, other-regardingness had the stamp of restraint and control, and it was the rationale for interference. Thus to uphold a new doctrine that made virtues of other-regarding conduct in a book celebrating liberty, apparently with few qualifications, would have undermined those arguments for liberty that served to implement the first, anti-Christian stage of Mill's plan for the reconstruction of the human intellect. . . .
>
> It is understandable that provision for restraints would be played down in a work that also defended liberty, spontaneity, and individuality, for to include it in *On Liberty* would have created an appearance of contradiction, and it would have reduced the impact of the liberty that Mill welcomed as a catalyst to the scepticism about Christian doctrine and the morality and the custom it sanctioned. Yet Mill's acceptance of restraints is clear in *Utilitarianism* and "Utility of Religion" [and perhaps even more dramatically in "Nature"], works written contemporaneously with *On Liberty*. This alerts us to what must have been Mill's deliberate obscurity regarding it in *On Liberty*.[44]

The recognition that *On Liberty* was designed to realize the first part of Mill's plan—to undermine Christianity—sheds light on what even the most devoted of Mill's disciples must recognize as the internal inconsistency of that essay: As Hamburger notes, Mill categorically condemns the use of public opinion as a social sanction (in Chapter II) while defending its use as a weapon against various forms of antisocial behavior (in Chapter IV). The reason is clear: Mill's actual target is not the *social* sanction of public opinion per se but the *religious* sanction as embedded in custom and prejudice. It is entirely appropriate and indeed necessary, Mill argues in Chapter IV, to express disapproval of undesirable behavior. One has a right to do so in any way short of legal persecution, including shunning the society of undesirables. Moreover, although Mill seems to be championing an unbridled freedom from the sanction of public opinion, he himself attaches overwhelming significance to public opinion as a regulating force in society. As we recall, in "Utility of Religion" and elsewhere, Mill, following Bentham, characterizes the all-important *human* sanction of public opinion as *the* governing force in any society, and he regards the shaping of the opinion underlying that sanction as the chief task of educators and moralists. All of this is in stark contradiction to the condemnation of the social sanction in certain sections of *On Liberty*. What this suggests, in light of all we know of Mill's aims and purposes, is that his argument in *On Liberty* against the legitimacy of coercive public opinion was chiefly directed against opinion shaped by traditional *religious* beliefs and not against such opinion in general. The aim of *On Liberty* was to destroy the conventional prejudice against the expression of heterodox religious views and the practices they engendered and sustained. Mill knew full well the importance of the "social stigma" to the regulation of human behavior, and he had no wish to declaw that sanction *except* in the case of traditional religious belief and the customs derived from it.

Although Mill seems to be attacking the "despotism of custom" in general, then, what he actually objects to is custom that derives from and that embodies traditional religious views (*OL*, 70). In *Utilitarianism,* as we shall see, Mill is more than willing to embrace customary morality, provided it is accepted as the result of utilitarian trials over time and not regarded as the revelation of a divine moral law. He fully intended that new customs, incorporating the nontheological morality and Religion of the Future, would take root and prevail: "I have said that it is important to give the freest scope possible to uncustomary things, in order that it may in time appear which of these are fit to be converted into customs" (*OL*, 67). Such was the very purpose of allowing "experiments in living." The Millian hero, akin to the superman of Nietzsche, was to establish the practices that would eventually become customs—customs derived, however, from a secular or human and not a theological standard (*OL*, 52). Mill also reiterates in *On Liberty* the "superior few" theory of the origin of customs (71) that he articulated in "Nature" (see Chapter 3, page 109).

In short, it seems that Mill's object in *On Liberty* was to champion a general freedom not, as it appears and is generally thought, from the restraints of all social convention, but merely from convention and custom derived from traditional religion. As discussed, such an interpretation is supported by the contemporaneously composed "Utility of Religion," which emphasizes the omnipotence of the *human* sanction of public opinion in governing human behavior. In that essay, Mill describes "the power of public opinion; of the praise and blame, the favour and disfavour, of [men's] fellow creatures; . . . [as] a source of strength inherent in any system of moral belief which is generally adopted, whether connected with religion or not" (410–11). As we recall, an emphasis on the power of the social sanction was central to the Benthamite-Millian attack on the allegedly selfish and immoral "posthumous" or religious sanction. Such an emphasis was also necessary to show the ease with which Christian belief and values may be replaced with those associated with the Religion of Humanity and nontheological utilitarianism; all that is required is a command over the means by which public opinion is shaped. Thus in

"Utility of Religion" Mill emphasizes the far-flung power of such opinion. Public opinion, he says, not only possesses a "deterring power" but can entail serious positive penalties as well, including ostracism, loss of favor, and even the means of subsistence, as well as "ill offices of various kinds." Mill also anticipates in that essay a solution to the problem of the socially recalcitrant, that is, those who require something more than the pressure of public opinion to change their moral outlook in accord with the new humanitarian religion. These, says Mill, may be "made to feel . . . [an] absolute obligation towards the universal good" by means of the "superadded force of shame" (410–11, 421). As these examples and others in his writings show, Mill was far from averse to employing the social sanction of public opinion in suppressing what he regarded as socially undesirable ("selfish") behavior and encouraging what he regarded as its opposite ("altruism").

This evaluation of the potential benefits of public opinion is dramatically at odds with that found in the early chapters of *On Liberty*, where conventional opinion is condemned for suppressing the development of individuality. The inconsistency of *On Liberty*, both internally and in relation to Mill's other writings, was demanded, however, by his rhetorical strategy in that essay. His aim was to invoke the maximum freedom from conventional social opinion regarding the expression of unpopular or heretical religious views. Accordingly, he was led to disguise or at least to deflect attention from his own genuine view—the indispensability of the social sanction of public opinion to effecting essential moral restraints. The religious agenda that governed the structure of *On Liberty* led Mill to champion a far-flung freedom from social opinion that he himself did not fully support.[45]

Mill's rhetorical difficulties in *On Liberty* were compounded by the methods he intended to use to establish mass belief in the new religion. Such methods were difficult, if not impossible, to reconcile with the valorization of individuality and the championing of expansive liberty in that work. For, as we shall see, Mill's new social morality and Religion of Duty would require the suppression of much self-regarding (selfish) behavior in service of the "absolute obligation towards the universal good." To draw attention to this in an essay ostensibly promoting a far-flung liberty was not politic.

Conscience and Restraint

In *On Liberty*, Mill is quite critical of the negative rules—the "thou shalt nots"—associated with traditional Christian morality. He especially condemns the inner restraints he attributes to Calvinism and its attempt to stifle spontaneity and the exercise of human will. As noted in Chapter 3, such views contradict Mill's own call for the utter emendation of human nature and his utter hostility to the "natural man" in the contemporaneously composed "Nature." Indeed, the ideas expressed in *On Liberty* and "Nature" are so inconsistent that only a rhetorical strategy of the kind suggested by Hamburger could make sense of them. As discussed, the purpose of *On Liberty* seems to have been to establish those conditions most conducive to the erosion of traditional religious belief and the customs derived from it. Thus, to avoid the most blatant inconsistency, Mill downplayed in that work the extensive role that social sanctions and various restraining rules were to play in shaping the new men of the future oriented toward the Religion of Humanity. As suggested, once the purpose of *On Liberty* is recognized, the conflicting views presented in that essay and "Nature" are at least comprehensible, if not more coherent.[46]

Further, despite Mill's attack in *On Liberty* on the conventional constitution of his fellows' conscience (one largely shaped by a traditional Christian ethos), he was most eager to enlist the support of conscience in service of the Religion of Humanity or Duty. Indeed, Mill fully anticipated that future adherents of the new religion and its neo-utilitarian moral standard would honor its precepts from an internalized sense of duty. That is, he intended that they would have a conscience shaped by the dictates of the new humanitarian utilitarianism. As he said, the "ultimate sanction" for utilitarian morality, as for any other standard, would be the "conscientious feelings of mankind," an issue to which we will return in the following chapter (*Util*, 229).

For now, let us note that Mill was most concerned with the formation of conscience and its role in regulating human behavior. In line with James Mill's associationist psychology, John Mill believed that the content of human conscience was essentially formed by an intense process of training and psychological association, and, as such, was utterly amenable to the ministrations of educators, parents, and other preceptors. He included the "internal inducement" or self-reproaches of conscience as one of the "punishments," along with law and the opinion of one's fellows, for failure to do one's duty. Hamburger points out the obvious: "[T]he fact that such a conscience would be a restraint, a kind of inner censorship, that reduced spontaneity and range of choice was not objectionable when it was in the service of his Religion of Humanity."[47] The principal conscientious restraints to which Mill seemed opposed were those associated with "theological morality," for the Religion of Humanity or Duty, as Mill presented it, required a formidable amount of self-restraint. As Mill says in "Nature": "[T]he duty of man is the same in respect to his own nature as in respect to the nature of all other things, namely not to follow but to amend it." Moreover, it seems that Mill's new Religion of Duty may require a good deal of restraint of other people as well as of the self. As he says in *On Liberty*, "All that makes existence valuable to any one, depends on the enforcement of restraints upon the actions of other people" (9). He is even more to the point in *Utilitarianism*: "It is a part of the notion of duty in every one of its forms, that a person may rightfully be compelled to fulfil it. Duty is a thing which may be exacted from a person, as one exacts a debt. *Unless we think that it may be exacted from him, we do not call it his duty.* Reasons of prudence, or the interest of other people, may militate against actually exacting it; but the person himself, it is clearly understood, would not be entitled to complain" (454). Despite what he appears to suggest in *On Liberty*, Mill was very far from advocating a spontaneous freedom from restraint or an unbridled development of individuality. Mill's failure to mention his new Religion of Humanity or Duty in an essay ostensibly promoting individual liberty is more than understandable.

There is, however, something disturbing and even sinister about Mill's combination of an intense intramundane religiosity and what amounts to Skinnerian behaviorist psychology. We may recall Mill's discussion in "Nature" of the notorious difficulty of acquiring the essential self-discipline of delayed gratification. That virtue, says Mill, is more capable than any other of being self-taught because it may be learned through personal experience, that is, because the "rewards and punishments" necessary to acquire it are administered directly by nature. "Nature does not of herself bestow [self-discipline or self-control], any more than other virtues; but nature often administers the rewards and punishments which cultivate it, and which in other cases have to be created artificially for the express purpose" ("Nat," 395). Mill suggests that in the case of all other virtues, the necessary rewards and punishments have to be "artificially created" by the Educator and other authorities.

What Mill called for, in effect, was a massive socialization of the populace oriented toward the "absolute" duty to serve humanity ("[u]nless we think that it may be exacted from him, we do not call it his duty"). As Hamburger describes Mill's conception, "All of an individual's experiences were to be organized to create and sustain a commitment to the new utilitarian ethic of the Religion of Humanity."[48] Lest this seem too strong a view to be attributed to the putative defender of liberty and individuality, here are Mill's own words:

> If we now suppose this feeling of unity to be taught as a religion, and the whole force of education, of institutions, and of opinion, directed, as it once

was in the case of religion, to make every person grow up from infancy surrounded on all sides both by the profession and by the practice of it, *I think
that no one, who can realise this conception, will feel any misgiving about the sufficiency of the ultimate sanction for the Happiness morality.* (*Util*, 436, emphasis
added)

The Religion of Humanity or Duty, in short, was to be generated and sustained through an intensive and comprehensive process of socialization
directed toward unity with all mankind, "whose service is to be the law
of our life." It is clear that Mill conceived this process as Bentham had:
It would use "laws and social arrangements" designed to place the happiness or interest (Mill often ambiguously conflated these two concepts)
of each individual in harmony with the general good or collective happiness. These laws would be supplemented by "education and opinion,
which have so vast a power over human character." As a result of each individual's intensive exposure to such a socialization process, he would
come to regard his own happiness as "indissolubly" bound up with the
good "of the whole." As Mill said, the hoped-for effect was "not only [that
the individual] may be unable to conceive the possibility of happiness to
himself, consistently with conduct opposed to the general good, but also
that a direct impulse to promote the general good may be in every individual one of the habitual motives of action and the sentiments connected therewith may fill a large and prominent place in every human being's
sentient existence" (*Util*, 418–19). The task of interpreting the constitution
of this "general good" was assigned to the utilitarian legislator or moralist. Nor is there an allowance for any allegiance higher than the general
good of humanity.

In light of the above considerations, it is difficult to dispute Hamburger's conclusion: "When one considers the accumulated effects of education, public opinion, and the trained conscience that internalizes the
morality of the Religion of Humanity, one is left with an individual that
was indoctrinated, socially pressured, and internally restrained."[49] One
in fact is left with the new "social"-ist man, trained to regard the collective good of the whole as paramount over the good of any particular individual, trained, moreover, to regard the good of this intramundane
whole as the *ultimate* value, and trained to disbelieve in the notion of
man's accountability to God. Mill was at pains to emphasize that the aim
of the new morality was emphatically *not* the good of the individual: "I
must again repeat, . . . that *the happiness which forms the utilitarian standard
of what is right in conduct, is not the agent's own happiness, but that of all concerned*" (*Util*, 418, emphasis added). And, as we have seen, the last words
Mill wrote on religion were meant to dispel the illusion of a justice beyond
the human.

"Miserable Individuality"

We have suggested that *On Liberty* should be understood as one of the instruments by which Mill sought to realize his long-standing religious purpose: to undermine Christianity and institute the Religion of Humanity. This purpose governed the structure and content of that work and led Mill to propound views at odds with his actual convictions. As we have seen, Mill did not wish to declaw coercive public opinion in general but only such opinion and sanctions that embodied traditional religious belief. *On Liberty* is thus far from representative of Mill's considered views on the subjects of personal liberty and individuality and, indeed, contains much that is in flagrant contradiction to his own ethical views and social aspirations.

Let us look at a final example of this incongruity, one that supports the notion that *On Liberty* was governed essentially by rhetorical considerations in line with Mill's antitheological aims. As we will discuss more thoroughly in the following chapter, one of the core moral elements of Mill's neo-utilitarianism and his Religion of Humanity is the condemnation of selfishness. On various occasions, Mill identifies selfishness with individuality, as well as with Christianity. For instance, in *Utilitarianism*, composed more or less contemporaneously with *On Liberty*, Mill identifies the "selfish egotist" as one who is "devoid of every feeling or care but those which centre in his own miserable individuality" (*Util*, 415). As Hamburger observes, such "miserable individuality" stands in stark contrast to the enthusiastic and celebrated promotion of individuality in Chapter III of *On Liberty*. In that essay Mill portrays the self-regarding realm as the realm of individual freedom and flourishing. In numerous other remarks, however, he is far less enthusiastic about self-regarding behavior. Examples include the mentioned reference to "miserable individuality" and his characterization of the moral end of the Religion of Humanity—the good of the whole and *not* the happiness of the individual. Moreover, Mill often identifies self-regarding activity with selfishness—the greatest sin of his social religion. Further, as we shall see, despite Mill's condemnation of "Christian self-denial" in *On Liberty*, he explicitly commends self-renunciation, the sacrifice of personal happiness, in service of the new "ideal object," Humanity. Such is not commonly associated with the spontaneous flourishing of individuality.

Mill was in fact quite contemptuous of the individuality of the common man. He often complained of the dismally low level of his contemporaries' moral and intellectual development, which he usually attributed to prevailing social institutions and the absence of qualified leadership. His remarks in the *Autobiography* give a good indication of his opinion of his contemporaries. There Mill condemns the

low moral tone of what, in England, is called society; the habit of . . . taking
for granted . . . that conduct is of course always directed towards low and
petty objects; the absence of high feelings which manifests itself . . . by general abstinence . . . from professing any high principles of action at all . . .
[and] the absence of interest in things of an unselfish kind. . . . [All of this,
in the English,] causes both their feelings and their intellectual faculties to
remain undeveloped . . . ; reducing them, considered as spiritual beings, to
a kind of negative existence. (62–63)

We may also recall Mill's evaluation of the quality of his fellow human beings in "Nature," where he complains about the kind of God who produced creatures as primitive as the likes of "Patagonians, or Esquimaux,"
and who could do no better than to endow them with merely the capacity for development. After centuries of struggle, this capacity has produced only a few human beings capable "of being improved in centuries
more into something really good" (390–91). As we have seen, Mill had no
great regard for the present stage of development of the mass of men.

Indeed, Mill indicates in *On Liberty* his unfavorable evaluation of the
actual individuality of the majority of his contemporaries, whom he describes as "starved specimens of what nature can and will produce" (60).
As he says in "Nature," the overwhelming majority may possess the
"germs" of virtues, but these germs require a great deal of artificial cultivation to produce human beings worth having (see page 109). Mill did
expect that, upon the establishment of the Religion of Humanity and
through decades of training and socialization, the masses might someday
be raised to the level of full-fledged human beings. But he did not seem
to regard their individuality as worth promoting in itself. Further, Mill's
characterization of human nature in "Nature" reveals his invective
against the "Calvinist theory" of human nature in *On Liberty* for the
rhetorical device it is. Calvinism is attacked in the latter essay for making
self-will "the one great offence of man" because this is useful to Mill's purpose in that particular passage—to promote what he calls "Pagan self-assertion" in contradistinction to "Christian self-denial" (*OL*, 62). This of
course serves the overall anti-Christian purpose of the essay.[50]

That Mill's aspirations for the common man were not for the free unfolding of his individuality but for his socialization in the direction of humanitarian ideals is further suggested by some remarks in *Utilitarianism*.
Mill is discussing how the "feeling of unity with mankind" may serve as
a satisfactory substitute for traditional religious aspirations. He knows
this may be difficult to imagine, especially considering the "actual feelings" of the majority of his contemporaries. "If differences of opinion
and of mental culture make it impossible for [an adherent to the Religion

of Humanity] to share many of [his contemporaries'] actual feelings—
perhaps make him denounce and defy those feelings—he still needs to be
conscious that his real aim and theirs do not conflict; that he is not opposing himself to what they really wish for, namely their own good, but
is, on the contrary, promoting it" (436). In other words, although one may
not actually be able to experience a "unity of feeling" with one's fellows,
one may console oneself with the fact that by helping to establish the Religion of Humanity one is helping those unenlightened fellows to achieve,
whether they know it or not, "their own good." Mill apparently knows
what his fellows "really wish for," whether or not they themselves are
aware of it. His remarks are not merely presumptuous, but chilling in their
political implications.

Mill's actual view of the "miserable individuality" of the mass of selfish men was prudently left unstated in *On Liberty*, for it would have been
impossible to reconcile with that essay's passionate plea for freedom from
social (religious) convention in the name of individuality.

"Purely Human" Morality

Hamburger points out that while Mill refrains for rhetorical purposes
from overtly advocating the Religion of Humanity and his neo-utilitarian
social morality in *On Liberty*, a careful reader will nevertheless find muted references to them. For instance, recall Mill's suggestion that "other
ethics than any which can be evolved from exclusively Christian sources"
must supplement the ethical principles embodied in Christ's life and articulated in his precepts; "other ethics," again, largely refers to nontheological utilitarianism. Mill, however, also expressly calls for the revival of
"Pagan . . . morality" and especially its conception of "duty to the State."
He reiterates the view he expressed in "Utility of Religion" of the superi-
or morality embodied in pagan civic virtue. Indeed, Mill sounds like no
one so much as Rousseau in his indictment of Christian morality for the
fact that it "scarcely notice[s] or acknowledge[s] . . . that grand department of duty. . . . What little recognition the idea of obligation to the public obtains in modern morality, is derived from Greek and Roman sources,
not from Christian; as, even in the morality of private life, whatever exists
of magnanimity, highmindedness, personal dignity, even the sense of
honor, is derived from the purely human, not the religious part of our education, and never could have grown out of a standard of ethics in which
the only worth, professedly recognised, is that of obedience."

Mill, then, explicitly differentiates the purely human ethics he advocates from Christian morality, which, he says, "should rather be termed

theological morality" (*OL*, 50). It is thus clear that the principal distinction between the morality he rejected and that he propounded, as Mill himself understood it, was between a morality believed to have its source and end in God, on the one hand, or in Man, on the other. As this work has aimed to show, the dichotomy between theological and purely human morality structured Mill's thought and religious aspirations from his first conversion to Benthamism through his final advocacy of the Religion of Humanity in "Theism." The enemy, as Mill conceived it, was transcendent, theologically based ethics, whether represented as traditional Christian morality, moral-sense theory, "in-itself" or transcendental morality, or intuitionism along the lines of Hamilton. His own ideal was a purely human, secular, nontheological ethics, one constructed by the best and the wisest specimens of humanity, which was itself conceived as the ultimate ground and end of value. Once Mill's overriding purpose—to replace theological with human morality in the sense just described—is recognized, the notorious contradictoriness and inconsistency of his work is reconciled. His work is consistent in that it all aimed to realize this governing purpose. Indeed, as suggested in Chapter 1, the replacement of God with Humanity was one of the governing purposes of Mill's public career.

Promethean Self-Assertion

Let us examine Mill's contention in *On Liberty* that Christian morality "is essentially a doctrine of passive obedience." This, he says, stems from the fact that the ideal of Christian or theological morality is

> negative rather than positive, passive rather than active, Innocence rather than Nobleness; Abstinence from Evil, rather than energetic Pursuit of Good: in its precepts . . . "thou shalt not" predominates unduly over "thou shalt." In its horror of sensuality, it made an idol of asceticism. . . . It holds out the hope of heaven and the threat of hell, as the appointed and appropriate motives to a virtuous life: in this falling far below the best of the ancients, and doing what lies in it to give to human morality an essentially selfish character, in disconnecting each man's feelings of duty from the interests of his fellow-creatures, except so far as a self-interested inducement is offered to him for consulting them. (*OL*, 51)

For Mill, Christianity is the religion of the selfish. The Religion of Humanity, the implicit alternative, is, by contrast, fundamentally concerned with "connecting each man's feelings of duty with the interests of his fellow-creatures." We will discuss Mill's long-standing dichotomy between the bad of "selfishness" and the good of the "social" more thoroughly in the following chapter.

What is of present interest is Mill's condemnation of Christianity for its inculcation of passivity and his related elevation of the virtue of "Pagan self-assertion." Mill warns of the "grave practical evil" that has arisen from education based solely on Christian doctrine. He is particularly concerned that a one-sided Christian education tends to eviscerate the human will and human agency: "Any attempt . . . to form the mind and feelings on an exclusively religious type, and discarding those secular standards . . . which heretofore co-existed with and supplemented the Christian ethics, . . . is even now resulting [in the formation of] a low, abject, servile type of character, which, submit itself as it may to what it deems the Supreme Will, is incapable of rising to or sympathizing in the conception of Supreme Goodness" (*OL*, 52). We might recall that Mill seemed to claim knowledge of the constitution of the "supreme goodness." As he says in "Theism," those who accept his limited probable god are "enabled to form a far truer and more consistent conception of Ideal goodness, than is possible to any one who thinks it necessary to find ideal goodness in an omnipotent ruler of the world" (486).

As noted previously, Mill was far from immune to the Promethean impulse that impelled Marx and Nietzsche and various other nineteenth-century titans. How he rails against the "Calvinist theory" of human nature, which conceives "the one great offence of man [as] Self-will" and which thinks human nature requires no other capacity than "that of surrendering . . . to the . . . alleged . . . will of God." How he decries the "pinched and hidebound type of human character which [Calvinist theory] patronises," the "cramped and dwarfed" human beings it produces by "wither[ing] and starv[ing] their capacities." The result is not only an incapacity for strong desires or pleasure but the complete evisceration of human nature. In short, in the Calvinist view, "[a]ll the good of which humanity is capable is comprised in obedience . . . [to] authority." (As Mill's contemporaries observed, however, the evidence stands in blatant contradiction to Mill's assertions. Calvinism produced some of the most active and energetic personages to grace Anglo-American history, including, we might add, both the Mills, neither of whom suffered from lack of strong desire or excessive passivity.) Against such a warped view of human nature, Mill sets the "Greek ideal of self-development"—the "cultivat[ion] and unfold[ing] of human nature toward excellence." Mill here assumes a pronounced Aristotelian stance. He waxes eloquent over the possibility of creating a human being who is a "noble and beautiful object of contemplation," one capable of "high thoughts and elevating feelings." Mill's humanitarian-utilitarianism, however, is never far from the scene. He points out the beneficial social consequences of honoring such an ideal of self-development: It would "strengthen . . . the tie which binds every individual to the race, by making the race infinitely better worth belonging to" (*OL,* 62–63). This is important, of course, since the Great Being of Humanity will inevitably become the ultimate source and end of value.

The explicit praise of individuality and self-development in *On Liberty* poses a problem for the Mill interpreter who is aware of Mill's contempt for the so-called individuality of the common man. It may be helpful to recall in this context Mill's fluid, or perhaps kaleidoscopic, character. His acquaintance Henry Cole recounted a conversation in which Mill "talked about his own personal character which he bore with other people. With utilitarians, said he, he was a mystic—with mystics a Utilitarian—with Logicians a sentimentalist and with the latter a Logician."[51] With Calvinists, it seems, Mill was an Aristotelian. Aristotelianism was quite useful to the Mill of *On Liberty.* As discussed, Mill's aim *was* to advocate liberty of discussion, for this, he believed, would further erode conventional religious belief and custom. To do so in the name of individuality was undoubtedly a better strategy to employ among his *liberal* contemporaries than overtly to acknowledge his actual purpose. (Alexander Bain reported that in 1854, while *On Liberty* was being conceived and planned, Mill "told Grote that he was cogitating an essay to point out what things society forbade that it ought not, and what things it left alone that it ought to control. Grote repeated this to me, remarking—'It is all very well for John Mill to stand up for the removal of social restraints, but as to imposing new ones, I feel the greatest apprehensions.'"[52]) The valorization of freedom from social restraint in the name of individuality was well served by an emphasis on the spontaneous unfolding of human nature; thus the implicit appeal to Aristotle.

It may be useful to recall that *On Liberty,* more than any of Mill's other writings, was shaped and informed by the views of Harriet Taylor. Mill said this essay "was more directly and literally our joint production than anything else which bears my name" (*Auto,* 174). Certain of Taylor's youthful writings express profoundly Nietzschean themes, such as the demand for the most untrammeled freedom from convention for the superior few, the Great Souls, the Romantic geniuses. Her voice resonates throughout *On Liberty* and especially in its call for the widest possible freedom for the development of individuality. Moreover, Mill's praise of individuality was, in some fashion, undoubtedly sincere: He did aim to create the most propitious environment for the exercise of "Pagan self-assertion" by the superior few. As we have seen, the vigorous exercise of human will and agency by this elite was to provide the energy and activism needed to order this disordered world, which was governed, if at all, only by an inept if well-meaning God. The masses, on the other hand, were to be indoctrinated from infancy in the values and ethics created by the best and the wisest specimens of humanity.

In light of Mill's religious aims and aspirations and in light of the role he intended *On Liberty* to play in their realization, Hamburger suggests that his famous essay is most properly regarded not as a celebration of liberty and individuality but as "something of a religious tract."[53] The only thing we might add to this perceptive characterization is that, in one way or another, all of Mill's writings, and not merely *On Liberty,* were designed to realize his religious purposes. They were all, in their way, "religious tracts."

Utilitarianism

[U]tility is not only not a godless doctrine, but more profoundly religious than any other.

—*J. S. Mill*, Utilitarianism

I think [Comte] has superabundantly shown the possibility of giving to the service of humanity, even without the aid of belief in a Providence, both the psychological power and the social efficacy of a religion, making it take hold of human life, and color all thought, feeling, and action, in a manner of which the greatest ascendancy ever exercised by any religion may be but a type and foretaste . . .

—*J. S. Mill*, Utilitarianism

The observation with which we concluded the previous chapter is emphatically true of Mill's *Utilitarianism* (1863):[1] This work, like *On Liberty*, is most properly regarded as a religious tract. We have identified the essence of Benthamite utilitarianism as its nontheological character and have seen the extent to which Mill experienced Benthamism as a religion "in one among the best senses of the word." We have also seen the depth of his commitment to the replacement of Christianity with a Religion of Humanity. Thus it is not surprising that one of the pronounced, if implicit, subtexts of Mill's famous "revision" of utilitarianism is identical to that of *On Liberty*—its antitheological or anti-Christian theme. Indeed, *Utilitarianism* is Mill's most carefully crafted effort at proselytization and conversion on behalf of his new humanitarian faith. Its argument was specifically constructed to meet the prevailing objections of Mill's contemporaries to Benthamite utilitarianism and its aim throughout is to insinuate the new secular ethics and social "religion without a God" into the minds of its readers. Any comprehensive interpretation of the work must take Mill's religious purposes into account.

One of the chief problems Mill faced in his effort to replace both traditional Christian and utilitarian Christian ethics with a nontheological utilitarianism spiritually sustained by the Religion of Humanity was the prevailing negative attitude toward Benthamite utilitarianism. The majority of Mill's contemporaries regarded Bentham's philosophy as not only novel, but also as vulgar, immoral, and godless. It was thought not only to violate common sense and the inherited maxims of morality it embodied, but also to encourage both hedonism and selfishness and to remove God from moral considerations. It was such attitudes that shaped Mill's strategy in *Utilitarianism*. In order to make Benthamism more palatable to his contemporaries, he revised it to meet these common objections.[2]

The first important revision entailed the assimilation of common-sense morality into Mill's "neo-utilitarianism."[3] Despite his long-standing contempt for common-sense morality, Mill now argued that inherited moral rules embody the utilitarian lessons learned by previous generations and, as such, would remain valid under the new nontheological utilitarian dispensation.[4] His second and more well-known tactic was to meet the charge of vulgarity by incorporating the most elevated and refined pleasures of intellect and taste into the utilitarian calculus. Mill responded to charges of selfishness by emphasizing the "social feelings" wedded to the utilitarian ethos, or, as Hamburger puts it, "by associating the Comtean values of 'altruism,' 'fraternity,' and 'unity with others,' . . . [values] that were at the core of the Religion of Humanity," with the new ethos.[5] Utilitarianism, Mill said, would "establish in the mind of every individual an indissoluble association between his own happiness and the good of the whole" (*Util*, 418). Finally, Mill responded to charges of godlessness by boldly asserting that "utility is not only not a godless doctrine, but more profoundly religious than any other" (423). By such arguments, Mill aimed to create a more inviting version of Bentham's doctrine, one designed to allay his contemporaries' fears and meet their common complaints.

Mill begins by specifying his topic—the age-old controversy over the "foundation of morality," the "criterion of right and wrong," the nature of the *summum bonum*. Mankind, he says, is unfortunately no "nearer to being unanimous on the subject, than when the youth Socrates listened to the old Protagoras, and asserted . . . the theory of utilitarianism against the popular morality of the so-called sophist."[6] Mill assumes an Aristotelian framework for the discussion: "All action is for the sake of some end, and rules of action, it seems natural to suppose, must take their whole character and colour from the end to which they are subservient" (*Util*,

401–2). The end Mill has in mind is the Benthamite pursuit of a strictly immanent and temporal collective happiness.

Mill's opening move is to draw the battle line in the contemporary controversy in moral philosophy: The contest, as always for Mill, is between the intuitive and the inductive schools of ethics. As previously discussed, the intuitionists or moral-sense philosophers regarded the principles of morality as a priori, self-evident, in some manner *given* to human consciousness; they believed that human beings possess a "natural faculty, a sense or instinct, informing us of right and wrong" (*Util*, 402). Or, as Mill says, his opponents believe in the "immutable, ineffaceable, and unmistakable dictates of justice, which carry their evidence in themselves, and are independent of the fluctuations of opinion" (*Util*, 460). Inductivists such as Mill maintained, on the contrary, that the principles of morality, like all other human knowledge, are generalizations from experience. As Mill frames the issue, "According to the one opinion, the principles of morals are evident a priori, requiring nothing to command assent, except that the meaning of the terms be understood [that is, recognized]. According to the other doctrine, right and wrong, as well as truth and falsehood, are questions of observation and experience" (*Util*, 403).

What is equally important, the enemy school also contends for traditional "in-itself" morality, that is, for the conviction that an action may be intrinsically good or bad, and not, as the utilitarians maintain, good or bad because of the consequences it tends to produce. Mill allows that there is common ground between the "in-itself" and consequentialist moralists. Both schools not only believe in the possibility of a "science of morals" but also "recognise the same moral laws." Moreover, both believe that particular moral rules can be reduced to general principles and that individual moral acts involve not merely "direct perception" but the application of a law or principle to a particular case. Of greater interest, however, is the difference, as Mill conceives it, between himself and his opponents: The two schools "differ as to their evidence, and the source from which they derive their authority" (*Util*, 403). It is clear, in short, that the fundamental issue for Mill is not the *content* of moral rules—both the utilitarians and the antiutilitarians "recognise the same moral laws"—but their *source.* This—the ultimate source of morality—is what is at stake in Mill's lifelong battle with the "in-itself" moralists. As discussed, the essence of nontheological utilitarianism, in both its revised Millian and original Benthamite forms, is its rejection of transcendent or theologically grounded morality. Mill and Bentham will have a purely human morality, grounded in the good of humanity and oriented toward its service. Humanity replaces God not only as the ultimate object of allegiance but also as the ultimate source and sanction of morality.

Mill also complains that the a priori moralists, despite their claims to believe in a science of morals, do not try to reduce the various moral precepts or maxims they accept to "one first principle, or common ground of obligation." This of course was not true inasmuch as they regarded the "common ground of obligation" as obligation to God. Mill, however, aiming to eviscerate the notion of accountability to God, charges that his opponents either "assume the ordinary precepts of morals as of a priori authority, or lay down some generality not obviously authoritative. . . . Yet to support their pretensions there ought either to be some one fundamental principle or law, at the root of all morality, or if more than one, there should be a determinate order of precedence among them; and the one [first principle] or the rule for deciding between the various principles when they conflict, ought to be self-evident." Mill adverts to his lifelong belief that nonutilitarian morality, that is, traditional theological morality, is nothing more than arbitrary preference. As said, one of Mill's fundamental articles of faith was that the morality promoted by the Christian Church was a mere cover for the imposition of subjective feelings in the guise of moral law. As he says in the present context, the "nonexistence of an acknowledged first principle has made ethics not so much a guide as a consecration of men's actual sentiments." Moreover, the "absence of any distinct recognition of an ultimate standard," of an acknowledged "root of all morality," is a serious problem. It has "vitiated" or "made uncertain . . . the moral beliefs of mankind." Mill's purpose is to rectify the existing defect by the introduction of the indispensable and strictly objective "first principle"—the "root of all morality," the "ultimate standard . . . [or] source of moral obligation"—the principle of utility, or greatest happiness principle. (The discussion provides a good example of Mill's special strategy with respect to God and religion—"to deal with [a] subject as if religion did not exist." He merely omits reference to the first principle or "root of all morality" that would be in the minds of most of his readers—God. He will employ this strategy repeatedly in *Utilitarianism*.)

Mill further insists that the ultimate standard he proposes is not, despite appearances, a novel introduction. For, though they may be unaware of the fact, men do follow—and have always followed—the principle of utility in practice.

[It would] be easy to show that whatever steadiness or consistency . . . moral beliefs have attained, has been mainly due to the tacit influence of a standard not recognised. Although the nonexistence of an acknowledged first principle has made ethics not so much a guide as a consecration of men's actual sentiments, still, as men's sentiments, both of favor and of aversion, are greatly influenced by what they suppose to be the effects of things upon their happiness, the principles of utility, or as Bentham latterly called it, the greatest happiness principle, has had a large share in forming the moral doctrines even of those who most scornfully reject its authority.

Everyone really knows, Mill claims, that "the influence of actions on happiness is a most material and even predominant consideration in many of the details of morals, however unwilling to acknowledge it as the fundamental principle of morality, and the source of moral obligation" (*Util*, 403–4, 427).

What Utilitarianism Is

As said, Mill's aim in *Utilitarianism* was to present a revised version of Bentham's doctrine, revised to meet the various objections prevailing among his contemporaries. Mill is thus at pains to clarify precisely what utilitarianism is, for, he says, misunderstanding of the meaning of that doctrine is the main obstacle to its general reception.

The first misunderstanding of utilitarianism concerns its conception of pleasure. Utility, Mill explains, is neither opposed to nor exclusively identified with pleasure. Nor is it to be identified with gross pleasures. Utility includes the useful, the agreeable, the ornamental, beauty, amusement, and all the higher pleasures of the mind and feeling. Mill offers a succinct definition of utilitarianism: "The creed which accepts as the foundation of morals, Utility, or the Greatest Happiness Principle, holds that actions are right in proportion as they tend to promote happiness, wrong as they tend to produce the reverse of happiness." Happiness, he further explains, means pleasure and the absence of pain; unhappiness is identical to pain and the "privation of pleasure." The philosophical basis or ground of the doctrine is the "theory of life" that "pleasure, and freedom from pain, are the only things desirable as ends; and that all desirable things . . . are desirable either for the pleasure inherent in themselves, or as means to the promotion of pleasure and the prevention of pain." Note how Mill appropriates the notion of "pleasant-in-itself" to the consequentialist cause, a feat he will also accomplish with "virtuous-in-itself."

Mill first addresses the popular objection that the utilitarian conception is base and ignoble, for he is aware that utilitarianism excites "inveterate dislike" in many minds for this reason. "To suppose that life has . . . no higher end than pleasure—no better and nobler object of desire and pursuit—they designate utterly mean and groveling, as a doctrine worthy only of swine." Mill, who was convinced of nothing so much as his superiority to the common herd, was more than prepared to meet such a challenge. In response to those who characterize utilitarianism as a degraded conception of life and action, Mill stands firmly on the "higher ground" of taste and refinement. To those who think "human beings [are] capable of no pleasures except those of which swine are capable" he answers that human pleasures are far more elevated than those of a beast. Because human beings have more elevated faculties, they require more elevated pleasures to gratify them—the higher pleasures of "the intellect, of the feelings and imagination, and of the moral sentiments."[7] Against the common misconception of Benthamism, Mill contends that utilitarianism is entirely compatible with the fact "that some kinds of pleasure are more desirable and more valuable than others." Quality is as important as quantity in the estimation of pleasures. Mill proposes his celebrated test for the evaluation of pleasures: "Of two pleasures, if there be one to which all or almost all who have experience of both give a decided preference, irrespective of any feeling of moral obligation to prefer it, that is the more desirable pleasure. . . . [It is an] unquestionable fact that those who are equally acquainted with, and equally capable of appreciating and enjoying, both, do give a marked preference to the manner of existence which employs their higher faculties." The issue is closed. There is no further appeal beyond the judgment of the more experienced, or the majority of them if the experienced cannot achieve unanimity. "[T]his verdict of the only competent judges" must be accepted as "final" (*Util*, 406–11).

It may be noted that the common view of Benthamism that Mill is here refuting was indeed a caricature of Bentham's, and James Mill's, actual views. Both of these men personally acknowledged, as well as lived, their belief in the superior pleasure attainable through the cultivation of the mind over the senses. Mill describes his father's views in this regard in his *Autobiography*; James Mill, he says, "never varied in rating intellectual enjoyments above all others, even in value as pleasures, independently of their ulterior benefits" (*Auto*, 55–56). Bentham made numerous remarks along the same lines. His famous quip about "pushpin" being as good as "poetry" was just that, a quip, and not a settled philosophical conclusion. He often spoke of the pleasures of knowledge. John Mill's "revision" of utilitarianism may not have been the result of a significant new discovery but rather, as suggested, a more or less calculated response to popular objections to the doctrine, one designed to win converts to the utilitarian creed.

Mill is at his most characteristic in *Utilitarianism*, speaking in a lofty moral tone from the commanding heights of experience and wisdom. The essay is marked by a vigorous and confident self-assertion and was published during a period when Mill was at the height of his influence, enjoying his status as "mentor to the world."[8] *Utilitarianism*, like *On Liberty*, resonates with the voice of Harriet Taylor Mill. For instance, it was long one of the Romantic Harriet's decided views that, as Mill puts it, a "being of higher faculties requires more to make him happy, is capable probably of more acute suffering, and certainly accessible to it at more points, than one of an inferior type."[9] Such a "superior being" would "never really wish to sink into what he feels to be a lower grade of existence." The elevated desires of superior natures may arise from various causes: pride, love of liberty and independence, love of power, and love of excitement, "but its most appropriate appellation is a sense of dignity, which all human beings possess in one form or other."[10] In any event, although the superior being, graced with exceptional endowments and capacities, may be susceptible to both greater pleasures and greater pains, he is undoubtedly "happier than the inferior." If the inferior—those with lower capacities of enjoyment—appear happier, this is only because they are more easily satisfied: "[A] highly endowed being will always feel that any happiness which he can look for, as the world is constituted, is imperfect. But he can learn to bear its imperfections, if they are at all bearable. . . . It is better to be a human being dissatisfied than a pig satisfied; better to be Socrates dissatisfied than a fool satisfied. And if the fool, or the pig, are [of] a different opinion, it is because they only know their own side of the question. The other party to the comparison knows both sides"[11] (*Util*, 409–10).

The End of Collective Happiness

So much for the gross misunderstanding of the utilitarian conception of pleasure. Mill now turns to address the charge that utilitarianism is a doctrine of selfishness. His discussion will highlight the tension between his lingering classical-liberal impulse to defend individual liberty and individuality and his passionate yearning for a full-fledged social religion to replace traditional theological religion. The question at issue is how utility or happiness is to serve as the universal "directive rule of human conduct." Mill addresses the problem of how adherence to the utilitarian standard can produce the greatest net balance of general happiness if superior natures not only require more elevated pleasures to realize happiness but also have a greater capacity for suffering. This capacity may substantially reduce the net balance of happiness in a world governed by utilitarian principles. Mill's response is straightforward. The possibility that certain superior individuals may not achieve happiness through the embrace of the utilitarian standard poses no obstacle to its universal acceptance. For that standard, he emphasizes, is *not* concerned with the happiness of the individual: "[T]he utilitarian standard . . . is not the agent's own greatest happiness, but *the greatest amount of happiness altogether*" (*Util*, 412, emphasis added). Accordingly, even if the nobler characters are not themselves happier in a world governed on utilitarian principles, the fact is that their great contribution to humanity's well-being raises the total net sum of happiness in the world, and this is sufficient to realize the utilitarian ideal—"the greatest amount of happiness altogether."

We have emphasized, however, that one of the essential elements of nontheological utilitarianism was its emphatic truncation of human aspirations and ends—the restriction of the pursuit of happiness to that "confined within the limits of the earth"—with its implicit invalidation of any conception of happiness that incorporates an otherworldly dimension of experience. This should be kept in mind when interpreting Mill's explanation of the greatest happiness principle:

> According to the Greatest Happiness Principle, . . . the ultimate end, with reference to and for the sake of which all other things are desirable (whether we are considering our own good or that of other people), is an existence exempt as far as possible from pain, and as rich as possible in enjoyments, both in point of quantity and quality . . . This, being, according to the utilitarian opinion, the end of human action, [it] is necessarily also the standard of morality; which may . . . be defined [as], the rules and precepts for human conduct, by the observance of which an existence such as has been described might be, to the greatest extent possible, secured to all mankind; and not to them only, but, so far as the nature of things admits, to the whole sentient creation. (*Util*, 413)

The "ultimate end" of Mill's new religion is (collective) temporal happiness, the elimination of all earthly suffering. Mill is a forerunner of the various modern expressions of this view, from the social gospel movement to modern "liberation theology"—of all religious movements that conceive the ultimate end of religion as the radical elimination of earthly suffering. Indeed, as we will see, Mill's vision resembles in many respects the socialist and communist dream that inspired the great ideological movements of the last century.

Self-Renunciation

Utilitarianism presents a telling discussion of Mill's views on the subject of self-renunciation or self-sacrifice and its relation to his new purely human ethic and humanitarian religion. Mill, following Bentham, denounces the Christian conception of self-renunciation in service to God as pathological asceticism. He himself, however, valorizes a similar conception of self-renunciation, one oriented not toward God but toward his proposed replacement—Humanity. Mill's strategy is characteristic, if oblique.

According to Mill, his (unnamed) opponents regard self-renunciation as a "necessary condition of all virtue." This Mill emphatically denies. He recognizes that human beings have long lived—and that most continue to live—without happiness, but he denies that renunciation of that end is of any intrinsic value. In line with his policy of dealing with the subjects of his public writings as if religion did not exist, Mill never explicitly mentions the Christian view of self-sacrifice that he pointedly, if implicitly, condemns. Moreover, he deliberately mischaracterizes the view he implicitly opposes—the Christian ideal of self-renunciation. Mill was undoubtedly aware that such an ideal was never regarded as an end in itself but as the sacrifice of worldly happiness in humility toward God and in service of eternal life. In any event, Mill says, any "sacrifice which does not increase, or tend to increase, the sum total of happiness [in this world is] wasted" (*Util*, 418). What he undoubtedly means to suggest is that renunciation in service of the transcendent God, which does not necessarily produce any visible increase in the sum total of temporal happiness, is "wasted."

Having denied any intrinsic value to self-sacrifice, and having implicitly condemned the traditional Christian conception of that virtue, Mill resuscitates the virtue of self-sacrifice in service to the Religion of Humanity. Although self-sacrifice has no inherent value, there is a form of self-sacrifice that Mill not only allows but in effect sanctifies: absolute self-sacrifice in service of the ultimate utilitarian end—the temporal happiness of others. His aim is to reorient the traditional virtue of self-renunciation away from service to God and toward service to Humanity. Renunciation in service of the traditional God is wasted, but is of the highest value when it is for the sake of the new humanitarian ideal. Mill in fact utterly embraces the renunciation of self and happiness in his own case and that of his peers.[12] The following passage is transparently self-referential.

[Renunciation of self and personal happiness] often has to be done voluntarily by the hero or the martyr, for the sake of something which he prizes more than his individual happiness. But this something, what is it, unless the [temporal] happiness of others or some of the requisites of happiness? *It is noble to be capable of resigning entirely one's own portion of happiness, or chances of it: but, after all, this self-sacrifice must be for some end; it is not its own end* [emphasis added; note again the bad faith expressed here: Mill knew that religious renunciation was never regarded as an end in itself]; and if we are told that its end is not happiness, but virtue, which is better than happiness, I ask, would the sacrifice be made if the hero or martyr did not believe that it would earn for others immunity from similar sacrifices? Would it be made if he thought that his renunciation of happiness for himself would produce no fruit for any of his fellow creatures, but to make their lot like his, and place them also in the condition of persons who have renounced happiness? *All honour to those who can abnegate for themselves the personal enjoyment of life, when by such renunciation they contribute worthily to increase the amount of happiness in the world; but he who does it, or professes to do it, for any other purpose, is no more deserving of admiration than the ascetic mounted on his pillar* [emphasis added]. He may be an inspiriting proof of what men *can* do, but assuredly not an example of what they *should*.

Though it is only in a very imperfect state of the world's arrangements that anyone can best serve the happiness of others by the absolute sacrifice of his own, yet so long as the world is in that imperfect state, I fully acknowledge that the readiness to make such a sacrifice is the highest virtue which can be found in man. I will add, that in this condition of the world, paradoxical as the assertion may be, the conscious ability to do without happiness gives the best prospect of realising, such happiness as is attainable. (emphases added)

Mill again claims the very highest moral, and religious, ground for non-theological utilitarianism:

[L]et utilitarians never cease to claim the morality of self devotion as a possession which belongs by as good a right to them, as either to the Stoic or to the Transcendentalist. The utilitarian morality does recognise in human beings the power of sacrificing their own greatest good for the good of others. It only refuses to admit that the sacrifice is itself a good [as, Mill implies, Christians believe]. A sacrifice which does not increase, or tend to increase, the sum total of happiness, it considers as wasted. (*Util*, 416–18)

This passage has been reproduced at length for two reasons. First, it clearly reveals Mill's strategy—to reorient traditional religious aspirations away from the transcendent God and toward the new intramundane object of service, Humanity. Mill's approach is again two-pronged: to disparage the traditional Christian conception of self-sacrifice for the sake of God and eternal life (anyone who professes self-renunciation for any other purpose than "to increase the amount of happiness in the world . . . is no more deserving of admiration than the ascetic mounted on his pillar"); and to reorient that virtue in service of his new social religion. Self-renunciation or self-devotion toward God is to be replaced by self-renunciation in service of the temporal good of humanity. Mill claims the very height of moral sublimity for his humanitarian ethic. Utilitarians, no less than transcendentalists, are capable of the most absolute self-sacrifice. The only difference is that their self-renunciation and self-devotion are not wasted.

Second, the passage yields insight into Mill's personal reasons for embracing the Religion of Humanity and highlights the pseudoreligious fulfillment he sought to find in that embrace. Mill was a troubled and unhappy, indeed, an alienated man who longed for meaning and purpose, for a God, but who could not or would not accept any of the traditional religious alternatives available to him. His powerful will and hubristic rationality seem to have precluded the humble submission requisite to genuine religious faith. The result was the misdirection of his spiritual or religious impulses toward the inappropriate and ungodlike abstraction of Humanity. Mill's discussion of the hero or martyr who renounces his own happiness for the sake of others' happiness is, as said, transparently self-referential. In the *Autobiography* he tells how, as a youth, he had discovered the futility of seeking happiness as an end in itself. The only way to realize some semblance of happiness, he learned, is indirectly, as a by-product, so to speak, of the pursuit of some other worthy end.[13] This is no doubt a common experience and in itself unobjectionable. The problem in Mill's case is that he had been trained from birth to find happiness not in the cultivation of his personal abilities and talents but in the improvement of the world. Indeed, he had been taught to identify his "entire happiness" with this object. Take the chronic dis-ease of a person unable to achieve satisfaction through the cultivation of self but only through the reformation of society, combine it with powerful but unfulfilled spiritual aspirations and a Promethean reach unbounded by humility or wonder, and the result is a messianic reformer seeking quasi-religious fulfillment through the improvement of the world and its inhabitants. Reforming, indeed transforming, other human beings became a substitute religion for Mill. His inability to find a God who could meet his intellectual and moral requirements resulted in the investment of his own reformist ambitions with religious or ultimate significance. All of the meaning and purpose he was unable to find through communion with a real God was to be achieved through perfecting mankind. The vehicle he sought to create in order to realize this end was a full-bodied social religion—the Religion of Humanity—invested with all the moral urgency and passion of a soul in search of salvation and unlimited in its reach by the belief in or experience of a higher authority. The probable limited god of Mill's imagination—the inept, ineffective, and untrustworthy "hypothesis"—posed no obstacles to his reformist ambitions. Indeed, his invented god served only to fuel those ambitions inasmuch as he urgently *needed* Mill's help and energetic agency. Mill yearned to transcend his selfish ego. Unable or perhaps unwilling to renounce that ego in humble alignment with the givenness of the order of being, Mill seemed to mask his egotistical ambition to control reality behind a self-deceiving, if not self-serving, service to humanity.

In *Utilitarianism*, as in *On Liberty* and "Theism," Mill employs his technique of enlisting Christ in service of his own social and religious purposes. Christ, he suggests, is the very embodiment of the utilitarian standard: "In the golden rule of Jesus of Nazareth, we read the complete spirit of the ethics of utility." The "ideal perfection of utilitarian morality," he further explains, is identical to Christ's precept "[t]o do as you would be done by, and to love your neighbour as yourself." Mill does not emphasize in this context that the concrete determination and application of Christ's "utilitarian" precept is to be made by the nontheological utilitarian moralist or legislator in line with exclusively intramundane utilitarian ends. He does explain, however, how this "ideal perfection" is to be made socially effective: through the three means we encountered in "Utility of Religion" and elsewhere—laws and "social arrangements," education, and public opinion. The first means, as noted, is purely Benthamite: "[L]aws and social arrangements should place the happiness, or . . . interest, of every individual, as nearly as possible in harmony with the interest of the whole . . . " The other two means of realizing Christ's "utilitarian" precept are identical to those prescribed by James Mill and Helvetius: "[E]ducation and opinion, which have so vast a power over human character, should so use that power as to establish in the mind of every individual an indissoluble association between his own happiness and the good of the whole . . . " (*Util*, 418). There is no suggestion that a real Christ might be involved in the "ideal perfection" of utilitarianism.

Mill cannot conceive that anyone could regard the "social morality" of his nontheological utilitarianism as anything short of perfection. He cannot conceive "what more beautiful or more exalted developments of human nature any other ethical system [that is, Christianity] can be supposed to foster, or what springs of action, not accessible to the utilitarian, such systems rely on for giving effect to their mandates" (*Util*, 419). In other words, Mill cannot conceive that the God of the Christians could possibly constitute a better "spring of action" than the desire for unity with Humanity. The blindness or willful arrogance is breathtaking. (Mill is somewhat more honest in "Theism." There, as we recall, he does acknowledge one decided advantage the Christian religion has over the neo-utilitarian Religion of Humanity—the "particular advantage" of a real and not merely an ideal god.) Mill of course claimed for utilitarianism, as for all his views, a "disinterested character." In fact, however, we know that Mill was not only passionately convinced of the superiority of his purely human utilitarianism to theological morality from at least the time of his first "conversion" to Benthamism, but was also passionately devoted to the propagation of the new secular or antitheological creed. Moreover, all his philosophical activities were guided by his overarching religious purpose as characterized throughout this work.

The Appropriation of Common-Sense Morality

As mentioned, one of the chief popular objections to Benthamism that Mill sought to answer in *Utilitarianism* was its putative dismissal of common-sense morality and the accumulated store of inherited wisdom embodied therein. Mill thus appropriates the whole stock of popular maxims and precepts for utilitarian morality. This was despite the fact that he regarded common-sense morality—a morality saturated with traditional religious connotations, one "round which custom has . . . thrown . . . [a] halo" (*Util*, 429)—as subjective feeling and prejudice posing as moral law. For the purpose of winning converts to utilitarianism, however, no sacrifice was too great, and Mill now claims that the stock of inherited moral rules is actually the result of utilitarian trials conducted over the course of human existence. The suggestion is that utilitarianism is in no way incompatible with and in many respects identical to the traditional body of received wisdom. Throughout the course of history, Mill says, "mankind have been learning by experience the tendencies of actions; on which experience all the prudence, as well as all the morality of life, are dependent." Men have learned not to interfere with the life or property of others; they have learned that lying and theft have socially pernicious consequences. Mill claims to be fully satisfied that "all rational creatures go out upon the sea of life with their minds made up on the common questions of right and wrong." In any event, the "matter is now done to his hand. It is truly a whimsical supposition that, if mankind were agreed in considering utility to be the test of morality, they would remain without any agreement as to what *is* useful, and would take no measures for having their notions on the subject taught to the young, and enforced by law and opinion." Mill again stresses the triumvirate powers of education, law, and opinion. As usual, however, what Mill gives with one hand he takes away with the other. He will accept the view that inherited morality embodies knowledge of a kind, but such morality is really appropriate only "for the multitude": "[M]ankind must by this time have acquired positive beliefs as to the effects of some actions on their happiness, and the beliefs which have thus come down are the rules of morality for the multitude, and for the philosopher until he has succeeded in finding better."[14] Having been forced to acknowledge the utilitarian value of traditional and customary morality despite his lifelong opposition to such a morality, Mill immediately tips his hand. He feels compelled to point out that *"philosophers might easily do this [find better moral rules], even now, on many subjects; [for] the received code of ethics is by no means of divine right;* and . . . mankind have still much to learn as to the effects of actions on the general happiness" (emphasis added).

Mill's successful appropriation of common-sense and traditional moral rules—what he refers to as "secondary principles" or "intermediate generalizations," in contradistinction to the "first principle" of utility—for utilitarianism countered one of the long-standing objections to that doctrine. As such, it had a significant positive effect on the eventual acceptance of nontheological utilitarianism in English society. What should be emphasized, however, is that Mill's concession to the dictates of popular morality and its "secondary principles" reveals that his fundamental concern was not the *content* of moral rules but their *source*. His aim was to shift the ultimate ground or "first principle" of morality away from "divine right" or a transcendent God and toward the purely human principle of utility. He could afford to lose the minor battle—to make some temporary concessions to customary morality—for the sake of the larger war: the establishment of utility as "the ultimate source of moral obligations" (*Util*, 425–27).

Utility: "The Ultimate Source of Moral Obligations"

Having addressed the charges of vulgarity and selfishness and having demonstrated the utilitarian capacity for devotion and self-renunciation, as well as the compatibility of utilitarianism with common-sense morality, Mill turns to the charge of godlessness. His discussion is remarkable for the transparency with which he reveals the pseudoreligious character of the utilitarian creed as well as his own conviction of moral and religious superiority. Against the "vulgar" charge that "utility is a godless doctrine," Mill replies with characteristic haughtiness that "utility is not only not a godless doctrine, but more profoundly religious than any other." The reason seems to be that God, if he is good, must be a utilitarian, that is, he must desire above all other things what Mill himself desires—the happiness of all his creatures. As Mill explains:

> [I]f it be necessary to say anything at all against so mere an assumption [that utility is a godless doctrine], we may say that the question depends upon what idea we have formed of the moral character of the Deity. If it be a true belief that God desires, above all things, the happiness of his creatures, and

that this was his purpose in their creation, utility is not only not a godless doctrine, but more profoundly religious than any other. If it be meant that utilitarianism does not recognise the revealed will of God as the supreme law of morals, I answer, that a utilitarian who believes in the perfect goodness and wisdom of God, necessarily believes that whatever God has thought fit to reveal on the subject of morals, must fulfil the requirements of utility in a supreme degree.

What is Mill saying? Does a utilitarian believe the revealed will of God to be the supreme law of morals? Mill answers that a utilitarian who believes in God's perfect goodness and wisdom (which, we may note, Mill does not; his probable limited god may be perfectly good but we have no assurance he is perfectly wise) "necessarily" believes that God's revelation with respect to morality must meet the criteria of the utilitarian standard. That is, any allegedly revealed moral rule that does not serve to promote the greatest happiness of the greatest number, as conceived by the non-theological utilitarian moralist, cannot be regarded as authentic revelation. The implication seems to be that utilitarianism alone provides the objective standard that permits one to decide between authentic and counterfeit revelation.

Mill continues: "But others besides utilitarians have been of opinion that the Christian revelation was intended, and is fitted, to inform the hearts and minds of mankind with a spirit which should enable them to find for themselves what is right, and incline them to do it when found, rather than to tell them, except in a very general way, what it is; and that we need a doctrine of ethics, carefully followed out, to *interpret* to us the will of God." That is, Christianity may be fit to engender the proper spirit needed for the determination of what is right, as well as the motivation to act rightly, but it does not, except very generally, provide guidance as to what is right. This is the task of (nontheological) utilitarianism—"to interpret to us the will of God." Mill seems to know what the Christian God actually intends. "Whether this opinion is correct or not, it is superfluous here to discuss; since whatever aid religion, either natural or revealed, can afford to ethical investigation, is as open to the utilitarian moralist as to any other. He can use it as the testimony of God to the usefulness or hurtfulness of any given course of action, by as good a right as others can use it for the indication of a transcendental law, having no connection with usefulness or with happiness" (*Util*, 423). Nontheological utilitarians, Mill suggests, can "use" Christianity as they wish. They can "use it," for instance, to claim God's sanction for their own conception of morality, as Mill indeed proceeds to do. He will, he says, show that anything revealed by a perfectly good God must "fulfil the requirements" of utilitarian morality and that utility (and not God) is "the ultimate source of moral obligations." He can do so, he claims, "by as good a right" as those who "use it" in support of their belief in a "transcendental law." Religion is a tool of moral philosophy. Needless to say, Mill was aware that there is a world of difference between an entirely secular or naturalistic rule of action and a transcendent moral law.

As we have seen, one of Mill's aims, perhaps his fundamental aim, was to claim for utility the status of "the ultimate source of moral obligations." Utility was also intended to serve as the ultimate standard or arbiter of morality. Mill acknowledges that those with different standards of morality will have correspondingly different conceptions of what does and does not violate the "moral law." Such differences of opinion existed long before utilitarianism, however, while that doctrine does at least supply a "tangible and intelligible" means of resolving them (*Util*, 422). In short, Mill proposes the principle of utility as the only available, or indeed possible, objective standard by which to choose among competing conceptions of the moral law. What is urgently needed is "an ultimate standard to which conflicting rights and duties can be referred. . . . Though the application of the standard may be difficult, *it is better than none at all*" (emphasis added). Existing moral standards, Mill suggests, in fact provide no standard at all. The problem, he says, is that "in other systems, the moral laws all claiming independent authority, there is no common umpire entitled to interfere between them." If utility is recognized as "the ultimate source of moral obligations," however, it may be invoked to decide between conflicting rights and duties when their demands are incompatible. Utility, in short, is to serve as the common umpire among competing ethical systems, "all claiming independent authority" but in actuality "rest[ing] on little better than sophistry, and unless determined, as they generally are, by the unacknowledged influence of considerations of utility, afford a free scope for the action of personal desires and partialities" (*Util*, 428). It is perhaps unnecessary to point out that there is no conceivable moral doctrine that provides a freer "scope for the action of personal desires and partialities" than the utterly amorphous notion of serving the greatest temporal happiness for the greatest number.

Utility: The Ultimate Sanction

Mill next tackles the difficult question of "the ultimate sanction" of the principle of utility. What is the binding force of its morality? As he says, people may recognize that they are bound not to murder, but why should they feel bound to promote the general happiness, "especially if [they think their] own happiness lies in something else"? Mill emphasizes that the identification of the ground of obligation is not a problem peculiar to utilitarianism but one confronted by any new and unfamiliar doctrine that people are called upon to adopt. The real problem, he says, is that "the customary morality, that which education and opinion have consecrated, is the only one which presents itself to the mind with the feeling of being *in itself* obligatory." Any moral standard "round which custom has not thrown the same halo" must fight an uphill battle for acceptance (*Util*, 429). Apparently, the obligation to promote the general happiness or to regard utility and not God as "the ultimate source of moral obligations" was not as self-evident to his contemporaries as it was to Mill.

Mill attributes their reluctance to embrace utilitarianism to faulty upbringing and education. The reason people are unable to recognize their obligation to serve the collective happiness is that their moral sense has not been shaped with a view to this end but has been shaped instead on the old (theological) model. They do honor some of the secondary principles of utilitarian morality, such as the prohibition of murder and theft. But the ultimate foundation of those principles, utility, has yet to become "in men's minds invested with as much sacredness as any of its applications." The task of would-be improvers of humanity is thus clear: to form the moral sense around the "sacred" and "ultimate" principle of utility:

> If the view adopted by the utilitarian philosophy of the nature of the moral sense be correct [that it is wholly shaped by circumstances and by training and education inculcated from infancy], this difficulty will always present itself, until the influences which form moral character have taken the same hold of the principle [of utility] which they have taken of some of the consequences [the secondary moral principles, such as the prohibitions against killing or robbing]—until, by the improvement of education, the feeling of unity with our fellow-creatures shall be (what it cannot be denied that Christ intended it to be) as deeply rooted in our character, and to our own consciousness as completely a part of our nature, as the horror of crime is in an ordinarily well brought up young person. (*Util*, 430)

Note first how Mill once again follows Saint-Simon in attempting to utilize Christian symbols—indeed, Christ himself—in service of his new religion.[15] Christ, claims Mill, intended mankind to embrace the Religion of Humanity—"the feeling of unity with our fellow-creatures." Once again, Mill's strategy appears to have been two-pronged: first, to recast traditional Christian symbols and beliefs, including its most significant symbol, Christ himself, in the image of utilitarianism; and second, to manipulate the sentiments of Christian believers with the aim of bringing them into the fold of the new humanitarian religion. As we may recall, Mill regarded the supernatural hopes and reverential feelings of Christian believers as "excellently fitted to aid and fortify that real . . . religion, . . . the Religion of Humanity."

The second striking feature of the above passage is the depth of conviction it evinces with respect to the utter malleability of the human conscience and moral sense. Mill is committed to the project of making a new kind of man, one in whom the "feeling of unity with our fellow-creatures" will be as a second nature. All selfish propensities are to be extirpated. This is to be achieved through the "influences which form moral character"—education and training, the intensive socialization process described in Chapter 1. The implications evoke visions of a brave new Skinnerian world.

Note also that Mill has not, as promised, provided any ultimate sanction for the new human morality. That is, he has not yet provided any moral reason why men should, in fact, feel obliged to promote the greatest happiness for the greatest number and regard utility and not God as "the ultimate source of moral obligations." All he says is that men will wish to do so once the Educators have managed to form the moral sense in the desired fashion. All the humanitarian educators need, we may recall, is to obtain the necessary power, the command over the resources heretofore controlled by religion and customary authority.

Mill does, however, leap into an extended discussion of what he understands is meant by the term *sanction:* external and internal inducements.

> The principle of utility either has, or there is no reason why it might not have, all the sanctions which belong to any other system of morals. These sanctions are either external or internal. . . . [T]he external sanctions . . . are, the hope of favour and the fear of displeasure, from our fellow-creatures or from the Ruler of the Universe, along with whatever we may have of sympathy or affection for them, or of love and awe of Him, inclining us to do his will independently of selfish consequences. There is evidently no reason why all these motives for observance should not attach themselves to the utilitarian morality, as completely and as powerfully as to any other.

Note again the bad faith involved in such appeals to Christian sentiments. Mill elsewhere and often—indeed, in the contemporaneously composed "Utility of Religion"—condemns "the hope of favour and the fear of displeasure" of God as immeasurably selfish and slavish and, moreover, explicitly denies the personal or social efficacy of the posthumous sanction. He seems, however, to have recognized that the condemned and allegedly inefficacious religious sanctions, as well as the ingrained Christian sentiments attached to them, may have potential use and value for the non-theological utilitarian cause. That is, as he suggests in this passage, "the hope of favour and the fear of displeasure . . . from the Ruler of the Universe" are motives perfectly well suited to "attach themselves to the utilitarian morality, as completely and as powerfully as to any other." We are familiar with his strategy in this regard.

Mill, then, apparently felt free to either condemn or invoke the posthumous sanction depending on the requirements of the argument at hand. Whatever the reason, Mill now claims that the posthumous sanctions of religion can, like their human counterparts, "become available to enforce the utilitarian morality":

> With regard to the religious motive, if men believe, as most profess to do, in the goodness of God, those who think that conduciveness to the general happiness is the essence, or even only the criterion of good, must necessarily believe that it is also that which God approves. The whole force therefore of external reward and punishment, whether physical or moral, and whether proceeding from God or from our fellow men, together with all that the capacities of human nature admit of disinterested devotion to either, become available to enforce the utilitarian morality, in proportion as that morality is recognised; and the more powerfully, the more the appliances of education and general cultivation are bent to the purpose. (*Util,* 430–31)

In other words, anyone who believes in God's goodness, as of course do the Christians, and, moreover, believes that goodness tends to the promotion of the general happiness, must necessarily believe that the Christian God sanctions utilitarian morality—that is, the notion that utility is the "ultimate standard" and the "ultimate source of moral obligations." The Christian God is invoked to validate Mill's contention that the ultimate ground of moral obligation is something other than that God himself.

The Internal Sanction: "Conscientious Feelings"

Mill next discusses the "internal sanction" of duty or conscience. This sanction, he says, is "a feeling in our own mind; a pain, more or less intense, attendant on violation of duty, which . . . rises . . . into shrinking from it as an impossibility. This feeling, when disinterested, and connecting itself with the pure idea of duty, and not with some particular form of it, or with any of the merely accessory circumstances, is the essence of Conscience . . . " Conscience, in short, is a painful feeling—one, however, "encrusted over with collateral associations" derived from various sources: sympathy, love, fear; from all the forms of religious feeling; from the recollections of childhood and one's past; from self-esteem; from desire for the esteem of others; and so on. Mill admits that this variety of sources of associations makes the identification of the actual constitution of conscience a matter of "extreme complication." Indeed, it is this complexity of the phenomenon of conscience that accounts for its "mystical character," that is, for mankind's propensity to associate the voice of conscience and the sense of moral obligation with God:

> [This complexity is] the origin of the sort of mystical character which . . . is apt to be attributed to the idea of moral obligation, and which leads people to believe that the idea cannot possibly attach itself to any other objects than those which, by a supposed mysterious law, are found in our present experience to excite it [that is, God's moral law]. Its binding force, however, consists in the existence of a mass of feeling which must be broken through in order to do what violates our standard of right, and which, if we do nevertheless violate that standard, will probably have to be encountered afterwards in the form of remorse. Whatever theory we have of the nature or origin of conscience, this is what essentially constitutes it. (*Util*, 431)

Mill was no doubt aware that the majority of his potential converts did not in fact hold a "theory . . . of the nature or origin of conscience." Traditional believers certainly regarded the "binding force" of conscience as much more than a "mass of feeling" engendered by naturalistic forces or causes. Mill seems to be following his old strategy of dealing with a subject "as if religion did not exist."

Having broached the subject of the "mass of feeling" that is conscience, Mill finally reveals the long-awaited ultimate sanction of not only the utilitarian, but of "all morality": "*The ultimate sanction . . . of all morality (external motives apart) [is] a subjective feeling in our own minds[.]* I see nothing embarrassing to those whose standard is utility, in the question, what is the sanction of that particular standard? We may answer, the same as of all other moral standards—the conscientious feelings of mankind" (emphasis added). There is no higher moral sanction than mankind, indeed, the "feelings" of mankind. There is no reason to believe, as the transcendental moralists suggest, that "this sanction will not exist in the mind unless it is believed to have its root out of the mind"—that is, in an objective, God-given, moral law. For "moral obligation," Mill has found, is "entirely subjective, having its seat in human consciousness only" (*Util*, 431–32).

Mill claims, then, that the ultimate sanction of utilitarian morality—"the conscientious feelings of mankind"—is identical to the sanction of "all other moral standards." This of course is not true, certainly not in the sense he intends. Although the traditional ultimate sanction of morality in the West since the time of Christ—moral obligation to the transcendent God—was bound up with conscientious feelings inspired by that obligation, the feelings of mankind were never thought to constitute the sanction of moral obligation, nor are all such feelings equivalent, as Mill suggests. As has been emphasized, however, Mill always regarded traditional religious morality and the feelings it inspired as arbitrary and subjective, having been created merely because the power of education and the control of public opinion had long been in the hands of religious authorities. In short, the traditional religious conscience was, in Mill's view, nothing more than "a subjective feeling in our own minds," a feeling, moreover, which could easily be reoriented away from a transcendent God and toward the proposed replacement, Humanity. One kind of conscientious feeling could serve as well as another. Nor is there any sanction beyond mankind's conscientious feelings. All of this was no doubt intended to advance the goal of replacing God with Humanity and theological with purely human morality. It passes belief that Mill could perceive no difference between the feelings inspired by the transcendent God of the Western religious tradition and those inspired by potential union with Humanity.

Mill also makes the extraordinary claim that those people who refuse to acknowledge conscientious feelings of unity with mankind as the ultimate basis of conscience have in fact no governing conscience at all: "Undoubtedly this sanction [conscientious feelings] has no binding efficacy on those who do not possess the feelings it appeals to [feelings of duty to and unity with humanity]; but neither will these persons be more obedient to any other moral principle than to the utilitarian one. On them morality of any kind has no hold but through the external sanctions." In other words, those who do not experience a conscientious feeling of duty to promote the collective happiness of humanity will not be any more obedient to other internal promptings of conscience, such as those inspired by traditional religious belief. For "morality of any kind has no hold" on those "who do not possess the feelings [humanitarian utilitarianism] appeals to." Mill continues: "Meanwhile, the feelings [that constitute conscience] exist, a fact in human nature, the reality of which, and the great power with which they are capable of acting on those in whom they have been duly cultivated, are proved by experience. No reason has ever been shown why they may not be cultivated to as great intensity in connection with the utilitarian, as with any other rule of morals" (*Util*, 432). As said, conscientious feelings are utterly malleable. Religious authority has managed to shape them in the direction of a transcendent God, but Mill saw no reason why they could not be shaped in the direction of unity with mankind (as Christ allegedly intended).

There can be no doubt that Mill regarded Christianity as the chief rival to utilitarianism. This is indicated by his frequent references to Christian revelation and the frequent parallels and contrasts he draws between utilitarianism and Christianity. For instance, to rebut the objection that utilitarianism cannot provide a practical rule of action because it is impossible to perform a utilitarian calculus prior to every act, he points to Christianity. If the objection is valid, he says, it must likewise be impossible to guide one's conduct by Christianity, because "there is not time, on every occasion on which anything has to be done, to read through the Old and New Testaments" (*Util*, 425). Mill's principal strategy in *Utilitarianism*, however, is to reduce traditional Christian moral beliefs to the status of subjective feeling and questions of ontology to mere "opinion." The implication is that the objective reality of the Christian God is more or less irrelevant to the issue of moral obligation.

> There is . . . a disposition to believe that a person who sees in moral obligation a transcendental fact, an objective reality belonging to the province of "Things in themselves," is likely to be more obedient to it than one who believes it to be entirely subjective, having its seat in human consciousness only. But whatever a person's opinion may be on this point of Ontology, the force he is really urged by is his own subjective feeling, and is exactly measured by its strength. No one's belief that duty is an objective reality is stronger than the belief that God is so; yet the belief in God, apart from the expectation of actual reward and punishment, only operates on conduct through, and in proportion to, the subjective religious feeling. The sanction, so far as it is disinterested, is always in the mind itself; and the notion therefore of the transcendental moralists must be, that this sanction will not exist in the mind unless it is believed to have its root out of the mind; and that if a person is able to say to himself, "This which is restraining me, and which is called my conscience, is only a feeling in my own mind," he may possibly draw the conclusion that when the feeling ceases the obligation ceases, and that if he find the feeling inconvenient, he may disregard it, and endeavour to get rid of it. But is this danger confined to the utilitarian morality? Does the belief that moral obligation has its seat outside the mind make the feeling of it too strong to be got rid of? The fact is so far otherwise, that all moralists admit and lament the ease with which, in the generality of minds, conscience can be silenced or stifled. The question, "Need I obey my conscience?" is quite as often put to themselves by persons who never heard of the principle of utility, as by its adherents. Those whose conscientious feelings are so weak as to allow of their asking this question, if they answer it affirmatively, will not do so because they believe in the transcendental theory, but because of the external sanctions. (*Util*, 432–33)

What Mill is saying is that the question of the objective reality of God is irrelevant to feelings of moral obligation. Moreover, he suggests that the equivalence of utilitarian and transcendental morality is evinced by the fact that all men, utilitarians and transcendentalists alike, are weak and by the fact that conscience often fails to govern—two issues that are of course unrelated. Mill suggests, however, that because traditional Christians sometimes fail to honor their moral obligations, utilitarian morality will serve just as well. The weak of either faith, transcendental or utilitarian, require "external sanctions"; the conscientious do not, for their subjective feelings will effectively guide their behavior. The point of the passage, as said, is to make the objective reality of God irrelevant to the question of moral obligation. A mundane faith is equivalent to a transcendent faith. What matters is the existence and strength of the requisite subjective feelings, not the reality or truth of the object of worship or the source of moral obligations. One's opinion with respect to ontology is beside the point.

The strictly human "external sanctions" of reward and punishment are more easily disposed of than the "internal sanction" of conscience: "[T]hose [external inducements] which refer to our fellow creatures are sure to [attach themselves to the utilitarian morality]; for whether there be any other ground of moral obligation than the general happiness or not, men do desire happiness; and however imperfect may be their own practice, they desire and commend all conduct in others towards themselves, by which they think their happiness is promoted" (*Util*, 430).

The Appropriation of Intuitionism

As mentioned, *Utilitarianism* is Mill's most carefully crafted effort at proselytization on behalf of the new humanitarian faith; his aim throughout is to bring everyone, and especially wavering Christians, into the utilitarian fold. As he was willing to repress his contempt for customary morality by characterizing it as utilitarian, and this against his settled view, so he also adopts a new approach to his age-old enemies the intuitionists. More particularly, rather than attacking the notion of a moral sense or of innate or intuitive knowledge of moral principles, Mill now suggests that intuitively apprehended moral principles, like the secondary principles of common-sense morality, may actually "coincide" with utilitarianism:

> It is not necessary, for the present purpose, to decide whether the feeling of duty is innate or implanted. Assuming it to be innate [for purposes of argument], it is an open question to what objects it naturally attaches itself; for the . . . supporters of that theory are now agreed that the intuitive perception is of principles of morality and not of the details. If there be any-

thing innate in the matter, I see no reason why the feeling which is innate should not be that of regard to the pleasures and pains of others. If there is any principle of morals which is intuitively obligatory, I should say it must be that. If so, the intuitive ethics would coincide with the utilitarian, and there would be no further quarrel between them. Even as it is, the intuitive moralists, though they believe that there are other intuitive moral obligations, do already believe this to be one; for they unanimously hold that a large *portion* of morality turns upon the consideration due to the interests of our fellow-creatures. Therefore, if the belief in the transcendental origin of moral obligation gives any additional efficacy to the internal sanction, it appears to me that the utilitarian principle has already the benefit of it. (*Util*, 433)

The first point that should be emphasized is Mill's admission that those who believe in the transcendental origin of moral obligation "unanimously hold that a large portion of morality turns upon the consideration due to the interests of our fellow-creatures." This resembles his earlier admission that the quarrel between utilitarianism and common-sense morality does not concern secondary principles or commonly accepted moral rules. On a practical level, it seems, there was a general consensus in Victorian society with respect to the substantive content of morality. Thus, as previously noted, it is obvious that the real point at issue for Mill was not practical moral precepts but the ultimate ground of moral obligation. Mill's real concern was to transfer that ground from the traditional transcendent God to the intramundane, nontheological, purely human principle of utility.

The passage also suggests that Mill was attempting to characterize the intuitionist position in such a way as to make it appear to support the utilitarian agenda, precisely as he portrayed the Christian God as a staunch supporter of nontheological utilitarianism and the Religion of Humanity. As he says, "[I]f the belief in the transcendental origin of moral obligation gives any additional efficacy to the internal sanction [that is, the mass of conscientious feelings], it appears . . . that the utilitarian principle has already the benefit of it." This, we recall, would follow from the fact that the intuitionists "hold that a large portion of morality turns upon the consideration due to the interests of our fellow-creatures," as utilitarianism recommends. Because both the intuitionists and transcendentalists believe that human beings should be concerned with others, the intuitionists implicitly acknowledge the truth of the utilitarian position. In other words, according to Mill, one who admits concern for one's fellow human beings implicitly concedes the truth of nontheological utilitarianism. What the discussion indicates is Mill's willingness to obscure the real issue at hand—"the ultimate source [and sanction] of moral obligations"—while simultaneously attempting to lead his readers to accept utility as that source and sanction.

Although Mill was willing to enlist the views of the intuitionists in support of his neo-utilitarianism, we know that he vehemently rejected their belief in an innate moral sense. All moral feelings and ideas are, in Mill's view, acquired through the force of education and training. This, however, creates certain problems for the moralist and educator, for human beings can all too easily acquire false notions through improper training. Indeed, under the influence of traditional religious and parental authority, this is precisely what has occurred:

> Unhappily [the moral faculty] is also susceptible, by a sufficient use of the external sanctions and of the force of early impressions, of being cultivated in almost any direction: so that there is hardly anything so absurd or so mischievous that it may not, by means of these influences, be made to act on the human mind with all the authority of conscience. To doubt that the same potency might be given by the same means to the principle of utility, even if it had no foundation in human nature, would be flying in the face of all experience. (*Util*, 434)

The silver lining, then, is that conscience can be salvaged from the wreckage that has been created by false (religious) opinions. There can be no doubt that "sufficient use of the external sanctions" and other forms of training can give the "same potency" to the principle of utility as traditional religious views have enjoyed in the past.

Mill also responds to the charge that utilitarianism may be too elevated and too noble a standard to be capable of realization by the mass of humanity. Critics had contended that it is too much to expect that "people shall always act from the inducement of promoting the general interests of society" and not their personal interest. Such an eminently realistic objection, says Mill, displays a gross misunderstanding of the "very meaning of a standard of morals." It "confound[s] the rule of action with the motive of it." Mill clarifies his meaning: The point of ethics is "to tell us what are our duties, or by what test we may know them; but no system of ethics requires that the sole motive of all we do shall be a feeling of duty." Utilitarianism recognizes that people act from many different motives, and not solely from "a feeling of duty"; this is perfectly acceptable so long as people do not violate the "rule of duty."[16] Mill denies that utilitarianism requires people to "fix their minds upon so wide a generality as the world, or society at large," despite the fact that this is precisely what he asserts in other remarks.[17] Mill is at his proselytizing worst here: "The great majority of good actions are intended not for the benefit of the world, but for that of individuals, of which the good of the world is made up; and the thoughts of the most virtuous man need not on these occasions travel beyond the particular persons concerned, except so far as is necessary to assure himself that in benefiting them he is not violating the rights, that is, the legitimate and authorised expectations, of anyone else." Very few people have occasion to be "public benefactors," that is, to multiply the happiness of others on an extended scale, to be concerned with "public utility." Normally, people need only attend to the "interest or happiness" of their acquaintances.[18] "Those alone the influence of whose actions extends to society in general need concern themselves habitually about so large an object," Mill explains. The great masses, once properly socialized, can serve humanity through action within their intimate circles; only the elite need consider humanity as a whole. People may bestow benefits exclusively within their intimate circles so long as they understand their "duties" in nontheological utilitarian terms. Mill also explains that the "ground of the obligation" to abstain from a certain action is the fact that "the action is of a class which, if practised generally, would be generally injurious . . . " This entails no greater regard for the public interest than any other moral system, for all of them prohibit behavior injurious to society (*Util*, 419–20).

Such thoughts would have had a reassuring ring to Mill's traditional liberal audience, but they are somewhat disingenuous if Mill's other statements concerning the Religion of Duty are to be taken seriously. For if the object of Mill's utilitarianism is not the world at large but merely the "interest or happiness" of one's immediate fellows, and if "the amount of regard for the public interest" needed for the widespread embrace of utilitarianism is not more than is "demanded by every system of morals," why is it necessary to train everyone from birth not only to have the strongest possible "direct impulse" toward serving the general good but also to be "unable to *conceive* the possibility of [personal] happiness, consistently with conduct opposed to the general good" (emphasis added)? Why is not a steadfast regard for the constitutional traditions of one's country sufficient to ensure the realization of the general interest? Why is it necessary to establish the "feeling of unity with Humanity at large" or posit Humanity as the ultimate object of reverence and service? Why may not the general interest be secured through the traditional Christian injunction to love one's neighbor as oneself while maintaining the Christian God as the ultimate locus of allegiance and accountability? The answer is that, despite the above rhetoric, Mill's new social morality requires far more devotion to the public good than traditional Christian ethics or liberal political morality finds desirable. It should not be forgotten that, for Mill, the general good is identical to the collective happiness. As he reiterates, "[T]he happiness which forms the utilitarian standard of what is right in conduct, is not the agent's own happiness, but that of all concerned" (*Util*, 418). Traditional theological morality is far too self-interested for Mill; from first to last he condemned Christianity as the religion of the selfish. Mill's settled view was that allegiance to the Christian God encouraged a selfish concern with mere personal salvation, with personal accountability to God, and not with the social salvation of the whole. Moreover, Mill, like Rousseau, seems to have apprehended that allegiance to the Christian God would draw off the emotional intensity or sentiment necessary to fuel the new humanitarian "religion without a God." We have heard Mill's frequent complaints about the failure of Christian morality to engender a proper concern for "duty to the State." The social religionists apprehended traditional Christian belief as a rival to the Religion of Humanity. They recognized that the former must be eviscerated if the latter is to achieve its end—the creation of a new purely human moral and social order religiously oriented toward humanitarian service, "confined within the limits of the earth."

The Social Religion: The Religion of Humanity

Mill addresses the possibility that the utilitarian attempt to create a "moral association" between utility and the "feeling of duty" may appear forced and contrived, as a "wholly artificial creation." As such, it may dissolve under the harsh light of rational analysis. Mill himself had experienced precisely such a dissolution of the association that his father had tried to form in his mind between his own happiness and the happiness of mankind; the consequence was the celebrated "mental crisis" of his young adulthood. It seems the mature Mill found a solution to this problem. For he had discovered that the association requisite to utilitarian morality—the association between personal and general happiness—while of course acquired and thus to some extent "artificial," in fact rests on a "firm foundation" or "natural basis," namely, "the social feelings of mankind; the desire to be in unity with our fellow-creatures." As previously discussed, Mill had discovered one innate quality in human nature—the "germ" of "social feeling":

> But there *is* this basis of powerful natural sentiment; and this it is which, when once the general happiness is recognised as the ethical standard, will constitute the strength of the utilitarian morality. This firm foundation is that of the social feelings of mankind; the desire to be in unity with our fellow creatures, which is already a powerful principle in human nature, and

happily one of those which tend to become stronger, even without express inculcation, from the influences of advancing civilisation.

Man becomes ever more social as civilization progresses and this through the development of an ever more "riveted" association of self with society. Mill has seen the future and it is "social"-ist:

> The social state is at once so natural, so necessary, and so habitual to man, that, except in some unusual circumstances or by an effort of voluntary abstraction, he never conceives himself otherwise than as a member of a body; and this association is riveted more and more, as mankind are further removed from the state of savage independence [Mill again sounds curiously like Rousseau]. Any condition, therefore, which is essential to a state of society, becomes more and more an inseparable part of every person's conception of the state of things which he is born into, and which is the destiny of a human being. (*Util*, 434–35)

The "social state" of the future will be one in which the interests of all people will be consulted. The object of utilitarian education is to form people in such a way that they will be unable to conceive a state in which they can totally disregard other people's interests. As earlier noted, Mill has already conceded that transcendental morality is extremely concerned with "the interests of our fellow-creatures." Thus his enthusiasm for the social "germ" in human nature suggests that he has something more intensive in mind than concern for the interests of our fellows. Such indeed is the case. The new men to be formed on utilitarian principles will be unable even to think of disregarding other people's interests. They will identify their feelings more and more with the good of others, until concern for the good of others becomes as a second nature. Every member of society will be concerned to assist in this process of mutual socialization. As Mill puts it, "[W]hatever amount of this feeling a person has, he is urged . . . to demonstrate it, and to the utmost of his power encourage it in others; and even if he has none of it himself, he is as greatly interested as any one else that others should have it." The new men will feel one another's interests as their own interests. They will not only become more cooperative but even capable of "proposing to themselves a collective, not an individual interest as the aim . . . of their actions." Mill is beside himself with enthusiasm for the glorious vision of the men of the future unfolding behind his eyes:

> Consequently the smallest germs of the feeling [the natural desire for unity with others] are laid hold of and nourished by the contagion of sympathy and the influences of education; and a complete web of corroborative association is woven round it, by the powerful agency of the external sanctions [that is, punishment].

> This mode of conceiving ourselves and human life, as civilisation goes on, is felt to be more and more natural. . . . In an improving state of the human mind, the influences are constantly on the increase, which tend to generate in each individual a feeling of unity with all the rest; which, if perfect, would make him never think of, or desire, any beneficial condition for himself, in the benefits of which they are not included.

Why the germ of social feeling—the allegedly natural desire to be in unity with our fellow-creatures—is accorded privileged status is not clear. As Mill was at pains to emphasize in "Nature," the fact that nature has endowed human beings with a feeling does not "legitimate all its promptings." Nor is it clear why such a feeling should be cultivated to an infinite degree in service of the general happiness. One may instead apprehend in such a feeling a dangerous reversion to an atavistic collectivist impulse, one that requires, as much as any other natural feeling, to be regulated by reason or tradition. Mill, however, greatly approves of the natural social feeling, essential as it is to his ethical doctrine and religious ends. He thus exempts it from his general condemnation or suspicion of natural feeling.

Mill is leading up to the centerpiece of his vision—the unnamed Religion of the Future, the religion of unity with and service to humanity: "[T]his feeling of unity [can] be taught as a religion, and the whole force of education, of institutions, and of opinion, directed, as it once was in the case of religion, to make every person grow up from infancy surrounded on all sides both by the profession and the practice of it" (emphasis added). Mill makes the genesis and substance of his vision of the unnamed religion of humanitarian service perfectly clear: He explicitly identifies their source in Auguste Comte.

> To any ethical student who finds the realisation difficult, I recommend, as a means of facilitating it, the second of M. Comte's two principal works, the *Traite de politique positive* [*Système de politique positive*]. I entertain the strongest objections to the system of politics and morals set forth in that treatise; but I think it has superabundantly shown the possibility of giving to the service of humanity, even without the aid of belief in a Providence, both the psychological power and the social efficacy of a religion; making it take hold of human life, and colour all thought, feeling, and action, in a manner of which the greatest ascendancy ever exercised by any religion may be but a type and foretaste; and of which the danger is, not that it should be insufficient but that it should be so excessive as to interfere unduly with human freedom and individuality. (*Util*, 435–36)

The towering height of Mill's religious ambitions could not be more clear. The new Religion of the Future—unity with and service to humanity, "even without the aid of belief in a Providence"—is certain, he believes, to achieve a greater ascendancy over "all thought, feeling, and action" than any religion to which human beings have previously adhered.

Mill now creates a difficulty for his interpreters. From the time of his initial conversion to Benthamism in 1821 until the end of his life, Mill claimed to be a strenuous opponent of emotivist ethics. He always characterized utility as the indispensable objective standard necessary to arbitrate among the various subjective feelings or preferences posing as moral law. Nothing could be more unphilosophical and pernicious in practice than to make mere feeling the basis of ethics. We now discover, however, that feeling—indeed, "social feeling"—is to "constitute the binding force of the utilitarian morality" of the future. As observed in the preceding chapter, Mill is aware that this may be difficult to conceive, especially considering the "actual feelings" of the majority of his contemporaries. The passage is worth repeating: "If differences of opinion and of mental culture make it impossible for [an adherent to the Religion of Humanity] to share many of [his fellows'] actual feelings—perhaps make him denounce and defy those feelings—he still needs to be conscious that his real aim and theirs do not conflict; that he is not opposing himself to what they really wish for, namely their own good, but is, on the contrary, promoting it" (*Util*, 436). Let us also repeat our conclusion from earlier in this chapter: Mill seemed able to disguise his desire for control over social reality by the self-deception that his true desire was to "serve" his fellows. Mill knows "what they really wish for," whether they themselves are aware of this or not. He will serve them for "their own good." Whatever this is, it is not classical liberalism. In this regard, we may also recall Mill's discussion of "duty" for the light it sheds on the potentially coercive implications of his new Religion of Humanity or, as he sometimes calls it, the Religion of Duty: "It is a part of the notion of duty in every one of its forms, that a person may rightfully be compelled to fulfil it. Duty is a thing which may be exacted from a person, as one exacts a debt. Unless we think that it may be exacted from him, we do not call it his duty" (*Util*, 454). Potential members of the Church of Humanity or Duty are forewarned. It may be necessary to "exact" service to humanity from those who have insufficiently internalized the proper "social feelings." For, as Mill says, "[u]nless we think that it may be exacted from [them], we do not call it [their] duty."

The Sin of Selfishness

[T]he great purpose of moral culture [is] the strengthening of the unselfish and weakening of the selfish element in our nature . . .
—J. S. Mill, "Utility of Religion"

For Mill, the opposition between moral evil and moral good coincided, on the whole, with the opposition between the selfish and the social. The rigid moral dichotomy between the bad or "selfish" and the good or "social" was not only one of the core themes of the Benthamite ethos but also, even more radically, of Comtean ethics and its opposition between selfish egoism and selfless altruism. The long-standing dichotomy in Mill's mind between the selfish and the social structured his thought and his aspirations in several ways. First, the war against the sin of selfishness was part and parcel of his war against Christianity, which he always characterized as a religion that promoted selfishness. As he said in *On Liberty*, Christianity "give[s] to human morality an essentially selfish character, in disconnecting each man's feelings of duty from the interests of his fellow-creatures" (51). As has been discussed, Mill, with Bentham, portrayed divine justice—the "posthumous sanction"—as a scheme of bribes, promises, and threats devised to appeal to selfish interests. Such an appeal leads a man to regard his duties to others chiefly as "a means to his own personal salvation." The good of the "social," on the other hand, was embodied in the Religion of Humanity, which was characterized by its commitment to the values of altruism, fraternity, and unity with others. The Religion of Humanity, in contrast to Christianity, is fundamentally concerned with *connecting* each man's feelings of duty *with* the interests of his fellow-creatures. It embodies, moreover, the very essence of religion—the "direction of the emotions and desires toward an ideal object, recognised . . . as rightfully paramount over all selfish objects of desire" ("UR," 421–22). The nontheological Religion of Humanity embodies a superior ethos in its selfless concern for the good of the whole over the concern for a particular and personal salvation centered on the "miserable individuality" of the average person. Mill's remarks in "Utility of Religion" provide a nice summation of his settled view. As we saw in Chapter 3, Mill believed that Christian ethics, and especially its conception of divinely administered rewards and punishments and its emphasis on personal salvation, taints moral action by encouraging self-interested behavior or outright selfishness. The social Religion of Humanity, by contrast, is disinterested, that is, "unselfish":

> It carries the thoughts and feelings out of self, and fixes them on an unselfish object, loved and pursued as an end for its own sake. The religions which deal in promises and threats regarding a future life, [by contrast,] fasten down the thoughts to the person's own posthumous interests; they tempt him to regard the performance of his duties to others mainly as a means to his own personal salvation; and are one of the most serious obstacles to the great purpose of moral culture, the strengthening of the unselfish and weakening of the selfish element in our nature. ("UR," 422)

The war against the evil of selfishness was also bound up with Mill's call for the radical emendation of human nature in "Nature." As we recall, in that essay Mill, having discussed what he, with Bentham, refers to as the "self-regarding" virtues, turns to an examination of their opposite, the "social virtues." These, he says, are exclusively the product of artifice and cultivation, for "it . . . is the verdict of all experience that selfishness is natural" (394). The observation of Henry Reeve is to the point: Mill, said Reeve, "aimed at a radical reform of human nature itself, when men were to care far more for the interests of the community than those of the individual."[19]

Another illustration of Mill's views in this regard is provided in his explanation for the unhappiness of those who "do not find in life sufficient enjoyment to make it valuable to them." The reason for their unhappiness, Mill tells us, is that they "car[e] for nobody but themselves." Selfishness is the cause of unhappiness while, conversely, highly developed "social feelings" realize the ultimate end of utilitarian morality, "collective" or "general" happiness. The crucial relation between social feeling and happiness in Mill's thought is thus related to his intense concern for cultivating the social feelings of humanity. Mill, as we know, had found what little happiness he did precisely in the thought that his own service to humanity was moving him closer to "unity of feeling" with that abstract collective. As he says, those "especially . . . who have . . . cultivated a fellow-feeling with the collective interests of mankind" remain vigorous and vital to the end of their days. Mill's view, as we have seen, was that the realization of such a fellow feeling with humanity's "collective interests" could provide a spiritual substance capable of fulfilling all of mankind's religious needs (*Util*, 415).

Mill refuses to concede that human unhappiness is an ineradicable part of the nature of things. Unhappiness is caused mainly by selfishness, as well as by insufficient "mental cultivation." There is no reason, he says, why each person may not be provided with "an amount of mental culture sufficient" to achieve happiness nor is there "an inherent necessity that any human being should be a selfish egotist, devoid of every feeling or care but those which centre in his own miserable individuality." The proper sorts of social affections and the proper kind of interest in the public good, says Mill, are available "to every rightly brought up human being." We may recall that Mill, like his father before him, was enchanted by the possibilities of perfecting human nature en masse through the art and skill of the Educator and Legislator. As he says in *Utilitarianism*, "Something far superior to [the miserable individuality of most existing men] is sufficiently common even now, to give ample earnest of what the human species may be made." Not, we may emphasize, what they may make themselves through self-cultivation, as the youthful Mill at the height of his Romantic reaction might have put it, but what they "may be made" by training ("from infancy") and especially through the formation of the right psychological associations. As James Mill had taught his son, through such training "we might make as many good men as almost as we please." In "a world such as this," devoid of moral order, organized by a God who could do no better than create people the likes of Eskimos or Patagonians or engineer his other "clumsy" contrivances, there is, as Mill says, "so much . . . to correct and improve."

Indeed, Mill envisioned possibilities for the amelioration of human existence that were breathtaking in their scope: "[N]o one whose opinion deserves a moment's consideration can doubt that most of the great positive evils of the world are in themselves removable, and will, if human affairs continue to improve, be in the end reduced within narrow limits." Mill specifically identifies poverty, which "may be completely extinguished by the wisdom of society," combined, he reassures his traditionalist readers, "with the good sense and providence of individuals." Disease too will assuredly be "indefinitely reduced" by education and the progress of science. Nor will Mill countenance submission to the "vicissitudes of fortune." These, he declares, are usually

> the effect either of gross imprudence, of ill-regulated desires, or of bad or imperfect social institutions. All the grand sources, in short, of human suffering are in a great degree, many of them almost entirely, conquerable by human care and effort; and though their removal is grievously slow—though a long succession of generations will perish in the breach before the conquest is completed, and this world becomes all that, if will and knowledge were not wanting, it might easily be made—yet every mind sufficiently intelligent and generous to bear a part, however small and unconspicuous, in the endeavour, will draw a noble enjoyment from the contest itself, which he would not for any bribe in the form of selfish indulgence consent to be without. (*Util*, 415–16)

This latter is an implicit reference to Christianity, the system of bribes to the selfish. The remarks that precede it—about the fulfillment each person will achieve through bearing his part, however small, in perfecting the society of the future, in helping to realize the final end of temporal human suffering and effort—implicitly refer to the Religion of Humanity. Religious fulfillment is to be gained through making this world what, "if will and knowledge were not wanting, it might easily be made." This, in short, is the "social" meaning and purpose Mill hopes to install in place of the meaning and purpose offered by transcendent faith and its hope for eternal fulfillment in God. A fulfilled and meaningful life need not wait for some uncertain and perhaps imaginary hereafter. All can find it here and now, taking their "unconspicuous" part in perfecting the inevitable future society and finding complete—religious—fulfillment in "the contest itself." There is no need to dwell on the ominous resemblance of Mill's vision to that which inspired the mass slaughter of the past century.

It may not be impertinent to ask why a morality based upon the love and fear of God and even upon the expectation of a final judgment is any more intrinsically selfish than Mill's own proposed "social morality." For the latter is based upon the love and fear of Mill's proposed *human* replacements for the traditional God, upon the expectation of *human* judgment. Despite his condemnation of the selfish system of rewards and punishments that is divine justice, Mill's own ultimate inducement for good behavior and sanction for bad behavior is precisely the threat of punishment, not one administered by God in the world beyond but here and now at the hands of purely human agents. Mill's intended replacement for transcendent justice makes it clear that his real concern is not with the selfish regard for one's personal salvation, as he claims, but with insuring ultimate control for the *human* "judges, preceptors, or parents, [who] administer reward and punishment as such" (*Util*, 450) and for whom the traditional God is an intrusion and a rival.

Mill adverts to his old moral dichotomy between the evil of the selfish (associated with Christianity) and the good of the social (associated with the Religion of Humanity). One problem faced by those who will establish the new social religion, he says, is that for most people social feeling is less developed than the propensity toward selfishness; for some, social feeling is altogether lacking. Nevertheless, there is hope. For Mill knows from personal experience that for those who do have the requisite "social feeling," such as Mill and his wife, "it possesses all the characters of a natural feeling." Mill is thus certain that people can be socialized to such an extent that this artificial creation will seem natural—a view, as noted, not only ominous but particularly strange from a thinker often regarded as a champion of the dignity of rational human choice and rational liberty. As Mill explains, however, the "social feeling" as he experiences it "does not present itself to [the mind] as a superstition of education, or a law despotically imposed by the power of society, but as an attribute which it would not be well . . . to be without. *This conviction is the ultimate sanction of the greatest happiness morality*" (emphasis added). Not God, not reason, not the ability to choose one's moral rules, obligations, or one's ultimate or even provisional commitments, but a "social feeling" or "conviction" so deeply internalized as a result of an intensive process of socialization that it seems like a second nature—this, Mill claims, is to be the "ultimate sanction," the "powerful internal binding force," of the utilitarian religion (*Util*, 437). Mill aimed for nothing less than the power to form souls, to shape the human mind and spirit in the direction of his new and superior humanitarian religion.

The Question of Proof

Mill, in contrast to his usual intense preoccupation with the issue of proof, is willing to tread somewhat softly when it comes to proving that the principle of utility is the "first principle" or ultimate ground of moral obligation. After all, he now argues, assuming an Aristotelian stance, neither first principles nor "questions of ultimate ends . . . admit of proof." One cannot prove that the medical art is good unless one assumes, without proof, that the goal, or end, of health is a good. We know, however, that health is a good by the fact that all people desire it, and we thus know that health is an end because "[q]uestions about ends are . . . questions [about] what things are desirable." All of this holds as well for the ultimate end of the utilitarian morality—happiness. We know happiness is the end of all action because we know that all people desire happiness. And since an end of human action is the same thing as what is desirable to the agent, we know that happiness is the end of human action. Indeed, Mill argues, utility or happiness is not only desirable, but "the only thing desirable, as an end; all other things being only desirable as means to that end"[20] (*Util*, 438). The question is why this should be accepted as true.

Mill's difficulty is not so much with proving that happiness is the ultimate end of human action. While people may quibble over what this actually entails—for example, the relative importance of temporal and eternal happiness, whether virtue promotes happiness or is an independent end, and so on—it is not difficult to so frame an argument and so appeal to common experience that the majority will concede that all people do desire happiness. Mill's problem, which he never solves, is to show from the fact that all people desire their own happiness that all people necessarily desire "the general happiness." Mill concedes that "[n]o reason can be given why the general happiness is desirable, except that each person, so far as he believes it to be attainable, desires his own happiness." He immediately leapfrogs over all possible difficulties and objections, however, and pronounces that because "each person's happiness is a good to that person, . . . *the general happiness [is], therefore, a good to the aggregate of all persons*" (emphasis added). In fact, however, there is no logical or experiential relationship between the two ends. Desiring one's own happiness is a realistic and concrete aim, but except in the most abstract or metaphorical sense there is no such entity as "the general happiness" that individuals may hope to realize. Nor is there any such entity as a sentient, thinking, willing "aggregate of all persons" who could enjoy the general happiness even if it were attained. This is all the more strange from a thinker like Mill, who sometimes characterized himself as a nominalist.[21] Mill, however, like the other ostensible nominalist Bentham, had a peculiar and inexplicable tendency to hypostatize general conceptions, as in his notorious hypostatizations of "society" in *On Liberty* and of "nature" in "Nature."[22] Indeed, Mill implicitly concedes that there is no necessary relation between personal happiness and the general happiness when he takes pains to emphasize that the aim of the greatest happiness doctrine is *not* in fact the happiness of the individual: "I must again repeat, . . . that the happiness which forms the utilitarian standard of what is right in conduct, is not the agent's own happiness, but that of all concerned" (*Util*, 418). Mill simply ignores the illogic of leaping from the fact that individuals desire their own happiness to the assertion that they therefore desire the general happiness. "Happiness," he says, "has made out its title as one of the ends of conduct, and consequently one of the criteria of morality," thereby skirting the important issue of whose happiness is involved, that of "the aggregate of all persons" or that of the individual. He also qualifies or contradicts by this statement his previous assertion that happiness is not only desirable but "the only thing desirable, as an end" (*Util*, 438–39).

Mill does acknowledge the validity of certain objections, for instance, that happiness, while an acknowledged end of human action, is not its sole end. People may desire virtue and the absence of vice as much as they desire pleasure and the absence of pain. Utilitarianism certainly admits that virtue is desired and desirable. Indeed, "[i]t maintains not only that virtue should be desired, but that it is to be desired disinterestedly, for itself." Having claimed this fundamental ground, Mill proceeds to appropriate all the virtues of a priori, in-itself morality for nontheological utilitarianism. For utilitarians, he says,

> recognise as a psychological fact the possibility of [virtue] being, to the individual, a good in itself, without looking to any end beyond it; and hold, that the mind is not in a right state, not in a state conformable to Utility, not in the state most conducive to the general happiness, unless it does love virtue in this manner—as a thing desirable in itself, even although, in the individual instance, it should not produce those other desirable consequences which it tends to produce, and on account of which it is held to be virtue. *This opinion is not, in the smallest degree, a departure from the Happiness principle.* (emphasis added)

Of course, it is the antithesis of the happiness principle, but Mill can explain this away on utilitarian grounds. More precisely, he can reconcile the seeming contradiction between the utilitarian view that virtue should be "desirable in itself" and its view that "actions and dispositions are only virtuous because they promote another end than virtue" on the grounds of the associationist psychology he inherited from his father (*Util*, 439–40).

Utilitarians, Mill says, fully acknowledge that certain activities, such as virtuous actions or pleasure attained through music, are "desired and desirable in and for themselves" and not merely "as means to a collective something termed happiness." The solution to this seeming puzzle is that virtue and other entities or activities usually regarded as good in themselves, while "not naturally and originally part of the end, [are] capable of becoming so." That is, through a process of association, activities "originally indifferent, but conducive to, or otherwise associated with, the satisfaction of our primitive desires, become in themselves sources of pleasure more valuable than the primitive pleasures." There is a psychological law of association that makes things originally desired as means to the end of pleasure become desired as ends in themselves. Mill illustrates this principle of association with the common instance of the love of money. While money is originally desired as a means to the various pleasures it can obtain, eventually it comes to be desired in itself. People forget the original end for which it was desired and come to regard its possession as a good-in-itself. The same process obtains for the love of virtue. Originally "desired as an instrument for the attainment of happiness," it too can "come to be desired for its own sake." In fact, one of the chief purposes of education and training is to create precisely such an association in the trainees' minds, so that, while they originally perform virtuously for the pleasure or reward it brings, eventually the association becomes so strongly established that they come to "love [virtue] disinterestedly . . . [It] is desired and cherished, not as a means to happiness, but as a part of their happiness." In short, with respect to the love of virtue-in-itself, as for any other thing desired as good in itself, there is actually "no original desire of it, or motive to it, save its conduciveness to pleasure, and especially to protection from pain. But through the association thus formed, it may be felt a good in itself, and desired as such with as great intensity as any other good" (*Util*, 440–41). In short, there is no natural desire of good or of God. All men desire only pleasure but can be trained to associate pleasure with virtue.

Mill, despite his criticism of the morality-intoxicated Comte, was every bit as devoted to the reign of virtue. Those people, he says, who have cultivated "the disinterested love of virtue" provide the greatest blessings to society. Thus, "the utilitarian standard, while it tolerates and approves [various] acquired desires" such as love of money, power, fame, and so forth, "up to the point beyond which they would be more injurious to the general happiness than promotive of it, enjoins and requires the cultivation of the love of virtue up to the greatest strength possible, as being above all things important to the general happiness." Moral slackers need not expect an easy time in the society of the future oriented toward the Religion of Duty.

Mill rests the ultimate proof of utilitarianism on the psychological considerations just developed. If these views are "psychologically true—if human nature is so constituted as to desire nothing which is not either a part of happiness or a means of happiness, we can have no other proof, and we require no other, that these are the only things desirable." Much rests on this statement. For, as Mill says, if it is true that "happiness is the sole end of human action, and the promotion of it the test by which to judge of all human conduct; . . . it necessarily follows that it must be the criterion of morality, since a part is included in the whole." Mill's confident assertion sounds plausible, but does not withstand a close examination. For, while it may be true that happiness in some sense or another is "the sole end of human action," it is not also necessarily true, as Mill suggests, that "the promotion of it [is] the test by which to judge of all human conduct." Nor is there anything compelling, morally or psychologically, about Mill's notion of happiness "confined within the limits of the earth" ("UR," 421). Many people throughout history have hoped to attain eternal happiness in God through obeying his moral law. Testing or judging one's behavior by its conformity to Mill's utilitarian rules would serve little purpose if this sort of happiness were one's end.

As may be expected, Mill contends that the question of whether all men desire that which produces pleasure and shun that which produces pain is "a question of fact and experience, dependent, like all similar questions, upon evidence." The requisite evidence, moreover, is to be gained through "practised self-consciousness and self-observation, assisted by observation of others" (*Util*, 442–43). This passage draws attention to Mill's employment of a double standard concerning "proof." As we saw in our discussion of "Theism," Mill, when dissecting and refuting the so-called "argument from consciousness" for the existence of God, ruled out of court the evidence of those who claim to have experienced an "inner light" or some other form of direct intuitive experience of God. Because Mill could find no such evidence within his own consciousness, he dismissed it. But when attempting to prove his own favorite principle— utility—he is perfectly willing to accept the validity of "practised self-consciousness and self-observation." This may be a small point, but it is characteristic.

Utility and Justice

The final chapter of *Utilitarianism* presents Mill's well-known discussion of the utilitarian conception of justice. The purpose of the chapter is to defeat what is perhaps the most important objection to utilitarian morality, namely, its apparent inability to account for the transcendent significance that most people attribute to justice. The special severity and weight that men have historically attached to that virtue seem, Mill says, to "point to an inherent quality in things," to suggest "that the just must have an existence in Nature as something absolute . . . " In short, the singular feeling attached to "the idea of justice" points, above all, to God and his moral law. As Mill believes, however, "[m]ankind are always predisposed to believe that any subjective feeling, not otherwise accounted for, is a revelation of some objective reality [that is, God. Accordingly, Mill's] object is to determine whether the reality, to which the feeling of justice corresponds, is one which needs any such special revelation . . . " Mill's task is clear. Following his long-established rule, he will attempt to find another (naturalistic) way to account for the transcendent feeling attached to justice.[23] If he succeeds, so he believes, the traditional association of justice with a transcendent moral law (and God) will have been seriously undermined, if not refuted. As we shall see, Mill not only does not trace the "imperative" quality of justice to a transcendent origin, but does not even locate its source in a strictly human reason, as one might expect from the Saint of Rationalism and disciple of the narrowly rationalistic Bentham. Mill, indeed, demotes the "sentiment" of justice to the level of the subhuman and subrational. The peculiar intensity of the sentiment of justice, he contends, is derived from its animalistic quality, for mankind's sense of justice turns out to be nothing more than "the animal desire to . . . retaliate," moralized by the "social feelings." We are a long way from the Greeks that Mill professed to admire.

Mill, then, will explain away, on naturalistic and even animalistic grounds, the seemingly transcendent significance of the idea of justice. This is essential because throughout human history the special significance attached to justice has proved an obstacle to the embrace of the utilitarian ethic. Most people have been unwilling to accept the doctrine that utility, or happiness, is the criterion of right and wrong because they have thought that justice points to God. Or, as Mill puts it, because "the subjective mental feeling of justice is different from that which commonly attaches to simple expediency, and [is generally] far more imperative in its demands, people find it difficult to see, in justice, only a particular kind or branch of general utility, and think that its superior binding force requires a totally different origin." To show that the "peculiar" feeling attached to justice does not require or even point to a transcendent source, Mill first attempts to identify the defining attributes of justice and injustice, that which is "always present" when men call something just or unjust. Once the defining attribute of justice has been identified, it should be possible to determine whether it "would be capable of gathering round it a sentiment of that peculiar character and intensity by virtue of the general laws of our emotional constitution, or whether the sentiment is inexplicable, and requires to be regarded as a special provision of Nature" (*Util*, 446–47). If the former should turn out to be the case, Mill believes, the issue will have been resolved. We can anticipate his findings. (We may note that to this point Mill has not once mentioned the idea of God, which is the real target of the analysis. This is yet another instance of his long-established procedure of dealing with a subject "as if religion did not exist.")

Mill adopts the nominalist approach in searching for the essence or defining attribute of justice: "To find the common attributes of a variety of objects, it is necessary to begin by surveying the objects themselves in the concrete." Justice, apparently, may be an attribute of either actions or "arrangements"; Mill will examine the various "modes of action, and arrangements of human affairs" that are usually classified as just or unjust. He identifies six classifications of "things well known to excite the sentiments associated with those names [Just and Unjust]." First, justice involves the protection of a person's *legal rights;* injustice in this case is thought to involve a breach of law. Second, a law itself may be regarded as unjust, and this when it is thought to violate a person's *moral rights.* The third sense of justice—which, Mill revealingly suggests, is "perhaps, the clearest and most emphatic form in which the idea of justice is conceived by the general mind"—is that of *desert*: "It is universally considered just that each person should obtain that . . . which he deserves . . . " Fourth, it is unjust to *break faith* with anyone, to disappoint legitimate expectations.

Fifth, justice generally involves *impartiality*, although this is absolutely required only "where rights are concerned." For Mill also thinks that impartiality can mean "being solely influenced by desert; as with those who, in the capacity of judges, preceptors, or parents, administer reward and punishment as such." Mill suggests that a desert-based justice can be impartial: "Impartiality, in short, as an obligation of justice, may be said to mean, being exclusively influenced by the considerations which it is supposed ought to influence the particular case in hand; and resisting the solicitation of any motives which prompt to conduct different from what those considerations would dictate" (*Util*, 448–50). Such an interpretation leaves considerable leeway for a wide variety of interpretations of exactly what "impartiality" dictates in any particular case. It may, for instance, mean "being solely influenced by desert" and not by the objectivity of law. Mill's defense of desert-based justice is emphasized here because, as has been discussed, his ideal was a perfectly transparent desert-based justice, a conception that in part accounts for his lifelong attraction to socialist economic arrangements (see Chapter 8).

Mill's sixth and final classification of justice is based on the notion of *equality*. This, he observes, is often "allied to the idea of impartiality" and, indeed, "in the eyes of many persons, constitutes its essence" (the classical-liberal understanding of equality under the law). Mill points out, however, that the relation between equality and justice is extremely controversial and varies dramatically among people—variations, he says, which "always conform . . . to their notion of utility." That is, "[e]ach person maintains that equality is the dictate of justice, except where he thinks that expediency requires inequality." For instance, some people think it expedient to uphold "social privileges" for certain classes such as the wealthy, or different rights for different groups, such as masters and slaves. Mill concludes that "there are as many questions of justice as there are differences of opinion about expediency." Moreover, "the sense of natural justice [the animal desire to retaliate] may be plausibly appealed to in behalf of every one of these opinions," because it can ally itself with any intellectual or moral conception (*Util*, 451).

Mill is looking for the "mental link" that unites all of the above understandings of justice. Etymology provides a clue. The history of the word *justice* "points distinctly to an origin connected with the ordinances of law," which, Mill says, can further be traced to a belief in a divine source of law: "There can . . . be no doubt that the idée mere, the primitive element, in the formation of the notion of justice, was conformity to law. It constituted the entire idea among the Hebrews, up to the birth of Christianity; as might be expected in the case of a people whose laws attempted to embrace all subjects on which precepts were required, and who believed those laws to be a direct emanation from the Supreme Being." What this suggests to Mill's mind is that the Jews (and, by implication, the Christians) did not have and could not have had the conception of an unjust law, because they thought all law was ordained by God and, as such, just. The notion of an unjust law, and indeed the development of the higher-law tradition in general, he further suggests, was bound up with the discovery that law is man-made:

But other nations, and in particular the Greeks and Romans, who knew that their laws had been made originally, and still continued to be made, by men, were not afraid to admit that those men might make bad laws; might do, by law, the same things, and from the same motives, which if done by individuals without the sanction of law, would be called unjust. And hence the sentiment of injustice came to be attached, not to all violations of law, but only to violations of such laws as ought to exist, including such as ought to exist, but do not; and to laws themselves, if supposed to be contrary to what ought to be law. In this manner the idea of law and of its injunctions was still predominant in the notion of justice, even when the laws actually in force ceased to be accepted as the standard of it. (*Util*, 452)

By such an "argument" Mill in effect transfers the source of the higher-law tradition from God to man. It goes without saying that the conception of a higher law was based precisely on the belief in a source of law higher than man. It was precisely because God's law transcended and ordered human law that man-made law could be resisted as unjust when it violated the higher, divine law. Mill not only ignores this fact, but twists the argument in the direction he desires. The notion of an unjust law, he says, arose because men knew, first, that they themselves made law; second, that they themselves could sometimes be partial and unjust; and thus, third, that a law, as made merely by men like themselves, could be partial and unjust as well. This is one of the clearest illustrations of Mill's willingness deliberately to distort an argument to serve his purposes. He well understood the source of the higher-law tradition in divine law. His aim in the above passage is not to conduct a philosophical inquiry but to draw a veil over the notion of a transcendent source of law, indeed, to so confuse and manipulate the reader as to lead him to embrace the conclusion Mill wishes to establish. All law, and all justice, he would insist throughout his life, are man-made.

Mill recognizes that the idea of a higher law—"the idea of the breach of what ought to be law"—lingers in the minds of his contemporary audience. But this lingering commitment to the notion of a higher law Mill will explain away on a naturalistic and psychological basis, drawing, indeed, on his own personal experience—on his own simultaneous terror and pleasurable anticipation of the administration of punishment. We approach a rather dark mental landscape.

Punishment

"Mistrust," said Nietzsche, "all in whom the urge to punish is strong." He may have had Mill in mind. For Mill believed he had identified the reason for mankind's belief in a higher law, not, as said, in the human apprehension of God's law, but in the pleasurable anticipation of punishing wrongdoing. The "essence of law," Mill says, is "the idea of legal constraint," which is related to the belief that a wrongdoer "ought to be punished." He explains, *It would always give us pleasure, and chime in with our feelings of fitness, that actions which we deem unjust should be punished . . . "* For various reasons, he acknowledges, people do not always think it "expedient" that their desire to punish wrongdoing should be fulfilled through public authorities. Nevertheless, but for incidental inconvenience and inexpediency, says Mill,

> [w]e should be glad to see just conduct enforced and injustice repressed, even in the minutest details, if we were not, with reason, afraid of trusting the magistrate with so unlimited an amount of power over individuals. When we think that a person is bound in justice to do a thing, it is an ordinary form of language to say, that he ought to be compelled to do it. We should be gratified to see the obligation enforced by anybody who had the power. If we see that its enforcement by law would be inexpedient, we lament the impossibility, we consider the impunity given to injustice as an evil, and strive to make amends for it by bringing a strong expression of our own and the public disapprobation to bear upon the offender.[24] Thus the idea of legal constraint is still the generating idea of the notion of justice, though undergoing several transformations before that notion, as it exists in an advanced state of society, becomes complete. (*Util*, 453)

The remarkable views expressed in this passage say very much about Mill and very little about justice. First, there is of course no universal "pleasure" in punishing wrongdoing, which may in fact be undertaken with sincere regret and even pain that coercion or restraint is necessary. Mill, however, not only asserts that delight in punishing is a universal fact of experience, but goes so far as to ground the very idea of justice in such delight. Right and wrong, he says, are necessarily bound up with the idea of punishment:

> [T]here is no doubt that th[e] distinction [between deserving and not deserving punishment] lies at the bottom of the notions of right and wrong; that we call any conduct wrong, or employ, instead, some other term of dislike or disparagement, according as we think that the person ought, or ought not, to be punished for it; and we say, it would be right, to do so and so, or merely that it would be desirable or laudable, according as we would wish to see the person whom it concerns, compelled, or only persuaded and exhorted, to act in that manner. (*Util*, 454)

To blame people is to think them "proper objects of punishment." To call an action wrong, says Mill, means that we think someone "ought . . . to be punished for it." Indeed, to call an action right also implies punishment or coercion, that is, "we would wish to see the person whom it concerns compelled . . . to act in that manner." In short, according to Mill, both right and wrong *always* involve the idea of compulsion. There is no law, moral or legal, absent a *human* sanction, absent the punishing or exhorting hand of the parent, preceptor, or magistrate. Let us recall in this context Mill's vehement condemnation of the servility and selfishness of the Christian expectation of divine punishment. Mill would destroy the notion of divine justice, of man's accountability to God. In its place he would put the revolting and ominous notion that right and wrong are solely defined by the coercive sanctions of various human agents. Apparently a slavish and servile fear before such human agents was less distasteful to Mill than the thought of submission to divine law.

Mill's conviction that right and wrong—justice—is necessarily bound up with the idea of legal constraint and anticipated delight in punishing wrongdoing is, then, bound up with the legal positivism he absorbed from Bentham and Austin. The "essence of law," he says, is "the idea of penal sanction." There is no law without punishment. This is bad enough, of course, but Mill takes the idea even further—not just legal obligation, but "moral obligation in general," he says, involves the idea of "legal constraint" or "penal sanction," that is, punishment: "For the truth is, that the idea of penal sanction, which is the essence of law, enters not only into the conception of injustice, but into that of any kind of wrong. We do not call anything wrong, unless we mean to imply that a person ought to be punished in some way or other for doing it; if not by law, by the opinion of his fellow-creatures; if not by opinion, by the reproaches of his own conscience" (*Util*, 453).

Mill's writings reveal a deep preoccupation with the subject of punishment, which assumes preponderant significance in his psychological and social theory. As we have seen, for Mill, the ordinary idea of what is right—"that a person is bound in justice to do a thing"—is necessarily bound up with the feeling "that he ought to be compelled to do it." It is perhaps unnecessary to point out the fallaciousness of this assertion. One often regards an action as right without in any way believing that a person should be compelled to so act. It is right to be trustworthy. It is right to be truthful and sincere. It is right to respect one's parents and to revere life. Very few people, and certainly few classical liberals, believe such states of being should be compelled or, indeed, that it is even possible to compel them. There is an obvious and tremendous distinction between what one regards as right-in-itself and what one regards as justifying compulsion. A person of questionable integrity may call forth our contempt or our pity, but not an instantaneous desire to punish him for his low ethical standards or compel him to do better. In any event, it is clear that the desire to punish is peculiar to a certain kind of person and is far from a universal fact of experience, as Mill asserts.

Mill's own anticipation of the delight of punishing and the fury he invested in the administration of a strictly human justice are transparently related to his equally fierce rejection of divine justice, of the contemptible "posthumous sanction." Having rejected the possibility of ultimate divine justice, the only justice available to him is that administered by human agents in present existence. A person who believes that the ultimate moral order of existence is not in human, but in God's hands, will not feel it appropriate to sit in judgment of all other human beings or to call them to account for their moral shortcomings, let alone to punish them for such and take pleasure in that act. For one, however, such as Mill, who is without the sense that the rightness of existence is ultimately in the hands of a higher authority, the urgency to administer total justice now or, as Mill puts it, "to see just conduct enforced and injustice repressed, even in the minutest details," assumes a frightening intensity.

Mill's identification of the idea of justice with "legal constraint" obliterates man's spiritual conscience and his relationship to a higher source along with the notion of higher law. For Mill, the human conscience is formed exclusively by the socialization process. There is no law above man-made law, and all such law is essentially defined by a coercive sanction. In-itself morality, and the associated sense of a *given* moral order, despite Mill's associationist maneuvers, are obliterated as well. Finally, Mill would eliminate divine justice merely to transfer the power of ultimate justice to human beings, to the various human judges, preceptors, and parents who loom in ominous and godlike proportion in Mill's imaginative scheme of things. In that scheme, there is ultimately nothing beyond their power of punishment, whether effected through the means of law, opinion, or the individual consciences they have formed. As previously remarked, in entering Mill's world, we enter a brave new world far, far beyond freedom and dignity.

Let us turn our attention to Mill's studied omission of divine justice from his account of punishment in *Utilitarianism*. A human being, he says, may fear punishment "by *law*, by the *opinion* of his fellow-creatures; . . . [or] by the reproaches of his own *conscience*" (emphases added). It is perhaps not accidental that Mill has omitted from his enumeration of possible penal sanctions the one kind of punishment that preoccupies him elsewhere—posthumous punishment by God. As we have seen, one of Mill's missions, from the time of his immersion in Bentham's *Analysis* through his writing of "Utility of Religion," was to undermine the belief in the efficacy of the posthumous sanction and to portray belief in that sanction as servile and selfish. Mill, however, has somehow forgotten even to mention the possibility of divine punishment in the context of his extensive discussion of punishment in *Utilitarianism*. This is yet another illustration of Mill's deliberate strategy, articulated in his correspondence to Comte, to ignore, when possible, questions of religion and God, in order not to draw his readers' attention to that which he was trying to obscure.

Justice: The Animal Desire to Retaliate

Mill finally identifies the defining attribute of justice as the notion of a "right in some person"—"a claim on the part of one or more individuals, like that which the law gives when it confers a proprietary or other legal right." Accordingly, the two things necessary for injustice to occur are a wrong done to someone who possesses a right and an "assignable person who is wronged." Justice, in short, always involves something a person can claim from another as his "moral right."

Having identified the defining attribute of justice, Mill returns to the chief purpose of the chapter, that is, to provide a naturalistic explanation for the transcendent significance that human beings attach to the virtue of justice. Or, as he says, the aim is to determine "whether the [special] feeling, which accompanies the idea [of justice], is attached to it by a special dispensation of nature, or whether it could have grown up, by any known laws, out of the idea itself; and in particular, whether it can have originated in considerations of general expediency" (*Util*, 455–56). Mill recapitulates his findings: "[T]he two essential ingredients in the sentiment of justice are, the desire to punish a person who has done harm, and the knowledge or belief that there is some definite individual or individuals to whom harm has been done." He returns to what he has identified as the foundation of justice—the desire to punish. This desire, he says, is a "spontaneous outgrowth from two [natural] sentiments, . . . which either are or resemble instincts; the impulse of self-defence, and the feeling of sympathy." As Mill explains, it is entirely natural to "resent" and to attempt to "repel or retaliate" any harm done or threatened to be done to ourselves or "those with whom we sympathize." It is not necessary, he says, to discuss the origin of this sentiment. The desire to retaliate may be an instinct or it may be "a result of intelligence"; in any event, we know that it is "common to all animal nature; for every animal tries to hurt those who have hurt, or who it thinks are about to hurt, itself or its young." In this respect, human beings differ from animals only in that, first, they can sympathize with a wider sphere of creatures, indeed, with "all sentient beings"; and second, they are more intelligent and thus have a wider range of sympathies, both "self-regarding" and "sympathetic." This is important, because man's superior intelligence and superior range of sympathy allow him to extend his instinct or natural desire to retaliate to the community at large. As Mill puts it, they make him

> capable of apprehending a community of interest between himself and the human society of which he forms a part, such that any conduct which threatens the security of the society generally, is threatening to his own, and calls forth his instinct (if instinct it be) of self-defence. The same superiority of intelligence, joined to the power of sympathising with human beings generally, enables him to attach himself to the collective idea of his tribe, his country, or mankind, in such a manner that any act hurtful to them, raises his instinct of sympathy, and urges him to resistance.

Mill, as we know, was at pains, in "Nature" and elsewhere, to discountenance the notion that a natural feeling is in any way entitled to moral approbation. Indeed, in "Nature" he counsels the strict regulation and even extirpation of such natural feelings. The "animal desire to . . . retaliate," however, like the "germ" of "social feeling," is a natural attribute that Mill has every interest in promoting.

Mill further identifies the desire to punish—as we have seen, a predominant element of the "sentiment of justice"—with "the natural feeling of retaliation or vengeance . . . applicable to those injuries . . . [or] hurts, which wound us through, or in common with, society at large." This natural desire for retaliation, Mill admits, is in itself amoral. The moralization of this animal desire occurs only by means of its "exclusive subordination . . . to the social sympathies, so as to wait on and obey their call." Mill explains: "For the natural feeling [by itself] would make us resent indiscriminately whatever any one does that is disagreeable to us; but when moralised by the social feeling, it only acts in the directions conformable to the general good: just persons resenting a hurt to society, though not otherwise a hurt to themselves, and not resenting a hurt to themselves, however painful, unless it be of the kind which society has a common interest with them in the repression of" (*Util*, 456–57).

The "sentiment of justice," in short, is the "animal desire to . . . retaliate" moralized by subordination to the "social feelings." Mill answers those who might object that the sense of justice is most often outraged not by harm done to society at large or to any "collective interest" but by a concrete violation of an individual's right. Mill acknowledges that this is a common experience, but he denies it is commendable or moral to feel outrage over a merely individual injustice. It is natural, he says, to feel resentment merely because we have suffered pain, but a person whose resentment is really a moral feeling, that is, who considers whether an act is blamable before he allows himself to resent it—such a person, though he may not say expressly to himself that he is standing up for the interest of society, certainly does feel that he is asserting a rule which is for the benefit of others as well as for his own. . . . If he is not feeling this—if he is regarding the act solely as it affects him individually—he is not consciously just; he is not concerning himself about the justice of his actions.[25]

Justice *requires* a self-conscious feeling for society.

Mill conceives the rule he has just pronounced—that a person "feel that he is asserting a rule which is for the benefit" of everyone—as equivalent to Kant's categorical imperative: "So act, that thy rule of conduct might be adopted as a law by all rational beings."

[Kant] virtually acknowledges that the interest of mankind collectively, or at least of mankind indiscriminately, must be in the mind of the agent when conscientiously deciding on the morality of the act. Otherwise he uses words without a meaning: for, that a rule even of utter selfishness could not possibly be adopted by all rational beings [is implausible]. . . . To give any meaning to Kant's principle, the sense put upon it must be, that we ought to shape our conduct by a rule which all rational beings might adopt with benefit to their collective interest.

Mill refines the "idea of justice" in line with the development of his argument: This idea, he now says, "supposes two things; *a rule of conduct, and a sentiment which sanctions the rule*" (emphasis added). The first element of justice—the rule of conduct—"must be supposed common to all mankind, and intended for their good." Mill does not say how or by whom the substance of the rules of justice is to be determined; he is undoubtedly thinking of utilitarian legislators and moralists. The second element, the "sentiment," is the desire to punish—the "desire that punishment may be suffered by those who infringe the rule." We now have Mill's final identification of the "sentiment" or "idea" of justice: "[T]he sentiment of justice appears to me to be, the animal desire to repel or retaliate a hurt or damage to oneself, or to those with whom one sympathises, widened so as to include all persons, by the human capacity of enlarged sympathy, and the human conception of intelligent self-interest" (*Util*, 457–58).

Mill explains that the morality of justice derives from the latter element, the ability to sympathize with all mankind. He is concerned that his naturalistic account will not satisfy those for whom the transcendent significance of justice points to a divine moral law, that is, that utility may not "convey a sufficient feeling of the strength of the obligation." He thus reiterates that the "peculiar impressiveness, and energy of self-assertion" of the sentiment of justice derive from the fact that this feeling is composed of "not a rational [element] only, but also an animal element, the thirst for retaliation . . . " The "intensity" of this thirst, "as well as its moral justification," is derived from the "extraordinarily important" utility it concerns—security—which everyone feels to be the most important of all human interests: "All other earthly benefits are needed by one person, not needed by another; and many of them can, if necessary, be cheerfully foregone, . . . but security no human being can possibly do without; on it we depend for all our immunity from evil," and all our plans for the future. Justice and rights, in short, involve the most important claims that people can make on their fellows—"to join in making safe for us the very groundwork of our existence." And it is this universal importance attached to personal security, Mill proposes, that partly accounts for the self-assertive "energy" of the sentiment of justice and the related notion of rights, that is, their "character of absoluteness, that apparent infinity, and incommensurability with all other considerations . . . The feelings concerned are so powerful, and we count so positively on finding a responsive feeling in others (all being alike interested), that *ought* and *should* grow into *must,* and recognised indispensability becomes a moral necessity, analogous to physical, and often not inferior to it in binding force . . . "

Mill's account of the relation between the moral intensity historically associated with the virtue of justice and the indispensability of security is plausible so far as it goes. That is, it may account for the vigor with which people defend (or once defended) their own, and others', rights of person and property. It does not, however, account for Mill's own main justice-related concern, that is, his concern with social, distributive, or desert-based justice. Such conceptions of justice do not have to do with security of person and property but with ensuring a "moral" distribution of the goods of this earth or an equivalence between material goods and moral desert. That Mill's strong concern with justice was not primarily related to security but to moral and distributive matters—to what he was among the first to call "social justice"—is evinced by the illustrations he provides. His first example involves cooperative industrial associations, which have little to do with self-preservation and security of person and property. Mill's reason for introducing this topic is not to illustrate the fundamental need for security but to argue that "social utility alone can decide the preference" between competing forms of industrial organization. His second example involves the justice of taxation. This *is* related to security of property, but not in the same sense as theft, assault, and so forth. Moreover, Mill traces the feeling that it is unjust to charge different prices for the same article not to the threat such action poses to personal security but to the alleged fact that "it conflicts so strongly with man's feelings of humanity and of social expediency." The animal desire to retaliate is not mentioned. Again, Mill's principal aim is to show that from the various conflicting views of just taxation, "there is no other mode of extrication than the utilitarian" (*Util*, 464). How the happiness principle is objectively to resolve such matters is unclear. Mill's contemporary critics had made the obvious objection that utility is an "uncertain standard, which every different person interprets differently" (*Util*, 460).

Indeed, Mill's concern for "social justice" is far more related to his religious and metaphysical views than to an animal desire for retaliation. More particularly, his rejection of the idea of a providential order, his related belief that what goodness and justice are to be realized in existence must be the work of human agency and will, and his rigid conception of justice as a transparent correspondence between moral goodness and temporal success lead straight to the demand for a humanly devised order of desert-based justice wherein temporal rewards and punishments are distributed in accordance with obvious moral merit. Mill's naturalistic explanation, in short, does not account for the high moral demands he himself makes for "just" institutions or his frequent complaints about the alleged injustices of society (such as permitting the inheritance of landholdings or wealth beyond a certain moderate amount). It is difficult to see a security issue involved in such demands.

Mill closes the chapter with a ringing proclamation that "justice is a more sacred thing than policy." Despite his naturalistic account of the origin of justice and utilitarian morality in general, he insists that utilitarians regard justice as fully as sacred and absolute as do those nonconsequentialist moralists who adhere to an "imaginary standard . . . not grounded on utility." Mill was not a person to take a backseat to anyone in the department of moral sublimity.

> [N]o one of those who profess the most sublime contempt for the consequences of actions as an element in their morality, attaches more importance to the distinction [between the just and the merely expedient] than I do. While I dispute the pretensions of any theory which sets up an imaginary standard of justice not grounded on utility, I account the justice which is grounded on utility to be the chief part, and incomparably the most sacred and binding part, of all morality. (*Util*, 465)

Again, however, Mill accounts for the sanctity of justice, its "character of indefeasibility," on naturalistic, utilitarian grounds: "It appears from what has been said, that justice is a name for certain moral requirements, which, regarded collectively, stand higher in the scale of social utility, and are therefore of more paramount obligation, than any others . . . " The moral rules classified under the "name" of justice are rules involved with the most essential aspects of human well-being, "in which we must never forget to include wrongful interference with each other's freedom." As such, they are "of more *absolute obligation*, than any other rules" (emphasis added). The same holds for "the essence of the idea of justice"—the notion of "a right residing in an individual" (*Util,* 465, 469). In such passages, the classical-liberal Mill rears his dusty head. As we have seen, Mill's eclecticism allowed him to pick and choose among moral and political philosophies at will. The result is the universally remarked and maddening inconsistency of his thought. One could make a career of quoting Mill against himself, which in part accounts for the myriad of interpretations of his work and legacy. He himself, however, seemed oblivious to the tension and even irreconcilability between his inherited attachment to traditional liberal convictions and his promotion of the collectivist and potentially invasive Religion of Humanity or Duty, an issue to which we will return in the concluding chapter.

Mill concludes *Utilitarianism* with a nice summation of its argument and a clear statement of its antitheological purpose. He emphasizes that he has resolved "the only real difficulty in the utilitarian theory of morals," that is, how to account for the transcendent value attached to justice and the peculiar intensity of that sentiment without falling back on the notion of a transcendent origin. His remarks are to the point:

> If this characteristic sentiment has been sufficiently accounted for; if there is no necessity to assume for it any peculiarity of origin [the still-unnamed origin is of course God]; if it is simply the natural feeling of resentment, moralised by being made coextensive with the demands of social good; and if this feeling not only does but ought to exist in all the classes of cases to which the idea of justice corresponds; that idea [the transcendent significance of justice] no longer presents itself as a stumbling-block to the utilitarian ethics.
>
> Justice remains the appropriate name for certain social utilities which are vastly more important, and therefore more absolute and imperative, than any others are as a class . . . and which, therefore, ought to be, as well as naturally are, guarded by a sentiment not only different in degree, but also in kind; distinguished from the milder feeling which attaches to the mere idea of promoting human pleasure or convenience, at once by the more definite nature of its commands, and by the sterner character of its sanctions. (*Util,* 469–70)

Mill believes he has vanquished the foe—transcendental, in-itself, or intuitive morality, morality derived from a divine source and the God to whom it points. He is triumphant in his conviction that he has removed the last remaining "stumbling-block" to the widespread embrace of non-theological utilitarianism—the enduring conviction of a transcendent source of order and justice. The chief purpose of *Utilitarianism,* a purpose it shares with a preponderant portion of Mill's corpus, has been realized.

Consequences and Implications

From now on, any definition of a successful life must include service to others.

—*George H. W. Bush*

The worst difficulties of the present time arise, I am sometimes tempted to think, even less from lack of vision than from sham vision. Otherwise stated, what is disquieting about the time is not so much its open and avowed materialism as what it takes to be its spirituality.

—*Irving Babbitt*, Democracy and Leadership

One of the more remarkable, if controversial, developments in Anglo-American society over the past century has been the transformation of liberal politics from a commitment to limited government toward the progressive expansion of governmental direction of the social process. Mill was a pivotal figure in that transformation. His self-avowed eclecticism allowed him to retain something of a commitment to classical liberalism, and he never completely abandoned the belief in a limited political sphere that characterizes that outlook. But Mill muddied the waters of classical-liberal philosophy and practice with his conviction that the end of government is the all-encompassing "improvement of mankind" and not the preservation of individual liberty under law, as well as with his self-conscious embrace and advocacy of the "social"-ist moral ideal. Moreover, Mill's ambition as elucidated in this study—to replace the theologically oriented society of the Western tradition with one grounded in and oriented exclusively toward humanity—necessarily entailed a departure from classical liberalism. For individual liberty under law, as historically understood in the West, is crucially and inseparably wed to the belief in a law higher than the enactments of mankind, as well as to the sanctity of the person that derives from his or her source in God. In short, Mill's attempt to replace God with Humanity not only eviscerates the higher-law tradition crucial to the preservation of individual liberty and limited government but their spiritual foundation as well. For it is the transcendent spiritual purpose of each human being that, historically and existentially, has engendered and sustained resistance to the pretensions of merely political power. When Humanity is elevated to the ultimate source and end of value, the political rulers become, in effect if not in name, the new gods.

Mill's influence on the development of the liberal tradition, then, is crucially bound up with the religious views and issues brought to light in this work. As said, Mill's successful incorporation of the doctrines associated with French radicalism into the Anglo-American liberal tradition is related to the transformation of liberalism from classical-liberal constitutionalism to advanced-liberal progressivism. This in turn is related to the tension in Mill's thought between his lingering commitment to a classical-liberal defense of individual freedom and limited government and his even more passionate commitment to the establishment of an intramundane social religion. As Maurice Cowling has suggested, in the end a proper evaluation of Mill's thought turns on the question of whether his apparently libertarian politics are not in fact "subordinate to the religious Mill."[1] As we have seen, Benthamite/Millian utilitarianism was in continuity with the attempt of various French thinkers to create a secular, social, or political "religion" to provide the spiritual substance thought to be essential to the maintenance of social unity and political order. It should not be forgotten that the precursor of Millian humanitarianism was the religious skepticism of the eighteenth-century philosophes and the radical anti-Christianity of the French Revolution. Through Mill's influence, this rampant hostility to traditional religion was incorporated into the Anglo-American tradition. In short, Benthamite/Millian utilitarianism should be regarded as a less virulent manifestation of the same antitheological impulse that led revolutionary forces in eighteenth-century France to overthrow Christianity in the name of the Goddess Reason and "Humanity." Mill's goal, like that of his predecessors, involved the implicit divinization of humanity as well as the elevation of "service to Humanity" to the *ultimate* end of religious aspiration. It also involved the equally important, if less dramatic, insinuation of Benthamite/Comtean altruism and its notion of the superiority of social to personal morality into modern Anglo-American consciousness.

Mill's attempt to weave the "social"-ist aspirations of the Continental thinkers into the essentially individualist tradition of Anglo-American liberal thought accounts for much of the notorious inconsistency of his corpus, for the tradition and ideal are irreconcilable.[2] The result of this attempt was the curious and unstable hybrid of modern liberalism, which attempts to promote the socialist moral ideal of collective service to humanity through expansive, activist government and this in the name of the very individual freedom that classical liberalism was concerned to secure. It is not surprising that Mill's views are most vigorously championed by modern liberals, for the spiritual and moral ethos he championed has impelled the rise of modern-liberal collectivism. Mill, in perhaps his most important incarnation, is the first modern liberal.

"The Meeting of the English and the French Mind":[3] The Transformation of Liberalism

F. A. Hayek is one of the chief proponents of the view that modern liberalism is an incoherent and unstable hybrid engendered by the conflation of two essentially distinct and opposing traditions, namely, what he, with Mill, refers to as Continental and Anglo-American liberalism.[4] At the age of fourteen, Mill was sent to spend a year in France with the family of Sir Samuel Bentham, Jeremy Bentham's brother. To this experience, Mill said, he owed not only a command of the language but also "a strong and permanent interest in Continental Liberalism, of which I ever afterwards kept myself au courant, as much as of English politics: a thing not at all usual in those days with Englishmen, and which had a very salutary influence on my development, keeping me free from the error always prevalent in England, and from which even my father with all his superiority to prejudice was not exempt, of judging universal questions by a merely English standard" (*Auto*, 51).

Opinions may differ with respect to the salutariness of the Continental influence on Mill's development. There is no question, however, that Mill played a significant role in the mingling of the two liberal traditions and must receive a prominent place in any research that attempts to disentangle them. He was a close student of French political developments and wrote a series of weekly articles on French politics for *The Examiner* during the 1830s, establishing himself as the preeminent English expert on French affairs. He wrote extensively on Armand Carrel, Jules Michelet, François Guizot, and Alfred de Vigny, as well as on the French Revolution (Mill had originally planned to write its history, but eventually turned over all his material to Carlyle, whose book on the subject established his reputation). Mill rushed to Paris at the outbreak of the July Revolution in 1830, impelled by apocalyptic expectations—he thought the Time of Man had arrived. Years later, he responded to Tory critics of French developments with his "Vindication of the French Revolution of 1848."

The correspondence between Mill and Comte indicates that a merger of what Mill regarded as the essentially competing traditions of English antirationalism and French rationalism was one of both men's explicit goals. In 1842, Mill wrote to Comte about "another idea to which, almost alone among my compatriots, I have always adhered: like yourself, I am thoroughly convinced that the combination of the French and the English spirit is one of the most essential requirements for our intellectual renewal. . . . The French spirit is necessary so that conceptions may be generalized; the English spirit to prevent them from being vague." Mill found the "lucidity and systematic spirit which are truly French" more to his taste than the plodding practicality of his English compatriots. What Mill loved was "abstract speculation," which he identified with French thought (*Corr*, 60). He often reproached the English for their lack of interest and sympathy toward French speculative thought, and especially toward the philosophies of history developed by such Continental thinkers as Saint-Simon and Comte and that played such a prominent role in Mill's own thought. For Mill, his fellow Englishmen, fouled as they were by the "stench of trade," were little more than a dead weight on his soaring rationalist-Romantic spirit.[5] Perhaps most important, Mill was the chief carrier of the illiberal ideas of Saint-Simon and Comte into Anglo-American society. Saint-Simon is widely seen as a fountainhead of totalitarian ideologies that flourished in his wake, and even Mill would finally renounce Comte's schemes as "spiritual despotism."[6]

We have suggested that the conventional characterization of Mill as the last great spokesman for the classical-liberal tradition is misleading. Victorian England did of course represent the heyday of classical liberalism. Moreover, Mill's deep immersion in that tradition, as well as his self-conscious eclecticism, ensured that his philosophy and outlook were informed by various authentically liberal elements. Nevertheless, as Hayek says and as Mill himself acknowledged, Mill was very far from representative of his age and tradition and, indeed, was often in violent opposition to them. As Mill wrote to Comte in 1846, "I have stood for quite some time in a kind of open opposition to the English character, which arouses my animosity in several respects; and all in all, I prefer the French, German or Italian character" (*Corr*, 365). Leslie Stephen described Mill as "an alien among men of his own class in English society." Hayek thinks Mill "acquired . . . contempt . . . for English society, . . . [as well as] for contemporary development of English thought."[7] Joseph Hamburger identifies Mill as the prototype of the modern "alienated intellectual," as hostile to the false consciousness of the bourgeoisie as any latter-day Marx-ist. Mill's contempt for his English compatriots was truly profound. As we recall, in the *Autobiography* Mill condemns the

> low moral tone of what, in England, is called society; . . . the absence of high feelings which manifests itself by sneering depreciation of all demonstra-tions of them, and by general abstinence . . . from professing any high prin-ciples of action at all; [and,] among the ordinary English, the absence of in-terest in things of an unselfish kind, . . . [All of this] causes both their feelings and their intellectual faculties to remain undeveloped . . . ; reducing them, considered as spiritual beings, to a kind of negative existence.

The English scarcely had reality for Mill.

Mill was as laudatory of the French as he was condemnatory of the En-glish. He speaks of

> the difference between [the English] manner of existence, and that of . . . the French, whose faults, if equally real, are at all events different; among whom sentiments, which by comparison at least may be called elevated, are the current coin of human intercourse, . . . and . . . are . . . kept alive . . . by con-stant exercise, and stimulated by sympathy, so as to form a living and ac-tive part of the existence of great numbers of persons . . . [In France,] the general culture of the understanding, which results from the habitual exer-cise of the feelings, . . . is . . . carried down into the most uneducated classes of several countries on the Continent, in a degree not equalled in England among the so-called educated . . . In France, . . . the general habit of the peo-ple is to shew, as well as to expect, friendly feeling in every one towards every other . . . (*Auto*, 62–63)

And so on.[8]

Henry Reeve's portrait of Mill in the *Edinburgh Review* is entirely in keeping with the image of the alienated intellectual sketched by Ham-burger. Over the years Mill became increasingly reclusive, generally shun-ning social intercourse, even with his own family. Both John and Harriet Taylor Mill preferred to avoid close contact with a society they regarded as vulgar and contemptible.[9] One result of their self-imposed quarantine, as well as of Mill's peculiarly isolated upbringing, was that, as Reeve put it, Mill was "totally ignorant . . . of English life" and society. His disserta-tions on the English character and society were not derived from thor-oughgoing immersion in the social life of his time but from an imagina-tive comparison with his perfectionist ideal. Human beings, English or otherwise, were always something of an abstraction for Mill. As Reeve put it,

Mill never lived in what may be called society at all. . . . In later life he affected something of the life of a prophet, surrounded by admiring votaries, who ministered to him largely that incense in which prophets delight. . . . [M]ankind itself was to him an abstraction rather than a reality. He knew nothing of the world, and very little of the play and elasticity of human nature. It would have been of incalculable value to his philosophy if he had condescended to touch the earth, and to live with men and women as they are; but that was a lesson he had never learned, a book he had never opened.[10]

Mill himself acknowledged that actual human beings did not figure largely in his scheme of things. As he said in *Auguste Comte and Positivism:* "As M. Comte truly says, the highest minds, even now, live in thought with the great dead, far more than with the living; and, next to the dead, with those ideal human beings yet to come, whom they are never destined to see" (136).

Mill's alienation from liberal Victorian society is not the only factor that places him outside the classical-liberal tradition. Equally significant is the towering reach of his ambition, that is, his aspirations for the *total transformation* of not only English political institutions, but also the English mind and thus society. Mill was at various points in his career a true revolutionary—socially, culturally, politically, religiously. Although some allowance must be made for his youth, Mill's remarks in a letter to his friend John Sterling, written when he was twenty-five, certainly portray him in a rather different light than the image of studied moderation he cultivated throughout his career. The context is the agitated environment that would lead to the Reform Bill of 1832:

If the ministers flinch or the Peers remain obstinate, I am firmly convinced that in six months a national convention chosen by universal suffrage, will be sitting in London. Should this happen, I have not made up my mind what would be best to do: I incline to think it would be best to lie by and let the tempest blow over, if one could get a shilling a day to live upon meanwhile: *for until the whole of the existing institutions of society are leveled with the ground, there will be nothing for a wise man to do which the most pig-headed fool cannot do much better than he.*[11] (emphasis added)

Mill's radical aspirations for total transformation mark a real break with the classical-liberal tradition as represented by a Burke, a Madison, or a de Tocqueville. His turn toward French radicalism, anticipated by Bentham and James Mill, interjected an alien activist element into the Anglo-American political tradition that has fueled the transformation of classical-liberal constitutionalism into modern-liberal progressivism. Such a recognition suggests that the conventional view not only of Mill but also of the liberal tradition requires reinterpretation. It suggests that English liberalism, generally seen as moderate, pragmatic, and sympathetic to traditional religion, was shaped in part by a militant ideology wholly informed by the anti-Christian humanitarianism of the French philosophes and their revolutionary descendants. As said, the result has been the transformation of the Anglo-American political tradition under the dispensation of the new god of Humanity: the birth of an incongruous "liberalism" that ostensibly seeks to promote individual liberty through the illiberal collectivist means of massive centralized government, dispensing benefits and sanctions through the godlike (and Benthamite) power of legislation. Nor is it coincidental that modern liberalism is very often hostile to traditional religious values and beliefs. As we have seen, such hostility was the essence not only of Benthamite "liberalism" but, even more, of the "advanced liberalism" of John Stuart Mill. As this study has shown, the putative secular ethic of modern-liberal humanism was regarded and experienced by its founders as a new religion, one that established its identity and claimed superiority precisely by its self-conscious opposition to its chief rival, Christianity. Indeed, Mill would insist that the Religion of Humanity is "more profoundly religious" than any that had heretofore governed mankind. In short, the intense intramundane religiosity that Mill incorporated into the Anglo-American political tradition casts a new light on the nature of modern "secular" liberalism, the chief political carrier of the new secular religiosity in the American context.

"The Religion of Secular Humanism"

Our interest is in the relationship of Mill's religious thought and aims to the development of the liberal tradition. Mill is often regarded not only as the last of the great classical-liberal thinkers but also as the prototypical secular liberal. Alan Ryan speaks of "Mill's utterly secular, this-worldly temperament." Even as perceptive a Mill scholar as Hamburger characterizes the impulse behind Mill's advocacy of the Religion of Humanity as "rational and secular."[12] Such interpreters, we may suggest, fail to see the true nature of Mill's enterprise. Mill was very far from a secular thinker if "secular" is understood as areligious, more or less indifferent to spiritual matters and preoccupied with mundane considerations. The true nature of the allegedly secular liberalism that stems from Mill is more accurately glimpsed by the surprising depth of his animus toward traditional religion, theology, and metaphysics disclosed by this study.

We have suggested that the conventional view of the process of secularization as a gradual lessening of the influence of religious authority, creeds, and the like is misleading, certainly with respect to Benthamite utilitarianism and its descendants. What occurred, certainly in the case of Mill, is not "secularization," if that term is understood as a movement away from a religious toward a nonreligious ethic and politics, but the emergence of a new religiosity in secular garb. Mill was quite clear that the negative philosophy of the eighteenth century, which merely eviscerated traditional religious belief, was radically insufficient to fulfill mankind's spiritual needs. What was required was the creation and establishment of a new and full-bodied religion. And Mill, like his French predecessors and compatriots, was never in doubt that his Religion of Humanity fully met such a requirement.

Mill's nature was not, as Ryan thinks, "utterly secular" and "this-worldly," but an essentially religious nature in search of a god. Mill's contemporaries saw this more clearly than later interpreters. As a contemporary critic put it, "[T]here was something in Mill which, whether you call it mysticism or not, was of a totally different cast from his honestly-professed opinions. . . . [Mill often] used the language of religion rather than of philosophy."[13] Indeed, Mill was, above all, a religious thinker and the impulse behind his militant advocacy of the Religion of Humanity, however distorted and misconceived, was of the same character. What all of this suggests is that the modern secular humanism that stems from Mill is, as both its proponents and opponents have recognized, itself akin to a religion. Moreover, it is a religion *defined* in its origin by its animus toward Christianity and, more generally, toward the notion of a transcendent source of order and obligation. As one contemporary adherent to "the religion of secular humanism" summarizes one of its basic tenets, "Man is his own rule and his own end."[14] This is a concise expression of Mill's two-pronged message. What should be emphasized is that the type of secularism that stems proximately from Mill and ultimately from his French sources was developed in explicit opposition to theological (Christian) morality and beliefs. This fact has been obscured in this century and with the general assimilation of the ethos that Mill championed. The anti-Christian roots of secular humanism uncovered in the course of this study may help explain why that creed, as its critics have sometimes alleged, seems tolerant of all religions except Christianity.

If this work succeeds in recovering the religious dimension of Mill's thought, as well as the nature and strength of his religious aspirations, so curiously neglected in Mill scholarship, its chief object will have been realized. An attempt has been made throughout to avoid the imposition of any preconceived interpretive perspective on Mill's writings, to allow his corpus to speak for itself. It is inevitable that assessments of Mill's thought and legacy will vary. Committed secular humanists will undoubtedly laud Mill's efforts, while people of traditional faith are certain to hold quite another view.

Nor has this work attempted to explain the ultimate reasons behind Mill's vehement rejection of transcendent faith, although they are far from self-evident. There is a well-developed literature tracing what Eric Voegelin famously characterized as the progressive "immanentization" of existence—the progressive eclipse of the transcendent dimension of reality—over the course of modernity. Others have written of the "drama of atheist humanism" enacted in the nineteenth century and the "revolt against God" such a drama represented. Although such views are persuasive, a critical analysis of them is beyond the scope of this study. It is clear, however, that whatever the ultimate explanation for the trend toward immanentization or the metaphysical revolt against the order of being, John Stuart Mill was a full participant in that process. Although Mill may not have taken as extreme a position as a Comte or a Marx, his aims and intentions were shaped by a similar impulse—to replace God with Humanity and to elevate mankind, however implicitly, to the status of divinity. This is what it meant to establish humanity or utility as the *ultimate source* and end of moral obligation and value. Indeed, Mill's efforts in this regard may have been more socially effective than those of the more radical carriers of the same impulse. Precisely because they appeared more moderate and were clothed in the idiom of the liberal tradition he knew so well, Mill's antitheological animus was able to insinuate itself into Anglo-American consciousness in a way that the more radical and essentially alien Continental expressions of that animus could never hope to do. Anglo-American society did not become self-consciously Marxist or positivist. It became, instead, modern-liberal—secular, humanistic, positivistic, collectivistic, relativistic—committed not to the establishment of the communist paradise or the final positivist state but to a mundane "service to Humanity" and the pursuit of a chimerical "social justice." Christianity was of course not destroyed but relegated, as Bentham and Mill had long intended, to the innocuous position of private or subjective preference. Mill's evisceration of the traditional God, precisely because it was less extreme and thus less threatening than the militant atheism of a Marx, was all the more socially effective. Yet for all practical purposes, the probable limited god that Mill offered his descendants was a god as dead, as effectively neutralized, as Marx's or Nietzsche's.

The Social Religion and Immanentist Consequentialism

The most far-reaching aspect of Mill's endeavor to incorporate the anti-Christian humanitarianism of the French radicals into the Anglo-American liberal tradition has been its success. Mill's Religion of Humanity and the concomitant social morality he absorbed from both Bentham and Comte have been more or less assimilated by large segments of contemporary Anglo-American society and, arguably, constitute the dominant public ethos.[15] While Mill's vision of a social religion has been only partially realized, the moral views he championed are so extensively assimilated that they have become seemingly self-evident. All good people today are expected to serve humanity, to realize social justice, to have a social conscience and a concern for social problems. As former President George H. W. Bush succinctly if unwittingly expressed the new humanitarian ethos, "From now on, any definition of a successful life must include service to others."[16]

The replacement of traditional theological morality with a humanity-centered social morality has entailed far-reaching changes in contemporary society. It is intimately related to what is widely decried as the accelerating decline in personal moral standards as well as to the emergence of the expansive-government form of liberalism discussed above. Traditionally, morality has been regarded as an attribute of an individual agent: A just person is a person who *is* just, who acts justly, and this because to do so is right in itself, in alignment with the moral law or the order of being. A decent or just society is the outcome of the just behavior of the individual members of that society. Such a conception of morality is antithetical to the social consequentialism championed by Mill and especially to the conception of social justice he advanced. Social or distributive justice is largely unrelated to the personal moral characteristics of individuals—the just and unjust alike can pursue a politically imposed agenda intended to realize someone's preferred conception of social justice. Perhaps even more important, Millian social justice cannot be realized by an individual agent but requires organized collective—political—action.

As said, Mill's immanentist consequentialism, wedded to the social ethos of Comtean altruism and service to humanity, contributed significantly to the evolution of the spiritual and moral ethos that has impelled the rise of expansive-government liberalism throughout the past century. The tension produced in Mill's liberalism by his simultaneous embrace of a "social religion" and his lingering classical-liberal impulse to defend individual liberty is brought to the surface by his repeated emphasis that utilitarianism is *not* concerned with the happiness of the individual. Both

Bentham and Mill explicitly elevated the social well-being of the collective over individual happiness. As Mill emphasized, "[T]he happiness which forms the utilitarian standard of what is right in conduct, is not the agent's own happiness, but that of all concerned" (*Util*, 418). As Bentham expressed the same view, when one discovers utility to be "the test and measure of all virtue, . . . the obligation to minister to general happiness [is found to be] an obligation paramount to and inclusive of every other."[17] As suggested, the immanentist consequentialism that derives from Benthamite utilitarianism, combined with the religious valorization of the "social" in the thought of Mill, was one of the stepping-stones toward the development of a full-blown "social"-ist or collectivist ethic in the Anglo-American context. The tendency of this social consequentialism was to shift the locus of morality from the person to external consequences or arrangements, that is, to displace the person as the bearer of moral agency in favor of society and social institutions. As Bentham put it in describing the superiority of his ethical system over that of the "religionists": "The laws of perfection derived from religion, have more for their object the goodness of the man who observes them, than that of the society in which they are observed. Civil laws, on the contrary, have more for their object the moral goodness of men in general than that of individuals."[18] Bentham's relocation of moral agency from the individual to "men in general," as well as its simultaneous projection of moral agency onto society and social institutions, resembles the transfer so prominent in the thought of Rousseau and Marx.

It has long been recognized that Benthamite utilitarianism is one of the roots of British socialism. What should be emphasized is that the root of *that* root is the very conception of a consequentialist ethic. When an action is judged moral or immoral on the basis of its consequences (especially its social consequences) and not on its inherent rightness or wrongness, justice inevitably moves in the direction of an outcome-based justice. Such a justice is antithetical to liberal constitutionalism, bound up as it is with rule-based or procedural concerns. Liberal constitutionalism is inseparable from the rule of law as historically achieved in the West—the universal observance of general rules, an observance that does not and cannot produce foreseeable concrete outcomes.[19] Accordingly, if what matters is the outcome of an action and not its inherent moral rightness or wrongness, the rule of law that sustains limited government and individual freedom is undermined. The pursuit of social justice is incompatible with the traditional rules of just personal behavior that sustain the classical-liberal order of limited government and market exchange. Apart from the theoretical issues involved, the rise of a consequentialist ethic has led historically in Anglo-American society to the demand for a Millian social justice. Mill championed a social consequentialism that evaluates the morality of an action by its temporal social effects—its contribution to the collective or general happiness, as determined by the utilitarian moralist and legislator. It is but a short step from this to a full-fledged socialist ethic demanding a social justice that entails, however implicitly, the imposition of a politically determined concrete pattern of distribution. Mill furthered such a development not only by his consequentialism and his religious valorization of the "social," but also by his infamous assertion that economic "distribution" is utterly amenable to human will. The ethical roots of Anglo-American collectivism, of the social religion that was to sweep Anglo-American society in the late nineteenth and early twentieth centuries, are firmly embedded in the Benthamite/Millian utilitarianism that substituted for the traditional conception of morality—doing what is right for its own sake—the notion that the morality of an action is to be determined by its social or temporal consequences. Mill's successful "revision" of Benthamism, his successful attack on the "in-itself" morality of the transcendentalists, and his successful promotion of Comtean altruism made him a major carrier of the consequentialist, "social"-ist ethic into the Anglo-American liberal tradition.

We have seen that Mill's ethics involved a rigid dichotomy between the bad of "selfishness" or self-interest, represented by Christianity, and the good of the "social," associated with the Religion of Humanity. As is widely known, what Comte offered in place of self-interest was the motive of altruism or, as the famous positivist slogan would have it, "liv[ing] for others." Mill was greatly attracted to Comte's altruistic or social ethic and would preach the good of "social"-ism over the evil of selfishness all his life. Mill not only disparaged traditional morality, bound up, as he thought, with the selfish Christian concern with personal salvation, but also invested its alleged opposite, social morality, with an intense religiosity. It is not coincidental that the social sciences have replaced what were called in Mill's era the "moral sciences," for as a result of the efforts of Mill and his compatriots, the social has become identified with the moral. Hayek enumerates over a hundred different uses of what he calls the "weasel word" *social* in modern ethical and political discourse. Terms like *social justice, social conscience, social morality, social duty, social democracy, social problems, social service,* and so on, have been thoroughly assimilated into Anglo-American moral consciousness. Social aims have assumed the character of the self-evidently good, having supplanted in many quarters the traditional personal or in-itself morality that shaped the evolution of Western liberal society.

All of this is no doubt related to the successful battle against such transcendental or antiutilitarian morality conducted by Mill in the name of nontheological utilitarian consequentialism. The "social" having become the "moral," classical liberalism, wedded to the notion that morality inheres in the personal agent and not in the social outcome—that is, in a rule-based and not an outcome-based justice—has been shaped in the direction of a modern-liberal "social"-ism that tends to judge the morality of actions in terms of their social effects. Such a view underlies, for instance, the contemporary communitarian call for a "personal" justice that takes account of particular circumstances and concrete outcomes, as well as the modern-liberal assumption that all right-thinking people should desire and pursue various "social (political) goods"—universal government-provided education, child and health care, "social safety nets," and so on. We have alluded to the decline in personal morality that has accompanied the widespread embrace of social morality. If what matters morally is the collective production of a predetermined social good and not the personal morality of the agent, then one may behave in any manner one wishes provided one supports or forces others to support the correct social causes.

The Political Religion: The Politicization of Society

Mill's partly successful endeavor to replace Christianity with a secular or social religion is also bound up with what is widely apprehended as the thoroughgoing politicization of contemporary American society.[20] This is related to the fact that Mill's promotion of a social religion shades off into the sacralization of the state and thus to the establishment of a full-fledged political religion. As has been emphasized, Mill was not concerned merely to dismiss or ignore God and religion; he was not a "secular" thinker. His aim was to found a new religion. Its realization did require the evisceration of the transcendent God of the Western tradition and of the belief in a morality and justice grounded in transcendent truth. But what is of special significance with respect to political developments is that it also required the *reorientation* of spiritual aspirations and yearnings away from that God and toward the intramundane substitute, Humanity. The result, as discussed, was the quasi-religious valorization of "service to Humanity." Mill's labors did not issue in the secularization of society but in the investment of religious or *ultimate* value in humanitarian service. The explicit aim was to engage the religious fervor formerly oriented toward a transcendent source and redirect it toward service of this-worldly humanitarian ends. Not only does such collective "service" implicitly require organized political action, but Mill also explicitly elevated the collective pursuit of humanitarian ends over comparable individual activities. As he said in *Auguste Comte and Positivism*, "[n]o efforts should be spared to associate the pupil's self-respect, and his desire of the respect of others, with service rendered to Humanity—when possible, collectively" (115). If this is not possible, he will allow such service to be performed individually. Again, despite Mill's lingering if qualified commitment to the classical-liberal ideal of limited government, his even greater desire to "improve" mankind and his elevation of an all-encompassing collective or social good over the good of the individual inevitably pushed his politics in the direction of expansive government.

While a full examination of Mill's contribution to the development of Anglo-American collectivism is beyond the scope of this work, there is no doubt that he played a significant role in the leftward shift of liberal politics over the course of the late nineteenth and twentieth centuries. Mill expressed his complete sympathy with the ultimate aims of socialism, going so far as to explicitly label himself a "Socialist."[21] Nevertheless, his legacy in this regard is a mixed one. He never accepted the socialists' proposals for the abolition of private property (although he did call for the nationalization of land; this, he said, should be regarded as a common resource of humanity) and never ceased, as he put it in *Principles of Political Economy*, "utterly [to] dissent from the most conspicuous and vehement part of their teaching, their declamations against competition."[22] Perhaps more important than his concrete proposals, however, Mill claimed the *moral* high ground for the socialist ideal. Although he believed contemporary human nature was still far too selfish and self-interested to allow the present establishment of socialist institutions, he believed that the man of the future, with proper education and training, would certainly become a more "social" creature concerned above all with the good of the whole. We may get a glimpse of Mill's influence in this regard from his remarks in *Auguste Comte and Positivism* concerning the "true moral and social ideal of Labour," which, as he says, was first articulated by Comte:

> [T]he proper return for a service to society is the gratitude of society; and ... the moral claim of anyone in regard to the provision for his personal wants is not a question of quid pro quo in respect to his cooperation, but of *how much the circumstances of society permit to be assigned to him*, consistently with the just claims of others. To this opinion we entirely subscribe. The rough method of settling the labourer's share of the produce, the competi-

tion of the market, may represent a practical necessity, but certainly not a moral ideal. Its defense is that civilisation has not hitherto been equal to organising anything better than this first rude approach to an equitable distribution. . . . But in whatever manner [the] question [of equitable distribution] may ultimately be decided, the true moral and social idea of Labour is in no way affected by it. *Until labourers and employers perform the work of industry in the spirit in which soldiers perform that of an army, industry will never be moralised* and military life will remain what, in spite of the antisocial character of its direct object, it has hitherto been—the chief school of moral cooperation. (emphases added)

Mill also champions "another idea of M. Comte which has great beauty and grandeur." This is "that every person who lives by any useful work should be habituated to regard himself not as an individual working for his private benefit, but as a public functionary, and his wages . . . not as the remuneration or purchase-money of his labor, which should be given freely, but as the provision made by society to enable him to carry it on" (*ACP*, 116–17). The notion that all people are public functionaries employed by society cannot by any stretch be regarded as an authentically liberal view. It is, however, a full-bodied expression of the socialist ideal.[23]

One result of Mill's endeavor to "immanentize" spiritual aspirations has been the growth of a centralized government charged with godlike power and duties and the thoroughgoing politicization of social life. Modern government has replaced God as the object of petition and the bestower of blessings. Government, like the former transcendent God, is asked to rectify every alleged social ill and, indeed, to provide the existential meaning and purpose formerly gained through transcendent faith. Politics has become religion—the Religion of Humanity—institutionalized not in the temples of humanity that once graced the Anglo-American landscape, but in what one contemporary scholar refers to as the liberal church universal.[24] In short, one outcome of Mill's endeavor to replace God with Humanity has been the quasi-religious pursuit of collective political ends. This has led to the implicit sacralization of politics (the realm of organized coercion), to a politics beyond which there is nothing higher and that is unrestrained by the recognition of a law higher than that enacted by human agents. The pursuit of political agendas ostensibly designed to serve humanity has itself become the "religion" that Mill intended, supplying existential meaning and purpose for many of his advanced-liberal and progressive descendants. These may be regarded as a shadowy manifestation of the modern spiritual power of which Mill dreamed, the "philosophical elite" of adherents to the Religion of Humanity, who, he hoped, would achieve an authority comparable to that of the medieval clergy. All of this is pernicious enough from the perspective of classical liberalism. But what is worse, when man is conceived as the *ultimate* source of moral order, when humanity is conceived as the *ultimate* object of service or reverence, when the only god that may be real is so limited and enfeebled as to become practically irrelevant, the human "servants of Humanity" become, in effect if not in explicit pronouncement, God. There is no source of appeal beyond the dictates of their judgment. The foundation of individual liberty and limited government is undermined. The replacement of the transcendent God of the Judeo-Christian tradition by the intramundane abstraction Humanity undercuts the spiritual foundation of the individual freedom that Mill at times seemed concerned to secure.

It is not merely hindsight that reveals the tendency of Mill's intramundane social religion toward the sacralization of politics. Mill himself implicitly and explicitly advocated such a development. If, as he says, "Rome was to the entire Roman people . . . as much a religion as Jehovah was to the Jews," there is no reason, he implies, why contemporary human beings cannot gain the same religious satisfaction in devoting their own ultimate allegiance to the state ("UR," 420). Moreover, as we saw in Chapter 3, Mill certainly believed that duty to the state or devotion to the good of one's country or humanity can serve as a full-fledged religion: "When we see and feel that human beings can take the deepest interest in what will befal [sic] their country or mankind long after they are dead, and in what they can themselves do while they are alive to influence that distant prospect which they are never destined to behold, *we cannot doubt that if this and similar feelings were cultivated in the same manner and degree as religion they would become a religion*"[25] (emphasis added).

That such is the logical and intended end of Mill's intramundane religion is further suggested by his high enthusiasm for the glory he associates with the classical devotion to the state and by his elevation of the good of the country and even of the world to the "grand duty of life," to the highest human allegiance: "When we consider how ardent a sentiment, in favourable circumstances of education, the love of country has become, we cannot judge it impossible that the love of that larger country, the world, may be nursed into similar strength, both as a source of elevated emotion and as a principle of duty." Mill admits that the morality of the ancients may have been deficient in certain respects, but not as concerns duty to their country, to which the ancients were ready to "sacrifice life, reputation, family, everything valuable . . . " Mill pointedly draws his conclusion: "If, then, persons could be trained, as we see they were, not only to believe in theory that the good of their country was an object to which all others ought to yield, but to feel this practically as the grand duty of life, so also may they be made to feel the same absolute obligation towards the universal good" ("UR," 421). Such an obligation is embodied in the Religion of Humanity, "which sometimes calls itself the Religion of . . . Duty," and interpreted in line with Mill's nontheological utilitarian standard. To grasp the fullness of Mill's idea it is essential to recall his understanding of duty: "It is a part of the notion of Duty in every one of its forms, that a person may rightfully be compelled to fulfil it. Duty is a thing which may be exacted from a person, as one exacts a debt. *Unless we think that it may be exacted from him, we do not call it his duty.* Reasons of prudence, or the interest of other people, may militate against actually exacting it; but the person himself, it is clearly understood, would not be entitled to complain" (*Util*, 454, emphasis added).

We may gather an idea of what Mill's proposed society of the future, oriented toward the Religion of Humanity, would look like from his frequent praise of the moral and social life of the ancients, and especially the Spartans. We have seen the utter subordination of religion to social or political ends in James Mill's proposed "State religion." John Mill's view is similar. He holds up the Spartan model for our edification:

> It was not religion which formed the strength of the Spartan institutions: the root of the system was devotion to Sparta, to the ideal of the country or State: which transformed into ideal devotion to a greater country, the world, would be equal to that and far nobler achievements. Among the Greeks generally, social morality was extremely independent of religion. The inverse relation was rather that which existed between them; the worship of the Gods was inculcated chiefly as a social duty . . . Such moral teaching as existed in Greece had very little to do with religion. . . . For the enforcement of human moralities secular inducements were almost exclusively relied on. ("UR," 409–10)

Needless to say, Mill's proposed replacement for allegiance to God— the elevation of the "ideal of the country or State," expanded, indeed, into "ideal devotion to a greater country, the world"—rests in uneasy tension with his alleged concern for the individual and his liberty. This is especially problematic in light of the fact that Mill aimed for the elimination or at least the evisceration of any supranatural or world-transcendent allegiance that, historically and existentially, served as the basis of spiritual resistance to secular or political power. The "whole course of ancient history," Mill insists, provides a "lesson on this subject"—that the good of the country is "an object to which all others ought to yield." We heirs to the twentieth century have had a good lesson on this subject as well and have been given a hard look at the results of attaching quasi-religious emotion to the notion that one's ultimate duty is to the state. Mill was certainly correct: "Objects . . . confined within the limits of the earth . . . have been found sufficient to inspire large masses . . . with an enthusiasm capable of ruling the conduct, and colouring the whole life" ("UR," 420–21). The gruesome aspect that such "enthusiasm" has assumed in the past century points emphatically to the dangers of repudiating world-transcendent spiritual allegiance while simultaneously investing any form of intramundane phenomena with *ultimate* value. When such is the case, not only is the pursuit of earthly ends impelled by all the terrifying energy of disoriented souls in search of salvation but the essential basis of spiritual resistance to political power is destroyed as well.

Let us again emphasize the innerworldly object of Mill's religion: to reform the world in the here and now, not to achieve eternal life beyond time and space. The fusion of the temporal sphere of politics and the spiritual sphere of religion in Mill's thought is obvious, as are the quasi-religious roots of his politics and philosophy. The "improvement" and indeed the "regeneration" of the world became the central purpose of his life, the carrier of all meaning. It was to provide a substitute for the meaning and purpose lost upon rejection of faith in a transcendent God. Mill's yearning is akin to the yearning that led many people in the earlier decades of the last century to embrace socialism and communism, and indeed, Mill's new god ominously resembles "the god that failed."[26] Accordingly, Millian utilitarianism should be understood as a precursor of the more virulent antitheistic ideological movements—communism, revolutionary socialism—as well as a forerunner of the more benign manifestations of the same impulse, such as Fabian socialism, American progressivism, and modern collectivist liberalism.[27]

The True Believer

We have discussed the remarkable sweep of Mill's ambitions for moral, intellectual, social, political, and religious reform. Mill wanted to create a new world, peopled by new men. We have also seen his personal experience of the existing world as a reckless chaos, devoid of goodness or justice. We have glimpsed his fear in the face of a world he could not rationally comprehend, a fear that issued in the intense desire radically to amend or control that world and its inhabitants. Mill would do so not through the overtly political means of coercion but through the intensive socialization of the populace. His aim was to shape human beings internally, to shape mind and soul through the socialization process and not through draconian legislation or violent terror. A deep immersion in

Mill's thought leaves one with the decided impression that his aspirations for human beings were not for the flowering of their unique individuality but for their conformity to his personal ideal of value and service. Mill, often portrayed as the great liberal defender of individual liberty, was not, we may suggest, a true friend of liberty. As we have seen, he seemed able to hide his aspirations for power and control—control over a fearful reality not fully transparent to the reasoning mind as well as over his fellows, the majority of whom fell far short of his conception of a full-fledged human being—behind the image of himself as a selfless servant of humanity. The perceptive insight of Irving Babbitt springs to mind: "If we attend to the psychology of the persons who manifest such an eagerness to serve us, we shall find that they are even more eager to control us."[28] One obtains a glimpse of such an aspiration in Mill's occasional private musings, for instance (as we saw in Chapter 3), in his ruminations over the injustice of the fact that such a being as his wife must die like all lesser creatures:

> If human life is governed by superior beings, how greatly must the power of the evil intelligences surpass that of the good, when a soul and an intellect like hers, such as the good principle perhaps never succeeded in creating before—one who seems intended for an inhabitant of some remote heaven, and *who wants nothing but a position of power to make a heaven even of this stupid and wretched earth*—when such a being must perish like all the rest of us in a few years.[29] (emphasis added)

What should be emphasized is the pretentious sweep of Mill's reformist ambitions and their divorce from any higher allegiance or recognition of limits. Mill, like the Grand Inquisitor, will correct God's work. He, unlike the inept god of his imagination, is motivated *solely* by the universal (temporal) good of humanity. He will enable "the mass of mankind" to realize the end that the bungling god of possibly divided purposes has failed to secure (*Util*, 414). Mill's eviscerated god will allow Mill himself to become like a god. He will make new men of a better and less selfish nature, and he will provide the goodness and justice that this disordered world so sorely lacks. The self-aggrandizement implicit in such ambitions would be merely pathetic if we heirs to the twentieth century had not witnessed the consequences of the attempt to achieve self-transcendence in the manner Mill recommends. Governments controlled by communists and other cadres of supposed self-sacrificing benefactors of humanity murdered a hundred million of their citizens in the past century, fueled by a drive similar to that which impelled Mill—to order and perfect a reality seen as in radical need of emendation. We have had a good hard look at the reality of the humanitarian heaven on earth, whether manifested as the communist paradise, the social gospel's Kingdom of God, or the "universal happiness" achieved through modern-liberal socialization.

Bruce Mazlish has perceptively characterized James Mill as the prototype of the modern "revolutionary ascetic." His son fit the pattern of the communist or socialist "true believer" in many critical respects.[30] John Mill's new god, as said, created by a similar combination of disoriented spiritual aspirations masking an unacknowledged will to power, was akin to the god that failed so many others who sought their salvation in an intramundane socialism divorced from any transcendent allegiance. Mill, like such socialists, sought collective salvation through the perfection of what he took to be the very imperfect creation that is the actual world. Having rejected the possibility of fulfillment beyond the world of time and space, he felt that perfection *must* be achieved in this existence. Mill, unable to find lasting happiness in his present life, projected all his dreams and hopes into the promised land of the future. Nor could he take any pleasure in the actual human beings he encountered. As we have seen, "man" was always something of an abstraction for Mill; the only men he could love were the ideal men of the future to whom he clung in his imagination. The thought that he was helping to "make" such men enabled him to endure the distasteful imperfection of actual human beings and actual life. "Oh, for something better!" was how he characterized his lifelong yearning.[31] To endure the miserable reality of the existing state of mankind and society, Mill consoled himself with the dream of his special mission: his (self-)appointed task to "improve" other human beings and to establish the means by which humanity would advance toward the "hoped-for heaven."

Mill, while bearing a certain family resemblance to his more virulent communist and socialist cousins, is not, however, Lenin. The reason has to do with those elements in his constitution and "mental history" that served as moderating forces. Mill's eclecticism, while maddening, was in some ways his saving grace: Think of such factors as his thorough immersion in the tradition of English liberalism, the lingering restraining influences of the Christian tradition against which he so largely rebelled, and his attraction to the stoicism his father also admired. As Mill put it in discussing the virtue of stoicism:

> For nothing except that consciousness can raise a person above the chances of life, by making him feel that, let fate and fortune do their worst, they have not power to subdue him: which, once felt, frees him from excess of anxiety concerning the evils of life, and enables him, like many a Stoic in the worst times of the Roman Empire, to cultivate in tranquillity the sources of satis-

faction accessible to him, without concerning himself about the uncertainty of their duration, any more than about their inevitable end. (*Util*, 417–18).

So Mill consoles himself in his more sober moments.

On the other hand, such factors were no more than a moderating force. The primary thrust of Mill's temperament was Promethean and Romantic, strongly colored by a gnostic pretension to infallibility and what can only be regarded as a breathtaking personal arrogance. Mill always asserted the most absolute moral authority, staked his claim on the very highest moral ground. His pronouncements assume the moral superiority of utilitarianism and the Religion of Humanity to traditional ethics and religion.

God and Social Justice

Let us recall Mill's peculiarly rigid and static conception of justice: "If the law of all creation were justice and the Creator omnipotent, then, in whatever amount suffering and happiness might be dispensed to the world, each person's share of them would be exactly proportioned to that person's good or evil deeds; no human being would have a worse lot than another, without worse deserts; accident or favouritism would have no part in such a world, but every human life would be the playing out of a drama constructed like a perfect moral tale" ("Nat," 389). Mill always conceived true justice to entail a perfect correspondence between moral desert and temporal reward. He also thought the reality of omnipotent goodness would necessarily entail a morally perfect world. As he said in "Theism": "If we reason directly from God's goodness to positive facts, no misery, nor vice nor crime ought to exist in the world" (479).

We have seen the difficulty of reconciling Mill's tenacious adherence to such perfectionist standards with his putative advocacy of individual freedom and flourishing. There is something disturbing about Mill's failure to recognize the most obvious reason for the imperfection of the world: It is not, as Mill suggests, various unknown obstacles to the exercise of divine omnipotence, but the fact of human freedom, moral and creative. It is difficult to understand how a philosopher who truly values human freedom could fail to see that connection. Mill's blindness to the relation between human freedom and the imperfection of existence is comprehensible, however, in light of what we have seen to be his predominant aim—to replace a theological with a purely human orientation. We have seen that Mill's understanding of moral agency was permanently shaped by the deterministic "doctrine of circumstances" he absorbed from his father. More important, however, he found it necessary to deny the fact of genuine—"uncaused" or "spontaneous"—moral freedom because, within his context, this pointed all too clearly to the source of that freedom—the free will granted by the Christian God. A God-given moral freedom was in fact the foundational assumption of Mill's Christian-voluntarist opponents such as Hamilton and Mansel, the "free-will theologians and philosophers" he attacked in the *Examination*. As Ryan says, "Hamilton's theology rested on human freedom. In effect, he held that the existence of a nonnatural origin of action was the chief ground for supposing that there was a personal Creator, rather than, say, a material First Cause or a Platonic Form, at the origin of the universe. . . . [For] unless human agency is somehow outside the ordinary natural course of events, there is no reason why the universe should not be thought of as having a wholly natural origin."[32] As a result of his antitheological agenda, Mill found it necessary to deny free will. Consequently, he did not have recourse to the traditional and obvious way to reconcile the imperfection of the world with omnipotent goodness—the fact of human freedom. Unwilling to accept the reality of a God who granted moral freedom to man, Mill was unable to accept the imperfection engendered by such freedom.

Mill's willful refusal to recognize the relation between moral freedom and the imperfection of existence is all the more remarkable in light of the fact that the reconciliation of omnipotent goodness and existing imperfection is implicit in the sort of trial-and-error "experiments in living" that Mill ostensibly advocates in *On Liberty*. That is, one may easily conceive of God as voluntarily restraining himself in the interests of individual development, refusing to intervene in any dramatic way, in order to allow human beings the opportunity to learn. For we may need to learn our spiritual, moral, and creative lessons precisely through a process of trial and error, through *concretely* experiencing the consequences of our beliefs and actions, as Mill himself seemingly advocates. Accordingly, the world at any moment in time would not and could not appear perfect in Mill's narrow sense. Human moral, spiritual, and creative growth has long been understood to require moral, and thus practical, freedom. Love and growth commanded or determined are not genuine, nor is theoretical understanding alone sufficiently compelling. As said, Mill's inability to reconcile existing imperfection and omnipotent goodness, as well as his blindness to the relation between freedom and imperfection, stemmed from his concern to eviscerate the God long regarded as the source of that freedom. His inability to perceive such a self-evident relation casts further doubt on the authenticity of his putative commitment to individual freedom. As we have seen, there are reasons to believe that Mill in fact regarded such freedom, at least for the masses, as a provisional necessity only, necessary in the short run to cut out the theological roots of the old order.

Mill's refusal to recognize the connection between human freedom and the imperfection of existence is, however, quite consistent with his frequent demands for a visible and transparent "social justice," that Trojan horse of Anglo-American collectivism. As said, Mill's demand for social justice derived from his lifelong conviction that perfect justice would require a perfect correspondence between moral desert and temporal rewards and benefits: "If the law of all creation were justice . . . , then, in whatever amount suffering and happiness might be dispensed to the world, each person's share of them would be exactly proportioned to that person's good or evil deeds." Or, as Mill put it in *Utilitarianism*, "[I]t is a duty to do to each according to his deserts . . . [S]ociety should treat all equally well who have deserved equally well of it, that is, who have deserved equally well absolutely. This is the highest abstract standard of social and distributive justice; towards which all institutions, and the efforts of all virtuous citizens, should be made in the utmost possible degree to converge" (468). Note, first, the ominous implications of the thought that "the efforts of all virtuous citizens, should be *made* in the utmost possible degree to converge" in the pursuit of social justice, and, second, Mill's strange, if characteristic, personification of "society," the suggestion that society is a thinking and willing mind or being.

As suggested, Mill's demand for social justice was intimately related to the religious issues brought to light in this work. More particularly, such a demand was related to Mill's sense of existential disorder, his hubristic rejection of the very possibility of Providence, and his insistence that *all* justice and goodness are products of human will and agency. As said, Mill's demand for "social" and "distributive" justice derived from his yearning for a desert-based justice—Mill *wanted* temporal success and failure to correspond with obvious moral merit and its opposite. Such a justice has historically been interpreted as the conscious arrangement of market and other social outcomes in a way that appears to meet someone's conception of merit or desert. There is, however, no correspondence between moral merit and economic success in a free society coordinated through market exchange; the wicked often prosper. Moreover, in a free or classical-liberal society wherein the coordination of human activities occurs through market-governed exchange, no one "distributes" the outcomes of social and economic activity. These are determined by impersonal social and market forces; they are unintended consequences of the observance of personal rules of just conduct. Although Mill himself did not plead for the institutionalization of the economic and political arrangements implicit in his demand for social justice—an arrangement wherein temporal rewards and punishments are meted out by a presumably all-knowing human "distributor" of some kind—such an implication was obvious and drawn by his descendants, as evinced both historically and contemporarily.

The mystery of the market was as unacceptable to Mill as the corresponding mystery of Providence. A free society, however, may require an acceptance of some such mystery, as well as the abandonment of the notion that *economic* success in any way reflects *moral* merit. This was undoubtedly difficult for a person such as Mill who not only sought to control a reality he experienced as fearful but who also held a perfectionist, and utterly unrealistic, conception of what goodness and justice must look like in a world such as ours and who, moreover, would not accept the possibility of transcendent reconciliation. A trust in both Providence and its secular expression, the "spontaneous order" of the market, may require the willingness to rest in the assurance that somehow there is an order, whether or not it is transparent to the limited reasoning mind. This Mill could not or would not do. Nor would he countenance the belief that each person has an internal source of order, a consequence of his or her source in God, or allow the possibility that the realization of *ultimate* justice is not in human hands. Lacking trust and humility, and consumed by an overweening hubris of will and intellect, Mill ignored the limits of the human mind, as his conception of goodness ignored the concrete reality of human existence and its inevitable imperfections. Having rejected faith in an all-wise, all-good, and, indeed, all-powerful governor of the universe, Mill felt that he and other human agents like himself must consciously design and impose the moral order that his inept if well-meaning god could not or would not achieve.

The material brought to light in this work, it is hoped, will inspire a far-reaching reevaluation of Mill's contribution to the development of the liberal tradition. Almost alone among Mill scholars, Hamburger and Cowling have attempted to draw attention to the fact that "Mill's politics are impregnated with religion."[33] Neither Mill's own work nor his legacy can adequately be comprehended without taking account of his religious aspirations—to usher in a new moral world in which Humanity has replaced God as the ultimate source and end of value. Nor can they be understood without an awareness of the extent to which Mill's views were permanently shaped by the most illiberal thinkers of his day—Saint-Simon and Auguste Comte.

Mill's is a confused and confusing legacy. He spoke the language of the liberal tradition while radically eviscerating its spiritual ground—a transcendent source of existence and value that alone sustains the value of the individual—as well as its moral and legal foundation—a law that is given and not man-made. In addition, individual liberty, limited government, and the rule of law cannot be sustained without a resurrection of the "in-itself" morality that Mill despised, the belief that an action is right or wrong in itself—because it violates the order of being and not because of its "social consequences." Of greatest importance, however, is the rejection of Mill's central religious tenet—the fantastic presumption that Humanity can replace God. The preservation of human liberty and the limited government that secures that liberty politically may require, on the contrary, the acknowledgment that each human being has a spiritual purpose and allegiance far greater and far more important than duty to country or even service to humanity. For only a recognition of the inviolable sanctity of the person that stems from his source and end in God can secure his freedom from organized coercion in forced servitude to pseudo-ultimate ends devised by all-too-human agents. Such a recognition is also essential to sustain the personal spiritual resistance that, historically and existentially, has served to limit the pretensions of political rulers and their clients. Mill claimed to desire the truth, as well as liberty. It may well be, however, that both truth and liberty require the recognition of precisely that which Mill took such pains to deny—whatever its merits, Humanity is surely not God.

Notes

Introduction

1. Interest in Mill's religious thought, however, does seem to be growing. A reprint of Mill's *Three Essays on Religion* was published by Prometheus Press in 1998, and a collection of his contemporaries' responses to the 1874 publication of that work appeared in 1997. *The Cambridge Companion to Mill* (1998) contains an article by Alan Millar entitled "Mill and Religion." Joseph Hamburger's *John Stuart Mill on Liberty and Control* (1999) also attends to the religious dimension of Mill's thought. Although Hamburger's chief concern is to examine the relationship of Mill's religious thought to his liberalism and not to examine that thought in depth, his conclusions are largely in accord with those of this book.

2. "Real, though purely human religion": "The," 488; "religion without a God": *ACP*, 133.

3. Alan Ryan perceives something of Mill's intense religiosity. He refers to Mill as the head of the "secular trinity" composed of Mill, Bertrand Russell, and John Dewey.

4. Mill to Comte, December 15, 1842, *Corr*, 119.

5. Mill, diary, January 24, 1854, CW 27:646.

6. Mill to Comte, dated January 28, 1842, but actually written in 1843, *Corr*, 129.

7. Jacob L. Talmon, *The Rise of Totalitarian Democracy*, 21.

8. Leslie Stephen, *The English Utilitarians*, 3:449.

1. Early Influences: James Mill and Jeremy Bentham

1. Mill's *Autobiography*, although inevitably selective and incomplete, provides a concrete glimpse into the daily life of the young Benthamite-in-training, especially with respect to Mill's precocious intellectual achievements. Ruth Borchard, in *John Stuart Mill, the Man*, and Michael St. John Packe, in *The Life of John Stuart Mill*, also present interesting and insightful accounts of Mill's life.

2. "Proud as Lucifer," said Bentham of James Mill (cited in Hamburger, *Intellectuals in Politics: John Stuart Mill and the Philosophic Radicals*, 16). Bruce Mazlish views James Mill as the prototype of the modern "revolutionary ascetic" (*The Revolutionary Ascetic: Evolution of a Political Type*). See also Robert A. Fenn, *James Mill's Political Thought*.

3. James Mill, "The Church, and Its Reform" (cited hereafter as "The Church"). Luther was in fact James Mill's moral hero. Mill regarded Luther as nothing less than "the greatest benefactor of the human race" (258).

4. John Mill worked in the Examiner's Office of the East India Company from 1823 until 1856, ultimately rising to the position of examiner, more or less equivalent to undersecretary of state.

5. F. F. Miller, "William Ellis and His Work as an Educationist," 236.

6. As John Mill put it, "[T]hough direct moral teaching does much, indirect does more; and the effect my father produced on my character, did not depend solely on what he said or did with that direct object, but also, and still more, on what manner of man he was" (*Auto*, 55).

7. Mill, early draft of *Auto*, CW 1:179.

8. Packe, *Life of Mill*, 25. According to Mill's sister Harriet, their maternal grandmother "was a truly excellent and religious woman and taught us [the Mill children] to pray, etc. . . . My father never interfered and as quite children we girls used to go to church" (Harriet Taylor to the Rev. J. Crompton, October 26, 1873, cited by Packe, 25).

9. It has been suggested, however, that the Mills themselves revived a gnostic perspective on existence. Christopher Budzisz argues that John Mill's religious speculations are best characterized as an "exercise in gnostic speculation" ("John Stuart Mill, Auguste Comte, and the Religion of Humanity"). Eric Voegelin wrote extensively on the gnostic character of modernity. Although he does not mention Mill in this connection, he does discuss Auguste Comte and his Religion of Humanity at length (*From Enlightenment to Revolution*). As we shall see, what may be said of Comte's endeavor to replace God with Humanity applies equally to Mill.

10. As discussed in Chapter 5, Mill did qualify his father's denial of evidence for God's existence by admitting the Argument from Design as probable evidence for a Benevolent Demiurge.

11. Borchard, *Mill, the Man*, 34.

12. Certain of Mill's contemporary reviewers drew attention to his lack of self-knowledge, particularly with respect to his inability to perceive a relation between his early indoctrination and his later views. See Anonymous, review of Alexander Bain, *John Stuart Mill: A Criticism, with Personal Recollections*.

13. In an early letter from the boy John Mill to his aunt, he does wax enthusiastic about "the two greatest books—Homer and the Bible" (Packe, *Life of Mill*, 25).

14. Mazlish, *James and John Stuart Mill: Father and Son in the Nineteenth Century*, 67. Fenn points out that James Mill's refusal to discuss "origins" extended to his own background as well (*James Mill's Thought*, 28). John Mill suggests that he knew very little about his father's upbringing in Scotland (*Auto*, 26). Not until late in life did he learn that his father had once been ordained as a minister. It is thus worth noting that Mill's discussion of his father's background and early views in the *Autobiography* was based to some extent on hearsay.

15. Mill continues: "He [James Mill], at the same time, took care that I should be acquainted with what had been thought by mankind on these impenetrable problems. . . . [A]t an early age he made me a reader of ecclesiastical history; . . . and taught me to take the strongest interest in the Reformation, as the great and decisive contest against priestly tyranny for liberty of thought" (*Auto*, 52). One may question whether a study of ecclesiastical history can shed much light on the quest for man's source. James Mill's point in encouraging such studies was probably to emphasize the conflicts created by religion.

16. James Mill, cited in Fenn, *James Mill's Thought*, 27.

17. Talmon, *Rise of Totalitarian Democracy*, 31.

18. As Talmon describes this conception:

> It is for the Legislator . . . to discover means of placing men under the necessity of being virtuous. This can be achieved with the help of institu-

tions, laws, education and a proper system of rewards and punishment. . . . The object of the laws is to teach man his true interest, which is after all another name for virtue. This can be done if there is a clear and effective distribution of rewards and punishments. A proper system of education in the widest sense would fix firmly in the minds of men the association of virtue with reward, and of vice with punishment, these embracing of course also public approval and disapproval ["opinion"]. . . . It is a question of external arrangements and of education at the same time. (Ibid., 33)

19. Ibid., 33–34.
20. Ibid., 34.
21. *Ham*, chap. 26, "Freedom of the Will."
22. Mill, diary, January 22, 1854, CW 27:645.
23. John Mill's own vehement attack on the natural man in "Nature" (see Chapter 3) is permeated by a similar Calvinist pessimism.
24. Mill's remark is noteworthy because his celebrated differentiation of higher and lower pleasures in *Utilitarianism* is usually seen as a substantial revision of the creed he inherited from Bentham and his father. As the *Autobiography* makes clear, however, James Mill also elevated intellectual pleasures above the sensual, as did Bentham himself. As discussed in Chapter 7 (p. 273), Mill's differentiation of pleasures did not represent a dramatic departure from Benthamism but seems to have been a rhetorical strategy intended to defeat various popular objections to Benthamite utilitarianism.
25. Bentham had attacked the clergy, whom he described as "quacks" who prescribed "nostrums," as early as the 1770s. Over the years, and especially after his conversion to "democracy" in the early years of the nineteenth century, his attack on religion became increasingly immoderate. Bentham's most virulent antireligious writings stem from this period and were inspired by the opposition of the Anglican clergy to his plans for what he called a "Chrestomathic School" that would provide a "sound education of proper Utilitarian tendencies to the upper and middle classes." Bentham was irritated by the Church's opposition, and he responded by exposing and attacking Church abuse and corruption in *The Church of Englandism and Its Catechism Examined* (1819). "The main root of all abuse in the field of religion and Government, [he would say, is] an Established Church" (cited in James E. Crimmins, "Religion, Utility, and Politics: Bentham versus Paley," 141). Bentham's other important antireligious works are *An Analysis of the Influence of Natural Religion on the Temporal Happiness of Mankind* (1822), compiled by George Grote and published under the pseudonym of Philip Beauchamp, and *Not Paul, But Jesus* (1823), published under the pseudonym of Gamaliel Smith, Esq.
26. Theodore Fantl, "Jeremy Bentham and John Stuart Mill on Religion," 1. Bentham, like the Mills, regarded the Anglican clergy as self-interestedly opposed to reform: "Anti-reform is the line of conduct marked out for them by their situation: for their fears teach them, that a discerning and improving spirit, once received, may be contagious; and may awaken men's minds out of . . . religious debility." Bentham also attacked clerical involvement in politics. Clergyman, he said, were bad legislators because of their "interest in propagating . . . despondency and ill-opinion of the times. . . . [Moreover, because of their] habits of humility and deploration, nothing great and liberal is to be expected from them in the way of legislation" (Bentham, cited in Fantl, "Bentham and Mill on Religion," 18, 35).

27. Hamburger, "Religion and *On Liberty*," 145.

28. Cf. John Mill, "The Church," debating speech, February 15, 1828.

29. The younger Mill seemed to enjoy tweaking the noses of English Protestants by his public recognition of the positive role historically played by the Catholic Church, especially during the Middle Ages. His views in this regard were derived from the Saint-Simonian and Comtean philosophy of history. Nevertheless, Mill, like his father, was a lifelong opponent of the evils of "priestcraft" and in *Auguste Comte and Positivism* he rebukes Comte for his failure to appreciate the special contributions of Protestantism.

30. Mill, diary, February 25, 1854, *CW* 27:656, 657.

31. Note the implicit identification of the will of God with the utilitarian end— the "good of mankind." John Mill would employ the identical tactic (see Chapter 7, p. 282).

32. Wilford N. Paul, "The Religious Views of John Stuart Mill," 17.

33. James Mill, cited in Mazlish, *James and John Stuart Mill*, 65. It was James Mill's firm teaching, Mazlish explains, "that actions are based on opinions, and opinions formed on evidence. Therefore, the weighing of evidence is crucial." Mazlish comments: "There is a kind of transplanted Calvinistic concern and anxiety manifested here. The 'evidences' are not about one's salvation directly, but, in good Utilitarian fashion, about the 'saving' of one's fellow men by having the correct opinions."

34. The Benthamites' condemnation of such inducements (the hope of heaven and fear of hell), a recurring theme in the work of John Mill, aimed to undermine the belief in a posthumous divine justice, in man's accountability to God. The issue of the alleged immorality of Christian "inducements" is discussed further later in this chapter.

35. See D. G. Charlton, *Secular Religions in France, 1815–1870*.

36. This work did not appear in English until 1864, as *Theory of Legislation*.

37. Mary Warnock, introduction to *Utilitarianism, On Liberty, Essay on Bentham*, 8; John M. Robson, introduction to *Auto*, 4.

38. It is noteworthy that in the early draft of his *Autobiography* (1850–1857; the finished work was published in 1873), Mill had written "in the best sense of the word, a religion" (*CW* 1:171). There is ample testimony to the effect that Benthamism served as a "religion" for other young philosophical radicals besides John Mill, especially those drawn into the circle of James Mill. The Benthamites spoke of the "true Radical faith"; critics spoke of their sectarian zealotry and doctrinaire fanaticism (see Hamburger, *Intellectuals in Politics*, 22–28, and the quote from Henry Reeve that begins part II of this chapter).

39. In fact, the young Mill found Bentham's aspirations far too moderate. Bentham "deprecat[ed] and discountenanc[ed] as reveries of vague enthusiasm many things which will one day seem so natural to human beings. . . . But, in my state of mind, this appearance of superiority to illusion added to the effect which Bentham's doctrines produced on me, by heightening the impression of mental power [reason]" (*Auto*, 69).

40. Robson, introduction to *Auto*, 8.

41. John Plamenatz, *The English Utilitarians*, 56.

42. Bentham, *Fragment on Government*, cited in Warnock, introduction to *Utilitarianism*, 14. As Warnock remarks, Bentham "in fact . . . appears somewhat to have simplified, if not misunderstood, what Hume actually said." Hume employed utility as a general explanation for the existence of law and government. He suggested that inherited institutions are adaptations to the nature and cir-

cumstances of human existence, such as human beings' limited benevolence and
the inevitable scarcity that accompanies existence. Hume recognized the func-
tional utility of historically evolved social institutions such as law, morals, and
language in adapting human beings to the requirements of the kind of world in
which they live and in maintaining social order.

43. The origin of this phrase is usually assigned to Francis Hutcheson (*An Inquiry into the Original of Our Ideas of Beauty and Virtue*, 1725). The "greatest number" qualification has also been traced to Helvetius. As Voegelin points out, Helvetius did not use the phrase to convey moral approbation but merely to refer to
the simple force or power of the numerical majority. Bentham said he first came
across the phrase in 1768 in Joseph Priestley's pamphlet *Essay on Government*
(Warnock, introduction to *Utilitarianism*, 7).

44. Ernest Albee, *A History of English Utilitarianism*, 65.

45. William Paley, cited in Plamenatz, *English Utilitarians*, 53.

46. Ibid., 62. As Plamenatz explains, Paley's answer to the question "Why am I
obliged to do what is right?" is: "I am urged by a violent motive resulting from
the command of another. . . . The violent motive is the expectation of a posthumous reward, and the command is God's" (53). John Mill was in revolt against
precisely this understanding of God—the God of Will and Power who rules by
fiat or command and through the agency of fear.

47. Crimmins, "Religion, Utility, and Politics," 130.

48. Ibid.

49. Ibid., 131. Bentham attacked Paley in various works. In *The Church of
Englandism and Its Catechism Examined* (1819), he attacked Paley's attempt to vin-
dicate England's Episcopal hierarchy and his position on subscriptions to articles
of faith. In the *Analysis* (1822), Bentham challenged Paley's argument from design
(later defended by John Mill), and in *Not Paul, But Jesus* (1823) he violently attacked Paley's laudatory interpretation of St Paul. John Mill followed suit by attacking Paley in his first published article on moral philosophy, "Sedgwick's Discourse" (1835), *CW* 10:31–74.

50. Paley grounded the authority of the Anglican Church on its utility, that is,
on its usefulness in inculcating the principles of Christianity and in the support
it gave to secular government.

51. Crimmins, "Religion, Utility, and Politics," 131. Paley, however, was also to
some extent a secular thinker. As Crimmins explains, "Within the ranks of the cler-
ics, he typified the eighteenth-century effort of the church to make its religion
more accessible to its congregation. There is . . . in Paley's thought a shifting of
weight from revelation and other-worldliness to reason and considerations of
temporal welfare" (132).

52. Mill tells us that an aspect of the *Traités* that made a deep impression on him
was Bentham's classificatory skill, or, as he put it, "the manner in which Bentham
put into scientific form the application of the happiness principle to the morality
of actions, by analyzing the various classes and orders of their consequences. . . .
[W]hat struck me at that time most of all, was the Classification of Offences, . . .
[for I had] a strong relish for accurate classification" (*Auto*, 67). Mill thus offers a
rationalistic explanation for an emotional experience that he says was equivalent
to a religious conversion. Mill's lack of insight into his own motives has already
been alluded to; the same deficiency is indicated by this curiously unpersuasive
explanation for his "conversion" to Benthamism.

53. See Chapter 6 for a discussion of the penalties attached to the expression of
anti-Christian opinion in England at this time. One of the ways Bentham and

Grote aimed to avoid social censure or legal prosecution for the publication of the *Analysis* was to insist that it treated only "natural religion" or deism, that is, religion "apart from the peculiarities of any special Revelation." They also claimed the work dealt merely with the utility of religion and not its truth or falsity. As Leslie Stephen pointed out, however, this was mere prudential disingenuity designed to give the appearance of impartiality, for the unquestioned aim of the work was to undermine both natural and revealed religion (Leslie Stephen, *English Utilitarians*, 2:340). The extent to which the Benthamites feared repercussions for the public avowal of their antireligious views is indicated by Grote's decision, when he published a reprint of the *Analysis* in 1866, to again do so under the pseudonym he used in 1822.

54. Accordingly, the *Analysis* has been called the "first systematical attempt to apply utilitarian criteria in order to determine the utility of religious belief" (Leslie Stephen, *English Utilitarians*, 2:348).

55. Crimmins, "Religion, Utility, and Politics," 131–32.

56. Ibid., 138.

57. Bentham, cited in Fantl, "Bentham and Mill on Religion," 17.

58. Mill elaborated this argument most extensively in "Utility of Religion," which is examined in Chapter 3.

59. Fantl, "Bentham and Mill on Religion," 20.

60. See Douglas G. Long, *Bentham on Liberty: Jeremy Bentham's Idea of Liberty in Relation to His Utilitarianism*, for a discussion of the parallels between Benthamite psychology and Skinnerian behaviorism.

61. As Bentham said in the *Analysis*, the sensation of pain is always more intense than the sensation of pleasure and thus the threat of punishment is always a more effective inducement than the anticipation of pleasure. John Mill repeats Bentham's views in this regard in *An Examination of Sir William Hamilton's Philosophy*; see the section on punishment in chap. 26, "Freedom of the Will."

62. Crimmins, "Religion, Utility, and Politics," 139.

63. Jacob Viner, *The Role of Providence in the Social Order: An Essay in Intellectual History*, 55.

64. Mill, diary, January 1854, *CW* 27:647.

65. Crimmins, "Religion, Utility, and Politics," 140.

66. Leslie Stephen, *English Utilitarians*, 2:348.

67. Bentham, 1801, cited in Warnock, introduction to *Utilitarianism*, 9. John Mill, unaware of Bentham's prior use of the term, believed he himself was the first to apply the term *Utilitarianism* to the new movement. Mill also implicitly pointed to the anti-Christian roots of the term. In the *Autobiography* he describes how he arrived at the name of the debating club he formed in the early 1820s—the Utilitarian Society. Mill says he first encountered the term in a novel by John Galt, *Annals of the Parish* (1821). He further mentions that the passage he refers to appears in a scene in which one character warns another not to abandon the Gospel and become a "utilitarian." In short, in its very origin the term was intended to convey an anti-Christian connotation.

68. See Charlton, *Secular Religions in France.*

69. Talmon, *Rise of Totalitarian Democracy*, 21.

70. A rough sketch of the foundations of Bentham's positivistic "social science" may be helpful.

> [Bentham's] social science assumes a universe in which all "real" entities are either discrete physical objects or else ultimately reducible to other

such "real" entities. . . . [Bentham also believed that] descriptive language can make these intelligible free from the verbal foibles, mysticism and fictions which commonly pose obstacles to . . . human understanding. These assumptions, plus classification and analysis, provide the empirical data (in law, economics, politics, or theology)—upon which utility, the greatest happiness principle, is then applied as the one, true test of social value. (Crimmins, "Religion, Utility, and Politics," 132)

One also discerns Mill's positivism in embryo in what Viner describes as Bentham's "penchant for the scientific, . . . his rejection of superstition, idealism and abstraction in favour of the strictly perceptible, verifiable and useful" (*Role of Providence*, 36).

71. As Plamenatz observes, Bentham's greatest happiness principle is a close cousin of Comtean "altruism" (*English Utilitarians*, 62).

2. The Spirit of the Age: Mill and French Immanentism

1. See Henri de Lubac, S.J., *The Drama of Atheist Humanism;* Frank E. Manuel, *The New World of Henri Saint-Simon;* Charlton, *Secular Religions in France;* Voegelin, *From Enlightenment to Revolution;* Talmon, *Political Messianism* and *Rise of Totalitarian Democracy.*

2. Manuel, *New World of Saint-Simon,* 123.

3. *The Correspondence of John Stuart Mill and Auguste Comte* is the first English translation of Mill's complete correspondence with Comte. It consists of eighty-nine letters written between 1841 and 1847.

4. See Richard K. P. Pankhurst, *The Saint Simonians, Mill, and Carlyle: A Preface to Modern Thought,* and Iris Wessel Mueller, *John Stuart Mill and French Thought.*

5. Mill to Harriet Taylor, January 1855, CW 14:280.

6. "M. Comte's philosophy . . . might be compendiously described as Catholicism *minus* Christianity" (Thomas Henry Huxley, *Agnosticism and Christianity and Other Essays*).

7. Mill to John Pringle Nichol, December 1841, CW 13:491.

8. Mill, diary, January 24, 1854, CW 27:646.

9. Charlton, *Secular Religions in France,* 27.

10. Mrs. George Grote to Francis Place, August 16, 1837, Add. MSS 35, 150, f. 279.

11. There is in Mill a kind of aggressiveness vis-à-vis the thought of other philosophers. What Hamburger says of Mill with respect to Tocqueville—that he "absorbed what supported his position and rejected what did not" ("Mill and Tocqueville on Liberty," 103)—applies more generally as well. Mill seemed little inclined to contemplative reflection for its own sake; the paramount importance he attributed to his own purposes always directed his reading and his interpretation. Moreover, as various commentators have pointed out, Mill at times distorted or otherwise manipulated the views he appropriated in order to force them into service of the nontheological utilitarian cause. For this reason he at times does violence to others' thought, as in characterizing Socrates and Christ as utilitarians. One may even suspect that Mill's embrace of Comtean positivism was instrumental to his own purposes and thus highly selective. He readily accepted those aspects that dovetailed with his own religious purpose while rejecting those that did not. Comte seemed to recognize this. As he said to Mill soon before their final break, "Littre's [Comte's French disciple] adherence to positivism is really

more complete and explicit today than yours" (*Corr*, 359). If this interpretation is valid, it would explain Mill's intimate and extensive collaboration with Comte, whose views were in so many respects antithetical to his own. Cf. T. H. Irwin, "Mill and the Classical World," and Mill's peculiar interpretation of Coleridge's notion of the clerisy (see pp. 72–73).

12. See Charlton, *Secular Religions in France*, and Talmon, *Rise of Totalitarian Democracy*.

13. Mill required a systematic philosophy to live by. As he said: "[W]hen I found the fabric of my old and taught opinions giving way in many fresh places, . . . I never allowed it to fall to pieces, but was incessantly occupied in weaving it anew. I never, in the course of my transition, was content to remain for ever so short a time, confused and unsettled. When I had taken in any new idea, I would not rest till I had adjusted its relation to my old opinions, and ascertained exactly how far its effect ought to extend in modifying or superseding them" (*Auto*, 127).

14. Mill himself connected his recovery from the depression with his introduction to the poetry of Wordsworth.

15. Mill to John Sterling, April 1829, *CW* 12:29–30.

16. See Mill's letters to d'Eichthal, November 7, 1829; November 23, 1829; April 30, 1830; August 27, 1831, *CW* 12:38–43, 48, 52, 72.

17. D'Eichthal to Mill, in Eugène d'Eichthal, ed., "Unpublished Letters of John Stuart Mill to Gustave d'Eichthal," in *Cosmopolis* 6:20.

18. Mueller, *Mill and French Thought*, 55. See also Pankhurst, *The Saint Simonians, Mill, and Carlyle*.

19. The two most important Saint-Simonian and Comtean works that Mill undoubtedly absorbed at this time were *Doctrine de Saint-Simon: exposition: premiere année, 1828–29*, and Comte's essay "Prospectus des travaux scientifiques nécessaires pour réorganiser la société" ("Plan of the Scientific Operations Necessary for Reorganizing Society"), first published in 1822 as a pamphlet and republished under the title *Système de politique positive* in 1824. This short work contains in embryonic but complete form the essential ideas that Comte would elaborate in his treatises over the years, which were eventually published under the same title. See F. A. Hayek, *The Counter-Revolution of Science: Studies on the Abuse of Reason*, 235–62.

20. This aversion was a reaction to his youthful Benthamite zealotry. Sectarianism, he now came to believe, was a "character above all to be avoided by independent thinkers."

21. Mill to d'Eichthal, March 1, 1831, *CW* 12:70–71.

22. Mill to d'Eichthal, February 19, 1830, *CW* 12:47.

23. Mill to d'Eichthal, August 27, 1831, and January 25, 1832, *CW* 12:72–73, 94–95.

24. Mill to d'Eichthal, November 30, 1831, *CW* 12:88–89. In his "Comparison of the Tendencies of French and English Intellect," Mill had described himself as "an Englishman, himself no Saint-Simonian, and agreeing with the Saint-Simonians partially on almost all points, entirely perhaps on none" (*Monthly Repository* 7 [November 1833]: 800).

25. Saint-Simon, cited in Manuel, *New World of Saint-Simon*, 221.

26. Ibid., 227.

27. As late as 1870, Mill restated his view that Saint-Simonism was "an important event in history, both the evidence and the cause of a new tone of thinking and feeling in France" (Mill to Carlyle, April 11–12, 1833, *CW* 12:153–56; Mill to d'Eichthal, May 24, 1870, *CW* 17:1725–26). See Mueller, *Mill and French Thought*, 52.

28. Mill also shared his father's view that the traditional aristocracy, whose

"business is pleasure" and who were "enervated by lazy enjoyment," stood in the way of the formation of a new "aristocracy of intellect." They must thus "be divested of the monopoly of worldly power . . . [and so yield to the] most virtuous and best-instructed of the nation" (*Spirit*, 44, 90–93). See James Mill, "Aristocracy."

29. Mill could not stomach the ludicrous antics of the cult and especially its advocacy of free love and its notorious search for the "female messiah" in the harems of Egypt. By 1831 or so, the Saint-Simonians had become a source of popular entertainment, their group home in the Parisian suburbs a favorite site for weekend tourists. Mill, ever concerned with reputation, muted his public praise of their doctrines. But even at the height of the egomania of "Père Enfantin," the leader of the sect, Mill was writing sympathetic letters to d'Eichthal, asking him to give his regards to Enfantin and his co-leader Bazard, as well as providing introductions and advice to the Saint-Simonian proselytes in England. And in 1831 he published "The Spirit of the Age," which, while not mentioning the Saint-Simonians by name, was intended to bring their doctrines, and especially their philosophy of history, to the English public. Nor was Mill put off by the extravagantly sentimental religiosity of the Saint-Simonian Religion of Love; while it may have been ridiculous, it was at least entirely "terrestrial."

30. Carlyle, cited in Mueller, *Mill and French Thought*, 57.

31. Mill to Carlyle, October 5, 1833, CW 12:180–82.

32. Mill, diary, April 10, 1854, CW 27:667.

33. Hayek's preface to *Spirit*, viii.

34. See Mueller, *Mill and French Thought*.

35. Manuel, *New World of Saint-Simon*, 230.

36. Ibid., 230–31.

37. Ibid., 230.

38. Comte's philosophy of history is essentially an elaboration of Saint-Simon's. Comte served as Saint-Simon's secretary for seven years, an experience crucial to the formation of his own later views. For our purposes, their philosophies of history may be regarded as more or less equivalent.

39. See the discussion of the movement toward closure in Mill's thought in Chapter 6.

40. Mill to d'Eichthal, February 9, 1830, CW 12:48.

41. Comte found proof of Mill's sympathy with his views in the fact that, according to Comte, the two thinkers "spontaneously chose . . . th[e] indispensable appellation, positivism" to represent their new school of thought and this independently of one another (*Corr*, 212). There is an interesting parallel here with the fact that both Bentham and Mill had independently coined the term "utilitarianism" as a label for the "new religion."

42. The title was coined by the English statesman William Gladstone.

43. Peter Gay, *The Party of Humanity: Essays in the French Enlightenment*. One consequence is the modern "social consciousness" that seems to define individual and collective morality and thus politics for a large segment of contemporary Anglo-American society (see Chapter 8). Positivist or humanitarian "social morality" has also been assimilated by traditional religious communities. See Charles D. Cashdollar, *The Transformation of Theology 1830–1890: Positivism and Protestant Thought in Britain and America*, for a good discussion of the manner in which Anglo-American Protestantism was transformed in the direction of the "social gospel" by its dialectical engagement with positivism throughout the latter half of the nineteenth century.

44. Hamburger, *Intellectuals in Politics*, 80.

45. This behavior was typical for Mill. Carlyle, the Saint-Simonians, Comte, and others initially apprehended a potential convert in the seemingly open, pliable, and yielding demeanor of Mill. In the end, their expectations were always disappointed. At some point Mill always turned cool and distant, reasserted his independence and stature, and broke off relations, generally leaving his would-be leaders perplexed and sometimes angry.

46. Mill is referring to Comte's "Plan of the Scientific Operations Necessary for Reorganizing Society" (see note 19).

47. Mill recommended the *Cours* to a friend as "one of the most profound books ever written on the philosophy of the sciences" (Mill to John Pringle Nichol, December 21, 1837, *CW* 12:363–66).

48. Mill's explanation for his interest in Comte seems on a par with his explanation for his "conversion" to Benthamism and his account of his allegedly areligious upbringing. That is, it evinces the same curious lack of insight into his actual motives.

49. As Morley put it, "Probably no English writer that ever lived has done so much as Mr. Mill to cut at the very root of the theological spirit" ("The Death of Mr. Mill," 105).

50. Vol. 4 of Comte's work presents "The Dogmatic Part of Social Philosophy"; vol. 5 presents "The Historical Part of Social Philosophy, in everything that concerns the Theological State and the Metaphysical State." Vol. 6 presents the "Completion of the Historical Part of Social Philosophy, and General Conclusions" ("Contents of the *Cours*," in *The Essential Comte*). See *ACP* for Mill's elaboration of Comte's theory.

51. Voegelin describes Comte's writing of the *Cours* as a "spiritual practice," an insight supported both by Mill's method of absorbing the material and his intense response to it (Voegelin, *From Enlightenment to Revolution*, 143). Mill meditated long and hard on the work. As he told Comte, it was "by successive rereadings of your work at my leisure . . . [that] I reached my final and decisive conception [of it] that was not only stronger but essentially new, since it is primarily of a moral nature." He discovered that Comte "had sown in the previous volumes such fertile seeds for all the main concepts of the last that even the most extraordinary ideas I read there seemed like friends I had always known" (*Corr*, 118). Mill's deep immersion in the *Cours* seems akin to the "spiritual practice" that Comte undertook in writing the work. Moreover, as a result of reading this work, Mill would substantially revise certain sections of his *System of Logic*, most notably book 6 ("On the Logic of the Moral Sciences"), which is essentially an elaboration of Comte's views.

52. See Alan P. F. Sell, ed., *Mill and Religion: Contemporary Responses to* Three Essays on Religion, for a representative selection of the responses of Mill's contemporaries to his religious views. See Borchard, *Mill, the Man*, for a discussion of Mill's influence at the height of his career, especially the chapter "Mill as Mentor to the World." See Cashdollar, *Transformation of Theology*; Robson, *The Improvement of Mankind: The Social and Political Thought of John Stuart Mill*; Ryan, *The Philosophy of John Stuart Mill*; and Pedro Schwarz, *The New Political Economy of John Stuart Mill*, for favorable evaluations of Mill. See Maurice Cowling, *Mill and Liberalism*, and Hamburger, "Religion and *On Liberty*," "Mill and Tocqueville on Liberty," "Individuality and Moral Reform: The Rhetoric of Liberty and the Reality of Restraint in Mill's *On Liberty*," *Intellectuals in Politics*, and *Mill on Liberty and Control* for a less rosy view of Mill.

53. Hayek, *John Stuart Mill and Harriet Taylor: Their Correspondence and Subsequent Marriage*, 16.

54. Cowling, "Mill and Liberalism," 353.

55. Mill adds: "The same kind of motive, though less compelling, has caused me sometimes to retain (what I probably would not have done in France) certain expressions of metaphysical origin; I always attempt to lend them a positive connotation and to eliminate . . . as far as possible all expressions that today cannot simply be considered as abstract terms for [observable] phenomena" (*Corr*, 42).

56. Mill further remarks that he himself has always followed this practice. Through his journal writing, he says, he "gave a kind of preliminary education" to future readers of his *Logic* (*Corr*, 304).

57. See Mill's discussion in the *Autobiography* of his responsibility for introducing Comte to the English-speaking public (205). See also Cashdollar, *Transformation of Theology*.

58. Mill does refer to his new "religion without a God" in *Auguste Comte and Positivism* (1865).

59. Comte had reason to fear the enmity of the "scientists." After the appearance of his 1822 essay on the "spiritual power" (see part III of this chapter), the philosopher Benjamin Constant had charged Comte with attempting to replace the religious with a scientific hierarchy—with attempting to construct a "scientific theocracy." As a result, Comte was careful to couch his discussion of the spiritual power in language that would disarm such critics and to revise the Saint-Simonian scheme accordingly. No longer were the scientists to acquire exclusive control and direction of the "temporal power"; that power would now be shared by artists and intellectuals, as well as scientists. As Comte put it, his public conflict with the scientists was "particularly indispensable for the influence of my philosophy, for it completely obviates the most dangerous reproach one could address to our new school, that of being simply directed at transferring the old power of priests to today's scientists." Constant's accusations, said Comte, "threatened to discredit the new philosophy from the very start." In order to attract disciples, Comte recognized, it was necessary to allay their fears that some type of "despotism will arise [when positivism is established. That is why] . . . I developed . . . the idea of the inevitable struggle of the new philosophic spirit [positivism] against today's scientific spirit [the false positivists]" (*Corr*, 275). Comte himself was of course a virtuoso strategist.

60. At one point Mill was instrumental in rounding up potential financial backers for Comte, and he solicited the help of George Grote in the project. As Mill told Comte: "[Grote] felt it would be more fitting to address himself only to minds completely emancipated in religious matters, judging that no one else can appreciate you sufficiently" (*Corr*, 142). This issue of financial support became another bone of contention as the relationship between the two men deteriorated. It centered around Comte's feeling that he was entitled to continuing financial support from Mill's friends Grote and William Molesworth. Mill, who had been tireless in securing financial support for Comte in the early years of their collaboration, did not believe Comte's English benefactors had a moral obligation to continue their assistance.

61. Mill suggests as much in a curious and revealing remark in his essay "Nature." Contemplation of the heavens, he observes, immediately subdues all notions of rivalry. The thought of rivalry would never cross the mind of the great majority of human beings. See Chapter 3, p. 97.

62. Diderot, cited in Talmon, *Rise of Totalitarian Democracy*, 21.

63. From the Saint-Simonians, Mill learned not only that his was an age of "transition," he also learned of the "provisional" nature of all social institutions, such as private property, and of the necessity of regulating inheritance in the interests of what Mill called "social justice." See Schwarz, *Political Economy of Mill*.

64. Mill worked sporadically on the *Logic* throughout the 1830s, while deeply engaged with political activity and his efforts to lead the philosophical radicals in Parliament. Disillusioned with politics by the end of the decade and recognizing that men's opinions had to be reformed before any lasting or significant change in social or political institutions could be effected, Mill rapidly brought the *Logic* to completion in 1841. The first edition appeared in 1843. See Hamburger, *Intellectuals in Politics*, chap. 2.

65. Mill also remarks in this letter that he can "only blame the deplorable imperfection of our social structure" for the fact that Comte's *Cours* has not yet been published in its entirety. It seems the "principal fault [of the social structure] toward men of the first rank is . . . that it forces them to use up their strength and spend most of a life, already too short, seeking by the most menial occupations to eke out the barest means of livelihood" (*Corr*, 82). Revolutionary socialists were not alone in resenting the existing social structure.

66. That is, according to the editor of the *Correspondence*, "those critical of theology like the philosophes, not Kant" (144).

67. Mill also complains that the English are less ready to accept the "positive science of history" than other advanced nations. "Social physics," he says, "was bound to originate and grow in France, because French civilization . . . comes ever closer to the normal type of social evolution, while English history strays ever further from ordinary progress," as Comte had observed. In England, "this exceptional development and eminent insularity have caused the national character to evolve quite abnormally, with the result that we are quite indifferent to continental history; we have the unscientific custom to consider ours fundamentally separate" (*Corr*, 68).

68. Set forth in Coleridge's *On the Constitution of the Church and State according to the Idea of Each* (1830).

69. H. B. Acton, *The Idea of a Spiritual Power*, 3, 9–10.

70. Ibid., 4.

71. Ibid.

72. Mill to John Sterling, October 20, 1831, *CW* 12:88.

73. Saint-Simon was the first to formulate the idea of a modern spiritual power, in *Letters from an Inhabitant of Geneva to His Contemporaries* (1803). He distinguished three social classes: owners, workers without property, and the class of savants and artistes (the "intellectuals"). This latter class was responsible for whatever genius was produced and was thus, as Saint-Simon and Comte believed, entitled to public financial support for the benefits it conferred on society (the liberal Mill demurred from this aspect of their program). Saint-Simon's vision for the "spiritual power" involved the establishment of a "Council of Newton" composed of the "leaders of humanity," who were to be elected to the Council by each of the three social classes. The Council would thus represent all the main branches of science and art and, in addition to their scientific and literary responsibilities, would preside at temples containing models of Newton's tomb. Comte's vision of the spiritual power was similar in substance if not in detail.

Saint-Simon eventually came to believe that God himself had arranged for the decline of the traditional spiritual power of the Catholic priesthood, who had allowed themselves to be dominated and absorbed by the temporal power, as well as for its replacement by the modern intellectuals. Indeed, he would come to regard the Council of Newton as "the new priesthood of art and intellect, . . . [as God's] representative on earth." Saint-Simon also thought that the "temporal power," presently predominant, will naturally be reduced to its rightfully subordinate position once the modern spiritual power has consolidated its authority in the persons of the men of science.

Comte, despite his eventual repudiation of Saint-Simon and the bitter hostility he came to feel for him, adopted his views more or less wholesale. In 1820 Comte published an essay, under Saint-Simon's name, entitled *A Summary Estimate of the Whole of the Modern Past.* Its general theme was that just as the new "temporal capacity" of industry is replacing the old military-feudal power, so the new "spiritual capacity" of science is replacing the old spiritual power based on theology. Comte develops the theme further in an 1826 essay, *Considerations on the Spiritual Power,* written after his acrimonious break with Saint-Simon (Acton, *Idea of a Spiritual Power,* 6–8).

74. Mill also reveals what "representative government" meant to him at the time and within the framework of a society organized on Comtean lines. The "only two spheres which could conceivably [belong to the subordinate classes] . . . in the future" under representative institutions involve, first, the "matter of political education for the masses," and, second, their ability to use representative institutions "as a regular instrument for giving or refusing popular support to the general regulations issued by the leadership" (*Corr,* 110). This too is far from reassuring to either democrats or liberals. Comte himself thinks Mill's concerns are premature; before such matters can be resolved, "spiritual reorganization" must be achieved. Temporal measures are not only far less important than spiritual matters, but can only "be appropriately conceived . . . once . . . [spiritual] regeneration has taken place" (*Corr,* 115). For Comte as for Marx, what is important is spiritual transfiguration; the details of the new utopia can be attended to later.

75. As Hamburger observes, "John Mill's wish to gain 'worldly power' for an intellectual elite was to remain a prominent feature of his political thought" (*Intellectuals in Politics,* 86).

76. Throughout his life, Mill was highly critical of "laissez-faire" arguments. Under the influence of Saint-Simonian doctrines, he came to regard the institution of private property as merely provisional and destined to undergo fundamental and dramatic transformation in the future. As Mill said, "[I]t was partly by [Saint-Simonian] writings that my eyes were opened to the very limited and temporary value of the old political economy, which assumes private property and inheritance as indefeasible facts, and freedom of production and exchange as the *dernier mot* of social improvement" (*Auto,* 141). In 1833 he wrote of the laissez-faire system: "That principle like other negative ones has work to do yet, work, namely, of a destroying kind. . . . [P]eace with its ashes when it does expire, for I doubt much if it will reach the resurrection" (Mill to Carlyle, April 11–12, 1833, *CW* 12:153–56). See Chapter 8 for a discussion of Mill's contribution to the ascendancy of "social"-ist moral and ethical ideals.

77. That Mill's advocacy of a modern spiritual power was aimed in part against traditional religious authorities is suggested by his 1840 article "Coleridge," wherein he gave his support to Coleridge's conception of a nationally endowed "clerisy." Mill emphasized that it would be in keeping with this notion that "the

Royal Society might claim a part of the Church property with as good right as the bench of bishops" (*CW* 10:150–51). The scientific authorities would replace the religious authorities.

78. In 1842, Mill described his public reputation to Comte as that of a "kind of political figure who belongs to the moderate revolutionary party and who has at times written philosophically on questions of contemporary politics." As such, he explained, he is "completely unknown to the public at large, and consequently [does] not hold the least moral authority." In the late 1830s, as will be discussed, Mill reoriented his energies toward theoretical and philosophical work, the first major fruit of which was the *Logic,* published in 1843. Its appearance, he told Comte, would permit him soon to "discover how far my purely philosophic activities . . . can exert a real influence on the march of ideas in our country. . . . [T]he *Logic* . . . will probably place me among the recognized intellectual leaders and will enable me to judge . . . the degree of influence I am capable of exerting on the movement of ideas as well as the best ways to make use of it" (*Corr,* 53). As Mill anticipated, the remarkable success of the *Logic* and, a few years later, of *The Principles of Political Economy* (1848) did indeed gain him the authority he sought. From the mid-1840s until his death in 1873 he was a force to be reckoned with in Victorian society.

79. Comte explicitly touted his theory of the separation of powers as a useful weapon in the "philosophical revolution" required to institute the positive society. As he said, "I believe that our separation of the two powers [political and philosophical] will help us greatly . . . [in the task of] the formation and establishment of the new [positivist] school of philosophy." This was based on his belief that the joint pursuit of "intellectual and moral regeneration" and political reform created unnecessary impediments to social regeneration, to reaching the "final solution in the realm of politics": "It is because people insist on advancing the political and the philosophical movements jointly that the latter encounter so many natural obstacles" (*Corr,* 124–25, 127).

80. Mill to John Sterling, October 21, 1831, *CW* 12:79.

81. Mill, early draft of *Auto, CW* 1:189–90. These views were elaborated in *Spirit,* 17–21, 24–31, passim.

82. Acton, *Idea of a Spiritual Power,* 18.

83. Mill, "De Tocqueville on Democracy in America," in *Dissertations and Discussions: Political, Philosophical, and Historical,* 1:111n; Acton, *Idea of a Spiritual Power,* 9.

84. John Roebuck, ed., "Democracy in America," *Pamph, P* (no. 20, October 22, 1835): 3–4. Mrs. Grote complained of "that wayward intellectual deity John Mill" (see note 10 above). See also Bain, *Mill: A Criticism,* 57n.

85. Mill will present quite another evaluation of common sense thirty years later in *Utilitarianism* where he seeks to draw common-sense morality into the utilitarian camp. See Chapter 7.

86. Mill to John Sterling, October 20, 1831, *CW* 12:84.

87. Such remarks may point to the root of Mill's hatred of the aristocracy—his belief that they do not morally deserve their comfortable positions. All his life, Mill would crave a visible and rationally transparent desert-based justice.

88. That Mill's revolutionary aspirations were no mere passing fancy of his youth is indicated by Comte's 1842 remark to Mill: "You believe . . . that an English 1789 is basically indispensable." Comte did not agree, for he thought the French Revolution was representative for all of Europe: the "revolutionary up-

heaval in France [was] carried on for the benefit of the entire European republic, England, France, Italy, Germany and Spain. . . . The decline of the old order . . . [was] a necessary prelude [to final renewal]. . . . France accomplished this for all, in a sense" (*Corr*, 47).

3. "Nature" and "Utility of Religion"

1. Helen Taylor, introduction to *Three Essays on Religion*, vii–ix.
2. Morley, "Mr. Mill's Three Essays on Religion."
3. See Anonymous, "Religious Opinions of John Stuart Mill," and Sell, ed., *Mill and Religion*.
4. Mill to Harriet Taylor, August 29, 1853, *CW* 14:110–11.
5. Mill to Harriet Taylor, January 19, 1854, *CW* 14:141–42.
6. Mill to Harriet Taylor, February 7, 1854, *CW* 14:152.
7. Harriet Taylor to Mill, February 14 and 15, 1854. Mill responded on February 20: "Your program of an essay on religion is beautiful, but it requires you to fill it up—I can try but a few paragraphs will bring me to the end of all I have got to say on the subject." Hayek, *Mill and Harriet Taylor*, 195–97.
8. See H. O. Pappe, *John Stuart Mill and the Harriet Taylor Myth*; Hayek, *Mill and Harriet Taylor*; and Packe, *Life of Mill*, for conflicting views of Harriet Taylor's influence on the development of Mill's thought.
9. The careless and incoherent use of the terms *nature* and *natural* in moral and political philosophy, says Mill, has been "one of the most copious sources of false taste, false philosophy, false morality, and even bad law" ("Nat," 373).
10. Mill, diary, February 2, 1854, *CW* 27:649.
11. "The conception which the ethical use of the word Nature implies, of a close relation if not absolute identity between what is and what ought to be, . . . derives part of its hold on the mind from the custom of designating what is, by the expression 'laws of nature,' while the same word Law is also used . . . to express what ought to be" ("Nat," 378).
12. For instance, William Arthur, in *On the Difference between Physical and Moral Law*.
13. Nietzsche, Marx, and Comte come immediately to mind. See de Lubac, *Drama of Atheist Humanism*.
14. Much of this passage resonates strongly with the views of Harriet Taylor Mill. The most extreme and gnostic statements in "Nature" are of her inspiration; some of them were taken verbatim from her letters to Mill (see *CW* 14 and Hayek, *Mill and Harriet Taylor*). Harriet had a horror of childbirth and was obsessed with the issue of violence, especially domestic violence (Mill wrote numerous articles on that subject at her behest). It is perhaps not inappropriate to mention in this context that the unanimous view of Mill scholars is that he and his wife never consummated their marriage. Each had a horror of the "animal function of sex" and regarded their mutual chastity as setting an example to the world of the possibility of true friendship between a man and a woman.
15. See Hayek, *The Mirage of Social Justice*, vol. 3 of *Law, Legislation, and Liberty*.
16. Mill, diary, February 14, 1854, *CW* 27:654.
17. See Chapter 7, p. 282, for a more extensive discussion of Mill's identification of his utilitarianism with the will of God.
18. "[I]n the times when mankind were nearer to their natural state, cultivated observers regarded the natural man as a sort of wild animal, . . . and all worth of

character was deemed the result of a sort of taming. . . . The truth is that there is hardly a single point of excellence belonging to human character, which is not decidedly repugnant to the untutored feelings of human nature" ("Nat," 393).

19. Note the implicit identification of "self-regarding" with "selfish." Mill's moral thought was always structured by a rigid dichotomy between the bad or "selfish" (identified with Christianity) and the good or "social" (identified with the greatest happiness principle and later with the Religion of Humanity). Such a dichotomy was one of the core themes of the Benthamite ethos and, even more radically, of Comtean ethics and its juxtaposition of selfish "egoism" with selfless "altruism." See Chapters 6 and 7, pp. 260 and 295, respectively, for a discussion of the significance of Mill's antithesis between the selfish and the social for the development of a "social"-ist ethic.

20. Mill's remarks are ironic in light of the fact that certain of his contemporaries regarded his relationship with Harriet Taylor as an example of precisely l'égoïsme à deux that he here criticizes. See Reeve, "Autobiography of Mill."

21. Mill also cannot leave unchallenged Rousseau's assertion that veracity is a virtue characteristic of the natural man: "[T]his is a mere fancy picture, contradicted by all the realities of savage life. Savages are always liars. . . . They have [no] . . . notion of truth as a virtue." What they have is merely a kind of morality, "growing out of [the] characteristic circumstances . . . of the savage state." Such a morality is particular and concrete and it consists "mainly . . . in not injuring those to whom they are bound by some special tie of obligation." In any event, Mill says, savages and primitives certainly do not value truth for truth's sake or consider truthfulness itself a virtue. In this respect, he adds, they are like "the whole East, and the greater part of Europe" ("Nat," 395–96). Mill is sure that only a very small minority of human beings possess or honor truthfulness in itself.

22. The authentically liberal aspect of Mill's eclectic philosophy does surface from time to time: "[T]he man who takes pleasure in the mere exertion of authority, apart from the purpose for which it is to be employed, is the last person in whose hands one would willingly entrust it" ("Nat," 398).

23. Delight in cruelty, Mill says, is evinced "in the East and in Southern Europe." He adds that it may not only be our "duty" to "extirpate this hateful propensity . . . [but perhaps] to suppress the man himself along with it" ("Nat," 398). Mill would have little sympathy for the concerns of some in our day for the rights of criminals.

24. Mill also condemns the implicit approval of a feeling because it is regarded as natural, that is, because it is "ordinarily found in human beings"—as when we say it was "natural to feel that way" ("Nat," 400). Mill's condemnation is more or less selective, however, for he will commend and indeed seek to cultivate the natural feeling of retaliation or revenge, which he regards as the "natural basis" of the sentiment of justice (see Chapter 7, pp. 313–17). As noted, he also fully approves of the "natural" germ of sympathy.

25. Mill, diary, February 15, 1854, CW 27:654.

26. Mill's remarks are transparently autobiographical. He had attributed his original "mental crisis" of 1826 to an excess of training in criticism and analysis that prevented the proper development and expression of feeling.

27. Mill, diary, February 7, 1854, CW 27:642.

28. It is perhaps of interest that while Mill adopts and follows the argument of Bentham/Grote's Analysis, and while he acknowledges his debt to Bentham and Comte, he never specifically mentions the Analysis. This may be related to the fact that many of the ideas in "Utility of Religion" are identical to those found in the

Bentham/Grote treatise, with only a few minor changes and qualifications. Or it may be due to Mill's "policy of prudent concealment" and his desire to not draw attention to the Benthamites' unorthodox religious views.

29. As Mill puts it, one must investigate whether the "usefulness of the belief is intrinsic and universal, or local, temporary, and, in some sense, accidental; and whether the benefits which it yields might not be obtained otherwise, without the very large alloy of evil, by which, even in the best form of the belief, those benefits are qualified" ("UR," 405).

30. Both Comte and the Saint-Simonians had vigorously defended the relative value of religion, and especially Catholicism, at earlier stages of human development.

31. Mill, diary, February 25, 1854, CW 27:646.

32. See Hayek's Preface to *Spirit.*

33. It is clear that Mill regarded the public contestation of "received systems of belief" as one of the ways, if not *the* way, to undermine traditional beliefs, especially traditional religious beliefs. His plea for freedom of discussion in *On Liberty* should be understood in light of this strong conviction (see Chapter 6).

34. Mill, diary, March 17, 1854, CW 27:660.

35. Mill will argue in *An Examination of Sir William Hamilton's Philosophy* that the strongest "passion" or "desire" always does and necessarily must determine human action (see chap. 26, "Freedom of the Will," 452–53). James Mill had also believed that men are driven by the desire for the good opinion of others as well as by the desire for power over others. He was a thoroughgoing Hobbesian, as were all the Benthamites.

36. One hears too the voice of Harriet Taylor, snubbed by society for her unusual relationship with Mill, behind Mill's simultaneous valorization of and attack on the power of public opinion. Her voice also rings out in Mill's emphasis on the extreme difficulty of holding on to the conviction that one is in the right when all the world thinks one wrong. Both the Mills were extremely anxious of their reputation. They were both, and especially Harriet, preoccupied with achieving Victorian respectability while, however, simultaneously flouting the social conventions of the day. Harriet Taylor resented the fact that her special relationship with Mill was not appreciated for the noble model she and Mill thought it was. One result was their attack on public opinion, which they claimed to hold in contempt, and an exaggerated emphasis on its importance: "When once the means of living have been obtained, the far greater part of the remaining labour and effort which takes place on the earth, has for its object to acquire the respect or the favourable regard of mankind; to be looked up to, or at all events, not to be looked down upon by them" ("UR," 411).

37. Bentham argued that Paul was the actual founder of organized Christianity and responsible for the corruption of Christ's message.

38. Speaking of the poetry of Wordsworth, Mill said: "I seemed to draw from a source of inward joy, of sympathetic and imaginative pleasure, which could be shared in by all human beings. . . . I needed to be made to feel that there was real, permanent happiness in tranquil contemplation" (*Auto,* 121). See Robson, *The Improvement of Mankind,* 27–30.

39. This last sentence is a direct quote from Harriet Taylor.

40. The inscription on the tomb of Harriet Taylor Mill, written by John Mill, reads in part: "Were there even a few hearts and intellects like hers, this earth would already become the hoped-for heaven."

41. See Mueller, *Mill and French Thought,* and Pankhurst, *The Saint Simonians,*

Mill, and Carlyle. See also the section on "The Meeting of the English and the French Mind" in Chapter 8, pp. 322–26.

42. Comte of course coined the term *altruism.* As we have seen, Bentham's greatest happiness principle was in all essentials identical to Comte's conception of an altruistic service to humanity. Both conceived the good of the Great Being as the *ultimate* ground of morality and service to it as the *ultimate* end of moral action. See Chapter 7, p. 298, for a discussion of Mill's lifelong sense of the dichotomy between the bad of the "selfish" and the good of the "social."

43. James Collins, *God in Modern Philosophy,* 288. As Collins says, "This recognition of a finite God, on an interim basis, constituted [Mill's] chief amendment of the Comtean religion of humanity."

44. Mill to Carlyle, January 12, 1833, *CW* 12:206–7.

45. It is difficult to refrain from remarking on the absurdity of this view. Happy people do not normally commit suicide or long for an end to existence. Mill will go to incredible lengths in his efforts at conversion.

46. Mill adopted this view from his father.

47. Mill, diary, March 19, 1854, *CW* 27:662.

4. Sir William Hamilton and the Mansel Controversy

1. Collins, *God in Modern Philosophy,* 289.

2. Especially Hamilton's *Discussions on Philosophy.*

3. Robson, textual introduction to *Ham,* lxxiv.

4. Collins identifies Hamiltonian "Belief" with Kantian practical reason (*God in Modern Philosophy,* 298), although Hamilton himself does not employ that terminology. As Mill wrote to Alexander Bain: "By the way, is it not surprising that Hamilton sh [*sic*] have believed & made the world believe, that he held the doctrine of the relativity of human knowledge? As held by him the doctrine is little better than a play upon the word knowledge, since he maintains that a great mass of Belief, differing from Knowledge in the mode but not in the certainty of conviction, may philosophically & ought morally to be entertained respecting the attributes of the Unknowable" (January 1863, *CW* 15:816).

5. A priorism thus included the mathematical a priori rationalism derived from Descartes and Leibnitz and various other forms of that belief which Mill lumped together under the heading of intuitionism. What these beliefs had in common was the assumption that there are "truths which can be known by direct intuition of the mind and which need not be tested by sense-experience" (Karl Britton, *John Stuart Mill,* 111–12). As Ryan describes it, for Mill, a priorism represented a "psychological approach which refers our most important beliefs about the world, and our moral principles, too, to instincts or to innate capacities or dispositions" (introduction to *Ham,* xxiv).

6. Warnock, introduction to *Utilitarianism,* 11. See also *Auto,* 162–63; Bernard Vise Lightman, "Henry Longueville Mansel and the Genesis of Victorian Agnosticism," 203; Britton, *John Stuart Mill,* 111; Ryan, introduction to *Ham,* x–xi; and Robson, textual introduction to *Ham,* lxxiv.

7. *Ham,* 295; Ryan, introduction to *Ham,* xi. In the *Autobiography,* Mill calls Hamilton "the great fortress of the intuitional philosophy in this country" (203).

8. Mill to Carlyle, July 5, 1833, *CW* 12:157.

9. Mill, though invariably referred to in the literature as a member of the British empirical school, was concerned to distance himself from that school to some degree. He considered himself a follower of Bacon, who, he believed, had given the world the true scientific method of induction. But he also believed that "the En-

glish mode of thought"—that is, its commitment to what it took to be Baconian empiricism—was "in reality a slovenly misconception of [Bacon,] leaving on one side the whole spirit and scope of his speculations. The philosopher who laboured to construct a canon of scientific Induction, by which the observations of mankind, instead of remaining empirical, might be so combined and marshalled as to be made the foundation of safe general theories, little expected that his name would become the stock authority for disclaiming generalization, and enthroning empiricism, under the name of experience, as the only solid foundation of practice." Mill was throughout his life enamored of systematic philosophy and especially "French speculation" (*Ham*, 485).

10. Lightman, "Mansel and Victorian Agnosticism," 200.

11. According to Mill, there is nothing inherent in the structure of the human mind that makes it necessary for 2 + 2 to equal 4. Mill explained our seeming conviction of this alleged necessity as the result of the Law of Invariable Association, one of the linchpins of James Mill's psychological theory. John Mill argues that we apprehend that 2 + 2 must equal 4 only because in our experience whenever two groups of objects containing two items apiece are conjoined, four items appear. But if we lived in a world where every time two such groups were conjoined, a fifth object appeared, we would believe that 2 + 2 = 5. As a critic pointed out, however, this latter world would not be one in which 2 + 2 = 5, but one in which every time two groups of two were joined, a fifth element automatically appears. See W. G. Ward, "Mr. Mill's Denial of Necessary Truth," 285–318.

12. Lightman, "Mansel and Victorian Agnosticism," x; Mill to Harriet Taylor, February 4, 1854, *CW* 14:149.

13. Mill characterized this dichotomy more fully in *Utilitarianism*. See Chapter 7, p. 270.

14. An intramundane consequentialist ethic such as Mill proposed is one of the roots of the modern socialist ethic of an outcome-based justice. Traditional in-itself morality is correspondingly associated with the classical-liberal conception of the rule of law. See Chapter 8, p. 330.

15. Ryan, *Philosophy of Mill*, 78; Britton, *John Stuart Mill*, 111.

16. Ryan, introduction to *Ham*, xi.

17. See *Ham*, chap. 26, "Freedom of the Will."

18. Lightman, "Mansel and Victorian Agnosticism," 8. Mansel's lectures were published as *The Limits of Religious Thought* in 1858, and went through five editions by 1867.

19. Henry L. Mansel, *The Limits of Religious Thought*, cited in Lightman, "Mansel and Victorian Agnosticism," 88.

20. Alexander Campbell Fraser, cited in Lightman, "Mansel and Victorian Agnosticism," 88.

21. Ryan, introduction to *Ham*, xxxiii.

22. William Hamilton, *Discussions*, cited in ibid.

23. Later in his career, Mansel delivered a series of lectures on "The Gnostic Heresies," which were published as a book in 1875.

24. Lightman, "Mansel and Victorian Agnosticism," 9, 205.

25. Mansel, *Prolegomena Logic*, cited in ibid., 41.

26. Mansel, *Limits of Religious Thought*, xliii.

27. Collins, *God in Modern Philosophy*, 296.

28. Ryan, introduction to *Ham*, xxxvi.

29. Ibid., xxi.

30. Mansel, *Limits of Religious Thought*, cited in *Ham*, 101.

31. Mill paraphrases Mansel's argument: "In other words, it is necessary to sup-

pose that the infinite goodness ascribed to God is not the goodness which we know and love in our fellow-creatures, distinguished only as infinite in degree, but is different in kind, and another quality altogether. When we call the one finite goodness and the other infinite goodness, we do not mean what the words assert, but something else; we intentionally apply the same name to things which we regard as different" (*Ham*, 101).

32. Mansel, *Limits of Religious Thought,* cited in *Ham*, 101.

33. Mansel, *Limits of Religious Thought,* 28.

34. Mill to Alexander Bain, January 1863, *CW* 15:817.

35. Ryan, introduction to *Ham*, xxxv, xxxvii.

36. Lightman, "Mansel and Victorian Agnosticism," 285.

37. Mansel, *Philosophy of the Conditioned,* cited in Ryan, introduction to *Ham*, xxxvii.

38. David Berman, *A History of Atheism in Britain: From Hobbes to Russell,* 235.

39. In a chapter entitled "Great Men and Their Environment," where James is more or less defending the "great man" theory of history, he says, "[T]he singular moderation which now distinguishes social, political, and religious discussion in England, and contrasts so strongly with the bigotry and dogmatism of sixty years ago, is largely due to J. S. Mill's example" (William James, *The Will to Believe and Other Essays in Popular Philosophy,* 234).

40. The view of God implied here is similar to that implied in the discussion of Kantian ethics in "Theism" (see Chapter 5, pp. 186–89). There Mill suggests that counseling obedience to mere divine fiat is immoral; he approaches the apprehension that God *is* law. Such intimations in Mill's thought make it all the more strange that he did not seek other traditional understandings of God than the God of Will and Power that he rejected. One is led to suspect that Mill was more interested in asserting himself against God than in apprehending his reality.

41. Mansel questioned the thoroughness of Mill's knowledge of traditional natural theology. Ryan thinks that Mansel was probably right to do so because "Mill thought traditional metaphysics was pointless and nonsensical" (introduction to *Ham*, xxxv).

42. Ryan, introduction to *Ham*, xxxvii.

43. Mansel, *A Lecture on the Philosophy of Kant,* 4.

44. Morley, "Mill's Three Essays," 648. Morley also observes that Mill's attack was "declared . . . with a vehemence that startled many of his readers."

5. "Theism"

1. Morley, "Mill's Three Essays," 648.

2. The "softened temper" of "Theism" may also be accounted for in part by the fact that this is the only of Mill's essays on religion conceived and written free of the influence of his wife, who died in 1858. One suspects that the more militant tone of Mill's earlier essays was partly due to the influence of the radically antireligious Harriet.

3. As Mill himself does in "Nature."

4. Mill is deeply impressed by the interconnectedness of events: "[N]othing takes place in the world of our experience without spreading a perceptible influence of some sort through a greater or less portion of Nature, and making perhaps every portion of it slightly different from what it would have been if that event had not taken place" ("The," 432).

5. This is why monotheism may be regarded as the "representative of Theism in the abstract" ("The," 432).

6. As Mill put it in his diary entry of February 27, 1854: "The doctrines of free will and of necessity rightly understood are both true. It is necessary, that is, it was inevitable from the beginning of things, that I should freely will whatever things I do will" (*CW* 27:647). As said, the deterministic element of Mill's outlook was pronounced.

7. Note Mill's implicit disapproval of such believers, a striking departure from his usual insistence on the indispensability of authority. The authority of which Mill disapproved was traditional religious and political authority, which posed one of the remaining obstacles to the establishment of the authority he himself favored—the modern or positivist "spiritual power."

8. "The appearances in Nature point indeed to an origin of the Kosmos, or order in Nature, and indicate that origin to be Design but do not point to any commencement, still less, creation, of the two great elements of the Universe, the passive element and the active element, Matter and Force" ("The," 452).

9. See *Ham*, chap. 26, "Freedom of the Will."

10. Note that Mill somewhat distorts his opponents' views. They did not believe they "found the belief in themselves without knowing from whence it came"; they believed it to have been implanted by God. Mill also ignores, for instance, Socrates' "inner voice," his daimon, which he did not claim to rationally comprehend and which could readily be conceived as intuitive knowledge.

11. See Manuel, *The Eighteenth Century Confronts the Gods* and *The Changing of the Gods.*

12. Mill's own peculiar idealization of his wife and of various other persons he admired testifies to his firsthand knowledge of the value of this attribute. The following passage from his *Autobiography* conveys something of his susceptibility to Romantic hyperbole: Mill describes his wife as one "whose sensitive as well as her mental qualities would, with her gifts of feeling and imagination, have fitted her to be a consummate artist, as her fiery and tender soul and vigorous eloquence would certainly have made her a great orator, and her profound knowledge of human nature and discernment and sagacity in practical life would, in the times when such a *carriere* was open to women, have made her eminent among the rulers of mankind" (147). Commentators are universally agreed that Mill was alone in perceiving the allegedly extraordinary abilities of his wife.

13. Kant, "the most discriminating of the *a priori* metaphysicians, . . . saw the inconclusiveness . . . of all arguments from the subjective notion of Deity to its objective reality. . . . He kept the two questions, the origin and composition of our ideas, and the reality of the corresponding objects, perfectly distinct" ("The," 445). This, Mill thinks, describes his own approach as well.

14. Mill says that William Paley's example of a watch, the classic proof of evidence of design in nature, "puts the case much too strongly. If I found a watch on an apparently desolate island, I should indeed infer that it had been left there by a human being; but the inference would not be from marks of design, but because I already knew by direct experience that watches are made by men." Mill thinks that the same inference Paley drew from a watch could be drawn as confidently from a "foot print" ("The," 445). Mill, however, misinterprets Paley's argument. Paley did not maintain that finding a watch on a deserted island leads to the inference that it "had been left there by a human being" but that it was an artifact deliberately designed by a conscious mind.

15. Mill explains the difference between induction and analogy: "[B]oth argue that a thing known to resemble another in certain circumstances (a and b) will resemble it in another circumstance (c). But the difference is that in induction, a and b are known, by a previous comparison of many instances, to be the very cir-

cumstances on which c depends." In the absence of many such comparisons, we only know there is a probability of c where a and b exist, stronger or weaker as the "known points of agreement" [circumstances a and b] are more numerous and the "known points of difference" fewer. This argument can "never be equal in validity to a real induction."

An inductive argument may be tested by the canons of induction, the rules which establish, as Ryan puts it, "inferential license." There are four such rules or methods, corresponding to the four classes of inductive arguments: the methods of agreement, of difference, of residues, and of concomitant variations. The design argument falls under the method of agreement, which, Mill says, is "the weakest of the four, but the particular argument is a strong one of the kind" ("The," 447–48).

16. Collins, *God in Modern Philosophy*, 288.

17. Mill, diary, March 7, 1854, *CW* 27:659.

18. In "Nature," as we recall, Mill had condemned the admiration of nature as a vulgar and immoral worship of power and might (p. 97).

19. It should again be emphasized that Mill's imagination was fixated on the idea of the "Almighty." He is utterly uninterested in exploring other traditional conceptions of the Christian God, for instance, the God of Thomas Aquinas, who is thought to be limited precisely by "conditions of possibility."

20. There can be little doubt that Mill is engaged in what Voegelin and others term "gnostic speculation" (Budzisz, "Mill, Comte, and the Religion of Humanity"). Mill too dreams of one day acquiring what heretofore has been the defining characteristic of God—the ability to create human life, to *make a man*. One may infer that Mill would approve of modern efforts in that direction—cloning, genetic engineering, and so forth.

21. "The reign of law" was a popular phrase of the day and its relationship to free will and to God was much discussed.

22. Mill seems to suggest that there is a fixed and predictable amount of good and evil in the world, which is in line with his views on the stability and consistency of statistical data concerning crime. More or less the same number of murders and other kinds of criminal acts seem to be committed each year, he writes, regardless of circumstances and other contingent factors. This allows planners and others to act with certainty (*Ham*, 425).

23. Note the irreconcilability of this passage with the views expressed in "Nature."

24. The term *organization* was used by Comte and others to refer to the physical constitution of the body.

25. Mill goes on to define *substance* as "but a general name for the perdurability of attributes: wherever there is a series of thoughts connected together by memories, that constitutes a thinking substance. This absolute distinction in thought and separability in representation of our states of consciousness from the set of conditions with which they are united only by constancy of concomitance, is equivalent in a practical point of view to the old distinction of the two substances, Matter and Mind" ("The," 462).

26. Mill, diary, March 24, 1854, *CW* 27:663.

27. Mill seems to be employing his "canons of induction" far less stringently with respect to the issue of immortality than, say, with respect to the necessity of a first cause. When discussing the argument for a first cause, Mill insisted that it is impermissible to believe in the necessity of a Divine Mind because we have no experience of any mind which did not have a beginning in time. With respect to

immortality, as Mill says, we similarly have no experience of any existing mind that is not affiliated with a physical organism. Moreover, we have no evidence either of an Originating Mind beyond space and time or of an existent soul not affiliated with a physical body. The two cases appear identical, on Mill's grounds. Nevertheless, he will allow the possibility of immortality but not of an Originating Divine Mind. Why is our allegedly universal experience that minds begin in time sufficient to reject the argument for an Originating Mind beyond time and space but our universal experience of an invariable association between mind or soul and a physical organism not sufficient to reject the argument for the immortality of the soul? Moreover, our universal experience, as Mill says, is that all things perish. Why does this not count against immortality if our universal experience of minds beginning in time is to count against an Originating Divine Mind, as Mill contends?

28. A few pages earlier, however, Mill had insisted that we cannot compare our present reality to posthumous reality, for we have no basis of comparison. Now he says we must assume that the same laws that govern this reality will also hold in the higher reality. In this reality, all things perish; if one is required to conjecture about posthumous reality on the basis of the laws that govern present existence, one would have to assume that there too all things eventually perish. Mill, said his contemporary Stanley Jevons, had "an essentially illogical mind." Although there may be truth to that evaluation, there was a kind of logic to Mill's shifting premises and assertions. His choice of argument was always governed by the purpose at hand, which was often to convert and not to conduct a philosophical inquiry. Mill was at war with traditional theological beliefs and especially with the notion of an ultimate, transcendent justice. All is fair in war.

29. This disclaimer seems on a par with Bentham/Grote's disavowal of any intent to criticize the Christian revelation in the *Analysis*. As we recall, Bentham and Grote also maintained that the sole aim of that work was to criticize natural religion, which was patently untrue.

30. Reeve, "Autobiography of Mill," 129.

31. This passage also caused consternation among some of Mill's close associates, such as his atheistic disciple John Morley. As Morley pointed out, in an earlier passage Mill suggests that God's plan involved the provision that Christianity would arise "at the appointed time by natural development" ("Mill's Three Essays," 639). In the present passage, however, Mill says that "a gift [Christianity], extremely precious, came to us which though facilitated was *not apparently necessitated* by what had gone before, but was due, *as far as appearances go*, to the peculiar mental and moral endowments of one man [Christ] . . . " (emphasis added). For Morley, these two statements are irreconcilable: Christianity cannot have been both a necessary emergence, designed to arise "at the appointed time by natural development" *and* "not apparently necessitated by what had gone before." Morley is not attending to Mill's qualification: "not *apparently* necessitated." It is possible to explain how, to Mill's mind, an "apparently" spontaneous or undetermined "unique" event could actually have been "determined" or "necessitated" and at the same time *seem* to arise spontaneously by the "natural development" of the human mind. The explanation involves Mill's deterministic conception of the world historical process. He allows that the order of nature and history may have been designed from the beginning, designed to unfold in accord with a strictly determined and naturalistic process of cause and effect. Mill's worldview allowed very little room for genuine creative freedom and the unpredictability such entails. In Mill's necessitarian view, God or the Demiurge could have de-

signed the unique event of Christ's appearance to occur precisely at the moment it did occur, and this in step with the predetermined mental development achieved by the human race at that point in time. The Designer could have achieved this by the right collocation of the initial circumstances. Once set in motion, these produce the process of history, a process that is essentially the gradual unfolding of a predetermined chain of naturalistic or phenomenal cause and effect. Every seemingly spontaneous human volition may actually be preordained. Mill's Calvinist roots were deep. See Mill's 1854 diary entry in note 6 above.

Morley, to his alarm, interpreted Mill's remarks on Christianity as an "appeal to a mystic sentiment which in other parts of the book he had shown such good reason for counting superfluous. With all profound respect and unalterable affection for Mr. Mill's character and memory, I for one cannot help regarding the most remarkable part of the book as an aberration not less grave than the aberrations with which he rightly charged Comte" ("Mill's Three Essays," 637).

32. Mill to Carlyle, 1833, *CW* 12:182.

33. We late moderns subjected to an endless barrage of such revolting "associations"—for instance, Pachelbel's Canon as background music to an automobile commercial—can fully sympathize with this heartfelt complaint. Mill, by the way, was a rather accomplished musician who often composed pieces on the piano for relaxation and enjoyment. Music and walking seem to have been two of his very few pleasures.

34. As Mill said in the *Autobiography*, "Her memory is to me a religion, and her approbation that standard by which, summing up as it does all worthiness, I endeavour to regulate my life" (183). Such remarks should be taken seriously. Mill had more in common with Comte than their mutual desire to establish the final positivist realm and their mutual hostility to traditional religion and transcendent ethics.

35. There is no need to dwell on the fact that Mill's own work, as numerous commentators have pointed out, is riddled with inconsistency. Hamburger explains Mill's facility for advancing conflicting beliefs (such as advocating socialist moral ideals while strenuously insisting on the indispensability of economic competition; championing the most far-flung and spontaneous development of individuality while calling for the utter emendation of human nature; simultaneously promoting and condemning the use of the "social sanction"; validating and rejecting the notion of Providence, and so on) by his ability to project his fantasies and ideals into the future, thereby not having to face the fact that they were either incompatible with other of his values or incapable of realization ("Mill and Tocqueville on Liberty," 117). As suggested in Chapter 6, however, there may be a logic behind Mill's apparent inconsistency. It may be explicable in light of his overriding and utterly consistent purpose: to replace a theological with a purely human orientation.

36. This may be one of the reasons why Mill is at pains to allow for the probability of a God and future existence in his later writings. Such a belief, he seems to think, may add to the appeal of the Religion of Humanity, which it remains his chief purpose to promote.

37. Mill took this idea from Comte. See *ACP*, 134.

6. *On Liberty*

1. Isaiah Berlin, "The Notion of 'Negative' Freedom," 78.
2. Hamburger, "Religion and *On Liberty*."
3. Exceptions include Cowling, *Mill and Liberalism*, and Hamburger, "Mill and

Tocqueville on Liberty," "Individuality and Moral Reform," *Mill on Liberty and Control,* and "Religion and *On Liberty.*"

4. See "Utility of Religion" and diary entries of 1854, *CW* 27.

5. Mill, diary, January 22, 1854, *CW* 27:645.

6. Pankhurst, *The Saint Simonians, Mill, and Carlyle,* 93, 95.

7. See Chapter 2, p. 71, for a discussion of the "social experiment" of Saint-Simon and Comte as a forerunner of Mill's "experiments in living."

8. Indeed, Mill suggested that all the fundamental truths in science had already been discovered: "The physical sciences . . . are continually growing, but never changing: in every age they receive indeed mighty improvements, but for them the age of transition is past" (*Spirit,* 19–20).

9. Mill to John Sterling, July 1833, *CW* 12:168.

10. Mill was a typical modern intellectual, hostile to bourgeois values. He complained of the "stench of trade" (Mill to Carlyle, March 9, 1833, *CW* 12:144) and of the fact that "[t]here is now scarcely any outlet for energy in this country except business" (*OL,* 70). See Chapter 8, pp. 323–25.

11. Hamburger, "Religion and *On Liberty,*" 144–45. In addition to the laws against blasphemous libel, Mill and his cohort were also vulnerable to legal prosecution on the basis of various other laws governing religious opinion, for instance, laws that granted authority over such matters to the ecclesiastical courts (ibid., 146).

12. For instance, Richard Carlile, who was convicted of such conduct several times during the 1820s. As Mill explained: "[T]he prosecutions of Richard Carlile and his wife and sister for publications hostile to Christianity, were then exciting much attention, and nowhere more than among the people I frequented. Freedom of discussion even in politics, much more in religion, was at that time far from being, even in theory, the conceded point it at least seems to be now [1873] and the holders of obnoxious opinions had to be always ready to argue and reargue for the liberty of expressing them. . . . I wrote a series of five letters, under the signature of Wickliffe, going over the whole length and breadth of the question of free publication of all opinions on religion, and offered them to the *Morning Chronicle.* . . . Three [were] published in January and February 1823; the other two, containing things too outspoken for that journal, never appeared at all" (*Auto,* 82–83).

13. James Fitzjames Stephen, cited in Hamburger, "Religion and *On Liberty,*" 145.

14. Ibid., 141.

15. Mill, "Fonblanque's England," *CW* 6:354.

16. Reeve, "Mill's Essays on Theism," 4, 8.

17. Hamburger, "Religion and *On Liberty,*" 140.

18. Hamburger, "Mill and Tocqueville," 111–12.

19. Mill and his father believed that writers of "periodical literature" were obliged not to "profess and inculcate the opinions already held by the public to which it addressed itself, [but to] rectify or improve those opinions" (James Mill, "The Church," 85).

20. Hamburger, "Mill and Tocqueville," 111; Mill citation from "Rationale of Representation," *London Review* (1835): 367.

21. Hamburger, "Mill and Tocqueville," 111. See Hamburger's *Intellectuals in Politics* for a full account of Mill's early political activism.

22. Mill to Macvey Napier, July 30, 1841, *CW* 13:483. Mill's rejection of active politics at this time was anticipated during a brief period in 1830–1831, when he experienced a similar distaste for political engagement.

23. Hamburger, "Mill and Tocqueville," 112–13.

24. Mill to Edwin Chadwick, April 1842, *CW* 13:516; Mill to Robert Barclay Fox, December 19, 1842, *CW* 13:563.

25. The early draft of Mill's *Autobiography* was composed during the same years as his "mental pemican" for thinkers of the future, that is, between 1850 and 1857.

26. Mill, early draft of *Auto*, *CW* 1:244, 246.

27. Mill, diary, February 18, 1854, *CW* 27:655.

28. Hamburger, "Religion and *On Liberty*," 158–59. Quotations from Mill are from the early draft of *Auto*, *CW* 1:244, 246.

29. Hamburger, "Religion and *On Liberty*," 161–64.

30. One may object that, on Mill's own grounds, the need to defend Christianity against its aggressive opponents would tend to revitalize Christian belief. Mill, however, does not allow for this possibility. I thank Howard Maxwell for this insight.

31. Mill, "On Genius," *CW* 1:337.

32. Hamburger, "Religion and *On Liberty*," 161.

33. Ibid.

34. This sounds fine, but the devil is of course in the details. Mill certainly meant much more by his nontheological utilitarianism than the Golden Rule. See Chapter 7.

35. Mill also enlisted Aristotle in the utilitarian camp; he speaks of the "judicious utilitarianism of Aristotle" (*OL*, 27).

36. As Hamburger puts it, Mill, in advancing his conception of Christ-as-model, "conceded nothing of his entirely rational and secular understanding of the Religion of Humanity" ("Religion and *On Liberty*," 162). Whether this is an accurate characterization of Mill's engagement with the Religion of Humanity is debatable, a point to which we will return in the concluding chapter.

37. Ibid., 161.

38. Ibid., 162.

39. Mill, diary, January 23, 1854, *CW* 27:645–46.

40. Mill says in *On Liberty* that "some of those modern reformers who have placed themselves in strongest opposition to the religions of the past, have been nowhere behind either churches or sects in their assertion of the right of spiritual domination: Monsieur Comte, in particular, whose social system, as unfolded in his *Système de politique positive*, aims at establishing (though by moral more than by legal appliances) a despotism of society over the individual, surpassing anything contemplated in the political ideal of the most rigid disciplinarian among the ancient philosophers" (17).

41. Mill, diary, January 24, 1854, *CW* 27:646.

42. For an account of the various meanings of the term *religion* in Mill's work, see Britton, "John Stuart Mill on Christianity," 21–23.

43. Hamburger, "Religion and *On Liberty*," 164. The *Examination, Utilitarianism,* and "Nature" spring immediately to mind.

44. Ibid., 167–68.

45. The major thrust of *On Liberty* is to suggest that all public disapproval based on customary moral grounds is illegitimate, and this is how the essay has been received by many of Mill's descendants. The most significant legacy of *On Liberty* may be the effectiveness of its all-encompassing attack on custom and tradition, religious and otherwise.

46. "Nature," as we recall, had quite a different purpose: chiefly to attack the "irrational" deist conception of a "Providence manifest in general laws." Thus Mill was concerned to portray nature as a reckless disorder—certainly not as a spontaneous unfolding—and to emphasize the need for self-restraint.

47. Hamburger, "Religion and *On Liberty*," 165–66.

48. Ibid., 165.

49. Ibid., 166.

50. Note the incongruity between Mill's advocacy of "Pagan self-assertion" in *On Liberty* and his valorization of self-renunciation in service of his new Religion of Humanity in *Utilitarianism*. See Chapter 7.

51. Henry Cole, diary, 1827–1834, entry of November 23, 1831, Victoria and Albert Museum.

52. Bain, *Mill: A Criticism*, 103–4.

53. Hamburger, "Religion and *On Liberty*," 169.

7. Utilitarianism

1. The work was originally published in 1861 in three installments in *Fraser's Magazine*.

2. Crimmins, "Religion, Utility, and Politics."

3. This label was introduced in 1870 by Joseph B. Mayor. See John Grote, *An Examination of the Utilitarian Philosophy*, ed. Joseph B. Mayor, 221.

4. See the discussion of common sense in Chapter 2, p. 83.

5. Hamburger, "Religion and *On Liberty*," 101–2. Such social values, as we have seen, were already implicit in Bentham's own elaboration of the utilitarian doctrine.

6. Note the concern with unanimity, still the desiderata for Mill in 1861.

7. Mill's vigorous defense of the "higher pleasures," of the "mental" over the "bodily" pleasures, although it superficially resembles the classical reverence for the contemplative over the active life, moves beyond that tradition in its severe— one is tempted to say gnostic—disparagement of matter. Mill's contempt for man's "animal nature" knew no bounds (*Util*, 410, 412). Throughout his life he engaged in a vigorous campaign against population growth; as a young man he was arrested for distributing handbills promoting contraception in the working-class section of London. With his father, moreover, Mill fully anticipated that the animal desires and pleasures stemming from man's sexual nature would wither in desirability and intensity over time, assisted, of course, by proper training and education. Mill was particularly hostile to the male nature and often expressed his hope that men would eventually become more like women, capable, as he believed women already were, of subordinating the sexual impulses to reason.

8. Borchard, "Mill as Mentor to the World" in *Mill, the Man*.

9. Carlyle once characterized Harriet Taylor as "a living Romance heroine."

10. One hears too the voice of modern liberalism in this profound elevation of the "sense of dignity," which seems to have become the *summum bonum* of modern-liberal ethics.

11. Mill's argument was formulated earlier, in his diary entry of March 23, 1854:

> The only true or definite rule of conduct or standard of morality is the greatest happiness, but there is needed first a philosophical estimate of happiness. Quality as well as quantity of happiness is to be considered; less of a higher kind is preferable to more of a lower. The test of quality is the preference given by those who are acquainted with both. Socrates would rather choose to be Socrates dissatisfied than to be a pig satisfied. The pig probably would not, but then the pig knows only one side of the question: Socrates knows both. (*CW* 27:663)

12. Whether or not the masses are to be admonished toward self-sacrifice in service to humanity is not clear. Mill suggests that this would be fine, so long as their self-renunciation tends to increase the sum total of happiness in this world. This is unquestionably true of the superior natures, while the value of self-sacrifice for the lesser folk probably depends on the height of the contribution they are capable of making.

13. As a young man, Mill had embraced what he called the "anti-self-consciousness theory" of Carlyle.

14. Note Mill's ambiguous use of the term *finding*, which suggests that moral rules are somehow given. As Mill makes clear in other contexts, however, he does not mean God-given.

15. See Manuel, *New World of Saint-Simon*, especially the chapter "The New Christianity," for a good discussion of Saint-Simon's method in this regard.

16. Indeed, utilitarianism above all other ethical systems affirms that "the motive has nothing to do with the morality of the action, though much with the worth of the agent" (*Util*, 419). It is right to save a person from drowning whether one's motive is a sense of duty or the expectation of reward. Betraying a friend is likewise wrong, regardless of the motive.

17. For instance, as Mill says in "Utility of Religion": "When we consider how ardent a sentiment, in favourable circumstances of education, the love of country has become, we cannot judge it impossible that the love of that larger country, the world, may be nursed into similar strength, both as a source of elevated emotion and as a principle of duty" (431).

18. Note the identification of interest with happiness, as in Chapter 6 (p. 260). If Mill meant *interest*, why didn't he use just that word? Perhaps his confusing identification of interest with happiness stemmed from a desire to appeal to the long-standing positive resonances of the term *self-interest* within English political culture. His aim, however, is not to promote this value but to eradicate the selfish pursuit of self-interest.

19. Reeve, "Autobiography of Mill," 127.

20. Mill goes on to say: "[T]here is in reality nothing desired except happiness. Whatever is desired otherwise than as a means to some end beyond itself, and ultimately to happiness, is desired as itself a part of happiness, and is not desired for itself until it has become so. Those who desire virtue for its own sake, desire it either because the consciousness of it is a pleasure, or because the consciousness of being without it is a pain, or for both reasons united; as in truth the pleasure and pain seldom exist separately, but almost always together, the same person feeling pleasure in the degree of virtue attained, and pain in not having attained more" (*Util*, 438).

21. See R. P. Anschutz, *The Philosophy of John Stuart Mill*, for a characterization of Mill as a Platonist and not a nominalist. See Harry Settanni, *The Probabilist Theism of John Stuart Mill*, for a discussion of Mill's occasional nominalism.

22. Crimmins has also drawn attention to this aspect of the nominalist Bentham, to what he describes as the "curious tension . . . between Bentham's nominalism with its regard for discrete entities and the emphasis he places on the abstract and collective notion of 'men in general'" ("Religion, Utility, and Politics," 139). The same holds for Mill's long-standing habit of attributing purposive intent to abstractions such as "society" and "nature."

23. Mill will employ an identical approach in *An Examination of Sir William Hamilton's Philosophy* with respect to the sense of moral accountability or responsibility. That is, he will account for this sense on naturalistic grounds. His aim in

the *Examination* is to defeat Hamilton and the other intuitionists who argued that man's sense of moral accountability, bound up as it is with free will, points directly to God. Mill, on the contrary, traces the sense of moral accountability to early childhood training and especially punishment. See *Ham*, chap. 26, "Freedom of the Will."

24. As noted, such remarks sit ill at ease with Mill's demand for freedom from conventional social sanctions in *On Liberty*.

25. Mill limits morally justifiable resentment to the times when a person "considers whether an act is blamable before he allows himself to resent it." It is not clear, however, what such a consideration has to do with justifying or moralizing resentment. The most obsessive paranoiacs undoubtedly brood intensely before concluding that their resentment is justified. There is nothing in such consideration that permits the objective differentiation of justified or unjustified moral resentment.

8. Consequences and Implications

1. Cowling, introduction to Mill, *Selected Writings*, 11.

2. Modern liberalism and its notion of the mixed economy, or, in contemporary jargon, the "third way," attempts to promote the collectivist ideal of social justice by employing, in a qualified way, the classical-liberal means of individual freedom and the market. This is an inherently contradictory and self-defeating task. For a thorough discussion of why this is so, see Hayek, *The Constitution of Liberty* and *Law, Legislation, and Liberty*.

3. Comte to Mill, *Corr*, 67.

4. Hayek, *Constitution of Liberty*.

5. Mill to Carlyle, March 9, 1833, CW 12:144.

6. Georg G. Iggers, *The Cult of Authority: The Political Philosophy of the Saint-Simonians, a Chapter in the Intellectual History of Totalitarianism*.

7. Leslie Stephen, *English Utilitarians* 3:16; Hayek's Preface to *Spirit*, vi–vii.

8. Mill grew to love France, or at least his romantic idealization of it, above all other places; he and Harriet planned to resettle in that country after his retirement from India House. During one of their trips to France, Harriet died, suddenly and unexpectedly. Mill purchased a cottage near her grave in Avignon, where he lived out his final years in company with his stepdaughter Helen Taylor. Upon his death in 1873, he was buried next to Harriet in their beloved Avignon.

9. As Hayek puts it, the effect of Mill's relationship with Harriet Taylor was that "he entirely withdrew from social life and become the recluse he remained for the rest of his life" (Preface to *Spirit*, xii).

10. Reeve, "Autobiography of Mill," 121.

11. Mill to John Sterling, October 20, 1831, CW 12:78.

12. Ryan, introduction to *Ham*, xxi; Hamburger, "Religion and *On Liberty*," 162.

13. Anonymous review of Bain, *Mill: A Criticism*. Leslie Stephen observed, "Truly, Mill was nearly qualified for a place among the prophets" (*English Utilitarians* 3:449).

14. J. Wesley Robb, *The Reverent Skeptic: A Critical Inquiry into the Religion of Secular Humanism*, 6. Robb identifies several of the leading tenets of the contemporary "Religion of Secular Humanism": 1) "There is no entelechy, no built-in pattern of perfection. Man is his own rule and his own end"; 2) "A philosophy founded on the agreement that 'man is the measure of all things' can have no room for belief in the intervention of non-material postulates"; 3) "[W]e have in-

creasing knowledge of our world, and . . . there is no need to postulate a realm beyond it"; 4) "Humanism believes that the nature of the universe makes up the totality of existence and is completely self-operating according to natural law, with no need for a God or gods to keep it functioning" (ibid., 6–7). These postulates are similar, if not identical, to various of Mill's teachings.

15. See Cashdollar, *Transformation of Theology*.

16. Bush made this remark at several commencement ceremonies and on a number of other occasions.

17. Bentham, cited in Warnock, introduction to *Utilitarianism*, 15. Bentham had defined utility as that "property *in* an object [whereby it] tends to produce benefit, advantage, pleasure, good or happiness" (more or less equivalent in the Benthamite lexicon) and this for the community as a whole: "An action is conformable to utility when the tendency it has to augment the happiness of the community is greater than any it has to diminish it" (ibid.). Bentham regarded the general or collective happiness as not only objective but as quantifiable and measurable.

18. Bentham, from his *Commonplace Book*, written between 1781 and 1785, in *The Works of Jeremy Bentham* 10:143. Crimmins points out that Bentham's "shift in focus" from individual goodness to that of men in general "clearly distinguishes the central aim of his work from that of the religious exponents of utility." The Christian utilitarians, while in some sense concerned with the long-term consequences of their actions in the eyes of God, remained committed to the belief that the person is the bearer of morality and that individual actions are what matter. Such a view was inseparable from a concern with personal salvation ("Religion, Utility, and Politics," 21).

19. See Hayek, *Rules and Order* and *The Mirage of Social Justice*, vols. 2 and 3 of *Law, Legislation, and Liberty*.

20. See Jacques Ellul, "Politization and Political Solutions."

21. Mill, *Principles of Political Economy*, ed. W. J. Ashley.

22. Ibid., 792.

23. It is indeed doubtful whether Mill ever fully embraced classical-liberal ideals. We have seen his contemptuous dismissal of classical liberalism in the 1830s and the extent of his commitment to the illiberal schemes of Saint-Simon and Comte well into the 1840s. We have examined the motives behind the apparent libertarianism of *On Liberty*. The extent of Mill's commitment to socialist ideals is evinced by the fact that a full-fledged socialist such as Sidney Webb regarded Mill as his spiritual "godfather" (Shirley Robin Letwin, *The Pursuit of Certainty: David Hume, Jeremy Bentham, John Stuart Mill, Beatrice Webb*). According to Borchard, "Mill's *Political Economy* did more than any other single book to bring about socialism in England" (*Mill, the Man*, 99). And various of Mill's socialist-leaning descendants, such as Mueller and Schwarz, unabashedly celebrate Mill's movement toward socialism (see *Mill and French Thought* and *Political Economy of Mill*, respectively).

24. Paul Edward Gottfried, *After Liberalism: Mass Democracy in the Managerial State*, 28, 101–2.

25. Mill, diary, March 17, 1854, *CW* 27:660.

26. See Richard Crossman, ed., *The God That Failed*, a collection of autobiographical writings by ex-communists.

27. For a discussion of Bentham's legacy to totalitarianism, see Richard A. Posner, "Blackstone and Bentham," 599.

28. Irving Babbitt, *Democracy and Leadership*, 314.

29. Mill, diary, February 14, 1854, *CW* 27:654.

30. Mazlish, *The Revolutionary Ascetic*; Eric Hoffer, *The True Believer: Thoughts on the Nature of Mass Movements*.

31. Mill, diary, March 25, 1854, *CW* 27:663.

32. Ryan, introduction to *Ham*, lx. See also *Ham*, chap. 26, "Freedom of the Will."

33. Cowling, introduction to Mill, *Selected Writings*, 11.

Bibliography

Acton, H. B. "Comte's Positivism and the Science of Society." *Philosophy* 26:99 (October 1951): 291–310.

———. *The Idea of a Spiritual Power.* London: Athlone Press, 1974.

Albee, Ernest. *A History of English Utilitarianism.* New York: Macmillan, 1957 [1901].

Allen, R. T. *Beyond Liberalism.* New Brunswick: Transaction Publishers, 1998.

Anonymous. "Religious Opinions of John Stuart Mill." *Quarterly Review* 5:2 (April 1875): 279–92.

Anonymous. Review of Alexander Bain, *John Stuart Mill: A Criticism, with Personal Recollections. The Nation* 34 (June 8, 1882): 884.

Anschutz, R. P. *The Philosophy of John Stuart Mill.* London: Oxford University Press, 1963.

Arthur, William. *On the Difference between Physical and Moral Law.* London: T. Woolmer, 1883.

———. *Religion Without God: Positivism and Mr. Frederick Harrison.* London: Bemrose and Sons, 1888.

Attfield, Robin. *God and the Secular.* Cardiff, Wales: University College Cardiff Press, 1978.

Babbitt, Irving. *Democracy and Leadership.* Indianapolis: Liberty Fund, 1979 [1924].

Bain, Alexander. *John Stuart Mill: A Criticism, with Personal Recollections.* New York: Augustus M. Kelley Publishers, 1969 [1882].

Baker, Rannie Belle. *The Concept of a Limited God.* Washington: Shenandoah Publishing House, 1934.

Bakunin, Michael. *God and the State.* New York: Dover Publications, 1970.

Bentham, Jeremy. *The Church of Englandism and Its Catechism Examined,* 1819.

———. *A Fragment on Government.* Cambridge: Cambridge University Press, 1990.

———. *An Introduction to the Principles of Morals and Legislation.* In *The Utilitarians.* New York: Anchor Books, 1973.

————. *Not Paul, But Jesus.* [Gamaliel Smith, Esq., pseud.] London: printed for John Hunt, 1823.

————. *The Theory of Legislation.* Ed. C. K. Ogden, trans. Richard Hildreth. London: Routledge and Kegan Paul, 1959.

————. *The Works of Jeremy Bentham.* 11 vols. New York: Russell and Russell, 1962.

Berlin, Isaiah. "The Notion of 'Negative Freedom.'" In *Limits of Liberty: Studies of Mill's* On Liberty, ed. Peter Radcliff. Belmont, Calif.: Wadsworth Publishing, 1968.

Berman, David. *A History of Atheism in Britain: From Hobbes to Russell.* London: Croom Helm, 1988.

Bill, Thomas Lee, C.S.C. "The Theory of Nature in John Stuart Mill." Ph.D. diss., Saint Louis University, 1963.

Billington, James H. *Fire in the Minds of Men: Origins of the Revolutionary Faith.* New York: Basic Books, 1980.

Blackley, W. Lewery. "Compulsory Providence as a Cure for Pauperism." *Contemporary Review* 35 (April–August 1879): 608–29.

Bonar, James. *The Tables Turned.* London: Macmillan, 1931.

Borchard, Ruth. *John Stuart Mill, the Man.* London: Watts, 1957.

Brackenbury, Edward. "Brackenbury's Discourses on Christianity." *Literary Journal* (October 1806): 517–22.

Braithwaite, R. B. *An Empiricist's View of the Nature of Religious Belief.* Cambridge: Cambridge University Press, 1955.

Braunthal, Alfred. *Salvation and the Perfect Society.* Amherst: University of Massachusetts Press, 1979.

Britton, Karl. *John Stuart Mill.* New York: Dover Publications, 1969.

————. "John Stuart Mill on Christianity." In *James and John Stuart Mill/ Papers of the Centenary Conference,* ed. John M. Robson and Michael Laine. Toronto: University of Toronto Press, 1976.

Budd, Susan. *Varieties of Unbelief: Atheists and Agnostics in English Society, 1850–1960.* New York: Holmes and Meier Publishers, 1977.

Budzisz, Christopher. "John Stuart Mill, Auguste Comte, and the Religion of Humanity." M.A. thesis, Southern Illinois University at Carbondale, 1996.

Bultmann, D. Rudolf. *History and Eschatology.* Edinburgh: University Press, 1957.

Burns, H. "Jeremy Bentham: From Radical Enlightenment to Philosophical Radicalism." *Bentham Newsletter* 8 (1984): 4–14.

Burston, W. H. *James Mill on Philosophy and Education.* London: Athlone Press, 1973.

Butler, Joseph. *Analogy of Religion, Natural and Revealed, to the Constitution and Nature.* 3d ed. Charlottesville, Va.: Ibis Publishing, 1986 [1736].

Caird, Edward. *The Social Philosophy and Religion of Comte.* New York: Kraus Reprint, 1968 [1885].

Carlyle, Alexander. *Letters of Thomas Carlyle to John Stuart Mill, John Sterling, and Robert Browning.* New York: Haskell House Publishers, 1970.

Carr, Robert. "The Religious Thought of John Stuart Mill: A Study in Reluctant Scepticism." *Journal of the History of Ideas* 23 (1962): 475–95.

Cashdollar, Charles D. "The Social Implications of the Doctrine of Divine Providence: A Nineteenth-Century Debate in American Theology." *Harvard Theological Review* 71 (July–October 1978): 265–84.

———. *The Transformation of Theology, 1830–1890: Positivism and Protestant Thought in Britain and America.* Princeton: Princeton University Press, 1989.

Castell, Alburey. *Mill's Logic of the Moral Sciences: A Study of the Impact of Newtonism on Early Nineteenth-Century Social Thought.* Chicago: University of Chicago Libraries, 1936.

Chadwick, Owen. *The Secularization of the European Mind in the Nineteenth Century.* Cambridge: Cambridge University Press, 1975.

Charlton, D. G. *Secular Religions in France, 1815–1870.* London: Oxford University Press, 1963.

Claeys, Gregory. "Justice, Independence, and Industrial Democracy: The Development of John Stuart Mill's Views on Socialism." *Journal of Politics* 49 (1987).

Clifford, W. K. *The Ethics of Belief and Other Essays.* London: Watts, 1947.

Cohn, Norman. *The Pursuit of the Millennium.* New York: Oxford University Press, 1970.

Collingwood, R. G. *Faith and Reason: Essays in the Philosophy of Religion.* Chicago: Quadrangle Books, 1968.

———. *The Idea of Nature.* London: Oxford University Press, 1945.

Collini, Stefan, Donald Winch, and John Burrow. *That Noble Science of Politics: A Study in Nineteenth-Century Intellectual History.* Cambridge: Cambridge University Press, 1983.

Collins, James. *God in Modern Philosophy.* Chicago: Henry Regnery, 1959.

Comte, Auguste. *The Catechism of Positive Religion.* London: Kegan Paul, Trench, Trubner, 1891.

———. *Cours de philosophie positive.* Trans. Abraham S. Blumberg. New York: AMS Press, 1974.

———. *The Essential Comte.* Ed. Stanislav Andreski, trans. Margaret Clarke. New York: Barnes and Noble Books, 1974.

———. *A General View of Positivism.* New York: Robert Speller and Sons, 1957.

———. *Introduction to Positive Philosophy.* Ed. Frederick Ferre. Indianapolis: Hackett Publishing, 1988.

———. "Plan of the Scientific Operations Necessary for Reorganizing Society." In *The Crisis of Industrial Civilization: The Early Essays of Auguste Comte,* trans. and ed. Ronald Fletcher. London: Heinemann Educational Books, 1974 [1822].

———. *Système de politique positive, ou Traité de sociologie instituant la religion de l'humanité.* 4 vols. Paris: Carilian-Goeury et Vor Dalmont, 1851–1854.

Courtney, W. L. *Life of John Stuart Mill.* London: Walter Scott, 1888.

Cowling, Maurice. *Mill and Liberalism.* Cambridge: Cambridge University Press, 1963.

———. "Mill and Liberalism." In *Mill: A Collection of Critical Essays,* ed. J. B. Schneewind. New York: Anchor Books, 1968.

———. Introduction to *Selected Writings of John Stuart Mill.* Ed. Maurice Cowling. New York: New American Library, 1968.

Cox, Harvey. *The Secular City: Secularization and Urbanization in Theological Perspective.* New York: Macmillan, 1966.

Crimmins, James E. "Religion, Utility, and Politics: Bentham versus Paley." In *Religion, Secularization, and Political Thought: Thomas Hobbes to J. S. Mill,* ed. James E. Crimmins. London: Routledge, 1990.

———, ed. *Utilitarians and Religion.* Bristol, U.K.: Thoemmes Press, 1998.

Crossman, Richard, ed. *The God That Failed.* New York: Bantam Books, 1954 [1949].

Cumming, Robert Denoon. *Human Nature and History: A Study of the Development of Liberal Political Thought.* Chicago: University of Chicago Press, 1969.

Diman, J. Lewis. *The Theistic Argument as Affected by Recent Theories.* Boston: Houghton, Mifflin, 1881.

Durham, John. "The Influence of John Stuart Mill's Mental Crisis on His Thoughts." *American Imago* 20 (1963): 369–84.

Edwards, Rem B. *Reason and Religion.* New York: Harcourt Brace Jovanovich, 1972.

Eisenach, Eldon J. *Two Worlds of Liberalism: Religion and Politics in Hobbes, Locke, and Mill.* Chicago: University of Chicago Press, 1981.

Ellul, Jacques. *The Politics of God and the Politics of Man.* Ed. and trans. Geoffrey W. Bromley. Grand Rapids: William B. Eerdmans Publishing, 1972.

———. "Politization and Political Solutions." In *The Politicization of So-*

ciety, ed. Kenneth S. Templeton Jr. Indianapolis: Liberty Press, 1979.

Fantl, Theodore. "Jeremy Bentham and John Stuart Mill on Religion." M.A. thesis, California State University, 1969.

Fenn, Robert A. *James Mill's Political Thought*. New York: Garland Publishing, 1987.

Foote, G. W. *Theological Essays*. London: Progressive Publishing, 1885.

Freeman, Kenneth D. *The Role of Reason in Religion: A Study of Henry Mansel*. The Hague: Martinus Nijhoff, 1969.

Gay, Peter. *The Party of Humanity: Essays in the French Enlightenment*. New York: Alfred A. Knopf, 1964.

Geivett, R. Douglas, and Brendan Sweetman. *Contemporary Perspectives on Religious Epistemology*. New York: Oxford University Press, 1992.

Gottfried, Paul Edward. *After Liberalism: Mass Democracy in the Managerial State*. Princeton: Princeton University Press, 1999.

Gray, John, and G. W. Smith, eds. *J. S. Mill's* On Liberty *in Focus*. London: Routledge, 1991.

Grote, George [Philip Beauchamp, pseud.]. *An Analysis of the Influence of Natural Religion on the Temporal Happiness of Mankind*. London: R. Carlile, 1822.

———. *Review of the Work of Mr. John Stuart Mill, Entitled, "Examination of Sir William Hamilton's Philosophy."* London: N. Trubner, 1868.

Grote, John. *An Examination of the Utilitarian Philosophy*. Ed. Joseph B. Mayor. Cambridge, U.K.: Deighton, Bell, 1870.

Haac, Oscar A., ed. and trans. *The Correspondence of John Stuart Mill and Auguste Comte*. New Brunswick: Transaction Publishers, 1995.

Halloran, Walter E., S.J. "Development of John Stuart Mill's Religious Thought." M.A. thesis, Saint Louis University, 1950.

Hamburger, Joseph. "Individuality and Moral Reform: The Rhetoric of Liberty and the Reality of Restraint in Mill's *On Liberty*." *Political Science Reviewer* 24 (1995): 7–70.

———. *Intellectuals in Politics: John Stuart Mill and the Philosophic Radicals*. New Haven: Yale University Press, 1965.

———. *James Mill and the Art of Revolution*. New Haven: Yale University Press, 1963.

———. *John Stuart Mill on Liberty and Control*. Princeton: Princeton University Press, 1999.

———. "Mill and Tocqueville on Liberty." In *James and John Stuart Mill/ Papers of the Centenary Conference*, ed. John M. Robson and Michael Laine. Toronto: University of Toronto Press, 1976.

———. "Religion and *On Liberty*." In *A Cultivated Mind, Essays on J. S. Mill*

Presented to John M. Robson, ed. Michael Laine. Toronto: University of Toronto Press, 1991.

———. "Utilitarianism and the Constitution." In *Confronting the Constitution,* ed. Allan Bloom. Washington: AEI Press, 1987.

Harp, Gillis J. *Positivist Republic: Auguste Comte and the Reconstruction of American Liberalism.* University Park: Pennsylvania State University Press, 1995.

Hawkins, Richmond Laurin. *Auguste Comte and the United States, 1816–1853.* Cambridge: Harvard University Press, 1936.

———. *Positivism in the United States, 1853–1861.* Cambridge: Harvard University Press, 1969.

Hayek, F. A. *The Constitution of Liberty.* Chicago: University of Chicago Press, 1960.

———. *The Counter-Revolution of Science: Studies on the Abuse of Reason.* Indianapolis: Liberty Press, 1979 [1952].

———. *John Stuart Mill and Harriet Taylor: Their Correspondence and Subsequent Marriage.* Chicago: University of Chicago Press, 1951.

———. *Law, Legislation, and Liberty.* 3 vols. Chicago: University of Chicago Press, 1973–1979.

———. *New Studies in Philosophy, Politics, Economics, and the History of Ideas.* Chicago: University of Chicago Press, 1978.

———. Preface to *The Spirit of the Age,* by J. S. Mill. Chicago: University of Chicago Press, 1942.

Hick, John, ed. *Classical and Contemporary Readings in the Philosophy of Religion.* Englewood Cliffs, N.J.: Prentice-Hall, 1964.

———. *The Existence of God.* New York: Macmillan, 1964.

———. *God and the Universe of Faiths: Essays in the Philosophy of Religion.* London: Macmillan, 1973.

Himmelfarb, Gertrude. *On Liberty and Liberalism: The Case of John Stuart Mill.* San Francisco: ICS Press, 1990.

Hoffer, Eric. *The True Believer: Thoughts on the Nature of Mass Movements.* San Bernardino, Calif.: Borgo Press, 1951.

Hollinger, Robert. *The Dark Side of Liberalism.* Westport, Conn.: Praeger, 1996.

Horowitz, David. *The Politics of Bad Faith: The Radical Assault on America's Future.* New York: Free Press, 1998.

Huxley, Thomas Henry. *Agnosticism and Christianity and Other Essays.* Buffalo: Prometheus Books, 1992.

Iggers, Georg G. *The Cult of Authority: The Political Philosophy of the Saint-Simonians, a Chapter in the Intellectual History of Totalitarianism.* The Hague: Martinus Nijhoff, 1958.

Irwin, T. H. "Mill and the Classical World." In *The Cambridge Companion to Mill,* ed. John Skorupski. Cambridge: Cambridge University Press, 1998.

James, William. *The Will to Believe and Other Essays in Popular Philosophy.* London: Longmans, Green, 1917.

Jevons, W. Stanley. *Pure Logic and Other Minor Works.* London: Macmillan, 1890.

Jonas, Hans. *The Gnostic Religion.* Rev. ed. Boston: Beacon Press, 1958.

Justman, Stewart. *The Hidden Text of Mill's* Liberty. Savage, Md.: Rowman and Littlefield Publishers, 1991.

Kennedy, Gail. *The Psychological Empiricism of John Stuart Mill.* Amherst: Metcalf Publishing, 1928.

Kinzer, Bruce L., Ann P. Robson, and John M. Robson. *A Moralist in and out of Parliament: John Stuart Mill at Westminster, 1865–1868.* Toronto: University of Toronto Press, 1992.

Koenker, Ernest B. *Secular Salvations: The Rites and Symbols of Political Religions.* Philadelphia: Fortress Press, 1965.

Kries, Douglas, ed. *Piety and Humanity.* New York: Rowman and Littlefield Publishers, 1997.

Laine, Michael, ed. *A Cultivated Mind, Essays on J. S. Mill Presented to John M. Robson.* Toronto: University of Toronto Press, 1991.

Laird, John. *Theism and Cosmology.* New York: Books for Libraries Press, 1969 [1940].

Lasky, Melvin J. *Utopia and Revolution.* Chicago: University of Chicago Press, 1976.

Letwin, Shirley Robin. *The Pursuit of Certainty: David Hume, Jeremy Bentham, John Stuart Mill, Beatrice Webb.* Cambridge: Cambridge University Press, 1965.

Levi, Albert William. *A Study in the Social Philosophy of John Stuart Mill.* Chicago: University of Chicago Libraries, 1940.

Lewes, C. H. "Comte and Mill." *Fortnightly Review* 6:34 (October 1, 1866): 385–406.

Lewis, C. S. *Miracles: How God Intervenes in Nature.* New York: Macmillan, 1960.

Lewy, Guenter. *Religion and Revolution.* New York: Oxford University Press, 1974.

Lightman, Bernard Vise. "Henry Longueville Mansel and the Genesis of Victorian Agnosticism." Ph.D. diss., Brandeis University, 1978.

Lindbom, Tage. *The Myth of Democracy.* Grand Rapids: William B. Eerdmans Publishing, 1996.

———. *The Tares and the Good Grain: or the Kingdom of Man at the Hour of Reckoning.* Macon, Ga.: Mercer University Press, 1983.

Lipkes, Jeff. "Politics, Religion, and the Fate of Classical Political Economy: John Stuart Mill and His Followers, 1860–1875." Ph.D. diss., Princeton University, 1995.

Loen, Arnold E. *Secularization: Science without God?* Philadelphia: Westminster Press, 1967.

Long, Douglas G. *Bentham on Liberty: Jeremy Bentham's Idea of Liberty in Relation to His Utilitarianism.* Toronto: University of Toronto Press, 1977.

———. "Censorial Jurisprudence and Political Radicalism: A Reconsideration of the Early Bentham." *Bentham Newsletter* 12 (1988): 4–23.

Löwith, Karl. *Meaning in History.* Chicago: University of Chicago Press, 1949.

Lowry, Charles W. *Communism and Christ.* New York: Morehouse-Gorham, 1952.

Lubac, Henri de, S.J. *The Drama of Atheist Humanism.* Trans. Edith M. Riley. Cleveland: World Publishing, 1963.

Lynch, William F., S.J., *Christ and Prometheus.* Notre Dame: University of Notre Dame Press, 1970.

Mackay, Thomas, ed. *A Plea for Liberty: An Argument against Socialism and Socialistic Legislation.* Indianapolis: Liberty Fund, 1981 [1891].

Mackenzie, J. S. *Lectures on Humanism.* New York: Burt Franklin, 1971 [1907].

Manent, Pierre. *The City of Man.* Trans. Marc A. LePain. Princeton: Princeton University Press, 1998.

Mansel, Henry L. *A Lecture on the Philosophy of Kant.* Oxford, U.K.: John Henry and James Parker, 1856.

———. *The Limits of Religious Thought.* 4th ed. Oxford, U.K.: Clarendon Press, 1859.

———. *Prolegomena Logic.* Oxford, U.K.: William Graham, 1851.

Manuel, Frank E. *The Changing of the Gods.* Hanover, N.H.: Brown University Press, 1983.

———. *The Eighteenth Century Confronts the Gods.* Cambridge: Harvard University Press, 1959.

———. *The New World of Henri Saint-Simon.* Cambridge: Harvard University Press, 1956.

———. *The Prophets of Paris.* Cambridge: Harvard University Press, 1962.

Mascall, E. L. *The Secularization of Christianity.* New York: Holt, Rinehart and Winston, 1965.

Mazlish, Bruce. *James and John Stuart Mill: Father and Son in the Nineteenth Century.* New York: Basic Books, 1975.

———. *The Revolutionary Ascetic: Evolution of a Political Type.* New York: McGraw-Hill, 1976.

McGee, John Edwin. *A Crusade for Humanity: The History of Organized Positivism in England.* London: Watts, 1931.

McLellan, David, and Sean Sayers, eds. *Socialism and Morality.* New York: St. Martin's Press, 1990.

M'Cosh, James. *An Examination of Mr. J. S. Mill's Philosophy.* New York: Robert Carter and Brothers, 1869.

McTaggart, John McTaggart Ellis. *Some Dogmas of Religion.* New York: Kraus Reprint, 1969 [1906].

Megill, Allan D. "J. S. Mill's Religion of Humanity and the Second Justification for the Writing of *On Liberty.*" *Journal of Politics* 34 (1972): 612–29.

Meyer, Frank S. *In Defense of Freedom and Related Essays.* Indianapolis: Liberty Fund, 1996.

Milbank, John. *Theology and Social Theory: Beyond Secular Reason.* Cambridge, Mass.: Basil Blackwell, 1990.

Mill, James. "Aristocracy." *London Review* 2 (January 1836).

———. "The Church, and Its Reform." *London Review* 1:2 (1835): 257–95.

———. *Political Writings.* Ed. Terence Ball. Cambridge: Cambridge University Press, 1992.

Mill, John Stuart. *Auguste Comte and Positivism.* Ann Arbor: University of Michigan Press, 1968 [1865].

———. *Autobiography.* Ed. John M. Robson. New York: Penguin Books, 1989 [1873].

———. "The Church." Debating speech. CW 26:418–27.

———. *Collected Works of John Stuart Mill.* 33 vols. Toronto: University of Toronto Press, 1963–1991.

1 *Autobiography and Literary Essays.* Ed. John M. Robson and Jack Stillinger. 1981.

2, 3 *Principles of Political Economy.* Ed. John M. Robson. With an introduction by V. W. Bladen. 1965.

4, 5 *Essays on Economics and Society.* Ed. John M. Robson. With an introduction by Lord Robbins. 1967.

6 *Essays on England, Ireland, and the Empire.* Ed. John M. Robson. With an introduction by Joseph Hamburger. 1982.

7, 8 *System of Logic: Ratiocinative and Inductive.* Ed. John M. Robson. With an introduction by R. F. McRae. 1973 [1843].

9 *An Examination of Sir William Hamilton's Philosophy.* Ed. John M. Robson. With an introduction by Alan Ryan. 1979.

10 *Essays on Ethics, Religion, and Society.* Ed. John M. Robson. With introductions by F. E. L. Priestley and D. P. Dryer. 1969.

11 *Essays on Philosophy and the Classics.* Ed. John M. Robson. With an introduction by F. E. Sparshott. 1978.

12, 13 *Earlier Letters, 1812–1848.* Ed. Francis E. Mineka. 1963.

14, 15, 16, 17 *Later Letters, 1848–1873.* Ed. Francis E. Mineka and Dwight N. Lindley. 1972.

18, 19 *Essays on Politics and Society.* Ed. John M. Robson. With an introduction by Alexander Brady. 1977.

20 *Essays on French History and Historians.* Ed. John M. Robson. With an introduction by John C. Cairns. 1985.

21 *Essays on Equality, Law, and Education.* Ed. John M. Robson. With an introduction by Stefan Collini. 1984.

22, 23, 24, 25 *Newspaper Writings.* Ed. A. P. Robson and John M. Robson. With an introduction by A. P. Robson. 1986.

26, 27 *Journals and Debating Speeches.* Ed. John M. Robson and Bruce L. Kinzer. With an introduction by Bruce L. Kinzer. 1988.

28, 29 *Public and Parliamentary Speeches.* Ed. John M. Robson and Bruce L. Kinzer. With an introduction by Bruce L. Kinzer. 1988.

30 *Writings on India.* Ed. John M. Robson, Martin Moir, and Zawahir Moir. With an introduction by Martin Moir. 1990.

31 *Miscellaneous Writings.* Ed. John M. Robson. 1989.

32 *Additional Letters.* Ed. Marion Felicia, Michael Laine, and John M. Robson. With an introduction by Marion Felicia. 1991.

33 *Indexes.* Ed. Jean O'Grady with John M. Robson. With an introduction by Jean O'Grady. 1991.

———. *Considerations on Representative Government.* Ed. H. B. Acton. London: J. M. Dent and Sons, 1972.

———. "De Tocqueville on Democracy in America." *London Review* 2 (October 1835).

———. *Dissertations and Discussions: Political, Philosophical, and Historical.* 2 vols. New York: Haskell House Publishers, 1973 [1859].

———. *Early Draft of Autobiography.* Ed. John M. Robson. New York: Penguin Books, 1989.

———. *The Letters of John Stuart Mill.* Ed. Hugh S. R. Elliot. New York: Longmans, Green, 1910.

———. *The Logic of the Moral Sciences.* La Salle, Ill.: Open Court, 1987 [1843].

———. *On Liberty and Other Writings.* Ed. Stefan Collini. Cambridge: Cambridge University Press, 1995 [1859].

———. *Principles of Political Economy.* Ed. Sir W. J. Ashley. New York: Longmans, Green, 1909 [1848].

———. *Principles of Political Economy and Chapters on Socialism.* Ed. Jonathan Riley. New York: Oxford University Press, 1994.

———. *Selected Writings of John Stuart Mill.* Ed. Maurice Cowling. New York: New American Library, 1968.

———. *The Spirit of the Age.* With a preface by F. A. Hayek. Chicago: University of Chicago Press, 1942.

———. *The Subjection of Women.* Cambridge: M.I.T. Press, 1974 [1869].

———. *Three Essays on Religion.* With an introduction by Helen Taylor. Westport, Conn.: Greenwood Press, 1969 [1874].

———. *Utilitarianism.* In *The Utilitarians.* New York: Anchor Books, 1973 [1863].

———. *Utilitarianism with Critical Essays.* Ed. Samuel Gorovitz. New York: Bobbs-Merrill, 1971.

Mill, John Stuart [alleged author]. *On Social Freedom.* With an introduction by Dorothy Fosdick. New York: Columbia University Press, 1941.

Millar, Alan. "Mill on Religion." In *The Cambridge Companion to Mill,* ed. John Skorupski. Cambridge: Cambridge University Press, 1998.

Miller, F. F. "William Ellis and His Work as an Educationist." *Fraser's Magazine,* n.s., 25 (1882): 236.

Mineka, Francis E. *The Dissidence of Dissent: The Monthly Repository, 1806–1838.* Chapel Hill: University of North Carolina Press, 1944.

Molnar, Thomas. *Twin Powers: Politics and the Sacred.* Grand Rapids: William B. Eerdmans Publishing, 1988.

———. *Utopia: The Perennial Heresy.* New York: Sheed and Ward, 1967.

Morison, James Cotter. *The Service of Man: An Essay towards the Religion of the Future.* London: Kegan Paul, Trench, 1887.

Morlan, George. *America's Heritage from John Stuart Mill.* New York: Columbia University Press, 1936.

Morley, John. *Critical Miscellanies.* 3 vols. London: Macmillan, 1886.

———. "The Death of Mr. Mill." In *Nineteenth-Century Essays,* ed. Peter Stansky. Chicago: University of Chicago Press, 1970.

———. "Mr. Mill's *Autobiography.*" In *Nineteenth-Century Essays,* ed. Peter Stansky. Chicago: University of Chicago Press, 1970.

———. "Mr. Mill's Three Essays on Religion." In *Nineteenth-Century Essays,* ed. Peter Stansky. Chicago: University of Chicago Press, 1970.

———. *Recollections.* 2 vols. New York: Macmillan, 1917.

Mueller, Iris Wessel. *John Stuart Mill and French Thought.* Freeport, N.Y.: Books for Libraries Press, 1968.

Neusch, Marcel. *The Sources of Modern Atheism.* New York: Paulist Press, 1977.

Oakeshott, Michael. *Religion, Politics, and the Moral Life*. New Haven: Yale University Press, 1993.

O'Dea, Thomas F. *Alienation, Atheism, and the Religious Crisis*. New York: Sheed and Ward, 1969.

Orr, James. "John Stuart Mill and Christianity." *Theological Monthly* 6 (1891): 8–21.

Packe, Michael St. John. *The Life of John Stuart Mill*. New York: Macmillan, 1954.

Pankhurst, Richard K. P. *The Saint-Simonians, Mill, and Carlyle: A Preface to Modern Thought*. London: Sidgwick and Jackson, 1957.

Pappe, H. O. *John Stuart Mill and the Harriet Taylor Myth*. Parkville: Melbourne University Press, 1960.

Patton, Francis L. *Antitheistic Theories*. N.p., 1880.

Paul, Wilford N. "The Religious Views of John Stuart Mill." Ph.D. diss., University of New Mexico, 1972.

Pickering, Mary. *Auguste Comte: An Intellectual Biography*. Cambridge: Cambridge University Press, 1993.

Pike, Nelson, ed. *God and Evil: Readings on the Theological Problem of Evil*. Englewood Cliffs, N.J.: Prentice-Hall, 1964.

Plamenatz, John. *The English Utilitarians*. Oxford, U.K.: Basil Blackwell, 1966.

Posner, Richard A. "Blackstone and Bentham." *Journal of Law and Economics* 19 (October 1976).

Radcliff, Peter, ed. *Limits of Liberty: Studies of Mill's* On Liberty. Belmont, Calif.: Wadsworth Publishing, 1968.

Raison, Timothy, ed. *The Founding Fathers of Social Science*. Baltimore: Penguin Books, 1969.

Rajapakse, Vijitha. "Early Buddhism and John Stuart Mill's Thinking in the Fields of Philosophy and Religion: Some Notes toward a Comparative Study." *Philosophy, East and West* 37 (July 1987): 260–85.

Reardon, Bernard M. G. *Religious Thought in the Nineteenth Century*. Cambridge: Cambridge University Press, 1966.

Rees, J. C. *Mill and His Early Critics*. Leicester, U.K.: University College, 1956.

Reeve, Henry. "Autobiography of John Stuart Mill." *Edinburgh Review* 139 (1874): 91–129.

———. "Mill's Essays on Theism." *Edinburgh Review* 287 (January 1875): 1–31.

Robb, J. Wesley. *The Reverent Skeptic: A Critical Inquiry into the Religion of Secular Humanism*. New York: Philosophical Library, 1979.

Robson, John M. *The Improvement of Mankind: The Social and Political*

Thought of John Stuart Mill. London: Routledge and Kegan Paul, 1968.

Rommen, Heinrich A. *The Natural Law: A Study in Legal and Social History and Philosophy.* Trans. Thomas R. Hanley, O.S.B. Indianapolis: Liberty Fund, 1998.

Rorty, Richard. *Achieving Our Country: Leftist Thought in Twentieth-Century America.* Cambridge: Harvard University Press, 1998.

Ryan, Alan. *Liberal Anxieties and Liberal Education.* New York: Hill and Wang, 1998.

———. *The Philosophy of John Stuart Mill.* 2d ed. Atlantic Highlands, N.J.: Humanities Press International, 1987.

Saint-Simon, Henri de. *Social Organization, The Science of Man, and Other Writings.* Ed. and trans. Felix Markham. New York: Harper and Row, 1964.

Schall, James V., S.J., and Jerome J. Hanus, eds. *Mill's Ethical Writings.* New York: Collier Books, 1965.

———. *Studies on Religion and Politics.* Lanham, Md.: University Press of America, 1986.

Schwarz, Pedro. *The New Political Economy of John Stuart Mill.* Durham: Duke University Press, 1972.

Segal, Robert A., ed. *The Allure of Gnosticism.* La Salle, Ill.: Open Court, 1995.

Sell, Alan P. F., ed. *Mill and Religion: Contemporary Responses to Three Essays on Religion.* Bristol, U.K.: Thoemmes Press, 1997.

Semmel, Bernard. *John Stuart Mill and the Pursuit of Virtue.* New Haven: Yale University Press, 1984.

Settanni, Harry. *The Probabilist Theism of John Stuart Mill.* New York: Peter Lang, 1991.

Shaw, G. Bernard. *Fabian Essays in Socialism.* London: Fabian Society, 1889.

Sidgwick, Henry. *Miscellaneous Essays and Addresses.* London: Macmillan, 1904.

Skorupski, John. *John Stuart Mill.* New York: Routledge, 1989.

Smith, James M., and Ernest Sosa, eds. *Mill's Utilitarianism.* Belmont, Calif.: Wadsworth Publishing, 1969.

Smith, Ronald Gregor. *Secular Christianity.* New York: Harper and Row, 1966.

Sokolowski, Robert. *The God of Faith and Reason: Foundations of Christian Theology.* Washington: Catholic University of America Press, 1995.

Steintrager, James. "Language and Politics: Bentham on Religion." *Bentham Newsletter* 4 (1980): 4–20.

Stephen, James Fitzjames. *Liberty, Equality, Fraternity.* Ed. Stuart D. Warner. Indianapolis: Liberty Fund, 1993.

Stephen, Leslie. *The English Utilitarians.* 3 vols. New York: Peter Smith, 1950 [1900].

————. *History of English Thought in the Eighteenth Century.* 2 vols. New York: Harcourt, Brace, and World, 1962 [1876].

————. "The Religion of All Sensible Men." *North American Review* 130 (1880): 438–61.

Talmon, Jacob L. *Political Messianism.* New York: Frederick A. Praeger, 1960.

————. *The Rise of Totalitarian Democracy.* Boston: Beacon Press, 1952.

Taylor, Helen. Introduction to *Three Essays on Religion,* by J. S. Mill. Westport, Conn.: Greenwood Press, 1969 [1874].

Templeton, Kenneth S., Jr., ed. *The Politicization of Society.* Indianapolis: Liberty Press, 1979.

Thomson, J. Radford. "Auguste Comte and the Religion of Humanity." *Present Day Tracts* 47 (1876).

Turner, Frank Miller. *Between Science and Religion: The Reaction to Scientific Naturalism in Late Victorian England.* New Haven: Yale University Press, 1974.

Turner, James. *Without God, Without Creed: The Origins of Unbelief in America.* Baltimore: Johns Hopkins University Press, 1985.

Vernon, Richard. "J. S. Mill and the Religion of Humanity." In *Religion, Secularization and Political Thought,* ed. James E. Crimmins. London: Routledge, 1989.

Viner, Jacob. *The Role of Providence in the Social Order: An Essay in Intellectual History.* Princeton: Princeton University Press, 1972.

Voegelin, Eric. *From Enlightenment to Revolution.* Ed. John H. Hallowell. Durham: Duke University Press, 1975.

————. *New Science of Politics, an Introduction.* Chicago: University of Chicago Press, 1952.

————. *Political Religions.* Trans. T. J. DiNapoli and E. S. Easterly III. Lewiston, N.Y.: Edwin Mellen Press, 1986.

Walsh, David. *The Growth of the Liberal Soul.* Columbia: University of Missouri Press, 1997.

Ward, W. G. *The Ideal of a Christian Church.* London: James Toovey, 1844.

————. "Mr. Mill's Denial of Necessary Truth." *Dublin Review* (October 1871): 285–318.

Warnock, Mary. Introduction to *Utilitarianism, On Liberty, Essay on Bentham,* by J. S. Mill. Ed. Mary Warnock. Cleveland: World Publishing, 1962 [1863].

Watson, John. *Comte, Mill, and Spencer.* New York: Macmillan, 1895.

Weithman, Paul J., ed. *Religion and Contemporary Liberalism.* Notre Dame: University of Notre Dame Press, 1997.

Westcott, Brooke F. "Aspects of Positivism in Relation to Christianity." *Contemporary Review* 8 (May–August 1868): 371–86.

———. "Comte on the Philosophy of the History of Christianity." *Contemporary Review* 6 (September–December 1867): 399–421.

Whittaker, Thomas. *Comte and Mill.* New York: Dodge Publishing, 1934.

Woods, Thomas. *Poetry and Philosophy: A Study in the Thought of John Stuart Mill.* London: Hutchinson, 1961.

Wright, T. R. *The Religion of Humanity: The Impact of Comtean Positivism on Victorian Britain.* Cambridge: Cambridge University Press, 1986.

Contemporary Journal Reviews of Mill's Writings

Autobiography (1873)

Anonymous. "The *Autobiography* of John Stuart Mill." *Contemporary Review* 23 (1874): 53–65.

———. "John Stuart Mill, 1869–1873." *Cosmopolis* 5:15 (1874).

———. "John Stuart Mill's *Autobiography.*" *London Quarterly Review* (January–April 1974). American edition.

Morley, John. "Mr. Mill's *Autobiography.*" *Fortnightly Review* 17 (1875): 103–31. In *Nineteenth-Century Essays,* ed. Peter Stansky. Chicago: University of Chicago Press, 1970.

Reeve, Henry. "Autobiography of John Stuart Mill." *Edinburgh Review* 139 (1874): 91–129.

An Examination of Sir William Hamilton's Philosophy (1865)

Anonymous. "John Stuart Mill on the Philosophy of Sir Wm. Hamilton." *Westminster Review* 85 (January–April 1866): 1–18.

———. "Mill's Review of Hamilton." *Christian Examiner* (November 1865): 301–27.

———. "The Philosophy of the Conditioned: Sir William Hamilton and John Stuart Mill." *Contemporary Review* (January–February 1866): 31–49.

Spencer, Herbert. "Mill versus Hamilton—The Test of Truth." *Fortnightly Review* (1865): 531–50.

Three Essays on Religion (1874)

Anonymous. "Religious Opinions of John Stuart Mill." *Quarterly Review* 5:2 (April 1875): 279–92.

Crane, C. B. "John Stuart Mill and Christianity." *Baptist Quarterly* 8 (1874): 348–62.

Morley, John. "Mr. Mill's *Three Essays on Religion*." *Fortnightly Review* 16 (1874): 634–51. In *Nineteenth-Century Essays*, ed. Peter Stansky. Chicago: University of Chicago Press, 1970.

Reeve, Henry. "Mill's Essays on Theism." *Edinburgh Review* 287 (January 1875): 1–31.

Sell, Alan P. F., ed. *Mill and Religion: Contemporary Responses to* Three Essays on Religion. Bristol, U.K.: Thoemmes Press, 1997.

Upton, Charles P. "Mill's Essays on Religion.—II. 'Theism.'" *Theological Review* (April 1875): 250–72.

Miscellaneous

Anonymous. Review of Alexander Bain, *John Stuart Mill: A Criticism, with Personal Recollections. The Nation* 34 (June 8, 1882): 884.

———. Review of Mrs. Grote, *The Personal Life of George Grote. Edinburgh Review* 138 (July 1873): 112–26.

Index

Analysis of the Influence of Natural Religion on the Temporal Happiness of Mankind (Bentham / Grote): influence on Mill, 28–33; and legal censure, 349n53

Anthropomorphism: and nature, 97–99; of Mill, 98–99; and origin of belief in gods, 170, 183, 184

Argument from design: as support for the conception of a limited god, 100, 141, 183, 189–93, 197, 199, 346n10; and Paley, 365n14. *See also* Evidences of theism

Aristotle: utilitarianism of, 370n35; mentioned, 41, 111, 129, 265, 266, 302

Associationism: and making new men, 7, 12, 300, 366n20; and James Mill, 12–13, 22, 146; and education, 12–14; and Mill, 14, 146, 148, 204; and Skinner, 34; and training of natural man, 112, 152; and conscience, 258, 286–87; and utilitarianism, 294; and unity with society, 294–96; and in-itself morality, 304; mentioned, 306, 312

Atheism: James Mill and, 8; Mill and, 11, 64–66, 163, 222, 242, 333; Comte and, 41, 64–66

Austin, John, 187, 241, 311

Authority: Mill on, 78–82, 173, 182, 365n7; as source of morality, 118–19

Bacon, Francis: empiricism of, 362n9; mentioned, 94, 95, 182

Bentham, Jeremy: on Church of England, 16, 347nn25,26; nontheological utilitarianism of, 25–28, 30; rivalry with Paley, 27; antitheological intent of, 28, 35; *Analysis,* 28–33, 349n53; on religious sanctions, 30–33, 124; on pleasure, 273, 347n24; on collective happiness, 330, 374n17; and Hume, 348n42; and totalitarianism, 374n27; mentioned, 2, 4, 6, 13, 17, 23–25, 116, 242, 255, 260, 279, 306, 311, 322, 323, 326

Bentham, Sir Samuel, 322

Benthamism: Mill's conversion to, 2, 23–25, 28, 41–42, 126, 246, 251, 264, 268, 280, 297, 349n52, 354n48; as religion, 22, 34, 37, 348n38; antitheological immanentism of, 28, 34–36; concealment of religious views, 29, 349n53; and religious sanctions, 30–33, 104, 256, 285–86, 298, 348n34; and Saint-Simonism, 45

Blackstone, William, 27

Buddhism, 144

Burke, Edmund, 25

Butler, Joseph: *Analogy of Religion,* 9; and deism, 90

Carlyle, Thomas, 45, 50, 75, 140, 147, 221, 241, 371n9

Catholicism: and Comte, 351n6; mentioned, 17, 96, 356n15

Christ: as model, 110, 227–30, 250; Mill on, 126–28, 134, 136, 138, 221, 227–33, 247–51, 263, 264, 288; as messenger of God, 230, 251; as ethical ideal, 249; usefulness of, 250;

and utilitarian morality, 251; and
Religion of Humanity, 284–85; mentioned, 41

Christianity: Mill on, 1, 11, 14, 18, 46,
102, 126–27, 136–37, 162–63, 165,
166, 187, 221–22, 247–52, 257–58,
263–65, 268, 275–77, 279, 282–83,
286, 367n31, 369n12; and the philosophes, 5, 116, 168; James Mill and,
8, 10–11; and divine justice, 29, 30–
31; utility of, 29–30, 101, 113; selfishness of, 31, 33, 36, 134, 135–37,
142–43, 261, 264–65, 294, 300, 301,
331, 360n19; attack on, 40–41, 45–
46, 114; and social reconstruction,
101; and Paulism, 126, 127, 221, 229,
361n37; benefits derived from, 126–
27; moral perversions of, 127, 138;
and law of the three stages, 132;
pernicious effects of, 136–37; conception of God of, 137–38, 200; and
philosophy of history, 168; omnipotent God of, 195; improvement of,
195, 221–22, 249, 250; revelation of,
219, 282; and miracles, 220; as support of Religion of Humanity; 221,
230–32; compared with Religion of
Humanity, 228; advantages of, 228–
29, 279; and freedom of discussion,
242, 248, 249; and On Liberty, 247–
52, 255, 257–58, 262, 370n30; partial truth of, 249–50; and English
society, 262, 323–25, 339; and selfsacrifice, 275–77; and utilitarianism,
282–83, 289, 326; rivalry with Religion of Humanity, 294, 301; and
French Revolution, 321; and secular
humanism, 327–28; as subjective
preference, 328; and Bentham's
Analysis, 349n53; mentioned, 32,
125, 128, 332

Christian utilitarianism: of Paley, 25–
27, 30–31; and Bentham, 26–28,
374n18; appeal of, 31; mentioned,
33, 149

Christian voluntarism, 175, 178, 180,
191, 341

Church of England: Bentham on, 16,
347nn25,26; Benthamite attack on,
16–17; James Mill on, 16–18; Mill
on, 17–19; Paley's defense of, 27;
and deism, 90

Church of Scotland, 8, 61

Common sense: Mill on, 83, 280–81,
358n85; school of, 155, 168; and utilitarianism, 269; appropriation of
common-sense morality, 269, 280–81

Comte, Auguste: and Religion of Humanity, 1, 3, 23, 36, 37, 38, 39–40;
antitheological intent of, 28, 39, 40,
51, 58, 66; positivist religion of, 28,
38; Mill's critique of, 39–40, 184,
252–53, 333–34, 351n11, 370n40;
and atheism, 41, 64–66; philosophy
of history of, 48–49, 67, 153, 353n38;
correspondence with Mill, 50–72;
on the role of women, 62–63; "two
powers" doctrine of, 76, 358n79;
and the spiritual power, 78–79,
355n59, 357n73; on deism, 90, 93; on
Mill's positivism, 351n11; and altruism, 351n71, 362n42; mentioned, 2,
6, 116, 134, 167, 171, 241, 244, 304,
313, 328, 329, 343. See also Positivism

Conscience: socialization of, 152, 312;
and restraint, 257–60; formation of,
258; and Religion of Humanity, 258;
and associationism, 258, 286–87;
malleability of, 284–85, 288, 290,
312; as internal sanction, 286–90;
as subjective feeling, 286–87

Consequentialist ethics: opposed to
in-itself morality, 149, 150, 270–71;
and social religion, 329–32; and displacement of moral agency, 330; and
justice, 330–31; and socialism, 330–
31, 337, 363n14; mentioned, 272, 344

Conversion: Mill's conversion to Benthamism, 2, 23–25, 28, 41–42, 126,
246, 251, 264, 268, 280, 297, 349n52,
354n48; Mill's conversion strategy,
5, 35–36, 141–42, 232–33, 250–51,
284–86, 288, 290, 291–93, 362n45;
Mill's conversion to the Religion of
Humanity, 28, 37, 53–55, 67, 251,
354n51; Mill on, 124

Cosmos: origin of, 176–77, 178–79, 180–81, 193

Custom: origin of, 109; Mill on, 256, 284; and *On Liberty*, 370n45

D'Eichthal, Gustave, 43–44, 241

Deism: refutation of, 89–90, 115; Comte on, 90; sentimental deists, 92; and "Theism," 169–70; and the "watchmaker god," 173; and Bentham's *Analysis*, 349n53; mentioned, 3, 4, 8, 9, 56, 129, 185, 195. *See also* Natural religion; Natural theology

Descartes, René, 185–86

Determinism: of Mill, 14, 152, 179, 219, 340, 365n6, 367n31; of James Mill, 14, 175. *See also* Doctrine of circumstances; Necessitarianism

Doctrine of circumstances, 13, 152, 340–41

Education: and associationism, 12–14; and the philosophes, 12–14; and morality, 119–21; power of, 120

English society: Mill's opinion of, 261–63; Mill and, 322–26, 339, 356n67, 373n9; mentioned, 243, 265

Epistemology: and Mansel, 4, 145–46, 153–54, 155, 157, 165; Mill and relativity of knowledge, 146, 156, 157, 159; Mill's denial of necessary truth, 150–52; and theology, 150–52, 154; Mill and pretense of knowledge, 164–66; mentioned, 162

Evidences of theism: argument for a first cause, 174–81; argument from the general consent of mankind, 182–85; argument from consciousness, 185–86; argument from marks of design in nature, 189–91, 199. *See also* Argument from design

Evil, problem of, 155, 160

Evolution, 180, 191

Freedom of discussion: and religious belief, 5, 235, 247–49, 253, 361n33; in France, 56, 71; and *On Liberty*, 59, 236, 237; in an age of transition, 70–

72; Mill on, 81, 84, 237; as a provisional necessity, 235–39; Saint-Simonians on, 236–37; Comte on, 237; and Christianity, 242, 248, 249

God: as demiurge, 4, 106, 138, 140, 175, 178, 193, 194, 195–97, 200–201, 206, 210, 223, 367n31; Mill's judgment of, 4, 103, 144, 155–65, 201–2; Mill's conception of, 5, 21, 101, 102, 104–8, 111, 138–42, 158–61, 166, 172, 176, 187–89, 191–203, 208–11, 222, 278–79; as hypothesis, 21, 140–42; as probable, 21, 138, 140–42, 189; man's accountability to, 29, 30–33, 251, 260, 271, 293, 294, 298, 311, 348n34; as limited, 104–8, 111, 138–40, 189, 191, 192–98, 200–201, 208–9, 278, 328; origin of belief in, 129–30, 170–72, 182–85; Christian conception of, 137–38, 200; evidences for, 139, 141, 174–91; as interim god, 140, 232, 362n43; permissible realm of belief in, 141; hope in, 141, 210, 223–27; as the Unknowable, 154; Mansel on nature of, 156; Mill on attributes of, 156, 191–203; as the Absolute, 157, 158, 159; as the Infinite, 157, 158; Mill on the goodness of, 158–59, 160–61, 166, 194–95, 200–201, 208–9, 219; as Being, 187; as benevolent utilitarian, 200–201, 281–82; as ground of moral obligation, 271; objective reality of, 289–90; and justice, 306; and social justice, 340–43

Great Being of Humanity, 23, 36, 40, 50, 134–35, 252, 266

Grote, George: and Bentham's *Analysis*, 28, 29, 113–14, 349n53, 360n28, 367n29; and *On Liberty*, 266; and religious emancipation, 355n60; mentioned, 90, 123, 241

Hamburger, Joseph: and *On Liberty*, 235; on Mill's "plan," 235, 247; on libel laws, 240; on Mill's silence on religion, 241; on socialization, 260;

on Mill's liberalism, 345n1; mentioned, 242–69 passim

Hamilton, Sir William: and intuitionism, 90, 146–50, 372n23; philosophy of the conditioned, 145, 153, 154, 155; mentioned, 67, 68

Hegel, G. W. F., 41, 158

Helvetius, 13, 279

Historicism, 169

Humanitarianism: as religion, 40, 51, 142, 232, 252, 268, 275, 285, 294, 297, 302, 332–33; precursor of Millian humanitarianism, 321; and Christianity, 329; mentioned, 34, 78, 140, 231, 249, 257, 258, 262, 276, 326, 353n43

Hume, David: on utility, 25; on origin of belief in gods, 129, 130; on miracles, 215; and Bentham, 348n42

Idealism, 205–7, 214

Imagination: Mill on, 141, 186, 214, 224–27; and religion, 224–25, 227; regulation of, 224–26

Immortality: Mill on, 142–44, 203–11, 226; and Christian belief, 143; and spirits, 207–8; grounds for hope in, 210, 226

Individuality, 112, 257, 259, 261–63, 265–66, 323–25, 338–39

Innateness, 150–53, 183

Intuitionism: Mill's attack on, 90–91, 108, 115, 129, 145, 146–50, 180, 182–83, 185–86, 191, 214, 264, 270, 290–94, 319, 372n23; and defense of theological morality, 148–49; opposed to nontheological utilitarianism, 149; pernicious consequences of, 150; and givenness, 150–53; and Mansel and Hamilton, 155; and science, 174; and sensory evidence, 214; appropriation of, 290–94; mentioned, 68

James, William, 164, 364n39

Justice: divine, 29, 30–33, 103–4, 123–25, 137, 149, 156, 202, 210–11, 260, 298, 301, 306–19; man-made, 100, 202; desert-based, 102–4, 194, 239,

307–8, 316–17, 342–43; Mill's conception of, 103, 313–17; social, 103, 316–17, 328, 330–31, 340–43; distributive, 104, 316, 342; and utility, 306–19; transcendent significance of, 306–7, 313, 315, 318–19; defining attributes of, 307–8, 313, 315; essence of, 310; and legal constraint, 310; animal desire to retaliate, 313–17; and social feeling, 314–15; and security, 316; rule-based, 330, 332; and consequentialist ethic, 330–31; outcome-based, 330–31

Kant, Immanuel, 186–89, 315, 364n40

Law: higher law, 6, 309–10, 312, 320–21, 334, 344; of nature, as conceived by Mill, 93–95; of distribution, 104, 331; common, 115–16; universality of, 126, 170–73, 197, 215–16, 231; of contradiction, 158; Kant and, 186–89, 315, 364n40; essence of, 311; rule of, 330–31, 344; God as, 364n40. See also Natural law

Law of the three stages: in Saint-Simon, 47; and Mill, 48, 170–72, 184; and religious development, 132, 168, 170–72, 183; mentioned, 3, 73

Liberalism: development of, 2, 5, 320–21, 323, 325–26, 329–31, 333, 343, 373n2; and Mill, 2, 7, 39, 75, 77–78, 81–82, 297, 308, 318, 320–26, 328, 329–35, 343, 344, 345n1, 357n76, 360n22, 374n23; Mill on insufficiency of, 75, 357n76; and On Liberty, 234; of Victorian society, 243; and religion, 326; and social morality, 329–32; mentioned, 293

Liberty: individual liberty, 56, 175, 259, 261, 321, 329–30, 335, 336, 338, 340–42, 344; provisional value of, 235–39

Locke, John, 182

Luther, Martin, 7, 173, 345nn2,3

Manichaeism: James Mill and, 10–11, 104–5, 111, 139; Mill and, 11, 104–5, 111, 138–39, 140, 196–98, 231–32

Mansel, Henry Longueville: and epistemology, 4, 145–46, 153–54, 157;
and the limits of religious thought,
153; Mill's critique of, 153–66; on
nature of God, 156; on Providence,
159–60; Mill's distortion of views
of, 164–65

Martyrdom, 62, 125

Marx, Karl, 12, 41, 132, 171, 244, 265,
328

Mill, Harriet Taylor. *See* Taylor,
Harriet

Mill, James: influence on his son, 7–
22, 138, 164, 166, 169, 241, 346n15;
charisma of, 8; education of, 8; religious views of, 8–12, 180; on evil of
religion, 10; and Christianity, 10–11,
19, 137; and Manichaeism, 10–11,
104–5, 111, 139; on self-making, 12;
on source of existence, 12, 346n14;
associationist psychology of, 12–13,
22, 146; on malleability of human
beings, 12–13; on education, 12–14,
279; doctrine of circumstances of,
13, 152, 340–41; determinism of, 14,
175; and the Greeks, 14–15, 120,
143, 265, 309; and reign of virtue,
14–16; on emotion, 15, 131; on pleasure, 15, 273, 347n24; on Church of
England, 16–19; concealment of religious views, 17, 19; on prayer, 18–
19, 172; on evidence, 20–21, 348n33;
on state religion, 21–22; on religious
sanctions, 123–24; and liberty, 175;
mentioned, 2, 4, 6, 223, 325

Mill, John Stuart: on Christianity, 1, 11,
14, 18, 46, 102, 126–27, 136–37, 162–
63, 165, 166, 187, 221–22, 247–52,
257–58, 263–65, 268, 275–77, 279,
282–83, 286, 367n31, 369n12; overriding aim of, 1–2, 78, 112, 126, 145,
151, 163, 235, 264, 280, 294; conversion to Benthamism, 2, 23–25, 28,
41–42, 126, 246, 251, 264, 268, 280,
297, 349n52, 354n48; and liberalism,
2, 7, 39, 75, 77–78, 81–82, 297, 308,
318, 320–26, 328, 329–35, 343, 344,
345n1, 357n76, 360n22, 374n23; and
secular humanism, 2, 163, 327,
373n14; and secularism, 2, 163, 326–
28, 332–33; attack on Providence, 3,
58, 90, 91, 92, 93, 96, 97, 99–101, 105,
107, 109, 111, 129, 137–38, 165, 166,
268, 296, 342, 343, 370n46; experience of disorder, 3, 9, 91, 97–102,
166, 337, 342; and philosophy of history, 3, 47–50, 84, 85, 183–84, 245,
323; silence on religion, 3, 17, 19, 39,
50, 55–59, 64, 65, 86, 239–43, 254,
360n28; on judgment of God, 4, 103,
144, 155–64, 165; conception of God
of, 5, 21, 101, 102, 104–8, 111, 138–
42, 158–61, 166, 172, 176, 187–89,
·191–203, 208–11, 222, 278–79; conversion strategy of, 5, 35–36, 141–
42, 232–33, 250–51, 284–86, 288,
290, 291–93, 362n45; and individual
liberty, 5, 6, 175, 259, 261, 321, 329–
30, 335, 336, 338, 340–42, 344; as religious founder, 6, 41, 66, 113, 151,
232, 234, 332; mental development
of, 7, 12, 22–23, 113; influence of
James Mill on, 7–22, 138, 164, 166,
169, 241, 346n15; religious upbringing of, 9–11; and atheism, 11, 64–66,
163, 222, 242; and Manichaeism, 11,
138–39, 140, 196–98, 231–32; and
associationism, 14, 146, 148, 204; determinism of, 14, 152, 179, 219, 340,
365n6, 367n31; and necessitarianism, 14, 173, 219, 220, 365n6, 367n31;
on emotion, 15–16, 115; on Church
of England, 17–19; rhetorical strategies of, 20, 50, 129, 167, 254, 257–59,
261, 262, 263, 266, 269, 284, 285–86,
289, 309, 313, 318, 347n24, 368n36;
on evidence, 21, 169; and Saint-
Simonism, 24, 27, 43–50, 72, 352n19,
353n29, 356n63, 357n76; antitheological intent of, 28, 38, 40, 51, 55,
58, 66, 77, 151, 261, 280, 328, 354n49;
conversion to Religion of Humanity,
28, 37, 53–55, 67, 251, 354n51; religious nature of, 35, 50, 51, 157, 327,
332; critique of Comte, 39–40, 184,
252–53, 333–34, 351n11, 370n40;
Prometheanism of, 41, 95–97, 164,
188, 264–67, 278, 340; and the spiri-

tual power, 47–50, 75, 76–77, 79–82,
118, 200, 237, 253, 334, 357n77,
365n7; correspondence with Comte,
50–72; and advancement of positivism, 56–65, 69, 145–46, 184,
351n11, 355n59; on the role of
women, 62–63; on the clerisy, 72–
73; on unanimity and authority, 76,
77, 78–84, 237–38, 253, 371n6; early
illiberalism of, 81–82, 374n23; and
valorization of human agency, 92,
95, 100–101, 103, 104–5, 198, 200,
201–2, 231, 265, 266, 338, 342–43;
and social justice, 103, 316–17, 328,
330–31, 340–43; perfectionism of,
103–4, 340–43; on inheritance, 104,
356n63; on self-making, 108, 202; on
selfishness, 109–10, 136–37, 142–43,
261, 269, 297–302, 331–32, 360n19;
on human nature, 109–12, 152; on
individuality, 112, 257, 259, 261–63,
265–66, 323–25, 338–39; on sources
of morality, 118–23, 125–28; on education, 119–21, 236; on religious
conversion, 124; on revelation, 126,
138, 161, 191, 203, 211–22, 282–83,
289; on Christ, 126–28, 134, 136, 138,
221, 227–33, 247–51, 263, 264, 279,
288; on the origin of belief in gods,
129–31, 170–72, 182, 183–85; on
hope, 141, 144, 189, 220, 223–27; on
imagination, 141, 186, 214, 224–27;
on immortality, 142–44, 203–11, 226;
denial of necessary truth, 150–52;
denial of givenness, 150–53; and
Mansel controversy, 153–66; and
pretense of knowledge, 164–66; and
historicism, 169; on eternity of the
universe, 176–77, 180–81, 193; on
evolution, 181, 191; on inward light,
186, 305; on the creation of life, 196;
on making new men, 196, 285, 299,
337, 338, 339; on the soul, 203–4; on
the relation between mind and matter, 205–7; propensity for literalism
of, 214, 226; on sensory evidence,
214; movement toward closure of,
239; as political activist, 243–45,

325–26, 356n64; and reconstruction
of the human intellect, 245–47; reformist ambition of, 245–47, 325–
26, 356n64; and behaviorism, 259,
284–85; on his contemporaries,
261–63, 265, 323–25, 339; on morality, 263–64, 270, 275, 280; and inductive ethics, 270; on individual and
collective happiness, 275, 330, 333;
on self-renunciation, 275–80, 371n6;
"mental" crisis of, 294, 360n26; and
amelioration of existence, 300; and
question of proof, 302–6; and reign
of virtue, 304–5, 371n7; and France,
322–25, 373n8; as revolutionary, 325;
and socialism, 330–31, 333–35, 337,
338, 357n76, 374n23; and political
religion, 332–40; as true believer,
337–40; and free will, 340–41,
365n6, 372n23; and representative
government, 357n74; and laissez-
faire, 357n76, 371n9; and empiricism, 362n9
Mind and matter, 205–7, 214
Miracles: and revelation, 212; evidences for, 212–20; Hume on, 215;
and reign of law, 215–17; and Providence, 217; and Christianity, 220;
hope in, 220–21
Monotheism, 170–71, 183, 184, 364n5
Morality: common-sense, 83, 269,
280–81, 358n85; social, 109, 125, 257,
293–94, 301, 320, 331–32, 336,
353n43; Christian, 117, 126, 128, 134,
135, 263–65, 271; sources of, 118–23,
213; ultimate origin of, 125–28, 270;
improvement of, 127–28; consequentialist, 149, 150, 270–71, 272,
329–32, 337, 344, 363n14; in-itself,
149, 150, 264, 270–71, 303–4, 312,
319, 329, 331, 344, 363n14; transcendental, 149, 150; theological, 249,
263–64; pagan, 263, 265–66, 371n50;
purely human, 263–64; foundation
of, 269; ultimate sanction of, 287–88;
emotivist, 297
Morley, John: on "Theism," 87,
367n31; on Mill–Mansel controver-

sy, 166, 364n44; on Mill's antitheological intent, 354n49; on Mill's necessitarianism, 367n31; on Mill and
Comte, 368n31; mentioned, 241

Natural law: and Bentham, 16; attack
on, 90, 91, 93, 129; as conceived by
Mill, 93–95; mentioned, 3, 8, 24, 52,
187, 202. See also Law
Natural religion: utility of, 30, 115,
197, 203, 209. See also Deism; Natural theology
Natural theology: and Mansel, 155,
161; and "Theism," 169–70; mentioned, 4, 178, 183, 192, 195, 198,
199, 212. See also Deism; Natural
religion
Nature: emendation of, 89, 128; as
reckless disorder, 90, 97–99, 165,
166, 195–96, 337; defined, 91–93,
105, 107, 111, 137; control of, 96, 97,
99, 100, 106, 112; anthropomor-
phization of, 97–99; malevolence of,
98, 101; as devoid of justice, 102–3;
human nature, 109–12, 152; and
reign of law, 170–73, 197, 215–16,
231, 366n21; amorality of, 199–200,
202
"Nature" (Mill), 87–113
Necessitarianism, 14, 173, 219, 220,
365n6, 367n31
Nietzsche, Friedrich: and death of
god, 12, 41; and Millian hero, 256;
mentioned, 265, 266, 309, 328
Nominalism: of Mill, 11, 157, 161, 163,
303, 372n21; of Bentham, 302,
350n70, 372n22
Nontheological utilitarianism: as new
religion, 7, 35, 36, 326; of Bentham,
25–28, 30, 31; antitheological impetus of, 34–36; essence of, 35–36,
275; and Mill, 39, 149; and intuitionism, 149; moral superiority of, 201;
and self-devotion, 277; and the will
of God, 282; and Christianity, 282–
83; mentioned, 23, 33, 50, 78, 80, 107,
123, 128, 232, 256, 319. See also Religion of Humanity; Utilitarianism

On Liberty (Mill): and freedom of discussion, 59, 236, 237; and undermining of religious belief, 234–35, 248,
370n30; and "Spirit of the Age," 236;
and philosophy of history, 236–37;
existential urgency of, 242–43; and
Christianity, 247–52, 255, 257–58,
262, 370n30; and the social sanction,
254–57; as religious tract, 267
Ontology, 289–90

Paley, William: Christian utilitarian-
ism of, 25–27, 30–31, 349n46; on
Church of England, 27; rivalry with
Bentham, 27; on design in nature,
365n14
Paulism, 126, 127, 221, 229, 361n37
Philosophical radicals, 8, 43, 244, 245,
356n64
Philosophy of history: Mill's embrace
of, 3, 47–50, 84, 85, 183–84, 323; of
Saint-Simon, 46–48, 353n38; of
Comte, 48–49, 67, 153, 353n38; and
Christianity, 168; and religious development, 168; and On Liberty,
236–37; and the English, 356n67;
mentioned, 64, 76, 343
Plato: demiurge of, 4, 106, 138, 175,
178, 182; mentioned, 22, 88, 203
Political religion: and utilitarianism,
321; and politicization of society,
332–37; mentioned, 5, 120, 134. See
also Religion of Humanity; Social
religion
Polytheism, 170–71, 183, 184, 197
Positivism: antitheological intent of, 3,
28, 50, 52, 57, 61; as basis of new religion, 51, 52–53, 62; Benthamism as
precursor of, 52; advancement of,
56–65, 69, 146, 184, 355n59; La revue
positive, 57; of Mill, 59, 145–46,
351n11; and the spiritual power, 76;
legal, 109, 187, 311; origin of term,
353n41; and social gospel, 353n43;
and Benjamin Constant, 355n59;
mentioned, 171
Posthumous religious sanction: Benthamite attack on, 30–33, 104, 256,

285–86, 298, 348n34; Mill's repudiation of, 31, 32–33, 210–11; James
Mill on, 31–32; inefficacy of, 116,
123–25; and justice, 312–13

Principles of Political Economy (Mill),
69–70, 245

Prometheanism, 41, 95–97, 164, 188,
264–67, 278, 340

Providence: Mill's attack on, 3, 58, 90,
91, 92, 93, 96, 97, 99–101, 105, 107,
109, 111, 129, 137–38, 165, 166, 268,
296, 342, 343, 370n46; Christian
apologists for, 109, 137–38; Mansel
on, 159–60, 165; special and general, 173, 216, 218; and miracles, 217

Public opinion: power of, 119, 122,
124, 255, 256–57; and morality, 121–
23; and Harriet Taylor, 361n36

Punishment, 309–13

Reeve, Henry: on the Benthamites, 22,
241; on sensory evidence, 214; on reform of human nature, 299; on Mill
and English society, 324–25, 356n67

Religion: Mill's silence on, 3, 17, 19,
39, 50, 55–59, 64, 65, 86, 239–43,
254, 360n28; James Mill on, 21–22,
336; utility of, 28–30, 32, 113–44;
and Bentham's *Analysis*, 28–33;
temporal usefulness of, 28–33, 116–
18; as social bond, 74; Harriet Taylor
on, 113, 364n2; truth of, 114, 168–69;
improvement of, 117, 249; as source
of conflict, 117, 346n15; nature of,
128–32; natural history of, 129;
and consolation for suffering, 131;
equivalence to poetry, 131; essence
of, 135; skepticism in England, 153;
and science, 168, 169, 171, 172; and
imagination, 224–25

Religion of Duty, 5, 15, 73, 142, 257,
258, 259, 293, 297, 318. *See also* Religion of Humanity

Religion of Humanity: and Comte, 1,
3, 23, 36, 37; superiority of, 4, 41, 66,
113, 132–38, 142, 188, 201, 228, 230,
253, 264, 277–80, 298, 340; Mill's

conversion to, 28, 37, 53–55, 67, 251,
354n51; Mill's embrace of, 40, 278–
79, 281–83; intramundane character
of, 115, 132, 133, 140, 337; rewards
of, 134–35; as "real religion," 135,
253; and supernaturalism, 139; incorporation of Christianity of, 221,
230–31, 249–50; compared with
Christianity, 228; establishment of,
251–54; and socialization, 259–60,
284–85; moral end of, 261, 275;
and self-sacrifice, 276–77, 371n50;
and Christ, 284–85, 291; rivalry
with Christianity, 294, 301; as social
religion, 294–97, 301; unselfishness
of, 298, 360n19; and amelioration
of existence, 300; and religious fulfillment, 300–301; collectivism of,
318, 333; and secularization, 327; assimilation of ethos of, 329; and the
good of the social, 331, 360n19; as
political religion, 334–35; mentioned, 15, 33, 39, 64, 73, 89, 128,
236, 256

Religion of the future, 127, 232, 233,
236, 251, 256. *See also* Religion of
Humanity

Revelation: Mill on, 126, 138, 161, 191,
203, 211–22, 282–83, 289; moral perversions in, 138; and Mansel, 153–
54, 155; evidences of, 211–22; imperfections in, 212; and miracles, 212–
20; of Christianity, 219, 282; and justice, 306; mentioned, 180

Rousseau, Jean-Jacques: deism of, 90,
92; and man's natural goodness,
108–10, 360n21; and dependency,
122; on Christianity, 136; and Mill,
263, 294, 295, 331

Saint-Simon, Henri de: New Christianity of, 38, 43; aim of, 39; philosophy of history of, 46–48, 353n38;
and the spiritual power, 72–78,
355n59, 356n73; mentioned, 2, 6,
284, 323

Saint-Simonism: and Mill, 24, 27, 43–

50, 72, 352n19, 353n29, 356n63, 357n76; antitheological intent of, 45; and the spiritual power, 46, 72–78; critique of religion, 116

Sanctions: and *On Liberty*, 254–57; defined, 285–90; and utilitarianism, 285–90; internal, 286–90; external, 288, 290, 295

Secular humanism: Mill and, 2, 163, 326–28, 332–33, 373n14; religion of, 326–29, 373n14; and Christianity, 327–28

Secularization: nature of, 34–35, 326–28; in France, 136; and Mill, 326–28, 332–33; and utilitarianism, 327

Secular religion: nature of, 34–36, 38, 40, 326–28, 332–37; in France, 38, 42, 45; differentiated from transcendent religion, 41

Selfishness: of Christianity, 31, 33, 36, 135–37, 142–43, 251, 264–65, 294, 298; Mill on, 109–10, 136–37, 142–43, 261, 269, 297–302, 331–32, 360n19; and desire for immortality, 143; and utilitarianism, 269, 274, 281, 285; sin of, 297–302; opposed to the social good, 298; and emendation of human nature, 299

Self-renunciation: and Christianity, 275–77; Mill's valorization of, 275–80, 371n6; and Religion of Humanity, 275–80; mentioned, 281

Service to humanity: as "law of our life," 135; as religion, 296–97, 299, 321, 332–33; mentioned, 6, 36, 80, 133, 232, 251, 268, 276, 278–79, 328, 329, 344

Skepticism: in England, 153; as the only rational attitude, 222–23

Skinnerian behaviorism: and Mill, 259, 284–85; and Benthamite psychology, 350n60; mentioned, 34

Smith, Adam, 69

Socialism, 330–31, 333–35, 337, 338, 357n76, 374n23

Socialization: of conscience, 152, 312; and belief in an afterlife, 208; and

Religion of Humanity, 252, 259–60, 267, 284–85, 292, 293; and associationism, 294–96; toward unity with humanity, 295–96; of social feeling, 301; and Mill, 337; mentioned, 339

Social justice: Mill on, 102–4, 194, 239, 307–8, 316–17, 328, 330–31, 342–43; and God, 340–43. *See also* Justice

Social religion: and social feelings, 294–97, 299, 301; and Mill, 321, 332, 335; and utilitarianism, 321; and consequentialism, 329–32; and social gospel, 353n43; mentioned, 274, 277, 278, 298. *See also* Religion of Humanity

Spiritual power: Saint-Simonism and, 46, 72–78; Mill on, 47–50, 75, 76–77, 79–82, 118, 200, 237, 253, 334, 357n77, 365n7; Saint-Simon on, 72–78, 355n59, 356n73; Comte on, 78–79, 355n59, 357n73

Spontaneous order: of nature, 96; of the market, 343

Stephen, James Fitzjames, 240

Supernaturalism, 135, 136, 139

System of Logic (Mill): instrumental to positivist cause, 59–60; and method to achieve unanimity, 79–81; and attack on intuitionism, 148; mentioned, 4, 21, 245

Taylor, Harriet: collaboration with Mill, 3, 88–89, 266, 361n39, 364n2; antireligious intent of, 88; described by Mill, 105, 147, 338, 361n40, 365n12, 368n34; on the finer natures, 110; and utility of religion, 113; moral intuition of, 147; as model of moral perfection, 227, 368n34; and *On Liberty*, 266; and *Utilitarianism*, 274; and English society, 324; on nature, 359n14; and public opinion, 361n36; and "Theism," 364n2; Carlyle on, 371n9; death of, 373n8; mentioned, 4, 131, 205, 241, 359n8, 360n20

Taylor, Helen, 87, 199

Theism, 173–91. *See also* Argument from design; Evidences of theism

Unanimity: desirability of, 76, 77, 78–82, 83–84, 237–38, 253, 371n6; and method, 79–81

Utilitarianism: as a new religion, 7, 35, 36, 281–83, 326; and pleasure, 14–16, 272–73, 347n24, 371n7; of Paley, 25–27, 30–31, 349n46; nontheological (Bentham's), 25–28, 272; antitheological thrust of, 28, 318, 321; and godlessness, 269, 281–83; Mill's definition of, 272–74; and selfishness, 274, 281; and collective happiness, 274–75, 293–94, 302–3, 330, 333; and individual happiness, 275, 302–3; and common-sense morality, 280–81; and sanctions, 285–90; and Christianity, 289, 326, 350n67; and social feeling, 297; and proof, 302–6; as social religion, 321; and immanentist consequentialism, 330, 353n14; origin of term, 350n67. *See also* Christian utilitarianism; Nontheological utilitarianism; Utility

Utilitarianism (Mill): antitheological theme of, 268; as religious tract, 268

Utility: as ultimate source of moral obligation, 271, 281–83, 284, 285, 291, 328; as ultimate standard of morality, 271, 283; ultimate sanction of, 283–86; and justice, 306–19. *See also* Utilitarianism

"Utility of Religion" (Mill), 113–44; and Bentham's *Analysis*, 360n28

Voltaire: deism of, 90; mentioned, 8

Voluntarism. *See* Christian voluntarism

Will: as causal agent, 175, 178, 180; free will, 340–41, 365n6, 372n23. *See also* Mill: valorization of human agency